HUMAN RESOURCE MANAGEMENT

A Case Study Approach

Editors

**Michael Muller-Camen,
Richard Croucher & Susan Leigh**

JAICO PUBLISHING HOUSE

Ahmedabad Bangalore Bhopal Bhubaneswar Chennai
Delhi Hyderabad Kolkata Lucknow Mumbai

Published by Jaico Publishing House
A-2 Jash Chambers, 7-A Sir Phirozshah Mehta Road
Fort, Mumbai - 400 001
jaicopub@jaicobooks.com
www.jaicobooks.com

Published in arrangement with
Chartered Institute of Personnel and Development
151 The Broadway
London SW19 1JQ

HUMAN RESOURCE MANAGEMENT:
A CASE STUDY APPROACH
ISBN 978-81-7992-933-9

First Jaico Impression: 2008
Sixth Jaico Impression: 2014

Printed by
Pashupati Printers
1/429/16, Gali No. 1, Friends Colony
Industrial Area, G. T. Road, Shahdara, Delhi - 95

Contents

List of Figures and Tables

Contributors

CHRIS BREWSTER

Chris Brewster is Professor of International Human Resource Management at the University of Reading in the UK. Previously he held the same title at Henley Management College and before that at London South Bank and Cranfield Universities. He has conducted extensive research in the field of international and comparative HRM; and published twenty-five books and over a hundred articles. In 2002 Chris Brewster was awarded the Georges Petitpas Memorial Award by the practitioner body, the World Federation of Personnel Management Associations, in recognition of his outstanding contribution to international human resource management.

MICHAEL BROOKES

Dr Michael Brookes is a Senior Lecturer in Economics at Middlesex University Business School. He became an academic relatively late in life, having for many years taught Economics and Business Studies in a number of secondary schools. His research interests include labour market discrimination, industrial relations and comparative HRM and he has already published a number of articles in each of these areas.

TRICIA CHASE

Patricia Chase is a graduate member of the CIPD and former programme leader for MA HRM at Middlesex University with experience of working in the Public Sector. Her special interests cover issues relating to violence in the workplace, diversity and performance.

TRACEY COCKERTON

Dr Tracey Cockerton is Associate Director in the School of Health and Social Sciences at Middlesex University and a Chartered Occupational Psychologist and Coaching Psychologist. She teaches selection and assessment methods and theories of personality and individual differences. Her research interests include: psychometric evaluations of various tools for assessing individual differences, coping and psychological well-being at work; emotional intelligence and personality; learning styles; attitudes to mental illnesses.

PETER CRITTEN

Dr Peter Critten is a Principal Lecturer at Middlesex University Business School and coordinates and teaches on the subjects aligned to Human Resource Development. Prior to joining Middlesex University he had 25 years' experience of introducing and evaluating training and development systems, mainly in service industries. His experience was written up in *Investing in People: Towards Corporate Capability* (1993). His current professional and research interests involve work-based-learning and the Doctorate in Professional Practice programme at Middlesex.

RICHARD CROUCHER

Richard Croucher is Professor of Comparative Employment Relations and Associate Dean: Research at Middlesex University Business School. He earned his PhD from the University of Warwick and was previously Senior Research Fellow at

Cranfield University. His research interests are in regulation of the employment relationship in different national, sectoral and workplace regimes and his work has been published in journals such as the *European Journal of Industrial Relations, Industrial Relations, International Journal of Human Resource Management, International Journal of Labour Law* and *Work, Employment and Society*. He has held research grants from the Economic and Social Research Council, the Leverhulme Trust, the Anglo-German Society for the Study of Industrial Society, the Department of Trade and Industry, the Low Pay Commission and the British Academy. Richard is a Fellow of the Royal Society of Arts.

PAUL ELLIS

Paul Ellis has worked for the Ministry of Defence since 1990 in 18 different countries. As Assistant Director at the Defence Leadership and Management Centre, part of the Defence Academy of the UK, he leads on the use of coaching with strategic leaders in the Armed Forces and Ministry of Defence. His main interests are the application of coaching, leadership, and organisational development.

IAN FAVELL

Ian Favell is a Visiting Professor at Middlesex University Business School, where he has designed and delivered undergraduate and postgraduate programmes for many years. He is a Chartered Fellow of CIPD, Chief Verifier Professional Assessment for CIPD, a member of the CIPD Membership & Education Committee, and a CIPD Quality Panel Chair. His main interests are professional management development, personal, organisational and work-based learning, and the accreditation of professional experience.

MATT FLYNN

Dr Matt Flynn is a Senior Lecturer at Middlesex University Business School. His main area of expertise is age management. He has carried out research for the UK government (Department for Work and Pensions, Department for Trade and Industry and the South East of England Development Agency) on age discrimination and retirement; and participated in an EU-funded project on age and knowledge management in the automotive industry (ESF); older workers as a vulnerable occupational group (EQUAL); and the relationship between gender, qualification and work in later life (HE-ESF).

PHILIP FRAME

Dr Philip Frame is Principal Lecturer in Organisational Development and Director of Work Based Learning Programmes at Middlesex University Business School. He is both a Middlesex and a National Teaching Fellow. Philip's first degree in Social Anthropology was followed by eight years with the Race Relations Board. He subsequently obtained an MSc in Organisational Development and a PhD in Management Studies. He is a Fellow of both the RSA and the Higher Education Academy, and is co-chair of SEDA's publishing committee. He has provided staff development workshops and published on student induction, work-based learning, managing diversity and business ethics.

SEBASTIAN FUCHS

Sebastian Fuchs is a Lecturer in Human Resource Management at Middlesex University Business School. Sebastian holds a BA (Hons) in HRM and Marketing from Middlesex University, and an MSc in HRM from the London School of Economics and Political Science. Currently, he reads for a PhD at King's College London, where he looks into the concept of Organisational Identification from a comparative perspective. Prior to his academic career, he worked for the Daimler AG in his native Germany, and gathered international working and teaching experience in Brazil, Peru and China.

MARY HARTOG

Dr Mary Hartog is a Principal Lecturer at Middlesex University Business School and Head of the Department of Human Resource Management. She has been awarded a National Teaching Fellowship for teaching excellence. Her research interests include the use of self-study for professional development; Critical reflective practice; Ethics and Professional Development; and Productive Diversity in teaching and learning. Mary has taught at Middlesex on both undergraduate and postgraduate Business & Management programmes since 1990. Mary also undertakes consultancy and research assignments through the university. Prior to joining Middlesex University, Mary worked as an HRD practitioner in local government, an employment law consultant for a publishing company, and before that, she had a career in community development and social work.

PAUL HIGGINS

Dr Paul Higgins is Senior Lecturer in Human Resource Management. He has worked on research projects funded by the European Social Fund and the Higher Education Academy and has published research papers in such journals as *Work Employment and Society, Public Money and Management* and *Local Government Studies*. His main research interests are employee relations, public sector reform and work-based learning.

CAROLINE HORNER

Dr Caroline Horner is an experienced coach and Director of an international coaching consultancy, i-coach academy. Prior to becoming a coach, she had over 12 years international experience in the technology, telecommunications and financial services sectors. In addition to her 1:1 coaching practice, Caroline facilitates post-graduate courses in coaching for both academic and corporate programmes, and is the Director of the Africa Centre for Individualised Learning and Coaching at the University of Stellenbosch Business School. Her research interests focus on the development of a professional coaching practice.

TERENCE JACKSON

Terence Jackson is Professor of Cross Cultural Management at Middlesex University. Before becoming an academic he was manager and internal training and development consultant in NatWest Bank. He has published widely in the area of Cross-cultural management and International HRM, is editor of the *International Journal of Cross Cultural Management* and has more recently directed projects on people management in Africa.

PHIL JAMES

Philip James is Professor of Employment Relations at Oxford Brookes University and a Visiting Professor at Middlesex University Business School. He has researched and published widely in the fields of both human resource management and occupational health and safety. In the second of these areas, he has acted as a Specialist Adviser to the Work and Pensions Select Committee and is Deputy Editor of the journal *Policy and Practice in Health and Safety*.

ANNA KYPRIANOU

Anna Kyprianou is the Dean of Middlesex University Business School. She has worked with the strategic development of organisations and their management teams for more than fifteen years. Her areas of specialism are organisational behaviour, managing people and learning and development with a particular emphasis on managing and developing people in the virtual organisation. She has extensive research experience in survey design and data analysis at organisational, national and international levels.

SUSAN LEIGH

Susan Leigh is a Senior Lecturer in the department of HRM. She joined Middlesex University in 1997 as a Research Fellow and then progressed on to being a lecturer. For a number of years she was the programme leader for the Postgraduate Diploma in HRM. She is Chair of the North London Branch of the CIPD and is on their academic quality panel. She is also on the membership upgrading panel of the CIPD. Her research interests are the psychological contract and managing absence and retention.

DAVID LEWIS

David Lewis is Professor of Employment Law and member of the Centre for Legal Research at Middlesex University. David has considerable experience as a consultant and is an ACAS arbitrator. He is also a member of the editorial board of the *Industrial Law Journal* and an elected member of the executive committee of the Industrial Law Society.

SUZAN LEWIS

Sue Lewis is Professor of Organisational Psychology at Middlesex University. Her research focuses on work-personal life issues and workplace practice, culture and change in different organisational and social policy contexts. She has published numerous books and papers on these topics and is a founding editor of the international journal Community, Work and Family. She has advised governments and worked with employers and policy makers on work-life issues in Europe, the USA and Japan.

ANDREW MAYO

Andrew Mayo is Professor of Human Capital Management at Middlessex University Business School with particular research interests in people-related measures. He is also a Fellow of the Centre for Management Development at London Business School, and designs and directs executive programmes for companies. He spent 28 years in international industry, and is the author of five books including *The Human Value of the Enterprise – Valuing People as Assets* (2001) and *Creating a Learning and Development Strategy* (2004). He is Chartered Fellow of the CIPD and is President of the HR Society.

CLIVE MORTON

Dr Clive Morton OBE is Professor of Corporate Governance at Middlesex University Business School. He is a corporate development director with an impressive record of achieving successful change in revitalising an unusually broad range of major organisations in private, public and not-for-profit sectors, offering specialist knowledge of HR at the cutting edge, and consults to organisations on change management. He is the author of four books including *Becoming World Class*, (published in 1994), *Leading HR* (published in 2001) and *By the Skin of Our Teeth* (published in 2003). He is a former Vice President of CIPD and a Chartered Companion of CIPD.

MICHAEL MULLER-CAMEN

Michael Muller-Camen is Professor of International Human Resource Management at Middlesex University Business School and has formerly worked at the International University in Germany, DeMontfort University in Leicester and the University of Innsbruck. His main research interests are the comparative study of human resource management, age diversity and sustainable human resource management. He has held research grants from the Anglo-German Foundation, the European Union (Marie Curie) and the ESRC and has published widely in academic journals such as *British Journal of Industrial Relations, Human Relations, Human Resource Management Journal, International Journal of Human Resource Management,* and *Organisation Studies.*

ALEXANDROS PSYCHOGIOS

Dr Alexandros G. Psychogios holds an MSc in Public Policy & Public Finance from the University of Athens, an MA in Public Services Management from the University of York and a PhD in Industrial & Business Studies from the University of Warwick. Currently, he is a Lecturer on Management, Organizational Behaviour and Human Resources and an Academic Research Coordinator at the Department of Business Administration & Economics of City College in Thessaloniki, Greece (Affiliated Institution of the University of Sheffield). He has published several articles in academic journals concerning contemporary issues of management.

IAN ROPER

Dr Ian Roper is Principal Lecturer and Director of HRM Programmes at Middlesex University Business School where he teaches employee relations and contemporary issues in HRM. His main research interests are concerned with (1) the government regulation of the employment relationship, and (2) the employment implications of public service reform, particularly in relation to UK local government. He has published widely in academic journals and has co-edited two books: *Modernising Work in Public Services* (2007) and *Contesting Public Sector Reforms: Critical Debates, International Perspectives* (2004).

MALCOLM SARGEANT

Malcolm Sargeant is Professor of Labour Law. He specialises in the implementation of EU labour law and has written widely on such subjects as transfers of undertakings and age discrimination in employment. He is author and co-author of a number of books including being co-author of *Essentials of Employment Law* and joint consulting editor for *Employment Law for People Managers*. Prior to his career as an academic he was HRM Manager of a large financial services company and helped run a specialist recruitment consultancy for a number of years.

LESLIE T. SZAMOSI

Leslie Szamosi is a Senior Lecturer and Academic Director of the EMBA at City College in Thessaloniki, Greece (Affiliated Institution of the University of Sheffield) and has published extensively in the areas of change management and human resource management practices. He has consulted extensively in both North America and South-Eastern Europe and his main research interests are in the areas of change management and international management practices.

MARTIN UPCHURCH

Martin Upchurch is Professor of International Employment Relations at Middlesex University Business School. His research interests cover trade unions, industrial relations and the political economy of work in the UK, Germany and transformation economies. He is editor of *The State and Globalization* (Mansell 1999), co-author of *New Unions, New Workplaces* (Routledge 2003), *Partnership and the High Performance Workplace* (Palgrave 2005), *The Reality of Workplace Partnership* (Palgrave 2008 forthcoming) and *The Crisis of Social Democratic Trade Unionism in Western Europe* (Ashgate 2008 forthcoming). He has held research grants from the Leverhulme Trust and British Academy and was Principal Investigator for an ESRC-funded major project on the Future of Work. He is currently undertaking research into workplace transformation, the international financial institutions and social dialogue in the former Yugoslavia funded by the British Academy.

DOIREAN WILSON

Doirean Wilson is a Senior Lecturer, HR Professional Practitioner, and member of the HRM Department at Middlesex University Business School. Her research is in the area of culture, diversity, gender disparity, leadership and management. She is also studying for a Doctorate in Professional Studies at Middlesex. She has been author and co-author for several academic papers and is lead compiler for a consultancy book based on a third-year undergraduate consultancy module for which she is module leader. Doirean, who is a former business consultant, journalist and television presenter, is also a Fellow of the CIPD.

GEOFFREY WOOD

Geoffrey Wood is Professor in HRM in the School of Management at the University of Sheffield. Previously he was Professor and Director of Research at Middlesex University Business School. He has authored/co-authored/edited seven books, and over one hundred articles in peer-reviewed journals (including journals such as *Work, Employment and Society, Organization Studies, International Journal of Human Resource Management, British Journal of Industrial Relations* and *Human Resource Management* (US). His current research interests centre on the systematic testing and development of contemporary institutional theory in the light of large-scale survey evidence. This has encompassed assessments of variations in industrial in different institutional settings, the relative fortunes of organized labour in emerging markets, and developments and extensions of regulationist theories.

Book Map

LEARNING OUTCOMES

Learning outcomes enable students to focus what they should have learned by the end of the chapter and evaluate their progress.

CASE STUDIES

At least two case studies per chapter, taken from a wide range of sources, help students make links between theory and real-life, practical examples.

Starter case studies establish the significance of the topic under discussion and stimulate thinking around it.

Main case studies incorporate a wider range of issues and illustrate complex issues facing HR professionals.

Each case study is accompanied by a set of questions or tasks encourage students to analyse the example in groups or individually.

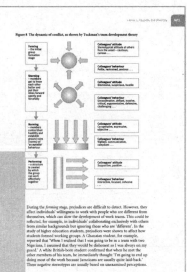

FIGURES AND TABLES

Visual learning aids scattered throughout the text illustrate key concepts, including tables relating British practice to that in other major European countries.

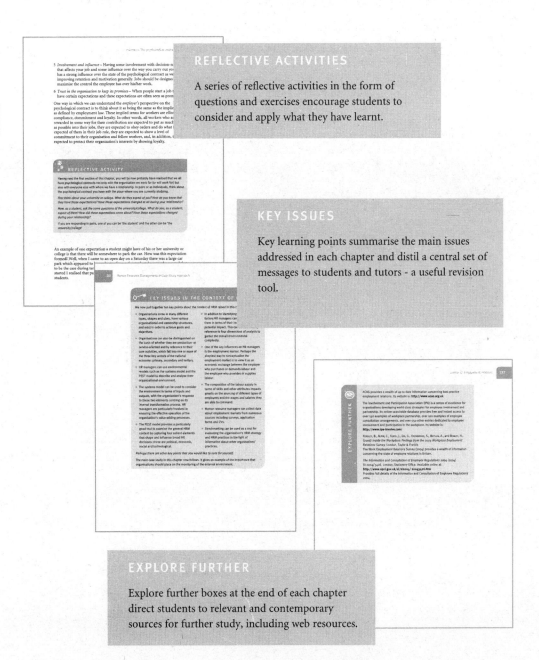

REFLECTIVE ACTIVITIES

A series of reflective activities in the form of questions and exercises encourage students to consider and apply what they have learnt.

KEY ISSUES

Key learning points summarise the main issues addressed in each chapter and distil a central set of messages to students and tutors - a useful revision tool.

EXPLORE FURTHER

Explore further boxes at the end of each chapter direct students to relevant and contemporary sources for further study, including web resources.

REFERENCES AND FURTHER READING

A comprehensive list of references at the end of the book pulls together the main works cited in each chapter and encourages students to build on their knowledge.

COMPANION WEBSITE

Comprehensive and interactive websites for students and tutors include features such as multiple choice questions for each chapter, allowing students to test their knowledge, and weblinks to help develop understanding. Go to **http://www.cipd.co.uk/letures/student/tsmfs/**

CHAPTER 1

Introduction

Richard Croucher, Susan Leigh *and* Michael Muller-Camen

This textbook is aimed to fulfil a need the contributors have experienced in their own daily practice as teachers of HRM at undergraduate level. We believe that it meets a need for a specific type of textbook, built around case studies, which is both practical and yet theoretically informed. It is anchored in the British national context while also seeking to place British practice within the wider global situation. Above all, this book aims to be accessible and yet challenging.

The textbook provides a comprehensive and practical text for use in the classroom and for background reading, aimed mainly at undergraduates with some preliminary knowledge and understanding of HR. Its overarching aim is to provide a clear exposition of practical issues that confront the HR practitioner, without over-simplifying or ignoring wider debates. It is therefore suitable for undergraduates at or around second-year level or for students embarking on their professional studies who have only a limited amount of knowledge of HR. We have attempted to recognise the busy and even pressured reality that many teachers and students find themselves in by providing a text that is comprehensive, systematically structured, accessible in language, and which is conceptually clear and easy to use. The chapters which describe subjects in an introductory way are grouped together in the book's earlier sections. Those requiring more background knowledge, which introduce more theoretical issues, or are more critical in approach, are in the last section. The text is also useful for a wider group of students than second-year undergraduates because of the inclusion of case studies in each chapter.

The case study approach is central to the text. Each chapter contains two case studies, to encourage students to think about issues in a concrete way that connects with contemporary realities. The case studies are derived from real-life situations, allowing teachers and students to use them in a range of different contexts and in their own way, bringing their own insights to the situations described. It is recognised that students will have a variety of cultural backgrounds; they may well not be native speakers of English and may have only minimal practical experience. There are also many opportunities to apply the knowledge that has been acquired in the 'Exercise' features that have been positioned at important points in each chapter. References have been kept to a minimum, to promote clarity of exposition and presentation. Furthermore we have tried to prioritise clarity of exposition and ease of use. For these reasons, some topics are touched on in more than one chapter, but these cases are always cross-referenced and the most in-depth treatment is to be found simply by looking for the chapter with the appropriate title. The emphasis has also been on establishing the practical significance of all the topics covered from the outset, and to provide multiple opportunities for relating general and theoretical concepts to practical situations. The text may appear dauntingly large, but it has been designed to allow a 'mix and match' approach by teachers and students, so that particular chapters may be selected as they appear relevant. We hope that these features will help teachers to use the book as the basis of a wide-ranging discussion on HRM's central issues.

Each chapter follows a similar pattern, with the following common features:

- an initial set of clearly articulated intended learning outcomes
- an introductory or 'starter' case study at the beginning of each chapter designed to establish the significance of the topic under discussion and to stimulate thinking around it
- a main case study at the end of each chapter intended to incorporate a wider range of issues and designed to illustrate the dilemmas and complexity often faced by the HR professional
- reflective activities, interspersed throughout, designed to help students make links between theory and practice
- illustrative tables systematically showing how British practice relates to that in other major European countries, in order to illustrate national variations in HR practices; we have generally sought where possible to include illustrative material from a range of countries
- a list of key learning points at the end of each chapter, designed to sum up major 'take-away' points and to allow busy students and teachers to distil a central set of messages.

The illustrative material provided in each chapter adds a distinctive dimension by taking an important practice and showing its incidence in a selection of European countries. They are taken from Cranet data (which one of the editors and a chapter author played a part in collecting) and the British Workplace Employment Relations Survey (WERS). Cranet is a network of academics spread across some 40 countries that has conducted surveys of HR practices in those countries since 1989. It asks the most senior HR practitioner in each surveyed organisation a wide range of questions about HR practices. WERS, by contrast, is a more detailed survey of employment relations practices conducted since 1980 that asks questions of both managers and employee representatives. Both surveys completed their most recent iterations in 2004. Further details of the surveys are available in Brewster and Hegewisch (1993), Tregaskis, Mahoney and Atterbury (2004) [both for Cranet] and Kersley, Alpin, Forth, Dix, Bryson and Bewley (2005) [for WERS].

At the very end of the book is a list of references and works for further reading, intended to show the main works in each area and to build on the insights offered herein.

The chapters are grouped in sections to allow teachers and students to select them for study both by subject and approach. In terms of their subject matter, the first section deals with both societal and corporate contexts and facilitates discussion of how these impact on the work of HR professionals. The second group of chapters provides a bridge with the third, by discussing issues linked with resourcing, which we think of as being positioned at the interface between external contexts and the workplace practices that occupy HR professionals. The third section deals with these latter issues, and is concerned with the important topics of employee development and performance management through reward and appraisal systems. The fourth section is about areas that potentially bring practitioners into contact with employee representatives, such as communication, employment relations and health and safety. Our fifth section contains more discursive and theoretical discussion, dealing as it does with subjects that we think of as of great contemporary significance (such as CSR) or at the borders between HR and other subjects such as organisational behaviour (including work organisation). A further characteristic of many of the chapters in these intermediate sections is that authors such as Terence Jackson on cross-cultural management and Peter Critten on HRD have taken novel and stimulatingly alternative perspectives on their subjects. The sixth and final section contains only a shortish chapter that looks at possible future developments in the HRM context.

The text's underlying philosophy is that of the 'collaborative' rather than the 'calculative' view of HR, which emphasises employees' as participants in a project based on commitment and participation (Gooderham, Nordhaug and Ringdal, 1999). To this extent, it takes a European rather than a US or 'calculative' view. It is therefore in the 'human relations' tradition discussed by several chapter authors. Although a further theme is the necessity to relate all HR issues to the business needs, we also recognise that businesses should be meeting the needs of all stakeholders, including employees. While there is still room to debate the precise contribution HR makes to the 'bottom line', there is in our view little room for debate on whether employees should be treated as more than simply a 'resource'. The text also recognises the continued relevance of the industrial relations tradition, largely because of that tradition's awareness of the possibility of conflicting interests in the employment relationship. Finally, there is a general concern in the text with issues of diversity, ethics and sustainability.

The book is the product of a group of teachers, most of them based at or associated with Middlesex University Business School, with long practical experience of HR issues and with considerable collective experience of teaching HRM at undergraduate and postgraduate level. The editors would like to thank many people for their help in what has been a considerable undertaking. We would especially like to thank Dr Michael Brookes, who compiled the tables in each chapter and Dr Pauline Dibben who led the project initially. The CIPD's staff have been supportive and unfailingly helpful. We also thank our six anonymous external readers for taking the time to read through and comment on the text, and Heike Schröder and Sebastian Fuchs for help with editing. Finally, we thank our students, for without them the experience that the book draws on would not exist – nor would the future of HRM look as positive as it does. Thank you also to Kate McClunes for her contributions to the website.

SECTION 1

HRM in Context

CHAPTER 2

The context of HRM

Paul Higgins *and* Philip Frame

INTRODUCTION

This chapter concerns the context of HRM within an organisation's environmental setting. It involves a critical examination of the key environmental factors that influence and shape organisations and the practice of HRM within them.

LEARNING OUTCOMES

By the end of this chapter readers should be able to:

- identify the key characteristics of organisations
- describe and analyse the key environmental factors that influence the HRM process within different types of organisations
- critically discuss ways in which organisations can monitor these environmental influences with particular reference to labour markets
- identify sources of information that can help HR managers to gain a detailed understanding of what is happening in employment markets affecting their organisation.

After the starter case study we identify the key characteristics of organisations by reference to their common features, ownership type, orientation and size. This part concludes with a discussion of the role of the HR process within organisations (there is more information on this subject in Chapter 20), and also provides the chance to test the reader's understanding of some of the key characteristics of organisations.

In the second part of the chapter, attention turns to the organisational environment and in particular how it can be described and analysed. We explore two models: the systems and the PEST model, using examples taken from a variety of different organisational settings, and pay particular attention to the HRM process. During this part the chance is afforded readers to apply these models to organisations known to themselves. We conclude with a summary of the environment in its entirety.

The third part of the chapter then builds upon the frameworks provided by the systems and PEST models by outlining and critically examining the ways in which organisations can monitor both potential and actual changes that they have identified in their environment. This is considered from the perspective of the monitoring of labour markets and the impact they have on the HR function within different types of organisations. Again, during this part, readers are asked to apply their knowledge to the various issues raised.

The chapter concludes with the main case study.

Reference sources named within the chapter may be looked up in the *References and further reading* section at the end of the book.

STARTER CASE STUDY

John, the HR manager has just arrived, and joins the team for its weekly meeting, a standing item for which is the latest instructions from headquarters. The team comprises John himself, his assistant Julie and their three administrators: Gary, Keith and Michelle. Headquarters is in London, but their outpost is located in the north-east of England. There is a general feeling that headquarters is ill-informed about outlying branches and that often its directives are totally irrelevant to local conditions. As a result, the team actively tries to avoid as many of these directives as it can without putting its members' future or that of the branch in danger.

Today's directive concerns the environment. There is a new requirement that branch employees actively monitor the local external environment. Something has happened at another branch which evidently came as a complete surprise and initially posed a significant threat to the branch's continued operations there. Headquarters does not want any more such surprises! The organisation intends to include this requirement in each and everyone's job description, but before it does so, it intends to try out a pilot scheme.

Members of the team are a little uncertain of what 'the environment' means. Is it about green issues and carbon footprints? There is general agreement that they are doing their bit on the recycling front, with ink cartridge and paper re-use. Most of the branch's products are produced locally, so the carbon issue is of no great significance, it is felt. So what is left and how can they find out? And then 'monitoring' – what does that mean, and how are they to go about it? Someone suggests that it is similar to what the sensible person might do when thinking about buying something new and major, such as a car – you'd ask your friends and neighbours and look at relevant consumer magazines. In other words, you would try to get as much information as possible before making a decision on what to do. But no, monitoring is not just focused on the customer, it is suggested, although the methods might be the same. And everyone who works at the branch is felt to be doing something similar, but on a private basis, not as an employee. Think of the impact if this personal activity is used for the organisational good.

The resources just aren't there, it is strongly asserted. And 'We have enough to do already' without additional tasks, the outcomes from which may well be difficult to quantify, which will make it difficult to sell to the staff because it seems unrelated to the outcomes-oriented focus of everyone's annual performance review. 'We are a small organisation here, unlike the bureaucracy in London.' Yet it is suggested that there may well be some advantages to becoming more aware of what is going on locally . . . over and above reducing the likelihood of surprises.

Questions for discussion

1 What do you think is meant by the term 'environment'?

2 How do you find out about or 'monitor' the outside world? Think of as many sources of information as you can and make a note of them.

3 What might the benefits of supplying local knowledge to headquarters be?

1 CHARACTERISTICS OF ORGANISATIONS

Organisations have been a key feature of human society for many years. They come in many different types, shapes and sizes, have various organisational and ownership structures, and exist in order to achieve goals and objectives (Mullins, 2007). Despite this, there are thought to be three major elements common to all organisations. These are ownership type, orientation and size.

OWNERSHIP TYPE

The broad strategic direction that managers take on behalf of the organisation depends in many respects on the type of organisational ownership. Ownership could be public, charitable/independent or private. The type of ownership is important to strategic direction because it helps to determine the purpose and financing of the organisation (Needle, 2004).

Firstly, the public sector is a broad area covering central government departments, local government departments, universities, schools, hospitals and public sector corporations. Organisations of this type are funded mostly by taxation and exist to serve society as a whole. Considered in terms of the UK government and society as a whole, the most important body is the state, which is normally thought of as: the executive, Parliament, the civil service, the judiciary, the armed forces and the police. Its purpose is to establish a legal framework, to develop economic policies, to provide basic services and infrastructure, and to protect the vulnerable and the environment.

Secondly, organisations from within the charities/independent sector, meanwhile, are non-governmental, non-profit-making in orientation, their funding coming from donations, government grants, user charges, subscriptions and merchandising. Charities tend to focus on particular areas of need. They therefore specialise in these chosen beneficiaries rather than seeking to serve society as a whole. Some organisations from this sector also take responsibility for services contracted or tendered out by such government organisations as health and local authorities (Hodge and Greve, 2005; Dibben, James, Roper and Wood, 2007).

Thirdly, private organisations are owned and financed by individuals, partners or shareholders, and they are principally accountable to these owners, their duty to society being regarded as very much a secondary responsibility, although this is currently changing (see Chapter 25). Their main aim is commercial in nature – to make a profit. In the UK context, three main types of private organisations can be identified: these are sole traders, partnerships and limited companies. Of these, limited companies comprise both public limited companies (plc) and private companies (ltd). The main difference between these two is that a plc has shares that are available for the general public to buy and the company is quoted on the stock market whereas the ltd does not and is not. Shares in private companies tend to be owned by the founders, family interest and/or current management. In both cases, the owners' liability is restricted to the amount that they have invested in the company, usually in the form of shares. Meanwhile, a sole trader is the most common form of ownership in the UK and is found in most small business start-ups. A key feature here is that of unlimited personal liability, which means that any debts are the responsibility of the owner. Finally, a partnership is essentially a collaboration for the shared interests of partners, and is found most commonly in such professions as law, accountancy and medicine. Ownership is shared on the basis that each partner puts capital into the firm, which is then taken out according to that share given when the partner leaves or retires. In common with sole traders, partnerships also have unlimited personal liability.

ORGANISATIONAL ORIENTATION

In addition to ownership, organisations can be distinguished on the basis of whether they are production- or service-oriented. Products relate to physical, material goods that can be seen and touched and which remain with the customer. Services, meanwhile, are called 'intangible' in the sense of being consumed at the point of delivery. Services cannot be stored, therefore, and estimations of their quality are influenced by users' subjective perceptions and expectations. A user's estimation of service quality also involves reference to service output and delivery, such as the consumption of a meal at a restaurant.

The orientation of an organisation can also be gauged by reference to its activities, which fall into the three key sectors of the national economy. These are the primary sector, the secondary sector and the tertiary sector. The primary sector refers to agriculture, fishing and the extraction of natural resources, such as oil and minerals. The secondary sector refers to manufacturing industry: the production of industrial products and the processing of commodities such as food. The tertiary sector, finally, refers to service industries, including distribution, hotels and restaurants, transport and communications, finance and business services, public administration, education and health.

ORGANISATIONAL SIZE

Organisations vary according to size. At the lower end of the scale are micro-businesses. These are organisations with fewer than 10 employees. In the middle range are those of small to medium size, with fewer than 250 employees. At the high end are those organisations with thousands of employees. These include such large public sector organisations as the NHS and local government and multinational organisations. Some famous brand companies exist in name only, their operating functions passed on to subcontractors (Kaletsky, 2006). At the same time, core and committed HR departments are more likely to be found in larger organisations where the problems of co-ordination and control of large and very varied groups of employees become important (Kersley et al, 2006).

Larger organisations are more likely to have someone like an employment relations or industrial relations manager who spends more than half his or her time on employment relations issues – as Table 1 shows. Readers may find more about employment relations in Chapter 17.

Table 1 The existence of an employee relations specialist within different types of organisation

Organisational characteristic	Employee relations specialist at the workplace or higher (%)
10–99 employees	17
100–999 employees	74
1,000–9,999 employees	91
10,000 or more employees	91
Stand-alone organisation	18
Part of a larger organisation	77
Private	53
Public	82

Source: Kersley *et al* (2006; p.41)

REFLECTIVE ACTIVITY

Look at Table 1.

What reasons can you give to explain the different percentage figures for employee relations specialists in stand-alone organisations and those in a part of larger organisations?

Likewise, why is it that a greater proportion of public sector organisations have employment relations specialists at the workplace level or higher, do you think?

2 DESCRIBING AND ANALYSING THE HRM CONTEXT

Having examined the key characteristics of organisations, we can now move on to consider the environmental factors that shape and influence their actual behaviour. Every organisation is influenced by factors in the environment which it is unable to fully control. These factors can be grouped and conceptualised in various ways so as to construct environmental models. HR managers can use these models to describe and analyse their organisational environment with a view to ensuring that the functions that they are responsible for are shaped accordingly, or that they take action to influence the environment in which they operate.

In this section we focus on two environmental models: the systems model and the PEST model. We then conclude by considering the environment as a whole.

THE SYSTEMS MODEL

HR managers can use the systems model to consider the environment in terms of inputs and outputs – the organisation's response to these two external elements is derived from its internal transformation process. The organisational transformation process is what adds value to the inputs so that as reformed outputs they can becomes sales to customers, or services to clients, and is therefore extremely important (Haslam, Neale and Johal, 2000).

Thus, taking for example the hypothetical car manufacturing organisation shown in Figure 1, we can see how it utilises such inputs as human resources, materials, finance, technology and information from the environment which it then transforms through its operational processes – such as manufacturing and servicing – to deliver these resources once more to the environment as goods and services.

Figure 1 A systems model of car manufacturing and servicing

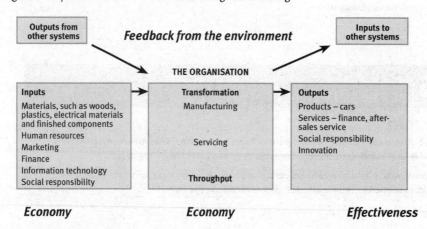

Source: adapted from Needle (2004, pp.38–9)

It is important to note in this model that although for many years it has been the function of car manufacturers to produce cars, the general oversupply and low margins associated with making cars has led many to focus on more profitable areas, such as finance for purchase. Many cars are no longer purchased in cash but are bought with financing deals such as loans or hire purchase. Thus the outputs of car producers, in addition to cars, are the financial packages they offer (Haslam *et al*, 1994). Of course the other feature that car producers spend vast amounts of money on – in addition to research and development – is marketing and advertising, as indicated in Figure 1.

In larger organisations it tends to be the task of HR managers to facilitate the process of efficient value adding, or transformation, by making sure that they hire the correct human resources and then retain them (see Chapters 7 and 8). In addition to this, human resource managers have also to provide training and development courses to ensure that employees can do their job (see Chapter 14); they must ensure that staff are provided with sufficient compensation and rest that they feel motivated to work hard, and ensure too that they are given appraisals and promotion opportunities for further development (see Chapters 12 and 13).

REFLECTIVE ACTIVITY

Apply the systems model to a service provider known to you.

What would the inputs, throughput and outputs be for your chosen organisation?

How does it add value to its inputs?

THE PEST MODEL

Another way to describe the external environment is by using the PEST model. The PEST model provides a particularly good tool to examine the general HRM context because it captures four important elements that shape and influence broad HR decisions. These elements are the Political, Economic, Social/Cultural and Technological aspects (see Figure 2), and each is considered in turn below.

Figure 2 The PEST model

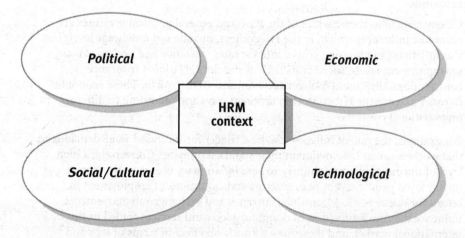

Political

The political environment is generally very important to HR managers, not least because included within it is the state and government. These have the power to make law and, therefore, to regulate the employment relationship between capital and labour, which trained HR managers are required to mediate (see Chapter 5). For example, the introduction of the National Minimum Wage by the Labour Government in 1999 determines minimum pay levels for UK workers, which HR managers must follow (Croucher and White, 2007). In addition, the law also shapes the bargaining power of employees and employers by detailing strike procedures, statutory recognition procedures and the minimum levels of employee information and consultation required in different types of organisations (see Chapter 19). Government laws and polices also shape the HRM context in less direct ways. Thus, for example, a policy of privatisation could provide a threat or an opportunity to an organisation depending on whether it faced the threat of losing contracts or had the opportunity to gain new markets (Domberger and Jensen, 1997).

In addition to national and local political factors there is also a wide range of international political factors. These too help to shape the general HRM context. Depending on the type of organisation, its ownership, size and activities, international political factors could involve the actions of the United Nations, such as an army or food agency; the activities of the World Trade Organisation (WTO), which might directly influence the operations of multinational corporations by opening up new markets and removing tariffs and other barriers to trade; and the activities of the European Union (EU), through such legal Directives as the Working Time Directive and the Part-Time Workers Directive. Finally, organisations might also be influenced by the activities of political pressure and interest groups that operate on the local, regional, national and international levels, and which may support or object to the organisation's intentions or behaviour.

Economic

Closely aligned to the activities of the state and general political pressures are economic influences which, in the HR context, include not only wage levels but also inflation (and housing costs), interest rates, currency and exchange rates, unemployment levels, social costs such as pensions, National Insurance contributions, direct and indirect taxation, and GDP growth. These economic factors influence the HR context in different ways and according to differing organisational contexts.

For example, the rate of inflation can be a trigger for increased wage demands so that workers can at least maintain their standard of living. Conversely, a high level of unemployment might help to ease inflationary pressures because unemployed people accept poorer terms and conditions of employment in return for scarce work. Meanwhile, currency and exchange rate movements influence the competitiveness of domestic goods and services traded in the international market, and these have a knock-on effect in terms of jobs and prosperity (Rugman and Collinson, 2006). Thus, for example, a strong currency would make a country's exports more expensive to overseas importers – with perhaps negative consequences for the security of jobs – whereas the country's imports would become cheaper. Finally, gross domestic product (GDP) growth and distribution might offer HR managers an insight into the strength of the economy and their confidence of it in the future. Under good conditions managers might try to expand through recruiting more workers, for example.

Social/cultural

The third part of the PEST model is social or social/cultural. This factor relates mainly to shifts in values and lifestyle, and in the HR context could involve a consideration of employees' attitudes to work and leisure, a consideration of wider demographic changes and potential pension costs, and general cultural values towards age, gender, sexuality and mobility, which may have an impact on recruiting strategies (see Chapters 6 and 8). The public's opinion towards Third-World debt, pollution, ethical trading and national competitiveness also helps to shape the general environment which HR managers are a part of.

Technological

Technological factors relate to the application of available knowledge and skills to create and use materials, processes and products. Technological change is very relevant to the HRM context. It can lead both to the displacement of labour by machines and to the creation of new jobs that require the skills to work with new technologies and jobs in companies making and supplying technological equipment. Indeed, in terms of job creation the emphasis has, in recent years, been put on the importance of employees' having transferable skills and of maintaining 'employability' as the opportunity for a 'job for life' disappears and as technological advances demand a skilled and trained labour force.

At the same time, technological advances have raised issues about the impact of e-/mobile communication between managers and the workforce and the surveillance of employees via sophisticated logging-on procedures for Internet use at work. It has also led to concerns about its impact on stress factors and tiredness, particularly amongst employees who are always on demand and contactable via email and mobile phone technology.

Teleworking, whereby employees use ICT to perform work at some distance from the organisation, can also add to the issues that HR managers should be aware of, and can bring advantages and disadvantages to the employee. For example, although teleworking can offer advantages to both employees (flexibility, reduced travelling costs) and employers (reduced costs), it does bring changes to the relationship between workers and the organisation that have to be carefully managed. These include potentially reduced promotion prospects caused by a lack of being visibly present, reduced chances for peer and professional development, reduced job security, confusion over the boundaries between home and work that influence social relationships, and greater feelings of social isolation that can lead to low motivation.

REFLECTIVE ACTIVITY

So far we have considered the PEST model from the perspective of the HRM environment.

Now apply the four factors of the PEST model to an organisation known to you.

For each of the four factors consider the respective influences.

PRIORITISING EXTERNAL INFLUENCES

When identifying key environmental factors, they must additionally be prioritised in terms of their importance and potential impact. In doing this, it is important to recognise that the nature of these influences changes both on a daily basis and, more seriously, as shocks to the system arise, often unexpectedly. There are four dimensions of analysis that can be employed to get a general feel of the organisation's overall environment: these are shown in Figure 3.

Figure 3 Dimensions of environmental analysis

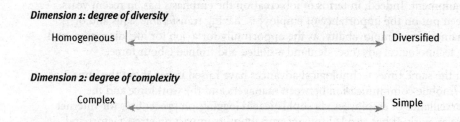

The first dimension, the degree of diversity, draws attention to the degree of diversity in the organisation's market. For example, a firm who supplies a single product to a single customer would have a homogeneous market. Conversely, a multi-product conglomerate serving a diverse group of clients would have a diversified market. Homogenous markets tend to be simpler to monitor than diversified markets.

The second dimension measures the degree of complexity. This dimension focuses on a) the number of significant environmental factors, and b) the degree of similarity or diversity between them. The greater and more diverse the number of significant environmental factors, the more complex is the environment.

The third dimension is concerned with the degree of routine. It concerns environmental change and the extent to which elements in the organisation's environment stay the same over time. In other words, is the organisation's environment static or dynamic? In making judgements about the degree of routine, much will depend on the degree of predictability or uncertainty in the organisation's environment and the rate of change within it.

The fourth dimension measures the degree of hostility and especially how far the environment supports or undermines the organisation's activities. A supportive or hostile environment could emerge as a result not only of favourable and unfavourable government policy but also as a result of the activities of a pressure group which might be supportive or hostile to an organisation's activities and behaviour.

REFLECTIVE ACTIVITY

Drawing upon the same organisation you applied the PEST model to earlier, consider its overall environment by reference to the four dimensions of analysis.

3 MONITORING ENVIRONMENTAL INFLUENCES

So far we have identified two useful ways to describe and analyse the general HRM context – the systems and the PEST models. We have also noted how managers can consider the overall complexity of the environment by referring to four further dimensions of analysis. Attention can now be turned to how organisations monitor changes in their identified environmental influences. For it is one thing to know what the most significant environment factors faced by organisations are, but it is quite another to know how to monitor and to respond to them.

In considering how organisations monitor changes in their environment, we remain focused on the HRM context and, in particular, examine the impact of labour markets on planning and strategic choice in HRM (see Chapters 3 and 7). The reason for this focus is that the labour market influences the supply and demand of one of the most important organisational resources – the human resource. This section therefore continues by first providing a brief and simplified overview of the labour market and then by investigating the implications of changes in it for HR managers. It ends by identifying the sources of information that can help HR managers to obtain a detailed understanding of changes in the labour market so that they can orientate their organisational strategy accordingly.

THE EMPLOYMENT MARKET

The simplest way to conceptualise the labour market is to see it as an economic exchange between two equal parties comprising the employer and the employee. The former buys or demands labour and the latter provides or supplies labour.

The demand for labour – the number of jobs offered by employers – is the total number of employees in employment plus the number of unfilled jobs. The extent of demand for labour depends on the amount of goods and services produced by the employer in a specific market. When the demand for the organisation's goods and services increases, the organisation's demand for labour rises, and when the demand for goods and services falls, the organisation's demand for labour also falls.

The supply of labour, in contrast, is the total number of people of working age (between school-leaving and state retirement ages) who are in employment and the number of hours that they are able and willing to work. In real terms, the amount of labour available to firms at any one time is influenced by the number of people of working age who are in employment or are *seeking* employment, and these people as a whole are classified as being *economically active*. Not everyone of 'working' age is therefore in employment at any one time because there are always some people who are not in work or seeking work. This part of the workforce is described as *economically inactive* and it typically includes those with caring responsibilities for children or other dependants, those who have retired from work, and people who are incapacitated through ill health or disability.

In addition to describing the potential size of the workforce in terms of economically active and inactive people, the actual workforce can be considered in terms of employment and unemployment. The employed segment of the workforce contains those in paid work, including those working full-time or part-time, temporarily or permanently, and as employees, workers or on a self-employed basis. In contrast, the term 'unemployed' is used to describe those people who are currently not in work but would like to be. Unemployed people can generally be classified in three different ways. Firstly, they might be classified as structurally unemployed – those who are unemployed as a result of the loss of whole industries such as (in Western Europe) mining and ship-building. Secondly, they might be classified as frictionally unemployed – those who are temporarily out of work because they are between jobs. Thirdly, the unemployed might be classified as being seasonally unemployed, which affects those who have no work during non-active seasons such as winter or summer.

Nationally, the unemployment rate in the United Kingdom stands at between 4 and 5% (2005–2007), or at about 1·5 million people. Although this figure might appear to be fairly high, it is less than half the amount of unemployment that was registered in 1993, when the number of people out of work was around the 3 million mark. It is also less than half of the equivalent rate in Germany and France. However, much of the explanation behind the relatively low levels of unemployment in recent years is a result of tightening definitions of unemployment and the increasing use of non-standard employment, including self-employment, part-time work, temporary agency work, temporary or fixed-term contracts, and home-working (Grimshaw, Marchington, Rubery and Willmott, 2005). In 1993, for example, 40% of the UK workforce was employed on either a part-time, self-employed or temporary basis. Another significant development in the supply of labour has been the growing feminisation of the labour force. Women's share of total employment increased from about one third (33%) in the late 1950s to 42% in 1980 to nearly half (50%) in 1998. Although this has contributed to greater levels of employment and lower levels of unemployment, the work undertaken by women remains largely distinct from that undertaken by men: the majority of women workers are engaged not only in clerical, serving and cleaning work but also often on a part-time or temporary basis.

REFLECTIVE ACTIVITY

What is the difference between being economically active and economically inactive and being employed or unemployed – and how does this affect the work of HR professionals?

SOME IMPLICATIONS OF CHANGING EMPLOYMENT MARKETS FOR HR MANAGERS

At an organisational level the composition of the labour supply in terms of skills and other attributes greatly affects the sourcing of different types of employees and the wages and salaries they are able to get. In industries where employers have recruitment difficulties and skill shortages, such as those dependent on new technologies, it is very important for the HR managers concerned to target their recruiting efforts accordingly. Another strategy that HR managers can use to deal with skill shortages is to focus on candidates' potential rather than current ability. In this way, candidates with the potential to perform to the desired standards can be recruited and then trained until they are sufficiently qualified. HR managers can also analyse the employment market from the perspective of its current workforce so as to gain a fuller understanding of such problems as low employee retention, particularly if current employees are being 'poached' or lured away by other employers.

The age structure of the population is also an important determinant of labour supply as firms draw labour from the portion of the total population that is of working age. The overall trend in the UK, Japan and Germany is of an ageing population, with increasing numbers of people aged over 65 and decreasing numbers of children under 16. For HR managers the implications of changes in the age structure of the population are many. For example, there could be more competition amongst employers for young workers. Likewise, as the average age of the working population increases, HR managers will be asked to develop employment strategies which succeed in attracting and retaining older workers (McNair and Flynn, 2005). They will also have to develop sophisticated means to manage sickness absence.

In addition to the age and skills of people, what other issues should HR managers be aware of when considering the potential impact of employment markets on HRM?

What can they do to plan for the issues identified?

RESPONDING TO CHANGES IN EMPLOYMENT MARKETS

At an organisational level, HR managers are required to ensure that their demand for suitably qualified staff is matched with what is available to them in terms of supply. In seeking to attract and retain suitably qualified staff, this balancing process involves a variety of HRM activities including recruitment, induction, appraisal, promotion, training, reward, retirement and redundancy. Such human resource planning can be seen to lie at the heart of the HRM function's recognising the importance of people to organisational strategy and performance.

Conventionally, human resource planning involves forecasting the supply and demand of labour so that the necessary actions can be implemented to rectify situations of labour shortage or surplus. The most common approach to this is managerial judgement whereby managers estimate the human resources necessary for the achievement of corporate goals. Estimates are likely to be based on a combination of past experience, local knowledge and instinct.

HR planners will also collect data from local, national and international labour markets, depending on the nature of jobs and the skills required, helping them to make these judgements. Data can be collected by formal or informal means, including national and local surveys, and information provided by applicants on application forms and CVs. Analysis may also relate to the ways in which human resources are currently managed – for example, to the extent that the current workforce structure, job design and reward system enhance or restrict productivity and performance levels.

In addition to specific labour market data, HR managers tend also to find out about general changes in environmental conditions by reading newspapers, industry publications and business periodicals. Of these, the latter tend to capture news items and developments within a fairly focused but still broad area of interest such as economics, law and HRM. Industry publications, meanwhile, are journals specific to particular industries such as nursing, accountancy and engineering.

Benchmarking also has a central role in understanding organisational performance within a particular labour market because by definition it involves managers' learning and adopting best (or at least better) HR practices by comparing their own practices with those of other more successful organisations. In undertaking HR benchmarking, HR managers must first identify which practice they wish to benchmark. This could be, for example, HR training, recruitment or reward systems, or the collecting of productivity and performance data. Managers must then identify suitable benchmark partners who not only use recognised best practices but who are also prepared to participate in the benchmarking exercise. Chosen benchmark comparators may include internal departments or external competitors and non-competitors in the same industry, national organisations or international organisations. Following analysis of benchmarking data, managers should thirdly identify the performance gaps between the way things are currently undertaken within their own organisation and the desired or best practice of others. Action plans should then be created so as to enable their organisation to close the gap between the current and desired performance.

REFLECTIVE ACTIVITY

List industry publications and business periodicals that HR managers might regularly read to keep them informed of changes in the HR environment.

How would you, as an HR manager, seek to monitor changes in the type and supply of labour sourced from university graduates?

KEY ISSUES IN THE CONTEXT OF HRM

We now pull together ten key points about the context of HRM raised in this chapter:

- Organisations come in many different types, shapes and sizes, have various organisational and ownership structures, and exist in order to achieve goals and objectives.

- Organisations can also be distinguished on the basis of whether they are production- or service-oriented and by reference to their core activities, which fall into one or more of the three key sectors of the national economy: primary, secondary and tertiary.

- HR managers can use environmental models such as the systems model and the PEST model to describe and analyse their organisational environment.

- The systems model can be used to consider the environment in terms of inputs and outputs, with the organisation's response to these two elements centring on its internal transformation process. HR managers are particularly involved in ensuring the effective operation of the organisation's value-adding processes.

- The PEST model provides a particularly good tool to examine the general HRM context by capturing four salient elements that shape and influence broad HR decisions: these are political, economic, social and technological.

- In addition to identifying key environmental factors HR managers can also prioritise them in terms of their importance and potential impact. This can be achieved by reference to four dimensions of analysis to garner the overall environmental complexity.

- One of the key influences on HR managers is the employment market. Perhaps the simplest way to conceptualise the employment market is to view it as an economic exchange between the employer who purchases or demands labour and the employee who provides or supplies labour.

- The composition of the labour supply in terms of skills and other attributes impacts greatly on the sourcing of different types of employees and the wages and salaries they are able to command.

- Human resource managers can collect data about employment markets from numerous sources including surveys, application forms and CVs.

- Benchmarking can be used as a tool for evaluating the organisation's HRM strategy and HRM practices in the light of information about other organisations' practices.

Perhaps there are other key points that you would like to note for yourself.

The main case study in this chapter now follows. It gives an example of the importance that organisations should place on the monitoring of the external environment.

Look at the description of the case set out below. Then decide on the recommendations that you would make as an HR manager for dealing with the issues raised. Try to think beyond the level of a 'quick fix' or simple solutions by developing a longer-term strategy as well as responding to the immediate issue.

Atif is sitting in the staff lounge of the white goods company where he works, reading the local paper. It's his mid-morning break and he's on his own – which is a pity, he thinks, because there is something really interesting on page 4 which he'd like to tell his colleagues about, not least because items of interest are few and far between in the *Coketown Times*.

Back once more in the HR section of the open-plan office, Atif starts talking to his four colleagues: two administrators like himself, Garry and Alice, the HR assistant Shilpa, and their manager Darren. They all find the news he's spotted equally interesting and decide to book a meeting-room to discuss the issue properly without attracting the glares of their open-plan colleagues.

The story is about the Council's decision to agree to a change of use, from office accommodation to retail, for a town centre property following some lengthy and not-so-subtle lobbying on the part of a rival white goods firm. And it has come as a bit of a surprise to Atif and his colleagues. But is it a threat? Or is it perhaps even an opportunity?

Alice says that her next-door neighbour knows a councillor and they have been complaining about the time taken in meetings to listen to different stakeholders' arguments, whatever development was proposed for the town centre.

'It won't affect us. We've been here for years, and our reputation's good,' says Darren cheerfully.

'They sell discounted stuff, though – cheaper than us,' counter Gary and Shilpa.

Darren replies, 'But people buy from people at the end of the day, and we've got some real selling experts.'

'Well, they might drive us under unless we do something,' suggests a rather gloomy Atif.

'So what is this something we need to do?' is what Alice wants to know.

They agree to raise the matter with the director responsible for HR issues and to make recommendations for action, both for the immediate future and the longer term.

Questions for discussion

1 What is the potential impact of this development on Atif and his colleagues, both as HR specialists and as employees?

2 Recalling the work you did on sources of information for the starter case study of this chapter, what sources are Atif and his colleagues using, and what others could they use?

3 Why has the development described come as a surprise?

4 What range of responses to this development should be recommended to the director?

5 What long-term strategy would you recommend?

EXPLORE FURTHER

BROOKS, I., WEATHERSTON, J. and WILKINSON, G. (2004) *The International Business Environment.* Harlow, Prentice Hall/Financial Times
This is a very useful book which provides a broad coverage of the external environment confronted by both large and small organisations in an international context. It is particularly strong on PEST analysis and considers competitive, ecological and legal issues too.

MORRISON, J. (2006) *The International Business Environment: Global and local marketplaces in a changing world.* Basingstoke, Palgrave Macmillan
This slightly more up-to-date textbook again charts the key dimensions of the international business environment, highlighting transitional and developing economies as well as advanced economies.

MULLINS, L. (2007) *Management and Organisational Behaviour.* Harlow, Prentice Hall/Financial Times
This book provides a thorough overview of organisational behaviour and management, large chunks of it devoted to organisations, the management of human resources and the organisational environment.

NEEDLE, D. (2004) *Business in Context.* London, Thomson Learning
This excellent textbook provides a detailed and rounded examination of the business environment, drawing upon many useful examples and case studies.

CHAPTER 3

People and human resources strategies

Andrew Mayo

INTRODUCTION

'Strategy' is a much overused word, but essentially it is about making choices. Typically, these are choices about which direction the organisation should take in order to meet a goal. Strategies then also have to be implemented through practical plans, sometimes called 'tactics'. When we talk about 'HR strategy' it can have two meanings. The first meaning is a strategy for 'people management', which should follow clearly from the organisational or business strategy, because – as mentioned at the beginning of Chapter 2 – this is what makes HRM different from personnel management. The second meaning corresponds to a strategy for the HR function itself – how it will be structured, what it will or will not outsource, what skills and software support it needs. Readers may have encountered phrases like 'being linked with' (eg Boxall and Purcell, 2003; p6), 'being aligned to' (Holbeche, 2001), and 'being driven by' the business strategy. The last one of these is the closest to how it should be. Ulrich and Brockbank (2005; p.150) phrase HR's primary deliverable as 'organisational capability' – the capability to meet the business strategy.

In formulating any strategy we have to decide what we will do and why, what we will *not* do (the difficult bit) and why, and how we will implement it. All of these involve *choices* – and that is what strategies are about.

LEARNING OUTCOMES

By the end of this chapter readers should be able to:

- explain the basics of strategy formulation in general
- identify the factors that have to be considered in order to create or revise a strategy for people management
- explain the steps to be undertaken to develop such a strategy
- list and explain the factors to be considered in building a strategy for the HR function itself.

The chapter is divided into two parts. Part 1 is about how we create a strategy for people in an organisation. This leads to determining what HR activities – both ongoing and specific initiatives – are the *right* things to do. Part 2 is about a strategy for the HR function itself – for example, how it will be organised, what professional tools it will use – in order to deliver the people strategy.

Reference sources named within the chapter may be looked up in the *References and further reading* section at the end of the book.

STARTER CASE STUDY

ABC Software is located in south London. The founder, now chairman, created a unique software product 10 years ago that does geographic profiling based on postcode. Customers buy the product once, but they need to buy annual updates to maintain its usefulness. This is a very profitable business model. After considerable success in the UK, the company has since expanded into some European countries, Australia and the USA. Today, about 15% of revenues come from international operations and the five-year plan is to move this to 50%.

The company has about 350 people. Of the 310 in UK, about 90 are in sales and marketing, 150 in product development and support, 30 in customer service, and the rest in senior management and support functions. In addition to London, there are offices in Birmingham and Manchester, which have about 25 people between them. Headcount growth over the next five years is expected to be about 60 net, and to involve some jobs in the UK being eliminated and more being created abroad.

The chairman recruited a CEO early on and let him get on and run the company. However, he has liked to interview every new recruit to make sure they 'fitted' the culture he wanted to build. He did this until the company reached about 250 staff. The average age of the staff is just over 30, and a strong culture has been created which might be described as 'work hard, play hard'. Unlike many software companies, everyone comes to work in suits, even developers, and employees generally join in the many social events organised by the company.

Your task

You have just joined as the first HR director reporting to the director of support services. There are two HR people, looking after administration and recruitment but with little time for anything else. The CEO has asked you to prepare a people strategy for the company as soon as you have settled in.

What questions do you need to ask, and of whom?

1   BUILDING A PEOPLE STRATEGY

UNDERSTANDING WHAT WE MEAN BY 'STRATEGY'

There are many words connected with planning that can cause confusion. We have goals, objectives, values, visions, missions, plans, strategies, targets and policies – how do all these fit together coherently?

- *A mission* describes what the purpose of the organisation is and what it is there to do.

- *A vision* is an end point of where we want to get to in the long term – maybe what we will be known for or a position we will attain.

- *Goals* are specific targets on the way to the vision, usually over a time period of two to five years.

- *Targets* are the measures that apply to the goals.

- *Strategies* are the routes we have chosen to achieve the goals.

- *Values* are the ways in which we want to behave in achieving our goals. This may (and should) include beliefs and principles about how we will do business – how we will treat our employees, our customers, our suppliers and/or the public.

- *Policies* are about how we will do certain things, consistent with our values.

- *Plans* are detailed actions for implementation in the foreseeable period ahead.

All of these can apply to an organisation as a whole, or to a part of it. Usually one organisation shares the same values and policies. Visions and missions may be written for parts of an organisation as subsets of 'umbrella' statements.

REFLECTIVE ACTIVITY

Jot down on a piece of paper all the options you have to travel from your home to your place of study. One will be your preferred option. We might call this your 'travel strategy'.

What factors did you weigh up and balance to make your choice?

In the case of the exercise above you probably made your choice based strongly on the *resources* available. There is an important lesson here – that chosen strategies have to be implementable. The secret with strategies does not lie with analysis but with the ability to turn strategy into practical plans and then to do what we have decided.

Organisations have to decide their main business strategies, and then departments put together their own, which support the main strategy. In the commercial world the strategy will be about how to achieve goals of revenue, profit and market share. The public sector is more about implementing policy – either political policy or to meet the needs of the section of the public it serves. This is another important lesson – that all the supporting strategies must be *driven* by where the organisation itself wants to go. We do not write a people strategy based purely on our own beliefs and what we know is good practice in HR.

This assumes that organisations do have a strategy. Whether it is written down or not, choices have been made. Often the strategy is not written down but emerges in an opportunistic way. Frequently, organisations have formally articulated neither their beliefs nor their principles. We will come back to that later, but clearly it makes life more difficult if there is nothing openly agreed and written. Table 2 shows some data about the existence of strategic plans in UK workplaces.

Table 2 The existence of strategic business plans in British organisations

	Percentage of organisations with no strategic plan
All workplaces	30
Organisation size 10–99 employees	53
10,000 or more employees	7
Manufacturing	46
Hotels and restaurants	50
Financial services	7
Public sector	6

Source: Kersley *et al* (2006)

This data has changed very little since 1998 and suggests that smaller organisations in particular often have no formal strategic plans.

SOME BASIC TOOLS FOR CREATING A STRATEGY

Thousands of books have been written on strategic planning and this is not the place to go into them in detail. Figure 4 captures the steps needed very well (Davies, 1993).

We must start with understanding where we are and where we want to get to. There are then a series of steps to go through. The first set is about formulating

Figure 4 A model of the strategic planning process

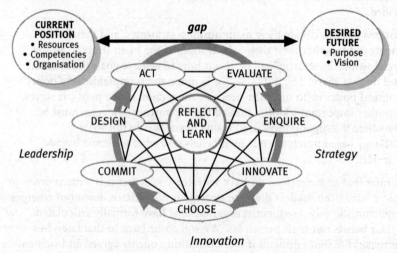

Source: Davies (1993)

the strategic options – evaluating the situation, researching and analysing, being creative and breaking out of the past – all to generate the choices. The second set of steps is about making the choices happen.

There are two well-known tools to use in the first phase. One looks predominantly at the external environment and is the PEST framework (see Chapter 2). The second useful tool is called SWOT analysis. It is a simple evaluation of our Strengths, Weaknesses, Opportunities and Threats in relation to what we want to achieve. It is more directed to looking internally at our capability, although opportunities and threats will look externally as well. Normally, it is drawn up on a page as four quadrants, with relevant items placed in each. What we want to be able to do is to see how we can harness the positives and mitigate the negatives.

Why would we want to write a strategy?

It is important to think through the *purpose* of writing a strategy and the *audiences* for it. The obvious answer is 'to decide systematically what we are going to do'. But there are other goals to be achieved too. A strategy may be demanded by an internal process or by external 'masters' (such as parent companies or governments). If we do not see benefits for ourselves in doing it, we will be tempted to do the minimum. It can be an important communication vehicle. We can use it to explain to others what we are doing and why, not least the HR people themselves. Furthermore, a strategy can be a means of seeking endorsement and resources. If it is logically argued from the business strategy and designed to support it, it can be powerful. Finally, it can provide visibility and credibility for colleagues and for external partners.

The style and tone of any document (or part of it) would be conditioned by its audiences. Note that a lot of people strategies or HR strategies look as if they have come straight from a textbook, using vague generalisations of 'good things' to do with people. They could refer to any organisation. A people strategy should be designed for *your* people in *your* organisation and be distinctive and specific. The methodology that follows will help readers do that. We also have to be realistic about what we can achieve – we have culture and traditions, and particular types of employees, and these things do not change easily or quickly: they take time.

A MODEL FOR DECIDING OUR PEOPLE STRATEGY

In practice we never start from nothing. You might tell me that you do not have a people strategy – meaning that it is not written down. But in fact you are doing some things and not doing others. So when we talk about 'creating' a people strategy it is more likely to be 'revising' – taking a new look at where we are, where we are going and how to get there.

Figure 5 illustrates the key drivers of our strategy. This is modelled on Schuler (1992; p.20), who then leads the analysis into a '5P' set of HR activities – HR philosophy, policies, programmes, practices and processes.

As we have said, the business strategy itself is key. We then have to think about the external factors – using PEST – from the point of view of HR and people. These are usually significant: there is always changing legislation about employment and

Figure 5 The drivers of an HR strategy

external factors affecting the labour market. Thirdly, there are internal issues. Every organisation has problems – things that do not run as well as they might. We may have morale, turnover or absentee problems: processes like performance management that are not working well, lack of skills to do a good job, conflicts in the organisation, and so on. Finally (and it *is* finally), the last influence is HR professional practice. Developments in HR practices must be watched to see if they would benefit *our* organisation. All these are encased in our values, beliefs and principles. If these are diverse and not commonly held, we will lack coherence in the implementation of any strategy. When we examine any one driver we have one simple question to ask. What are the implications of values, principles and beliefs on people in the organisation, specifically in six areas of HRM? These are:

- organisation and culture
- rewards and recognition
- communications and employee relations
- resourcing
- general HR policies, and
- learning and development.

Let us take three examples. Suppose that one of the values of the organisation is 'teamworking'. Tables 3, 4 and 5 show some possible implications of this for our strategy in people management. You might have thought that none of these examples had much to do with HR, except perhaps the first. Wrong! Every manager's objective and every problem has people implications. Even plain financial forecasts have them.

Table 3 HR implications of business strategy: example 1

SUPPORTING: the value of teamworking	
Organisation and culture	• organisation structure team-based • building a culture of teams helping one another • 'the team is as important as the individual'
Rewards and recognition	• team bonus schemes • team awards • reduced emphasis on individual performance
Communications and employee relations	(not affected)
Resourcing	• a promotion factor would be team orientation
General HR policies	(not affected)
Learning and development	• effective teamworking, inter-team facilitation, being a team leader • multi-skilling

Table 4 HR implications of business strategy: example 2

SUPPORTING: EMEA division's target to grow market share in Africa	
Organisation and culture	• new team needed, based in Nigeria
Rewards and recognition	• review incentive scheme • local packages, salary and benefits
Communications and employee relations	(not affected)
Resourcing	• recruit local salespeople • appoint experienced international manager
General HR policies	• review foreign service policy • create local policies as needed
Learning and development	• sales training • African culture training

Did you notice that each table of Tables 3 to 5 supports a different *level* of issue? (See Mayo, 2004; pp13–14.) They have quite different time-scales. Each one fits on the continuum below in a different place:

Today's problem	*Current targets*	*The way we want to be*
Reacting	**Proacting**	**Continuing**
(Table 3)	(Table 4)	(Table 5)

The 'continuing' strategy fits with our mission, vision, values, beliefs and long-term business goals. It incorporates the key principles of people management, with processes and programmes that we operate each year. It is not of course continuing for ever. We would revise it every time there was a significant change

Table 5 HR implications of business strategy: example 3

SUPPORTING: reducing problem of customer complaints in large store	
Organisation and culture	• test general culture towards customers • check analysis of complaints to see if caused by organisational process inefficiencies such as shortages • conflicts between store needs and head office targets? • jobs suitably designed?
Rewards and recognition	• check rewards not a source of employee dissatisfaction • consider awards based on customer feedback
Communications and employee relations	• ensure all staff are aware of volume and reasons for complaints • institute regular 'service quality' groups
Resourcing	• enough staff? • shift patterns?
General HR policies	• review why people leave • check whether any policies (such as flexible working) are a source of discontent
Learning and development	• customer focus training needed? • personal skills training needed?

in the nature of the organisation itself, and from time to time we would test it for still being relevant. (In practice, whenever the CEO of an organisation changes, or the HR director, it is natural for them to review and often change the strategy in order to make their mark.)

The 'proacting' strategy is a set of initiatives to support the business units or departments in what they are seeking to achieve. It will include resourcing needs, and then specific initiatives, projects and learning programmes to support them.

The 'reacting' strategy is not really a strategy at all. Nevertheless, we still have to make choices. Every organisation has problems that are people-related – HR has to decide which are the priority ones to address and feed them into its plans. Since all strategies must lead to implementation plans, we cannot ignore this often very important category.

 EXERCISE

Imagine you are the HR director in a significant garden centre business. This year the company has decided to go online and offer its products for customers to order and have delivered to their doorstep.

Draw up a table similar to Tables 3 to 5, and think through the implications for people of this decision.

What questions should be asked in each category?

THE 'CONTINUING' PEOPLE STRATEGY

When we try and put this together, or review where we are, what factors will guide us? We need to follow the general outline of Figure 5 but start with the business and move clockwise. There is a great temptation by ambitious and idealistic people in HR to want the 'perfect' people management strategy according to every good practice that has been read about. Particularly in the public sector one can find HR strategies so far from reality as to have lost all credibility. You just cannot move some deeply entrenched cultures very fast. It actually is counterproductive to publish aspirations and then for employees to see no signs of them in reality.

What are the factors to be considered in putting together this part of the strategy? They are the following, and each will be explained in more detail:

- the vision and values of the organisation
- the beliefs and principles we have regarding people management and development
- the long-term business goals and strategies
- the core competencies of the organisation that we want to maintain
- the general external factors that affect our kind of organisation.

Vision and values

If we assume that the organisation does want these to become a reality (and one sometimes wonders whether some organisations do), then HR must ask how it will help that to happen. The values must be supported in many ways, such as through recruiting people who share them (see Chapter 8); training people to live them in their jobs (see Chapter 24); arranging peer or manager feedback to employees (see Chapter 12); rewarding the right behaviours *and* sanctioning undesired behaviours; promoting and rewarding people who demonstrate the values (see Chapters 12 and 13); designing processes that exhibit the values; and reinforcing them in communications (see Chapter 19). All too often this does not happen. HR can have an enormous influence in this area, and this is not a one-off programme at the time of launching of the values. It is an ongoing part of the people management strategy.

REFLECTIVE ACTIVITY

You are the HR director and one of the values of your organisation is 'taking responsibility'.

How would HR support such a value?

Beliefs and values in people management

Beliefs and values are a very important subject. HR people are generally in HR because they care about people being respected, valued and treated well. Not all line managers share their perspectives, and they have pressures on them to deliver results. This causes conflicts. On the one hand idealistic HR people have to move more towards reality, and on the other managers may have to be educated to understand that well-treated people produce better results. A *shared* philosophy of the principles of people management is therefore important. And there *are* choices. Figure 6 shows some of these choices. Whichever one is chosen will significantly impact the work HR has to do and its priorities. It will affect the *kind* of training we do, the *kind* of pay systems, the *kind* of organisation, and the *kind* of policies we create.

Figure 6 Options in people management beliefs

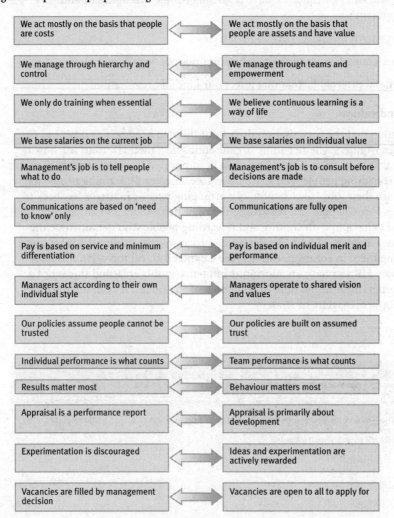

We act mostly on the basis that people are costs	We act mostly on the basis that people are assets and have value
We manage through hierarchy and control	We manage through teams and empowerment
We only do training when essential	We believe continuous learning is a way of life
We base salaries on the current job	We base salaries on individual value
Management's job is to tell people what to do	Management's job is to consult before decisions are made
Communications are based on 'need to know' only	Communications are fully open
Pay is based on service and minimum differentiation	Pay is based on individual merit and performance
Managers act according to their own individual style	Managers operate to shared vision and values
Our policies assume people cannot be trusted	Our policies are built on assumed trust
Individual performance is what counts	Team performance is what counts
Results matter most	Behaviour matters most
Appraisal is a performance report	Appraisal is primarily about development
Experimentation is discouraged	Ideas and experimentation are actively rewarded
Vacancies are filled by management decision	Vacancies are open to all to apply for

What is important is that HR does not itself decide what the beliefs should be. There is a great temptation to do so, and there is no reason why HR should not try to *exert influence* towards what it believes is the best philosophy. But the senior management team must decide –because they must 'own' and believe personally in what is decided. It is a good idea for the senior team just to write down a series of statements. The American pharmaceutical company Johnson & Johnson have a whole set of statements for all their stakeholders and call it their 'Credo' – here is the section for employees:

> *We are responsible to our employees, the men and women who work with us throughout the world. Everyone must be considered an individual. We must respect their dignity and recognise their merit.*
>
> *They must have a sense of security in their jobs. Compensation must be fair and adequate, and working conditions clean, orderly and safe.*
>
> *We must be mindful of ways to help our employees fulfil their family responsibilities.*
>
> *Employees must feel free to make suggestions and complaints.*
>
> *There must be equal opportunity for employment, development and advancement for those qualified. We must provide competent management, and our actions must be just and ethical.*
>
> *Extract from Johnson & Johnson's 'Credo'*

The long-term business goals and strategies

Long-term business goals and strategies are the third set of factors to consider. It may be that the organisation just plans to do more of the same (as today), hopefully better and more efficiently as years go by. But if it has ambitions – to acquire other companies, to create new subsidiaries, to expand internationally, and so on – we need to have 'the right people in the right place at the right time with the right skills' to meet the challenges. Some of these business goals might also require quite new HR policies and pay systems, for example.

Maintaining core competencies in the organisation

There are two different kinds of 'core competencies'. The first refers to the expertise that we need to have to be in our kind of business. If we are running an airline, for example, we have constant needs for pilots, yield optimisation experts and schedulers (to name a few). So we are constantly recruiting and training such people because it is our life. Another type of core competence is that which gives us a competitive advantage – we are better at them. Easyjet and Ryanair have all the experts other airlines do, but they are better at aircraft utilisation and it gives them a clear advantage. Our people strategy must be one that maintains all these core competencies.

External factors

Every organisation has its own external factors to take into account in the medium term – trends in the market or in regulation, for example, that must be considered in shaping our strategy. The PEST analysis (see Chapter 2) will help us identify these factors. For every factor we have identified under the five headings above, we are going to ask the same question as we asked earlier – what are the implications for the six areas of HRM? The implications may be of different kinds:

- they may shape our HR policies (the beliefs about people management may almost be policies in themselves, depending on how they are worded)
- they will shape sub-strategies for rewards, resourcing, organisation design and development and communications/employee relations
- they may lead to a long-term resourcing plan
- they may define a desired culture to aim for
- they may lead to people processes that we do not have
- they may lead to ongoing programmes of learning.

Bringing the 'continuing strategy' together

If we have done the above systematically, we will have a large number of tables such as Tables 3, 4 and 5 that need to be integrated into one. One way to do that is to have one sheet for each of the six HRM areas as shown in Table 6. Strategies often have just a series of intentions, such as the first (top) box in Table 6. But it is the other three boxes that will make it all work. Running the processes and developing short-term action plans which progress the strategy forwards will make a significant contribution to the question right at the beginning of the chapter-deciding 'what we should do and why'.

REFLECTIVE ACTIVITY

Go back to the garden centre we introduced in one of the previous exercises – the garden centre which serves both visiting and online customers. Imagine it has 250 employees, half of whom are part-time and/or seasonal, and 10 managers.

Go through the five areas to consider for putting together the 'continuing' strategy, with particular reference to the area of learning and development.

Draw up a table like Table 6 for learning and development.

Table 6 Example of an integrated sub-strategy for 'organisation and culture'

1 Policy statements
● We want an organisation that is agile and adaptable; therefore we will aim for a minimum number of layers between the front line and senior management.
● Wherever possible we will organise by process teams to maximise efficiency of flow and minimise hierarchy.
● We want to build a culture that truly reflects our values, and all stakeholders will experience them.
● It is essential for our business that new knowledge is rapidly shared. We will organise to minimise boundaries and generate a culture that is willingly and skilfully knowledge-sharing.
2 Processes
● We will have a steering committee on organisation design which will advise and approve all proposed changes in line with the policy statements.
● We will at least annually test our culture through perception surveys against the desired cultural template.
● We will set up a series of knowledge-sharing processes, such as communities of practice, project reviews, expert seminars and virtual discussion groups.
3 Supportive learning programmes
● We will have a section of new employee induction that emphasises the cultural behaviours expected.
● We will have regular programmes to learn effective knowledge-sharing techniques.
4 Resource requirements to implement this ongoing strategy
● The organisation steering committee will consist of part-time representatives from each main area of the business.
● An 'organisation development' team of two people within HR will be needed to facilitate this ongoing strategy.

THE 'PROACTING' AND 'REACTING' STRATEGIES

Some would say these are not really strategies but just plans and initiatives for the current year. Let us not worry about the words – we still need to make choices and priorities for what we will do in addition to running the 'continuing' strategy – supporting operational managers in their objectives and tackling problem areas.

Supporting operational managers (proactively)

It is normal in organisations for all managers to have current objectives and targets to go with them. HR typically might talk to each manager about a headcount plan and a training plan for the department concerned, but this approach starts off with many assumptions. A better way is to sit down with each manager when he or she has his/her objectives and go through a process of getting answers to questions like the following:

For each objective:

● What is the objective, and does it have a measurable endpoint?

● What factors are working for its achievement and what are working against it?

- Who (individuals or groups) are involved in these factors?
- What are the implications (if any) for each set of people in the six areas of HRM?

After doing this for all the objectives one by one:

- Which of all the actions and initiatives that we have noted would have the biggest impact on your goal achievement?

Note here that we are not talking about people generically, but specifically by group – or even by individual. What kind of actions might result? Examples are a recruitment task, a new bonus plan, special learning programmes, a new skill test, or some form of coaching.

Supporting operational managers (reactively)

Above, we sat down with managers to look forward and ask how we could support them in achieving their goals. At the same time we might ask another question: 'Are there any existing *problems* that you need help with?' If the organisation has a good metrics system (see Chapter 16), we might already have some data that would tell us about problems – signals coming from opinion surveys, labour turnover and attrition statistics, health and safety audits, and so on. But there may be problems less obvious to HR but still with people solutions. Problems with quality, productivity, project over-runs, compliance, budgets – all of these may benefit from professional HR attention. So we apply the five questions above in the same way – except that we substitute 'problem' for 'objective' and 'solution' for 'achievement'.

Integrating and prioritising

You can imagine that we might well end up with a long list of issues and potential initiatives as we go round all the managers. We will inevitably be limited to resources available and have to make choices. There will be items that we have no choice over and we just have to make a plan to get on with them – essential training or recruitment, for instance. But how do we decide about the rest? Figure 7 is a well-known method of helping to make prioritising easier. Look at the long list of all the things that could and should be done, and allocate them to one of the boxes in the figure. The two dimensions are the *impact* on the organisation's achievement and the *difficulty* of implementation. 'Quick wins' are always a temptation, especially for building credibility, and some are good – but it is the top two boxes that demand the most attention. Remember, it is fine to do the analysis and make statements of what we will do – the reality is in the detailed planning that implements it all. *Strategy should be 10% analysis and 90% implementation,* not the other way round. So all this has to be turned into practical, phased and resourced plans to make it happen.

We finally have to make sure that all the various initiatives do not conflict and that they support each other. This is called 'horizontal integration'. For example, we do not want to find that we have set cultural aspirations but are pursuing policies and processes in the reward sub-strategy that work against them.

Figure 7 Prioritisation of demands

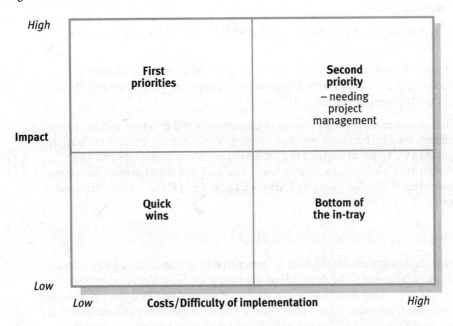

Lynda Gratton (2000) wrote a book called *Living Strategy*, which was about what she called 'the *path* of the journey'. It is about the environment in which our strategy will (or will not) be realised, and how to bridge philosophy or ideals to action. It is beyond the scope of this chapter to discuss the book in detail, but it is recommended for further reading.

Part 1 of this chapter has been about an organisation's people strategy – what policies, processes, programmes and projects we need for good people management and how HR and line managers can work in partnership to achieve this. These are all in addition to everyday administration which, as explained at the beginning of Chapter 2, is a fundamental part of HR work. Now it is time to look at the strategy for the HR function itself.

2 A STRATEGY FOR THE HR FUNCTION

The HR function, like other support functions (such as IT and Finance), exists to do the following:

- to carry out necessary administrative activities – in this case to do with people
- to ensure compliance and integrity with relevant legislation and company policies
- to represent the company externally on people issues as required
- to manage, usually jointly with line management, people management processes

- to apply professional knowledge to support the organisation and its managers in their goals

- to provide data and information that enables management to manage effectively.

The last three of these activities clearly interface with the people strategy discussed in Part 1. The function needs a strategy that will deliver all of these efficiently and effectively.

That means making choices about organisation of the function and the resources needed; the capabilities of people in the function; ongoing process evaluation and review; 'tools' to support the processes; people-related measures and standards of performance; involvement and dialogue with business managers; and external benchmarking and networking. Each of these is now examined in turn.

ORGANISATION AND RESOURCES

How the HR department should be structured is an important strategy choice. One key influence is the demands of the people strategy, but another is also the approach we want to take to resourcing. Historically, an HR department would have seen three main roles – administration, the professional generalist and the professional specialist. The *generalist* would look after a section of people – usually linked to a business or division – and the role often included some administration and specialist activity. The *specialist* would be dedicated to one area of HR.

Today, things are not so different in practice, but new words are in use and technology has had a big impact. Administration and quite a lot of what the generalist used to do is encompassed in the term 'transactional HR'. It includes all the routine tasks involved in employing people. Some of this can be made 'self-service' using intranet facilities; it is usually centralised today, and also is frequently outsourced.

'Shared services', as the centralised option is often called, may go beyond just administration and include legal advice, grievance support, training programmes and a lot of day-to-day activities that an HR generalist used to do. The new generation of generalists is more likely to be called 'advisers' or 'business partners', and their role is more to support business priorities and take initiatives that will help their dedicated area of the organisation. It is more of an 'organisational effectiveness' role than traditional HR, and is sometimes referred to (somewhat pretentiously) as 'transformational HR' or 'strategic HRM'. Line managers need some time to adjust to the fact that they now have to go to more than one HR person for their needs. Meanwhile the 'specialist' roles (experts in our six areas of HRM) still continue and may be supplemented by consultants as needed.

A CASE STUDY OF A SHARED SERVICE MODEL

A large London-centred law firm used the Peoplesoft HR system to provide a technical base for moving to a new HR operating model. The model comprised three parts. An HR solutions group was established to deal centrally with the vast majority of HR enquiries concerning people. All routine transactions were centralised and standardised to give a consistent and responsive HR service across the firm. They used a 'contact management tool' to capture and progress all enquiries. This enabled the senior HR managers to provide a more strategic HR service through developing and implementing specific strategies for the practice areas. In addition, a new centre of expertise was established, consisting of specialists in areas such as resourcing, benefits and rewards whose aim was to ensure that HR policies and processes for the firm were of best HR professional practice. This change saved the firm £1 million in reduced staff costs in the HR function.

CAPABILITIES

The changes to HR departments outlined above have been driven not only by the continual desire for cost reduction and by technological opportunities, but very much by the inspiration given to the HR profession by Professor Dave Ulrich of the University of Michigan. He maintained that the delivery of the strategy depends on the capability of HR people. Ulrich (1997; p.253) illustrated the requirements under four headings. At the heart we have 'personal credibility'. HR people have lots of ideas, and indeed an often idealistic view of what managers and organisations should be like. But if they want to be listened to, they must have some fundamentals in place. These include:

- efficiency, responsiveness and reliability – they do what they say they will do, and do it well

- realism, recognising the pressures that managers have from day to day

- using language that is free from jargon

- demonstrating that they really care about what the business and its managers are trying to achieve.

Then we have 'business mastery'. 'Mastery' is a strong word and perhaps too strong, because if you have chosen HR as your profession and not worked operationally in the business, you cannot expect to master all the intricacies of a business. But it does mean that at least the 'business partner' professionals:

- understand the basics of the financial model of the business and the effect on costs of initiatives we propose

- are able to do credible 'return on investment' calculations

- know what people *do* in the organisation – what the different roles entail

- can discuss the business objectives and ask intelligent questions.

Thus 'human resource mastery' refers to professional knowledge of HR, or at least having access to it.

'Change and process mastery' is essential if we want to play the role of change catalyst and facilitator, and in order to ensure that our own processes are effective. It means we understand:

- process design and re-engineering

- measuring process effectiveness

- models of effective change

- helping people through change.

Our strategy will include a 'functional development strategy' – our priorities and goals for the development of our HR people in order to ensure that the value of our own human capital is maximised.

REFLECTIVE ACTIVITY

Go back again to the garden centre of the previous exercises – the garden centre which serves both visiting and online customers.

What kind of resource in HR do you think it could afford to have?

What do you think would be the top ten capabilities that the HR director should have to be effective?

PROCESS EVALUATION

Table 7 features a list of processes that HR would typically design and 'own', even though line management is jointly responsible for implementing most of them. We do not have to have every people process in the HR textbook, but we need those that will support our 'continuing' strategy. Other chapters in this book cover many of these processes in detail. There may be processes that we need but do not have, or we may have some that need revision. Criteria we might use to test whether a process is 'fit for purpose' include:

- Its purpose is clear.

- It makes the business more effective in some way – it adds value to one or more stakeholder.

- The cost and time of running the process is justified by the value it brings (as seen by line managers).

- The process is consistent with our values.

- The process has been recently examined for possible simplification.

Table 7 List of HR processes

Resourcing	Remuneration	Learning and development
Job profiling	Job grading	Personal development planning
Recruitment	Salary banding	Training needs analysis
Selection	Salary increases	Training design
Induction/Orientation	Variable pay/bonus systems	Training evaluation
Vacancy management	Market benchmarking	Knowledge management
Promotion	Recognition schemes	Further education
Succession planning	Performance management	Training authorisation
		Use of coaching and mentoring
Organisation and culture	**Communications/ER**	**HR policies**
Organisation design	Communication processes	Discipline
Organisation restructuring	Employee consultation	Grievance
Culture analysis	Suggestion schemes	Absence management
Workforce planning	Use of intranet	Poor performance
Opinion and engagement	Upwards communication	Sickness
surveys		Time off and leave
		Use of company equipment

Our strategy will include the 'map' of needed processes, and – resources permitting – our plans will include making sure they are all fit for purpose.

TOOLS WHICH SUPPORT PROCESSES

Perhaps the most important tool to support HR processes is technology. We need a human resources information system (HRIS) that will provide us with data and reports and that keeps track of our people. We need to decide how distributed it will be – what information managers and employees will have access to. We may use specialised software for particular processes also – such as performance management or talent management. The intranet provides us with many opportunities for communication (see Chapter 19), such as having policies and forms online. A whole part of our strategy will be how technology is deployed, and this is covered in Chapter 4.

Then there are professional tools which may or may not be automated. These are instruments that are purchased, or specially designed internally, to help a process work more effectively. HR is constantly bombarded by suppliers who offer tools and methodologies, and its choices have significant effects on resources. Table 8 gives some examples of the tools that may be used.

How would we evaluate the choices over tools to be used? Criteria we might use to test whether a tool is 'fit for purpose' include:

- It makes a process more effective.

- It is consistent with our values.

- It *works* – it fulfils its promise.

- The cost of purchase, development and implementation is justified by the value it produces.

Table 8 Some of the tools used in HR

Resourcing	Remuneration	Learning and development
Assessment centres	Job evaluation systems	E-learning programmes
Personality tests	Salary planning software	Development centres
Ability tests	Salary surveys	Competency frameworks
Web-based recruitment		Role specifications
Structured panels		Learning resource centres
Graphology (mainly in France)		Talent management software
Biodata questionnaires		Training management software
Application forms		360-degree assessments
Organisation and culture	**Communications/ER**	**HR policies**
Organisation design software	Web-based tools	Intranet and web-based tools
Culture surveys	Virtual discussion groups	
Questionnaires	Conferencing tools	
Workforce planning models	Satellite broadcasting	
	Pulse surveys	

- It is easily understandable by non-HR people.
- It preferably can be used in several processes.
- It is appropriate for our culture.

PEOPLE-RELATED MEASURES AND STANDARDS OF PERFORMANCE

Part of our HR strategy will be to measure and monitor our own effectiveness. This is covered in Chapter 16.

INVOLVEMENT AND DIALOGUE WITH BUSINESS MANAGERS

The business-oriented HR function cannot operate in isolation. We have already described the need for our people strategy to be driven by the business strategies and objectives. But our HR strategy must include regular contact with the operations.

A lot of angst appears in the HR media about 'having a seat at the top table' and 'being a member of the board'. A lot depends on the role of a board and the requirements of its members. The most senior HR person is more likely to be on a board sub-committee, such as the remuneration committee, than on the board itself, particularly for a holding or large parent company. The 'top table' should be interpreted as the 'executive committee', and it is clearly desirable for HR to be represented there. It is more the personal qualities and credibility of the individual that will bring this about than the 'right by job title'.

Nevertheless, there are many other opportunities to be involved in. HR can set up 'steering committees' of operational executives to advise it on some issues, such as management development and internal communications. Individuals can represent the function in project committees and task forces and be regular attenders at business reviews so that they pick up people-related issues. They may have to take the initiative for this to happen.

EXTERNAL BENCHMARKING AND NETWORKING

Finally, the HR strategy will include a part which is keeping up to date. The HR world offers many opportunities – perhaps too many – and a systematic choice of which to be involved in is important. The function may want to go in for the many awards and league tables that are on offer (such as the various annual 'great place to work' surveys), which can help build the employee brand. 'Benchmarking clubs' in the organisation's own commercial sector provide useful knowledge of good practices and comparative data. We may also want to participate in research projects, particularly in areas which relate to the initiatives we have decided to take in our main HR and people strategies.

KEY ISSUES IN PEOPLE AND HR STRATEGIES

We now pull together ten key points about HR strategies raised in this chapter:

- 'Strategy' means choosing routes to get to a goal. It merges into objectives and plans. It is important to remember that it also involves choices of what *not* to do.

- HR has to prepare two different strategies. One is the 'people strategy' and the other is a strategy for the HR function itself.

- The people strategy is one of the strategies that supports the business in maintaining its competitive advantage and achieving its goals. There are well-established processes for defining strategies and tools, such as PEST and SWOT.

- The key drivers that help us to define our people strategy are: the business strategy itself, our guiding principles and beliefs on people management, external factors we must take into account, and internal factors such as organisational problems.

- In deciding what should be in a people strategy, we can divide it into three parts. The first part is 'continuing' – the core policies and processes we want in place to achieve our ongoing goals in people management. The second is 'proacting' – specific initiatives that will support current business goals. Finally, we have things we should do as 'reacting' to problems and issues that need solving.

- The people strategy can be divided into six sub-strategies – organisation and culture, learning and development, rewards and recognition, communications and employee relations, general HR policies, and resourcing.

- We integrate the demands of these sub-strategies into policies, processes, learning requirements and resources, ensure that they are 'horizontally integrated', and then prioritise them. This leads us to practical implementation planning.

- The HR functional strategy is about choices it must make for itself. It includes how to organise, how to use resources, and how to debelop the capabilities of the in-house resources.

- Then we have to decide which processes and tools we need to deliver the people strategy, what technology will support us, how we will measure our performance, how we intend to keep close to the business and how we will keep track of the outside world.

- Finally, HR should do none of this in isolation. People management is a shared partnership between HR and managers, and all HR policies and programmes should be mutually agreed.

Perhaps there are other key points that you would like to note for yourself.

The main case study in this chapter now follows. It gives an example of the HR strategy of a British local government authority.

THE HR STRATEGY OF HERTFORDSHIRE COUNTY COUNCIL

Make an initial reading of the case study to gain an overview of the situation, and then read the questions that you will need to address. Now read the case study again, making notes of issues and facts that will help you in your analysis and responses to the questions. Remember to 'read between the lines' as well as picking out the obvious points, and also to consider what is not said as well as what is presented here.

This is an extract from the people strategy of Hertfordshire County Council (2001).

Introduction

The people strategy is the County Council's statement of how it will achieve its objectives through its people. The County Council has in place the infrastructure needed to achieve its promises to its communities. The 'Herts Connect' programme, the creation of new children's schools and family services and a new integrated adult care service are just a few examples of transformations in the way the County provides its services. However, infrastructure alone is not enough. To achieve successful change we need to engage, value and enthuse the unique contribution of all employees. At Hertfordshire we recognise that our success as an organisation is totally dependent upon the commitment and dedication of the very talented people who work here. This people strategy sets out how we will continue to value and develop our people in order to maintain our success in the future and mark ourselves out as the best-performing local authority in the country.

Bill Ogley, Chief Executive,
Hertfordshire County Council

Linking strategy to objectives: 20–20 vision

The County Council's promises to the people of Hertfordshire create the strategic objectives that will drive the County through the early years of the twenty-first century. These objectives also shape the people requirements for the organisation. Any people strategy must be closely aligned to organisational objectives in order to ensure that the right people are achieving the right things at the right time. Our starting point in developing this people strategy has therefore been an analysis of the people objectives contained within the following:

The promises: Four key promises have been made to the communities of Hertfordshire about how the County Council will improve their lives. These promises provide a framework for the planning and development of all services across the organisation. They will play an important role in determining the skills, competencies and behaviours needed from employees now and in the future so that we can:

- make Hertfordshire a better place to live and work

- improve education and promote prosperity

- help people to help themselves

- get better in all that we do, and involve and serve the public.

Herts Connect is a major county-wide initiative that is fundamentally changing the way we operate. So far it has resulted in:

- the introduction of an all-service call centre, a new interface with customers via the website (Herts Direct)

- a rationalisation of the way we use our property and transport and a focus of service delivery on the needs of our customers, a major structural change in the development of the new children's schools and family services and adult care services to focus service delivery on the needs of our customers.

These initiatives will all require employees to work more flexibly, in different ways, across professional boundaries and using new competencies.

Best value: Although a government initiative, the principles of best value are closely aligned to the principles of Herts Connect. Every service of the County Council will be fundamentally reviewed within the next five years. These reviews, along with advances in technology, will change the way that the County Council operates and the way that people work.

What you told us ...

In developing this strategy it was important that we listened to people across the organisation. We wanted to understand what the key people requirements for the business success were and to develop a common agreement on what the people strategy is aiming to achieve. This is what you told us:

- There are significant recruitment and retention difficulties that have arisen as a result of national skills shortages. These shortages are now impacting on the ability to deliver quality services.

- We need to do more to diversify our workforce.

- We need to become a more flexible employer.

- We need to develop more effective methods of rewarding contribution.

- We need to do more to enable our employees to embrace new communications technologies.

- We need to do more as an employer to actively demonstrate how we value our people.

- We need to develop new leadership capabilities.

- Departmental and professional silos need to be challenged so that people can work more effectively together.

Delivering the people strategy

The people strategy will form an organisation-wide framework for the delivery of people management objectives over the next three to five years. All departments of the County Council will be responsible for developing their own tailored strategy for delivering the five key people objectives identified in this document.

Strategic people objectives

The five strategic people objectives set out in this document are the building-blocks of our

people strategy. They will ensure that the work of the personnel function across the County Council is always closely aligned to organisational objectives. Our performance in achieving our strategic objectives will be closely monitored and measured. The value added by the personnel function will be identified through tangible performance measures.

The building-blocks of success

To be an employer of choice, we will aim to be an organisation that people aspire to work for by:

- creating flexible employment, development and reward packages that employees highly value

- creating a challenging and exciting working environment

- being a good employer and looking after our people.

To be a developer of people, we will develop the organisation through its people by:

- developing strong leaders

- promoting and assisting career development through coaching, mentoring, shadowing and secondment schemes

- developing a culture of learning through practice

- developing structured professional qualification strategies and personal development opportunities based on our development charter and organisational objectives

- ensuring that employees take responsibility for their own continuous development and lifelong learning.

We will enable all the elements of this strategy to be delivered by embracing new information and communication technologies. People practices in the organisation will become more effective and more efficient by our:

- making access to personnel services much easier for all our customers and partners

- communicating with people within and outside the organisation more effectively through a variety of communication and technology portals

- providing effective and timely management information on people-related issues.

We will continuously influence the success of organisational change by:

- involving and empowering employees to contribute to innovation and change within their services

- developing a performance culture

- recognising the importance of engaging employees in organisational change at the earliest opportunity to ensure effective culture change

- developing more effective partnerships with our trade unions and employees

- developing flexible employment packages that reflect the new paradigm of work.

We will value and embrace the creativity and uniqueness of all employees by:

- harnessing the diversity of our employees to improve service delivery

- enhancing Hertfordshire's reputation inside and outside the organisation by our actions, not just our words

- ensuring the fair and consistent treatment of all our employees

- monitoring personnel practice and workforce profiles and taking positive action to redress any imbalances found.

Note: These are followed by quite extensive lists of actions to be taken, with targets, performance indicators and accountabilities under each of the five building-blocks.

Questions for discussion

Consider and come to conclusions on the following questions, and be prepared to discuss your answers.

1 How does the above case study relate to the principles outlined in the chapter?

2 What do you think is particularly good about it?

3 If you were a consultant to the Council, would you suggest any areas the Council might consider adding or changing?

EXPLORE FURTHER

Armstrong, M. and Baron, A. (2002) *Strategic HRM*. London, CIPD
This draws on previously unpublished research to provide authentic voices from real-life managers discussing how they set about developing and implementing HR strategies. The research includes interviews with HR directors and chief executives from a variety of organisations, demystifying the concept and practice of 'strategic HRM', and placing it firmly within the context of the wider organisational strategy and business goals.

Boxall, P. and Purcell, J. (2007) *Strategy and Human Resource Management*. Basingstoke, Palgrave Macmillan
A thorough review of the literature and the evolution of strategic HRM thinking. The authors also develop a conceptual framework to provide an exploration of the the field.

Gratton, L. (2000) *Living Strategy*. London, Prentice Hall/Financial Times
Based on Gratton's experience leading a consortium of companies over the years in exploring added-value HR, this book shows how to design strategies that have meaning and purpose for people without whose commitment they remain drawings on the wallchart. It shows how to create a people vision, how to analyse gaps from where we are and where we want to be, and how to turn strategy into implementation.

Mayo, A. J. (2004b) *Creating a Learning and Development Strategy*. London, CIPD
Although focused specifically on learning and development, the methodologies in the book are very similar to this chapter. The ideas are developed more thoroughly and is written as a practical guide for HR professionals.

CHAPTER 4

HRM and technological innovation

Anna Kyprianou

INTRODUCTION

This chapter looks at the use of technology-based systems, applications and tools, often referred to as 'e-HR', and its impact on key HR functions and processes. It therefore looks at subjects also covered in other chapters (especially Chapter 20 on HR roles, Chapters 8 and 9 on recruitment and selection, Chapters 14 and 24 on workplace learning and HRD, Chapters 12 and 13 on performance management and reward, and Chapter 19 on communication), but offering a different perspective on all of those subjects.

LEARNING OUTCOMES

By the end of this chapter readers should be able to:

- define the concept of 'e-HR'

- explain the impact of e-HR on the HR role and function

- identify appropriate uses of e-HR for different HR issues

- evaluate the benefits and detriments of a range of e-HR practices.

This chapter is in two parts. The first discusses issues surrounding technological innovation, the emergence of e-HR and its impact on the HR role and function. The second part explores the use of e-HR in key HR processes.

We begin with a 'starter' or introductory case study. Unlike most case studies in this book, the case presents a futuristic view of the use of technology in HR in an attempt to get readers thinking about the changing nature of e-HR. The main case study at the end of the chapter uses a large company's experience to draw together some of the key issues.

Reference sources named within the chapter may be looked up in the *References and further reading* section at the end of the book.

It is 3am GMT and Julie George, talent strategist for the multinational technology organisation Global Industries, wakes up in a cold sweat having forgotten to deal with some urgent applications for the post of Global HR Director. She sits up in bed and immediately goes to her inbox on her videophone and downloads the applications. The five digital CVs she downloads are mapped onto her core competencies and corporate fit model for an initial pre-screen and the results reveal that three of the applicants have matches between 95% and 98%. Julie sends each of the three an email inviting them to a preliminary first interview, which will be conducted virtually, using video-conferencing. She also ensures that an automatic, yet personalised, 'rejection' letter is sent to the other two applicants who only scored a 70% and 75% fit respectively. Julie then goes back to sleep, feeling relieved.

The following morning, Julie logs on to the corporate employee portal to check how many people have chosen their flexible benefits for the year 2021–22. It appears that gym membership is proving more popular

than ever before and outstrips private healthcare. Julie thinks it is not surprising that staff are more interested in the way they look in that their average age is 25.

Julie has a four-year-old son and Global Industries' flexible working policy means that she works from home most days and as long as she completes her tasks by 3pm GMT, she can spend the rest of the time with her son. The last job on her electronic list is to train herself in voice recognition software. So she goes to her password-protected personal development folder on the employee portal and downloads the appropriate training module . . .

Questions for discussion

1 What would it be like to work for Global Industries? List the benefits and detriments for both Julie George and Global Industries.

2 What impact would such a heavy reliance on technology have on the HR function?

Source: adapted from S. Weekes and S. Beagrie (2002) *E-People*, Capstone Publishing

Some would argue that it is no longer possible for HR without technology to realise its strategic potential (see Chapter 20) and provide the necessary wide range of services and products that an organisation needs (Fein, 2001).

Just as HR's role is changing, technology has continued to evolve. If HR's role has come to be to deliver employee support and management based on the needs of the organisation, then technology's role has helped that. Technology can provide an effective and efficient way for organisations to capture, edit, store, retrieve and share the essential information about people. But the key to ensuring a streamlined information-sharing service is by integrating them into a robust HR network. It is important to note that there is no one technological solution or innovation that meets the needs of all organisations.

1   TECHNOLOGICAL INNOVATION IN HR: TOWARDS A DEFINITION

What is e-HR? Ulrich (2002; p.91) says:

E-HR means a lot of things ... I see it as a matrix with two columns: transaction – doing the administrative things faster and better; enabling employees to be self-sufficient and self-reliant; building employee portals, etc;

and transformation – becoming more strategic and building sustainable competitive advantage. My sense is that most of the e-HR work is in the transactional column, doing the administrative parts of HR systems.

At an advanced level, e-HR represents a fully integrated, organisation-wide electronic network of HR-related data, information, services, databases, tools, applications and transactions that are generally accessible at any time by end-user groups. Because e-HR does mean a lot of things, we now give a quick overview of the terms, often used interchangeably, relating to technology and HR.

A human resource information system (HRIS) is a system that helps an organisation 'acquire, store, manipulate, analyse, retrieve, and distribute information about an organisation's human resources' (Tannenbaum, 1990; p.28).

E-HR in its simplest sense refers to the use of technology within the HR function. E-HR in its broadest sense is 'the planning, implementation and application of information technology for both networking and supporting at least two individual or collective actors in their shared performing of HR activities' (Strohmeier, 2007; p.19).

Other terms, often used interchangeably, are:

- *virtual HR* (Lepak and Snell, 1998) – virtual HR refers to technology-mediated networks of different internal and external stakeholders that provide an organisation with the HR services needed, so obviating any requirement for a conventional HR department

- *web-based HR* (Ruel *et al*, 2004) – The use of Internet technologies

- *business-to-employee* (B2E) (Huang, Jin and Yang, 2004) – this focuses on internal stakeholders such as line managers, HR professionals and employees. In contrast e-HR has a greater reach in that it includes other, external, stakeholders such as applicants and consultants.

In this chapter, 'e-HR' is used in both its simplest and its broadest senses.

EVALUATING TECHNOLOGICAL INNOVATION IN HRM

Historically, HR was one of the first departments in organisations to automate its processes. This has sometimes led to a legacy of unconnected applications, systems and attitudes that has not helped the development of coherent technological HR strategies. Table 9 provides a brief historical outline of the relationship between technological innovations and HR.

Today's technology frees HR from its administrative history. The technology can range from simple spreadsheets to all-embracing integrated HRIS to web-enabled applications and systems covering all HR functions, processes and strategies.

As can be seen from Table 10, technology can extend HR services directly to managers and employees through self-service systems. Furthermore, technology can both facilitate the management of HR more efficiently and enable the adoption of practices across the whole organisation.

Table 9 Technological innovations and HR: a 40-year chronology

1960s	First payroll processing systems appear
1970s	Emergence of HR information systems with functional features such as compensation, benefits and pensions
1980s	HR begins to develop its own systems as desktop computers offer local solutions relatively cost-effectively
1980s	Cost-effective software facilitates the spread of HR information systems to an increasing number of organisations
1989	Creation of the World Wide Web enables the effective navigation of the Internet
1995	Online job boards are introduced
1996	ICL launches Café VIK, an employee portal designed to share knowledge
1998	The term 'e-business' is coined; major HR technology vendors move increasingly to the Internet; terms such as 'e-HR' and 'web-enabled HR' appear
1999	Outsourcing comes into its own; BP sign one of the biggest HR outsourcing deals
2000	Increasing number of business-to-employee (B2E) services emerge
2001	All major corporations embark on some form of e-HR

The use of technology in HR

Organisations are approaching the introduction and development of e-HR from several perspectives, often combining several elements. These elements include:

- HR transaction processing systems for employees

- knowledge servers for instructions and queries

- self-service tools

- information system tools for managers

- integrating systems to link different existing systems.

How far are these used? A CIPD survey in 2005 found that 77% of organisations used some sort of technology for HR-related activities. The 2003 Cranet survey found high levels of use, 82% of UK organisations having some form of HRIS. This survey also suggests that in terms of e-HRM use UK organisations are not necessarily ahead of those in other European countries. On the one hand, Table 11 shows that in 2003 only 18% of UK organisations surveyed reported no use of technology in HR compared to just under 30% in Slovakia. Interestingly, Germany, Greece and Slovakia reported greater integration of HR systems into wider management systems than Sweden and the UK – this may be explained by the time at which these countries began using HR-related technology (the earlier, the more likely that legacy systems are more important).

Table 12 shows the level of HR web development for those organisations that reported e-HR facilities. The UK and Greece mainly use e-HR for one-way communication with minimal employee access to personal information. Employee access to update personal data appears to be even less common. Complex HR transactions were indeed a rarity in 2003 across Europe.

The general application of technology in HR has spread. However, it remains on an administrative level, as Table 13 shows. Administrative tasks such as personnel records and payroll were clearly supported by technology across the countries surveyed, whereas advanced, complex strategic or decision-support applications had yet to be fully realised (Ball, 2001; Teo *et al*, 2001).

Table 10 The application of technology in support of HR

Recruitment	Learning and development	Core HR	Policies and procedures	Performance management
The enablers				
• corporate job boards • external job sites • applicant tracking and management systems • online candidate screening, testing, skills matching and ranking • task-specific skills matching	• e-learning • blended learning and community learning • knowledge management and best practice sharing systems	• self-service tools for employee transactions • online flexible benefits system • payroll systems • employee portals	• employee portal/corporate intranet for storing information • email for disseminating information • online induction	• internal incentive and reward systems • external incentive and reward sites • online flexible benefits systems • email for collaborative discussion on staff appraisal • online benchmarking against core competencies • online 360-degree feedback
Individual aim				
Reduce the cost and time to hire; more responsive recruiting; extend reach of candidate pool	Develop staff more effectively and cultivate, maintain and retain company knowledge	Reduce administration so HR can be strategic; empowered employees	Reduce administration for HR to become more strategic; improve corporate communications and empower employees	Tailored recognition and rewarding; more effective and collaborative performance assessment
Overall aim				
To create a strategic HR function and an empowered, motivated workforce, performing at optimum efficiency				

Source: adapted from Weekes and Beagrie (2002)

Table 11 'What type of HR Information System do you have?'

	UK	Sweden	Germany	Greece	Slovakia
No computerised HR information system	18%	13%	16%	12%	29%
Primarily independent HR system	57%	68%	52%	52%	39%
Integrated into wider management system	25%	19%	31%	36%	32%

Source: Cranet (2003)

Table 12 'If you have e-HR facilities, what is the level of HR web deployment?'

	UK	Sweden	Germany	Greece	Slovakia
One-way communication	65%	41%	48%	75%	50%
One-way, but allowing employee access to some personal information	15%	31%	35%	13%	27%
Two-way: employee is able to update simple personal information	11%	16%	8%	6%	8%
Two-way: employee is able to perform complex transactions	2%	9%	2%	5%	1%
Other more complex transactions	0%	2%	0%	0%	1%
Don't know	7%	1%	7%	1%	13%

Source: Cranet (2003)

Table 13 'In which of the following areas is the HR Information System used?'

	UK	Sweden	Germany	Greece	Slovakia
Individual personnel records	98%	46%	33%	97%	95%
Payroll	74%	96%	93%	95%	94%
Benefits	66%	72%	80%	80%	48%
Time registration and attendance	48%	20%	90%	86%	82%
Recruitment and selection	66%	19%	39%	60%	35%
Training and development	68%	38%	55%	69%	44%
Performance management	36%	12%	29%	52%	28%
Career planning/Succession planning	15%	12%	24%	30%	17%
Work scheduling	11%	54%	28%	64%	40%
Health and safety	21%	18%	24%	29%	29%

Source: Cranet (2003)

REFLECTIVE ACTIVITY

Look at Tables 11, 12 and 13 carefully and explore the similarities and differences of the data between the countries.

Can you provide reasons for the similarities and differences identified?

KEY DRIVERS AND BENEFITS OF TECHNOLOGY IN HR

The adoption of e-HR stems largely from the wish to improve the efficiency and effectiveness of HR-related activities. The three key drivers for the increasing importance of e-HR in the twenty-first century are (Snell, Stueber and Lepak, 2002; Kettley and O'Reilly, 2003):

- the need for *operational efficiency* – The increasing cost of administering HR throughout the 1990s has led HR to seriously consider ways of reducing costs and enhancing the speed and accuracy of data

- the *relational impact* – The increasing expectations and reported low levels of satisfaction of employees with HR has necessitated a change in the relationship between HR, managers and employees

- the *transformational impact* – It has been perceived necessary to change the HR role from primarily administrative to one of a strategic business partner.

Two technological applications have contributed to the timely delivery of accurate and detailed information: corporate intranets, and employee and manager self-service. Starting with the intranet – a 2005 CIPD survey found that 71% of organisations had an intranet providing HR information including policies, practices and HR forms. HR intranets have become one-stop shops for HR-related queries and routine transactions (through employee and manager self-service applications). Nevertheless, the complexity and content of HR intranets can vary. At the simplest, an HR intranet gives access to comprehensive HR policy content and associated guidelines and constitutes a means for employee communication. At a more sophisticated level, self-service applications allow HR transactions to be streamlined and devolved to line managers and employees. Intranets provide a *single repository for HR information.* They offer an alternative channel of communication with employees and line managers by carrying organisation-wide news stories and highlighting policy changes. Discussion groups allow employees to share knowledge, while colleagues with particular expertise can be found by using staff profiles in an online employee directory.

As for employee and manager self-service – one of the fastest-growing trends in the delivery of HR information is employee self-service. Again there are international differences: 80% of US organisations delivered some information to employees through self-service in 2000 whereas only 22% of UK organisations had such a system (CIPD, 2005). These applications help employees to access and maintain HR information about themselves. In organisations such as Nationwide and ICL, employees are able to select their own benefits package. Similarly, managers' self-service provides a variety of HR tools and information for managers thereby improving managerial effectiveness. Increasingly, employees can carry out some basic HR transactions using interactive self-service applications. By handing over primary responsibility to staff for maintaining their own personal details a major administrative burden can be removed from HR and the accuracy of records is often improved.

There are a number of drivers of e-HR, but how successful is it in fulfilling expectations?

Table 14 offers a comparative assessment by HR managers and gives an impression of relative success.

Table 14 Success in meeting objectives for the introduction of HRIS

Criteria	North America (%)	Rest of the world (%)
Improving data accuracy	92	82
HR staff acceptance	91	100
Employee acceptance	84	88
Manager acceptance	84	82
Employee services improvement	80	88
Meeting administrative cost savings goal	77	59
Enabling HR to be more strategic	76	81
Aligning workforce with organisational objectives	70	47
Accountability	70	63
Enabling organisation to recruit key talent	68	41
Enabling employees and managers to make better decisions	67	59
Revenue growth	42	59

Source: Cedar Crestone, 2006. Workforce Technology and Service Delivery Survey, 9th Edition

The evidence to support the claim that these benefits have indeed been fully realised is patchy – HR managers may give an optimistic picture. On the one hand some surveys have reported reductions of up to 60% in transaction costs, the length of time taken to deal with queries, reductions in enquiries directly to HR, and less HR administration. Other reports suggest, however, that e-enabled HR has not delivered its potential (Ruel *et al*, 2004).

REFLECTIVE ACTIVITY

In the light of the benefits of e-HR in freeing HR of burdensome administration and the evidence of the uptake of e-HR, consider the reasons why some argue that HR has yet to realise its full transformational potential.

Below are some practical considerations and challenges that may help us to understand why that potential may not be reached.

Practical considerations and challenges

Some organisations have used 'off-the-shelf' packages (packages that can be used in more than one organisation), whereas others have decided to tackle all elements through the development of a custom-made, coherent integrated e-HR system. Both types of system can have their problems, but the choice of technological solutions has shifted dramatically from the generic to the specific and customised. Whether to use off-the-shelf or customised e-HR solutions can only be decided by looking at the requirements of HR and the organisation and at what they want to achieve. For HR a key criterion is to consider which solution best streamlines administration and transaction processing tasks.

Dissatisfaction can come from a number of causes.

First, e-HR is still predominantly used by white-collar employees. This group of staff generally has personal access to a computer and is usually familiar with the technology. There is some risk, therefore, that although these staff are increasingly empowered, their blue-collar colleagues may be less so. In response, organisations are beginning to find alternative ways for making HR applications available to their manual workers. Among the options already being implemented are shared-access kiosks or PCs situated in communal areas.

Second, employees, line managers and HR itself must be convinced that such HR delivery is of real benefit to them and the organisation. Senior management are more likely to accept the benefits by projected cost savings. Employees can be persuaded of the benefits of self-service. However, line managers must be reassured that processes will be simplified and that the whole exercise is not just a case of work being transferred from HR to them. HR staff themselves may be the hardest to convince because technology often leads to a significant change in the role and structure of HR.

Third, staff and line managers have to be persuaded to use and keep using the technology and its associated applications once it is up and running. Above all, the system must be attractive, easy to use and well maintained. Making sure that it delivers practical benefits as well as cost reductions by removing unnecessary bureaucracy from routine transactions is vital.

The biggest challenge that HR faces with the many complexities and uncertainties around e-HR is to effectively adjust and learn to manage the world of technology at both transactional and transformational levels. As will be seen in Part 2 of this chapter, many functions and processes of HR have embraced technological solutions, at least at a transactional level. E-HR provides HR with the opportunity to take on the challenge of *transformation*.

2 E-ENABLED HR FUNCTIONS AND PROCESSES

There is clear evidence of the widespread use of a number of e-enabled functions and processes. What follows is a fuller discussion on a range of HR functions in which technology has had a large impact. We begin by looking at technology used in recruitment.

E-RECRUITMENT

Technology has dramatically changed recruitment practices. Some estimates are that 100% of large organisations currently use the Internet for recruitment purposes, with 82% using intranet systems to advertise posts internally (Cedar, 2002). E-recruitment practices include the use of recruitment pages on existing corporate websites, kiosks, specialist recruitment websites (job portals, online job boards), state-of-the-art online games, websites devoted to helping users make new friends, and podcasts offering career advice to attract job applicants. Interactive tools for processing applications (online applications, email auto-responding), and using online screening techniques such as online interviews or personality assessment further enhance e-recruitment.

Corporate websites are becoming more important in attracting candidates because they enable potential applicants to find out more than simply about the vacancies. They can also provide applicants with visuals on what offices, break areas and amenities look like. Add this to employee blogs and applicants can now get a better sense of what it is like to work for an organisation.

To make the most of corporate website recruiting it is important that it should include: a link to the careers section from the homepage, information on benefits and culture, separate graduate recruitment section, job search by job category, location, and keyword, urgent jobs highlighted, complete job descriptions, one click to apply, pre-assessment tools for each job, choice of cut-and-paste form or CV builder, attachment of formatted CV, application automatically connected to a job position, anonymous application, email to friend, job agent, profiling, re-use of candidate information for multiple applications and online user feedback (**www.recruitsoft.com**).

The popularity of websites such as Facebook, Bebo and Myspace, whose original intentions were to work as social sites, has been used by organisations with a desire to establish work-related interactions such as recruitment. Such taking over of social Internet spaces is further illustrated by the Yell Group which has undertaken a recruitment campaign in the virtual world of Second Life. Yell put up company posters and created three-dimensional characters wearing Yell T-shirts in the virtual world where they can be asked for more information on current vacancies. Some recruiters use mobile technology to notify candidates of potential job opportunities: a number of mobile access websites being have been developed enabling applicants to search, view and apply for positions directly from a mobile phone.

These practices have the potential benefit of reaching large numbers of qualified applicants globally (Gueutal and Stone, 2005; Stone *et al*, 2003). They can bring down recruitment costs, decrease cycle time, streamline administrative processes and enable organisations to more effectively evaluate their recruitment strategy – but e-recruitment is still seen by most employers as an add-on tool. E-recruitment has not replaced traditional methods of recruitment. Some have argued that there may be a number of detriments. For example, replacing traditional recruiters with computerised systems may make the recruitment process much more impersonal and inflexible and therefore have a negative impact on applicants' attraction and retention rates. Likewise, the use of online recruitment may have a negative impact on minority groups who may not have access to the Internet or possess the skills needed to use it. Applicants may think that online systems are more likely to invade personal privacy than other recruitment processes and may therefore be less willing to use e-recruiting systems than traditional systems to apply for jobs.

There is evidence that applicants still prefer traditional recruitment sources (especially newspaper advertisements and employee referrals) to e-recruiting, and surveys consistently indicate that the Internet is not the number one source of jobs for most candidates (Galanaki, 2002; Zusman and Landis, 2002). E-recruiting is more likely to be used by young, highly educated white job candidates than those who are older, less well-educated or members of ethnic minority groups (Galanaki, 2002; McManus and Ferguson, 2003). E-recruiting systems are more likely to produce candidates who appear to change their jobs frequently (McManus and Ferguson, 2003). Whereas e-recruiting systems may attract more applicants, those applicants are not always of higher quality than the applicants attracted by traditional recruiting systems (Chapman and Webster, 2003).

In one sense e-recruitment works too well, bringing a large response from applicants, many of them unqualified. An effective selection process that sorts these applications quickly without screening out good applicants is therefore essential (Capelli, 2005).

E-SELECTION

E-selection uses filtering tools to filter out unqualified applicants through online pre-employment testing and to apply selection and assessment tools, often tailored to each job, to match applicants to the job requirements. Such systems and tools may use a variety of specific strategies (eg interviews, ability tests, personality measures) to find out which applicants have appropriate levels of knowledge, skills and attitudes.

Organisations use online testing for a number of purposes. Some use it to assess the knowledge skills and attitudes of applicants in a cost-effective manner. For example, Home Depot placed kiosks in stores to test applicants and reported saving $135 per applicant in administrative costs. They also found an 11% reduction in turnover among candidates who were tested in kiosks (Gueutal and Falbe, 2005).

Other organisations use e-selection systems to do online interviews or simulations designed to find out the critical thinking or decision-making skills of applicants. One such interviewing tool is activ8's 'a8i Recruitment', a product that promises to offer 'the potential to remove the traditional face-to-face interview completely' with the help of artificial intelligence. Others provide applicants with the opportunity to complete online self-assessments of personality to assess the degree of fit between the applicant's traits and the organisation's culture.

Despite the increasing use of e-selection tools and systems, there is still little research on their effectiveness (Kehoe *et al*, 2005). The OPP survey of British HR professionals found that two thirds of respondents had reservations about using online personality tests at the recruitment stage. The main concerns were over lack of control – whether the candidates had understood the instructions properly, and not knowing who had completed the form (OPP 2001).

REFLECTIVE ACTIVITY

How can organisations overcome some of the concerns over e-selection tools that have been raised by the OPP survey?

E-LEARNING, TRAINING AND DEVELOPMENT

Of all HR processes, learning, training and development is the most technologically enabled. It has been argued that 'web-based training is replacing traditional training as the most effective educational tool' (Greengard, 1999; p.95). The use of such technology for learning includes shop-floor as well as white-collar workers.

Although computer-based training (CBT) continues to have a presence in organisations, the shift to web-based learning, training and development is inevitable. As Cohen (2001; p.137) states:

> *Unlike traditional, off-line classes, web-based training can typically be accessed on demand, so users have much more flexibility when scheduling sessions. And because of the interactive nature of the Net, classes are often far more engaging and lively. Beyond boosting the efficiency of training, the web can also make it affordable.*

Many organisations keep their own libraries of reference materials and some have their own virtual university. There are a number of examples of this. American Airlines has its own university where it provides learning and development for a wide range of staff across a variety of methods including computer- and Internet-based programmes. Biolink, a group of scientific companies in the south of England, has joined with academic partners to provide a virtual university for their members, where they can access a variety of resources connected to management development. The UK financial services company Egg has also launched a virtual university where its staff can have access to learning and development from around the world using the Internet.

What are the key drivers for these changes? We look at the question from three perspectives: the organisational, work team and individual perspectives.

Starting with the *organisational perspective*, there are two main advantages: cost and effective targeting. Firstly, learning materials can be purchased or designed in electronic format, bringing cost savings. Learning and training materials can be deposited on the organisation's intranet and employees can access them from their desks or from home as and when required. The organisation can also target particular learning specifically to the individual who needs it rather than designing events using a 'one-size-fits-all' approach for everyone. Learning materials can also be made available to remote staff, as is particularly relevant for large, global or virtual organisations. Secondly, effective targeting is an advantage, because organisations spend a great deal of money on learning, training and development without always knowing what the real return on investment is. One could go as far as to say that there is often no direct link established between learning, training and development and performance improvement. Technology provides the tools to create a skills database, track competencies and skills, identify gaps in employee knowledge and then create the necessary courses using appropriate learning technologies to address specific needs.

Adding the *work team perspective* to the organisational perspective, there are a number of advantages to the virtual classroom. People do not actually need to leave their place of work – they can 'attend' the event via their computer. They can also interact with others on the same programme through the use of:

- *online briefings* – Each person receives the same information at the same time from the person who is facilitating the event although he/she does not have to act on it at the same time. They can wait until their work pattern allows a convenient opportunity for them to focus on their learning. They can also make any response in their own time

- *discussion rooms* – These allow people to exchange ideas. They can be particularly useful for finding innovative approaches or for sharing experience. The 'rooms' are usually facilitated by a trainer, although informal networks can also be an effective vehicle for exchanging ideas. Discussion rooms can take several formats including real-time, where people are online at the same time, and noticeboards, where messages can be posted and responded to one at a time as people log on to the programme

- *conferencing* – 'Meetings' can be set up in which people in remote places can both talk and see each other simulating to some extent the networking and sharing of ideas often associated with a conventional training event where people turn up in person.

Finally, there are many benefits to the use of e-learning, training and development from the *individual perspective*. As Greengard (1999; p.95) states:

> An employee can log on and peruse a course syllabus, click to specific lessons to get an idea of what the course entails, and then sign up electronically. At that point, the student can receive lessons and coursework online, take tests and advance to the next level. Best of all, it's possible to study at home, at work or while sitting in a hotel room in Dubuque.

There are further advantages for individuals: tutor support and helplines from which learners can seek advice from their tutors on a one-to-one basis; access to other learners – learning networks can be established, providing an effective way of sharing knowledge and experiences; working at their own pace as and when appropriate and convenient; and easy access to information at any time.

Despite the advantages of e-learning outlined above, the value of traditional methods should not be overlooked. Learning works better when participants can physically meet and talk to each other. Social interaction and feedback are important. Maintaining participant motivation is problematic in programmes where there is little or no face-to-face contact. Computer and web-based training can be a lonely experience. Imaginative use of newsgroups, dedicated chatrooms and webcams can help reduce isolation. E-learning, training and development is an additional set of tools which when combined with traditional methods can provide powerful learning and development solutions.

REFLECTIVE ACTIVITY

Develop an action plan by which a 'blended' approach can be used to greater effect in relation to learning, training and development.

E-PERFORMANCE MANAGEMENT SYSTEMS

The main purpose of any performance management process is to manage and control employee behaviour, ensuring its alignment with organisational goals (see Chapter 12). E- systems enable managers to measure performance, write performance reviews and provide employees with feedback (Cardy and Miller, 2005; Stone *et al*, 2003). For instance, computerised performance monitoring (CPM) systems facilitate the measurement of performance by storing such information as number of items produced, time spent on tasks, and error and wastage rates. Some estimates indicate that CPM systems are used to monitor the work of over 40 million workers. One of the many reasons for organisations' using such systems is that they allow for greater spans of control and eliminate the need for managers to spend time observing the behaviour of employees and assessing their performance (Cardy and Miller, 2003).

E-performance management systems also help with writing appraisals and providing employees with feedback. One benefit is that employees can be appraised more frequently. The e-system simplifies the process of completing appraisal forms through the use of predefined sentences and paragraphs. Intranet systems are used for 360-degree feedback. Such systems send emails to evaluators and ask them to complete online evaluations of employees. The data are subsequently merged and feedback is provided for the appraisee. These systems also can be used to track and compare individual, team and organisational performance with respect to such areas as attendance, lateness, grievances and turnover (Stone *et al*, 2003). Such data can be used to identify specific performance problems, highlight exceptional performance, and more importantly provide managers with feedback on these in order for informed decisions to be made.

But many e-performance systems can only be used for low-level jobs with clearly definable objective performance standards. They often measure the quantity rather than the quality of products and services produced. Nor do they have any real capacity to assess organisational 'citizenship' and co-operation. Little research has focused on their overall effectiveness (Cardy and Miller, 2003).

E-COMPENSATION SYSTEMS

E-compensation systems are used for developing and implementing pay systems, providing benefits and evaluating the effectiveness of compensation packages. They facilitate the process in a variety of ways. First, they allow HR to collect job analysis data through online questionnaires. The systems automatically collect job analysis data from 'experts', summarise the data, and generate standardised job descriptions. In addition, they convert the job analysis data to job evaluation point scores. Furthermore, they integrate the job evaluation point scores with online labour market data. Then they use the data to create pay grades and establish pay levels in organisations.

E-compensation systems are also used to communicate data about benefits options to employees, and give them the opportunity to select benefit plans online (Gueutal and Falbe, 2005). Employees are not always aware of the types of benefits offered by organisations (Cascio, 2006), often because information is hidden in large employee handbooks. E-systems also facilitate the use of 'cafeteria' or flexible benefit packages. The typical use is through employee self-service systems that give employees the opportunity to alter their benefit packages as their needs change. Such systems may meet employees' needs to a greater degree than traditional benefits systems.

E-compensation systems also allow managers to model the impact of incentive systems and ensure the fairness of salary allocation decisions. These systems can be linked to e-performance management systems, increasing the likelihood that pay rises are based on performance. They can be used to make sure that rewards have internal and external equity. Research reveals that individuals have higher satisfaction and retention levels when pay systems are perceived as fair (Bergmann and Scarpello, 2002).

REFLECTIVE ACTIVITY

Consider how traditional HR practices compare with e-HR practices.

What are the benefits and drawbacks of each?

Consider how organisations need to rethink their HR functions, and what skills and competencies HR professionals would need to have in order to add real value using e-HR.

KEY ISSUES IN HRM AND TECHNOLOGICAL INNOVATION

Properly designed e-HR systems can increase organisational efficiency by increasing an organisation's ability to gather, access and disseminate information. Thus, e-HR can help the HR function to become more strategic, although there are still HR functions which are lagging behind due to poor data systems or poor web applications. The true value of technology is only realised when it is perceived as a tool.

We now pull together ten key points about HRM and technology raised in this chapter:

- E-HR strategies are a combination of the transactional and transformational. The first deals with traditional HR functions such as payroll and benefits. The second is more concerned with developing employees and building competitive advantage. It is the automation of the former that facilitates the latter.

- Operational efficiency, relational and transformational impact are key drivers for the growth of e-HR.

- Consideration of organisational culture, processes and understanding the business are essential in developing e-HR.

- There is no one technological innovation or solution that meets the needs of all organisations.

- Technology is not the major driver of change for HR – rather, it is the desire to integrate its multifunctional nature that technology enables.

- An intranet can be a powerful platform for an organisation to deliver effective e-HR.

- Self-service and employee portals are critical to any online HR strategy.

- Technology offers new opportunities for delivery of HR services such as recruitment, learning, performance management and reward and compensation.

- Individuals can access learning and development materials in a convenient manner.

- Blended HR systems that combine e-HR with traditional systems have a greater chance of success.

The main case study in this chapter now follows. It is based on the experience of ICL and the development of their employee portal, Café VIK.

ICL, the IT solutions organisation owned by the Japanese Fijitsu Group, has brought all of its web-enabled processes into what they refer to as e-ICL. An integrated web-enabled e-HR system is a key aspect of ICL's vision to put into practice the values and vision of the organisation.

ICL was one of the first organisations to create an organisation-wide intranet in 1996. The intranet is seen as much more than just an HR tool – it is seen as a business tool. The knowledge-sharing initiative was branded as Café VIK ('valuing ICL knowledge'). Café VIK is a set of portals which enable employees to access a range of information and services. By its first anniversary in November 1997, Café VIK was already being used by about 50% of ICL's 19,000 employees. As awareness of the service spread, the number continued to grow. Key staff state that 'It's helping HR to play a leading role in developing strategy and managing people. After that, the next phase will be to use it as a management tool.'

In 1998, a number of cross-function groups were set up to explore how the company could get more staff involved with the intranet. During 2000, ICL re-launched the intranet to allow greater personalisation of content (introduction of My Café VIK tool) and to encourage employees to share their knowledge through online communities. The second-generation model was housed on a single server which brought to an end the duplication of materials associated with the original version. The search facilities were improved and the new HR intranet became far more interactive. The self-service application has reduced the administrative activity of the HR function and has encouraged employees to take greater responsibility for keeping their data up to date by entering it directly onto the HR database.

Employees can view their current employment terms and benefits online, update personal details directly on the HR database via the Café VIK interface, and can order equipment that they need for their jobs, such as IT kit and mobile phones via an online authorisation process. Café VIK also incorporates a flexible benefits system which allows employees to make choices on their benefits package and view its value at any time. The range of benefits can be tailored to suit individual lifestyles or circumstances, and they can be exchanged and traded online. Employees can trade up to three days' holiday for their cash value. The benefits are elected annually and staff are given a four- to five-week window to decide on them. Staff with 30 days' holiday who find that they can not use it all tend to trade down. Employees can choose from a range of discounted benefits such as travel insurance and health club membership, and company-provided schemes such as life assurance and dental cover – pet insurance is also on the menu. ICL uses its buying power to get good rates to pass on to employees.

The learning gateway provides a single portal to all available learning and development opportunities. Learning programmes are supplied by the e-learning provider KnowledgePool. The portal features a database of information of over 5,000 learning options including online, CD-ROM and classroom-based courses, books and videos. A community homepage has links to a range of additional material such as management development information and online libraries. A system of online professional and knowledge communities has established Café VIK as the centre for knowledge management throughout the organisation.

By 2002, 35% of ICL's employees were mobile workers, and its growing number of remote workers can access the intranet to ensure that they can operate effectively from home or wherever via the Extended Connected Office which gives them access to mobile phone networks and fixed lines, email facilities, the Internet and the Café VIK intranet. These are available on laptops, PCs, PDAs or WAP phones. New joiners to the organisation can access a short walk-through on general information about ICL, its values, employment policies and key information about being an ICL employee.

ICL is continually improving the transactional scope of Café VIK for its employees. It is, however, clear that some staff do not make the time to browse through the HR intranet and to take advantage of its knowledge-sharing capabilities. In fact, some staff have not registered on My Café VIK and are therefore missing out on the advantages it offers and reducing the operational scope of the intranet.

Questions for consideration and discussion

1 Using your knowledge of this chapter and the case, what are the benefits of such an e-HR system to ICL, its managers and individual employees?

2 Why do you think that some employees fail to use Café VIK?

3 And what recommendations can you make that will help ICL boost the user rate of applications such as employee self-service?

EXPLORE FURTHER

CIPD (2005) *Technology and People Management: The opportunity and the challenge*. London, CIPD

CIPD (2006) *HR and Technology: Beyond delivery*, Change Agenda. London, CIPD

CIPD (2006) *The Changing HR Function: The key questions*, Change Agenda. London, CIPD
This selection of CIPD material concerning technology in HRM provides a professional overview of the development and issues of the topic. Written in a very accessible style, they are useful for students and practitioners alike.

CIPD (2007) *HR and Technology: Impact and advantages*. London, CIPD
This latest report from the CIPD examines the use of technology in nine public, private and not-for-profit sector organisations, focusing on its impact on the delivery and support of HR activity and processes, employee communications and engagement, and the changing role and skills of HR and other managers.

ASHTON, C. (2001) *E-HR: Transforming the HR function*. London, Business Intelligence
This is an in-depth report on how organisations are making the shift to e-HR. It features a survey of 91 organisations and case studies including Cisco, IBM, Oracle, BP, BT and Nokia (see **www.businessintelligence.co.uk**).

GUEUTAL, H. G. and STONE, D. L. (2005) *The Brave New World of e-HR: Human resource management in the digital age*. San Francisco, Jossey-Bass
This textbook offers an overview of the major technological trends in e-HR and shows how to use technology to enhance organisational effectiveness.

CHAPTER 5

Labour law

David Lewis *and* Malcolm Sargeant

INTRODUCTION

This chapter is about the legal and policy contexts of HR management, or, put another way, how the labour market is regulated and what the objectives of such regulation are. In this way, it goes beyond the previous chapter and also lays an important basis for most of the following chapters. 'Regulation' is the way that the state sets rules for how people are treated at work, through laws and the other tools such as funding that it can use to manage the national economy. It is important for HR professionals to understand these state policies and laws because they are expected to advise other managers on how they apply. If you work in HR, one of your major responsibilities will be ensuring that your organisation complies with current employment law. This chapter talks about the law as it is currently, but there are always changes and updates. You should therefore be prepared to make use of the Internet links at the end of this chapter to keep yourself up to date.

LEARNING OUTCOMES

By the end of this chapter readers should be able to:

- explain the different elements that make up the national policy on employment regulation
- explain the role of the public and the private sector in the labour market
- give an account of employment law relating to equalising employment opportunities.

This chapter is structured in three parts. The first part deals with the policy context, and employment services in particular. The second part examines discrimination at the workplace. The third part considers the legal status of workers in the labour market.

The chapter concludes with the main case study.

Reference sources named within the chapter may be looked up in the *References and further reading* section at the end of the book.

Patricia Dacas was a cleaner who had a 'temporary worker agreement' with an employment agency, Brook Street Bureau. This agreement stated that its terms 'shall not give rise to a contract of employment between Brook Street and the temporary worker, or the temporary worker and the client'.

Brook Street had a contract with Wandsworth Borough Council to provide agency staff. This set out the agency's responsibilities and provided that the Council would pay Brook Street on the receipt of invoices. These invoices were calculated from timesheets completed by the agency staff supplied to the Council.

For a number of years Ms Dacas worked exclusively at a hostel run by the Council. The Council had day-to-day control over her work and supplied her with cleaning materials, equipment and an overall. She worked fixed hours for five days a week. The agency fixed her pay rate and paid her wages out of the sums received from the Council. Brook Street also deducted PAYE and National Insurance contributions and issued payslips. Ms Dacas arranged her holidays and notified any sickness absence to the agency.

As a result of a dispute between Ms Dacas and a visitor to the hostel, the Council requested that she be withdrawn from the contract. In the light of this incident and a previous one when she was thought to have been rude, Brook Street notified her that it would no longer be finding work for her. Ms Dacas claimed unfair dismissal on the basis that she was an employee either of the agency or the Council.

Questions for consideration and discussion

1   Would an employment tribunal be entitled to conclude that Ms Dacas was employed by neither the agency nor the Council?

2   Should an employment tribunal be free to look at the reality of the relationship between Ms Dacas and Brook Street and disregard the label that the parties put on their contract?

3   Alternatively, would a tribunal be entitled to decide that even though there was no written contract between Ms Dacas and the Council, a contract of employment could be implied between them?

4   What requirements would have to be met for a contract of employment to be implied?

When you have considered how you might answer these questions, it is recommended that you read the Court of Appeal's judgment in *Dacas v Brook Street Bureau*. The case citation is [2004] IRLR 358.

1   THE POLICY CONTEXT

The United Kingdom Government has a national plan for employment. This is part of a wider European employment strategy for employment organised by the European Union. Some of the UK targets are therefore influenced by European policies. An example of this was set out in 'the Lisbon strategy' in 2000. This established a ten-year plan to make Europe 'the most dynamic and competitive knowledge-based economy in the world, capable of sustainable economic growth with more and better jobs and greater social cohesion, and respect for the environment'. The Lisbon strategy called for governments to – amongst other matters – develop policies with the intention of increasing the total employment rate to 67% by 2005 and 70% by 2010; increasing the female employment rate to 57% by 2005 and 60% by 2010; and increasing the employment rate of older workers to 50% by 2010. It was a policy of combining economic growth with a concern to advance social cohesion (see *Facing the Challenge: The Lisbon strategy for growth and employment*, Report from the High-Level Group chaired by Wim Kok, November 2004).

In order to help achieve this and its own policies, the UK Government has set a number of objectives, which include developing:

- active labour market policies, including help for those without work

- policies that make work pay – such as incentives to work, paid through the tax and benefits system

- policies that reduce barriers to work, such as those concerned with education, skills development and training.

One way of implementing these objectives is by a programme of promoting training and lifelong learning – this is about increasing the skills and the qualification levels of the working age population (less than 15% of the population now have no qualification).

THE ROLE OF THE PUBLIC AND PRIVATE SECTORS

Since the 1980s, the UK Government has given many of the functions relating to labour market regulation and other public service areas to executive agencies and similar bodies. These bodies are usually financed by a parent department of the civil service and are responsible for carrying out many aspects of the public sector's contribution to the regulation of the labour market. The Government's review of executive agencies describes their role thus (in *Creation, Review and Dissolution of Executive Agencies, April 2004*: Cabinet Office, 2004):

> *Executive agencies were created to enable executive functions within government to be carried out by a well-defined business unit with a clear focus on delivering specified outputs within a framework of accountability to Ministers.*

By the mid-1990s the agency model had become the principal organisational type for public service delivery. And by 1997, when most of the 'creation' phase was over, some three-quarters of all civil servants were working for executive agencies. The present Government has continued to develop this policy. Examples of such bodies in the employment sector are Jobcentre Plus and the Learning and Skills Council. There is an agencies and public bodies website which provides more information on such agencies. It can be found at **www.civilservice.gov.uk/improving_services/agencies_and_public_bodies/ index.asp**.

The United Kingdom also has a history of the private sector playing an increasingly important role throughout the twentieth century in the employment field. This has been predominantly in the supply of temporary workers and candidates to fill permanent vacancies with client organisations.

PRIVATE EMPLOYMENT SERVICES

There is a long-established and active private sector concerned with the placement of people in permanent employment and with the provision of temporary workers. Today, some 500,000 workers use its services each week. The industry has been regulated since 1973, when the Employment Agencies Act 1973 came into force. This contained a system for licensing and regular inspections by the Department of Employment. The implementation of this Act was changed by the Conduct of Employment Agencies and Employment Businesses Regulations 2003 (SI 2003/3319), which came into effect in April 2004 (see **www.opsi.gov.uk**).

The 1973 Act and the 2004 Regulations distinguish between employment businesses and employment agencies. Employment businesses are those that are concerned with the supply of temporary staff, whereas employment agencies are those that are concerned with the supply of work-seekers to fill permanent vacancies with client organisations (see sections 13(1) to 13(3) Employment Agencies Act 1973). Many organisations are both employment businesses and employment agencies.

The main provisions of the Act and the Regulations are:

- Neither an employment agency nor employment business may charge fees to work-seekers for finding them work or seeking to find them work. Neither an agency nor an employment business may make help to a work-seeker conditional upon using other services which require a fee. There is a restriction on the terms that can be included in contracts between employment businesses and hirers which have the effect of preventing temporary workers from taking up permanent jobs unless a fee is paid to the employment business first.

- An employment business may not introduce a work-seeker to a hirer to perform the normal tasks carried out by a worker who is taking part in an industrial dispute or other industrial action, unless it is an unofficial strike or industrial action – ie one that does not take place within the rules governing such actions contained in the Trade Union and Labour Relations (Consolidation) Act 1992.

- Employment businesses are not able to withhold pay owed to a temporary worker just because the worker has not obtained a signed worksheet from the hirer.

- When an agency or business first offers to provide a work-seeker with services, the agency or business must supply the work-seeker with details of its terms of business and fees (if any). The agency or business will obtain the agreement of the work-seeker on fees, if any, and the type of work the agency or business will try to find for the work-seeker.

- Employment businesses must agree whether the work-seeker is, or will be, employed under a contract of service or a contract for services. The work-seeker will also be given an undertaking that the business will pay him or her for the work that he or she does, regardless of whether the business is paid by the hirer. Other terms of business will include the rate of remuneration paid to the work-seeker and the minimum rate of remuneration to be paid to the employment business, details of any entitlements to holidays and to payment in respect of holidays.

- Similar requirements are imposed upon employment agencies to explain to work-seekers what services will be provided and details of any fees to be paid to the agency for work-finding services, although fees may only be charged to work-seekers wanting work in such areas as sport, music, dance and theatre.

- Agencies and businesses are required to keep documentation showing the work-seeker's agreement to the terms of business and any changes to them. Neither an agency nor a hirer may introduce or supply a work-seeker unless the agency or business has sufficient information about the hirer, the dates on which the work-seeker is required and the duration of the work, the position to be filled and the experience, training and qualifications necessary to work in this position, including the rate of remuneration to be paid to the work-seeker. There are similar conditions concerning the finding out of information about a work-seeker before that person can be introduced to a hirer. Agencies and employment businesses must obtain references on job-seekers wishing to work with vulnerable persons.

- Every advertisement must carry the full name of the agency or business and state the nature of the work, its location and the minimum qualifications necessary when advertising rates of pay.

- Employment agencies must not introduce an employer to a young person under the age of 18 years if that person is attending school or has just left school, unless that person has received vocational guidance from their local careers service.

- There are strict rules on record-keeping.

Generally, the Act and the Regulations regulate the relationship between the hirer and the agency or business and the relationship between the job-seeker and the agency or business. They set down the requirements for communicating information between all the parties involved and the terms of the agreements between each of the parties.

Anyone who contravenes the prohibition on charging fees to work-seekers, fails to comply with Regulations to secure the proper conduct of the agency or business, falsifies records or fails, without reasonable excuse, to comply with a prohibition order, will be guilty of an offence and subject to a fine not exceeding £5,000. There is a further fine of up to £1,000 for obstructing any officer from carrying out enforcement functions. An employment tribunal may make an order prohibiting a person (or company) from conducting or being concerned with an employment agency or business for up to 10 years on the grounds that the person is unsuitable because of misconduct or any other sufficient reason.

In addition, terms of contracts with hirers or work-seekers which are invalid in terms of the Act or Regulations will be unenforceable. Any contravention of the Act or Regulations which causes damage, including death or injury, will be actionable in civil law.

REFLECTIVE ACTIVITY

Do you have any experience of private employment agencies?

How important are they and the rules regulating them to the work of an HR professional?

PUBLIC EMPLOYMENT SERVICES

Jobcentre Plus is an executive agency of the Department for Work and Pensions and provides the public sector part of the UK employment service (see **www.jobcentreplus.gov.uk**). The purposes of the Agency are outlined in its annual report. In summary, these are to:

- increase the effective labour supply by helping as many unemployed and economically inactive people of working age as possible to move into jobs or self-employment

- provide employers with high-quality demand-led services to help fill vacancies

- help people of working age in the most disadvantaged groups and areas to move closer to the labour market

- work towards parity of outcomes for minority ethnic customers

- ensure that people receiving working age benefits fulfil their responsibilities and are offered appropriate high-quality help and support

- pay people of working age the correct amount of benefit to which they are entitled.

Initiatives include Internet jobpoint terminals on its website, making it the most heavily used Government website; providing details of local job vacancies on digital television; building up direct payment of benefits (to individual bank accounts) so that these amounted to 2,648,182 such payments in April 2004.

2 DISADVANTAGED PEOPLE IN THE LABOUR MARKET

Other ways of improving the supply of labour include increasing the employment rate of those who are disadvantaged in the market.

WOMEN

The Commission for Equality and Human Rights provides the following information (**www.equalityhumanrights.com**): 44% of women and 10% of men work part-time. The average hourly earnings for women working full-time are 18% lower than for men; for women working part-time, earnings are 40% lower than for men working full-time. Women are the majority in administrative and secretarial and personal service jobs, whereas men hold the most skilled trades.

The Government tries to encourage women's participation in the labour market through various work–life balance initiatives, including improved childcare help, financial incentives and flexible working. Outlined below are some of the key provisions relating to flexible and part-time working and equal pay.

Flexible working

The Flexible Working (Procedural Requirements) Regulations 2002 (SI 2002/3207) and the Flexible Working (Eligibility, Complaints and Remedies) Regulations 2002 (SI 2002/3236) set out the rules for encouraging individuals to apply to their employer for more flexible work arrangements, and to have that request treated seriously. Employees have the right to:

- apply to work flexibly
- have their application considered in accordance with the procedures set out in the regulations
- be turned down only where there is a clear business reason for doing so
- be accompanied when having the meeting with the employer to discuss the application
- have a written explanation as to why it was turned down
- appeal and to complain to an employment tribunal if the Regulations have not been followed.

Employers have the right to reject an application when the work arrangements sought cannot be reconciled with the needs of the business.

Part-time work

The treatment of part-time workers is a discrimination issue, because the great majority of part-time workers are female (see *R v Secretary of State, ex parte Equal Opportunities Commission* [1994] IRLR 176 HL). In the United Kingdom, women represent 33% of all those working full-time and 81% of all those working part-time.

Evidence given by the Equal Opportunities Commission to the Education and Employment Committee of the House of Commons contained examples of how part-time workers were disadvantaged. Over 75% of female part-timers, for example, earn less than the average hourly wage. About 54% of male part-timers and 42% of female part-timers work for employers who do not have a pension scheme, compared with 25% of full-time employees. Part-time work is still mostly confined to the low-paid in a relatively narrow range of occupations. There appear to be limited opportunities for part-time employees to be promoted.

The Part-time Workers (Prevention of Less Favourable Treatment) Regulations which came into force on 1 July 2000 (SI 2000/1551) are an attempt to improve the situation of part-time workers. Regulation 2(1) of the Regulations identifies a full-time worker as someone who is paid wholly or partly by reference to the time worked, and, having regard to the custom and practice of the employer in relation to its other workers, is identifiable as a full-time worker. Regulation 2(2) has the same definition for part-time workers as this, except that they must be identifiable as part-time workers. To be an appropriate comparator, a full-timer must be:

- employed by the same employer under the same type of contract

- engaged in the same or broadly similar work having regard, where relevant, to whether he/she has similar levels of qualifications, skills and experience

- based at the same establishment or, if there is no full-time comparator at the same establishment, at a different establishment.

What happens if there is no full-time person who can meet the criteria? Where a workforce is made up entirely of part-time employees in a particular category, the Regulations will be of no assistance in enabling them to claim discrimination on the basis of being a part-time worker. (In *Wippel v Peek & Cloppenburg Gmbh* [2005] IRLR 211 the European Court of Justice suggested that a part-time casual worker might be covered by the Framework Agreement. However, Ms Wippel could not find a full-time comparator who worked on a casual basis.) One example might be a contract cleaning operation. All the employees concerned with cleaning might be part-time and all the supervisory, management and administration employees might be full-time. The result is that there is no full-time comparator.

Equal pay

The Equal Pay Act (EPA) 1970 came into effect in 1975. Although the legislation has undoubtedly had an impact on the relative pay of men and women, a significant gap still remains. In 2003 female employees who worked full-time earned 82% of the average gross hourly earnings of male full-time employees. This is an improvement, however, on the situation when the EPA was passed. In 1971, women earned only 63% of the average hourly earnings of full-time male employees (see Commission for Equality and Human Rights, *Women and Men in Britain – At The Millennium* (2000)).

Section 1(1) EPA 1970 implies an equality clause into all contracts of employment. According to section 1(2) EPA 1970, such a clause applies to all the terms of a contract under which a woman is employed, and not just pay. The clause has effect where a woman is employed on:

- like work with a man in the same employment

- work rated as equivalent with that of a man in the same employment

- work which, not being work in (1) or (2), is, in terms of the demands made upon her, of equal value to that of a man in the same employment.

In these situations any term of the woman's contract that is less favourable to the woman than the comparable man should be modified so as to be not less favourable. Similarly, if the woman's contract does not contain a term conferring a benefit on her that is contained in the comparable man's contract, the woman's contract will be deemed to include the term.

ETHNIC MINORITIES AND RACIAL DISCRIMINATION

Generally, people from ethnic minorities have lower levels of economic activity and higher levels of unemployment than white people. Ethnic minority households are more likely to suffer lower income levels. Pakistani and Bangladeshi homes have an average household income that is more than 50% below the national average income.

Protection from discrimination

The United Kingdom has the following legislative measures against race and sex discrimination:

- The Sex Discrimination Act (SDA) 1975 provides protection from discrimination on the grounds of gender, gender re-assignment, civil partnership and being married. Further protection for women is provided by the Equal Pay Act 1970 (see above).

- The Race Relations Act (RRA) 1976 provides protection from discrimination on racial grounds. Section 3(1) defines racial grounds as meaning 'colour, race, nationality or ethnic or national origins'. The Race Relations (Amendment) Act 2000 came into effect in April 2001. It amended the 1976 Act and, amongst other matters, it placed a statutory duty on a wide range of public authorities to promote racial equality and to prevent racial discrimination. Protection is provided against direct and indirect discrimination as well as against victimisation and harassment.

Both the SDA 1975 and the RRA 1976 provide for a situation where being of a particular sex or of a particular racial group is a genuine occupational qualification. There are certain situations where it is permissible to use sex or racial origin as a criterion in the selection of an applicant or in providing access to promotion and training. Section 7(2) SDA lists the situations in which being a man may be a genuine occupational qualification. These exceptions apply where only some of the duties of a job fall within the categories, as well as when all the duties do so. They apply where:

- 'The essential nature of the job would be materially different if carried out by a woman.'

- There are decency reasons for a job to be held by a man – such as a job involving physical contact with men where they might reasonably object to the job being carried out by a woman or where the men are likely to be in a state of undress or using sanitary facilities.

- The job concerns working in, or living in, a private home and the job has to be held by a man because of the degree of physical or social contact and the knowledge of the intimate details of a person's life.

- The nature or location of the establishment make it impracticable for the job-holder to live anywhere but on the premises supplied by the employer and there are no separate sleeping or sanitary provisions for men and women, nor is it reasonable to expect the employer to provide them.

- The nature of the establishment, or the part in which work is done, requires the job-holder to be a man.

- The job-holder provides individuals with personal services promoting their welfare or education, or similar services, and this can best be done by a man.

- The job has to be done by a man because it is likely to involve the performance of some of the work in a country where a woman would not be able to effectively perform the duties.

- The job is one of two held by a married couple.

Section 7A SDA 1975 provides similar rules to be applied in situations relating to gender reassignment, and section 7B provides that there is a further genuine occupational qualification concerning those who are planning a gender reassignment or are undergoing the process of gender reassignment. This exception includes jobs that are concerned with, firstly, being called upon to conduct intimate searches; secondly, with living or working in a private home; thirdly, where the location or establishment requires the person to live on the premises and there are not separate facilities for preserving decency and privacy; and, finally, where the job-holder is providing personal services for vulnerable individuals, promoting their welfare or similar, and where the employer decides that the services cannot be provided by someone undergoing gender reassignment.

Under the RRA 1976 there are fewer situations in which a genuine occupational qualification applies. These are where:

- authenticity in drama or other entertainment requires a person of a particular racial group

- the production of visual imagery in art or photography requires a person from a particular racial group for reasons of authenticity

- the job involves working in a place where food and drink is served to the public and membership of a racial group is required for authenticity

- the job-holder provides persons of that racial group with personal services promoting their welfare, and where those services can be most effectively performed by a person of that racial group.

DISCRIMINATION ON THE GROUNDS OF RELIGION, BELIEF OR SEXUAL ORIENTATION

The Employment Equality (Religion or Belief) Regulations 2003 and the Employment Equality (Sexual Orientation) Regulations 2003 were introduced to comply with the Framework Directive on Equal Treatment at Work (Directive 2000/78/EC).

'Religion' means any religion and 'belief' means any religions or philosophical belief. This is not a helpful definition because it provides no meaning to the terms 'religion' or 'belief'. It has been deliberately left to the courts, relying on Article 9 of the European Convention on Human Rights, to decide whether any particular religion or belief meets this definition. The Government guidance on these Regulations states that this definition is a broad one and will clearly include those religions that are widely recognised, such as Christianity, Islam, Hinduism and Judaism. Equally, it will apply to groups within religions, such as Roman Catholics and Protestants.

'Sexual orientation' is defined as a sexual orientation towards persons of the same sex, thus covering both gay men and gay women; opposite sex, which provides for heterosexual relationships; and same sex and opposite sex, which covers bisexual men and women.

Protection is also provided against direct and indirect discrimination, victimisation and harassment.

In the employment context, there is an exception for a genuine occupational requirement. This must be:

- a *requirement* of the job, which means that it must be essential for a person to be able to carry out the job

- a *determining* requirement – something that is crucial to the job

- an *occupational* requirement, meaning a close connection with the job in question

- a *genuine* occupational requirement and not one created just to avoid the regulations.

PEOPLE WITH DISABILITIES

The Disability Discrimination Act (DDA) 1995 was the first measure to outlaw discrimination against disabled people in the United Kingdom and included an obligation upon the employer to make adjustments (the approach prior to the DDA 1995 had been to establish quotas of disabled people in an employer's workforce – see Disabled Persons (Employment) Act 1944; this approach failed). The Act gives disabled people rights in employment and other areas. It is enforced by the Commission for Equality and Human Rights.

The need for action is illustrated by the fact that there are over 6.8 million disabled persons of working age in Great Britain (**www.equalityhumanrights.com**). They account for nearly one fifth of the working age population but only for one eighth of all those in employment. When employed, disabled people are more likely than the non-disabled to be working part-time or as self-employed. Disabled people are over six times as likely as non-disabled people to be out of work and claiming benefit. However, employment rates vary with the type of disability. Some types, such as those concerned with diabetes, skin conditions and hearing problems, are associated with relatively high employment rates. Other types, such as those associated with mental illness and learning disabilities, have much lower employment rates.

The DDA 1995 makes a number of forms of discrimination unlawful (see also Chapters 4 and 5 of the Code of Practice, which give a very good description of these types of discrimination with many examples, some of which are used here). These are direct discrimination, disability-related discrimination, victimisation and failure to comply with a duty to make reasonable adjustments. Each of these is now discussed in turn.

Direct discrimination

Direct discrimination results from treatment of a disabled person that:

- is on the grounds of the person's disability

- is treatment which is less favourable than that given to, or would have been given to, a person not having that particular disability, when

  - the relevant circumstances, including the abilities, of the person being used as the comparator are the same as, or not materially different from, those of the disabled person.

Thus the discriminatory treatment must be on the grounds of the person's disability. There is no requirement for there to have been a deliberate and conscious decision to discriminate. Indeed, much discrimination may be the result of prejudices about which the discriminator is unaware. The comparator must be someone who does not have the same disability and may be someone who is not disabled. It is important, however, that the comparator's relevant circumstances, including his or her abilities, are the same as, or not materially different from, those of the disabled person. It is not necessary to identify an actual person to use as a comparator. Where someone with similar relevant circumstances is not available, a hypothetical comparator can be used.

An example of direct discrimination given in the DRC Code of Practice is where a person who becomes disabled takes six months' sick leave because of his or her disability and is dismissed by the employer. A non-disabled fellow-employee also takes six months' sick leave, because of a broken leg, and is not dismissed. The non-disabled employee is an appropriate comparator because the relevant circumstances are the same – ie having six months' sick leave. Direct discrimination has occurred because of the less favourable treatment of the disabled person.

In relation to direct discrimination there is no justification defence for the employer. Treatment that amounts to direct discrimination cannot be justified, as it can in some other circumstances (see below).

Disability-related discrimination

Section 3A(1) DDA 1995 states that an employer discriminates against a disabled person when:

- it is for a reason related to his or her disability

- the treatment is less favourable than the treatment given, or would have been given, to others to whom the reason does not or would not apply, and

- the employer cannot show that the treatment in question can be justified.

The phrase 'disability-related discrimination' is not used in the Act, but is used in the CEHR Code of Practice to describe discrimination that falls under section 3A(1) DDA 1995 but that does not amount to direct discrimination. It therefore has a wider scope – and a good example of this is given in the CEHR Code of Practice:

> *A disabled woman is refused an administrative job because she cannot type. She cannot type because she has arthritis. A non-disabled person who was unable to type would also have been turned down. The disability-related reason for the less favourable treatment is the woman's inability to type, and the correct comparator is a person to whom the reason does not apply – that is, someone who can type. Such a person would not have been refused the job. In respect of that comparison, the disabled woman has been treated less favourably for a disability-related reason and this will be unlawful unless it can be justified.*

Importantly, this discrimination is not direct discrimination, because, in that case, the correct comparator would have been someone who did not have arthritis and who had similar disabilities – ie someone who could not type. This comparator would not have obtained the job either, so there would not have been less favourable treatment.

There are strict limitations to any justification defence. There may be situations when the employer will still not be able to justify the treatment, even if there are material and substantial justifications for the less favourable treatment. This may occur if the employer has failed in the duty to make reasonable adjustments (see below). The employer will, in such circumstances, have to show that the material and substantial circumstances would have applied even if the adjustments had been made.

Victimisation

An employer discriminates against an employee or another person if the employer treats that employee or other person less favourably than it treats or would treat other employees in the same circumstances because the employee or other person:

- brought proceedings against the employer or any other person under the DDA 1995, or

- gave evidence or information in connection with such proceedings brought by any other person, or

- otherwise does anything under the DDA 1995 in relation to the employer or any other person, or

- alleged that the employer or other person has contravened the DDA 1995.

Treating the employee or other person less favourably because the employer believes or suspects that the employee or other person has done or intends to do any of these actions is also unlawful. Unlike the other forms of discrimination outlawed by the DDA 1995, this form can be claimed by non-disabled people as well as disabled people. The treatment, however, will not amount to less favourable treatment if any allegation of the employee or other person was false and not made in good faith. There is also protection for ex-employees in a situation where there has been a relevant relationship between an employer and a disabled person that has come to an end. A relevant relationship is where there has been an employment relationship during which there was an act of discrimination or harassment. In such a situation it is unlawful for the ex-employer to discriminate against or harass the disabled person concerned.

Duty to make reasonable adjustments

The employer also discriminates against a disabled person if the employer fails to comply with a duty to make reasonable adjustments in relation to the disabled person. Thus, where the disabled person is placed at a substantial disadvantage compared to persons who are not disabled because of a provision, criterion or practice applied by or on behalf of an employer, or any physical feature of premises occupied by an employer ('physical feature' includes any feature arising from the design or construction of a building, approaches to it, access or exits, fixtures, fittings, furnishings, furniture, equipment or material in the building; section 18D DDA 1995).

It is the duty of the employer to take reasonable steps, in all the circumstances of the case, to prevent the provision, criterion, practice or feature from having that effect. This obligation applies in respect of applicants for employment as well as in respect of existing employees. There is, however, no obligation placed upon the employer if the employer does not know, or could not have reasonably been expected to know, that the applicant or employee had a disability. Provision, criteria or practice includes any arrangements. The arrangements referred to include, firstly, the arrangements for determining who should be offered employment, and, secondly, any term, condition or arrangements on which employment, promotion, transfer, training or any other benefit is offered. The arrangements referred to are strictly job-related. Employers are required to make adjustments to the way that the job is structured and organised so as to accommodate those who cannot fit into the existing arrangements. This appears to exclude providing assistance with personal arrangements and care so as to enable an individual to attend work (see *Kenny v Hampshire Constabulary* [1999] IRLR 76). Examples of steps which may have to be taken are making adjustments to premises, allocating some of the disabled person's duties to another person, or transferring the disabled person to an existing vacancy.

An example of the scope of the duty to make reasonable adjustments arose in *Archibald v Fife Council* [2004] IRLR 651 HL. This concerned an employee of Fife

Council who was employed as a roadsweeper. As a result of a complication during surgery she became virtually unable to walk and could no longer carry out the duties of a roadsweeper. She could do sedentary work and the Council sent her on a number of computer and administration courses. Over the next few months she applied for over 100 jobs within the Council, but she always failed in a competitive interview situation. Eventually she was dismissed because the redeployment procedure was exhausted. The issue for the Court was the limits of the duty to make reasonable adjustments. It was agreed that the DDA 1995 required some positive discrimination in favour of disabled people, but did this include finding them another job if their disability stopped them from performing their current one? The Court held that the DDA 1995, to the extent that the provisions of the Act required it, permitted and sometimes obliged employers to treat a disabled person more favourably than others. This may even require transferring them to a higher-level position without the need for a competitive interview. (This was one of the problems for the employer – most positions were at a higher level than that of a roadsweeper and the local authority assumed that it had an obligation to make all promotion interviews competitive.)

REFLECTIVE ACTIVITY

Do you have any experience of discrimination at work?

How important do you think this aspect of an HR professional's job is?

Harassment

It is unlawful for an employer to harass a disabled employee or a disabled job applicant. A person subjects a disabled person to harassment if he or she engages in unwanted conduct which has the purpose or effect of violating the disabled person's dignity, or creating an intimidating, hostile, degrading, humiliating or offensive environment for him or her.

Conduct will be seen as harassment only if, having regard to all the circumstances, especially the perception of the disabled person, it can reasonably be considered as having the effect of harassment. Thus, although there is a reasonableness test, it is not necessarily an objective test because the view of the disabled person affected by the conduct is important.

Section 53A of the Disability Discrimination Act provides for the Disability Rights Commission to give practical guidance on how to avoid discrimination in relation to the DDA 1995 and to promote equality of opportunity. The current Code of Practice was issued by the Disability Rights Commission and took effect in October 2004. Failure to observe the provisions of the Code does not in itself make a person liable to proceedings, but any provision of the Code that appears to be relevant to a question arising in any proceedings will be taken into account.

OLDER WORKERS

There is ample evidence that age discrimination takes place in the EU. One EU-wide indicative survey (Marsh and Sahin-Dikmen, 'Discrimination in Europe', *Eurobarometer*, May 2003) of people's perceptions of discrimination in relation to racial or ethnic origin, religion or beliefs, disability, age and sexual orientation found that the most often-cited ground for discrimination was age (5%) followed by racial or ethnic origin (3%), religion or belief, physical disability, learning difficulties or mental illness (2% each). In the same survey people were asked which of the following would have the most difficulty in finding a job, training or promotion: a person from another ethnic origin, a person with minority beliefs, a physically disabled person, a person with learning difficulties, a person aged under 25, a person aged over 50, or a homosexual. Some 87% of respondents thought those with learning difficulties would be the most disadvantaged, and some 77% thought that the physically disabled would be the next most disadvantaged. In third place was the over-50-year-old. Some 71% thought that such a person would have less chance. There was a significant variation between countries, though, ranging from 17% in Greece to 83% in Finland. The fourth choice, for information, was the person from another ethnic origin.

The Employment Equality (Age) Regulations 2006 (SI 2006/1031) provide protection against direct and indirect discrimination, harassment and victimisation. The definition of direct and indirect discrimination is the same as in the other equality enactments. However, unlike other forms of discrimination (except in relation to genuine occupational qualification), it is permissible to directly discriminate on the grounds of age in some circumstances. There is a requirement to show that the less favourable treatment is a 'proportionate means of achieving a legitimate aim'.

One major issue is whether making people retire is a form of age discrimination. The 2006 Regulations introduced a default retirement age but the Government proposes to review this after five years. Until then employers will be able to enforce retirement at the age of 65 years, and at other ages if this can be objectively justified. Retirement below the age of 65 years will have to be objectively justified. Section 98 of the Employment Rights Act 1996 is amended to add another fair reason for dismissal, which will be 'retirement of the employee'. There is, however, no requirement to go through any statutory dismissal procedure. This is replaced by a statutory retirement procedure as outlined in new sections 98ZA to 98ZF of the Employment Rights Act.

For retirement to be taken as the only reason for dismissal, it must take place on the 'intended date of retirement'. There is still the opportunity for the employee to claim that the real reason for dismissal was some other reason and that the retirement would not have taken place but for this other reason, or that the dismissal amounts to unlawful discrimination under the Regulations. This will not be easy and there will be a heavy burden of proof on the employee. The operative retirement date is the 65th birthday unless there is an alternative date which is the normal retirement age, in which case it is that date. There is then a procedure in which the employer and employee must participate. Failure on the employer's part may render the dismissal unfair.

3 THE LEGAL STATUS OF THE WORKER IN THE LABOUR MARKET

EMPLOYEES AND WORKERS

The legal status of the worker in the labour market is an important issue because some of the protection afforded by legislation affects only those who are employees and not, for example, the self-employed. Many organisations now 'outsource' a good deal of their work, sometimes to the self-employed (see Chapter 10).

One of the features of employment law in the United Kingdom is the distinction between employees and workers. The latter tends to have a wider meaning. The Employment Rights Act 1996 defines an employee as 'an individual who has entered into or works under (or, where the employment has ceased, worked under) a contract of employment'. The definition of a worker is broader – ie an individual who has entered into, or works under, a contract of employment or any other contract 'whereby the individual undertakes to do or perform personally any work or services for another party to the contract whose status is not by virtue of the contract that of a client or customer of any profession or business undertaking carried on by the individual'. Thus there are some individuals who are not under a contract of employment but are under a contract to perform personally any work or services for an employer. Often the latter are treated as self-employed, although they may be as dependent on one employer as those who are employees.

In *Byrne Brothers (Formwork) Ltd v Baird* [2002] IRLR 96 the Employment Appeal Tribunal (EAT) held that Parliament had intended to create an intermediate class of protected worker – one who is not an employee but also could not be regarded as carrying on a business. In this case the EAT concluded that self-employed sub-contract workers in the construction industry fitted into this category. The court stated:

> *There can be no general rule, and we should not be understood as propounding one; cases cannot be decided by applying labels. But typically labour-only sub-contractors will, though nominally free to move from contractor to contractor, in practice work for long periods for a single employer as an integrated part of his workforce.*

By way of contrast, in *Inland Revenue v Post Office Ltd* [2003] IRLR 199, the EAT decided that sub-postmistresses and sub-postmasters were not workers for the purposes of the National Minimum Wage Act 1998 because they had a choice whether or not to do the work themselves.

THE SELF-EMPLOYED

The numbers of self-employed workers has grown significantly in the last 20 years and, in 2004, amounted to approximately 3.5 million people, compared to almost 25 million employees. Over two thirds of the self-employed have no employees themselves and are dependent upon using their own skills and labour. For some workers, self-employment is an illusion. They will be dependent upon one employer for their supply of work and income, but may be lacking in certain employment rights because of their self-employed status.

There is then a real difficulty in distinguishing between those who are genuine employees and those who are self-employed, especially if they have the same dependence on one employer as do employees. To some extent this is recognised by the Government when certain employment protection measures are applied to workers and others to employees only. The Working Time Regulations 1998, for example, refer, in regulation 4(1), to a 'worker's working time', whereas the Maternity and Parental Leave etc Regulations 1999 apply only to employees.

There are a number of reasons why it is important to establish whether an individual is an employee or self-employed:

- Some employment protection measures are reserved for employees, although there are measures which refer to the wider definition of 'worker' including the Working Time Regulations 1998, the Sex Discrimination Act 1975 and the Race Relations Act 1976.

- Self-employed persons are taxed on a Schedule D basis, rather than the Schedule E basis for employed earnings. This allows the self-employed person to set off business expenses against income for tax purposes.

- Employers are vicariously liable for the actions of their employees, rather than for independent contractors.

- The employer also owes a higher standard of care to employees. This was demonstrated in *Lane v Shire Roofing* [1995] IRLR 493, where the claimant was held to be an employee rather than a self-employed contractor. As a result of this, damages in excess of £100,000 were awarded after a work-related accident which would not have been awarded if the claimant had been carrying out work as an independent contractor.

KEY ISSUES IN LABOUR MARKET REGULATION

We now pull together ten key points raised in this chapter:

- It can be seen that both the public and the private sectors are regulated as regards their relationships with employees. However, much of the regulation by the Government is of the private sector and is concerned with the protection of employees and equalising the balance of power in the relationship between employer and worker.

- It is important to note particularly the context in which labour market regulation takes place, such as the requirements of the national plan and the Lisbon strategy.

- Both public and private employment agencies are regulated, and details can be found in the relevant sections.

- Since 1970 there has been increasing protection for employees who have been disadvantaged in the past.

- Women and ethnic minorities were the first groups to be protected in the 1970s and disabled people have been protected since 1995. Age discrimination was outlawed in 2006.

- The anti-discrimination laws are frequently updated to take account of new situations. For example, sex discrimination now covers sexual orientation and gender reassignment. Regulations now protect against discrimination on the grounds of religion or belief.

- All HR activities are affected by anti-discrimination practices including recruitment, selection, promotion and access to training.

- Employees are protected from exploitation by numerous acts including the Working Time Directives, the Employment Act 2002 and its updates.

- In recent years, there have been a number of measures introduced to reduce illegal working such as the Asylum and Immigration Acts and the updates controlling workers from the new EU states.

- HR professionals must understand the importance of the type of employment status enjoyed by individual workers in order to respond appropriately.

Perhaps there are other key points that you would like to note for yourself.

The main case study in this chapter now follows. It gives an example of the possible legal implications of discrimination in the workplace.

MAIN CASE STUDY

Make an initial reading of the case study to gain an overview of the situation, and then read the questions that you will need to address. Now read the case study again, making notes of issues and facts that will help you in your analysis and responses to the questions. Remember to 'read between the lines' as well as picking out the obvious points, and also to consider what is not said as well as what is presented here.

This case study is based on a Court of Appeal decision in 2004. Lakhbir Rihal is an Indian-born Sikh who has been a UK resident for many years. He worked for the London Borough of Ealing as a surveyor in the housing department and then as a senior surveyor in the central technical team. The head of this team and the capital programmes subdivision was Ms Herman. In May 1996, Mr Relf, the acting head of the planned maintenance subdivision, retired. He was not replaced and Mr Rihal, who was as well qualified as Mr Relf, was not given that position. Instead, a white employee junior to Mr Rihal was promoted and shared Mr Relf's responsibilities with Mr Rihal.

In September 1996 Ms Herman retired and was replaced as head of the central technical team by a white man, Mr Foxall. The position of head of the capital programmes subdivision was filled on an acting-up basis by a Mr Gaffikan, who was white and had fewer qualifications and less experience than Mr Rihal.

In 1998 new posts were created as a result of a reorganisation. These were filled by a process of 'assimilation' whereby an existing employee whose post matched sufficiently closely to a new position was entitled to the new post, unless more than one person qualified on this basis, in which case there were competitive interviews. Mr Rihal unsuccessfully applied for a new managerial position as housing investment manager and for the two posts below that as investment planning and standards manager and programme delivery manager. In February 1999 he applied again for the post of investment planning and standards manager but this was given to Mr Gaffikan on the grounds that he had interviewed better. Mr Rihal then brought a grievance under the Council's procedure but this was not dealt with for over 14 months. Subsequently, he complained to an employment tribunal that he had been discriminated against on racial grounds.

Questions for consideration and discussion

1 In deciding whether there are racial grounds for less favourable treatment, is an employment tribunal entitled to look at evidence about the conduct of the alleged discriminator both before and after the act about which a complaint has been made?

2 Where there are allegations of direct or indirect discrimination by an employer over a substantial period of time, should the tribunal look at the individual incidents in isolation from one another?

3 If an employer has an arrangement which is racially discriminatory, does it make any difference that the manager in charge changes?

4 How relevant is it that there was 'a "force" in existence throughout that prevented Mr Foxall and others from picturing a turban-wearing Sikh with a pronounced accent in the managerial roles, which a person of the applicant's qualifications and experience could easily have achieved?'

5 Where a selection process focuses on experience, should any handicap which the employer has inflicted on a candidate by earlier discriminatory behaviour be taken into account?

6 Is a tribunal entitled to take into consideration the fact that a 'glass ceiling' operated in a particular department, which made it very difficult for those who were not white to obtain senior management positions?

7 Where direct or indirect discrimination is alleged, how relevant is the manner in which the complainant's grievance is dealt with?

8 If Mr Rihal had chosen to resign as a result of his treatment by the employer, could he have complained of unfair constructive dismissal?

[Note that a contructive dismissal occurs where an employee terminates the contract with or without notice in circumstances such that he or she is entitled to terminate it without notice by reason of the employer's conduct. Employees are entitled to treat themselves as constructively dismissed only if the employer is guilty of conduct which is a significant breach going to the root of the contract or which shows that the employer no longer intends to be bound by one or more of its essential terms.]

When you have considered your answers to these questions, you may wish to read the Court of Appeal judgment. The case citation is *Rihal v London Borough of Ealing* [2004] IRLR 642.

EXPLORE FURTHER

Advisory, Conciliation and Arbitration Service	www.acas.org.uk
Age Positive	www.agepositive.gov.uk
Basic Skills Agency	www.basic-skills.co.uk
Business Link	www.businesslink.gov.uk
Cabinet Office	www.cabinetoffice.gov.uk
Central Arbitration Committee	www.cac.gov.uk
Certification Officer	www.certoff.org
Commission for Equality and Human Rights	www.equalityhumanrights.com
Corporate social responsibility	www.csracademy.org.uk
Department for Business Enterprise and Regulations	www.berr.gov.uk
Department for Education and Skills	www.dfes.gov.uk
Department for Work and Pensions	www.dwp.gov.uk
Home Office	www.homeoffive.gov.uk
Information Commissioner	www.informationcommissioner.gov.uk
Job Centre Plus	www.jobcentreplus.gov.uk
Learning and Skills Council	www.lsc.gov.uk
Lifelong Learning	www.lifelonglearning.co.uk
Low Pay Commission	http://www.lowpay.gov.uk/
National Institute of Continuing Adult Education	www.niace.org.uk
Recruitment and Employment Confederation	www.rec.uk.com
Sector Skills Development Agency	www.ssda.org.uk
Small Business Council	www.smallbusinesscouncil.org
Small Business Service	www.sbs.gov.uk
Stationery Office	www.opsi.gov.uk
Statistics	www.statistics.gov.uk
Trades Union Congress	www.tuc.oug.uk

CHAPTER 6

Equality and diversity

Doirean Wilson, Matt Flynn *and* Philip Frame

INTRODUCTION

This chapter examines the management of equality and diversity in the workplace as a way of ensuring that organisations both operate within the law and make best use of workers' diverse skills and talents. As the previous chapter has shown, laws in Britain and many other countries now protect workers from discrimination on the basis of race, gender, disability, ethnicity, religion, sexual orientation and age. All employers are therefore obliged to make sure that their staff are not subject to workplace discrimination in how they are managed, how their pay, rewards and benefits are determined, or how decisions on training and development, promotion and dismissal are made.

Employers are also responsible under discrimination law for protecting their employees from bullying and harassment from colleagues and managers. See Chapter 5 in this book for an overview of discrimination laws in the UK.

Compliance with discrimination law is not the only reason why workplace equality and diversity are important. Discrimination has a demoralising effect on employees and can lead to poor work output and a waste of their skills and talents. However, employers who take steps to stop discrimination in the workplace could benefit by using fully the wide range of skills, talents, experience and cultural resources of their workers. In other words, equality and diversity are important to any well-run organisation.

In using the terms 'equality' and 'diversity', we note that they are often regarded as identical, but they are not in fact completely interchangeable. For example, 'equality' means not treating somebody less favourably on the basis, of for instance, his or her gender or age. Here, the focus is on the individual. 'Diversity', on the other hand, refers to approaches which employers can take to make sure that people from different backgrounds, and with different perspectives, are suitably represented, and valued in the workplace. Equality and diversity are closely associated since promoting equality is likely to lead to a diverse workforce; and an employer who promotes diversity is more likely to treat employees equally than one who does not. The first part of this chapter is about age equality, and the second examines cultural diversity.

LEARNING OUTCOMES

At the end of this chapter readers should be able to:

- describe ways in which discrimination can occur in the workplace
- discuss the negative impact that discrimination can have on workplace morale and performance
- adopt a positive approach to working with those of difference
- identify the organisational benefits of having strategies for equality and diversity
- list ways of embedding equality and diversity in all aspects of management
- describe ways in which to harness positive working relationships
- pinpoint ways in which to resolve workplace conflict.

This chapter is divided into two parts. Part 1 discusses the importance to employers of having a strategy for managing equality and diversity in the workplace. This is illustrated in the context of developing an age-positive workplace. In 2006, age discrimination in the workplace was made unlawful in Britain. Although most employers have equal opportunities policies, few have developed strategies for appropriately translating the policies into HR management. This chapter is not meant to give an overview of the new law – see chapter 5 for a detailed discussion of UK law and the Employment Equality (Age) Regulations 2006 – but to examine how an organisation's approach to equality and diversity can impact on how people are managed.

In Part 2 of this chapter we look at how equality and diversity policies can be used to improve team performance. This is demonstrated using the concept of 'cultural positivity' as a twenty-first-century tool for promoting, understanding and addressing conflict among those people who are different from each other, especially those working in teams.

This chapter also draws readers' attention to various diversity-related issues from a theoretical perspective, in order to broaden their knowledge and to encourage their support for a positive approach towards dealing with negative stereotypes. Although the issues raised in this chapter are illustrated by examples of age and cultural equality and diversity, the lessons learned can be used more widely, to tackle other forms of discrimination.

Consolidated Motors is a small manufacturer which supplies car parts to major automotive companies. Factory workers are divided into teams of five, and each team puts together a specific part. One of the teams is responsible for assembling wing mirrors. It is made up of four workers who are in their twenties and John who is 58. John has been with the company since it opened in the 1970s. He gets on well with his colleagues, and they often go out for a beer together at the end of the working day. John is considered the wise man of the team. When things go wrong with the machine, John is usually asked to sort things out. He appreciates that his experience is respected and enjoys the friendships he has at work. However, the job is very hard, and he has told his foreman that he might want to retire on a reduced pension when he reaches 60.

Earlier this year, one of the car companies began complaining about the quality control of the wing mirrors. Some were scratched and had to be returned. The quality control manager investigated and found that workers were not using the machines properly. He ordered the four younger workers to go through retraining. He also advised the HR manager to cancel their annual productivity bonus. John, on the other hand, was treated more leniently. The manager didn't want to embarrass John by making him relearn how to use a machine which he had operated for years, and didn't feel there was much point in training him, since he was going to retire the next year. Besides, there is a cost associated with training, and it did not make sense to waste money on someone who would be leaving soon anyway. He also let John keep his bonus as a 'retirement gift'.

Questions for discussion

1 How would John's colleagues feel about this situation?

2 Might John feel singled out by being treated differently from the others?

3 What might happen to the work team if one of them is singled out for better treatment?

4 Can John remain productive if he doesn't go through the same training as the others?

5 Is the quality control manager guilty of age discrimination?

Throughout, the reader is encouraged to reflect on his or her previous experiences of equality and diversity in work and learning.

The chapter concludes with the main case study.

Reference sources named within the chapter may be looked up in the *References and further reading* section at the end of the book.

1 EQUALITY: THE EXAMPLE OF AGE

The starter case study above shows that discrimination can often be unintentional, as demonstrated by the quality control manager, who probably had good intentions. However, the manager is clearly discriminating on the basis of age in that some workers are being treated less favourably because they are being denied a bonus in comparison to another employee because of their age. (Remember that age discrimination can affect young as well as older employees.) Under the new age discrimination laws, this is unlawful.

Consider the situation from John's perspective. His manager assumes that he will retire early, and decides not to provide training which is essential for him to remain productive. Perhaps he will later decide not to take early retirement; but without training it will be difficult for him to continue in his job. Even if he does keep his plans to retire early, he may still have a few more years of service which will be marked by worsening performance in comparison with his colleagues. Those colleagues may also resent the fact that he received a bonus when they did not – despite similar performances. He may therefore be pushed out of work with a sense that he is no longer a contributing team member.

The scenario described is often called allowing staff to 'coast into retirement', and is common to many organisations. It can appear to be the easy way to remedy performance problems of older workers, since uncomfortable discussions can be avoided, but is one of the factors that can lead to premature exit from the labour market.

THE POLITICAL CONTEXT

Governments across Europe have become increasingly concerned about age discrimination because of the effect it has on older people's employment. Both the EU and the UK have set targets for increasing older people's participation in work. The UK government wants 80% of the working age population (including 1 million additional older workers) to be economically active (European Commission, 2005). To achieve this goal, it has changed state pension rules, as well as tax regulations on occupational pensions, to restrict early retirement and make later retirement more attractive to workers (DWP, 2005).

All EU member states have strategies for increasing the number of older workers, although some are taking a different approach. Sweden, like Norway, has a state pension age of 65, but older workers have the right to continue in work for a further two years (OECD, 2003). Belgium, Germany and Italy are all countries with very low real retirement ages which are now focusing on state pensions and redundancy laws to restrict opportunities for early retirement (OECD, 2005). Finland has seen the sharpest growth in the number of older workers, which reflects employers' and unions' application of 'Workability' tools to help people remain economically active longer. The Workability model, developed by the Finnish Institute for Occupational Health (Ilmarinen, 1999), is used to identify factors early which might lead to premature exit from the labour market. Workers who are at risk of early exit through incapacity, for example, are given support such as changes to work design to help them stay in work. Across most of the EU, negotiations between employers' groups and unions have been shaping the scope and application of age discrimination regulations. In the UK, employers will be uncertain about how the new regulations will apply to them until the courts interpret the law – particularly on the justifications for discrimination (discussed below).

The age discrimination regulations are part of the Government's efforts to meet its 1 million older workers target. Much of the law is what the Government itself termed 'light touch' (DTI, 2005) employment regulation. Retiring employees now have the right, for example, to request an extension to their working lives and the right to request flexible working should they have eldercare responsibilities. Although neither right-of-request gives older workers any new employment rights, they do force employers to respond to employees' requests by considering (however superficially) the possibilities for facilitating the extension of working life.

Too often, employers' management of performance and development is built on expectations that older workers want to, or could at least be persuaded to, retire early. Measures which could be taken to help older employees, such as training or small changes to work design, are not considered cost-effective, as judged against when retirement could be assumed to take place. Yet a worker in his late fifties is likely to have as long a future with his employer as one in his twenties. Whereas the former may eventually leave through retirement, the latter is more likely to change workplaces.

A number of studies have found that most older workers would like to work beyond what they consider to be their normal retirement age, but they need support from their employers to do so (Owen and Flynn, 2004; Loretto, Vickerstaff and White, 2005; Loretto, Vickerstaff and White, 2006). One found that half of those who are retired now would have preferred to stay in their jobs but to work more flexible hours (McNair and Flynn, 2004). In the UK at the time the age discrimination regulations were coming into effect there was a dramatic increase in the real retirement age, which is now 64.2 for men (just below the state pension age) and 61.8 for women (just above). Changes to employers' behaviours as a response to the law can therefore have a direct impact on older workers' employment.

In the UK, part of the reason for the fact that ageism is to be found everywhere is that the age discrimination laws are so new, and employers have only recently been confronted with the need to define what unacceptable behaviour is. Half a century ago, employers who dismissed female employees when they married were not uncommon – the Civil Service itself was one! Now, after more than 30 years of sex discrimination law, almost everyone would consider the practice unfair and absurd. Age discrimination has, until very recently, gone unchallenged by the law, and practices which are long on discrimination but short on merit have been allowed to continue.

Many employers took steps to eliminate age discrimination before the regulations forced them to do so. In the UK, skills shortages and an expanding economy have persuaded employers to look for new ways to recruit and retain older workers (McNair and Flynn, 2005). According to the Cranet survey, 14% of British employers say that they have an action programme to encourage older workers to remain economically active longer. This is twice the proportion of employers who responded from Germany, where the economy is going through a period of high unemployment. Employers in London and the south-east of England are particularly likely to have policies for keeping older workers employed longer.

Leading efforts to encourage older people to stay in work are 'age champions' which include Barclays, British Telecom, Coca-Cola, Tesco and Nationwide. However, large employers are not the only ones who are benefiting from an increase in older workers' participation. In fact, many of the most innovative ways of addressing workplace ageism derive from small firms, which come from a range of sectors. The most common feature of age champions is a recognition that they need to recruit and retain skilled workers, and age discrimination is inconsistent with these objectives. In other words, age discrimination does not make business sense.

Perhaps one of the highest-profile age champions is B&Q. Rapid expansion in the early 1990s forced the company to look to recruit beyond the pool of their typical job applicants and to challenge the assumptions made about older workers' ability to work in DIY stores. They soon found that, with machines and technology, there are few tasks which are too physically demanding for a 60-year-old employee. The retailer has also found that its older employees have lower rates of absenteeism and turnover than their younger colleagues. Many of their older employers have experience working in a trade, and use their skills and knowledge to help customers. Today, 21% of B&Q front-line employees are over 50.

REFLECTIVE ACTIVITY

Think of an industry you are familiar with.

When do people normally expect to retire? Are employees expected to retire early? What does the employer do, if anything, to help or encourage people to stay on at work longer?

What are the costs to an employer, and the workforce, of operating ageist policies? What are the benefits of age equality?

A STRATEGY TO ELIMINATE DISCRIMINATION

The starting point for employers has often been establishing or amending an equal opportunities policy prohibiting discrimination in the workplace. However, simply drafting a statement into the staff handbook or annual report to say that the company does not discriminate does little to change workplace culture. With ageism, there is a real gap between what HR managers *say* corporate policy is, and what line managers *think* to be the case.

Equal opportunities policies require employers to review HR policies and practices in order to remove discrimination from the workplace and to make policy a working reality. The new age discrimination regulations have brought calls for employers to build 'integrated age strategies' (Walker, 1999) – that is, to have age policies which are pushed firmly into all aspects of HR policies and practices. They also require employers to raise awareness of age management within their workplaces, particularly amongst managers. In this way the barriers which older workers face in staying economically active are more likely to be removed.

Although age equality policies are common in the UK workplace, age strategies are more rare. According to WERS 2004 data, 73% of workplaces have equal opportunity policies (see Table 15). However, only a minority regularly review activities to eliminate ageism (see Table 16). Around 16% of employers regularly review their recruitment and selection procedures – and yet only one in 18 reviews pay rates to eliminate age biases in its pay system. Employers are almost as slow to review policies in order to eliminate other forms of discrimination. For example, only one in five reviews recruitment and selection procedures to identify discrimination on the basis of gender, ethnicity or disability.

Table 15 The incidence of equal opportunity policies in UK workplaces

	Equal opportunity policy (%)
All workplaces	73
Organisation size	
10–99 employees	46
10,000 or more employees	97
Industry	
Manufacturing	52
Hotels and restaurants	50
Financial services	96
Public sector	98

Source: Kersley *et al* (2006; p.238)

Table 16 The incidence of regular organisational reviews, by workforce characteristics

	Percentage of workplaces		
	Review recruitment and selection procedures	Review promotion procedures	Review relative pay rates
Gender	19	11	7
Ethnic background	20	11	5
Disability	19	10	4
Age	16	9	6

Source: Kersley *et al* (2006; p.248)

EMBEDDING EQUALITY INTO HR PRACTICES

Having integrated age equality strategies and practices to carry them out requires employers to consider the effect discrimination has on all aspects of management. Unlike other discrimination law, the age discrimination regulations allow some forms of direct discrimination which are determined by the courts to be objectively justifiable. For example, a restaurant manager may decide not to train any staff under 18 in bartending because it is unlawful for minors to serve alcohol. Although the manager's decision is based directly on age, there is a legitimate business reason for it.

The Government has set two criteria which employment tribunals will use in assessing whether an age discriminatory practice is objectively justifiable. Firstly, it needs to reflect a legitimate business objective; and secondly, it has to be proportionate – that is, the costs to the employee must be compared to the benefits to the employer.

The courts will decide exactly what practices are unlawful, but these criteria are a good starting point to think about age discrimination and HR practices. Think back to the starter case study. There, the manager decided not to send John on a training course because he expected that the company would not benefit enough to recoup the costs. Was this a legitimate business objective? In some circumstances, employers might have a valid reason for using an employee's proximity to retirement (or even the likelihood of his leaving for another job) in deciding whether to send him on a long or expensive training programme. The EU Directive from which the regulations come specifically gives the example of training costs as objectively justifiable. But is it proportionate? If you think of the cost of the training, and the benefits which John (not to mention the employer itself) would have gained through increased productivity and improved job prospects, the decision does not seem to be justifiable.

It is now worth thinking about some of the ways in which age discrimination can affect HR practices. We start with *appraisals and performance management*. We showed above how managers can allow problems with performance not to be looked at, hoping that poor performers will retire early (and often persuading them to do so). In contrast, older workers who have unmet skills needs are often reluctant to ask for additional training for fear of signalling to their employers that they have gone beyond their productive years and should therefore be encouraged to retire.

Age bias in *pay and benefits* is also common, although pay systems that are directly related to age are rare. Usually, such pay systems offer a lower rate to those at the younger end of the age scale. ('Development rates' for the UK National Minimum Wage remain lawful, for example.) Indirect age discrimination is more likely, such as pay scales which reflect length of service. Performance-related pay and individually negotiated remuneration packages can also reflect age bias if they are based on discriminatory ideas – for example, the idea that young people are generally undependable.

Turning to *working hours and job design*, research suggests that older workers would stay longer if their work could be designed to meet their individual circumstances, such as reducing their working hours or reducing the stress associated with their work. In addition, many older workers have caring responsibilities for elderly relatives or grandchildren. Older carers often have fewer opportunities to work flexibly, and the stress associated with balancing home and work responsibilities often accelerates their desire to retire. In 2007, the statutory right to request flexible working was extended to employees with eldercare responsibilities.

Age-related selection criteria for *redundancies* can work in both directions. Common compulsory redundancy procedures – such as 'last in, first out' – disadvantage younger workers (as well as workers from ethnic minorities) who tend to have shorter service. Voluntary redundancy schemes often provide financial incentives to older workers to retire early. In contrast, age equal redundancy systems focus on the skills and competencies which are needed for retention by the organisation, regardless of age.

Older workers are more likely to face age discrimination when applying for jobs, and unemployed people over 50 are among the least likely to find employment. We need to ask ourselves why, if ever, age should be a factor in *recruitment* decisions, and note the recent moves of many leading employers to remove requests for age-related information from application forms. Even when this is removed, selectors may still make negative assumptions about applicants' age, abilities and expectations. In order to deal with this problem many employers now use recruitment tools which are based on competencies rather than biographies in order to limit information (for example, whether someone sat a particular sort of examination that is no longer used) which could be used to guess age.

Employers have a duty to protect employees from *harassment and bullying* which is based on any form of discrimination, including age. Structures should be put in place to make sure that such claims are recognised as legitimate, and addressed effectively, fairly, and in a timely manner.

Perhaps the most difficult issue which the age discrimination regulations address is that of *retirement*. Employers can lawfully set a compulsory retirement age which is 65 or over without needing to justify it. However, an employee who remains in work beyond 65 is protected against *unfair dismissal*. It has been widely suggested that the default retirement age, as well as the statutory framework for handling retirement, are age discriminatory and do not fully implement the EU Directive from which the regulations derive. The European courts are currently considering this issue. Nevertheless, good age management practices should include clear and understandable criteria for handling requests to stay in work beyond retirement age.

The above list of issues highlights just some of the issues which employers and HR specialists must consider when developing strategies for promoting equality, including those related to age, in the workplace. What should be clear is that equality issues affect management at all levels of an organisation. Discriminatory practices could exist in all corporate HR policies (for example, pay scales with long-service-related higher pay), or could continue in the prejudices of individual managers. It is important, therefore, that employees – particularly those involved in HR decisions – are trained in equal opportunities, are aware of the organisation's policy, and appreciate how this should be reflected in HR decisions.

Many employers are using the introduction of age equality strategies to review other anti-discrimination policies to ensure their continued effectiveness and harmonisation. This is also a way to address multiple discrimination. It is easy to think of older workers as a uniform group, but this is not so. Those who experienced discrimination (for example, on the basis of gender or disability) at a younger age are more likely to be disadvantaged in later working life than those who did not. In summary, it is important not to consider age discrimination as separate from other equality issues.

REFLECTIVE ACTIVITY

As a manager, or potential manager, are there any assumptions you would make about employees or job-seekers based on their ages or, indeed, their other characteristics?

If there are, can you justify these assumptions?

2 DIVERSITY IN WORK TEAMS

In the first half of this chapter we noted the importance of having strategies for embedding equality and diversity in the management of employees. We will now show how equality and diversity strategies can be embedded into HRM practices, thereby enhancing the performance of managers and those people they manage.

One of the most important responsibilities of a manager is to foster the development of effective teams in which employees can work together to meet shared objectives. Daniels and MacDonald (2005; p.30) acknowledge that 'Teamwork also allows the strengths and weaknesses of individuals to be matched so that overall the team is stronger than the individuals who are within it.' This is something that tends to be fairly common among teams of students.

REFLECTIVE ACTIVITY

Were you ever part of a team where it was obvious that other individual members possessed particular team strengths or weaknesses?

Did these strengths or weaknesses have an impact on the team's performance – and if they did, how?

How could weaker members of a team be developed to improve their team performance, do you think?

As members of groups who have traditionally been under-represented in the workforce enter the labour market, work teams have become much more diverse than they were a decade ago. It should come as no surprise, therefore, to learn that 'No one is untouched by the impact of diversity' (Parvis, 2007; p.1). In a recent publicity article, WWP Training Limited (2007; p.1) acknowledged that 'The blending of skills from different cultures has become a major engine of human and corporate development.' Hence the potential benefits that can be gained from incorporating suitable diversity policies and procedures in an organisation.

For example, 'The Latino Employee Network at Frito-Lay, the snack division of PepsiCo, did just that, during the development of Doritos guacamole-flavoured tortilla chips. Members of the network provided feedback on the taste and packaging to help ensure that the product would be regarded as authentic in the Latino community.' This helped to make the product 'one of the most successful new launches in the company's history, generating more than $100 million in sales in its first year' (Rodriquez, 2006; p.1), which was indeed a positive outcome. It is also speculated that 'Diverse teams actually perform better than non-diverse teams because they have a greater range of knowledge and cognitive skills to draw on' (Daniels and MacDonald, 2005; p.31). However, it could be argued that this would depend on whether individuals in the team were working well together.

Diversity in the workplace can also present challenges which managers need to meet in order to maximise the performance of their work teams. Everyone holds stereotypes or assumptions about people who are different from themselves (whether, for example, they are different in terms of age, gender, ethnicity, race, sexual orientation or ability/disability). Usually these prejudices are not spoken, because social traditions and the law prohibit people from sharing their prejudices. False assumptions persist because they are usually not voiced and therefore remain unchallenged. But if we were to 'imagine a world without diversity, it would be hard to tell one person from another, because we would all look alike and have the same conversations since everyone would think alike. We couldn't have team sports because they require varied skills, and only one political party would exist' because there would be 'no need to vote on anything, since we would all see things the same way' (WWP Training Limited, 2007; p.2). When exploring this ideology, we would have to be mindful of the possible implications on societal development.

CULTURAL POSITIVITY

In the starter case study, we saw how a manager's action undermined a positive work team – the workmates who were of different ages got on well with each other until one was treated differently. Now we will discuss how managers can foster good relationships within a diverse team. We will do this by using a concept known as 'cultural positivity'. It is a method which facilitates collaborative working in an internationalised higher-education environment. Here, we will show how it can be applied in a workplace context as a means to break down cultural barriers.

'Cultural positivity' encourages an attitude shift from negativity or pessimism to one which builds a more positive and optimistic outlook. An additional aim is to acknowledge and celebrate cultural differences in order to build pride in self and ethnicity, while addressing potential conflicts that can occur when working with cultural diversity in practice. In America there are several similar culturally positive initiatives such as the Martin Luther King Junior Award and the NH Martin Luther King Coalition that is aimed at honouring 'young people who make diversity, civil rights and tolerance a part of their lives' (Powell, 2006; p.1).

The idea of cultural positivity came from observations made of the ongoing hostilities and conflict that could occur among students working with those who were from different backgrounds. Conflict can occur in any group with more than one team member, but is more likely to happen in teams that are large and diverse, particularly if there is a negative attitude to those from diverse backgrounds. Daniels and MacDonald (2005; p.30) noted that 'Diversity can lead to a reduced group cohesion and greater levels of conflict within the group.' In turn, this can have a negative impact on team relationships and morale, and thus, the standard of work produced.

REFLECTIVE ACTIVITY

Think back to a time when you worked or studied with people from backgrounds that were different from your own.

What was your initial impression of them?

Were your perceptions based on personal experiences or from what you had read, heard or been told?

Were these impressions based on reality?

Did your perceptions influence your approach towards those of difference – and if so, how?

Do you now tend to adopt a different approach when interacting with those from backgrounds that are the same or similar to your own – and if so, why?

How cultural conflict can manifest itself

Conflict in work teams can continue if managers are unaware of the impact that it is having on the members' ability to work together, or if they just don't care. Cultural differences, and the unresolved conflicts that result, are sometimes put down to 'clashes of personality'. But this may not always be the case and managers must be aware of the range of sources from which conflict may emerge.

A good way to analyse conflict is to use Bruce Tuckman's 1965 team development theory (Daniels and MacDonald, 2005; p.32; Tuckman and Jensen, 1977; pp419–27) by which he shows how conflict can emerge, peak, and, with proper management, be resolved (see Figure 8).

Figure 8 The dynamic of conflict, as shown by Tuckman's team development theory

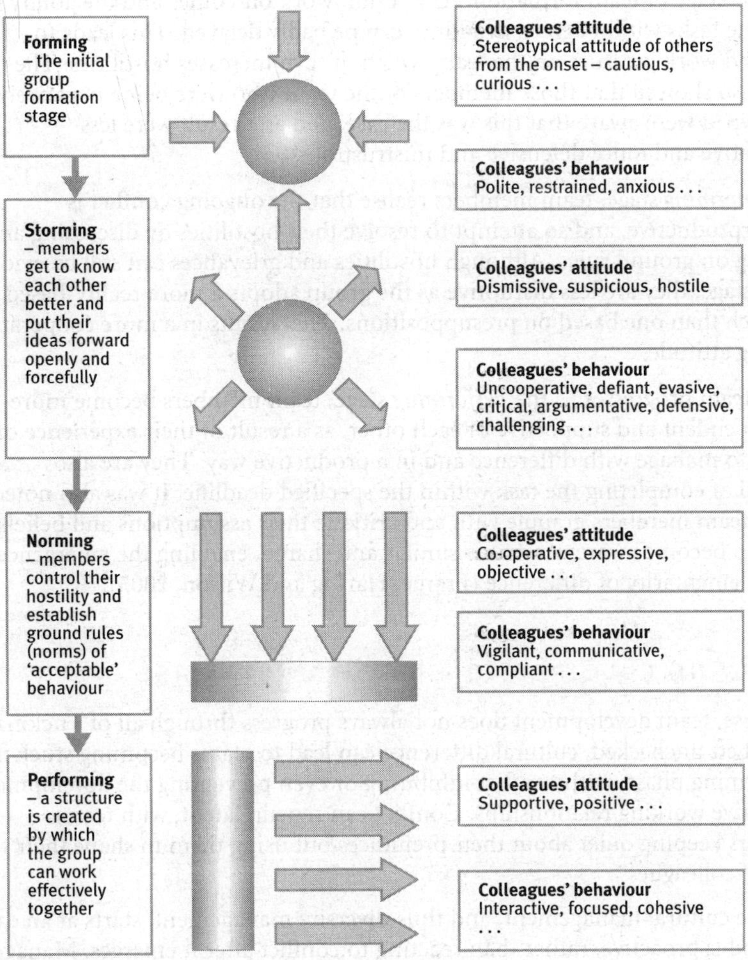

Forming – the initial group formation stage		Colleagues' attitude Stereotypical attitude of others from the onset – cautious, curious . . .
		Colleagues' behaviour Polite, restrained, anxious . . .
Storming – members get to know each other better and put their ideas forward openly and forcefully		Colleagues' attitude Dismissive, suspicious, hostile
		Colleagues' behaviour Uncooperative, defiant, evasive, critical, argumentative, defensive, challenging . . .
Norming – members control their hostility and establish ground rules (norms) of 'acceptable' behaviour		Colleagues' attitude Co-operative, expressive, objective . . .
		Colleagues' behaviour Vigilant, communicative, compliant . . .
Performing – a structure is created by which the group can work effectively together		Colleagues' attitude Supportive, positive . . .
		Colleagues' behaviour Interactive, focused, cohesive . . .

During the *forming* stage, prejudices are difficult to detect. However, they affect individuals' willingness to work with people who are different from themselves, which can slow the development of work teams. This could be reflected, for example, in individuals' collaborating exclusively with others from similar backgrounds but ignoring those who are 'different'. In the study of higher education students, prejudices were shown to affect how students formed working groups. A Ghanaian student, for example, reported that 'When I realised that I was going to be in a team with two Nigerians, I assumed that they would be dishonest so I was always on my guard.' A white British-born student confirmed that when he met the other members of his team, he immediately thought 'I'm going to end up doing most of the work because Jamaicans are usually quite laid-back.' These negative stereotypes are usually based on unexamined perceptions.

They can frequently result in conflict among team members, which occurs at the *storming* stage of team formation. As a result, work outcomes and the ability to complete tasks within agreed deadlines can be badly delayed. This leads to increased work pressure on the team which in turn increases hostilities. The study also showed that those members of the team who were being negatively stereotyped were aware that this was the case, and as a result were less cooperative and more defensive and mistrustful.

At the *norming* stage, team members realise that the ongoing conflict is counterproductive, and so attempt to resolve their hostilities by discussing and agreeing on ground rules. Although hostilities and grievances can still be evident at this stage, they are less disruptive as the group adopts a more reality-based approach than one based on presuppositions. This results in a more cooperative working attitude.

As the team progresses to the *performing* stage, team members become more interdependent and supportive of each other, as a result of their experience of having to manage with difference and in a productive way. They are also mindful of completing the task within the specified deadline. It was also noted that as team members grapple with and critique their assumptions and beliefs, they also become aware of what is similar and shared, enabling the emergence of a complementarity of difference (Frame, Hartog and Wilson, 2005).

RESOLVING CULTURAL CONFLICT — AN EXERCISE

Of course, team development does not always progress through all of Tuckman's stages. Left unchecked, cultural difference can lead to teams becoming stuck in the storming phase, with conflict inhibiting or even preventing the development of effective working relationships. Conflict can remain latent, with team members keeping quiet about their prejudices but using them to shape their views of colleagues.

Effective cultural management, and thus diversity management, starts at an early stage and is proactive, rather than reacting to conflict after it emerges. Managers must encourage good team relationships, particularly when cultural conflicts have the potential to act as barriers to effective working.

One exercise that has been used to achieve this in an academic context can be applied to a workplace setting. It is based on the approach of 'cultural positivity' detailed above. Participants are asked to form work teams which are based on mixed gender, ethnicity, age and location. The above criteria helped to ensure that there was a mix of members in each team, while also preventing them from being dominated by certain groups of individuals. The steps outlined in Figure 9 below can encourage a better awareness of difference, in addition to creating more trusting and harmonious working relationships, by helping to expose and address potential sources of team conflict. Each team was required to follow the three steps identified below and then present to the whole group.

When the model was first used, the audience watching each team presentation would gasp in surprise whenever members revealed things about themselves that

Figure 9 The three steps that encourage better awareness of difference

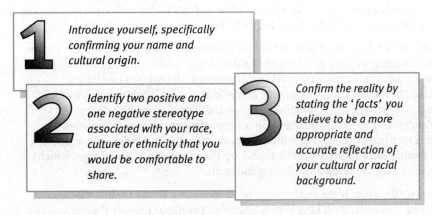

Introduce yourself, specifically confirming your name and cultural origin.

Identify two positive and one negative stereotype associated with your race, culture or ethnicity that you would be comfortable to share.

Confirm the reality by stating the 'facts' you believe to be a more appropriate and accurate reflection of your cultural or racial background.

did not match the stereotypical perception of them, which was, as is often the case, based on physical appearance. This was evident when a blue-eyed Caucasian-looking white female member of one team introduced herself as being a 'Jamaican whose parents and grandparents were also born and raised in Jamaica'. The audience was very surprised by this, especially in the light of the student's strong Jamaican accent. The reaction from the audience was the same when a female member of another team, who looked Asian, revealed that she was of 'mixed race with an Irish mother and an Afro-Caribbean father'.

This exercise challenged and undermined the pre-existing perceptions of participants based on physical appearance; the gasps were the oral representation of this. Since its introduction there has been a drop in the number of reported conflict among team members by as much as 50%. The exercise showed that there are clear benefits for the development of teams in addressing cultural issues in an open, direct and constructive manner:

- People generally welcome the opportunity to present themselves and their culture from a perspective of which they can feel proud.

- Although participants notice aspects of culture, these issues were less prominent between people of the same background.

- Participants discovered their similarities as well as their differences.

- Exercises like this can motivate participants to address negative stereotypes in a non-confrontational and positive way which can significantly undermine the stereotypes' power.

- Diversity exercises can make participants view those of difference from a less negative and guarded viewpoint, in addition to making them curious to learn more about the upbringing and background of the others.

- The same is true of the often unrealistic expectations associated with positive stereotypes.

- Diversity exercises can trigger a shift in the students' perception of others from one that was primarily influenced by culturally driven stereotypes to one that focuses on the individual and their 'here and now' behaviour.

Finally, and perhaps most importantly, the exercise demonstrated the significant role that managers have in taking the initiative and addressing cultural issues at an early stage of collaborative working. If ignored, stereotypes can have a negative effect on team development and effective working which can lead to subsequent management difficulties. When individuals can discuss their differences, and indeed similarities, in a supportive environment, positive cultural identities can emerge which support, rather than hinder, constructive team formation. Productive work teams are then more likely to emerge, which will have a positive impact on the organisation.

Of course, the same ideas can be applied to managing teams of different age, gender or disability. By taking action to enable people to present themselves in a positive way, managers can help to break down stereotypes of team colleagues and their abilities.

REFLECTIVE ACTIVITY

Have you ever been in a team or work situation in which you felt you were being disadvantaged because of your age, ethnicity, gender, background, disability or ability?

If you have, how did it affect you?

KEY CULTURAL POSITIVITY ISSUES

Finally, we turn to the four key 'cultural positivity' issues that must be considered before taking organisational action. When considering how to take action against discrimination in your work team, you should think about:

- your approach
- the timing
- the benefits of participation
- obtaining feedback.

Approach

This relates to the need to choose a suitable approach that is relevant and appropriate for encouraging involvement from participants. The approach chosen should focus primarily on the positive aspects of diversity, and on similarities as well as differences.

Timing

The timing for introducing 'culturally positive' diversity activities is important and should preferably begin at the *forming* stage of the team development relationship. Should this not be possible, a team process intervention at a later stage is advisable, along the lines noted above in Figure 9.

Participation

It is important to communicate the benefits of 'culturally positive' diversity activities from the outset, in order to secure involvement and commitment from participants.

Feedback

This relates to the need to obtain feedback from participants on the relevance and benefits of the diversity activities, and how these can be improved, as well as learning whether the activities resulted in an improvement in interpersonal relations.

Let's think about the difficulties that can arise with regard to the four key issues mentioned above. They include those outlined below.

Approach

A biased 'culturally positive' approach – that is, one that is partial rather than inclusive, in that it does not reflect the diverse backgrounds of all team members – can be counterproductive. Similarly, an inflexibility which results in an unwillingness to recognise the negative effects of positive stereotypes will undermine the effectiveness of this process. For example a manager who assumes that older workers don't need training is denying them opportunities to learn and remain productive.

Timing

An attempt to introduce positive diversity activities when conflict has become the norm within the team is likely to be viewed with suspicion or be met with some hostility. It is better to take a positive approach to diversity from the start rather than trying to make repairs when things go wrong.

Participation

If participants have already had negative experiences of working in teams with those from diverse backgrounds, it can make it more difficult to get their participation in 'culturally positive' activities – unless, of course, the benefits of such activities are made clear.

Feedback

If no action is taken following feedback obtained from participants regarding 'culturally positive' activities, it can lead to the suspicion that there is a lack of commitment on the organisation's part. This in turn can lead to an unwillingness to participate in future activities.

KEY ISSUES IN EQUALITY AND DIVERSITY MANAGEMENT

We now pull together ten key points about sustainable HRM raised in this chapter:

- Workplaces are becoming more diverse as people from different backgrounds enter the labour market. This can be good for business since diversity brings new ideas.

- Taking a positive approach to equality and diversity can benefit you and your organisation by encouraging employees to make best use of their talents and fostering positive working relationships.

- Ageism is the latest form of discrimination to be made unlawful, and most employers will find it a challenge to eliminate it from the workplace. Ageist attitudes are often hidden as 'common sense' and it is difficult to make people realise that they are discriminatory.

- Tackling ageism early can give an employer a competitive edge, since it can make use of an unused source of skilled and experienced labour.

- Discrimination, even if done with good intentions, is unlawful and can do more harm than good to a person whom you are trying to help. It can also have unintended consequences in the workplace.

- Simply having an equal opportunity policy is not enough to stop discrimination. You must make sure that all HR policies and practices treat people equally, and that employees understand that discrimination is not tolerated.

- Stereotypes can hurt team formation, as colleagues hold false assumptions about their colleagues.

- Stereotypes can be broken down by discussing them within a team, but dialogue must take place in a positive and constructive environment.

- It is better to take a positive approach to equality and diversity at an early stage rather than after things go wrong.

- Governments across Europe are taking steps to eliminate discrimination because it harms people and is bad for the economy.

Perhaps there are other key points that you would like to note for yourself.

The main case study in this chapter now follows. It is based on a team conflict situation.

MAIN CASE STUDY

Read through the case study and decide on the recommendations that you would make as an HR manager for dealing effectively with the issues raised.

A medium-sized niche retailer decided to start using the Internet to sell its products to a wider group of customers. The head of the marketing department was asked to put together a team to develop an online marketing strategy for the company. The project team needed a mix of skills, such as a range of information technology skills, design, manufacturing, commercial law, and, of course, marketing.

Because of the range of skills needed, a large team was formed, and conflicts between team members soon became apparent. The IT technicians, who were mostly the younger members of the group, wanted to use the firm's intranet system for collaborating, while other team members complained that they lacked the training and equipment to participate in this way. Older employees from the legal department said that they had had experience advising on earlier campaigns which could benefit this project, but their views had been ignored. People with childcare responsibilities had times when they could not work on the project, and others felt that they were not contributing their fair share. The team was also culturally diverse, and some team members were overheard making inappropriate remarks about colleagues. In addition, it became clear that some team members were working on the project out of hours, excluding others in their collaboration. Because the working relationships within the group broke down, the project team was unable to meet its objectives. The head of marketing had hoped to present a comprehensive online marketing strategy to the board of directors, but it was not achieved.

Questions for discussion

1   How could the conflict have been reduced? If you were managing this team, what would you have done to resolve these tensions?

2   At what stage would you intervene in order to reduce or avoid conflict? How might you raise awareness within the team of the challenges of working with a diverse group of colleagues? Is there a stage at which intervention is too late to avoid a breakdown of communications?

3   The 'cultural positivity' model which was described in Figure 9 was explained using a culturally diverse group of management students. In this case study, differences in the team can be seen in respect to gender, age, class and culture. How could the model be used in order to reduce conflicts based on these dimensions?

4   What are the costs of conflicts such as this? How might the team's performance be affected by the differences outlined above?

5   Are there benefits to team diversity? In this case, can the differences of background be used to the advantage of the team? How might the team be organised to encourage the participants to think about the positive aspects of diversity?

EXPLORE FURTHER

DANIELS, K. and MACDONALD, L. (2005) *Equality, Dversity and Discrimination*. London, CIPD

This book is relevant for various equality-and-diversity-type HR and business degree modules. Designed for those students taking such modules it includes case studies and useful real-life examples.

FLYNN, M. and MCNAIR, S. (2007) *Managing Age: A guide to good employment practice*. London, CIPD/Trades Union Congress

This guide explores in more detail the issues around age, work and retirement. It is focused on a practitioner audience and aims to support the development of good approaches to age management.

HARVEY, C. P. and ALLARD, M. J. (2005) *Understanding and Managing Diversity*, 3rd edition. London, Pearson/Prentice Hall

This book provides a combination of varied readings, real-life case studies and various thought-provoking exercises. Its treatment of the topic of workplace diversity helps to prepare students today for working in an environment where it is necessary to understand all the issues that relate to diversity.

TAYLOR, P. (2006) *Employment Initiatives for an Ageing Workforce in the EU-15*. Luxemburg, Office for Official Publications of the European Communities

This guide provides interesting examples of good practice that have emerged throughout Europe.

Employee Resourcing

CHAPTER 7

HR planning

Andrew Mayo

INTRODUCTION

'The right people in the right place with the right skills at the right time' is a fundamental goal of HRM. This chapter explores the balance between external and internal resourcing – both the strategic considerations and practical planning techniques. It also looks at the dynamics of internal movement and promotion, career patterns, types of potential and managing continuity for the organisation. The next chapter deals with the processes of recruiting – this one is about what leads up to that.

LEARNING OUTCOMES

By the end of this chapter readers should be able to:

- explain and apply the basic principles of workforce planning

- explain the different kinds of potential for growth that employees have and how these can be utilised in longer-term planning

- define the different steps needed in putting together a system of succession planning, and explain what is needed for it to operate successfully

- explain how individual career planning can be helped and encouraged, and how this interacts with succession planning.

Resourcing in today's organisations is much more complex than the recruitment and selection of permanently contracted employees. There are many ways by which a person may contribute to an organisation, and we see very different mixes from sector to sector. Especially desirable resources are described by Boxall and Purcell (2007; p.75) as 'valuable and scarce, inimitable (hard to copy), non-substitutable and appropriate (meaning that they are directly relevant to the purpose of the organisation)'.

The first part of this two-part chapter can be seen as 'macro' in that it analyses the organisational-level requirements for human resources in terms of numbers and skills. This will give us ways to ensure that each group of employees is correctly resourced at a given time, to meet the business plan. The future is always uncertain, but without a plan we are left merely reacting to events. The second part is more at the 'micro' level – seeing how individuals fit into the plan, and also what plans they should have for themselves.

The chapter concludes with the main case study.

Reference sources named within the chapter may be looked up in the *References and further reading* section at the end of the book.

STARTER CASE STUDY

The holding company of a series of retail brands left the operational side firmly in the hands of the local management of each subsidiary. However, the staff functions, such as Finance and HR, were strongly co-ordinated from the centre. The company made two or three acquisitions per year, and in addition its revenues grew organically at about 6% per year.

The Finance Director became increasingly concerned, despite having good compensation packages, that the company was constantly losing professional finance people. There were about 120 such positions across the Group and about 20 left each year. He often had to resort to interim appointments, because recruitment was a long process.

Questions for discussion

You are a consultant called in to help him solve this problem. What kind of questions would you ask?

1   THE RESOURCING STRATEGY

Organisations always have a choice of whether to plan for the future or whether to be agile, responsive and opportunistic based on the needs of the moment. There are risks in both approaches. The former can result in masses of analysis and lengthy papers which soon become out of date and in practice may not be used. If we do no planning, we risk being short of our most essential resource, people, and incurring expensive ad hoc recruitment or temporary staffing that eats into our budgets. The strategically minded HR professional will, however, want to look ahead and be prepared – both to meet the demands of the business plan and for emergencies should they arise.

There is also overwhelming evidence that companies that plan for *continuity* achieve more sustainable results and growth. Collins and Porras (1994), in a book called *Built to Last*, researched organisations that had been consistently successful for between 50 and 100 years to see what common characteristics there might be. They found that one was a focus on internal promotion. In a total of 1,700 years of corporate history of these great companies, only four occasions were found of hiring an external CEO. This is a long way from today's normal practice, where the average life of a CEO in public companies is less than three years. Planning for succession means planning development experiences for people over time. McCall, Lombardo and Morrison (1998; p.5) argue for the importance of systematically managing experiences as the fundamental source of executive learning. They assert (from their research) that 'companies viewed as better managed do more of this than less well-managed companies.'

Questions on which an organisation has to make crucial strategic decisions include:

● At different levels, in filling vacancies, what would be the ideal ratio of internal promotion to external recruitment?

It may be that strategically you need to attract in as much experience as you can from outside, or you feel you really do need a shake-up by bringing in new blood. But once things have stabilised, the desired ratio will generally be in the 80% internal promotion range.

● What should be the ratio of 'fixed' resource (employees with contracts) to 'variable' resource (sub-contract, temporary, interim people)?

This of course depends on the nature of the organisation – whether it is seasonal in its business or subject to other peaks and troughs. 'Interim' people are contracted for a short time to fill a job – typically for three to nine months – to cover (for example) a maternity leave or a lengthy recruitment period for a full-time person.

● Which positions are critical in terms of continuity?

These are the ones we want to plan succession for – we look at this in more detail later.

● How will our diversity policy influence resourcing?

Many organisations today positively seek to reflect the community in which they operate and/or their customers through their employment profile. This leads to setting targets at particular job levels.

WHAT CAN WE KNOW ABOUT THE FUTURE?

There are things we know and things we do not know – things that will happen and things that may never happen – but for which we want to be prepared. Figure 10 shows the factors that must be taken into account in resource planning.

Let us briefly look more closely at the factors involved.

● *The vision and strategy*, the goals of the organisation – Where is the organisation heading? Is it on a strong growth path? Expanding into new

Figure 10 Factors that affect a resourcing plan

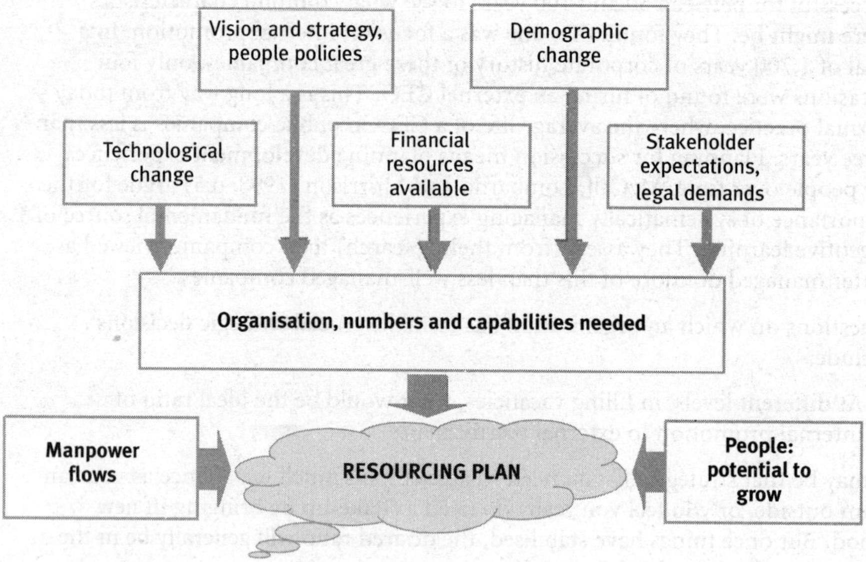

Source: based on Mayo (2004; p.115)

areas? Restructuring the organisation design (such as reducing levels)? Or planning to outsource functions in the future? What will all this mean for numbers and capabilities of people over, say, six monthly chunks ahead?

- *The people policies* – This is where the answers to the strategic questions outlined above come in. What are the policies on resourcing? If there are long-term diversity goals, what effect will this have on recruitment?

- *Demographic change* – Within our normal labour pools are there going to be enough skilled people available in the future?

- *Technological change* – Future technology changes the requirements for people, bringing in new capabilities and making redundant older ones. Planning enables us to reskill employees and reduces actual people redundancies, which both cause pain to people and cost a lot of money. Technology also affects productivity – we may need fewer people to get the same amount of work done.

- *The financial resources available* – Too often this is allowed to define the 'headcount' of an organisation on its own, taking a short-term view. Nevertheless, sometimes budgets are cut in both private and public sectors, and there are limits to what can be afforded. Activities have to be reduced or eliminated.

- *Stakeholder expectations and legal demands* – The law constantly changes and affects resourcing. Examples are the 48-hour week restriction, provision of holidays for long-term temporary staff, and extensions to maternity allowances. Customers are ever more demanding and may look for new services (such as internet purchases), and politicians both central and local make continually changing demands on public servants.

All the above are factors to take into account as an organisation looks ahead. Some will be more precise than others in their implications. But, job family by job family, we should be able to make estimates of how the numbers will change over time – and whether those families will need new capabilities to continue their role. Now, instead of looking to the future we want to look at history and the data we have at present about our employees.

- *Manpower flows* – Our organisation should be divided into job families, and for each we need to be able to answer a lot of questions (see below) to help us understand what is likely to happen to that family in the future. This analysis is essential to compare with the requirements of future resource needs,

- *People and potential* – Finally, at the individual employee level, assuming we are committed to internal development, we need to know the *potential* of people to grow and do different jobs in the future.

WORKFORCE PLANNING

'Workforce planning' is sometimes used wrongly to mean 'HR planning in general', but is actually the modern name given to what used to be called 'manpower planning'. Bennison and Casson (1984; p.8), who wrote still the best guide to this subject, said that 'A stand-alone manpower planning system must be replaced by manpower management.' In other words, any system is but a means towards more effective resource management. If we can do it effectively, it helps us to do the following:

- make a recruitment plan and be ahead of the game, so that vacancies are minimised

- specifically define the number of young entrants, such as graduates and trainees, that we need

- plan for continuity of key expertise and positions

- plan for individual career development to ensure that we have the managerial responsibility and technical/professional leadership to meet the needs

- plan for core competence training to be available as needed.

To do this we need to have a very good understanding of the internal demographics of the organisation – by function, division, location and staff category. For the latter it is useful to use the concept of *job families* – defined as groups of employees who share common characteristics in terms of entry requirements to the job, and a similar job market.

REFLECTIVE ACTIVITY

Think of a university as an organisation.

List as many job families as you can think of that work there.

What do we need to know about job families?

To help us with forward planning, we would like to know – from analysis of the factors that affect a resourcing plan (see Figure 10) – the expected number of people needed in this job family quarter by quarter, plus any critical capability changes. Benison and Casson (1984) talk of 'push' and 'pull' flows – the former being when people move into a job family and the latter when they move out. We therefore need to know:

- the distribution of length of service

- losses for, say, the last two years and the reasons for loss

- where people transfer to and from within the organisation

- the number of people expecting to retire

- the distribution of potential

- the map of key competency distribution.

Stephen Connock (1991) also recommends studying where employees live in relation to the location of the organisation as an additional factor in understanding employee movements.

This data, together with our forward look, enables us to get a picture of what is happening, and what we can predict will happen *within* a job family – but as we link job families together, we can also achieve a number of outcomes, such as:

- forecasting future flows out of, into, and within the organisation

- consequent decisions about young entrant recruitment and actions to reduce attrition in some areas

- planning accelerated development for some individuals

- strengthening of areas that are weak in potential and succession

- taking action on retention of key and potential staff

- creating new career paths

- planning significant capability shifts (and preparing for them).

Modelling a job family itself

Figure 11 illustrates the flows into and out of a job family group.

Figure 11 Flows in and out of a job family

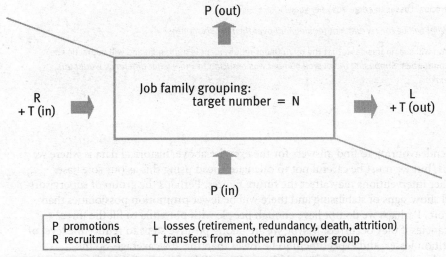

P (out)

R
+ T (in)

Job family grouping:
target number = N

L
+ T (out)

P (in)

P promotions	L losses (retirement, redundancy, death, attrition)
R recruitment	T transfers from another manpower group

Note: '*Attrition*' *is a word often used for people leaving the organisation. It may be voluntary or involuntary. '*Labour turnover*' *is a term used for the percentage of attrition compared with the total workforce.*

First, we decide our planning period – it might typically be six or twelve months ahead. The target number at the end of the period is N. We then feed in our predictions, based on history plus future expectations, of:

- **L**: losses out of the organisation (for which we are planning)
- **T (out)**: lateral transfers out of this group to other groups
- **T (in)**: lateral transfers into this group from another
- **P (out)**: promotions to the group above
- **P (in)**: promotions from the group below.

Finally, we can calculate the expected recruitment requirement (R) over the period ahead. If R turns out to be a negative figure, we will need to either increase the transfers out (if possible) or will need to manage some redundancies. Note that time takes care of many workforce changes, many organisations (especially in the public sector) just cut off recruitment, increase transfers and wait for the N to stabilise over time.

In endeavouring to find answers for the exercise above, historical data is where we start, but we must be careful not to calculate ahead using this as our sole base. Other interventions may affect the future figures. Perhaps the group of supervisors will show signs of stabilising and there will be fewer promotion possibilities than before. Perhaps we do not have enough people with potential to fill the three vacancies if they occurred. Maybe we are taking positive steps to reduce the level of attrition losses, and expect them to be lower than the 20% average. So the numbers we use will always be a judgement of all the facts available to us.

Figure 11 has four arrows in two directions which interact with other parts of the organisation. So we go on to integrate all the job families together, as shown diagrammatically in Figure 12. This is a simplification, especially at the

Figure 12 Integrating the manpower flows horizontally and vertically

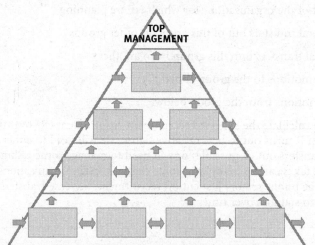

horizontal level, because the transfer arrows from one box may go in to more than one other. However, a model can be built up using Excel or special software that represents a particular organisation.

Using staffing ratios

One common technique in determining numbers needed is to use some guiding ratios. For example, in the exercise above, how many employees will we have per supervisor? The more we have, the lower our costs, but the more difficult it is for a supervisor to provide individual attention and feedback – a classic cost-versus-quality dilemma in staff planning. How many support staff do we need per salesperson? Answers to questions like this vary enormously with the business sector and how complex a sale is. How many employees per HR professional? With such ratios we always start with the bottom of the organisation, or the 'front line' and work inwards. So far we have concentrated only on the numbers. However, workforce planning is not just about the right number of people at the right time – but also about people with the right skills.

Capability planning

For each job family we need to identify the critical core skills essential for the job to be done. There may be others we wish to develop in people, but our business planning focus is on the core. To do this we must have a 'scale of expertise' – and this would typically be a description of four or five levels. Here is one such scale:

- A: Aware: knows what it means
- B: Basic: can talk about it
- C: Competent: can put it into practice
- D: Distinguished: people come and ask how
- E: Expert: teaches others.

One of several pictures we can build up about a job family is shown in the example in Figure 13. Note that this distinguishes between an 'entry level' – the minimum needed to get the job – and a 'fully competent level' – the level we would expect after training and experience. Under each person we have an estimate of his or her current level.

This profile describes our current situation: we can draw up a second one for how we would like it to be at the end of our planning period. Note that it takes time to grow capabilities and we may therefore use a longer planning period here. The comparison of the desired future and where we are now clearly informs our training requirements, but may also dictate the recruitment of specific expertise if we are short of it. No team can operate with every person at the 'entry level', for example. Also, our forward look may dictate *new* capabilities needed – required by technology change, for example.

The requirement for young entrants

For many jobs, the age of people we recruit is not important, and the law does not allow us to discriminate on this basis. Nevertheless, young people with

Figure 13 Core skill profile of assistants in a retail store

KNOWLEDGE OR SKILL	Entry level	Fully competent level	Person 1	Person 2	Person 3	Person 4
Product knowledge and demonstrations	A	C	D	B	C	C
Operation of discount/promotion schemes	A	C	C	C	C	B
Operation of guarantee and service	A	C	C	C	C	C
Sourcing of items	A	D	C	D	C	B
IT systems	B	C	C	D	C	C
Team cooperation	C	C	B	D	C	C
Personal customer delight skills	B	D	C	D	B	C

varying qualifications enter the job market all the time and we need a strategy for their recruitment. Some organisations will say that because young people rarely stay with them more than two or three years, it does not make sense to go to all the expense of recruitment and training just to lose them. It is better, therefore, they would say, to bring in people already trained. Others will say quite the opposite – that it is vital to get the best talent available from Day 1, immerse them in the culture, train them thoroughly and do the best to keep them. Deloittes, for example, is one of the large professional firms putting immense effort into recruiting the best possible graduates.

The range of qualified young entrants is large and we may need to consider several groups. These may include school-leavers with no qualifications other than GCSEs or A-levels, school-leavers with vocational qualifications, ordinary graduates, high-quality graduates, specialised Masters, MBAs, and PhDs. Each of these groups needs different recruitment approaches. Many organisations build up special relationships with academic institutions to ensure good access to the best students in order to regenerate their 'talent bank'. Where graduates have a choice, surveys repeatedly show that training schemes feature strongly in their priorities.

OPTIONS FOR RESOURCES

We naturally think of the people in organisations as employees, and indeed, all the models we have discussed above relate to such. However, in today's world reality is more complex, especially in the highly flexible UK environment. What we call 'employees' are those who have an employment contract with the organisation that makes them a part of the organisation and brings them under the umbrella of all the appropriate benefits, policies and disciplines. They may be 'full-time' or 'part-time' – the latter typically describing a stated number of hours per week. Some jobs may be shared by two part-time people. Because of this mix, the term 'full-time equivalents' or FTEs is often used as the basis of workforce planning. It is not the same as 'headcount' – which is the number of people actually on the payroll. The decision for part-time may be dictated by the workload or is often by employee request in line with their work–life balance.

For many reasons we may supplement the employees with additional people, sometimes called the 'contingent workforce' (see Chapter 10). Among these are temporary and interim contracts, typically used for filling absences, coping with temporary overload or leading a special change project; and sub-contract staff – people with specialised knowledge or skills used on projects. These both typically have a fixed-term contract, which may be renewed. They work within the organisation and after a time develop certain legal rights. In addition, there may be sets of consultants, doing research and analysis, providing advice, suggesting change, working to fixed deliverables rather than for a fixed time. The requirement for consultants is dictated primarily by the capability and capacity of the existing staff. In addition, they may be used to specifically tap into the external world, or for 'political' reasons – using outsiders to bring into the open uncomfortable truths.

REFLECTIVE ACTIVITY

Should we minimise or maximise the core resource – our employees?

List the advantages of dedicated employees on the one hand, and contingent workers on the other.

What kind of organisation would have a higher-than-average ratio of contingent workers?

2 PLANNING FOR THE INDIVIDUAL

THE POTENTIAL OF PEOPLE TO GROW

Figure 10 showed that an essential input to a resourcing plan is the knowledge we have about people's potential to grow and their ability to do something different in the future. Each job family needs a profile of the potential that exists within it. 'Potential' is often seen in very limited way as referring to those who have the ability to become future senior managers. Actually, this is very unlikely to exceed more than 1% of the workforce – and surely, we cannot say that 99% have *no* potential. Figure 14 illustrates three dimensions of potential. 'Height' is about the traditional high-flyers – people rising up through the management ranks. 'Depth' is about creating world-class expertise in core competences, the potential to

Figure 14 The three dimensions of 'potential'

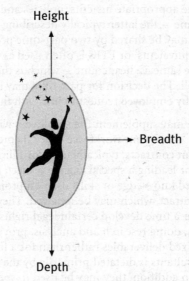

Source: Mayo (1994; p.118)

deepen knowledge and eventually provide technical leadership. 'Breadth' recognises the value that comes from individuals who can turn their hands to several different kinds of job – 'lateral' potential.

To achieve the profile of a group, we must have a system of classification – a shorthand. However, there are many dangers in 'labelling' people. After all, any classification is only a judgement at a point in time – and people change. A good term to use, therefore, is 'current perception of potential'. This also makes it much easier to have an open dialogue with individuals about it.

In choosing classifications, options for describing 'height' available include an assessment of the *speed* of rising responsibility (eg two levels within four years); an assessment of *levels* beyond the current one (eg able to rise two levels); and an estimate of the person's *ceiling* (eg 'will make Grade 15'). We will want a broader classification if we take the extended view of talent. The classification used by a young software company is as follows:

M1 = Able to progress to a senior management position within three years

M2 = Able to progress to take management responsibility

TP = Able to progress to a leadership role (not necessarily managing people) in his/her technological or professional expertise

L = Able to progress laterally and learn new skills outside of his/her current job

O = Likely to stay in present job at present level, and develop with the job

E = Ability not suited to the current position and level.

Should we classify certain groups only in the workforce, or everybody? Talent may lurk in unexpected quarters. Besides, it will be very useful to know the distribution of talent for the population as a whole – and where strong and weak pockets currently exist.

REFLECTIVE ACTIVITY

What do you think would be the key characteristics you would look for in deciding whether a person had the potential of 'height', 'depth' or 'breadth'?

POTENTIAL ASSESSMENT

How can we find out what a person's classification should be? We must not be confused by great performance in the current job. It is good news, of course, but is not a certain indicator of an ability to do a bigger job in the future. The problem is that we are trying to judge whether someone would succeed in a job he/she is not yet doing.

Figure 15 summarises some of the methods that can be used. One dimension is that of the number of assessors – the more we have, the better judgement we are likely to make. An 'assessment centre' is a series of simulated exercises reflecting the target job level, with trained multi-assessors and a systematic evaluation of required capabilities. As is often the case in professional HR, there is a trade-off between cost and quality. The second dimension is that of the observation period. Some methods take into account what we have observed over time.

Figure 15 Options for assessing potential

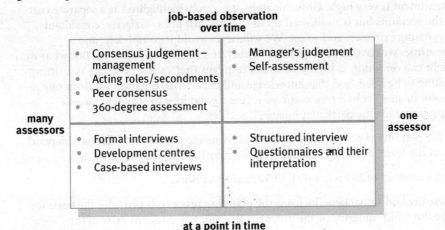

Others, like the psychologist interview and the assessment centre, take an in-depth look at a point in time. For a first evaluation, we would rely on a manager's judgement. We would deploy the more sophisticated approaches with those who are thought to have the highest potential (height or depth).

'TALENT MANAGEMENT'

'Talent management' is a term frequently heard. What does it mean? It refers to the processes of:

- recruitment: seeking the best people in the marketplace

- motivation: enabling them to give of their best

- retention: doing one's best to keep them in the organisation

- development: growing their capability

- career progression: meeting their career ambitions.

As applied to people judged to be 'talented' – ie capable of providing superior added value to the organisation and its stakeholders – the definition of 'talent' is key here. How broad will we make it? Will it include people who do a superb everyday job but who are not going to get promoted? Sadler (1993) talks of the 'talent-intensive organisation', and lists four main categories of talent: specialist expertise, the ability to lead, business-getting talent, and hybrid talent (a combination of the others).

There is a good argument for saying that if we apply these processes to *all* employees, we will avoid being discriminatory and open to accusations of favouritism – and still we will be looking after our 'talent'. Further, we will expand the pool of talent available beyond the narrow way it is often conceived of in organisations.

SUCCESSION, OR CONTINUITY, PLANNING

Organisations can survive without planning for the future, but they will almost certainly incur costs that they could avoid. Particularly at senior levels, the cost of recruitment is very high. Unfortunately, it is rarely highlighted as a separate cost in the accounts but is swallowed up in various cost lines – salaries, consultants, advertising expenses, and so on. We will never avoid it completely, and sometimes we have good reasons to deliberately bring in new blood. But what we might call *continuity* is highly valuable. It means that vacant posts are not sitting waiting to be filled, and that knowledge and experience is passed on from one person to another in a systematic way. It is a good idea to set some targets, appropriate for the particular business, such as:

- the percentage of vacancies to be filled by inside promotion (this may depend on the level in the organisation – so we may have several targets), or

- the number of key posts with identified successors.

There are additional benefits from the planning process. It provides the basis for a 'health audit' in terms of the potential that does or does not exist in the organisation, and also for individual discussions with people about their careers. It helps too in achieving diversity targets as we systematically audit and plan the development of people. This kind of planning is often called *succession planning*. The outcomes of the process are:

- a plan for filling unexpected vacancies
- a longer-term plan for providing continuity of posts and development of people
- an audit of continuity strength
- proactive career moves
- regular lists of people for whom action is required.

Selecting the jobs that need planning

It would be a bureaucratic overkill to plan succession for every job in an organisation. Some jobs are more critical than others in terms of the need for continuity. A 'critical position' is one where:

- success depends on an intimate knowledge of the organisation and its people, and/or
- a time gap in continuity of the position would have serious business effects (leadership and direction, customer relationships, key investment decisions, programme momentum), and/or
- the skill/experience is very hard to find.

Such positions could be individual jobs or generic jobs. Figure 16 shows an example of identifying the jobs for which long-term planning is needed. There are at least two 'planning horizons'. The first is 'now' – what we do in the event

Figure 16 Mapping critical positions in an organisation

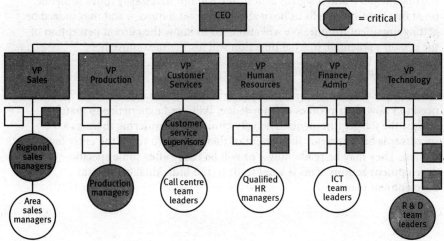

of an unexpected vacancy. The second is some time in the future – two years ahead, for example, or maybe both two years and five years. Note that today's organisation chart is unlikely to be the same in five years' time, but our future scanning – which we talked about at the beginning of the chapter – may help identify new positions that are anticipated and that require planning. It is the names that we are able to put in the longer-term slots that lead to proactive career and development planning.

The information that is needed

For each position we have identified, we need to know the following information:

- *the key requirements for the job: essential levels of knowledge, skills and experience*

  If we are recruiting from outside we will want the best and most experienced person we can find. Internally, however, all jobs are part of the process of development and are learning opportunities in themselves. So the level we look for does not need to be so high. Despite the temptation to pick someone who is already very capable, all jobs should be used as part of the process of continuing development. Each job therefore has a 'minimum entry' level and a 'maturity level' – the knowledge, skills and experience of someone who has mastered the job.

- *information about the person(s) in the job today*

  We will probably have a lot of information about all employees, but what we need specifically here is data related to the current job-holder's likelihood of moving on. There may be a planned retirement date, although this is by no means as cut-and-dried as it used to be. A judgement of the 'risk of leaving' is helpful – the higher we judge the risk, the more concerned we would be about succession. A particularly useful piece of data is 'earliest date for a move'. This will be based on the ideal time to be in a job – the higher or more complex the job is, the longer that will be. The date is then calculated based on the date of starting the job – and it signals action. We will not necessarily move someone on at that date, but it tells us he or she is ready for a move – and may indeed be getting impatient for one. We will also need to know the current perception of the person's potential: in what direction will his/her next move be?

- *information about the possible successors*

  For each possible successor, we need the above information as well. We also need to know their profiles of knowledge, skills and experience to match against the job requirements. The very choice of considering them as a successor is based on our judgement of their ability to reach the entry level of the job. They may be ready now – or will be ready after some specific development actions. This is what leads to the individual career and development plans.

A process to make it all work

It is no use doing all this planning if nobody takes any notice of it when a vacancy occurs. It cannot be a backroom task done in isolation by HR people, and must involve line managers. The most successful organisations are those in which the CEO chairs review and decision meetings, and requires a high standard of data and of commitment by all concerned.

An approach developed by ICL, now Fujitsu Systems, and subsequently widely adopted is one that integrates succession discussions with operational business reviews (see Mayo, 1994; p.267). Generally termed the 'organisational and management review' (OMR) or similar, it synchronises a formal review of issues such as succession, key people development, strategic training issues, and potential strength with the cycle of business reviews. Typically, this might take place every four to six months, being 'cascaded' upwards through business units and subsidiary companies, eventually reaching the CEO. Each level in the cascade generates information that feeds into the next level.

This approach puts the ownership with line management, links business performance with people capability, recognises the dynamism of organisational and people development, and provides continually updated succession information. Actions to close gaps or deal with problems can be taken regularly. Items that might be on the agenda of the meeting include:

- the current structure and people; the changes anticipated
- the distribution of potential
- who should be considered for a move in the next period
- who is at risk
- succession problems and gaps
- series of planned moves
- review of process and data – are they satisfactory?

HR has a number of key roles to play. It will be the designers and owners of the process, responsible for making it successful. It should try to ensure consistent standards of judgements and classification. HR is a broker and boundary-spanner – enabling successors to be considered from, and career moves to take place, across the whole organisation. Its personnel may also be counsellors and advisers to managers.

Several specialised software systems have been created, aimed at succession planning and talent management. Particularly useful for large, complex and changing organisations, they enable immediate identification of successors. However, whatever system is used, its strength is always dependent on the quality, reliability and recency of the data in the system.

PERSONAL CAREER PLANNING

So far we have looked at everything from the point of view of the organisation. But every individual also evaluates his or her own progress and ambition. Most people are not actually very ambitious in the sense of wanting to have a senior role. But they still care about their career – having a sense of moving forward in life.

Just as many organisations are opportunistic in respect of vacancies when they do not have good plans, so most individuals think most about their careers when a change is imminent. Is it better to have a plan, even though the future is uncertain, or not to bother? That is a personal decision, of course. But an organisation that believes in strategic resourcing would encourage employees to plan. The organisation should help individuals to look at options by making information available. The organisation should make information available about the nature of jobs and their requirements – the minimum entry levels referred to above. The organisation can be drawn diagrammatically in the form of a 'map of learning opportunities' showing which jobs provide particular areas of knowledge and experience. There are some career moves that are easier to make than others – so we can identify some typical career paths and acceptable 'bridges' across boundaries and functions. There will be more bridges at the lower levels of the organisation than further up, because specialised knowledge is less of a requirement. So each person should be able to see the options from his or her current job for where he or she could move next. This vision of possibilities is likely to be conditioned by the department the person is in – ie what he or she is familiar with. This additional information will broaden horizons.

The other kind of help is to enable people to understand themselves and their ambitions, using motivational and interest tests, perhaps career guidance events or skilled career counselling. To help them plan ahead, they should always be encouraged to look beyond the next step alone – five to seven years ahead with a clear aiming-point would be reasonable for most. Choosing the aiming-point (there could be two or three alternatives) is the critical and often the most difficult part. Once it is chosen, we can look at the routes to get there – some training perhaps, but mostly the focus should be on 'building-blocks of experience'. These will provide most of the knowledge, skills, contacts and, of course, experience itself that is needed to bridge the identified 'career gap'. Such experience derives not only in the form of job changes but may be achieved by secondments, job enlargement, assignments, projects, committee involvement, and so on.

Secondments are one of the most valuable forms of development, and essential in 'flatter' organisations. Relatively low-risk to all parties, they provide an opportunity for new learning through real-life experiences. This has been the traditional route for international assignments, and many organisations have deployed secondees on a broader basis – to project teams, to new departments, or from line to staff posts and vice versa. Herts County Council, in an effort to mitigate a reduction in traditional career opportunities, introduced a 24-page booklet entitled *Guidelines for Effective Secondments, Job Swaps and Job Shadowing.*

Career paths

In many national and corporate cultures, development is 'silo-driven' right up to high levels. This creates a problem because when people become senior, they lack an understanding of what other functions and operations do. However, there are several general models of career development, and one has to be chosen (or evolve). Models include (Mayo, 1994):

- *the Narrow T* – In this model people remain specialists until the highest level, managing groups of their own specialism but not working outside it. It is not until the top of the 'tree' that they take broader collegiate responsibilities

- *the Wide T* – This is a model more common in the UK, where beyond, say, the first ten years of specialism and junior management, people broaden across functional boundaries and become a 'management resource' thereafter

- *the I* – Here, young entrants are given a general knowledge of the organisation and its business for perhaps up to three years. They then specialise in a chosen area, and remain in that area until reaching senior management, when they become more general again

- *the Y* – Found in highly technical organisations, career opportunities and matching rewards exist to a more or less equally high level for both specialists and generalists.

Career development is an important policy decision that has to be matched with rewards, and that clearly influences people's ability to manage their own careers. It is a classic problem of naturally hierarchical organisations that good specialists become poor managers because there is no alternative route for progress. It is a double loss. An organisation that believes in the value of varied experience has to facilitate movements across boundaries. One large international pharmaceutical company had a policy of 'two functions plus two countries plus two business units' for future general managers. Its succession planning process enabled the right movements to take place to achieve this goal over time.

REFLECTIVE ACTIVITY

Many organisations believe it is unwise to discuss with individuals what is on the succession plan, in that it might create expectations that are never fulfilled. Others argue that openness is the only route.

List the points of argument for both sides.

On balance, which do you think is the stronger side?

Bringing personal and organisational goals together

The plans that are made must come together and match. This can only happen through open dialogue, sharing ambitions on the one hand and the collective view of potential on the other. At the end of the day we need an agreed development plan that both sides work together to put into practice. Who should conduct this dialogue? Many would say it is the job of a person's manager (and it is often expected at appraisal time) – but it could be a careers professional either within or outside the organisation. Nobody should leave an organisation because of uncertainty of the opportunities available or of how his or her potential is viewed. Sadly, such departures are all too often the case – the right dialogue has not taken place.

Vacancy management – how does succession management live alongside open job advertising?

There is an apparent dilemma between open access to jobs (via an intranet) and planned development, where the two might seem to be in conflict. This need not be so. Some organisations make it clear that above a certain level jobs will not be advertised. Others would say 'You are on the succession chart, but this is not a guarantee – it means you will be considered alongside any other suitable candidates who apply.' Some, especially in the public sector, advertise externally anyway – however, this is hard to justify if internal successors are available, and it only demotivates existing staff.

Whatever is done has to have credibility, and not appear be a showcase behind which selection is fixed. The more 'shared' the information about aspirations and perceived potential, the easier it is to have coherence between the planned and the open.

We now pull together ten key points about resourcing raised in this chapter:

- Organisational success is totally dependent on people – on having the right people with the right skills in the right place at the right time.

- Organisations have a choice of planning for their future or being reactive and opportunistic. Successful organisations invest in planning and make clear and consistent strategic decisions over resources.

- Workforce planning starts with scanning the future, looking both at where the business wants to go and at the environment in which it expects to operate.

- The organisation can be divided up into discrete job families to find out relevant data about the members of each family and the flows in and out of it.

- Selecting a planning period, and feeding in the knowledge available, we can predict the resourcing requirements – both in numbers and in capabilities.

- There are options for resourcing – decisions to be taken about the ratios of core and peripheral staff.

- A classification for potential is a vital tool – potential has several dimensions and is not just about ascending the management ranks. A range of methods are available for assessing this.

- Succession planning, sometimes called 'continuity planning', is a key process for critical jobs in an organisation, using two categories – 'availability in the event of an emergency' and 'longer-term successors' – for whom we will have a development plan.

- To facilitate succession planning we need career paths, and we can provide significant help for individuals in their own career planning – not least of which is talking to them about it.

- Finally, we need to ensure that our policy on vacancy notification and management is consistent with all other processes.

Perhaps there are other key points that you would like to note for yourself.

The main case study in this chapter now follows. It gives an example of career planning in one particular organisation.

MAIN CASE STUDY

Make an initial reading of the case study to gain an overview of the situation, and then read the questions that you will need to address. Now read the case study again, making notes of issues and facts that will help you in your analysis and responses to the questions. Remember to 'read between the lines' as well as picking out the obvious points, and also to consider what is not said as well as what is presented here.

The Limassol Manufacturing Company is based in Cyprus and produces technical equipment for the wine industry. It employs 4,000 people. The structure of this organisation is indicated by the organisational chart (see Figure 17). In addition you have got an overview of the talent pool (see Table 17).

Table 17 Talent pool: Limassol Manufacturing Company

Department and group	Level below VP	Total number	Potential A ready for move now	Potential A not yet ready for move	Potential B ready for move now	Potential B not yet ready for move	Potential C and/or D
Manufacturing							
Production managers	1	7	0	0	1	1	5
Senior staff roles	1	4	0	0	0	0	4
Supervisors	2	20	1	0	2	1	16
Purchasing							
Senior purchasing officers	1	4	0	0	1	0	3
Junior purchasing officers	2	6	0	0	0	0	6
Sales and marketing							
Regional sales managers	1	4	1	0	1	0	2
Area sales managers	2	12	0	0	1	1	10
Marketing managers	1	3	1	0	0	1	1
Marketing officers	2		1	0	1	0	3
Finance and IT							
Finance/IT managers	1	6	0	0	1	0	5
Accountants etc	2	19	2	2	2	1	3
IT team leaders	2	6	0	0	1	0	5
Human resources							
Senior HR managers	1	3	0	0	0	0	3
HR officers	2	7	0	0	0	0	7
Comms and government							
Communications officers	1	3	0	0	0	1	2
Technology							
Technology managers	1	4	0	0	1	0	3
Team leaders	2	8	1	0	0	1	6

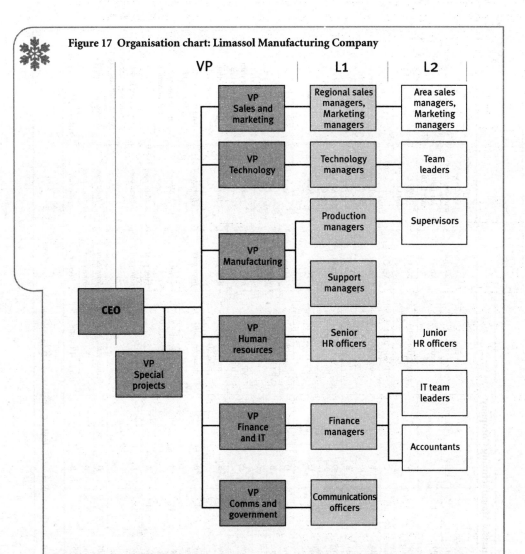

Figure 17 Organisation chart: Limassol Manufacturing Company

Your task

You are the Organisation and Manpower Planning Committee reviewing the attached succession plan (see Table 18). Consider the following issues:

1 What actions would you take if the VP for Finances and IT resigned?

2 How would you prepare Mr N for the position of VP Technology?

3 How would you prepare Mr O for VP Purchasing?

4 What would you do about succession to VP Communications and Government?

5 What do you conclude from examining the 'talent pool'? What actions would you place on the HR Director?

Table 18 Succession plan (January 2007): Limassol Manufacturing Company

Job title	Current holder, date app'ted, age	Expd date of move	risk	P'tial	Pf/inance	Planned next job and date	Emergency successors	Longer term-successors and date ready	Development required
Chief Executive	Dr A 9/01, 62	6/09	L			retire	Mr D	Mr D: 3/09 Mr I: 2013	
VP Manufacturing	Mr B 1/97, 54	now	L	D	**	early retire 2009	Mr C	Mr C Mr O: 2010	
VP Purchasing	Mr C 5/02, 46	now	M	C	****	VP Mfg 2009	Mr O	from pool	
VP Finance and IT	Mr D 3/02, 48	now	H	B	***	CEO 2009	None	Ms L: 2009 Mr I: 2009	customer involvement
VP Sales and marketing	Mr E 1/00, 51	now	M	B	***		Mr J	Mr K: 2009	
VP Human resources	Ms F 8/04, 43	Q4 07	M	D	***		None	Ms M: 2008 Ms Q: 2011	
VP Comms and government	Ms G 3/05 45	09	M	C	**		None	None	
VP Technology	Dr H 1/97, 61	now	L	D	**	retire 2010	None	Mr N	
VP Special projects	Mr I 6/05, 38	07	H	B	****	VP Finance 3/09	None needed		
Level 1 below VP: Potential A and B									
Regional sales manager	Mr J 3/01, 42	now	H	A	****	VP Sales and marketing	from pool	from pool	involvement with gov'ment sales
Regional sales manager	Mr K 2/99, 48	now	L	B	***	marketing role, 2008	from pool	from pool	needs marketing experience
Management accounting manager	Ms L 4/04, 41	now	M	B	***	IT manager, 2007	from pool	from pool	wider experience of finance/IT
Factory HR manager	Ms M 6/05, 36	08	H	B	***	Managemt developmt mgr, 1/08	None	None	involvement in HR strategy
Product marketing manager	Mr N 4/03, 45	now	M	A	****		from pool	from pool	
Production manager	Mr O 4/02, 47	now	L	B	***	?	from pool	from pool	more people mgt exper'nce staff role in Manufac'ing
Production manager	Mr P 5/04, 39	Q3 07	M	B	***	Senior staff, Mfg	from pool	from pool	appropriate courses
R&D manager, Tech dept	Mr R 4/99, 47	now	L	B	***		from pool	from pool	
Press relations officer	Ms Q 3/06, 27	6/07	M	B	****	Job in HR, 2008	Recruit	Recruit	HR generalist position

Notes   Risk: **H** high **M** medium **L** low
Potential (P'tial): **A** high potential; fast mover **B** some potential; move one level **C** lateral move **D** in the right job

EXPLORE FURTHER

BENNISON, M. and CASSON, J. (1984) *The Manpower Planning Handbook.* Maidenhead, McGraw-Hill

This is the classic textbook on workforce planning. It covers most of the areas we have examined, including a variety of other planning models. It also deals with creating strategies and has a chapter on managing careers. The chapter on analysing wastage is a classic.

McBEATH, G. (1992) *The Handbook of Human Resource Planning.* London, CIPD

This highly practical book examines the implications for organisations of rapid business change and of constant changes in manpower. It presents a systematic approach for analysing the flows and current skills of existing employees and for formulating strategies to acquire and develop skills for tomorrow from new and from existing staff.

MAYO, A. (1994) *Managing Careers – Strategies for Organisations.* London, IPM

This was the first book in Europe to look at career management from the organisation's perspective. It starts with looking at future needs and the influence of culture on the way careers work. It examines all the systems and data needed, and includes chapters on individual counselling and managing personal growth. Chapter 6 particularly discusses the data needed for the purposes of this chapter.

CHAPTER 8

Recruitment

Ian Favell

INTRODUCTION

Recruitment and selection is a core area of HRM (French, 2007), and is crucial to the successful functioning of an organisation (Pilbream and Corbridge, 2006). It is a critical mechanism to make sure that the organisation has the right skills, expertise and qualifications to deliver the key organisational objectives. This chapter looks at some of the important issues that should be considered in an effective recruitment process. It should be read in conjunction with Chapter 7 on HR Planning and Chapter 9 on Selection, because these go hand in hand – one being 'pre-' and the other being 'post-' the recruitment process.

LEARNING OUTCOMES

By the end of this chapter readers should be able to:

- list some of the factors that should be considered before starting a recruitment process

- identify a range of methods for reaching potential candidates

- explain aspects and approaches to advertising that can be critical to an effective recruitment process

- give an overview of the timing and topics that should be part of an effective induction programme.

The chapter is in three parts. Part 1 is an overview of the whole recruitment process, and the key steps involved. Part 2 then picks up some important but often glossed-over issues that should be considered in trying to attract the best applicants for a job. Finally, Part 3 considers effective induction, to make sure that the organisation keeps the good people who have been recruited.

The chapter concludes with the main case study.

Reference sources named within the chapter may be looked up in the *References and further reading* section at the end of the book.

STARTER CASE STUDY

Billy Brown's Butchers is a chain of seven butcher's shops preparing and providing fresh meat and cooked meat products for several small and medium-sized market towns in Hampshire. Each shop has a senior butcher, a junior butcher and a sales assistant. Three of the shops also have as part of the premises a small teashop that serves (for example) hot pies, sausage rolls and pasties. Following the recent retirement of the senior butcher in Fareham, the junior butcher at Lambton (who the owner had been watching with approval for some months now) was invited to move to Fareham to take over as the senior butcher as a replacement. This left a vacancy in Fareham for a junior butcher. One of the young women teashop assistants expressed interest in being trained up to take this vacancy, and the junior butcher at Liphook also asked to change branches to progress to this larger branch and build on his experience. However, the owner – always bullish in his approach – decided that the chain needed some new blood, and saw this as an opportunity to recruit externally, effectively cutting out the two existing members of staff who were interested.

The owner placed a small advertisement in the local paper for two weeks, and was pleased to find that a number of people applied. However, when looking through the applications, the owner was not pleased to find that most were inexperienced, and that some very unsuitable people had applied (including some who were obviously not

English and were therefore unlikely to understand the needs of a typical English family's meat requirements). Several of the applications also appeared to be from young women, who obviously had not considered the nature of the business and the strength required. He did, however, have one application from an ex-serviceman, who appeared to have worked in a kitchen on a battleship. He was appointed immediately, and started the following week.

Questions for consideration and discussion

1 What could have caused the number of poor applications? What could the owner have done to widen the range of applications?

2 How do you think the staff might have reacted to the appointment to the senior butcher posts from within the ranks? What are the issues about how this appointment was made?

3 How do you think the staff might have reacted to the external advertisement, when internal staff had expressed interest?

4 What was unlawful about the approach taken by the owner?

5 How far might such poor practice be present in your own organisation (or one you know well)?

6 How should the situation have been handled, for maximum effectiveness?

WHY IS EFFECTIVE RECRUITMENT IMPORTANT?

Organisations are only able to provide goods and services because of the efforts of the people employed by them. Without good people, working effectively together, the organisation is much less likely to be able to provide what is needed by its customers. Having the right person in the right job at the right time is therefore critical to success (Bilsberry, 1996).

Another point that many organisations do not yet realise is the importance of the link between effective recruitment and other processes within the organisation. If the recruitment process is weak, it is possible that a person recruited will not perform particularly well. This is likely to give rise to performance management issues, which in turn may lead to significant training and development to enable him or her to work effectively and efficiently. If the individual had been recruited effectively, this chain reaction would have been avoided, or at least minimised, saving time, effort and costs.

If the recruitment process is not effective, then as well as probably causing these issues, the individual concerned is likely to quickly become demotivated and may well leave, giving rise to a need to start the recruitment process all over again (Taylor, 2005b). Effective recruitment is therefore key to business success.

Who should be involved in the recruitment process?

Recruitment is usually undertaken for one of two reasons: either to fill a vacancy (Taylor, 2005b) or – as with many graduate schemes – to enable promising individuals to enter the organisation on a fixed-length work-based development programme leading to later permanency.

With a graduate programme, those involved are usually the HR department and specialist training managers or project managers, who recruit into the scheme and then as part of the ongoing programme arrange secondments in various parts of the organisation for those recruited. For a vacancy, however, much depends on the size of the organisation. In larger organisations, the HR department often has the most important role, the section manager taking part mainly in specifying the job to be done and attending the interviews. In a smaller organisation there may not actually be an HR department, so section managers are more likely to take full responsibility themselves, perhaps guided by a manager who has a specialist responsibility for people issues.

To ensure effectiveness in recruitment, it is important to identify the key parts of the recruitment process (see the box below). Although there is no exactly 'correct' approach, the following is drawn from a wide range of authors (for example, ACAS; Roberts, 1997; Taylor, 2005b) and is absolutely typical of what many organisations might use.

The effective recruitment process

- identification of basic need
- job analysis
- make the case and gain approval to recruit
- job description
- person specification
- decision regarding selection methods
- decisions regarding advertising and application methods
- design and place advertisements
- receive applications
- shortlist
- interviews and tests
- selection decision
- acceptance/rejection letters
- references
- contractual issues
- induction

REFLECTIVE ACTIVITY

Think about the approach taken by an organisation you know well.

To what extent does it include the elements listed in the box above? Are all the elements present? What might be the effect of having some missing, or perhaps in a different order? Are there any additional steps taken? In what ways do these add value and assist in making the process effective?

Identification of recruitment need

Before beginning any recruitment activity, the first step is to make sure that there is a need (Taylor, 2005b, particularly stresses this). There may well have been a previous post-holder, but that in itself does not necessarily mean that the person has to be replaced. Perhaps the components of the job are not required any more, or not in the same form, or maybe the work could be divided and spread between other jobs. Another option is to outsource the job perhaps overseas or to use agency staff to do the work as and when there is a need. It is important therefore to establish exactly what the work requirement is, and whether that is sufficient to give rise to a recruitment situation. Normally, once decided, this will need authorisation because organisations are rightly concerned to control recruitment

Job analysis, making the case and gaining approval

Having decided that there is indeed a need, the job or details of the activity should be analysed and examined to find out exactly what sort of requirement there is, so that a case can be made for finance or permissions and authority to undertake recruitment. Organisations of course vary in their approach. Some managers are given their budgets, and they are able to recruit as and when they see fit to meet the demands of their sections. This might be especially true in larger organisations where, for example, each region may be able to work autonomously. However, increasingly, organisations are trying to minimise the number of employees since people costs are some of the highest outgoings for an organisation (CIPD research, highlighted in Taylor, 2005b). As a result, it is becoming normal for permission to be requested to recruit, usually after a formal proposal, fully costed, is put forward to justify why recruitment is necessary. This is even the case in many organisations where a vacancy has occurred naturally – the replacement has to be justified and permission given before recruitment can begin. This permission is granted usually by senior managers, although in many organisations the decision may be devolved to HR and personnel departments, who manage the activity on a day-to-day basis (see Chapter 20 on HR roles).

Job analysis is a series of techniques used to explore exactly what the job entails. A job is unlikely to have remained static and it is advisable to take the time to find out what the current job requirements are before starting a recruitment process. There are a number of ways of gaining this information (Pearn Kandola, 1993; Armstrong, 1999; Taylor, 2005b), including watching someone doing the role, and talking to or interviewing current job-holders and their managers and, if possible, the person or people who have left. It may be better to utilise the services of a specialist consultant to analyse the jobs – and they will probably use a questionnaire-based approach. Once a job analysis has been completed and the recruiter has up-to-date knowledge of the job and the skills, experience and qualifications of the person required to do it, the job description and person specification can be drawn up.

Job description

Most authors agree that a detailed description of the job is then essential – to clearly spell out what it is the post-holder will have to achieve (for example, Taylor, 2005b; Lucas, Lupton and Mathieson, 2006). Note that a good job description is not a list of tasks (this is the historical approach, and is potentially quite constraining) but clear statements of targets, outputs or outcomes that the post-holder will be required to achieve.

Clearly, there are some jobs – especially operational jobs – where some of the activities are so essential that they do form part of the job description, and it is quite common to have specific tasks listed in the job description. However, it is not best practice to do this, because as soon as aspects of the job change (for example, with the introduction of a new machine, or a change of process), all of the job descriptions in that area may have to be revised (and this might also give rise to potential union argument and pay issues). With a job description that is worded in outcome-achievement format, the actual detailed tasks are left open, allowing changes to be made without making the job descriptions useless. It is important, though, that readers are aware that many job descriptions do not follow this good practice approach but continue to list the tasks to be undertaken, and many staff expect this to be the case, especially at more high-skills levels. The job description will lead to the person specification.

Person specification

Whereas the job description details the job to be done, the person specification details the characteristics of an ideal person who has the capability to do the job. This document therefore uses the job description to identify the skills, knowledge, experience, attributes and characteristics of the type of person that is needed to fulfil the job requirements (Lucas *et al*, 2006; Taylor, 2005b). It should contain clear, measurable statements of these attributes, because these will be the benchmark to decide whether a candidate is or is not suitable. Within the selection process the person specification is what determines whether an individual is capable of doing the job or not, and so the person specification is the key document at the point of selection.

There are three main approaches used for person specifications:

- focusing on the needs of the job, and the personal characteristics required for someone to do the job (and he or she is then expected to learn about the organisation and team, and develop to fit in with them)

- focusing on the organisation and team, and the person's abilities to fit in (and he or she is then expected to learn about and develop into the job itself)

- a competency approach, in which skills, attributes and behaviours required for both the job and the team are listed, and the applicant measured against them.

What is key for a person specification is that it should be used equally across all applicants in providing a basis for measuring the characteristics of each individual to determine the extent to which he or she fits that description.

Decision regarding selection methods

Now the selection method has to be decided. This is critical – there are many different ways of selecting candidates from among those who have applied. Chapter 9 of this book should help with more information on this topic.

Advertising and application decisions

There is no point in having an excellent selection system if no one applies. The first step towards getting applicants is to raise awareness of the vacancy and what is required in the job. Although there are a number of different ways of finding people to apply, all start with some form of awareness-raising, usually by advertising. (Where this is not the case, it is usually because agencies are used – but even these advertise.) There are a number of important issues with advertising, which are discussed more fully in Part 2 of this chapter.

Before even thinking about raising awareness and attracting applications it is essential that you should be clear on what applicants need to do to apply. This should, of course, be spelled out clearly in any advertisement. Often the application method is chosen to be part of the selection process. As Table 19 shows, different application methods might be used to check different issues.

Table 19 Application methods and their use

Application method	May be used to check (eg)
Completing an application form	• Ability to complete forms • Ability to summarise key points • Handwriting skills • Ability to understand key requirements
Writing a letter of application	• Handwriting skills, if relevant to the job • Ability to understand key requirements • Capability of constructing a structured document
Sending in a CV	• Capability of compiling a structured document • Ability to summarise key points
Telephoning for information and initial detail-giving	• Tone and quality of spoken voice • Use of the English language • Level of formality or customer service used • Image projected
Online questionnaire	• Experience, qualifications, factual understanding • Ability to use web-based applications

The next steps in the recruitment process are usually considered part of the selection process, and are examined in the following chapter.

2 SEEKING APPLICANTS

One of the key issues of recruitment is where to start to look for potential candidates. As the world becomes smaller, travel and mobility now being more the norm than the exception, the potential source of candidates is huge. In practice, though, many of these people are not actually easily available, and unless you are seeking a specialist or someone with a specific combination of skills that is unusual, it is more likely that you will first look locally or nationally.

So where should you look for candidates? It does of course depend very much on a number of important issues relating to the reason you are recruiting, and the job role you are intending to fill. There are five main areas to consider: the person needed, the job role you want him/her to undertake, your department and organisation, the wider context of your subject discipline and marketplace, and the details of the constraints on the recruitment process itself. For each of these areas there are a number of questions to think over before making any decisions about how and where to seek applicants. We now examine them in more detail.

About the person

The person specification should help to answer questions about the person you are looking for. Key questions should include:

- What experience, skills, qualities and other attributes are you looking for? This might affect whether you seek internally or externally, and how widely you need to look. The more specialised or focused your requirements, the more likely it is that you will need to look far afield or use multiple or national advertising methods to reach those who are likely to meet your needs.

- Which qualifications and other achievements would be ideal, or essential (like a Heavy Goods Vehicle driving licence, for example)? Answers to this question might point you towards specialist journals or particular national newspapers or professional bodies. At senior levels, some achievements or qualifications might need a specific search perhaps through a recruitment agency or head-hunters.

- How available should the person recruited be? This of course depends upon how quickly you must have him/her in the job – urgently, in a month or two, or later? This is likely to affect the extent to which you have time to advertise widely, since some journals need a significant time to prepare their publication. It may also affect the style and content of the advertisement.

About the job

Most authorities (for example, Bilsberry, 1996; Taylor, 2005b; Roberts, 1997) clearly state that the job description should provide information about the job. Key questions might include:

- Are you looking for someone who will be permanent, temporary, casual or on a specified contract? Apart from pointing towards different media for an advertisement, for all except permanent positions this might suggest a more local than a national approach.

- Is the main work long-term, short-term or perhaps only project-based? Again, this should cause you to consider local versus national methods of raising awareness of the vacancy.

- Part-time, full-time or variable?

- Day work, evening work, night work or shift work?

The following two questions should help you to define particular requirements and consider the extent to which advantage can be taken of how closely those who live within easy reach of the place of work. Local advertising might appear appropriate, but those from afar might be prepared to move to join your organisation. You will have to consider the implications for any moving costs and how these might be met by the organisation. Clearly, for more senior positions this may be necessary, but for relatively straightforward jobs this might be less important. Again, this should help you with the decision over whether advertising should be local or wider.

What about the physical and geographical location of the workplace, and its accessibility? Will the position be office-based, home-based or mobile? This should inform the extent to which your search for applicants is local or wider.

Are there any issues of resources or facilities needed by the job that might affect who you are seeking (use of a car or van, or own set of kitchen knives, or own guitar and amplifier, for example)? These are important issues for the job, but really only affect the search for applicants in terms of the practicality of their travelling to the place of work or removing to your location from far away.

About the organisation

Lucas *et al* (2006) note that the organisational context should be considered (see Chapter 2). The following questions are important in relation to an organisation that is seeking to fill a position:

- Is the organisation multinational, national, regional or local? This might affect people's perceptions of possible career paths, as well as geographical mobility potential. Decisions about advertising method and design may well be affected by your answers here.

- What is the profile of the organisation (for example, high-profile, well-known or small and relatively unknown)? A brand name can often influence people's wish to apply. Decisions about advertising method and design may well be affected by your answers here too.

- Multiple products or services or of specific focus? The issue of breadth versus depth of work potential can influence applicants. Specialists often seek out specialist firms, for example, whereas a generalist or person with uncertain career plans might favour a more diverse organisation. This should help you to think through whether a specialist journal or professional body will be needed for your advertisement, as well as the actual content of the advert.

- What is the structure and culture of the organisation? Much has been written about structure and culture (for example, Handy, 1993; Johnson and Scholes, 1999; Blundell and Murdock, 1997), and for most people the extent to which they perceive that they might 'fit' usually determines the extent to which they apply seriously (if at all). The design and content, as well as the medium chosen, should be delineated with care, because they will subconsciously convey some of the underlying philosophies of the organisation, and therefore its apparent attractiveness to individuals.

- How far is career progression available, expected and welcomed within the organisation? These days, knowing how they will progress (usually measured in financial and in status terms) is often important to people's willingness to explore job opportunities. Any advertisement may have to reflect such opportunities, for maximum effectiveness.

About the profession or business sector

The profession or business sector has also to be considered:

- Which sector are you in – for example: art, science or support? Clearly, this is a key point for placing advertisements to match the desired audience.

- What is the main job focus – for example, manufacturing, service, distribution or research? Similarly, the placing of any advertisements should be influenced by this point.

- Is the business environment highly regulated, restricted or very organic and freeform? Personal style and approach to work differs significantly, and this point ties in with the questions about organisational structure and culture. Some people cannot settle to work in a highly controlled or regulated environment, whereas others might struggle if the organisation and work is too organic and freeform. Care should be taken in the placing of an advertisement to reflect this aspect of the job content, and the wording itself must reflect any special focal points or requirements, to avoid many applications from those who are not of a suitable disposition.

The recruitment process itself

In order to plan an effective recruitment process it is necessary to ask a number of questions, many of which are listed below. The information obtained from the job analysis is helpful in finding out the answers to the questions, which is why it is advisable to plan recruitment with an up-to-date job analysis available.

- Is the position for internal applicants, external applicants or both? Ideally, of course, you should aim for the widest possible search for candidates by looking inside and outside the organisation. However, time-scales, experience or succession planning might cause you to decide to look internally first, and only look externally if a suitable internal candidate cannot be found. Alternatively, if your aim is to bring fresh blood or new ideas and experience into the organisation, external candidates should presumably be sought.

- What is the timeframe available – how soon must the person be in the post? Does that allow for enough time for the various steps necessary to achieve this result? Timing is one of the most important issues, and will most likely affect what you are able to do to raise awareness of the position and attract candidates. Wherever possible, you should allow enough time to be able to attract the best candidates, and so if you can, you should decide the recruitment methods first, and then work out the timing needed afterwards. In most situations, however, this is not possible, and you are likely to be under significant time pressures, and probably have to compromise your recruitment approaches to fit operational requirements.

- What is your resource availability – for example, how much can you spend? How easy is it to place advertisements? What steps internally do you need to undertake? Being clear about the time (as above), finance, people and physical resources required and available may also affect the approach you are able to take.

- What is the people situation – who must be involved in the process, and what limits are there on those people's availability? How will you establish the best combination of people to involve, and how will you get their participation and commitment to the process?

- What is the experience of the staff involved – are there any training issues or additional people that must be involved in the design or preparation of the process? Any such issues might also take up time and additional resources.

Before thinking about where to look for possible applicants, questions like these should be considered. The answers should help you to decide where to put your efforts in seeking out those you would like to apply.

REFLECTIVE ACTIVITY

List the key questions that would apply to a job you are familiar with. (Ideally, list responses to the questions too.) This should help you focus on the key issues that affect the recruitment process.

Now put questions (and responses) in priority order, to focus your thinking further.

FINDING YOUR APPLICANTS

So where can you find potential applicants? Having thought through the details of the situation, context and requirements, there are a number of options. The key issues here are whether you are going to focus on internal or external candidates, and also how far you wish to handle things yourself or work through others to help you. The WERS data on recruitment channels by workplace characteristics (see Table 20) identifies three distinct approaches to finding applicants. The data clearly shows that although workplaces do use informal methods and formal methods that use professional help, most organisations use the formal processes that they themselves devise and implement without professional assistance.

Table 20 Recruitment channels, by workplace characteristics

	Formal channel – professional help (job centres, careers services and private employment agencies)	Formal channel – no professional help (newspapers, specialist press, notices, replying to speculative applications, and Internet)	Informal channel (direct approaches to potential recruits, recommendation or enquiry by existing employees and word of mouth)
All workplaces with vacancies in core group of employees in previous year	69	88	64
Organisation size 10–99 employees 10,000 or more employees	68 71	80 95	70 60
Industry Manufacturing Hotels and restaurants Financial services Public sector	76 69 66 51	78 83 93 98	72 77 64 32

Source: Kersley *et al* (2006; p.73)

Let's look in detail at the different ways in which applicants might be found. Newell and Shackleton (2000) suggest that most private sector organisations attempt to fill vacancies internally before looking outside. Internal candidate search might, for example, be from within a single department, other departments, other geographical sites or partner sites and organisations. Internal methods of letting people know about the vacancy include word of mouth, organisational intranet or emails to all employees, staff newsletters, newspapers and bulletins, and noticeboards (paper or electronic).

An internal promotion or appointment can cause bad feeling among colleagues who were not selected, so managers in the area concerned will have to handle the transition carefully. Also, staying internal to the organisation does not bring in any new ideas from outside, even if it is perhaps cheaper and quicker to appoint from within. As the Cranet data suggests, internal promotion is more common in some countries than in others. Whereas in the UK and Sweden only about a third of organisations fill management positions internally, most do in Greece and Slovakia (see Table 21).

Table 21 'How are management positions most commonly filled?'

	UK	Sweden	Germany	Greece	Slovakia
Internally	37%	37%	44%	56%	56%

Source: Cranet (2003)

EXTERNAL — WORKING THROUGH OTHERS

There are many methods for letting people know about a vacancy by working through others (Taylor, 2005b). These include:

- word of mouth and personal contact
- previous applicants on file (usually held and accessed through those overseeing HR in the organisation)
- using job centres, careers services and youth and adult training schemes and placement programmes
- recruitment and employment agencies
- head-hunters (those who actively seek out suitable people in other organisations, to see if they can be encouraged to leave).

Of these, one of the most widely used is that of the recruitment agency, who can advertise on behalf of employers, and who also may well have a large file already of people looking for such an opening. However, an agency needs careful briefing, especially when using an agency that you do not really know, or that does not already know you and your organisation well. A clear briefing has to be backed up by an effective job description and person specification. If at all possible you should talk to the person who will be working on your case, and then ask to see the final brief that he/she builds in order to check that it really does meet your requirements.

Keep a close eye on the activities of the agency, because some may well not screen (or filter out) people very well, and send you people to interview on the off-chance that you will take them, rather than screening them properly first. This may happen particularly if your contract with the agency stipulates payment on finding someone, rather than for its services in general. Remember that just because you use an agency does not take away your responsibility for the effectiveness of the recruitment. It simply means that someone else is doing the detailed basic work for you. You should therefore be clear in dealing with the agency about what is and is not acceptable, and make sure you give it clear information about the criteria that you expect it to use in screening people. You might also ask it to give you details of those that it turns away (with its reasons for doing so) as well as those that it passes to you for the selection process, so that you can check that it is truly carrying out your wishes fully.

EXTERNAL – DEALING WITH IT YOURSELF

This largely involves some form of advertising, to let people know of the opportunity. The question here is where to choose to advertise – for example:

- a card in a shop window
- an advert in local paper
- an advert on local radio/TV
- a national advert in the press or a magazine or journal
- the Internet (passive information-giving – or interactive, perhaps even pre-checking suitability).

Additional issues that you will need to address include:

- exactly which professional journals, magazines, national and local papers you use, and your reasons for choosing those
- the format of the advertisement itself, involving:
  - the style of wording you use
  - the graphic layout and design of the advertisement
  - the actual detail and content of the message.

Below is a checklist you might use when you are putting an advertisement together:

About the job:

- title, rate of pay, location
- who reports to or is responsible for whom.

About the application:

- who to contact, how to apply, the deadline for doing so
- the address to send application to
- the telephone number for further enquiries
- when and where interviews will be held (if decided in advance).

About the person needed:

- the key must-have points from your person specification
- any special requirements.

About the writing style:

- Keep it brief and factual.
- Keep it professional.
- Keep it legal (see Chapters 5 and 6).

Time spent on getting the advertisement right will save you time later on, because the resultant applications should be exactly the kind you were looking for, rather than including a large number that are no real use to you because the advertisement did not explain your requirements properly.

REFLECTIVE ACTIVITY

In light of the ideas in this chapter so far, consider which of the various methods of recruitment would be most suitable for a job you know well – such as course tutor in a college or cashier at a supermarket. Be able to explain exactly why you think these are suitable, and why you have rejected the other methods.

If you decide to advertise, what issues are particularly important for you to remember?

Compare your decisions with what actually happens in the organisation. What changes or improvements would you make to ensure greater effectiveness?

EQUALITY OF OPPORTUNITY

Recruitment and selection are areas in which there are many pitfalls in terms of equality of opportunity, and if you are involved with recruitment in any way, you should always check the latest legal position before proceeding. (Chapter 5 deals with legal issues in general, and is a good starting point for this.)

You must certainly think about whether the method you choose might disadvantage certain types of people who might wish to apply for the job. For example, if you always advertise in a particular newspaper, only the people who read that newspaper will get to hear about the job. People who read a different newspaper (who might be – for example – of a different religion, ethnicity or social standing) will not have the chance to apply because they will not know about the vacancy. Word of mouth can have equal opportunities issues too, because it relies on people recommending friends and acquaintances. In this instance the pool of applicants is artificially limited, and certainly not necessarily inclusive or representative across religions, gender, age, race or disabilities.

REFLECTIVE ACTIVITY

What are the main equal opportunities issues that you should be aware of when seeking applicants? Where might such issues arise within the recruitment process?

In an organisation you know well, how much attention is paid to these sorts of issues?

What might you have to do to ensure compliance with the law, and to ensure that you receive the best applications?

3 INDUCTION

Induction (or 'orientation', as it is known as in many countries) is the name usually given to the process by which a new employee (or someone in a new position) is integrated into the organisation, the team and the work role. It is the method by which these people can effectively learn issues of organisational purpose, policies and procedures, and (for example) ways of working. The process should help them to become aware of the organisational culture, the skills, knowledge and behaviours required for the job, and to fully understand their responsibilities.

Although the induction process is often not considered to be part of the recruitment and selection process, it is actually key to success. After all, if you spend significant amounts of time and money on getting the right people into the organisation, it is clearly sensible to look after them once they arrive, so that they can not only feel at home quickly but they can become productive immediately. Indeed, a number of studies have shown a direct relationship between the effectiveness of the induction process and retention – the length of time a new employee stays with the organisation (Taylor, 2005b; Fowler, 1996; Reid, Barrington and Brown, 2004). Where induction has been well thought through and undertaken, there is a much higher likelihood that the new member of staff will settle quickly. Where the induction process is weak or absent, new staff often do not settle and may quickly move on. An effective induction is an essential part of the formation of a positive psychological contract, and a positive psychological contract reduces absence and turnover and maximises performance (see Chapter 11).

The induction programme is usually regarded as part of the new employee's development programme – which of course it is – but it is also the link between the recruitment process and the performance management process (see Chapter 12). The effectiveness of this link can easily set the tone for the new staff and show them the value that you place on their services and the way they will be managed in the future. It is for this reason that induction is key to effectiveness of the recruitment process, because a weak induction can undermine and completely devalue all the good work put into obtaining the services of those individuals in the first place. Where an effective induction programme is not present, there can be poor integration into the organisation, team and job role, leading to low morale for the individual and the team, and less effective performance. In turn, this may also lead to disillusionment, and eventually resignation of the new team member, which of course might then demotivate the team, and require the whole recruitment process to be gone through again, at significant cost.

Taylor (2005b) has suggested that a 'standard' process may not be as effective as a tailor-made process from the viewpoint of retaining those recently recruited. Again, perhaps you should consider how you might feel if you were 'processed' for your induction in a mechanical standard manner rather than in a more personalised and job role-related way.

Who needs an induction programme? Anyone who takes on a new role should have some form of induction. This includes new full-time, part-time and temporary staff, trainees (for example, on a graduate training scheme), and those appointed internally to a different role or those returning after a long absence (for example, after maternity/paternity leave or after recovery from long-term sickness). The principle can also be extended to those who are on secondment or attachment, or perhaps at the start of a medium- to large-sized project assignment. The variety of situations in which induction is useful is quite wide, and this further reinforces the need for induction programmes to be tailor-made rather than standard or 'off the shelf'.

An effective induction programme ensures that a number of issues are well covered. These should include the physical facilities of the workplace and details of the job role and how it fits within the larger organisational and team purpose and objectives. They should include health and safety information – this is a legal requirement: see Chapter 18 – and clear coverage of the terms and conditions of service that apply. In larger organisations an employee handbook is distributed which can be used to set out contractual and non-contractual information. The employee is often asked to sign to say that he or she has received this information, and it can be used in the future as a source of information provided it is kept up to date when there are changes.

There are other issues that can be covered in the induction, such as information about the organisation, perhaps its history, services and products, and mission, values and culture. Although they may not be essential elements of an induction, they are nonetheless very desirable to ensure full integration. Most writers on the subject of induction recommend that some form of mentor or 'buddy' is appointed in the early days, so that the new person has a specific point of contact for support and enquiries, and someone who can help to introduce him/her to others in the organisation as essential contacts, colleagues and potential friends.

The way in which the programme is constructed is critical to its success. Traditionally, organisations used to set aside a few days at the start of the employment contract for this activity, and then gave people large amounts of information, booklets, documents, visits to various areas, and introductions to everyone in the department (and anyone who happened to pass by). Overload was often the result, and even the most motivated and focused individual soon found that he/she was confused.

Some parts of this approach are of course essential within the first few days, but for real effectiveness the process is best spread over a much longer time, with a planned approach. In this way the required information can emerge gradually and in a structured manner for the newcomer in a way that enables him or her fully to understand each aspect. There should be a review meeting planned after the employee has been in post for some time at which the employee can ask for any further information or training if needed. This can form part of an annual appraisal meeting. It is not only helpful to the new employee, it also helps managers to evaluate the effectiveness of the induction and to make any changes for the benefit of future new starters.

Marchington and Wilkinson (2005) suggest that line managers should hold the responsibility for the effectiveness of the induction process for their staff. After all, they are the ones who need the staff, and the new member is one of their team, performing a role that contributes to their section's operational performance objectives and targets. However, in many organisations the induction programme is viewed as 'an HR issue', and therefore either left to HR to sort out or formally delegated to the HR department. This may be effective, but often is not, because induction can so easily be assumed to be only about meeting legal requirements, and about the rules and regulations, totally ignoring the integration issues discussed above. A good compromise is to have the induction programme designed by both line managers and HR in cooperation with each other, and then perhaps for the HR department to oversee its delivery (calling upon the line manager and team colleagues for input where needed).

So exactly what should be included? The actual content will vary according to the type of organisation, the person being inducted, his or her contractual terms and conditions, job role and prior experience of work, and the organisational context itself. There have been many books and articles written about effective induction, including lists of the specifics that should be included in the wider programme, which might cover, say, the first three months of service in the job. A good starting point to read further on this topic are the factsheets and checklists provided by ACAS, the CIPD and the CMI .

REFLECTIVE ACTIVITY

What are the effects of the induction process in an organisation?

How can any negative effects be minimised? What are the reasons that induction programmes can be less successful?

What legal requirements are there that should be included?

KEY ISSUES IN RECRUITMENT AND INDUCTION

We now pull together ten key points about recruitment and induction raised in this chapter:

- Effective recruitment is essential to ensure that the right people are brought forward for consideration for every job.

- The first step is to ensure that a job analysis is undertaken, leading to a clearly specified job description.

- The job description should be used as the basis for determining and clearly specifying the personal attributes and characteristics of the ideal individual for the job, written in a person specification.

- Finding the right applicants is an important step, and there are many ways of ensuring that people get to hear about a vacancy.

- Before advertising, a decision should be made on exactly how a potential candidate should apply.

- The content of an advertisement should reflect not only the core duties of the job, taken from the job description, but also details from the person specification of the key characteristics required.

- Agencies can be used to bring forward suitable applicants, but the process should be managed effectively from within the organisation to ensure that the agency does provide appropriate shortlisted applicants.

- Staff involved with the recruitment process should be fully trained to ensure that they take action that is effective and meets legislative requirements.

- Effective induction is essential to retain and make productive all those who join the organisation or commence new job roles.

- Only by effectiveness throughout the recruitment and induction processes is it possible to get and keep the best talent available for your organisation, upon which to build a sound and growing business.

Perhaps there are other key points that you would like to note for yourself.

The main case study in this chapter now follows. It gives an example of recruitment and induction issues faced by many organisations.

Make an initial reading of the case study to gain an overview of the situation, and then read the questions that you will need to address. Now read the case study again, making notes of issues and facts that will help you in your analysis and responses to the questions. Remember to 'read between the lines' as well as picking out the obvious points, and also to consider what is not said as well as what is presented here.

A large broadcasting organisation, operating on a 24-hours-a-day, seven-days-a-week basis, regularly recruits new operational engineers to operate specialist sound, lighting, vision and computer equipment. In this organisation recruitment occurs typically every two years to ensure that a good number of staff are properly trained and are available to apply when actual full-time operational post vacancies occur. It takes about two years' training for staff to become sufficiently proficient to take on regular

duties, and historically there is low turnover, so that a phased entry has worked well. Within the organisation, career opportunities to progress and diversify are readily available, and this form of succession planning has always previously been appropriate to ensure continuity of staff in the main operational areas, while at the same time providing seasoned practitioners to rise to more senior and specialist jobs.

Because the organisation has undertaken this recruitment exercise regularly over the last 20 years, a normal process has become established. When the due date arrives (determined by the date of the last recruitment round, usually the first week in July) the departmental manager confirms the wish to proceed, and HR looks out the job description and issues a standard advertisement, which is placed in the media section of the Tuesday edition of the Daily Blurb national newspaper for two consecutive weeks.

Are you what we need to join our next generation of Operational Engineers?

Major broadcasting organisation is seeking bright, lively, committed and enthusiastic people to join the pool of trainees that will eventually provide the backbone of our services. You will have a proven interest in engineering or operations in your current role or hobbies, an 'A'-level in physics, maths and English, and normal colour vision.

You will be working initially at our training centre in Kent, followed by a series of three- to six-month attachments and secondments at various locations throughout the UK. This will involve weekend, bank holiday, and shift working. A permanent operational unit position may be applied for at any time after the first year, and subject to satisfactory progress, is guaranteed at the end of Year 2.

Expenses are paid, and salary will initially be £18,000 pa, rising to £21,000 on successful completion of the training programme. Large city weighting is paid additionally for postings to the major conurbations.

For further information and an application form, please ring

Fiona Jarvis on 0208-123 45678

We are an equal opportunities employer, and welcome applications from all sections of society.

The advertisement contains details of the job prospects and salary (see above), and how to apply. HR collects the application forms that are sent in by candidates, which are then sorted into alphabetical order and sent on to the departmental manager for selection.

Four years ago, 54 people applied but most were found at selection to be unsuitable. Seven were appointed where 10 positions had been available. Two years ago, 23 people applied and not one was found to be suitable, so a second recruitment round was held six months later. Then, only a handful of applicants came anywhere near the required standard. Clearly, something was not going well. The departmental manager complained to the HR department, demanding that something be done to improve matters before the next round of recruitment commenced.

Once in the organisation, the new staff attended a two-day induction programme alongside other staff recruited around the same period from a range of departments. Staff records show that about 15% of those recruited did not stay in the organisation, although there was a higher level of retention in the technical departments (about 10% leaving within a year).

Your task

Consider the following questions, making notes of the key points of your responses. If you are studying in a group, discuss your responses, and come to an agreed set of answers. Then draft a short report to the department manager and HR manager, explaining and justifying your suggestions.

1   What are the factors that have contributed to the lack of success?

2   What changes should the HR department make to its recruitment processes?

3   What changes should the departmental manager make to the recruitment approaches and processes in the department?

4   What are the implications to be considered before making the changes you suggest?

5   To what extent does this organisation comply with legislation on equal opportunities?

6   What should the organisation do to increase the retention of those recruited?

EXPLORE FURTHER

CIPD (2005) *On-Line Recruitment*, Factsheet. London, CIPD
CIPD (2006) *Recruitment*, Factsheet. London, CIPD
CIPD (2006) *Induction*, Factsheet. London, CIPD
The three factsheets are aimed at the practitioner with an overview of the main issues involved in recruitment. Very accessible, and a great help to anyone who already works in HR or who wants to say something productive during a first interview on recruitment.

ROBERTS, G. (2005) *Recruitment and Selection*, 2nd edition. London, CIPD
This text provides a very comprehensive overview of the main issues involved in recruitment and selection, written in a clear and succinct style.

TAYLOR, S. (2005b) *People Resourcing*, 3rd edition. London, CIPD
A wider look at resourcing issues, with clear guidance on recruitment processes for both the practitioner and the academic.

CHAPTER 9

Selection

Tracey Cockerton

INTRODUCTION

This chapter considers the selection process as a means of predicting performance in the workplace. Identifying the right person for a position is essential for individual and organisational success. Planning, developing, implementing and evaluating a selection process can be time-consuming and costly, but the long-term benefits outweigh the costs of hiring an unsuitable candidate unable to perform well in the position. Both the organisation and the individual may suffer and the individual may need extra support.

LEARNING OUTCOMES

By the end of this chapter readers should be able to:

- describe the selection process and state how the organisational context can influence selection outcomes and in turn impact on organisational performance and development

- give an overview of the different methods of assessment for selection and the factors determining choice

- explain how selection can be a predictive process using the concepts of reliability and validity (particularly criterion-related validity)

- identify appropriate ways of evaluating selection strategies

- explain how to use psychometric tools within the required legal framework with sensitivity to issues of diversity.

The chapter is structured in two parts. The first part discusses the wider issues around choice and use of selection methods, and the second part focuses on the more technical issues of reliability, validity and evaluating selection procedures.

The introductory case study is drawn from a real-life situation and is designed to examine some of the common problems with selection procedures. There follows an investigation of the meaning of selection and the importance of considering selection within the organisational context. Next, we look at the range of selection and assessment methods available, with particular reference to those methods UK companies most often use. The following section describes the factors that determine the choice of selection procedures and the advantages and difficulties associated with each.

Part 2 defines the concepts of reliability and validity and discusses the technical issues surrounding the different types of validity and reliability, explaining also how selection can be a predictive process adopting a criterion-related validity approach. This leads on to a section on how to evaluate selection strategies that also examines some of the current issues in relation to the required legal framework with sensitivity to issues of diversity.

STARTER CASE STUDY

An HR administrator has convinced her boss that personality assessment would add value and objective information to the selection process for senior manager appointments, particularly in relation to identifying leadership qualities. She has obtained a copy of a well-known personality questionnaire from her postgraduate programme. Although she has never been trained in psychometric testing, she is permitted by her boss to administer it to candidates for a high-level and very responsible management position as part of the selection process. A job description documenting the responsibilities and outcomes of the position has been produced, but not based on a job analysis. A person specification or competency profile has not been finalised.

Senior manager candidates are interviewed at different times during the week by different interviewers, asking different questions. Unfortunately, organising a schedule for the administration of the personality questionnaire during a busy week proves difficult, and as a result, the candidates all undertake completion of the questionnaire on an individual basis, some before interview, some after interview, and not everyone is informed of the purpose of this part of the selection process. In addition to this, some candidates write their answers on the questionnaire booklet instead of the answer sheet. The HR administrator has only one copy of the booklet and some of the candidates' answers cannot be removed. However, she had photocopied the questionnaire booklet in advance and uses these photocopies with the remaining candidates. Her only problem is getting these back in time from her flatmates who asked to borrow them.

In due course it turns out that the personality questionnaire is an outdated version of the instrument. Moreover, due to time constraints the candidates receive no feedback on their responses, and the profile information produced by the HR administrator includes only brief summary information relating to each candidate's score. Also, the personality questionnaire is not one that is work-related. As the week of interviewing ends, there is little time to produce feedback summary reports, although all the information relating to each candidate, by name, is on computer and can be made available to the selection panel to help their decisions. However, the members of the panel are not trained in psychometric testing, nor do they have any understanding of that particular personality questionnaire or how it relates to the vacant management position.

Questions for discussion

1 How many examples of unprofessional practice can you find in this case study? List them.

2 What elements of the process would you keep – and what would you change, and how?

Notes:

There are many lessons to be learned from this case study and improvements can be made at every point in the process as described. Personality questionnaire assessments may provide additional and objective information for a selection process. However, the information will be most useful when there is evidence of a predictive relationship between particular personality characteristics and job performance (Furnham and Heaven, 1999). Inconsistent, ad hoc administration of personality questionnaires by an untrained individual can even then reduce the value of such personality information.

The chapter concludes with the main case study, which draws together most of the issues covered in the form of a real-life example of selection practice – albeit a very bad one!

Reference sources named within the chapter may be looked up in the *References and further reading* section at the end of the book.

1 SELECTION METHODS AND ORGANISATIONAL CONTEXT

Selection procedures are used to enable an employer to appoint the most 'appropriate' person for employment to a vacant post. Selection procedures are means of assessing individual candidates who have applied for a post against a set of agreed criteria which are deemed relevant. From an organisational perspective, selection procedures must be as fair, reliable, valid, objective, ethical, cost-effective and efficient as possible, while differentiating as accurately as possible between candidates to determine the right choice – ie someone who can perform most successfully in the post. However, the process of selecting the right person for the job adopting the person–job-fit model – which refers to the match between the abilities of the person and demands of the job (Edwards, 1991) – may not be as appropriate or as simple as it appears. Alternatively, the person–organisational-fit model (Kristof, 1996) acknowledges the wider two-way compatibility-matching process which may occur between a person and an organisation during selection and recognises the significance the organisational context may have on the selection process.

The culture of an organisation includes the organisation's philosophy, which can both explicitly and implicitly determine the approaches to recruitment and selection, selection decisions, and measures of successful performance at work. Organisational culture is also likely to be reflected in the organisation's identity, and this in turn will influence who applies for a vacant post. Selection does not occur in a vacuum. It takes place within an organisational context and the culture of the organisation may influence who applies, as well as the outcome. The assessments occurring during a selection process are not all one-way. Individuals also carefully select the organisation they apply to and evaluate the potential employer at each stage of the process.

Beyond the organisational context, there is the legal framework to consider. Selection processes have to be conducted appropriately to ensure that there is no unlawful discrimination on the grounds of sex, race, disability, age, sexual orientation, or religion or belief (see Chapter 5). In Britain and more widely in Western Europe, equality of opportunity is an integral part of the recruitment and selection process. Employers and HR practitioners have to regularly monitor the outcomes of each selection process stage for potential discrimination and address accordingly. Furthermore, as organisations adopt global resourcing strategies the recruitment, selection and assessment process becomes an ever-increasing challenge (see Sparrow, 2006).

SELECTION METHODS CURRENTLY USED IN EUROPE

A wide range of selection methods are currently available but differ considerably in frequency of application and according to the type and level of vacant position. The range includes application forms and CVs, biographical data, interviews, references, psychological testing, job or work samples, in-tray exercises, group assessment, presentations and assessment centres.

Table 22   Most popular selection methods used for managerial staff

	UK	Sweden	Germany	Greece	Slovakia
Interview panel	77%	59%	57%	21%	48%
One-to-one interviews	51%	72%	60%	87%	35%
Application forms	66%	34%	14%	39%	16%
Psychometric test	47%	66%	6%	17%	15%
Assessment centre	26%	12%	23%	18%	10%
Graphology	1%	3%	2%	7%	1%
References	79%	85%	45%	41%	24%

Source: Cranet (2003)

As is evident in Table 22, the most commonly used selection methods for management positions in the UK and many other countries are application forms, interviews and references. These are followed by psychometric testing and assessment centres for management positions. Despite the range of selection methods available, many organisations, large, medium-sized and small, employ the most long-standing approaches, such as interviews. Why is this? It may be because they are part of their custom and practice, and because without evaluating the effectiveness of a selection process it is difficult to know whether it is worth changing.

FACTORS THAT AFFECT THE CHOICE OF SELECTION METHOD(S)

Choosing the right selection method(s) depends on a number of factors:

- the available budget
- the time-scale for appointment
- the accuracy required
- the type, specialism and level of post to be filled
- previous custom and practice
- selection criteria for the post to be filled
- the acceptability and appropriateness of the methods
- the abilities of the staff involved in the selection process
- administrative ease.

Selection tools can assess a variety of individual characteristics such as knowledge, skills, abilities and attributes relevant to the vacant post. Perhaps one of the most significant steps in the design of a selection procedure is to ensure that the most applicable skills, abilities, knowledge and attributes are identified and accurately assessed according to the requirements of the vacant position. This raises the important question of a 'one-size-fits-all' approach versus individually tailored selection processes. To answer this, HR managers must focus on their organisation's strategic aims and thereby ensure that selection processes are part of an overall coherent and integrated approach reflecting the organisation's values and designed to meet the organisation's vision. On a practical level, HR managers may carry out a series of interviews or data-collection sessions with stakeholders, line managers and co-workers to find the capabilities required for successful performance, once they understand and agree on exactly what 'successful job performance' is and how it may relate to wider organisational values and behaviours. This is the key to ensuring that the selection process is a way of predicting performance in the workplace.

It is now quite common for external experts – 'head-hunters' – to be employed as professional recruiters (see Chapter 8). Head-hunters search out potential applicants and invite them to apply for vacant positions which they may not have considered or even been aware of. Applicants are then systematically screened and through a process of elimination reduced to a select few candidates presented to the recruiting organisation for further assessment. For the rejected applicants who were not considering the vacant post before they were encouraged to apply for it, the process can be demoralising. However, for organisations and for HR managers in particular, this service can guarantee, if managed properly (as discussed in Chapter 8), that they select candidates from a diverse and competitive pool of applicants, and is often essential when recruiting to specialist senior positions and/or key leadership roles.

2 SELECTION METHODS

We now examine the selection methods most commonly used, highlighting the pros and cons of each.

APPLICATION FORMS AND CVS

Application forms are produced by organisations to allow applicants to present essential information in a standardised format. They also provide an insight into the organisation – and the image they present to candidates may influence the response level and content provided by the applicant. Potentially successful applicants may be lost at this stage because they do not complete the application form; it may appear too long, too complicated, to require irrelevant information, or not to fit with the applicant's image of his/her ideal employer.

Application forms are rarely used as the only method of selecting candidates, but are useful for screening and identifying a short-list of suitable candidates to go forward for a further selection process. A well-designed application form, available online and used in conjunction with relevant short-listing criteria helps in reducing costs of the overall selection process. However, if the application form is unclear and/or the short-listing criteria are not relevant to the job, those rejected at this stage may include a number of potentially successful applicants.

Not all organisations rely on application forms. Some – particularly US, Australian and German organisations – request a CV or résumé from the applicant in addition to or instead of a completed application form. A CV is a summary document designed and produced by the applicant. CVs include information similar to that requested in application forms, but the content, presentation, order and wording are at the discretion of the applicant. The applicant may even include a photograph of himself/herself. A well-designed and presented CV can make an excellent impression although it is not necessarily an appropriate indication of job performance, particularly if the candidate received professional assistance in compiling the CV.

BIOGRAPHICAL DATA

Biographical data or 'biodata' uses a biographical inventory or questionnaire to collect factual information about a candidate's life history to build a profile of employees in a particular role. Candidates' responses are scored and matched against successful employees in a particular occupational role. Biographical data questionnaires may be presented in multiple-choice format and include both 'hard' items, which are easy to verify, and 'soft' items, which are easy to fake. Typical items cover educational background, previous work experience, educational background, hobbies and interests, aspirations and attitudes. Impression management scales may be included to deal with faking. There is no underlying theory determining the inclusion of questions. However, the empirical basis of biodata questionnaires has been the focus of considerable research, and they have generally been found to be a good predictor of job performance (Robertson and Smith, 2001). Biographical data may be used in the selection process in numerous occupations and questionnaires are more commonly used in the USA than the UK.

REFLECTIVE ACTIVITY

Which selection tool – application form, CV, or biographical data questionnaire – do you think is best at differentiating applicants and predicting performance at work in respect of each of the following occupations?

- construction worker
- librarian
- store manager
- company director
- call centre operator

Both application forms and biographical data are more discriminatory between applicants than CVs because they are standardised – they ask the same questions of everyone. However, whereas application form information is compared to job requirements and identified competencies (eg teamworking), possibly identified from job analysis, biographical data is collected and matched against biographical characteristics identified from statistical analysis of the profiles of successful employees. But statistical relationships between different biographical characteristics (eg living abroad before the age of 12) and job performance (eg as airline cabin crew member) may not reflect a causal relationship.

INTERVIEWS

Interviews may be carried out as one-to-one selection processes or involve a panel of interviewers. The interview itself may be unstructured and free-flowing or structured according to an ordered set of questions; these may relate to a criterion-based or competency-based interview format which includes questions focused on obtaining evidence against particular criteria or competencies. Interviews are the most used, most abused and also most well-researched selection procedure. So not only do we know why interviews are used so often, and how differently interviews can be designed and carried out, we also have some idea about how to enhance them to improve job performance predictions.

Interviews are relatively inexpensive compared to other methods, such as assessment centres or psychometric testing, although they are often wrongly assumed to require little training and preparation. Interviews by their nature are an exchange of views and therefore allow interviewers to become acquainted with the interviewees and assess a number of knowledge, skills, abilities and training requirements as part of one assessment process. Overall, interviews appear to be – and can be – cost-effective and efficient. Unfortunately, there is also a high price to pay if interviews are not well designed and conducted appropriately.

Interviews can be designed to assess relevant knowledge, skills, experience, abilities, training needs, aspirations and person–organisation fit, but quite often this approach is too broad and the quality of the experience and information obtained can be further undermined by a limited and relatively short time period allowed for the interview. Even well-designed interviews can be problematic since the skills of the interviewer are of great importance in determining interview outcomes. Interviewers may display their own nervousness, dominate the interview process, allow the interviewee to provide lengthy, irrelevant answers, be influenced by the physical appearance or communication skills of the interviewee, fail to remember important answers and be distracted by irrelevant information. Decisions can be reached too quickly or on the basis of irrelevant information, and undue weight may be placed on negative information provided by the candidate.

Unlike most other selection methods, interviews are interactive and allow an exchange of communications between two or more people. This means they are not only heavily influenced by the verbal and non-verbal communication skills of those taking part – the interviewees and the interviewers – but also by their thoughts, feelings and judgements. Social psychologists such as Anderson and Shackleton (1993) have focused on identifying factors that shape interview decision-making and understanding individuals' implicit personality theories, cognitive biases and judgement errors. Potential sources of error that can influence interviewer evaluations of candidates have been the focus of considerable research and are summarised in the list below (Taylor, 2005).

Expectancy effect

An excellent application form or reference can lead interviewers to expect and judge a candidate's interview performance as excellent and confirm the initial expectations.

First impressions

The first few minutes of an interview can have long-lasting effects and determine the final outcome – in either a negative or a positive way.

Stereotyping

This can occur when interviewees are evaluated against the interviewer's personal understanding of categories of interviewees – eg females, ethnic groups, a good applicant.

Halo and horns effect

This is a tendency to generalise one aspect of an interviewee's good (halo effect) or bad (horns effect) performance to all performance or perceived abilities.

Contrast effect

It can be difficult not to compare each interviewee with the previous one, contrasting them on certain aspects which may not be relevant to the selection process.

Leniency and harshness effect

This is a general tendency to judge people's performance favourably (leniency effect) or unfavourably (harshness effect).

Negative information bias

This occurs when an initial unfavourable piece of information is weighted more significantly than any following positive information. Bolster and Springbett (1961) suggested that it can take eight pieces of positive information to outweigh the damaging effect of one piece of negative information

'Similar to me' effect

This refers to a favourable bias towards interviewees who are judged by the interviewer to be similar to himself/herself.

ASSESSING INTERVIEW PERFORMANCE AND PREDICTING JOB PERFORMANCE

Robertson and Smith (2001) summarise some of the research on the job interview which has been extensively investigated. Briefly, interviews are more likely to accurately predict job performance when the interview format is structured, standardised and incorporates situational interviewing. This is where candidates are asked the same situation-specific questions relating to how they would do the job and are examined on their hypothetical performance. Answers are scored by specialists and interpreted according to a pre-defined set of criteria. Alternatively, behaviour description interviewing may be adopted, which focuses on the candidate's actual behaviour. However, although it has been said that past behaviour is the best predictor of future behaviour (Janz, 1989), the review by Robertson and Smith (2001) found that situational interviews tend to be slightly better at predicting successful job performance than behaviour description interviews (see Taylor and Small, 2002, for other recent research in this field).

Assessing individuals' performance in any context is difficult and requires precise definition of the main criteria behaviours as a starting point (see the above section on factors that affect the choice of selection method). One approach in appraisal contexts and selection processes includes the use of behavioural anchored rating scales (BARS) to improve objectivity in assessments by limiting biases and assumptions. However, using BARS will not ensure that the process of evaluation is objective. Assessors require understanding, training and practice in the use of BARS or any other behaviour rating system.

BEHAVIOURAL ANCHORED RATING SCALES (BARS)

BARS are hierarchical descriptions of behaviours which assessors use to evaluate candidates' responses to interview questions or behaviours demonstrated in job sample tests or assessment centre exercises. Developing BARS can be a lengthy process but uses the information collected from repertory grid and critical incident techniques and visionary interviews used for getting objective information about superior job performance. These techniques gather a lot of information and examples of ideal, good and poor performance which can be grouped into dimensions (eg communication or leadership or problem-solving) and specify the behaviours associated or expected of superior performers. These behaviours can be ranked and presented in a BARS format so that each point on the rating scale is tied to a behaviour description to make the rating as meaningful as possible. (See Cook, 2004, for further details on how to create a BARS and example.)

Training assessors to observe and then record what they have seen may seem like unnecessary skills to focus on, but observations and records of candidates' behaviours are often distorted by the biases and assumptions that can affect the selection process. To avoid such biases candidates' behaviours should be observed, recorded and then classified (or categorised) and finally evaluated. In many assessment situations candidates are observed and evaluated without behaviours being accurately recorded and classified.

REFLECTIVE ACTIVITY

How would you improve a one-to-one unstructured interview?

REFERENCES

As is evident in Table 22 above, references are widely used throughout Europe and particularly in the UK. References require applicants to provide details of the names, occupation and addresses of at least two individuals who can be contacted to provide a written or verbal statement about the applicant. Reference requests generally seek information in relation to the applicant's employment history and experience and to verify objective information such as the applicant's qualifications, rate of absenteeism, reliability, standard of work and achievements. Standardised reference forms are becoming more common to ensure consistency in information gathered about applicants.

References may be obtained as part of the assessment and selection process or at the end of the selection process and once a provisional offer has been made to the applicant. This means that the value and importance of references in determining the outcome of a selection process may vary considerably. The CIPD recruitment, retention and turnover survey (2006) found that 50% of organisations rate pre-interview employment references as one of the methods they use to select applicants.

Referees may be chosen by applicants to provide a positive assessment, although references from relatives and friends are rarely accepted. Usual practice requires that applicants' current and former employers are named as main referees. The information given in references must be carefully considered and as accurate as possible and not present a misleading impression of the applicant, overly favourable or otherwise. Under the Data Protection Act 1998 it can be possible for applicants to obtain copies of their references.

In terms of the usefulness of references, the findings from the Recruitment Confidence Index (RCI) produced by Cranfield School of Management (2006) reveal that 86% of HR managers who take up written references do not find them useful predictors of future success.

REFLECTIVE ACTIVITY

What value do you think references add to the selection process?

How would you try to ensure that references assist in predicting candidates' job performance?

PSYCHOLOGICAL TESTING

Psychological tests or instruments are sophisticated tools – usually developed by psychologists – for measuring individuals' characteristics such as personality, abilities, intelligence, interests and aptitudes (ie abilities to acquire further knowledge and skills). They are designed to measure psychological characteristics in a systematic way, according to standardised measurement dimensions, and for this reason are also known as psychometric tests. (Psychometrics is the theory and practice of psychological test construction.) Psychological testing is adopted for a variety of purposes, employment selection being a common use.

It is important to note that psychological tests invariably take considerable time and expertise to develop and refine to reach a high standard of acceptability, reliability and validity. HR practitioners must be familiar with the concepts of reliability and validity and understand the different types of reliability coefficients and validity coefficients and what they mean. Most psychological instruments are available through publishers who provide training for each particular test or questionnaire before they can be purchased. Manuals are also available, and these are necessary for in-depth information and future reference to ensure that they are used appropriately to provide standard and consistent assessment. Psychological tools are protected by copyright laws, which mean that they must not be reproduced without prior permission of the publisher.

Guidelines for using psychological tests in the selection process

Individuals who use psychological tests for assessment are expected to follow the British Psychological Society's Code of Good Practice for Psychological Testing. This means they should hold the relevant Certificate(s) of Competence in Psychological Testing, continue to develop their competence, and work within their competence.

Procedures for administration, scoring and interpretation should be followed in accordance with the appropriate test manual. The administration of psychological tests should be the same for everyone. This includes the same questionnaire booklets, answer sheets, time constraints, sequence in the selection process, environmental conditions, scoring of responses and interpretation. Unqualified individuals should not have access to the materials, and all information relating to the materials and individuals' responses and scores should be kept securely. Confidentiality must be respected.

All potential test-takers must be informed of the purpose of psychological testing and how their results will be used. They should also be provided with feedback. If all this guidance to ensure that psychological tests are used appropriately is followed, they can promote fairness and equality of opportunity. This is because they are designed to be as objective as possible. On the other hand, inappropriate use of tests or inadequate testing processes can lead to bias and unfair discrimination against some candidates.

In general, psychological tests can be divided into two main categories: personality questionnaires, and ability and aptitude tests.

Personality questionnaires

Personality questionnaires are not tests because there are no right or wrong answers. The use of personality questionnaires in the selection process has been the subject of some debate based on two main issues. Firstly, can personality be measured? And secondly, how important is personality in job performance? There are no simple answers to these questions but the case for personality assessment in selection continues to be argued (see Robertson, 1994). The underlying assumption in the adoption of personality questionnaires is that an individual's personality is relatively stable and can be accurately assessed using questionnaires to identify key characteristics which are thought to be of significant importance in determining successful job performance.

The type of personality characteristics assessed by questionnaires include interpersonal style, thinking style, management style, emotional responsiveness, sociability, independence, empathy, conscientiousness, self-discipline, decision-making, impulsivity, and so on. Each personality measure is based on a particular theory of personality – for example, the NEO-PI personality measure is based on the 'Big Five' theory of personality. The big five personality dimensions are **N**euroticism, **E**xtraversion, **O**penness, Agreeableness and Conscientiousness, and NEO-PI stands for the first three dimensions of personality theory measured by the **P**ersonality **I**nventory. However, occupationally related measures of personality reflect theory and research findings on the role of personality (behaviours, preferences and attitudes) in work performance and assist in assessing the suitability of an individual for a particular role. There are a wide range of occupational personality questionnaires.

Ability and aptitude tests

Ability and aptitude tests may measure general or specific abilities or aptitudes. In general, these psychometric tests are carefully designed to assess clearly defined concepts and skills. For example, specific ability tests look at individual abilities such as critical reasoning ability, numerical critical reasoning and spatial ability. Specific aptitude tests are designed to assess skills that are required for particular job activities or training, such as computer programming. Ability and aptitude tests are often developed to cover a range of ability levels and form part of a battery of several tests. They may be very general in application and applied in a selection process for a wide variety of different jobs, or be relevant to a specific skill set.

General ability tests, however, assess what is often referred to by psychologists as 'general intelligence'. Like the concept of personality, general intelligence has been the subject of considerable debate. General ability tests provide an overall measure of mental ability for a wide range of activities across a wide variety of situations, and this may not provide enough information on how well an individual will perform in relation to specific job requirements. Examples of ability tests commonly used in the selection process include the Watson Glaser Critical Thinking Appraisal test, the Employee Aptitude Survey, which is a set of employment tests designed to meet the practical requirements of a personnel office, and the Advance Assessment Series for Managerial and Graduate Tests VRT1 and NRT1 for verbal reasoning and numerical reasoning. The ABLE (Aptitude for Business Learning Exercises) Series is designed to measure aptitude for learning new competencies and to reduce the potential for discrimination against minority groups. As the WERS data indicates (see Table 23), the use of personality questionnaires for selection purposes is not as common as performance tests, and overall the popularity of these psychological tools has not increased a great deal since 1998.

Table 23 Selection tests, 1998 and 2004

	(1998)		(2004)	
	Personality questionnaires used routinely for some occupations (%)	Performance tests used routinely for some occupations (%)	Personality questionnaires used routinely for some occupations (%)	Performance tests used routinely for some occupations (%)
All workplaces	18	44	19	46
Organisation size				
10–99 employees	12	41	7	38
10,000 or more employees	22	48	29	58
Industry				
Manufacturing	12	44	17	37
Hotels and restaurants	15	23	20	33
Financial services	53	69	25	61
Public sector	16	56	18	63

Source: Kersley *et al* (2006; p.77)

JOB OR WORK SAMPLES

Standardised job or work samples may be the most appropriate, reliable and valid approach to selecting the best candidate for the job according to predetermined structured performance criteria, as reviewed by Robertson and Smith (2001) and Schmidt and Hunter (1998). However, practical constraints may prevent the inclusion of work samples in the selection process and may disadvantage those candidates lacking specific job-related knowledge or experience. It is also critical to carry out a job analysis to identify the content of the job that is to be sampled for selection purposes.

In-tray exercises

In-tray exercises are often used to assess individuals on some of the core administrative functions of a job and may be regarded as a sub-set of work samples. In-tray exercises may require candidates to produce a report based on an analysis of a variety of information or prioritising and co-ordinating various actions in response to a number of competing demands and requirements. Such tasks are intended to assess candidates' analytical skills, problem-solving ability, resourcefulness and initiative, etc. In-tray exercises can be assessed quite objectively with a clearly structured scoring system and are often included in assessment centres.

GROUP ASSESSMENTS

Where working with others is a fundamental aspect of a job, group discussions provide an opportunity to assess individuals' interpersonal and communication skills and the ability to work with or lead others in a social work-related situation. An analysis of the content and relevance of the discussion may also provide an evaluation of individuals' reasoning skills. Group discussions can be organised to focus on different aspects of individuals' verbal and non-verbal behaviour and communication skills, and – like in-tray exercises – group assessments are often included in assessment centres.

A common group assessment involves candidates' completing a task as a group exercise. This approach allows assessors to evaluate a wide range of abilities including problem-solving, initiative, creativity, teamwork, flexibility, and so on. Structured criteria for assessment are needed to ensure consistency and relevance in evaluating individuals' contributions in group discussion sessions or group assignments.

PRESENTATIONS

Managerial and leadership roles generally require a high standard of communication skills in all situations including presentations to large, possibly very diverse, groups of employees. Selection processes for this type of position therefore often involve a presentation on a specific topic which is formally assessed. Various aspects of the presentation can be evaluated, including the structure, content, style of delivery, persuasiveness, relevance, accuracy, and so on.

ASSESSMENT CENTRES

An assessment centre is not a place but an approach to selection that includes a number of exercises and assessment methods which simulate the main requirements of the job. A typical combination of assessment methods which compromise an assessment centre might include psychometric tests such as personality and aptitude tests, a criterion-based structured interview, an in-tray exercise, a group exercise, a group discussion and a presentation. Each assessment method will be carefully designed to evaluate particular competencies required for the job. Each part of the selection process is observed and evaluated by trained assessors to be as consistent and objective as possible in scoring candidates' behaviours. Assessment centres are an expensive selection process but increasing in popularity. Some 48% of organisations surveyed by the CIPD in 2006 then utilised assessment centres, compared to 34% in 2005. However, research studies (see Robertson and Smith, 2001) question whether cheaper methods could produce the same selection outcomes with the same, or better, chances of predicting the candidates' job success.

THE ACCURACY OF SOME METHODS OF SELECTION

The accuracy of different selection methods varies considerably. This means that some selection methods are better than others in identifying the candidate who will perform most successfully in the job. In general, various research studies suggest that assessment centres, work sample tests, ability tests and structured interviews tend to be more accurate than unstructured interviews and references.

REFLECTIVE ACTIVITY

Why are some selection methods better than others in identifying candidates who will perform more (or less) successfully in the job?

How would you know if a selection method was successful?

Different selection methods vary in how closely they match and measure the key abilities and skills required for the particular job. In other words, they vary in content validity (matching the tasks and duties of the job) and criterion-related validity (measuring performance on the tasks and duties). A statistical procedure such as correlation can help us evaluate the effectiveness of our selection processes or methods. The next section covers these key points in more detail.

3 SELECTION AS PREDICTION AND MEASURE OF SUCCESSFUL SELECTION

There are two concepts that are central to understanding what is meant by successful selection. These are validity and reliability. Valid means sound, authentic and genuine. A valid selection method accepts good applicants and rejects poor ones. Reliability, on the other hand, means consistent, unchanging and stable. A reliable selection method achieves the same outcome given the same circumstances and the same individuals.

VALIDITY

Validity is a most important concept. There are several types of validity. This means that a selection method may be or appear to be sound, genuine and authentic in different ways.

- *Face validity* refers to whether a selection method *appears* relevant, appropriate and acceptable to the selection participants. This is important. Yet face validity may result in false validity, because a selection method may appear appropriate when it is not. How is face validity assessed? By asking participants if they think the selection method is plausible.

- *Content validity* is present when the questions or items in a test *are* relevant, appropriate and measure what they are designed to measure. Content validity relies on job analysis to ensure that the content of the selection method is relevant and allows required skills, knowledge, experience, etc, to be demonstrated. How is content validity assessed? Experts in the particular area – eg individuals who perform in the role, managers or supervisors – are asked to assess the content in relation to breadth and depth of information covered by the selection method. It is a logical assessment, not a statistical one.

- *Construct validity* is concerned with concepts and overarching theories. Different ability tests, personality questionnaires, aptitude tests, intelligence tests, etc, are based on particular theories and are designed to measure concepts defined within such theories. For example, there are different theories of personality, which in turn means that each different personality questionnaire is built on a different theory of personality and attempts to measure the different constructs of each theory that predict how people behave. These predictions are reflected in the questions or items that make up the questionnaire. Construct validity is about analysing the meaning of the questions, items and the responses in relation to defined concepts or constructs to ensure consistency with the overarching theory. How is construct validity assessed? Statistical procedures such as correlation, t-tests and factor analysis are often employed to explore and offer evidence of construct validity.

- *Criterion-related validity* studies are at the heart of selection as prediction of successful job performance. Criterion-related validity studies compare performance assessed by the selection method (eg an ability test) to a relevant external measure of job success or 'performance criterion'. Criterion-related validity is high when the selection method identifies individuals who are or will be successful on the job as defined by the particular measure of job success chosen as the performance criterion – eg number of sales, supervisor rating, etc. Criterion-related validity can be assessed as *concurrent validity* or as *predictive validity*.

- *Concurrent validity* assessments are often carried out with current employees. The purpose is to identify highly successful and less successful performers according to a measure of job performance (eg manager ratings), which correspond well with a particular test or task (eg ability test) that can be used for selection purposes. Comparing individuals' test performance with another assessment – eg a job sample task – can also assess concurrent validity. Concurrent validation provides an assessment of individuals' current level of performance and is quicker and easier to conduct than predictive validity studies.

- *Predictive validity* is assessed by comparing or correlating results of assessments taken before individuals are employed and once they are in post. The aim is to predict future successful job performance at the point of selection. The main problem with assessing for predictive validity is identifying a relevant and meaningful job performance measure, and it may not be possible to use the same measure at the point of selection for various practical reasons.

RELIABILITY

Reliability refers to consistency, stability and equivalence. Selection processes must include reliable methods or tools to ensure that the assessments of individuals are consistent from one assessor to another, stable over time and can be repeated, so the same outcome decisions are obtained every time. Selection methods lack reliability if the same interview performance, for example, is rated high by one interviewer and low by another, and completely differently three weeks later. If there is a lack of consistency in the process, selection decisions will be unreliable.

The concept of reliability is mostly used in connection with statistical assessments of psychological tests. In most test manuals, information on the reliability of the test is reported as the correlation obtained between one set of test scores and another. However, the same approaches can be adopted for assessing any selection method, including structured interviews, job samples, in-tray exercises, etc, so long as there is a means of obtaining objective scoring for candidates' performance included in the process.

The most effective way to improve reliability of selection methods is to standardise the process – the interview, assessment exercise, job sample, etc – as far as possible. In effect this means ensuring that all candidates are treated in the same way – eg asked the same questions in the same way, under the same assessment conditions, with the same time constraints and with responses to questions observed, recorded, classified and evaluated according to a predefined rating system.

REFLECTIVE ACTIVITY

Which do you think is more important – validity or reliability?

Why?

EVALUATING SELECTION STRATEGIES

A selection strategy involves a process of selection using different methods – often application forms, references and interviews are included as a minimum – with the aim of identifying the candidate(s) who will perform most successfully in the post. But how do we know this aim is achieved and our selection strategy has been successful? We need to evaluate the selection methods adopting a predictive-criterion validity study design. This involves correlating the objective, reliable and valid scores obtained at the point of selection (eg test results or interview BARS results) with the valid and reliable job performance criteria collected once the employees are well established in their jobs (after between one and three years). This is often not done, even though the costs of using poor selection processes are high.

KEY ISSUES IN SELECTION

We now pull together ten key points about selection raised in this chapter:

- Selecting appropriate employees is a key activity in any organisation since failure is costly and can threaten organisational performance, development and even survival.

- Success depends on using appropriate and effective selection methods.

- It is important to remember that the selection process is two-way: applicants are also engaged in a selection and evaluation process of organisations and may reject offers from organisations if there is a lack of 'fit'.

- Selection processes reflect the organisation's culture and values.

- Different European countries adopt a different mix of commonly used selection methods which reflects different cultures and values.

- Various factors can determine the selection methods adopted because a 'one-size-fits-all' approach is not appropriate.

- Legal issues must be considered in the design of any selection process to avoid unlawful discrimination.

- The different psychological processes at play in interview situations must be controlled as far as possible.

- There are many psychometric tools available – however, the value of such tools may be lost if they are not chosen carefully nor used appropriately.

- Evaluation of the selection process itself, however simple, is a vital exercise to undertake.

Perhaps there are other key points that you would like to note for yourself.

The main case study in this chapter now follows. It illustrates some examples of good practice and highlights the importance of a well-designed, coherent approach to selection. In addition, it demonstrates the benefits of evaluating the selection methods and overall selection strategies, however simply.

This case study is based on a selection process developed by a large private sector employer based in the UK. Custom and practice relied on a structured interview method for assessment and selection of candidates to manager-level positions, most of whom were recruited locally or promoted from within the company. However, as the company expanded, struggled to keep step with technological advancements, strove to beat off international competition, and at the same time began to attract more highly qualified and more overseas applicants with additional experience and skills, it became apparent that the selection process was not sufficiently discriminatory. Inconsistent hiring decisions were made in different part of the company and there was no focus on future needs. In sum, the selection process was no longer adequate. Consultants were commissioned to review, design, train and implement a revised selection process.

The consultants began by taking account of the company's new strategic plan and involved discussions with senior executives, who were required to answer two key questions to drive the focus of the redesigned selection process: What sort of people does the company want? How does the company describe people who are really good? Job analyses were then employed to identify the main tasks and responsibilities of particular roles, how good performance might be measured, and how these roles might change in the future, and therefore what these people would be required to do in the future. The main criteria – skills, abilities, knowledge, etc – could then be described in meaningful terms for all senior executives and line managers to provide feedback on. Involving all key stakeholders in the organisation in the redesign of the selection process was an important contributory factor in its success implementation and in ensuring that individuals would be selected who 'fitted' with the organisation.

An online application form was designed that was carefully assessed against the company's recruitment needs and the requirements of the vacant positions. Successful applicants were then invited to a two-day selection process which included a group task, a job sample, a psychological test and a structured interview which has since become competency-based as candidates are now asked for specific examples of experience and how they have resolved difficult situations. Current interviewers are trained in on-going interviewing skills workshops on competency-based interviewing to improve objectivity and justifiable selection decisions against a tailored rating system. Performance on each of the selection methods is rated according to the agreed dimensions, such as working with others, communication and influence, technical orientation, problem-solving and drive to reach an overall selection decision. The same dimensions are used in the six-monthly appraisal system to track individual performance and can be used to evaluate the components of the selection process.

Your task

Not all organisations can afford consultants to construct the selection and evaluation process described above. If you were asked to create a selection process to recruit your new boss, what method(s) would you adopt, what steps would you take to establish the process, and how would you reassure yourself that you had chosen the right person?

EXPLORE FURTHER

BPS (2002) *Code of Good Practice for Psychological Testing*. Available from: **www.psychtesting.org.uk**
This provides clear guidance for the appropriate use of psychological tests for testers and test-takers.

Cook, M. (2004) *Personnel Selection. Adding value through people*, 4th edition. Chichester, John Wiley & Sons
A research-focused textbook written from the perspective that there is a clear link between selection and productivity.

Searle, R. H. (2003) *Recruitment and Selection: A critical text*. Milton Keynes, Palgrave/Open University Press
A research-focused textbook which aims to critically evaluate various practices in recruitment and selection.

Sparrow, P. (2006) *International Recruitment, Selection and Assessment*. London, CIPD
A research-informed report covering recruitment, selection and assessment issues facing HR professionals working in an international context.

CHAPTER 10

Flexibility and work–life balance

Suzan Lewis *and* Ian Roper

INTRODUCTION

This chapter is about matching the personal needs of employees outside of work with the operational and commercial needs of employers in the workplace.

LEARNING OUTCOMES

By the end of this chapter readers should be able to:

- explain what employers may mean when they refer to 'flexibility'
- explain the growing significance of 'work–life balance' as a key source of employees' need for flexibility
- identify where the apparently competing needs of employers and employees may be put together effectively
- recognise and challenge aspects of workplace culture that undermine flexible working arrangements
- understand that achieving mutual flexibility involves processes and not just policies.

The chapter is structured in four parts. The first part discusses the development of the term 'flexibility' in the field of HRM, comparing employer-oriented needs with those of workers. (The term 'employee' is not used here, specifically because one form of flexibility is the use of non-employment-based contracts.) The second part examines what employees want from flexibility; the third part focuses on work–life balance; and the final part looks at how these various issues can be integrated into HR best practice.

The starter case study highlights some uses of flexibility in a real-life organisational situation. The text then explains in more detail some of the different forms of flexibility that employers have sought to utilise, and examines one or two problems with some of these approaches. This is followed by a discussion of some more recent uses of the term 'flexibility', which appear to be more employee-led and strongly associated with the concept of work–life balance. The third part of the chapter then goes on to discuss the development

LonBoro is a London metropolitan borough council with a large and ethnically diverse workforce. In the period being described here, the Council had gone through a number of years of political turmoil resulting in some negative publicity. The political leadership was seeking radical restructuring of the organisation, moving away from a traditional bureaucratic model of management to one where much greater devolution was assigned to the services themselves. This strategy had a number of stages. First, services were turned into cost centres for which budget targets were delegated to service heads and managed accordingly. Service managers were therefore 'empowered' to make more decisions about staff issues than had been the case before. Combined with this there was a large reduction in the size of the workforce, together with a series of decisions to tender out, completely, a number of services to private contactors. Overall, this package of changes could be called a strategy based on *numerical flexibility* (which we explain later).

In the next stage of reform, LonBoro embarked upon an ambitious quality management project to enhance the reputation of its services. Service managers were encouraged to make innovations in working practices to realise this aim – a strategy that could be described as focusing on the *functional flexibility* of its staff (which we again explain later).

A further stage involved the decision to outsource all of what remained of in-house provided services, effectively transferring all the front-line staff over to private contractors bidding to run the services, leaving only

'strategic' commissioning units in the Council, In the end, however, much of this final stage was actually abandoned when LonBoro's political leadership changed in subsequent local elections.

The effects of these various changes were mixed. The early round of severe job cuts and outsourcing – through numerical flexibility – led to a steep downturn in staff morale. Later, however, the introduction of the quality policy – partly associated with functional flexibility – led to improved staff morale, albeit, in the light of the previous round of job cuts, described somewhat lugubriously by one manager who said that 'morale among the survivors' was good. This generally improved picture was further boosted by the enhanced reputation that LonBoro was receiving for the quality of its services – which further boosted morale. However, this virtuous circle was again broken by the further announcement of more outsourcing. Among other issues of concern, staff surveys were now reporting a perception of how this was all badly affecting LonBoro's previous commitment to equality issues and it was also leading to direct confrontation with the union. Figure 18 shows the effects of these changes on morale, as described by a senior manager.

Questions for discussion

Basing your response on what has been described in this case study, what would you say were the likely advantages and disadvantages of *numerical flexibility* and *functional flexibility*?

Figure 18 Staff morale at LonBoro

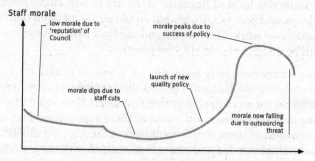

of flexible working arrangements within a work–life balance framework, using case study examples to illustrate the reason for their development, their advantages and limitations. In this section we explore an approach to flexibility that is both employer- and employee-led. The chapter then concludes with the main case study, which describes the introduction of work–life balance policies and practices into an organisation.

Reference sources named within the chapter may be looked up in the *References and further reading* section at the end of the book.

FLEXIBILITY FROM THE EMPLOYER'S PERSPECTIVE

WHAT IS FLEXIBILITY?

First we should explain some of the flexibility terms used and see how certain types of flexibility may be used in conjunction with others. One of the issues arising from the case study above is the definition of 'flexibility' being used. Quite clearly, there appear to be very different consequences involved in using *numerical flexibility* than in pursuing *functional flexibility*. Another issue is the question of who is intended to benefit from any particular type of flexibility. The word itself implies a call to be 'reasonable', and it is very hard see how anyone could object to being asked to be flexible. As Tailby (2003; p.490) has succinctly put it, when flexibility is

> applied to the world of work and employment, however, this obviously raises the issue of whose interests are at stake. Practices deemed to be rigid by management, for example, may be the source of stability and security for employees. Consequently, job protection rights and the employer's freedom to hire and fire may be a source of conflict between the parties.

For this reason we need to be precise about *who* is being expected to be flexible and *in what way*. Blyton (1996) provides a useful starting point for us here. He has consolidated many of the definitions of flexibility into four basic types: numerical, functional, temporal and financial flexibility. Each of these is now explained.

Numerical flexibility (as the name implies) is concerned with management's ability to make rapid adjustments to the number – and also the composition – of its workforce. We could think of how this has been traditionally used in seasonal industries like tourism: running a holiday camp at the seaside requires the recruitment of large numbers of staff during the peak season in the summer, but only a very basic skeleton staff during the winter. Being numerically flexible allows such an organisation to make these rapid adjustments to seasonal market conditions. Crucially, though, this type of flexibility works in *this* industry partly because it meets the expectations of the workers in it.

Fuctional flexibility refers (again as the name implies) to the functions that
employees carry out when employed. It implies a multi-skilled, multi-tasking
worker keen to carry out a range of duties. It is functional flexibility that has
been identified by numerous commentators to have been at the heart of Japanese
industrial success from the 1970s onwards and is credited as being equally crucial
to Japanese transplants such as Nissan and Toyota that came to Britain in the
1980s and 1990s (Oliver and Wilkinson, 1992). From an employee perspective,
functional flexibility would seem to be a much better option than that of
numerical flexibility – offering the possibility of getting skills that would be
transferable to other employers. However, critics have pointed to a bleaker side
to functional flexibility, often referred to as 'work intensification' – whereby it is
not so much responsibility and increased autonomy that are being improved, but
rather 'horizontal job loading' by which more tasks are added into the working
day. (See Chapter 11 on the importance of autonomy.)

A third type of flexibility is *temporal flexibility*. Yet again as the name suggests,
this is to do with adjustments to time – the working day or the working year.
Examples include the use of flexitime, annualised hours, or the use of termtime
working. It also extends to some more long-standing practices such as the use of
part-time work and even 'overtime' – although many of the innovations in
temporal flexibility are designed to reduce the need for employers to resort to
paying an overtime premium to cope with high peaks in demand.

The final form of flexibility defined by Blyton (1996) is that of *financial flexibility*.
Financial flexibility describes practices relating to variations to standard methods
of payment. A 'standard' method of payment could be assumed to mean payment

based on a flat rate for the job, based on hours worked. Flexibility, on this theme, might include performance-related pay – based upon some idea of management being able to adjust pay rates individually according to some method of assessing each individual's contribution (see Chapter 13). It may also involve the inclusion, within the pay package itself, of bonus schemes and employee share ownership schemes. Flexibility within the 'reward system' may also include a range of non-pay aspects such as variations in fringe benefits. More recently, innovations in 'flexible benefits' packages have involved organisations allowing employees to trade off various aspects of their benefits package to optimise to their own personal circumstances – trading in their company car allowance in favour of more generous holiday entitlement, for example.

COMBINING TYPES OF FLEXIBILITY: THE IMPACT OF (DE)REGULATION AND THE FLEXIBLE FIRM

We have so far examined and categorised different types of flexibility separately. In practice, however, firms are likely to use versions of these approaches to flexibility in combination. In 1984, John Atkinson proposed a model for an integrated approach to flexibility in the model known as 'the flexible firm'. This now well-known model compared the traditional firm – employing sufficient numbers of permanent full-time employees to enable the firm to carry out all activities at any given time – with an emerging flexible firm in which the long-term commitment of the firm to such large numbers of people was seen as impossible. In the flexible firm the workforce is divided into two elements. The first element is a 'core' workforce of functionally flexible employees on secure permanent employment contracts, typically being highly trained, qualified and on high salaries. Outside this core, however, is the second element, a 'periphery workforce' – based on the principles described under numerical flexibility. This group would conduct a whole range of activities not perceived to be of strategic importance to the core activity of the business. In the Atkinson model, this periphery is further divided into different peripheral sub-groups comprising different types of employment with varying degrees of job security.

Although there are some important criticisms that can be made of the flexible firm model, it is helpful in describing what most large UK organisations, private and public now look like, compared to how they may have looked, say, 30 years ago. However, this situation did not take place purely through the persuasive strength of the model alone. Making labour markets this flexible required changes to the external environment. During the 1980s, Britain experienced a step-change in the way that government treated employment regulation – one that was significantly different from past approaches and one that was significantly at odds with the way such matters were dealt with in continental Europe. The Conservative governments of this period were committed to making the labour market more flexible, as the following quote from their election manifesto indicates (Conservative Party Manifesto, 1983):

We shall go on reducing the barriers which discourage employers from recruiting more staff, even when they want to. And we shall help to make the job market more flexible and efficient so that more people can work part-time if they wish, and find work more easily.

Table 24 shows some examples of regulatory and deregulatory changes made during the 1980s and early 1990s, and how they impacted upon employers' use of flexibility.

Table 24 Changes to regulation and the impact on flexibility

Regulatory change(s)	Impact on flexibility
Restriction of trade union powers	Reduces collective employee resistance to introducing functional flexibility
Abolition of Wage Councils	Allows lower rates of pay for new job categories created by numerical flexibility
Reduction in unfair dismissal protection for employees	The reduced risk for employers incentivises a growth in the use of fixed-term temporary employment
Opt-out of EU Social Chapter	The reduced cost, through reduced rights for part-time and temporary employees, allows growth in non-standard employment
Forcing of public services to tender out series of activities to private contractors	Transference of the logic of the flexible firm into the public sector

In fact, if we look at figures from the WERS data, the evidence is mixed. For example, although the outsourcing of various peripheral functions is common, there are differences between functions. For example, whereas 59% of organisations outsource building maintenance, still only 12% outsource catering services (Kersley, Alpin, Forth, Dix, Oxenbridge, Bryson and Bewley, 2006); and it is public sector organisations that are more likely to make use of fixed-term contract workers (61% of workplaces) rather than what we might assume to be the more ruthless cost-conscious private sector equivalents, where only 23% used these types of contracts (*ibid*; p.80).

2 FLEXIBILITY FROM THE EMPLOYEE'S PERSPECTIVE

The case for flexibility that has been made so far has all been based on the perceived benefits to employers. From this logic it is assumed that if the business benefits from reduced costs and enhanced efficiencies gained from such flexibilities, then the employees go on to benefit too, through the enhanced job security and job prospects that they receive from this. However, it could be argued on the other hand that if *all* organisations can gain maximum flexibility from their workforces, no *single* workforce will be able to gain this added job security, because any one organisation will only be as efficient as all the other organisations. It was for this reason that in the early part of the twentieth century employers were constrained by government regulation in their ability to compete on the terms and conditions of their employees; to prevent, as Winston Churchill is reputed to have stated at the time, 'the good employer being undercut by the bad employer, and the bad employer being undercut by the worse employer'. The most recent example of this trait is probably the increasing concern being felt by those – in manufacturing and in services – unable to compete on cost terms with emerging economies such as China and India. For employees this is the 'race to the bottom' scenario: that in being so 'flexible' to the needs of employers, employees are now having their jobs outsourced, not to local sub-contractors with whom they might expect to obtain employment in the future but to remote locations thousands of miles away. The argument here is that such one-sided flexibility makes it increasingly difficult for employees to achieve personal financial stability to plan a normal family life outside of the workplace.

This brings us to the other side of flexibility – that of the increased employee demand for work–life balance. But before this, we should return to some more recent changes – and continuities – to the themes mentioned in the previous section.

It was noted that 'flexibility' was not just something that occurred as a result of 'best practice': it was positively encouraged by the government by various means. When the Conservatives left office in 1997, to be replaced by Labour, a shift occurred in relation to the attitude to regulation. It was not, however, a radical shift. The new government entered into office with a stated desire to improve basic employment rights and bring them more into line with European norms, but not in a way that undermined employers' basic desire for flexibility. The approach has therefore been to 'opt in' to the European Social Chapter, thereby bringing in regulations affecting equal rights, parental rights, working time issues and employee consultation rights. Some critics from employers' lobby groups have complained about the 'regulatory burden' involved in complying with such regulations, while other lobby groups representing employee rights issues have complained that the regulations that have been introduced have been significantly watered down when applied in Britain.

The effect of this has been mixed. Most observers agree that Britain still has the most flexible labour markets in Europe even though there are high costs to geographical mobility because of home ownership. It has the least employment protection and the longest working hours, for example. However, since the equalisation of rights for non-standard workers, the overall pattern of job growth in Britain has been in permanent full-time and part-time employment, with a decline in temporary employment. Table 25 shows the growth in temporary employment in the early 1990s compared with its decline in the late 1990s and 2000s.

Table 25 UK employment growth, 1992–2002

Employees	1992–1997		1997–2002	
Full-time	+234,000	+1.4%	+1,165,000	+6.9%
Part-time	+641,000	+12.5%	+409,000	+7.1%
Permanent	+410,000	+2.0%	+1,787,000	+8.5%
Temporary	+465,000	+35.9%	–213,000	–12.1%

Source: TUC (derived from Labour Force Survey data)

So to some extent, the agenda of merely providing flexibility for employers at employees' expense has been kept under control. However, the area of 'employee-led' flexibility that has grown most in recent years is probably that related to what has been termed 'family-friendly policies' or 'work–life balance'. The case can be made that raising children makes a significant contribution to the economy as a whole (even if we think, very crudely, of the future generations that will have to be in work in order to pay for our own pensions in future years), and that this burden has fallen too much on women in the past, in terms of the loss in direct earnings and career development. Government figures estimate that the average difference in lifetime earnings between an unskilled man and an unskilled woman with no children is £197,000. This may in itself be unfair. However, if both are parents of two children, this gap increases to £482,000. Even for graduates, the lifetime pay gap between a father and mother is £161,000 (DTI, 2000). If women are not able to contribute to the labour market in line with their qualifications and experience, there are also implications for the national economy (DTI, 2001).

There has consequently been a change in government policies to address some of these issues. At the most basic level, maternity rights have been steadily improved since 1997, providing more paid maternity leave. This agenda has also, however, attempted to affect wider cultural assumptions about childcare responsibilities, providing extended rights to extended parental leave, the right to take time off work to deal with 'family emergencies', the introduction of paid paternity leave – introducing, for the first time, the rights of fathers in the workplace equation. Most recently, the government's 'family-friendly' agenda has introduced the right for parents of children up to the age of six to request flexible working, with a duty on employers to consider it (see Croucher and Kelliher, 2005, for more details). Figure 19 shows evidence from WERS 2004 that some of these initiatives seem to have had some effect on British workplaces – at least at the level of policies.

3 AN INTEGRATED APPROACH TO FLEXIBILITY

Having considered what flexibility might mean from an employer's and from an employee's perspective, we now go on to examine how these two different agendas can potentially be integrated.

WHAT IS WORK–LIFE BALANCE?

Work–life balance has been defined (Employers for work–life balance, **www.employersforwork-lifebalance.org.uk**) as being

> *about people having a measure of control over when, where and how they work. It is achieved when an individual's right to a fulfilled life inside and outside paid work is accepted and respected as the norm, to the mutual benefit of the individual, business and society.*

However, the term 'work–life balance' is problematic. It has been criticised for a number of reasons (Fleetwood, forthcoming; Lewis et al, forthcoming). In particular it is argued that the concept (Lewis and Cooper, 2005):

Figure 19 Percentage of workplaces with flexible working arrangements, 2004

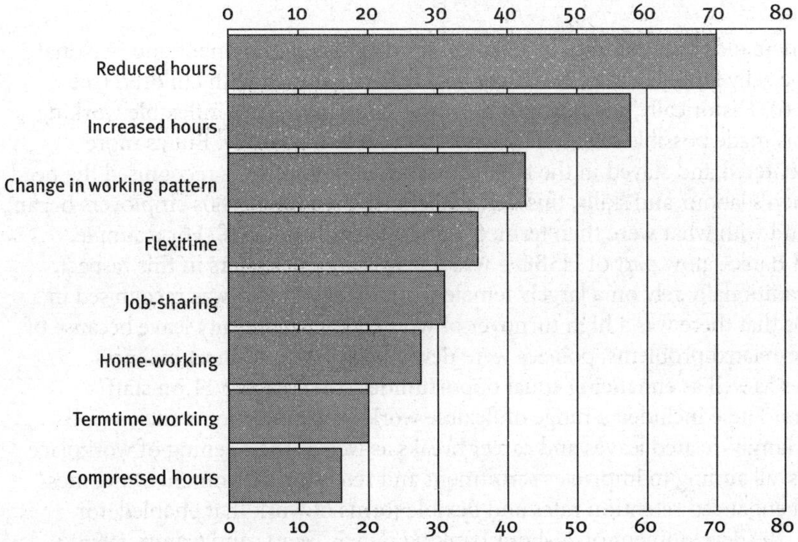

Arrangement	0	10	20	30	40	50	60	70	80

Reduced hours
Increased hours
Change in working pattern
Flexitime
Job-sharing
Home-working
Termtime working
Compressed hours

Source: Kersley, Alpin, Forth, Dix, Oxenbridge, Bryson and Bewley (2006)

- implies that work and life are separate spheres, rather than that work is a part of life
- is often interpreted as viewing lack of 'balance' as an individual rather than a workplace issue
- assumes 'balance' is always good and imbalance bad
- neglects workers' changing needs for different forms of 'balance' at different points in their lives
- as an approach tends to focus on policy rather than practice and culture change, which are necessary for policies to be effective.

Despite the ongoing discussion about the term, work–life balance has for many reasons – as explained below – become increasingly significant for organisations.

REFLECTIVE ACTIVITY

Consider your own circumstances and those of others in your group.

How much would your own home commitments affect the patterns of work you feel able to do? What differences emerge within your group?

What kind of work would not be suitable for some people's home commitments, and what might organisations be able to do to make it more suitable?

WHY HAS 'WORK–LIFE BALANCE' BECOME INCREASINGLY SIGNIFICANT FOR WORKERS AND FOR HRM?

At first, demands for flexibility to 'balance' or integrate employment and personal life – especially family demands – came largely from women with children (see Chapter 6). Historically, the norm of full-time, continuous and inflexible working hours was made possible for men by women's role in the family. But as more women entered and stayed in the labour market, and employers recognised the need for women's labour and skills, this was challenged. From the 1980s employers began to respond with what were then termed 'family-friendly policies'. For example, Midland Bank – now part of HSBC – was one of the early leaders in this respect. Banks traditionally rely on a largely female workforce. When it was recognised in the 1980s that there was a high turnover of women after maternity leave because of childcare-related problems, policies were developed to help to meet business objectives as well as enhancing equal opportunities (see Chapter 11 on staff turnover). These included a range of flexible working arrangements such as job-sharing, family-related leaves and career breaks as well as the opening of workplace nurseries, all aiming to improve recruitment and retention of women. Outcomes included enhanced retention rates and flexible forms of work that enabled, for example, the development of 24-hour banking (Lewis, Watts and Camp, 1996).

A move from a focus on 'family-friendly' to 'work–life balance' policies occurred from the mid-1990s associated with a number of trends:

- Family-friendly policies usually focused on women. But as families and social norms shift, men – especially younger men – also want or need to be more involved in families or just to have a life outside work.

- With the trends towards long working hours and an intensification of work, more people feel the need for some 'balance' between their paid work and the rest of their lives.

- The government developed a work–life balance campaign, partly in response to EU pressure (as noted above).

- Britain still has fewer employment regulations and statutory supports (such as state-funded childcare) than many other European countries for reconciling employment and family life. This leaves considerable room for employers to develop a competitive edge by developing work–life balance policies.

FLEXIBLE WORK ARRANGEMENTS

Development of flexible working arrangements is key to work–life balance strategies. Most of the flexible working arrangements developed under the work–life balance umbrella are a form of temporal flexibility. Some forms of flexible working arrangements, such as part-time work and some flexitime or shift systems, have a long history and were introduced as productivity or efficiency measures, although it is increasingly recognised that these strategies have implications for work–life 'balance'. Others are newer and are depicted as tools for reducing work–family conflict or enhancing work–life balance, but it is increasingly recognised that they are also beneficial to employers (Lewis, 2003). It makes a difference whether these initiatives are seen primarily as productivity or work–life balance measures.

For example, a company in Japan developed a career break scheme for carers and also a flexitime scheme. The carers' scheme was open to men and women but only women used it. The flexitime was presented as a productivity measure and both men and women used it. In fact, there were business advantages to both.

REFLECTIVE ACTIVITY

Write down your considered answers to the following questions.

1 *What difficulties do you see with the implementation of flexible working arrangements within a work–life balance framework rather than as a productivity measure?*

2 *Where might resistance come from, and why?*

3 *What other barriers might there be to the effective implementation of such arrangements?*

These issues are examined in detail later in this chapter.

Table 26 shows the percentage of full-time and part-time employees who use formal flexible working arrangements. There are of course many others, particularly in smaller businesses or in professional and managerial roles, who have opportunities for informal flexibility of working times and place.

Table 26 Percentage of employees with flexible working patterns, by sex, 2004

	Males	Females	All employees
Full-time employees			
Flexible working hours	9.2	14.6	11.3
Annualised working hours	5.0	4.8	4.9
Four-and-a-half-day week	1.5	0.7	1.2
Term-time working	1.2	5.5	2.8
Nine-day fortnight	0.3	0.3	0.3
Any flexible working pattern	*17.4*	*26.2*	*20.7*
Part-time employees			
Flexible working hours	5.3	8.1	7.6
Annualised working hours	3.1	4.3	4.0
Term-time working	4.2	11.2	9.9
Job-sharing	1.0	2.7	2.4
Any flexible working pattern	*15.0*	*27.0*	*24.7*

Note: Some of the percentages in this table are based on totals which exclude people who did not state whether or not they had a flexible working arrangement; respondents could give more than one answer.

Source: Labour Force Survey, Office for National Statistics

There are of course variations across countries, as illustrated by the Cranet-E data (see Table 27).

Table 27 'Does your organisation use the following working arrangements?'

	UK	Sweden	Germany	Greece	Slovakia
Weekend work	65%	65%	77%	68%	60%
Shiftwork	61%	74%	74%	85%	67%
Overtime	92%	99%	56%	89%	87%
Annual hours contract	26%	46%	30%	10%	66%
Part-time work	97%	99%	98%	48%	12%
Job-sharing	55%	34%	41%	7%	60%
Flexitime	48%	94%	90%	43%	60%
Temporary/casual	86%	94%	65%	51%	54%
Fixed-term contracts	75%	97%	97%	79%	7%
Home-based work	32%	34%	13%	7%	16%
Teleworking	20%	44%	43%	9%	45%
Compressed working week	29%	20%	26%	2%	0%

Source: Cranet-E (2003)

4 THE ROLE OF HR PROFESSIONALS IN WORK–LIFE BALANCE

The role of HR professionals in work–life balance is not limited to the development of policies. It includes assessing the needs of workers and the business and finding the best way of meeting both agendas. This is important for convincing senior and line management of the need for flexible working arrangements. HR professionals also have an important role to play in monitoring the effectiveness of work–life balance policies, including implementation and take-up rates, and for developing strategies for overcoming resistance to change amongst managers and others, and barriers to success.

REFLECTIVE ACTIVITY

How would you convince management that work–life balance policies are important for organisational effectiveness?

Below are listed some of the business benefits that have been proved to follow from policies that are well implemented:

- compliance with regulations, and using this to positive advantage – for example, treating the parents' right to request flexible working as a challenge and opportunity to innovate rather than as a threat
- better recruitment and retention
- becoming an employer of choice by keeping up with and possibly even exceeding the flexible options offered by other employers in the same sector, especially where there are skills shortages
- reduction in stress associated with conflicting demands at work and beyond
- reduced absenteeism (flexible working arrangements, for example, enable workers to make up time lost through family or other issues)
- raised morale – workers are more engaged if they feel that their needs are recognised and if they have more autonomy and control over their time
- good public relations
- attracting ethical investors who are increasingly asking about equal opportunities and related policies
- achieving mutual flexibility (give and take between workers and their manager), which makes for additional forms of flexibility, as noted below.

For example, in a small printing business (see Lewis and Cooper, 2005) workers were encouraged to learn multiple skills so that colleagues could cover for each other on a reciprocal basis if they took time off for any reason. Workers collaborated in finding flexible solutions that they saw as fair and which also sustained production.

REFLECTIVE ACTIVITY

Can you think of further scenarios in which the sort of flexibility associated with work–life balance enhances other forms of flexibility, or vice versa?

BARRIERS AND RESISTANCE TO THE EFFECTIVE IMPLEMENTATION OF FLEXIBLE WORKING ARRANGEMENTS

Evidence indicates that work–life policies can be successful up to a point, but much depends on how they are implemented and managed (Lewis and Cooper, 2005). They can, for example, improve recruitment but they do not necessarily maximise the use of women's (or in some cases, men's) skills. This is because flexible working policies are necessary – but not sufficient – to make the changes needed to enable all workers to develop their full potential at work and at home. Flexible working arrangements without culture change have limited impact. This is illustrated by the case of 'Proffco', a large multinational professional services firm.

Proffco has developed an impressive raft of work–life policies. They include not only family-related initiatives such as time off to care for dependants (recognising that staff have elder care and other care commitments and not just childcare-related issues) but also initiatives relating to other work–personal life commitments and aspirations. For example, a nine-day fortnight is used by some members of staff to participate in sport or other activities. The policies have increased the rate of return from maternity leave and improved scores on a staff satisfaction questionnaire. However, long working hours and inflexible work remains the norm, and those members of staff – mostly women – who do take up flexible working practices are often thought to be less committed than other employees. Consequently, most men and many women say they do not make use of flexible working arrangements because they know it would be career-limiting. Assumptions about ideal workers are deeply embedded in the culture. A woman who worked full-time, but flexibly, explained:

I am the first at work every day. Also, I usually work through lunch. The fact that I leave work on time quite often (even though I might have a caseful of work at peak periods) means that I get comments like 'I know that it's difficult for you to put in the hours, with the children.'

Those who do work flexibly believe that they are equally effective with – and in many cases, more effective than – their colleagues. Most of their managers agree with this. Yet despite the impressive policies and the success of flexible working arrangements in some departments, the organisational culture is very slow to change. People who are considered for promotion – often referred to as 'strong players' or those who 'are 'willing to go the extra mile' – are not those who use flexible working arrangements. Selection for promotion is thus made from a limited pool. Hence, the effectiveness of policies in helping all staff to work most effectively and to enhance career development is undermined. Turnover has been reduced but is still high because many employees leave to go to smaller, more flexible firms or to become self-employed.

Questions for discussion

HR professionals in many organisations will recognise the problems faced at Proffco.

Do you have any ideas about how to challenge workplace cultures in which ideal workers are still assumed to be those who do not need flexibility of working arrangements?

One possible approach is explored in the next section of text.

EMPLOYER- AND EMPLOYEE-LED: MUTUAL FLEXIBILITY

The previous sections showed how flexible working arrangements that focus on employee demands or needs are implemented for business reasons. This can be a win/win solution for employers and workers, but the effectiveness of these policies is limited if they are implemented without culture change. For example, the opportunities for reduced hours or flexible work have limited success if only full-time non-flexible workers are valued.

A further approach to flexibility is based on a dual agenda. That is, changes are implemented to meet the needs of both employer and employees, with both given equal weight. Initiatives based on the needs only of employers or only of employees are less effective (Rapoport, Bailyn, Fletcher and Pruitt, 2002). This approach stresses the importance of going beyond policy development to start a process which first challenges assumptions that sustain ineffective practices and then draws on collaboration to develop more appropriate and effective norms and practices. This is illustrated in the case of a Customer Administration Centre described below.

(See Rapoport *et al*, 2002, and Lewis and Cooper, 2005, for more details of this approach.)

CASE STUDY

At the Customer Administration Centre, where the workforce comprised largely women, many with family commitments, there were high levels of unexpected absence, resulting in problems of lack of cover. There was also high staff turnover. Management was attempting to shift the structure towards more empowered self-managed teams so that staff could manage their own absences ensuring cover at all times, but it was not working smoothly. Collaborative interviews with members of the team, including managers, revealed that employees were not trusted to manage their own time flexibly and sustain productivity. A culture of control by management was undermining the goal of empowerment. Although there was a range of flexible work policies available, managers were reluctant to allow employees to use them because they feared that it would 'open the floodgates' and undermine productivity. Consequently, employees had to make their own arrangements to try to juggle work and family commitments. Often these arrangements broke down, so they would have to call in sick or use holiday time, creating absence problems.

Bringing these assumptions, which were embedded in the culture and not just individual manager perspectives, to the surface enabled managers to reflect on their reluctance to give up control because of short-term productivity concerns. They came to understand why they were experiencing so much difficulty moving towards empowered teams. In response to this, the managers and employees worked together to design an experiment in which flexible working policies were made available to all, regardless of family situation or management discretion. There was, of course, some resistance and it was important to engage with this, again exploring the assumptions underpinning the culture of control. The experiment was implemented and ultimately there was a move away from individual accommodation to meet the needs of specific employees, towards a situation where flexibility became ingrained in the culture. The outcome was that teams came up with collective approaches to flexibility to meet productivity and personal needs. This resulted in a 30% decrease in absenteeism. In addition, customer responsiveness increased as times of coverage were extended. Employee satisfaction also improved. It became possible to move to more self-managed teams which gradually took on more responsibility and participated in decisions about work schedules.

The principles of this approach, illustrated in the case above, include:

- starting by looking at a key business need (in this case the need to reduce absenteeism and turnover by empowering self-managed teams)

- working together to develop mutual understandings of working practices, underlying assumptions and their impact on the dual agenda (employees' work–life needs and workplace effectiveness)

- keeping the dual agenda in focus at all times – dropping either perspective prevents positive outcomes
- working together to come up with innovative solutions
- experimenting with new ways of working
- engaging with resistance throughout.

The next stage is to evaluate interventions and communicate outcomes in order to diffuse learning within the organisation.

REFLECTIVE ACTIVITY

Think of a specific workplace situation where flexible working arrangements are not working, and consider how you might apply the dual agenda approach.

What difficulties might you face?

What strategies could you, as an HR professional, develop to overcome them?

KEY ISSUES IN FLEXIBILITY AND WORK–LIFE BALANCE

We now pull together ten key points about flexibility raised in this chapter:

- Flexibility became a popular concept in HRM from the 1980s.
- It is important to see that different types of flexibility result in different outcomes for employers and employees. It is important to understand *who* is being flexible and *in what way*.
- The initial emphasis in the popularity of flexibility was concerned with advantages for employers, rather than for employees.
- The types of flexibility being used by employers are related to government regulations. In the 1980s the emphasis was on numerical flexibility; from 1997 there has been a greater emphasis on work–life balance.

- Work–life balance policies are not just employee-led. They are usually introduced for business reasons.
- Solutions that meet the dual needs of employers and employees can be very effective.
- Work–life balance policies are just a first step. Good implementation and manager support are essential.
- Flexible working arrangements without culture change have limited impact.
- It is important to question assumptions that undermine mutual flexibility.
- Mutual flexibility is best developed through collaboration rather than top-down.

Perhaps there are other key points that you would like to note for yourself.

The main case study in this chapter now follows. It gives an example of how it is possible to advance from work–life policies to culture change. It also highlights some of the pitfalls and barriers to success.

MAIN CASE STUDY

Look at the description of the case set out below. Then decide on the recommendations that you would make as an HR manager for dealing with the issues raised. Try to think beyond the level of a 'quick fix' or simple solutions and to be wary of assumptions that undermine opportunities for mutual flexibility.

The company, which we are calling Peak, is a large insurance company that has undergone mergers, takeovers and restructuring in recent years. There is now a drive for flexibility: numerical (mostly through the use of agency workers but also some staff on temporary contracts), functional (via multi-skilling), and temporal (via flexible working policies) as well as culture change (primarily through management training and development).

Downsizing and reorganisation have brought increasing job insecurity and intensification of work for those who survived redundancies. The most recent merger/takeover was followed by a strategic drive to develop a distinctive culture for the new merged company, including a decision to develop policy, practice and culture change to increase flexibility of working hours. The goal was to move to a more people-focused culture, based on trust, mutual flexibility, autonomy and self-management at all levels, non-hierarchical, non-status-based relationships and collaboration and mutual responsibility between managers and employees. Traditional ways of working were challenged and there was wide talk of the value of two-way flexibility. In the new culture, ideal employees would be regarded as those who were flexible, adaptable and self-motivated.

A number of flexible working arrangements thus came into existence at Peak involving some major shifts in policy following the merger. In particular, there were changes to the existing flexitime system, which involved a shift from formal clocking-in to an informal trust-based flexitime system. This was viewed by management as consistent with the drive for culture change towards greater flexibility and autonomy. It was also justified in terms of financial savings, in that workers had previously been able to clock in 10 minutes early each day and build up days off, which was regarded as no longer beneficial to the

organisation. An on-site crèche at the main premises was also replaced with childcare vouchers throughout the company.

There was an implicit dual agenda of pursuing business needs by meeting staff flexibility needs. However, policy change solutions were not always reached collaboratively. Rather, decisions were often made at management level and communicated in a top-down way. Because of this, some workers did not understand the reasons for the new policies and resented them. For example, the change in flexitime system and loss of the crèche created major problems for some employees, making it more difficult for them to manage their work and private lives, and this was then associated with higher levels of absenteeism and turnover.

Similarly, some line managers had not accepted the rationales for the new policies even though managers underwent training and development to spread the new management values and style. Consequently, management support for mutual flexibility was patchy. Employees with 'new-style' supportive managers were very satisfied with the enhanced level of trust, autonomy and flexibility. However, the new values and discourses of empowerment raised expectations of support, so employees who worked under 'old-style' non-supportive managers were particularly resentful. Nor was the lack of change restricted to line managers. Some HR managers were very slow to take on and live by the new values.

The drive for a shift in culture, and the changes in structures and practices that this was intended to bring about, incorporated a deliberate questioning of deeply held assumptions that ideal workers were those who worked full-time and inflexibly. Although the effectiveness of flexible working arrangements was increasingly apparent, one assumption remained stubbornly intact. This was the belief that managers and supervisors must work full-time and long hours (although flexible working hours made it impossible for single managers to cover all the working hours of their subordinates). Many managers returning from maternity leave requested reduced working hours or other flexible working arrangements, and this was granted – but they were moved to non-managerial posts. Consequently, many managers and supervisors left the company after maternity leave. The failure to question assumptions about the nature of jobs involving people management, and the lack of trust implied in these assumptions, despite the high-profile drive for a trust-based culture shift, prevented Peak management from treating these requests as opportunities for learning and innovating.

So the current position is that on the positive side there is an understanding of the need to go beyond policy to changes in culture, structures and practice, and this is used strategically at Peak as a way of pursuing business aims in a rapidly changing and competitive environment. There is a concerted effort to train and develop managers as agents of change and to work towards putting espoused values into practice. These strategies have achieved some success, both in terms of workplace effectiveness and of satisfying the personal needs of some employees, but with some gaps and limitations. There has been some listening to employees' needs, but this falls far short of a collaborative approach. Above all, however, there has been limited questioning of assumptions about ideal workers, especially at more senior levels. At this point in time the longer-term impacts of the changing practices have not been monitored in terms of the dual agenda.

Your task

Imagine you are an HR professional working in Peak. Prepare a short report based on the information you have been given above, making recommendations to your colleagues about how the situation can be improved.

EXPLORE FURTHER

DTI (2001) *Work–life Balance: The business case*. London, Department of Trade and Industry
This report sets out the business case for introducing work–life balance initiatives in organisations.

LEWIS, S. and COOPER, C. (2005) *Work–life Integration: Case studies of organisational change*. London, John Wiley & Sons
A book of case studies using a work–life integration approach to bring about organisational change and flexibility. This provides a range of practical examples and has learning points at the end of each chapter.

RAPOPORT, R., BAILYN, L., FLETCHER, J. and PRUITT, B. (2002) *Beyond Work–family Balance: Advancing gender equity and workplace performance*. London, Jossey-Bass/John Wiley
A very detailed but readable account of an action research model of organisational change using a work–life balance lens.

STREDWICK, J. and ELLIS, S. (2005) *Flexible Working Practices*. London, CIPD
Using case studies from leading organisations and many practical tools, the authors show how to develop and implement effective and flexible working policies.

WOOD, G., HARCOURT, M. and ROPER, I. (2006) 'The limits of numerical flexibility. Continuity and change'. In G. Wood and P. James (eds) *Institutions, Production and Working Life*. Oxford, Oxford University Press
This chapter provides a comparative look at the use of numerical flexibility across Europe, highlighting its incompatibility with other forms of flexibility.

Managing Employee Performance and Development

CHAPTER 11

The psychological contract, absence and turnover

Susan Leigh

INTRODUCTION

This chapter discusses the psychological contract between employees and their employer, with special emphasis on its use to maximise employee contribution – a subject relevant to HR management anywhere in the world. The chapter also looks at one of the most important results of problems with the psychological contract: absence. There are two perspectives on workplace absence – temporary absence (authorised or unauthorised), and permanent absence in the form of people leaving their jobs, the measure or rate of which is called turnover. Turnover is usually perceived as negative, for reasons that are examined later in the chapter. People being away from their jobs temporarily or permanently can have a negative effect on productivity, so both types of absence are discussed here.

LEARNING OUTCOMES

By the end of this chapter readers should be able to:

- describe the psychological contract, understand why it is important, and suggest HR practices to improve its state
- identify the causes of absence and explain how it can be managed effectively
- understand the importance of managing turnover and discuss some strategies for keeping good performers in the organisation.

The chapter is structured in three parts. The first part introduces the psychological contract and explains why it is key to managing employee performance. The second part introduces absence management and discusses various way of managing it effectively. The third part covers labour turnover and examines how organisations can increase the likelihood that key employees will be happy to stay with the organisation.

STARTER CASE STUDY

Whitegoods plc has long been an established retail company selling kitchen appliances such as fridges, freezers and cookers from a chain of showrooms spread all over the UK. Over many years they built up a good reputation based on their competitive prices and knowledgeable sales staff. Customers liked to visit their local showroom to discuss their requirements with the staff there. Once they had placed their orders they knew they could rely on Whitegoods to deliver and even install their new appliance, if that was needed. In order to give this level of service, Whitegoods built up a team of talented managers and staff many of whom had been with the company for years. The company encouraged promotion from within – many of the managers started off as junior sales staff and worked their way up.

Pay and benefits were not much better than at other retailers but the staff discount was particularly valuable. Staff could get a discount of 30% on anything they bought, and the discount was also available to family members and friends. Another benefit much appreciated by the staff was time off to attend classes and tuition fees for those who wanted to improve their product knowledge.

After many years of successful trading, Whitegoods are currently finding that their sales are dropping despite the high level of customer service provided. Last year's trading figures revealed that Whitegoods plc was in serious financial trouble. As a result, the chief executive decided it was time to take early retirement and several senior managers also decided that it was time to either retire or go elsewhere. A new chief executive was found quite quickly – her name was Jennifer Smith and she had previously been in charge of the kitchen appliances division of one of the country's most successful retail chains. The reward package she demanded was very generous, but the board of Whitegoods decided that the right CEO could turn the company round and prevent branch closures.

Jennifer Smith quickly made changes. Firstly, she had the layout of the stores changed and new work practices introduced to increase efficiency. However, she did not consult the staff about these changes. Secondly, she cut the staff discount from 30% to 15% – and it was no longer available to their friends and family. No explanation was given for this. Thirdly, she introduced a profit-sharing scheme for senior managers which meant that they could earn substantial bonuses if the company's trading improved.

The staff working in the shops were furious at the changes, especially since they had not been consulted. Many felt that they should also have been consulted about the layout of the stores in which they worked, because they believed that they had a much better understanding of customers' requirements than anyone coming from outside the company. The new working practices included a requirement for staff to clock in and out at the beginning and end of their shifts. Up till now staff had been trusted by their managers to come in on time and to work a full shift. In addition, the staff had less flexibility about which shifts they worked. Previously, staff had been able to work flexibly by making their own arrangements with their colleagues to cover shifts. Now the store managers had to insist that staff worked the shifts they were contracted to do – and staff who did not work their contracted shifts were disciplined. Staff were particularly upset about the halving of their staff discount, and that senior managers were going to be entitled to large bonuses and profit-sharing while shopfloor staff were not was another source of disappointment. Many shopfloor staff wrote angry letters of complaint which they sent to head office. However, their letters were not acknowledged by head office and no one received an answer.

Questions for discussion

1 What has happened to the psychological contract as far as the staff are concerned in this case study?

2 What effect is the situation likely to have on employee engagement?

3 What advice would you give Jennifer Smith and the senior managers to help them manage the psychological contracts of their employees more effectively?

The chapter concludes with the main case study.

Reference sources named within the chapter may be looked up in the *References and further reading* section at the end of the book.

1 THE PSYCHOLOGICAL CONTRACT: THE KEY TO MAXIMISING EMPLOYEE PERFORMANCE

THE PSYCHOLOGICAL CONTRACT AND THE WRITTEN EMPLOYMENT CONTRACT

British employees receive a written Statement of Terms often (wrongly) called a 'contract' although the full contract, legally speaking, actually contains implied terms as well. The written statement normally includes the job title, the pay, the place of work, whether the job is permanent or temporary, full-time or part-time, and the number of hours to be worked. Other information can be included in the main terms and particulars such as holiday entitlements and sick pay arrangements or these can be presented in a different format such as an employee handbook. Some other contractual arrangements can be seen on noticeboards in large organisations. Regardless of the way the information is presented, it is in writing. This written statement of terms could be as simple as a letter confirming the job offer or it could be a series of documents (see Chapter 5). Nevertheless, can these written documents, or the legally implied terms (in English law, terms can be 'implied' by practice without ever being written), give the employee information on the expected behaviours and the culture of the organisation he or she has joined? They cannot: this is where experience of working in the organisation comes in, and the result is the psychological contract.

The psychological contract is developed between the employee and the organisation over an extended period of time. It starts with the experiences the candidate has when applying for the job, develops during the recruitment and selection process, and continues to be formed during the induction and settling-in period. The psychological contract is constantly being revised and adjusted throughout the period of employment. If this process of revision and adjustment is well managed, we can say that there is a positive, or good, psychological contract. If it is not well managed, we can say that there is a poor psychological contract. This is known as the 'state' of the psychological contract and, as is explained later in this chapter, the state of the psychological contract has implications for motivation, performance, attendance and retention.

What exactly *is* the psychological contract? First of all, it is subjective. This means that each employee and employer has his or her own view of what is expected. The psychological contract is a unique combination of beliefs held by an individual and his or her employer about what they expect of each other. This is in contrast to the written, legal contract, the Statement of Terms, which is likely to be the same for groups of employees doing the same job. The psychological contract consists of expectations and obligations as opposed to the tangible content of the written Statement of Terms.

The psychological contract is based on the idea of mutuality and exchange, which means that a good psychological contract depends on an agreement being made and understood as to what is expected and the idea that there is 'give and take'. With the written Statement of Terms there may not be agreement on both sides because the employee has to accept the terms and conditions offered by the employer in order to get the job. Although it is implied that the employee will work hard for the employer and be honest and protect the employer's interests in exchange for pay and benefits, this exchange is rarely set out in detail in the written Statement of Terms.

The psychological contract can be fulfilled or unfulfilled. If the expectations of the parties are met to their mutual satisfaction, it can be said that their psychological contract has been fulfilled. In reality, it is rare for all expectations to be fulfilled – but so long as most are, then a satisfactory balance is achieved. It is also important to understand that the psychological contract can be violated or broken. This happens when one party makes a significant change without first getting the agreement of the other party.

THE EMPLOYEE'S AND THE EMPLOYER'S PERSPECTIVES ON THE PSYCHOLOGICAL CONTRACT

There are two perspectives to the psychological contract – the employee's and the employer's or manager's. These two perspectives are different, and ensuring that the two perspectives are not *too* different is one outcome of a well-managed psychological contract.

Guest and Conway's (1997) research carried out for the CIPD found that the psychological contract from the *employee's* perspective consists of six parts:

1 *Fairness, equity and consistency* – Employees who see their managers treating members of their teams differently, by, for example, being lenient when one person is late but reacting harshly to another team member when he/she is equally late, are likely to have a less positive psychological contract.

2 *Security of employment* – Although most people realise that one can no longer expect a job for life, a certain amount of job security is expected. In cases where job security is in doubt, employees will have a poorer psychological contract compared to employees who feel that their jobs are not threatened.

3 *Scope to demonstrate competence* – A good psychological contract is more likely when employees are given the skills, knowledge and tools to do their job properly. A computer that is constantly giving problems but not replaced can have a very negative effect on the psychological contract.

4 *Career expectations and the opportunity to develop skills* – Although there are a few employees who do not wish to develop themselves and improve their career or job prospects, the majority are more likely to have a positive psychological contract if they see that there are opportunities for advancement.

5 *Involvement and influence* – Having some involvement with decision-making that affects your job and some influence over the way you carry out your work has a strong influence over the state of the psychological contract as well as improving retention and motivation generally. Jobs should be designed to maximise the control the employee has over his/her work.

6 *Trust in the organisation to keep its promises* – When people start a job they have certain expectations and these expectations are often seen as promises.

One way in which we can understand the *employer's* perspective on the psychological contract is to think about it as being the same as the implied terms as defined by employment law. These implied terms for workers are effort, compliance, commitment and loyalty. In other words, all workers who are being rewarded in some way for their contribution are expected to put as much effort as possible into their jobs, they are expected to obey orders and do what is expected of them in their job role, they are expected to show a level of commitment to their organisation and fellow workers, and, in addition, they are expected to protect their organisation's interests by showing loyalty.

REFLECTIVE ACTIVITY

Having read the first section of this chapter, you will by now probably have realised that we all have psychological contracts not only with the organisation we work for (or will work for) but also with everyone else with whom we have a relationship. In pairs or as individuals, think about the psychological contract you have with the place where you are currently studying.

First think about your university or college. What do they expect of you? How do you know that they have those expectations? Have those expectations changed at all during your relationship?

Now, as a student, ask the same questions of the university/college. What do you, as a student, expect of them? How did these expectations come about? Have these expectations changed during your relationship?

If you are responding in pairs, one of you can be 'the student' and the other can be 'the university/college'.

An example of one expectation a student might have of his or her university or college is that there will be somewhere to park the car. How was this expectation formed? Well, when I came to an open day on a Saturday there was a large car park which appeared to have plenty of room for students' cars, so I expected that to be the case during termtime. Has this expectation changed? Yes – when term started I realised that parking was only available for staff and postgraduate students.

REFLECTIVE ACTIVITY

Now think of some more expectations on both sides.

When you have thought of a minimum of six expectations on each side, write a paragraph about how this exercise made you feel.

If you are working or have had a job in the past, write another paragraph about your thoughts about the psychological contract you have/had with your employer.

WHO IS INVOLVED IN CREATING AND MAINTAINING THE PSYCHOLOGICAL CONTRACT?

As we have seen above, there are many different people and practices involved in creating the psychological contract, although it is usually the employee's line manager or supervisor who plays the major role in maintaining the contract once it is formed. It is usual for the manager to be seen as the organisation's representative even though, as we have seen, he or she is not the only person involved in this process. Co-workers also play an important part in the making of the psychological contract because new employees see how their co-workers behave and model their behaviour according to what they see. So if co-workers regularly come back late from lunch, it will be perceived as an acceptable part of the organisation's culture.

Top management also plays a major role in formulating the psychological contract because they set an example to middle managers who are generally the main architects of employees' psychological contracts. If an organisation wishes to change its culture, it must be done from the top down. Top managers must adopt the new behaviours first and cascade them downwards.

HR professionals also play a key role in creating the psychological contract because they are often the first contact a future employee has with the organisation and are usually involved with the employee's induction. Recruiters are the first point of contact with the organisation and the impression they make forms the basis of the psychological contract. Recruiters should present unfavourable as well as favourable aspects of the job so that expectations are realistic. During the selection process it is common for promises to be implied or made in order to encourage a good candidate to take up a job offer. For example, an interviewer may promise that an employee will be given training – but when he/she takes the job he/she finds that the department where he/she works is under-staffed and cover cannot be found to enable him/her to participate in the promised training.

Once the employee has settled in, HR's role is to help managers to manage the psychological contract effectively.

THE IMPACT OF HR PRACTICES ON THE PSYCHOLOGICAL CONTRACT

Most HR practices suggested in this book can influence the psychological contract positively. For example, a good induction, a fair and objective performance management system, the provision of training and development as well as good employee communication can have a significant impact on the state of the psychological contract (see Chapters 8, 12, 14 and 19). This is shown by Guest and Conway's (1997) research. Employees were asked about the HR practices in their organisations and the application of these practices was correlated with the state of those employees' psychological contract. These HR practices are listed in the box below, with the practice mentioned most frequently at the top and the practice mentioned least frequently at the bottom.

HR practices and the psychological contract

- providing opportunities for training and development
- *keeping employees informed about business issues and performance*
- providing employees with formal appraisal reviews
- ensuring that the job provides opportunities to learn new things
- *whenever possible trying to fill vacancies from within the organisation*
- *trying to make jobs as varied and interesting as possible*
- having a policy of single status
- *having a policy of avoiding compulsory redundancies and lay-offs*
- providing a bonus or merit payment if employees perform well
- having some form of workplace involvement

Note: Points in *italics* represent the strongest links to a positive psychological contract

Source: Guest and Conway (1997)

All the HR practices (or the absence of them) listed in the box above had an effect on the state of the psychological contract, but those printed in *italics* correlate most strongly. Organisations should therefore make sure that keeping employees informed, avoiding compulsory redundancies, filling vacancies from within and making jobs as interesting and varied as possible are given top priority.

Although HR policies and practices are only one input to a positive psychological contract, they have been found by researchers to have an important influence on organisational performance by motivating people and getting the best out of them. Guest and Conway (1997) make this clear in their research. They believe that *a positive psychological contract is worth taking seriously because it is strongly linked to higher commitment to the organisation, higher employee satisfaction and better employment relations. Again, this reinforces the benefits of pursuing a set of progressive HRM practices.*

More about the psychological contract is available on the CIPD website. Visit especially: **http://www.cipd.co.uk/subjects/empreltns/psycntrct/psycontr.htm? IsSrchRes=1**

2   MANAGING ABSENCE

One outcome of a poorly managed psychological contract can be persistent unauthorised absence. What is meant by absence? The broadest definition is that it is any time when an employee is not doing the job he or she is employed to do. A good deal of absence is by previous arrangement (annual leave, educational leave, medical appointments and trade union activities). These prearranged absences have to be monitored and recorded and should not cause major problems. It is the other two types of absence that cause problems – sickness and unauthorised absence – and we now consider these in detail.

Sickness absence is usually divided into three types. *Uncertificated* absence is when the organisation allows the employee to return to work without filling in any paperwork giving reasons for the absence. It is *self-certificated* when the organisation allows the employee to report the reasons for the absence without a doctor's certificate to back them up. In the UK, self-certificated absence is often permitted for the first few days but after a certain number of days – typically four to seven – a doctor's certificate is required. This is then *certificated* absence.

Sick pay is at the discretion of the organisation and there is a wide range of different provision made. Some companies pay absent employees their full wages or salary from the first day of sickness whereas others pay nothing for the first few days or even weeks of sickness. The length of time for which companies go on paying their sick employees also varies greatly. For example, some employees may be entitled to only a couple of weeks of sick pay whereas many public sector employees could be entitled to six or even 12 months of sick pay (although normally the second six are half-pay). Regardless of any company sick pay entitlement, after four days an employee may be entitled to Statutory Sick Pay which his or her employer may be required to pay for the first 28 days of sickness.

Many organisations distinguish between short-term and long-term sickness because they have to be considered differently. Longer spells of sickness are sometimes easier for managers to deal with because they may be possible to plan for, and cover can be arranged when, for example, someone has to go into hospital for an operation. However, most long-term sickness is unplanned.

THE EXTENT AND COSTS OF ABSENCE

Survey evidence for the UK suggests that the average figure for absence is just below 4%, equivalent to about 8.5 working days per employee based on a working year of 228 days. There are variations between different sectors and different sizes of organisations. Absence in the public sector is generally higher than in the private, and it is much lower in organisations with fewer than 100 employees than in large organisations employing more than 2,000. Most absence is short-term – approximately 60% is for five days or less, with a further 20% for six days to four weeks. The remaining 20% of absences last for more than six weeks.

Absence costs can be calculated from both the employer's and the employee's perspectives. From the employer's point of view there are direct and indirect costs. *Direct* costs include the sick pay and fringe benefits paid, the overtime payments to others doing the sick person's job, and the costs of having to employ extra staff to ensure that absences do not cause disruption. These costs are relatively easy to measure – but *indirect* costs must also be taken into account. These include disruptions or even shutdown due to frequent or prolonged absences, reduced productivity or lower productivity when staff are absent, and perhaps even loss of customers where there has been a good relationship between customers and an absent member of staff. There are also the indirect costs of extra management time needed to organise cover and supervise replacements, and the time needed to do return-to-work interviews, the extra administration cost to organise cover and deal with sick pay and sickness reporting, and possibly also the extra recruitment costs if an employee can no longer do the job because of sickness.

REFLECTIVE ACTIVITY

Think about a job that you have done or that you know well.

Estimate the cost to your employing organisation if you were to be absent for one month. Take both the direct costs and the indirect costs into consideration.

There are also costs to other employees though these cannot usually be calculated in monetary terms. However, they can have a very negative impact on motivation. These costs occur when staff have to cover for an absent employee and/or deal with the problems that arise because of that absence. There is likely to be resentment at having to do other people's work, poor performance due to the tiredness it causes or due to inexperienced staff having to do the absent person's work. If the absence continues for an extended period, there may be a decrease in morale generally. An outcome could be poor attendance due to stress and heavy workload and even increased turnover as a result of having to cover for an absent colleague too frequently.

REASONS FOR ABSENTEEISM

Certain types of work are more likely to cause illness due to the nature of the tasks involved. Any form of manual work, especially where there are heavy items to be moved or lifted, is likely to cause injury. Excessive use of a keyboard can cause repetitive strain problems. Miners and people who worked with asbestos frequently contracted illnesses because of their work before the links were established between coal dust and asbestos dust and their illnesses. Even people who have to fly long distances as part of their jobs can suffer from short-term medical problems due to jet lag or more serious problems due to deep vein thrombosis (see Chapter 18). A very British problem that leads to a lot of absence is poor job design. Jobs that are designed to give employees control over how they work and as much autonomy as possible will prevent boredom and make it less likely that an employee will be absent. Work–life balance can also be important. Very limited provision for family-friendly working is a major cause of absence in people who have caring responsibilities. Family responsibilities can cause significant absence when there are elderly relatives and young children to care for. Employers can respond with time off for family emergencies and other family-friendly policies, flexible working hours, baby and granny crèches, and so on.

Many of the above reasons for absence are linked to stress. Poor working conditions, shiftwork, work overload, poor relationships at work or lack of consultation in decision-making are among the most important causes of stress.

When employers are asked to list common reason for sickness absence in their organisations, the most usual cause of absence is minor illness – for example, coughs, colds and headaches. However, there is one very important factor that affects whether or not people stay away from work when suffering from minor ailments: the organisational culture. The attitude of the organisation to staying away from work with minor illnesses is extremely significant. New starters soon work out the organisation's attitude to calling in sick with minor complaints. They see managers and colleagues either coming in to work with a bad cold or even flu – or alternatively calling in sick with relatively small illnesses. In addition, the organisation's policies, practices and procedures relating to sickness absence may encourage or discourage an individual. If he/she believes that his/her manager or supervisor has a less than sympathetic attitude to absence due to minor illnesses, the unwell person is more likely to decide to attend.

The British Disability Discrimination Act (1995, and updates) is relevant in managing long-term sickness absence because an employer cannot just dismiss an employee because he or she is unable to work. If the sickness has resulted in a disability under the Act, the law requires employers to make reasonable adjustments to the job content or the workplace to make sure that the disabled person is not placed at any disadvantage in the workplace. This includes people applying for a job and employees who become disabled while in employment. In addition, information held about employees' disabilities is sensitive personal data and must be handled carefully to avoid contravening both the Disability Discrimination Act and the Data Protection Act. Finally, any issues concerning absence and pregnancy must be handled equally carefully to avoid contravening the Sex Discrimination Act.

In summary, the way in which managers handle absences amongst their staff can make a huge difference to the amount of unauthorised and non-genuine sickness absence. It has been found that if managers adopt the following guidelines these types of absence can be minimised.

DO:

- Make employees aware that they have been missed and insist on return-to-work interviews.
- Be sympathetic on the telephone to encourage employees to call in as soon as they know they will be absent.
- Go through the procedure with new employees at induction to ensure that they know exactly what to do if they cannot attend.
- Compile a computerised database and use the information to keep managers informed.
- Consider stress management training and minimise stress factors as far as possible. Consider allowing employees to access employee assistance programmes.
- Be flexible by allowing employees to take leave where appropriate.
- Be firm where necessary and use disciplinary processes in cases of unacceptable absence.
- Consider paying attendance bonuses or making other awards for a perfect attendance record.
- Consider using a potential employee's previous absence record as a selection criterion.
- Improve job design and the working environment.
- Examine the family-friendliness of work arrangements.

DON'T:

- Set a level of acceptable absence measured as a number of days so that employees treat up to that number of days as extra holidays.
- Allow individuals to leave messages with anyone except their line manager.
- Jump to conclusions about reasons for absence.
- Be inconsistent when granting leave – it is important to treat all employees equally when they ask for time off.
- Make taking leave so difficult that calling in sick is the easy answer.
- Let staff use up all their holiday in the first half of the holiday year so that they have no leave left for unplanned eventualities.

For more information about managing absence, visit the CIPD website, and especially: **http://www.cipd.co.uk/subjects/hrpract/absence/absncman.htm ?IsSrchRes=1.**

A poorly managed psychological contract can also result in high employee turnover. Employee turnover is the number of people leaving an organisation over a given period of time. Most organisations want to minimise employee turnover where the people who are leaving are good performers and have benefited from in-company training. To keep track of the number of people involved, most organisations measure their turnover rates on a month-by-month or year-by-year basis. The measurement commonly used is the crude turnover or wastage rate, which is based on a simple formula:

$$\text{Labour turnover rate} = \frac{\text{Total number of leavers over a given period}}{\text{Average number of employees in that period}} \times 100$$

THE EXTENT AND COSTS OF LABOUR TURNOVER

The CIPD recruitment, retention and turnover survey 2006 reported that the overall annual employee turnover rate for the UK is 18.3%. It varies considerably between industries. The highest levels (22.9%) are found in private organisations rather than the public sector where the average turnover rate averages 13.3%. In the private sector the highest annual levels of turnover are found in call centres, retailing, hotels and restaurants, where turnover often exceeds 50%. Turnover levels also vary between regions. The highest rates of turnover occur where unemployment is lowest. However, there is little evidence of any long-term trends towards higher staff turnover. Over the 10 years from 1996 to 2006 the average turnover rate was 18.4%. One third of UK employees have been in their jobs for more than 10 years, and 10% for over 20. As a proportion of total turnover the number of people leaving organisations as a result of redundancy is small. In the private sector about 8% of the turnover is due to redundancy, and in the other sectors (public, not-for-profit and manufacturing) it is about 5%.

When people leave an organisation and have to be replaced, substantial costs are incurred. These consist of *direct recruitment* costs, such as recruitment administration and selection costs. There are also *development* costs, such as those of training the replacement member of staff. The extra effort required from existing staff to cover while a new member of staff is recruited can result in pressure that makes them consider leaving too. Alternatively, existing employees may not go as far as resigning from their jobs but there is likely to be a reduction in their motivation and productivity as a result of increased turnover in their team.

Whether or not the levels of turnover are problematic depends on the type of labour market the organisation operates within and the types of jobs that are affected. In retailing, for example, it is relatively easy to find and train new employees to replace those who have left, so it is possible to keep good-quality levels of service despite having a high turnover rate. By contrast, where jobs involve skills that are relatively scarce, where recruitment is costly or where it takes a while to fill a vacancy, high turnover is likely to present problems for management and employees. This creates severe problems when staff are lost to direct competitors or where customers have built up relationships with particular employees. In 2005, 73% of the respondents in the CIPD's annual recruitment and retention survey reported retention difficulties, and the survey showed that managerial and professional staff are the most difficult to retain, especially in the public sector.

A limited amount of turnover is positive for organisations. It can enable a poor performer to be replaced by a more efficient employee or create an opportunity for career development and promotion when someone in a senior position leaves. A new employee can bring fresh ideas into the organisation. Also, payroll costs can be reduced if the new employee is paid less than the person he or she replaces. In situations were business is poor, a delay in replacing someone who has left can be an effective way of reducing payroll costs.

UNDERSTANDING THE EMPLOYEE TURNOVER STATISTICS

Crude turnover figures as described in the previous section are used by all the major turnover surveys. They represent all leavers, including those who leave involuntarily due to dismissal, redundancy or retirement. They also do not distinguish between functional (or beneficial) turnover and turnover that is dysfunctional and harmful to the organisation.

So in order to make sense of the turnover figures in an organisation it is important to do a more detailed analysis. This means looking at the turnover figures in the context of that particular organisation. For example, the average annual turnover figure for a supermarket chain might be 40% – but that is not much help if you are trying to find out what is going on in a particular store or with a particular group of employees. One store may have a turnover of 20% and another of 60%. This would make you want to investigate what was going on in the store with the low turnover, because it is obviously doing something right. This might help us understand any problems there are with the management in the store with 60% turnover. A similar logic applies to work teams. Crude turnover figures therefore have to be broken down by location, department and team.

It would also be useful to break down the crude figure to find out more about the types of people who were leaving. For example, turnover figures could be broken down by age, sex, ethnic origin, grade or job title and job tenure. If the people who are leaving have been in their jobs for less than a year, it may indicate a problem with poor recruitment decisions or perhaps with induction. In some cases it might be appropriate to look at the appraisal records or performance rating of the people who are leaving. If it is discovered that the good performers are leaving whereas the poor performers are staying, it would merit urgent investigation.

INVESTIGATING THE CAUSES OF TURNOVER

Well-managed organisations want to know why people are leaving their jobs, particularly if the people who are leaving are people who they would prefer to retain. However, most organisations make no attempt to find out the reasons for dissatisfaction until the employee has given in notice or has actually left. This is too late – there is no chance of getting a valuable employee to change his or her mind at that stage.

Usually, companies use exit interviews to discover why an employee is leaving, although exit surveys or word-of-mouth sources of information are used in some cases. These methods can be unreliable because the employee leaving is usually reluctant to tell the employer the real reason why he or she is leaving in case it jeopardises the chances of getting a good reference to take to his/her new employer. Exit surveys, or 'separation questionnaires' as they are sometimes called, can be equally unreliable unless the people filling them in feel confident that their answers are completely anonymous. This is difficult to achieve unless the organisation has a large number of people leaving all at the same time.

So what is the best way of finding out why people are leaving? It is continuously to monitor employee satisfaction throughout the entire employment relationship. In other words, to stop the problem in the first place. This can be done in two ways: by regular staff attitude surveys and, for particular groups of employees who you really want to keep, by conducting focus groups.

Staff satisfaction surveys have to be carried out regularly so that trends in staff satisfaction can be monitored. It is very important that management are seen to be responding to feedback from staff satisfaction surveys so that staff can see the benefit in giving their honest opinions on workplace issues. Benchmarking your organisation's turnover rates against that of similar organisations is a good idea. If similar organisations have similar turnover issues, there is less to be concerned about – but if your organisation has turnover rates that are considerably higher than average, it may be possible to look at the retention strategies of a successful organisation to see if anything can be learned from them.

REFLECTIVE ACTIVITY

Ask as many people as possible who have worked for an organisation and left the job voluntarily to tell you their reasons for leaving.

Make a list of the reasons and see which of the above categories they fall into.

(You will need to exclude reasons such as 'I moved away from the area,' or 'I left because I'd finished my studies,' in order to make this exercise more meaningful.)

RETENTION STRATEGIES

What can be done to encourage good employees to stay? Below, we examine four areas in which an organisation might invest to improve its retention record.

Improving corporate culture and management style

People are more likely to leave their jobs because of dissatisfaction with their manager than for any other reason. Organisations that wish to improve retention should therefore concentrate on improving their managers' people management skills. They should help managers to develop a management style that encourages staff participation, develops teamworking, promotes individual autonomy and provides regular communication. Managers must develop a leadership style that supports rather than commands, and give employees autonomy through empowerment. Managers need to be aware of the importance of explicitly recognising good employee performance and saying 'Well done.'

Investing in training and development

Many employees leave because of a lack of opportunity to develop their skills, knowledge or competencies. Strategies to improve retention could therefore include introducing a mentoring scheme, encouraging multi-skilling, improving career development opportunities and investing in succession planning. Many organisations also encourage their employees to make use of general development opportunities because these can develop transferable skills that can be used at work (see Chapter 14 and Chapter 24).

Improving work–life balance

As older employees move into retirement, often with elderly parents of their own to take care of, a degree of flexibility is needed (see Chapter 6). In addition, many more women and single parents are now working and a number of government initiatives are aiming at increasing the proportion of working mothers. All these groups need to have flexibility in their working hours, and this has been supported by legislation. Recent legislation gives parents of children aged under six the right to ask to work flexibly, and there have been extensions to maternity and paternity leave. Another possibility is to offer assistance with childcare to help a parent to work. It is not just people with eldercare and childcare responsibilities who may want to work flexibly. Some organisations offer career breaks after an employee has been working for a number of years, and this allows the employee to take time off while keeping his or her job open. A menu of different types of benefits can meet more employees' needs and can cater for all age groups and life stages. Older people might opt for an increased pension whereas younger people may prefer more time to travel. Parents of school-age children may prefer time off in the school holidays, and so on.

Improving pay and benefits

Dissatisfaction with pay and benefits is a major reason for employee turnover. Some organisations target rewards at key individuals and groups. However, this can cause resentment and demotivation of other employees and often has no lasting influence on retention. A simple pay increase is a useful strategy – it can put off someone's intention to leave ... but only for a short time if the real reason for dissatisfaction goes beyond pay issues. Other possibilities are to pay retention bonuses to stop people from leaving from hard-to-fill jobs or to develop share ownership plans or other rewards which benefit employees over the long term. To maximise retention it is important to ensure that market rates of pay are matched or bettered, although high pay alone is not always the answer to keeping key employees.

More information about managing retention is available on the CIPD website, and especially from **http://www.cipd.co.uk/subjects/hrpract/turnover/empturnretent.htm?IsSrchRes=1**.

KEY ISSUES TO DO WITH THE PSYCHOLOGICAL CONTRACT, ABSENCE AND TURNOVER

We now pull together ten key points relating to the psychological contract, absence and turnover raised in this chapter:

- The psychological contract is shaped by employment practices and employment experiences.

- The psychological contract influences employee attitudes and behaviour and, if well managed, can improve employee performance.

- There are considerable variations in the state of the psychological contract within different sectors.

- The most common causes of short-term absence are minor illnesses such as coughs, colds, headaches and back pain. Stress is a major reason for longer-term absence.

- Absence can be minimised by good management control and the use of return-to-work interviews.

- Employees are less likely to be absent if they have a positive psychological contract.

- The organisational culture has a major influence on employees' attitudes to attendance.

- The causes of turnover should always be investigated, preferably by using such techniques as performance appraisals, focus groups and staff satisfaction surveys.

- Retention can be improved through a number of different initiatives including offering opportunities for employee development, improving pay and benefits, improving work–life balance and by making the job content and work environment as interesting and comfortable as possible.

- Most people leave a job because the relationship between them and their supervisor or manager becomes poor. Considerable effort should therefore be put into training managers to manage their staff well if they want them to stay.

Perhaps there are other key points that you would like to note for yourself.

The main case study in this chapter now follows.

Look at the description of the case set out below. Then decide on the recommendations that you would make as an HR manager for dealing with the issues raised. Try to think beyond the level of a 'quick fix' or simple solutions.

Getwell Hospital is situated in a small town on the south coast of England. Many of the people who live in the town retired to the seaside, so the majority of the hospital's patients are aged over 60. The hospital is housed in a crumbling Victorian building which is difficult to keep clean and has big wards, unlike most modern hospitals. But as is usual with hospitals nowadays, accommodation is not provided for nurses or other staff, and the only places available to rent in the town tend to be bed-and-breakfast places which fill up with tourists in the summer. Because the hospital is in the centre of the town there are very few parking spaces for staff or visitors. The pay-and-display car parks in the town centre are a viable alternative for visitors but are expensive for staff to use if they need to stay for a full shift. There are no social amenities for the staff, and even if there were, many of the staff have to travel long distances and need to set off for home as soon as they finished their shift. Because the population of the hospital's catchment area consists mainly of retired people, there are no clubs and few shops of interest to younger people in the town.

The hospital's HR department has noticed that there are increasing problems in filling a number of key positions – in particular, finding enough qualified and experienced nurses to work on the crowded geriatric wards. There is also a shortage of other professionally trained staff, such as physiotherapists, pharmacists and radiotherapists. In fact, the only areas in which there are no shortages of staff are the hospital shop and refreshment counters, and these are normally staffed by volunteers anyway.

The problem does not lie in attracting the qualified staff the hospital needs. Because the NHS is currently making cutbacks to save money, there are fewer jobs about, so there is no shortage of good applicants for every job that is advertised. The problem is with getting them to stay. For example, the university in

the nearest larger town runs a course leading to a nursing qualification, and many nurses complete the practical part of their qualification at Getwell Hospital. On completing their qualification many of the nurses join the permanent staff – but most do not stay for very long. Once they have gained sufficient experience to allow them to apply for jobs in London or to work abroad, they resign from their jobs at Getwell Hospital and do not stay long enough for the hospital to benefit from the experience they have gained while working there. The same thing happens with other staff: they seem to be using Getwell Hospital as a stepping-stone to jobs elsewhere and only stay long enough to get the experience they need to move on.

The hospital decided to engage the services of a consultant, who designed a staff satisfaction survey. All members of staff, including the nurses, filled in the questionnaire, hoping that the managers would respond to their complaints. For example, days that had been set aside for training the new nurses often had to be postponed due to staff shortages and there seemed to be problems in some wards, with some nurses not getting on very well with the ward managers. When people went off sick, which happened rather frequently, the managers did not seem to be very interested in finding out why. Working on the wards was often very stressful due to staff shortages resulting from the high turnover and the demanding nature of the work. Elderly and infirm people need a lot of care and often become confused and disorientated when hospitalised. However, nothing changed as a result of the survey, and the turnover rate has since remained higher than that of other hospitals nearby.

The hospital has been experiencing many problems as a result of this high level of turnover. To keep the wards running at all, the management recruited a number of nurses from abroad. Although they were highly qualified and skilled, the nurses mostly spoke

English with an accent that the elderly people – many of whom had impaired hearing – had difficulty understanding. Another way of keeping the wards fully staffed has been to employ agency nurses, especially on the less popular shifts. Some of these nurses work only one or two shifts at the hospital and so never know much about the hospital's routines and certainly do not know any of the patients' names. In other cases, the 'agency' shifts are filled by the hospital's regular staff working double shifts to earn extra money. This makes it more likely that mistakes are made due to tiredness, and is not a satisfactory long-term solution.

Your task

What advice would you give the hospital's management team to improve retention generally, but particularly the retention of qualified and skilled nurses?

EXPLORE FURTHER

EVANS, A. and WALTERS, M. (2002) *From Absence to Attendance*, 2nd edition. London, CIPD
A useful book which covers all aspects of managing absence.

GUEST, D. and CONWAY, N. (1997) *Employee Motivation and the Psychological Contract*, IPD Report. London, IPD

GUEST, D. and CONWAY, N. (2000) *The Psychological Contract in the Public Sector*. London, CIPD
Two of a series of reports published by the IPD/CIPD looking at different aspects of managing the psychological contract.

TAYLOR, S. (2005a) *The Employee Retention Handbook*. London, CIPD
This book gives an insight into the best ways of retaining employees and helps readers understand the reasons why people leave their jobs.

CHAPTER 12

Performance management and appraisal

Patricia Chase *and* Sebastian Fuchs

INTRODUCTION

This chapter examines performance and how organisations assess and evaluate whether the performance levels of their employees are acceptable by utilising performance management systems and employee appraisals. It looks at how a performance management system can support an organisation's overall performance through maintaining or improving the performance of its employees. It offers key drivers that should be considered both when designing and when re-evaluating them.

LEARNING OUTCOMES

By the end of this chapter readers should be able to:

- describe the differences between a performance management system and a performance appraisal
- explain how customised performance appraisals can be used as a strategic tool in improving individual performance as part of a performance management system
- identify good practices and the different ways of assessing performance
- evaluate the effectiveness of systems already in place.

The chapter is divided into three main parts. Part 1 discusses performance, motivation and performance management systems in relation to the organisation. Part 2 looks at performance assessment in general and shows how it reinforces the strategic aspect of performance management. Part 3 considers performance management in relation to the balanced scorecard, coaching and 360-degree appraisal.

The chapter concludes with the main case study.

Reference sources named within the chapter may be looked up in the *References and further reading* section at the end of the book.

Metalik Creations [a fictional company] provides interior designers with metallic sculptures made from scrap metals and more recently has started a direct sales mail-order operation for anyone interested in owning one. The rapid rise in popularity of these sculptures due to the new service has led to a need to increase production to meet demand without losing creativity, innovation or quality.

Because production of the sculptures is team-based, the managing director has decided to involve two teams in increasing the production levels. He calls in the team leaders of Team A and Team B and informs them both that due to higher demand for the sculptures they are required to increase their levels of production over the next year to meet this increase without compromising on the build quality. Both team leaders are told they can interpret and communicate the new objectives set by the managing director to their teams.

Team A are told by their team leader that they are required to produce more sculptures to meet the increase in demand. As a result of this, the team agrees on the following measurements to assess their performance:

- how quickly the materials for producing the sculptures can be obtained

- who obtains the most scrap metal (for which an award would be given)

- how many sculptures the team produced.

Team B are told by their team leader that they are required to produce more sculptures of the same quality as those already being produced to meet the increase in demand. The team leader makes it clear that the

innovative nature, creative qualities and overall quality of the sculptures must be maintained despite having to produce more sculptures. The agreed performance measurements are as follows:

- the amounts of good-quality scrap metal found by the team and used in the sculptures

- the number of good-quality sculptures produced.

To help Team B in identifying their performance levels a bulletin board was set up to monitor their progress. The measurements agreed focused on the quality of the scrap metal obtained, the quantity effectively used against the wastage from each batch of work, and the successful identification of high-quality sources of materials. Team B also had an opportunity to assess their level of performance through regular feedback sessions during the year, and an incentive scheme was introduced based on the production levels of good-quality sculptures and the profits made.

Questions for discussion

Consider what the possible consequences might be from the way the organisation's goals and objectives are communicated downwards to the teams.

At the end of the year, what do you think the outcomes were specifically as a result of the way the team leaders communicated the objectives set by the managing director?

Answer first for Team A, and then for Team B.

1 PERFORMANCE, MOTIVATION AND PERFORMANCE MANAGEMENT SYSTEMS

To put the following discussion in context, sit for a moment and consider what it was like when you first started senior school, college, university or a job. There are features common to all of these that apply here, especially when starting in a new place where you do not know what is really expected of you. People who are new to any scene are often left feeling very isolated until they know what they need to do, how they should do it, what is expected of them and how their success is measured to show that they have reached the standards required.

Let us consider a simple example at this stage. A programme of study usually includes a syllabus and descriptors, which provide an outline of the quality of work for each grade of assessment. This determines a level of understanding of what might be expected of you. Different courseworks and examinations are set to test your ability to perform; the grades you receive are feedback on your performance.

When you see your teacher or tutor for feedback, that is the time when your performance is reviewed and, depending on your grades, for discussion on what you have done well and where you might improve. At the end of the session you may go away with an action plan to help you continue to perform well or improve your performance for the future. So, taking these analogies forward, let us look at what is meant by 'performance'.

The role of performance is a complex one. It is a mixture of inputs based on an individual's knowledge, skills and actions combined with the available organisational resources and/or support. The outcome can be a service or a product, or a combination of both. The quality of the outcome will be reflected in the expertise of the individual and the supporting resources. For example, the quality of call centre front-line operators' responses to customers on particular products and services will reflect their levels of knowledge, training and supervisory support. Equally, the quality of teaching and the level of resources available can impact on the overall performance of students.

In the case of the call centre front-line operators, the performance is directly linked to what their job descriptions are likely to entail: providing answers to questions and issues customers might have on a range of products and services. There are, however, many areas in organisational settings where employees' behaviour can have a positive impact on individual and organisational performance, even though it is not related directly to their jobs. For instance, convincing your friend that he or she should use the products and services offered by the company you work for is likely to have a positive – albeit small – effect on sales and ultimately on the performance of the organisation. This type of behaviour refers to contextual (as opposed to task) performance and relates to the idea that employees engage in 'citizenship behaviour' as one element of performance (Organ, Podsakoff and MacKenzie, 2006). Regardless of whether organisations want to improve task or contextual performance, we must look at what makes people engage in performance-related behaviours. Understanding employees' motivation to work is one important way of getting to grips with this.

WORK MOTIVATION

Part of generating higher levels of performance is recognising the uniqueness of each individual and what motivates him or her. To some extent the motivational process is within the individual's control.

REFLECTIVE ACTIVITY

Think of the times you have had coursework to do and left it to the last moment because there
were more interesting things to do.

What finally motivated you to do the work?

Individuals need to know that what is being offered to them not only has
purpose and direction but will be beneficial and provide a fair outcome for their
efforts. This may explain why motivators vary in their degree of effectiveness
over time. In 1943, Maslow suggested that a 'hierarchy of needs' exists.
According to his theory, once the basic physiological need has been satisfied to
some degree, the individual's concerns move in turn towards safety,
belongingness, self-esteem and self-actualisation (Arnold *et al*, 1995). His theory
is very popular with managers because it seems plausible that, for instance, once
you feel safe, you can start getting concerned with other things such as finding a
suitable partner. Moreover, it would be a convenient way of managing people
just to exhibit higher levels of motivation by passing people through these stages.
However, the theory was developed during a time of significant uncertainty in
many countries, and more basic things such as food and shelter were on people's
minds. There is not much conclusive evidence to suggest that people actually
function in a way where they climb from one stage to the next, nor do we know
whether people can switch between these different stages in short time-spans.

McClelland (1971) identified three related important needs – namely, 'power',
'affiliation' and 'achievement'. Identifying these helps us to understand the
impact of power relations – for example, management's behaviour, the necessity
of valuing individuals, and how achievement can be encouraged to enhance
performance through training.

Equity is also important – the need to be treated equally and fairly. Individuals
make comparisons between the levels of recognition and rewards they receive
with others giving the same level of effort. Should there be any differences, they
may decide to increase their efforts further to maintain a balance or,
alternatively, if they see this as not worthwhile, their effort may be reduced
(Adams, 1965). Thus, to some extent justice, transparency and the distribution
of rewards and other organisational resources determines the extent to which
people are motivated to perform.

The way performance is assessed can affect the level of motivation: the goals and
targets individuals are expected to achieve must be clearly set out and
challenging. So goal-setting is another motivational theory in that it clarifies,
specifies and prioritises what is expected of individuals at work. The attainment
of such goals closes the feedback loop and provides important feedback. This, it
is argued, encourages people to focus their actions on achieving these goals
(Locke, 1968; Latham and Locke, 1990). If you think about setting yourself

targets and goals in your academic or personal life, ideally 'SMART' ones (specific, measurable, attainable, realistic and time-bound), you are more likely to get results. For instance, creating the goal of completing your undergraduate studies within three years – so that you can finally start earning some money afterwards – is likely to get you through your degree smoothly. The same principle applies to organisations. Clear targets have been found to lead to an increase in goal attainment, and this, if designed in correspondence with the organisational strategy (see Chapter 3), is likely to increase organisational performance.

Expectancy theory is based on work by Vroom (1964). He suggests that 'valence', 'instrumentality' and 'expectancy' impact on how successfully individuals take up realistic and challenging goals. The successful outcome of goal-setting to some degree may depend on how individuals perceive the extent to which they have the ability to achieve these goals (expectancy), whether their performance is rewarded (instrumentality), and whether or not they value the reward being offered (valence). In other words, individuals expect certain outcomes (referred to as performance) to result from their efforts, and those efforts are made more strenuously when these outcomes are of personal importance to them.

REFLECTIVE ACTIVITY

Think of a time when you were faced with a challenge to produce a project or some coursework by a specified deadline.

What motivated you to do it – and how did it motivate you?

Try to consider some of the theories outlined above.

Once you have completed this exercise, look back at the starter case study and consider how you might relate your experiences to it.

To encourage higher rates of performance, organisations can use different performance measurement criteria within either a more overarching performance management system (PMS) or an appraisal system. These criteria can vary from results-oriented outcomes to competency-based assessments, or they may be combined. Although performance is managed in a variety of ways, it is still often used by managers in terms of 'objective-setting and appraisal', and where it focuses on individual performance it tends to be linked to talent management, succession planning, development or career management (CIPD, 2005).

Recognising that a performance management system strategically manages the inputs and outputs of individuals or teams by aligning the performance criteria with the business objectives is the first step to realising how important it is. For this, it is crucial:

- to understand the business of the organisation
- to have the ability to interpret the more abstract goals and objectives at board level into more practical operational goals and objectives at employee level to meet them – that is, to place in context the expected levels of performance required of employees, and to communicate them to them
- to practically align individual or team objectives with those of the organisation, including a review process to ensure that they are on track to meet the expected outputs
- to monitor the outputs to ensure that they achieve the required levels of service or quality and quantities of products.

The system's process creates a platform to develop better human resource plans, assess promotion potential and training needs and develop consistency in standards and performance. It is an on-going process requiring some flexibility so that adjustments can be made to maximise levels of performance.

REFLECTIVE ACTIVITY

Think of an experience you have had with customer services when purchasing a product or a service.

What was your overall impression of the service you received? Did the way in which you were dealt with provide any insight into the capabilities and motivation of those who served you?

THE PERFORMANCE MANAGEMENT SYSTEM CYCLE

Figure 20 shows corporate goals and objectives being communicated downwards to the divisional or departmental level, where they are interpreted in combination with the job description, person specification and work situation to provide operational-level performance criteria. Once agreement is reached between line managers and individuals on their performance criteria, action plans are drawn up to help them in their performance. Their performance is monitored and feedback provided on a regular basis, which at the end of the agreed reporting period results in a review feedback report. Feedback provides the opportunity to assess actual against expected performance and to identify any performance gaps or development needs. It can be used to deal with inefficiencies and poor performance by providing more focused performance criteria and frequent monitoring.

In conjunction with the cycle, the vertical integration of the performance management system with other processes (eg training, development, reward, etc) provides the focus for interpreting organisational goals as operational ones, so identifying for teams and individuals the levels of performance needed to ensure sustainable operations, including an opportunity for two-way feedback between management and individuals/teams.

Figure 20 The performance management system cycle

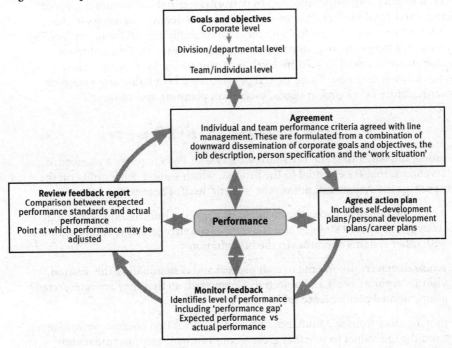

Although its horizontal integration provides a platform on which the organisation can either improve its performance or adjust it when necessary, the PMS recognises that any changes within the organisation can affect the process and that there should therefore be a degree of flexibility to accommodate such changes. A combination of both vertical and horizontal integration of the PMS ensures that the process incorporates elements in its design that allow it to support other processes and procedures within the organisation.

Effective use of technology is important in supporting these processes because essentially it allows for faster sharing of information on the local, national and global level, making it a powerful tool provided it is controlled and not in control. To design and produce a fully functional HR system requires input from all relevant stakeholders to ensure that it supports both the HR function and an effective PMS. It requires trained operators, on-going support and the recording and storage of relevant data, which are ideally linked to other systems within the organisation (eg the data controller).

In practical terms, the most difficult aspect of a PMS is managing people effectively to gain their commitment to perform. There are a number of major variables that can affect the process – for example, the type of organisation (eg retail, health sector, etc), the styles of leadership and management (transformational, autocratic, etc), the make-up of the workforce (eg full-time, part-time, professional, etc), motivation levels and the products or services being offered.

A key aim is thus to provide a clear recognition of levels of performance, and ways of dealing with inconsistencies in performance that will ensure improved outputs and commitment. Part of this process is to develop managers to the point at which they are able to think more strategically and add value by looking at ways to improve the overall performance (see Chapter 3). To assist them further, there is a need to identify levels of performance by providing clear performance indicators. These should provide for an equitable assessment of rewards, future development needs, succession planning and training.

CREATING A PERFORMANCE MANAGEMENT SYSTEM

Creating, implementing and operating a successful PMS requires a number of interventions that are essential to the process, which should concentrate on the 'purpose' of the system and not on the 'system' itself. These are:

- a clear alignment between the business strategy, the information technology strategy, the reward strategy and the human resource strategy, and integration with other systems operating in the organisation

- senior managers driving the overall process and disseminating the mission, vision, corporate goals and objectives downwards so that they are interpreted as operational performance indicators

- moving away from a 'command-and-control' ethos that coerces performance from the individual to one that creates commitment, empowerment and loyalty

- managers coming to a mutual agreement on the methods by which individuals will reach their set targets, on regular reviews to monitor their progress and on the ability to adjust the targets to match any changes

- providing an opportunity to bring about change – for example, creating a shift in culture or workforce attitudes by targeting them through the performance indicators

- a clearly structured review or appraisal process to ensure clearer channels of communication at all levels and provide a better understanding of the part each employee plays in the organisation. Translating organisational objectives and goals into individual ones allows for a better understanding not only of the relationship of reward to performance but the necessity of improving individuals' skills and knowledge. Where a more development-focused culture is encouraged, it provides a level of security in respect of multi-skilling employees, improving areas requiring further development and building on their strengths

- ensuring that line managers take early 'ownership' (CIPD, 2005) via training and provision of on-going advice and support, which reinforces and updates them

- providing informative feedback, action planning regarding work and career development, empowerment and recognition of good performance to create higher levels of job satisfaction and retention

- inculcating a context of Keep It Simple (KIS): if designed correctly it can assist in focusing on SMARTer working practices (CIPD, 2006)

- finally, monitoring and evaluating the system's progress and building into it the ability to adapt to changes caused by legislation, globalisation, social trends, political and economic change and technological developments created by internal and external factors that can impact on the design and delivery of the organisation.

REFLECTIVE ACTIVITY

Why is it important to consult with all interested parties when developing a performance management system?

List the parties who should be involved in the process, and provide justifications for your selection of parties.

There are key advantages in having a clearly structured PMS which incorporates an appraisal (as discussed in detail later on in this chapter). It provides for an equitable evaluation of wages, eligibility for rewards/promotion and feedback. It identifies for employees their level of performance, gives recognition of good practices and assists in clarifying and directing their work. It defines 'performance' and channels development to achieve this end, which helps in improving the quality or standards of the outputs and maximises task performance in relation to products or services. It can support management development and succession planning through identifying staff's management and leadership potential through their performance appraisals. This is especially important in developing future leaders, who can be groomed for top positions (high-fliers).

It supports human resource planning (see Chapter 7) in that it identifies the right people with the relevant skills and experience to do specific jobs. It also highlights skills and training gaps and assists in targeting training and development that will help in improving productivity and supporting the organisation's business. It can identify and resolve issues related to job structure through restructuring the way the work is done (this relates to the work profile described in the final section of this chapter, on appraisal).

Feedback and performance reviews provide a platform for drawing up action, personal development and career plans for developing individuals which can provide a positive impact on their perception of being valued members of the organisation. Clear recognition of individual and team contributions also aids this perception, which can be motivating and often lead to higher retention rates. Improving employee skills, knowledge and retention rates can have a positive impact on the reputation of an organisation, and, ultimately, on its performance.

However, a PMS also has some potential drawbacks:

- It can be a time-consuming and costly process.

- There may be problems where it is linked directly to pay and rewards, especially if it is an off-the-shelf package and not designed specifically for the organisation. The design of the rating scales can cause issues in respect of pay decisions and identifying good and poor performers, especially where it encourages a central tendency – managers taking the average of the rating scale due to reluctance to identify the true state of an individual performance – which may create difficulties. Pay expectations among employees may be unrealistically raised, creating discontent.

- Lack of support or clarity regarding performance expectations can result in lower retention rates because it may be seen as being unfair or inequitable in operation – especially if the assessments are too subjective and based on favouritism.

2   PERFORMANCE ASSESSMENTS

The way in which performance is assessed in organisations can provide a chance to identify individual and team potential and any skills and knowledge gaps, whether it is in terms of performance development reviews or staff appraisals. The performance indicators used may vary across the organisation as the targets of managers differ in relation to the staff they supervise. The assessment may involve the use of rating scales, objective setting, BARS or competencies, and where practicable, combinations of them.

In the light of the UK Government's initiatives regarding 'dignity at work' (ECU, 2007), the designing of the performance criteria (or indicators) should be clearly linked to diversity, equal opportunities policies and disability issues, and should moreover reinforce zero tolerance to conceivable negative behaviours. This should essentially reduce discriminatory behaviours against any one group in relation to, for example, race, age, sexual orientation or disability (see Chapter 6). Organisations have a great variety of performance indicators to choose from. The main ones are examined below.

Rating scales assess an individual's performance against a set of agreed descriptors that indicate the standard of work produced and whether he or she has fulfilled his/her main duties (from the job description) to a satisfactory level. The performance indicators can reflect certain employee characteristics that are needed to successfully perform the work; each may be rated on a scale ranging from 'unacceptable' to 'outstanding'. The scale may be linked to a numerical rating ranging from one to five, which can be used to provide an overall rating. This form of rating can cause problems with employees where the descriptors and rating provides a more subjective assessment, especially if it is linked to pay rewards and promotion prospects.

Orange recently experienced problems with using a numbered five-point rating scale where staff were having difficulties in accepting that a rating of 'three' meant they had 'met their objective and were doing a good job'. To solve the problem and make the ratings more transparent, the five-point scale was retained but in the form of descriptors ranging from 1 = 'unacceptable', 2 = 'getting there', 3 = 'great stuff' (used to reflect 'effective performance'), 4 = 'excellent' and 5 = 'exceptional', which is referred to as the 'Orange thing' (Johnson, 2006).

Objective-setting in management by objectives programmes monitors the feasibility or achievability of the objectives or targets set, and whether they have been successfully reached. Employee objectives should be aligned with organisational objectives. Because the objectives are focused on achievement of the work goals set, there is an opportunity for self-assessment and feedback during the reporting period. This is often used together with rating scales to provide a clearer overview of performance. The process does require management to recognise that situations can arise that are outside the control of the individual, which may affect achieving the set objectives and lead to suitable adjustments having to be made to the performance requirements.

Behaviourally anchored rating incorporates a number of rating scales that are customised to evaluate the expected performance levels that reflect the particular job in question. In deriving these ratings, managers first identify the key areas essential to successfully performing the job; descriptors are then drawn up that reflect varying levels of performance within each of the key areas. Once this process has been completed, the 'typical or expected' level of performance for each individual across the scale is drawn up by their appraiser (individual rating scale). This more focused approach is useful in identifying potential and development needs.

Competencies are a form of assessment that looks at the level of competence individuals display in respect of each of the competencies (standards to which individuals are expected to perform) they are being assessed on. Competencies may be measured in respect of a number of capabilities which can focus either on behaviours or functional/technical know-how, or a combination of these, within an agreed framework.

A good example of the competencies approach is the *transformational government initiative* The initiative has produced the *transformational government framework*, which provides a set of core competencies in order to improve performance, increase skills and expertise in the public services; it is seen as part of the way forward (Cabinet Office, 2007).

As part of this initiative, there is now a Chief Information Officer Council which is involved in developing the 'government gateway', which will provide services for sharing information across the public sector and with the public. To ensure that, for instance, IT professionals have the relevant specialist and technical skills and knowledge, a *core skills framework for IT professionals* has been developed consisting of five core competency groups, namely:

- architecture, information and innovation
- business change management
- solutions delivery and implementation

- service delivery
- procurement and management support

plus two competency groups for senior managers:

- delivery management
- enterprise strategy and architecture.

This enables IT professionals to identify their profiles and development needs, and it can be used as a part of the performance management or recruitment processes for IT specialists (CIO, 2007).

The British National Health Service is another example where a 'knowledge and skills framework' has been introduced to standardise performance criteria and encourage a learning and development environment as part of the broader agenda for change programmes. The framework's design incorporates regulatory-required competencies and identifies six *core dimensions* considered essential to the performance of all health staff covered by the framework; these are: 'communication', 'personal and people development', 'health, safety and security', 'service improvement', 'quality' and 'equality and diversity'. Support materials are provided for managers and staff online to assist them in using the framework and the development review process. Successful implementation of such frameworks arguably will depend on whether managers and employees alike understand and accept them.

THE PERFORMANCE APPRAISAL

The performance appraisal is an opportunity for employees to discuss their performance with their line manager. It provides a platform for clarifying the quality of performance through feedback on both an informal and a formal basis throughout the year. To ensure meaningful and effective feedback the performance targets must have been set as the employee commenced work. Some organisations use personal development reviews rather than appraisals – although there are similarities between the two, the personal development review tends to be more development-oriented.

The appraisal analyses employees' past performance over a set period of time and considers their future potential. The 2004 WERS survey suggests that even for non-managerial employees, regular appraisals are common (see Table 28). However, larger organisations are more likely to do them than smaller organisations, and there are also differences between industries, appraisals being more common (for example) in financial services.

Performance appraisals are part of a formal process which provides an opportunity to assess the individual's suitability for promotion, further training and/or development and appropriate levels of reward. It monitors:

- the quality of performance in relation to achievements and failures over the reporting period
- the work profile content, load and volume
- the agreement and setting of future objectives.

Table 28 Percentage extent of performance appraisals, by workplace characteristics

	Regular appraisals for 60% or more non-managerial employees
All workplaces	64
Organisation size	
10–99 employees	49
10,000 or more employees	82
Industry	
Manufacturing	41
Hotels and restaurants	48
Financial services	96
Public sector	77

Source: Kersley *et al* (2006; p.83)

Whether it is a stand-alone process or part of the performance management system, it provides performance indicators that reflect organisational goals and objectives, including at least two of the following three elements.

Performance review

This looks back on performance during a given period and whether or not performance objectives, goals or targets are being achieved or have been reached. The aim is to improve current performance. It should focus on the strengths of the individual/team to create a positive work ethos that encourages higher levels of commitment, proactivity and levels of achievement. Areas that need improvement should be approached with a positive attitude that allows the individual or team the opportunity to work with the appraiser on ways to improve. Current performance can be used to set the objectives for the coming year, especially where progress is on-going. This is an opportunity to be proactive and to set objectives that will reflect future needs as opposed to just the organisation's present needs. We can see clear links here with how organisations make use of goal-setting theoretical foundations in order to increase individual performance in the future.

Potential review

This part of the appraisal focuses on development needs and could be related to areas needing improvement which require a mutually agreed action plan that encourages and supports such improvement. It can also be used as part of the career plan whereby the future potential of the individual is identified and areas for development or 'opportunities for progression' are defined within the action plan. Where the performance management system focuses on development, this particular element is often dealt with in a separate session. The reasoning behind the separation is that although the appraiser may be focused on developing the employee, the employee's own focus may be more on whether or not his/her level of performance meets requirements and he/she receives the due reward.

Employees are less likely to admit to difficulties regarding their performance when there is a chance that any such admission on their part may affect their reward.

Reward review

There is evidence to suggest that the inclusion of the reward element in the appraisal can be demotivating. A leading police service has moved away from assessing reward and development within the same review because it has been identified as having a negative impact on performance. There are, however, national variations. The Cranet-E survey suggests that in the UK as well as in Continental Europe appraisals are most often used for development and training purposes (see Table 29). The link to reward is strongest in Sweden and Germany.

Table 29 'Is the performance appraisal system used to inform the following?'

	UK	Sweden	Germany	Greece	Slovakia
HR planning	64%	51%	46%	71%	44%
Analysis of training/development needs	98%	79%	87%	86%	51%
Career	86%	66%	87%	82%	35%
Pay determination	55%	87%	74%	80%	62%
Organisation of work	53%	43%	42%	65%	45%

Source: Cranet-E (2003)

The review session is also an opportunity for an exchange between the line manager (appraiser) and the employee (appraisee). The reviews should be undertaken on a regular basis and at least once a year. It is a way of making sure that performances are on target and of having the tools to deal with poor performance. The reviews can be both informal and formal. Having informal reviews on a regular basis allows for a closer monitoring of performances and gives an earlier opportunity for addressing any issues. The completed appraisal form is usually signed both by the appraiser and appraisee and countersigned by the appraiser's line manager to make sure that reporting is transparent.

A crucial factor in driving the appraisal system, which must be noted here, is the buy-in of line managers (appraisers) to the process. They not only need to take ownership of the process, which may be encouraged through making it one of their performance targets, they also need on-going training, advice and support to sustain it.

The appraisal also should be seen as being transparent and equitable, providing reporting consistency and regular feedback on performance. It should be simple, straightforward and easy to understand with objectives that are 'SMART' – ie specific, measurable, attainable, realistic and time-bound (Armstrong and Baron, 2005).

Issues can occur in relation to a poor buy-in to the system creating a lack of commitment. Poor training or the complete lack of it can encourage a mistrust of performance ratings, which may also not be clearly set out to provide a realistic reflection of performance. The system if seen negatively may be sabotaged through lack of active support.

The appraisal process requires a number of conditions to ensure that it is carried out effectively:

- There must be preparation prior to the formal review meeting on the part of both the reviewer (appraiser) and the reviewee (appraisee).

- Where appraisees are required to fill out a self-assessment form, the form should be given to the reviewer before the apparaisal meeting because it will allow the reviewer a useful insight into the reviewee's perspective of his/her performance.

- The reviewer should be familiar with the reviewee's performance record, and should therefore be comfortable with setting aside time in a quiet and private area to discuss it in confidence.

- The reviewer may start by discussing positive aspects of the reviewee's performance before going on to areas that may require further development.

- The reviewees should be encouraged to put forward their views and should be encouraged to do most of the talking while the reviewer listens carefully to the responses. This two-way communication should result in the preparation of a development or action plan which encourages and motivates the reviewee to meet agreed targets over the coming year.

- Reviews can take place both formally and informally: there are times where during the process issues may be highlighted that need further monitoring, especially where there may be grievance, disciplinary or counselling implications.

3 CURRENT ISSUES IN PERFORMANCE MANAGEMENT

THE BALANCED SCORECARD

The 'balanced scorecard', developed by Kaplan and Norton (1996), provides the organisation with a framework for communicating the company's vision and strategy by expressing them in the form of strategic objectives, measures and goals (Olve *et al*, 2001).

It facilitates the integration between different functional areas and translates the business mission, vision and goals to provide measurable short-term performance goals that relate to the long-term organisational ones. It translates strategic processes into operational ones and encourages continuous improvement and accountability mainly in respect of the team rather than the individual (Armstrong and Baron, 2005). It uses feedback as part of the learning and as a process for adapting strategies to improve organisational performance. This allows the company to deal with changes in the marketplace.

The overall business's performance is assessed through four different perspectives:

- *learning and growth* – which encourages 'self-improvement' both at the corporate and operational level

- *financial* – which looks at the importance of providing accurate and up-to-date financial data in support of the organisation's overall performance

- *customer* – which identifies the importance of retaining customers and making sure they are satisfied with the quality of services and products

- *internal/business process* – which focuses on the effectiveness of the business in its provision of goods and services.

The focus of the balanced scorecard relates to the alignment of the performance management system with other aspects of the business and how long-term goals are translated into short-term performances (Armstrong and Baron, 2005). Its design varies according to the focus of the mission, vision and objectives of the organisation. For instance, an airline's focus will differ from that of a public sector organisation.

Used correctly, it is an important instrument for expressing a vision and strategy in more concrete terms (Olve *et al*, 2001). The Highways Agency has developed a scorecard which contains five perspectives that mirror its objectives. These are *customer service, teamwork, improvement, diversity* and *best value*. It also includes *integrity* (Highways Agency, 2007). This has led to clearly defined performance indicators that have set the types of behaviours it requires to deliver a more effective service. Part of the process has been the introduction of the 'valuing employees reward'. The Highways Agency provides a good example of ways to move performance forward.

REFLECTIVE ACTIVITY

Access the Highways Agency website, **http://www.highways.gov.uk/ default.aspx** and look at the development plans and performance indicators there.

What is so interesting about them?

Another interesting example is Orange. Orange now links objectives to the balanced scorecard, translating them downwards to provide individual objectives that clarify the role of employees in the organisation. This is achieved through the 'strategy' and 'business excellence' teams working with HR to set the scorecard and translate strategy into operational targets along four dimensions:

shareholders, customers, partners, and people/the workforce (Johnson, 2006). This too is an on-going process.

360-DEGREE FEEDBACK

This may be referred to as '360-degree appraisal or multi-rater feedback' (DBA, 2002), and is a process that seeks to create more effective feedback on performance from a number of sources linked to the individual concerned (eg peers, supervisors, colleagues, project teams, internal and external customers) through raising his/her awareness of how his/her behaviour and performance is perceived by others. It measures competencies through the use of a questionnaire specifically designed to provide feedback relevant to the organisation and the individual. It requires trained raters, facilitators and managers so that the feedback can be effectively produced and interpreted.

A well-designed 360-degree feedback format can thus be used to measure the relevant knowledge, skills, abilities and/or competencies that are required to meet the organisation's needs. It can provide a unique opportunity for individuals to make an objective comparison of their self-assessment with the assessments of their peers, managers and customers or other interested parties involved in the process. Moreover, it provides assessed feedback from a number of sources that when combined present a clearer picture of an individual's overall performance.

It is particularly useful in the development of managers and senior managers because it gives an insight into how they are seen by others. It is a time-consuming process that needs a skilled interpretation of the results of the assessments obtained, but on the other hand it does provide a more accurate picture of an individual's performance. The person elected to provide the feedback for the individual concerned has an opportunity to discuss any development needs from a more informed perspective.

The Cranet-E data implies that 360-degree feedback is not yet widespread in European organisations. Table 30 suggests that appraisals are mainly based on the input of the supervisor and employee. In contrast, the review of subordinates, peers and customers count less.

Table 30 'Who is formally expected to input/provide data for the performance appraisal process?'

	UK	Sweden	Germany	Greece	Slovakia
Immediate supervisor	100%	100%	100%	100%	59%
Supervisor's superior	80%	69%	70%	89%	28%
Employee himself/herself	99%	89%	68%	74%	66%
Subordinates	22%	36%	19%	17%	18%
Peers	26%	26%	6%	17%	23%
Customers	15%	20%	9%	21%	25%

Source: Cranet-E (2003)

COACHING

Coaching appears to be increasing in popularity and managers are being encouraged to use it to assist in improving employees' performance. Coaching in the right hands can be a powerful tool in directing individuals and improving their performance. It sits comfortably with self-awareness and encourages coachees to look forward and be proactive in their own development. There are different types of coaching, which focus on different levels of the organisation. There are, for example, executive coaches and development ones. How successful the coaching is depends on a number of variables, including the coach's experience, the type of coaching, the type of intervention used and ultimately the coachee. It can – if used effectively – focus, improve and motivate an individual to move forward.

FURTHER CONSIDERATIONS ON PERFORMANCE MANAGEMENT

After examining a solid range of frequently used tools to measure performance in organisations, let us consider some of the major problems we still find in relation to performance. Perhaps you are doing a part-time job besides your studies and have already come across such tools. If so, what were the problems you encountered? In some jobs, such as in sales, task performance can be measured relatively easily: sales per day/shift/week/month/quarter/year. Other jobs, such as HR or marketing-oriented ones, for instance, are much harder to quantify. How can we set 'SMART' objectives for developing an effective human resource development system for these kinds of jobs?

Another problem is that some employees might visibly exert more effort than others, but it does not always increase actual measured performance. For instance, your teacher may try very hard to help students in their learning, but the final marks (as moderated by external examiners) may turn out to be very similar to those of students of another teacher who has been far less energetic in teaching. It is likely that anybody who puts in a special effort would prefer to be rewarded on the basis of that effort, whereas management generally deems output the more important criterion. This is likely to create ill-feeling, which in turn is likely to result in demotivation and disillusionment, and in reducing or withholding contextual performance.

There is also ample evidence that rater biases do exist and are difficult to minimise. People who are liked by the rater are often more favourably assessed – regardless of the final outcome – than those who have a weaker relationship with the rater. Moreover, appraisers may be reluctant to express severe criticism during a performance appraisal because it creates an unpleasant atmosphere and, after all, people generally have to go on working with each other. It has got to be awkward to spend the rest of the day (or week or month) in the same office with someone you have just told is not good enough at his or her job.

REFLECTIVE ACTIVITY

Think about the problems we have just outlined with regard to performance management in organisations.

To what extent might the methods we described in earlier sections of this chapter overcome such problems?

KEY ISSUES IN PERFORMANCE MANAGEMENT AND APPRAISAL

We now pull together ten key points about performance management and appraisals raised in this chapter:

- A clearly structured performance management system can improve organisational performance by providing simple and straightforward appraisals that monitor performance.
- The system must be aligned to the strategic plans. The performance goals must be clearly identified and set in relation to individuals, teams, processes, etc, and cascaded downwards.
- The system has to provide for the learning and development needs of individuals and teams. This includes coaching and mentoring, skills audit and succession planning.
- The appraisal should represent an opportunity to encourage the development of action, personal development and career plans.
- All parties with an interest in the process should be identified, because their commitment is an ingredient essential to the success of the process. This may include managers, individual or trade union representatives, customers and shareholders.
- The assessment design for individual or team performance should reflect the nature of the work concerned – the ratings must be objective to encourage confidence in the system.
- Line managers should be supported in developing the expertise to operate the system and encourage their staff to perform to higher levels.
- Performance management systems should be ethical and provide a platform for cultural and job profile changes, should promote the values of the organisation, and should be integrated into the HR process. There should be in-built monitoring and evaluating processes which allow improvements to be made to the systems through re-structuring and adaptations.
- Piloting or testing them on designated areas of the organisation to evaluate their effectiveness would provide an opportunity to modify or adjust them to ensure that they can be effectively implemented.
- There are some crucial problems which even well-designed performance management systems may not overcome.

Perhaps there are other key points you would like to note for yourself.

The main case study in this chapter now follows. It provides an example of how performance-related interventions can be used to engineer a change from a quantity- to a quality-oriented culture.

The production history of the Halewood plant, Merseyside, offers an insight into how one of the worst-performing car plants in the Ford portfolio was transformed into the exemplar of the Japanese-style Ford production system and six-sigma quality system, producing high-quality motor vehicles. Halewood's production of the Ford Escort (1968–2000) was plagued by poor industrial relations and poor build quality. During this time the British car industry was in flux to the extent that in 1989 Ford purchased Jaguar. During 1999 their Jaguar plant at Castle Bromwich, Birmingham, became operational and doubled their production of the S-type. In 1998, as part of increasing Jaguar's model productions it was decided to produce the new X-type at Halewood. This nearly did not happen in the light of the opposition that Ford experienced from the workforce.

Jaguar took over operation during this turbulent time and began the process of changing to Jaguar working practices. The Gateway Agreement, as part of the changes in working, was signed up to by the unions. Unfortunately, strikes ensued when management attempted to implement the Agreement. Because of these poor industrial relations, Ford threatened to pull out – but this was resolved when 90% of the workforce signed up to the Halewood charter and the rest took voluntary redundancy or early retirement. The changes in working practices relating to the move to producing Jaguars were supported by government grants for re-training the workforce.

The senior management team at Halewood sought to obtain buy-in by the workforce to the new more flexible working arrangements. It was important to move from being volume-driven to being quality-driven – which meant changing mindsets. The plant was shut down in 2000 for nine weeks for modification in readiness for production of the new module. This provided an opportunity for a series of interventions to be put into operation to support the new more flexible working practices and the reopening of the plant.

The creation of centres of excellence was part of the move to sustain quality. These centres delivered specific elements of the business, which focused on cultural change and improved quality. This, combined with the new processes and a more open management style, provided a platform whereby managers and the workforce alike were able to hold open discussions on the changes. Provisions were made for shopfloor workers to draft their job descriptions and for the creation of teams of six to eight workers whose team leaders were able to monitor quality control.

Assessment centres were used to identify new managers who would not only be committed to running the centres of excellence but be comfortable with the changes and with operating the new production processes. The successful operation of the new centres of excellence created a positive impact, which encouraged others to buy in to this more enthusiastic approach to work.

One intervention that really encapsulated the new approach was empowering the workers to stop the production line to deal with any quality issues. This freedom to act independently to some extent recognised the value of each worker in the production process and helped the drive for better-quality products.

All the training programmes set up during the closure of the plant were designed to support the change process. Senior managers and volunteers from the workforce underwent training to become facilitators so that they could deliver the new programme to the rest of the workforce. Production workers undertook college courses focused on IT, numeracy and literacy skills training to support their role in record-keeping. Community projects were set up to encourage the integration of the new production teams – this was initially viewed with caution by those concerned, but as the projects progressed, attitudes changed, and the experience appeared to have a positive impact.

Some operators and all supervisors and group leaders were seconded to the new S-type Jaguar plant to obtain an overview of the new production process and a level of expertise that they could take back to Halewood. Training on trial car-building runs enabled them to train other operators on their return by becoming product coaches.

The combination of interventions resulted in teams being formed that had a clearer idea of what performance levels and product quality were expected of them in the new teams and working conditions. Senior management recognised that to sustain performance the process needed on-going monitoring. Production started in 2001, and an audit of the new working practices has since provided a template that others might put into practice.

Source: Pickard (2002)

Questions for discussion

1 Why did this combination of interventions succeed in changing the performance record of the workforce from one of the worst to the best?

2 Analyse each intervention noting the individual aspects of each one that demonstrate good practice. Can they be used for similar changes elsewhere?

3 What else might you do to sustain high-quality performance?

Note: It is your response to Question 2 – asking yourself why individual aspects worked and whether different combinations of them might be used elsewhere to produce similar outcomes – from which you should be able to develop your ideas as recommendations in response to Question 3.

EXPLORE FURTHER

ARMSTRONG, M. and BARON, A. (2005) *Managing Performance – Performance management in action*. London, CIPD
These are useful in providing a base from which people management policies, procedures and process can be developed to contribute to the overall performance of the business.

CABINET OFFICE (2007) *Transformational Government Enabled by Technology*, Annual Report. Online version available at:
http://www.cio.gov.uk/documents/annual_report2006/ trans_gov2006.pdf
[accessed July 2007]
The Cabinet Office provides reports on a number of HR-related areas including the framework.

CIO (2007) *IT Skills Framework and the Focus of the Council*. Online version available at: **www.cio.gov.uk/about_the_council/index.asp** [accessed July 2007]

CIPD (2005) *Performance Appraisal*. London, CIPD

CIPD (2005) *Performance Management*, CIPD Survey Report. London, CIPD
The report looks at the performance management arrangements in different organisations and analyses the effectiveness of the activities that feature in them.

CIPD (2007) Performance management factsheet. Online version available at:
http://www. cipd.co.uk [accessed March 2007]WALTERS, M. (2005) *People and Performance: Designing the HR process for maximum performance delivery*. London, CIPD

HIGHWAYS AGENCY (2007) *Business Plan*. Online version available at:
www.highways.gov.uk/ aboutus/1283.aspx; general access:
http://www.highways.gov.uk/default.aspx [accessed July 2007]
These sites provide not only information on performance indicators and the balanced scorecard but also an insight into the activities of the agencies.

CHAPTER 13

Reward systems

Geoff Wood, Leslie T. Szamosi *and* Alexandros Psychogios

INTRODUCTION

This chapter aims to provide an introduction to and an overview of reward systems in the modern organisation. It takes a comprehensive look at recent developments in the deployment and administration of reward systems and examines the practical implications for organisations.

LEARNING OUTCOMES

By the end of this chapter readers should be able to:

- discuss the links between overall organisational strategies and reward systems in practice
- introduce and describe the limitations and uses of job evaluation in the modern organisation
- introduce and critically discuss the individual performance-oriented pay ('new pay') approach to reward systems
- appreciate the role of team pay and the contexts in which it may be the most appropriate
- provide an overview of key ethical questions in the deployment and use of reward systems.

The chapter is structured in two parts. The first part discusses the context of reward and the second part deals with different types of reward systems.

The chapter concludes with the main case study.

Reference sources named within the chapter may be looked up in the *References and further reading* section at the end of the book.

Central to the employment contract are questions related to reward (Snell, 1992). All jobs – even voluntary ones – are performed in the anticipation of some reward, whether as wages or in personal satisfaction. Quite simply, organisations have to take the process of reward seriously in order to attract and retain talented staff (Brewster, 1995). In looking at reward within an organisation, we tend to look at reward systems (Snell, 1992). These are the

In 1960, Northstar was one of five steel producers located in Oldstown, which, in all employed some 26% of the town's mill-age-eligible adult population. Today, it is the sole surviving steel producer, employing some 2% of the eligible adult male population. Traditionally, Northstar supplied the shipping industry but today it owes its survival to a gradual shift to smaller batch production, providing specialist products in niches of the market not covered by major Far Eastern steel producers.

As a result of this shift, Northstar has been forced to redefine the manner in which it manages its human resources. Most recently, senior management has begun to explore the possibility of adopting an employee involvement programme (EIP). It is hoped that such a programme will encourage commitment, facilitate further multi-skilling and ultimately enhance the quality of the products produced. Theoretically, the success of an EIP is predicated on both parties' adopting co-operative norms of power-sharing to a lesser or greater extent.

Work at Northstar has for many years been characterised by employee defiance of many of the rules imposed by the company (and in many cases, by the union as well). Workers 'know their jobs', and have committed their lives to making the world's best steel. However, they have also found time to redefine the work area to meet their own needs and norms. A workplace survey revealed that workers tended to see supervisors as incompetent, 'lacking family values' and big drinkers, and senior management seemed to be held in even lower esteem. Moreover, workers 'make their own tea breaks', engaging in recreational activity on company time – a practice that supervisors turn a blind eye to, within certain parameters. Finally, Northstar has always been dogged by high levels of petty theft of company property.

Questions for discussion

What changes to or reforms of the reward system might help solve some of the problems faced by management in this organisation?

overall structures and processes that are in place to ensure that each individual is adequately rewarded for his or her output or general contribution to the organisation. There must be some consistency in this process.

1 REWARD SYSTEMS

The employment contract is about an exchange relationship by which a specified amount of labour power is traded for various rewards – a tenet of all motivation theories. The *traditional approach* to motivation emphasises economic rewards linked to productivity (ie scientific management). The *human relations approach* emphasises non-monetary rewards as the prime motivating factor (eg the Hawthorne studies) while the *human resource approach* suggests that workers are motivated by many individualised reward systems (eg Theory X and Theory Y).

For almost all employees, the most important reward is monetary compensation. Wages are an *extrinsic* reward ('hygiene factors', according to Herzberg's two-factor motivation theory) – in other words, it is given for a certain amount of work, and does not directly constitute a part of the actual working experience. The other major extrinsic reward is job security. Most employees prefer secure employment in view of their personal and family commitments, or, at the very least enough notice period to make alternative arrangements should their employment end. On the one hand it could be argued that only incompetent staff will set a premium on job security – the best staff will have good externally marketable skills, and will rapidly be able to find another job. Organisations might thus become more flexible by concentrating extrinsic rewards towards pay only, and be able to rapidly cut or increase workforce sizes (and overall pay obligations) in the light of changing circumstances. On the other hand there is considerable evidence to suggest that job-seekers in a strong bargaining position will naturally demand some job security, if nothing else to reduce the costs incurred during employment transitions. It is perhaps telling that most executive board members in the UK ensure that they will receive generous payouts in the event of having to leave the organisation.

Intrinsic rewards are those that form part and parcel of the working day ('motivating factors', according to Herzberg's two-factor motivation theory). They could include issues such as recognition from peers and superiors, personal fulfilment from the nature of the tasks performed, celebrations on attaining work goals, and/or the sense of belonging to a community. Although a large proportion of the literature on reward systems concentrates on extrinsic rewards, the importance of intrinsic rewards should not be underestimated.

The reward that a worker takes from his or her efforts indicates whether his/her behaviour was appropriate and sufficiently compensated. Organisations must seek to determine the right balance of rewards to keep workers motivated. For example, in terms of the content theories of motivation (eg Maslow's hierarchy of needs, ERG Theory) needs must be satisfied and the appropriate reward linked to fulfilment of those particular needs. On the other hand, through Reinforcement Theory, rewards (and punishments) are used to immediately link behaviours and consequences.

REFLECTIVE ACTIVITY

Think of an organisation you know.

How important are/were intrinsic rewards in motivating employees?

It is difficult to accurately measure the exact worth of a particular amount of labour time, and, for that reason, there is inevitably some room for a conflict of interest between employer and employee. The employer naturally has an interest in closely tying perceived output – and the general value of the employee to the enterprise – to payment. Although employees are in employment precisely because they wish to be rewarded – above all, in the form of pay – they have an interest in a reward system that is predictable (in view of personal financial commitments), is fair, and does not impose undue amounts of stress.

So the manner in which organisations administer and distribute rewards reflects a desire to mould the behaviour of their staff. This would include the monitoring of their performance and/or the controlling of their output. In other words, companies administer reward systems in a manner that directs staff towards the realisation of organisational objectives. However, organisations may choose – or choose not – to empower staff with considerable room for manoeuvre in the way in which outputs may be attained. They may act unilaterally, or they may allow staff some input in the process of goal-setting, in the manner in which performance is measured, and in the nature and extent of the actual rewards given.

On the one hand, most organisations naturally seek to optimise their output (in terms of goods manufactured or services offered). This would including giving greater rewards to the most productive, skilled and/or capable employees (Koch and McGrath, 1996). On the other hand, too much emphasis on closely controlling the work of employees and/or the distribution of rewards in a manner that is perceived to be unfair or overly punitive will result in the migration of the most competent staff members to organisations where the quality of working life is better, leaving behind a discontent group of less capable and mobile staff who have to put up with the system in the absence of alternative options. The operation of reward systems may thus have effects opposite to those intended. Again, the close monitoring of employee performance may encourage dishonesty, with employees lying or systematically breaking rules to attain preset outcomes.

There is very much more to reward than output and moulding the behaviour of staff. Reward systems also aim to control costs, to be fair and to increase staff morale (Lado and Wilson, 1994). In addition, many countries prohibit pay discrimination on the grounds of gender and race – the operation of a reward system has legal implications. Organisations have to monitor pay rates to ensure that legislation is not being breached, even if inadvertently. Quite simply, reward is one of the key, fundamental policy-making areas of HRM.

REFLECTIVE ACTIVITY

What is more important in designing a reward system – controlling costs or promoting fairness?

STRATEGY, HR AND REWARD

Since the early 1980s, a growing emphasis has been placed on the strategic dimension of people management (see Chapters 3 and 20 for a more in-depth discussion of the issues that are only summarised below). Historically, personnel administration was just that – the administration of pay and reward systems and other elements of the personnel function in a predetermined manner according to formal rules and procedures. The increasingly turbulent global environment has forced firms to take *strategic* issues in the management of human resources more seriously.

There is a very simple reason for this. The resource-based view of the firm suggests that many of a firm's attributes cannot be readily bought or sold on the external labour market, and yet may be the source of sustained competitive advantage. For example, staff may have skills, attributes or knowledge specific to the organisation that may not have a commensurate value on the external job market, or even be known to competitors. So what a firm does with its people may be the key to greater organisational competitiveness: the manner in which they are rewarded may provide the basis of success, even if external conditions are bleak. Any inclusive HR strategy therefore has rewards as one of its core components. Ideally, reward systems should be linked directly to overall organisational strategies, and concern not just issues of motivation and control but also provide incentives for higher productivity.

In the early years of the Industrial Revolution, pay was generally set on the basis of output. In practice, pay-setting in early industrial organisations was often arbitrary. The rise of trade unions in Britain saw a shift towards pay rates for the job – in other words, all those doing a similar job were paid according to the same pay-scale. With the decline of unions in Britain, pay by results or performance has returned to popularity. Interestingly, many organisations have also tended to decentralise the operation of rewards systems away from a central HR department and towards greater involvement by line management. There is something of a contradiction here in that although there is a greater emphasis on the need for reward systems to be strategic – and hence, flexible – considerable attention in the literature has been focused on promoting 'best practices': customer-focused pay, variable pay linked to individual performance, and pay as the primary reward for good performance. Indeed, critics have charged that most HR systems are a collection of issues rarely integrated or designed from a 'total systems' perspective – that in the real world, pay systems are rarely integrated into overall HR, let alone internal organisational strategies (Drucker and White, 1997). After all, reward systems are often inconsistent even internally, reducing their general effectiveness.

Moreover, many companies create or maintain reward systems that are not linked with the overall organisational strategic aim (Kerr, 1975). When rewards are aligned with strategic goals, employees can coordinate and emphasise their efforts and their daily labours. The challenge is therefore to guarantee that the reward systems are enhancing strategic intent instead of being a drag on it. For this reason it would be appropriate to involve in the design process of the reward systems not only HR specialists but also those people that are fully aware of the strategic goals of the organisation (Meyer, 1994).

REFLECTIVE ACTIVITY

It is often argued that reward systems should be adjusted in line with changing organisational strategic objectives – yet in the real world, this is not often the case.

Why is that, do you think?

2 TYPES OF REWARD SYSTEMS

There are three basic approaches to reward systems. The first, and simplest, is to pay all individuals in the same job grade the same rate, or on a similar pay-scale (allowing gradual progression on the grounds of seniority). Secondly, individuals may be ranked in their own right, some individuals being judged superior, some average and some inferior; pay rates are adjusted accordingly. Thirdly, team pay is a variation of performance-related pay, allocated on the basis of teams of employees, rather than individuals.

TRADITIONAL APPROACHES TO PAY

As noted above, up until the 1980s most British organisations tended to make use of formal bureaucratic pay systems. Typically, staff were placed on predetermined pay-scales. The latter had often been pre-negotiated with a trade union, representing the outcome of a *collective agreement* that in turn represented the outcome of *collective bargaining* between the union and management. Today, only about a third of employees are covered by collective bargaining in the UK. The coverage is particularly low in private services, but relatively high in the public sector (see Table 31).

Table 31 Aggregate collective bargaining coverage, 1998 and 2004

	Percentage of employees	
	1998	2004
All workplaces	38	35
Industry		
Manufacturing	43	35
Hotels and restaurants	12	4
Financial services	49	35
Public sector	66	75

Source: Kersley *et al* (2006; p.187)

In the traditional approach, the pay scale is contingent on the job, and the individual's position on the pay-scale on seniority. The advantages of such systems include internal consistency, legitimacy (in the case of collective agreements), and administrative ease. Central to such a process is job evaluation – in other words, the ability to tell what a particular job really is about and worth, rather than the performance of the individual carrying it out.

Job evaluation

Job evaluation is the analysis of a particular set of roles typically performed in carrying out a job. Because it is specific to the job, it should be a process less prone to personal prejudice or discrimination than the assessment of a particular individual. There are two basic types of job evaluation. The first, 'non-analytical' ranking system assigns rank to a job as a whole, vis-à-vis others: in other words, what the job as a whole entails in relation to others. The second, 'analytical' approach breaks up a job into individual factors and elements, and looks at each in turn, which, in theory at least, should enable greater objectivity. Non-analytical systems leave more room for job stereotyping, which may reflect embedded gender, age or ethnic stereotypes, but does recognise that jobs represent more than simply packages of tasks, and may be harder to manage in the case of jobs that entail a wide range of duties.

Job evaluation simply is the process of deciding the relative contribution of a particular job to the organisation as a whole, and its worth both *internally* (that is in terms of the organisation) and *externally* (in terms of comparable jobs in other organisations). In other words, it is about finding out the relative worth of a job to assign pay to it. As such, it is distinct from *job analysis*.

Job analysis is essentially *the compilation of information on what a particular job really is about* – in other words, the duties attached to a particular job, and the context thereof. No job evaluation is possible without some form of job analysis in advance: one has to gather information about a job in order to evaluate it or decide on its relative worth. Job analysis is used not only for subsequent job evaluation but also to compile *job descriptions* (what a job entails), *job performance standards* (what is expected in a particular job) and *job specification* (what is required to do a particular job – eg skills, knowledge, physical and psychological attributes, etc).

Job evaluation is a somewhat subjective process, although it is also a formal and procedural one. Table 32 highlights some of the principal forms of job evaluation system. Job evaluation is about finding out the relative value of a job and assigning pay rates to it – not an individual, who may, at a particular time, carry out the job. On entering a particular job, individuals will be assured of a particular pay rate – either a simple fixed wage (eg the national minimum wage) – or a place on the pay-scale attached to the relevant job grade. The individual will then gradually progress on the scale (eg on the basis of seniority).

Table 32 Job evaluation systems compared

Type of system	System	Description
Non-analytical	Ranking	Places jobs in an order, from the least to the most important for the organisation
Non-analytical	Job grading/ Job classification	A number of possible job grades are identified, each attached to a particular pay-scale. These grades may be defined on skill, knowledge and responsibilities. Individual jobs are then slotted into these predetermined grades
Analytical	Quantitative methods	*Factor comparison schemes* identify a number of factors (scales), such as skill, responsibility, effort, etc. Each job is ranked on each factor, and pay is set accordingly per factor, ultimately leading to an overall pay package. A variation of this is the *point comparison system*, in which instead of assigning components of pay to each factor, points are assigned (eg 10 out of 100 for skill). Overall points assigned to a particular job are then added up, and this is used as a basis for differentiating pay

Critics have charged that such approaches are inflexible, and do not allow enough room to award individual excellence (or punish poor performance): 'old pay fits old bureaucratic organisations', whereas more modern flexible organisations require more modern pay systems. In other words, traditional pay rewards individuals according to their place in the organisation and their accomplishments, but is not congruent with 'knowledge- or quality-oriented organisations' (Allen and Killmann, 1999).

REFLECTIVE ACTIVITY

What do you think are the positive and negative aspects of job evaluation schemes?

(If you have had experience of a job evaluation scheme, draw on it for your answer.)

INDIVIDUAL PERFORMANCE-ORIENTED PAY

Often referred to as 'the New pay', a term coined by Edward Lawler, individual performance-oriented pay systems are depicted by their proponents as a more up-to-date strategic approach to pay and reward. It is argued that pay systems should be integrated and mutually supportive with other areas of HRM, and organisational strategies at large (Lewis, 1998). New pay is about flexibility, and a more direct linking of individual performance to reward (Heery, 1996; Dickinson, 2006). As such, it reflects the declining influence of unions and collective bargaining. New pay approaches argue that fixed base pay rates only reward a job, not the nature or quality of an individual's input; it is argued that, in an increasingly competitive world, it is necessary to tailor pay to what individuals *really* contribute to an organisation (ie both tangibles and intangibles). Person-based systems aim explicitly to promote the attainment of certain pre-decided organisational outcomes. 'New pay' systems focusing on the individual are a form of individual performance-related pay (PRP) – in other words, a system where an individual's pay is at least partly dependent on his or her performance appraisal or ranking (Kerrin and Oliver, 2002). Current research has shown, however, that traditional reward systems are still strong throughout Europe (Willems, Janvier and Henderickx, 2006).

Individual performance-related pay assumes that rewards can be adjusted to changes in organisational circumstances, enabling firms to become 'fast and nimble'. The literature on 'New pay' makes little reference to collective bargaining, and assumes that determining reward is ultimately the prerogative of management. New pay also argues that individual rewards should reflect both the state of the external market and the net worth of the individual staff member. As with any other benefits, pay rates should be flexible and readily adjustable to changes in circumstances, and encourage entrepreneurial behaviour among staff (Carraher, Hart and Carraher, 2003). However, in reality, the rate at which New pay systems have been adopted remains uneven, reflecting both an abiding reluctance by senior management to abandon tried and trusted measures and the continued popularity of job-evaluation-based reward systems. In part, the latter would reflect the effects of equal pay for equal work legislation (for example, legislation that outlaws differential pay on the basis of gender or ethnicity), which would encourage firms to become more, rather than less, consistent in the manner in which they pay their staff.

The adoption of an individual PRP system does not mean that the entire salary package should be based solely on performance. However, the base pay (that is, the set amount that is related to the job, rather than individual performance) should be kept at the bare minimum necessary to attract and retain key staff. Thereafter, performance-related payments would top up salaries, ensuring that the 'best' workers are the 'best rewarded'. This would also assist in motivating employees (eg Equity Theory).

It has been argued that the PRP model is most appropriate to more 'flexible' employment contracts, by which incumbents have lower degrees of job security, but with more room for redeployment, and, perhaps advancement (see Chapter 10). It represents a move away from the formal regulation of the employment contract, and, as such, may be most appropriate in cases where the ability of individuals to depart from preset norms is particularly valuable (ie thinking outside the box).

Proponents have argued that the new pay is particularly appropriate to firms operating in the high technology sector. Rapid change in such environments poses the risk that reward system will fall behind changing organisational needs (eg Twomey and Quazi, 1994). New pay assumes that wages should be variable; in practice, pay packages are often designed in such a manner that some indirect costs can be shifted on to the individual in the event of sub-optimal performance. This also turns fixed costs into variable costs thereby allowing easier budgeting and forecasting expenses. Such reward systems may be supplemented and improved by objective bonus plans and the availability of firm-specific training to increase the value of the employment relationship, making it more worthwhile for talented staff to stay with the organisation (Ichniowski and Shaw, 2003).

Critics have charged that this model is overly simplistic, and that it merely assumes there is a direct link between compensation strategy and individual performance, whereas classic theories of motivation (eg Vroom's Expectancy Theory) would point to more complex relationships between the two. In today's work environment these links may be becoming even more complex as workers also seek to balance work and family concerns against straight compensation. Individual PRP thus takes little account of the social context in which work takes place, which we are seeing as becoming even more critical in today's environment. Individuals may restrict their output in order to maintain good relations with their peers, or work together to ensure that targets are mutually attainable.

Again, New pay is based on the assumption that managers and employees have essentially the same interests – interests that can be readily reconciled. Through high-quality work, individuals contribute to the broader well-being of the organisation, and are also well rewarded through flexible pay systems (Scott and Dean, 1992; Dickinson, 2006). It has accordingly been referred to as *neo-unitarist* – that is, that managers and employees should have *united* interests.

Reward systems are investments to attract talented individuals and ensure that they perform well over time. Yet if rewards are seen as inequitable, individuals are more likely to leave, qualified individuals are also less likely to join, or staff may stay and produce at a lower level. In reality, there have been many cases where employees have opposed the introduction of new pay systems, and/or voted by their feet by choosing to move away from organisations where the administration of reward is seen as unduly coercive.

The introduction of New pay may be used as a device for undermining unions – employees are rewarded according to the perceived value they add, rather than through a collectively negotiated contract.

There are also other practical concerns. The evaluation of any staff member is necessarily a subjective process, based on managerial perceptions of customer satisfaction and/or the perceived quality of goods or services that are produced. This level of vagueness leaves management with a great deal of discretion, which may perpetuate existing inequalities in the organisation – for example, those on race or gender lines. Indeed, the introduction of individual PRP systems may raise equity and fairness concerns, contribute to employee anxiety, result in unduly negative evaluations of specific categories of employee, and inevitable injustices may contribute to perceptions of organisational inefficiency (Pearce, Branyiczki and Bakacsi, 1994). Because the New pay is individually (or at best, team-) focused, workers may lack an effective collective voice to challenge managerial judgements.

On the one hand, there is substantial evidence to suggest that large numbers of organisations have moved towards more flexible benefits systems – or redesigned existing systems – particularly in certain job categories. On the other hand, this may reflect the influence of external factors. The latter could include factors as disparate as changes in tax policy and declining union power – and hence, collective bargaining and centrally agreed pay-scales.

REFLECTIVE ACTIVITY

What would you say are the benefits and disadvantages of individual PRP in practice in organisations – in particular, in service and manufacturing industries?

TEAM-BASED PAY

Performance-based pay may be administered not only on the basis of individual effort and achievement but also, alternatively, on the performance of autonomous work teams (Cacciope, 1999). When firms cannot measure accurately the contribution of individual workers, group-based incentive pay may be particularly appropriate. This includes rewarding employees according to physical output or firm-wide profit-sharing (Ichniowski and Shaw, 2003). However, it can create the problem of 'free-riding', less productive workers relying on the efforts of others (Kerrin and Oliver, 2002). This has often led to a focus on small groups or teams of workers; work teams may boost group identity (Brown, 1996).

It may be difficult to decide on suitable measures of team performance in organisational settings other than manufacturing or frontline services. Even in the case of the latter, performance measures may have perverse effects. For example, the speed with which customers may be dealt with may result in difficult or time-consuming requests being deferred or ignored, with the bulk of attention being directed towards dealing with customers who can be speedily processed (even in cases where the potential revenue that may flow from the latter is less). There is also the problem of excessive competition between teams, which can undermine organisational solidarity and lead to employees being reluctant to share information with each other. Finally, team-based incentive systems are not always compatible with the use of individual bonuses or other forms of performance recognition – and in fact, if exercised, can cause catastrophic team dysfunction. This has meant that, in practice, organisations may choose to go for gestures or symbolic rewards for exceptional team performance, rather than completely redesigning reward systems on team lines (Cacciope, 1999).

Teams may be rewarded not only through the payment of bonuses but also through resetting base pay rates, through the future allocation of resources (including supporting infrastructure) and the allocation of work. The allocation of rewards may be uniform across the entire team, or be customised to take account of particular effort (or lack thereof). This is a complex process, and packages that work in one context may not work in another. Any package should be flexible, and capable of coping with structural and technological changes. Again, the process must be integrated into the process of building teams and reallocating individuals between teams. Finally, it seems that team-based pay can be also linked with overall organisational strategy. Because team-based rewards can be adjusted in line with the firm's strategic goals, team members' attention can be directed to follow specific strategic patterns (Meyer, 1994). This will enhance the fulfilment of strategic challenges that organisations face.

SHARE OWNERSHIP AND PROFIT-SHARING

Employees may also be rewarded through share ownership schemes or by profit-sharing. Table 33 compares and contrasts firm-level practices in a range of different national contexts, based on the findings of the Cranet-E survey (full details are supplied elsewhere in this volume). As can be seen, employee share schemes (in other words, schemes that assist workers in buying shares) and stock options (opportunities for employees to buy shares at favourable rates) are less common in Sweden and Germany – countries where there is a strong tradition of collaboration between firms and unions – than in the United Kingdom and, indeed, Greece – where there are traditions of more adversarial industrial relations (Table 33).

In other words, it is suggested that firms appear more likely to offer such schemes when unions are weaker. This would reflect the fact that such schemes closely tie workers to overall organisational performance as reflected by short-term share prices, the pursuit of which may undermine long-term job security and, indeed, collective bargaining between unions and employers as a means of pay-setting. This variation is also reflected at the level of managerial staff. Again,

Table 33 Profit-sharing, employee share ownership and stock options in different national contexts

Do you offer the following managerial staff?	UK	Sweden	Germany	Greece	Slovakia
Employee share schemes	25%	10%	15%	25%	15%
Profit-sharing	20%	21%	65%	16%	43%
Stock options	21%	11%	12%	30%	9%
Do you offer the following for manual staff?					
Employee share schemes	15%	5%	8%	8%	7%
Profit-sharing	11%	13%	23%	6%	13%
Stock options	2%	2%	2%	11%	1%

Source: Cranet-E (2003)

giving managers a strong interest in immediate share prices is likely to incentivise certain forms of behaviour: an immediate fascination with the bottom line and with factors likely to impact on the share price.

In contrast, profit-sharing was very much more common in Germany – where, in other words, workers were given a proportion of overall profits. Typically, this would be linked to collective bargaining and reinforce the collective identity of the workforce and effectively that of the union. This collective basis is also likely to make for greater long-termism – because the interests of all workers at all stages of their careers have to be considered – rather than where each worker seeks to maximise his or her own interests and/or the immediate concerns of the firm.

ETHICS AND REWARD SYSTEMS

The operation of reward systems raises a number of ethical and related concerns. Firstly, there are questions of *equity*. Reward systems have to take account not only of external equity (that is, prevailing rates for a particular job) but also of internal equity (fairness vis-à-vis others in the organisation) and individual equity (whether an individual is being fairly rewarded for his or her efforts). Balancing these three equity concerns may prove to be extremely difficult in practice. The issue of internal equity has become an increasingly important one. In Britain, the pay gap between senior managers and other employees has substantially widened since the 1970s. This is grounds for particular concern in that winning organisations in sustainable areas of economic activity, where competitiveness is particularly dependent on quality – such as high-value-added manufacturing (in which Britain performs particularly poorly) – have, in most contexts, had relatively narrow gaps between senior managers and rank-and-file. Greater quality, trust and employee commitment are more likely when pay differentials are muted (Baron and Cooke, 1992). There is little doubt that high pay inequality within an organisation greatly undermines notions of 'partnership' or 'mutual commitment' (Jansen and Glinow, 1985).

Again, although organisations are quick to penalise individual employees for poor performance, often senior managers are rewarded for poor performance with ever greater pay increases, and, at the worst, 'golden goodbyes' – substantial payments to encourage them to move on. Critics have charged that the New pay has allowed managers to transfer increasing amounts of risk to employees, who are blamed and punished for organisational failures. Senior managers optimise their own rewards while delegating many responsibilities.

REFLECTIVE ACTIVITY

Do you think it is possible for organisations ever to reconcile internal, external and individual equity concerns?

Secondly, there are questions of employee well-being. As noted earlier, the appraisal of performance depends, in the end, on the subjective judgement of managers. This may result in the perpetuation of existing organisational inequalities, on race and gender lines. It may also open up individual workers to bullying or harassment (at both ends of the spectrum – working too hard or not working enough) (Scott and Dean, 1992). Managers may use the additional power opened up by an appraisal in an inappropriate manner, even if their behaviour is illegal in terms of formal organisational rules. Again, most employees desire some stability and predictability in their earnings (in order to meet financial commitments such as bond payments, rent, loan repayments, etc); variable New-pay-inspired systems may challenge their ability to meet everyday financial commitments in a consistent way.

KEY ISSUES IN REWARD

We now pull together some key points about reward raised in this chapter:

- In the UK context, there has been a trend for the last 30 years towards more individually based reward systems, with pay being more closely linked to perceived performance.
- This trend has allowed organisations to better reward exceptional achievement and penalise failure.
- To critics, this has resulted in increasing internal inequality within organisations, and may undermine relationships with long-standing employees.
- Growing numbers of organisations are seeing reward as of *strategic* importance rather than simply a formal *administrative* function centring on the administration of predetermined pay rates.

Perhaps there are other key points that you would like to note for yourself.

The main case study in this chapter now follows. It gives an example of how the increasingly important issue of communicating with people who work for the organisation, but are not directly employed by it, can affect a company in practice.

Look at the description of the real-life case set out below. Then decide on the recommendations that you would make as an HR manager for dealing with the issues raised. Try to think beyond the level of a 'quick fix' or simple solutions.

The firm, making textiles and trimming, was established in 1964. The factory originated in a small building with one crochet loom machine, and a group of local people who were subsequently trained by the family on how to create hand-made trimming. In the last ten years the company has been growing at an average rate of 20% per year, and has become a major global player in the trimming business. The company exports 80% of its products to 71 countries worldwide. The major market is the US market, followed closely by the European market. The company is viewed today as one of the top three companies in the world within its field and provides employment for approximately 1,000 people. The success of the company has, according to management, been due to its being innovative, flexible and aggressive with regard to the export market. More specifically, by concentrating on specialised niche markets the firm has managed to survive the flooding of global markets by cheap textiles manufactured in the Far East. The firm received an Exporter of the Year award in 1994. Management are proud of the fact that many employees have been with the firm for many years and that the enterprise has one of the lowest staff turnover rates in the textile industry.

The organisation decided many years ago to focus and to become a leading force in the international arena. In the mid-1980s the organisation manufactured basic trimming that required a simple level of manufacturing. It made use of only 30 types of combinations of raw materials and colours. Today, this figure has expanded to over 350 types of yarns/colours. From a range of combinations of products in the region of 20,000 at the beginning of the 1990s, the organisation now deals with over 130,000 combinations of products. This ability to meet specialised niche demand, through the production of individualised batches, has, in part, insulated the firm from head-on competition with high-volume low-cost Far Eastern producers.

In the late 1980s and at the beginning of the 1990s, customers abroad bought large quantities of relatively few items. However, increased competition forced the firm to concentrate on niche markets. In the latter areas, it seems that a very real market break-up has occurred, many customers now demanding small quantities of very complicated items in thousands of combinations and variety of colours, whereas 15 years ago a much more limited range would have sufficed. In addition, the established lead time for delivery on handmade articles was 13 weeks in the late 1980s. By the onset of the 1990s customers expected a lead time of no longer than four weeks, probably on account of a desire for reduced inventory stocks. This diversification necessitated more flexible methods of production, hinging around a multi-skilled workforce. After making a survey of the international literature on multi-skilling, a formal training plan was formulated. Thereafter, extensive (and lengthy) consultation took place with departmental heads, shop stewards, and finally the employees themselves.

At the time of the case study, production was divided into four main divisions: i) crochet knitting, which produced mainly *crochet-knitted* decorative trimmings (for example, fringes), ii) the handmade division, where activities revolved around the assembly of decorative trimmings by hand (for example, tiebacks and tassels), iii) *twisting and component manufacturing*, and iv) *narrow weaving*, which manufactured woven material, such as ribbons and narrow-width decorative trimming.

Within the crochet knitting division, the set-up time on the machine for each article could take between a minimum of four hours and maximum of 12 hours (for a qualified mechanic). To produce 100 metres of knitted material could take within the region of one hour. As the market conditions changed and short runs had to be put through the machines, management decided to recast the division of labour on the shop floor. Prior to the implementation of the development initiative, the ratio of operators to mechanics was 10:1. Within this area, human resource development plans aimed to train all the operators to become mechanics – a process that is still on-going. This has not reduced employment, but it has enabled the organisation to produce shorter runs and to have many more changes of products in order to fulfil market requirements. An accurate list was undertaken of all employees' educational qualifications, and psychometric tests were then undertaken to evaluate their mechanical abilities, whereby they proceeded to choose the best potential operator. This operator was then assigned to a qualified mechanic as a trainee. Meanwhile, the most capable mechanics were then chosen to acquire additional skills in the engineering workshop.

The handmade division comprised two sections. The tassel fringe section consisted of workers manually tying tassels to the end of braids. The loose tassel section mainly assembled tiebacks and key tassels by hand. Even though the two operations of covering and tying yarn to different components seemed to be similar activities, they were, in fact, not compatible. During periods when there was a shortage of orders in one department, management attempted to transfer workers from one department to the other. This proved to be unsuccessful in the sense that, according to management, workers were unable to reach a reasonable level of productivity within a short time-frame. Thereafter, management decided to train new multi-skilled operators, capable of performing both tasks, from scratch. According to the departmental manager:

People who were used to performing certain hand movements for long periods found it difficult to change this habit.

However, a few existing employees proved capable of operating in both sections and, unlike their 'repetitive peers' enjoyed relatively high levels of job security.

Within the twisting and component manufacturing section, management saw multi-skilling as particularly desirable, in that it would enable any worker to operate all the machines should a peer be absent. Each operator has since been trained, or is currently undergoing training, to be able to operate all the machines. In both the cord-making and mould-covering sections, a single worker may have to operate between two to six machines at any one time.

The organisation therefore decided to train operators from cord-making and mould-covering to be able to function in each others' department. The entire department underwent assessment and evaluation to ascertain their ability and skill level. Those who were discerned to be 'more capable' were asked to undergo intensive training in order to be able to operate the other section's machines. Management motivated employees by stating that, due to being multi-skilled, their position within the organisation would be much more secure than that of their single-skilled co-workers.

Staffing levels in the narrow weaving division were extremely tight, each worker 'being trained to the maximum of his ability'.

Source: G. Wood and R. Sela (2000) 'Making human resource development work', *Human Resource Development International*, Vol. 3, No. 4, 451–64. Fuller information on the case can be found in the original article

Questions for consideration and discussion

1 What type of reward system would be most appropriate for this organisation and how would it differ (or not) between the four departments?

2 Assume there is a trade union in this organisation. How would this affect the choice of reward system?

3 How could a reward system best be integrated into teamwork in an organisation of this type?

EXPLORE FURTHER

ARMSTRONG, M. (2002) *Employee Reward*. London, CIPD
This CIPD textbook provides a comprehensive coverage of employee reward systems from an applied practitioner perspective.

CACCIOPE, R. (1999) 'Using team-individual reward and recognition strategies to drive organizational success', *Leadership and Organization Development Journal*, Vol. 20, No. 6, 322–31
This article provides a look at the role of team-based reward systems from a practitioner perspective.

HEERY, E. (1996) 'Risk, reward and the New pay', *Personnel Review*, Vol. 25, No. 6, 54–65
This article locates reward systems within a broader ethical framework.

ICHNIOWSKI, C. and SHAW, K. (2003) 'Beyond incentive pay', *Journal of Economic Perspectives*, Vol. 17, No. 1, 155–80
This theoretically rigorous account looks at the limitations of incentive-based reward systems and alternatives thereto.

KERRIN, M. and OLIVER, N. (2002) 'Collective and individual improvement activities: the role of reward systems', *Personnel Review*, Vol. 31, No. 3, 320–37
This article links theoretical questions to the practical implementation of reward systems.

CHAPTER 14

Training and development

Ian Favell

INTRODUCTION

This chapter is about learning in the workplace.

LEARNING OUTCOMES

By the end of this chapter readers should be able to:

- explain the range of different methods available for workplace learning
- describe some key issues of on-the-job and off-the-job methods of training and development
- identify the benefits and disadvantages of a range of different workplace learning methods.

The chapter is closely related to Chapter 24 on HRD, and is structured in three parts. The first part deals with formal training and development. The second part then turns to informal learning initiatives in organisations. The third part examines formal schemes based around a mixture of formal and informal learning methods, blended to suit the context of the individual and the subject. The final case study then shows a number of the ideas in operation within an organisational context, with mixed success and effectiveness.

Reference sources named within the chapter may be looked up in the *References and further reading* section at the end of the book.

Most organisations recognise the importance of learning and development for their staff, and usually have some form of training and development scheme. Many schemes are based around the organisation's performance management scheme (appraisal), in which development needs and aspirations are discussed and a development plan agreed for each individual each year (see Chapter 12 on performance management and appraisal). The plans will range in approach according to individual needs and the issues involved, and may call upon any appropriate training and development methods.

John leaves school with almost no qualifications. He has decided that he would like to work as an electrician. He applies to a number of local firms for a job. However, he is not even invited to interview by any of them. After several frustrating months he decides to talk to a local training provider about how he should train himself for his chosen career, in order that he might get on the first rung of the ladder. The provider, by chance, is one that offers qualifications that involve an Individual Learning Plan, associated with an apprenticeship. This involves some classroom attendance, for learning of theory and practical skills, and some work-placement for on-the-job practice and experience. John is overjoyed to find that for his workplace practical experience he is placed in one of the organisations that he had previously applied to, and that some of the assessment is competency-based in the workplace as well as at the training provider. At his Induction event, John is surprised to find an observer from an inspection agency.

At the training provider a learning resource centre is available, which provides a wide range of facilities, freely available, including e-learning packages, books, journals, videos,

practice tests, and other materials – everything that he needs to progress. As well as the written tests, his apprenticeship contains a vocationally based technical certificate, which confirms his competence in the basics of the job. Having successfully completed his training programme, John then accepts a paid secondment with the firm that he has been working with during his programme, to further his career, in the hope that if he is successful it will eventually take him on, on a full-time basis.

Questions for discussion

1 What are the key points about workplace learning that can be drawn from this case study?

2 What are the components of the final qualification that John will achieve?

3 Why do you think that the firm would not take John on initially?

4 How will the resource centre be helpful to John?

5 What problems might John experience if the resource centre was not available or so well equipped?

Learning and development in the workplace falls into one of two categories – formal schemes, and informal, more self-managed approaches, each on the job or off the job. Both are important, and the approach taken within organisations ideally should include both components (Blundell and Murdock, 1997; Lucas, Lupton and Mathieson, 2006; Marchington and Wilkinson, 2005). Nevertheless, both to be comprehensive and to aid comprehensibility in this chapter we separate them, examining formal schemes in Part 1 and informal ones in Part 2.

1   FORMAL SCHEMES

Any learning and development scheme that forms part of the formal processes within an organisation could be considered a formal scheme, especially if there is a prescribed approach or reporting mechanism in use. Formal schemes are most commonly found in the form of training courses, coaching and mentoring schemes, as well as job rotation and shadowing. Job rotation is widely used in some countries, such as Germany and Japan, where it is used for all staff and not just for graduate recruits. Each of these methods is examined in turn below.

TRAINING COURSES

Although (for example) a college course and qualifications may well help organisations and individuals, these are often not considered to be 'workplace learning' unless the programme of learning has been specially designed to support organisational needs or goals, and is sponsored by and/or run in conjunction with the organisation itself. There are of course exceptions to this, where individuals must get or maintain a qualification or licence in order to be operational, and staff are scheduled to attend external provision of training and examination. Examples of this include, in the financial sector, the qualifications that allow an individual to give mortgage or other financial advice, and in the building industry the qualification to allow an engineer to install and repair gas appliances.

Outside the formal college and qualification context, training courses in workplace learning are usually designed and delivered with specific focus on and in the specific context of the organisation and job roles. They are generally designed to last a couple of hours, half or a full day, or several days. They are most likely to be led by a trainer or tutor, who is a subject expert, with the main purpose of passing on knowledge or skills. There are two main types of framework for these training courses – they are meeting-based or activity-based.

A meeting-based course involves some presentation from the trainer or expert, and then discussions around the subject and how it relates to practical issues in the workplace. The activity-based approach is more likely to start with a practical work-related or simulation activity that is then analysed and discussed as a practical example of some aspect of work, often then generalised to make wider workplace learning points. Each approach can be trainer- or participant-focused, and it is frequently beneficial on longer courses to use a mixture of the two approaches. The decision over which is used is often made by thinking about how far those doing the training are experienced in learning, the subject matter under consideration, and whether the training centres on knowledge, skills or behaviours. However, the organisational structure and culture can often have a significant effect on the approach chosen, because it affects participant and trainer expectations and norms (Marchington and Wilkinson, 2005). A highly autocratic and hierarchical organisation is more likely to favour and therefore use a meeting approach (since it lends itself to a 'lecture' style of training) than a 'flatter', more collegiate organisation (which is more likely to favour an experiential, facilitative approach).

Many authors (for example, Lucas et al, 2006) explore the relative merits of formal education and training. Benefits of formal training courses include the fact that the content can be designed in advance, and checked as being appropriate before delivery. It can make sure that a consistent message is delivered in a structured manner to a large number of individuals over a long period of time. Costs and length are usually known in advance and therefore the approach may be useful in those situations where many staff are involved, or consistency is very important. Planning of the programme of courses is also relatively straightforward, because demand and requirements are largely known, or possible to anticipate.

Disadvantages of training courses include the fact that they can so easily be ineffective, the people attending only because they are required to, and the content and approach to delivery being somewhat fixed and potentially inappropriate to individuals' needs. The focus can also be more on attendance than on learning. Training courses can additionally be costly for the benefits gained.

REFLECTIVE ACTIVITY

Think about an organisation you know well, and the type of formal training that takes place.

How effective is this approach?

How might it be improved?

COACHING SCHEMES

Both formal and informal coaching schemes can be very effective for workplace learning (see Chapter 15 on coaching). In a formal scheme, expert staff are formally allocated or scheduled for a period to 'buddy' one or more members of staff, to oversee their activity and help them to become more effective at specific tasks or job activities. The coach does this mainly on regular occasions (often scheduled) when the staff being coached have opportunities to discuss problems and issues, to explore areas of uncertainty or inconsistent or poor performance, or to demonstrate an activity under the guidance of the coach. The coach then offers his or her expertise to suggest ways in which the performance can be improved or changed to be more effective.

In an informal scheme, coaching relationships are encouraged but not necessarily formalised or scheduled, and staff mutually support each other on an 'as required or requested' basis. They undertake coaching activities as above, but only for the issue under consideration that gave rise to the request. Most managers in organisations have this informal role built into their job descriptions, to oversee and guide their staff to effectiveness, although managers themselves do not necessarily undertake the coaching activity personally on every occasion.

Coaching schemes have the benefit that they are seen by staff to be highly relevant to their job, with the focus on what is required to assist them to become effective or maintain effectiveness. They are often cost- and time-effective, and can be used at all levels and at any time, as well as being scheduled for regular performance monitoring, updates or enhancements. However, the coaching approach does depend on the personal skills of the coach, especially in his or her ability to build a positive relationship with the staff he/she is supporting, and assumes that those who are coaching also have the expert knowledge and skills in the first place. Without these, of course, poor practice can so easily be reinforced and spread in the organisation.

MENTORING SCHEMES

Like coaching schemes, mentoring schemes can also be formal or informal, and involve one-to-one relationships between the mentor and the member of staff being supported (sometimes called the 'mentee' or the 'protégé[e]'). The key difference between mentoring and coaching is mainly in the focus of the relationship (Lewis, 2000). Coaching largely focuses on the work tasks to be completed, and is clearly job-role-related. Mentoring tends much more to have as its focus the individual and his or her personal development and growth needs which may relate to wider issues than just the current work role. It is common, for example, for lower-level managers to get career advice by this route. Whereas coaching is often undertaken by a colleague or line manager, mentoring is usually done by a senior manager or a manager in a different department or field altogether, to enable wider perspectives to be brought into consideration. As with coaching, the effectiveness of mentoring schemes is affected by the personal skills and expertise of the mentor, and also his or her organisational influence in being able to access wider perspectives, information and contacts (Lewis, 2000).

JOB ROTATION AND JOB SHADOWING

Job rotation and job shadowing are two simple techniques that are often used formally within a section or department to give variety in the work that an individual might do, while offering an opportunity to develop a wider understanding of the department and of other job functions. Job shadowing might take the form of sitting alongside another individual to 'shadow' them by watching what they do, how and when (Mumford, 1996). Much can be learned about the other job from the individual undertaking it, although one obvious potential disadvantage is that the technique assumes that the person being watched is fully effective in the job that he or she is displaying to the visiting shadow.

Job rotation takes a similar form to the technique of secondments and attachments discussed below, except that it occurs usually internally within a section or department, and several people change job roles on a planned and sometimes regular basis.

REFLECTIVE ACTIVITY

Think about an organisation you know well.

To what extent is job rotation or job shadowing undertaken?

In what ways does job rotation/shadowing support individual development?

How might mentoring help further?

2 INFORMAL SCHEMES

Although formal schemes are still used significantly within organisations, training and development schemes are increasingly focusing upon more informal methods of workplace learning. These might include working through a series of workbooks, or electronic (eg online, CD-ROM, DVD) packages or private reading. Such self-managed schemes are occasionally provided as part of a formal development programme but are much more likely to be found as informal individual learning. The packages usually give key information on a topic and include a way of checking understanding, or in some cases formally testing knowledge or responses.

There are several benefits to such individual learning packages. One is location, because individual learning packages can be worked through in a variety of different locations, such as a normal workstation or desk, in a specially provided area or resource centre, while travelling or at home. Another is context flexibility. Individual learning packages can be used in a range of different ways, such as individually to suit specific time-scales, requirements and learning style; in small groups, with review points set along the way; in a classroom setting, with a tutor providing monitoring and support. Also, they can be provided and updated relatively quickly and delivered to large numbers of people at the same time. With informal learning and development in the workplace there are usually many more options. These can also include coaching, mentoring, self-selected and self-directed reading (which can include the packages described above), and action learning from reflection on workplace activities or projects (Lucas *et al*, 2006).

E-LEARNING PACKAGES

With the arrival of the Internet and in-house intranets, increasing use is now being made of e-learning packages (Sloman, 2007; Marchington and Wilkinson, 2005). These have a significant advantage in that they can be worked through at the individual's workstation at his or her own speed, with opportunities to go back over the work to review, refresh and summarise if wanted. Furthermore, with some packages it is possible to score or mark the work done in a way that can contribute to a final score and even to a formal qualification.

However, e-learning has several important disadvantages (Sloman and Rolph, 2003). For example, the learner has to be self-motivated. A less committed or very busy individual might not start or complete the package, or may enter into it half-heartedly. Also the work is largely unsupervised, and so tutors and trainers are less likely to be available to answer questions, clarify issues or develop themes further. This often means that learners can become 'stuck' at a given point, and give up because of the lack of easily available help. A further issue is that technology is fine when it works, but from time to time creates problems that can disturb the learning or even put a participant off completely – and of course the individual undertaking the development cannot carry on if the package, or the equipment, is for some reason unavailable.

Blended learning

The expression 'blended learning' describes a mixture of formal and informal learning, using a range of different learning media and methods such as described in this chapter. It is thought by learning professionals and participants alike to offer an effective approach, because it enables the selection of the method most appropriate to each individual aspect that has to be learned, and of a delivery method that most suits the organisation, the department, the team and the individuals concerned. The main disadvantage is that it is much more difficult to plan (needing attention to each individual and each topic) and more difficult to monitor progress across the many methods in use. It can also be more expensive, because a wider range of options might be used than would be the case if a more specific approach were to be used.

Links to appraisal

One area that is used particularly for workplace learning and development is that of a performance management (appraisal) system. Many systems exist, and some are more successful than others (see Chapter 12). However, an organisation that truly wishes to embed effective workplace learning and development into its culture and operations will need an effective appraisal system that has a forward-looking positive focus and developmental approach to performance measurement and support (Pedlar, Boydell and Burgoyne, 1991).

REFLECTIVE ACTIVITY

Think about your own organisation or one you know well.

In the organisation, is the focus more on formal or on informal leaning and development? Why is this, do you think?

What facilities are there in the organisation to support informal learning and development?

TRAINING IN CONTEXT

The WERS data (see Table 34) shows that there are some clear differences in the way in which different organisations and sectors use formal or informal learning methods. For example, the data indicate that across all organisations surveyed, only 47% of them use formal off-the-job training for the majority of their core workforce, and of those organisations that do, the larger organisations are more likely to use this approach than the smaller organisations. The WERS data also shows some clear differences in approach across the industries too, with a very marked difference in responses. Manufacturing and catering industries are shown to use relatively little off-the-job training compared to public sector and financial institutions, which are reported to use it significantly.

Table 34 Off-the-job training in British organisations

	Percentage of organisations with off-the-job training for 60% or more experienced core employees
All workplaces	47
Organisation size	
10–99 employees	35
10,000 or more employees	59
Industry	
Manufacturing	28
Hotels and restaurants	27
Financial services	77
Public sector	72

Source: Kersley *et al* (2006; p.83)

Much is therefore dependent on a number of issues, and when thinking through the range of workplace learning methods in order to make a selection, matters such as the availability of resources, the size and type of business, the internal training capability and the structure and culture of the organisation should be considered. Each of these is examined in turn below.

Firstly, how much an organisation has of significant resources to put into workplace learning will clearly affect the organisational provision. Key issues in this area are particularly the time and money to fund what might be needed, although the location and space for physical resources are also important. Examples of this include whether a learning centre can be provided, whether time off can be given to key employees to further their learning, and whether the cost and time for the design and delivery of formal workshops and courses is within acceptable parameters.

Secondly, as the WERS data has indicated, the size of the organisation can be important because a small organisation may be less likely to be able to find a high level of resource than a larger organisation. Also, a smaller organisation may not have the space (or potential use) of other supporting facilities, nor the ability to release staff for training sessions.

Thirdly, the type of business is worth considering. Some businesses operate in a highly regulated context (for example, legal services, financial services, gas and petrochemical operations). To meet the needs of the regulators and legislative requirements, formal training courses (often followed by examinations) are a requirement, and much of the learning and development initiative in these organisations is likely to have this as a focus. This might go some way to explain the bias in the WERS data for those sorts of organisations towards the use of off-the-job training. However, other businesses operate in arenas that are less regulated, if at all (for example, fashion and design, publications, performing arts). Here there might be some formal courses, but much of the learning and development may well be informal and even fully self-driven in approach (and, for that matter, not necessarily fully business-focused). Again, the infrequent use of off-the-job training in the catering and manufacturing areas reported in the WERS data may well be because of the highly skills-based nature of the work, and the fact that there may be a need for some learning to be done in a practical sense on-the-job where first-hand and live experience can be used as the basis for performance improvement.

Fourthly, whether the workplace learning is formally based or informally based, on-the-job or off-the-job, one key issue to be considered is how far the organisation has experienced and qualified training and learning facilitators on the staff or easily available. Without skilled trainers and learning facilitators, formal on- or off-the-job training programmes are less likely to be considered or possible. However, they could be outsourced or bought in if resources are available.

Fifthly, the way in which the business is organised can also play a part in how learning and development takes place. For example if the organisation is structured as a tall hierarchy (ie with many different levels of staff, the real power strongly concentrated at the higher levels, as described by, for example, Handy, 1993), then particular types of training or subject areas may only be open to those at particular levels or positions in the organisation. This might be associated with different needs at different levels, or a sense that a certain level of seniority is required before certain areas of training are appropriate (even though this judgement is often incorrect). However, in a flatter structure an organisation might be more willing to enable every individual to undertake development at any point that he/she, or the organisation, feels it to be useful.

Finally, the general style and culture of the organisation also often greatly influences the approach to learning and development (Lucas *et al*, 2006). Some organisations may well have a supportive coaching and developmental approach to the whole of their activities. In this case, there may well be a formal framework in which informal learning takes place all the time, both on-the-job and off-the-job components being brought together into a programme of learning that supports both individual and organisational goals. At the other extreme might be an organisation that is rather formal, traditional, and with the business bottom line as the whole driver of all activities. In this case there is a much higher likelihood that learning and development will only be focused on activities to meet specific business needs, and will probably only take the form of formal 'courses', and these may not be optional or available to all because selection for attendance is only based upon demonstrable business needs. In some organisations, legally appointed union learning representatives may operate, seeking to encourage employees who might have reservations about 'going back to school' (see Chapter 17 on employment relations). They may also play a role in helping to change both employees and managements towards being more open to different types of learning.

3 LEARNING WHILE WORKING

Although most aspects of workplace learning can be described as formal or informal, there are many schemes that combine these two approaches within an overall formal (and sometimes externally funded) programme. Such programmes can be for those not yet in employment, as a way of starting their career, or for those already employed who need to expand or change their role. This section looks at some of the most well-known and widely used of such programmes. It starts with induction, since this usually combines both the formal and informal, and is a process that almost all new staff come across.

INDUCTION

One key learning occasion for every employee is the induction process. Without a successful induction, not only will the new member of staff not come up to speed so quickly, it is more likely that he or she will not be so effective and may not settle well into the new job. Indeed, there is plenty of evidence that organisations that suffer from high turnover of staff do so because they do not put sufficient effort into their recruitment and selection *and induction* processes.

Ideally, induction is a process that is on-going, rather than (as many organisations seem to think) a single event (Marchington and Wilkinson, 2005). If all of the details are contained in a single event, the new member of staff is likely to become 'overloaded', and be unable to remember or take on board much of what is covered. In an ideal situation, the induction programme is spread over a number of weeks or perhaps months, and blends naturally into the organisation's learning and development programme.

APPRENTICESHIPS

The importance of this type of learning varies over different countries. In many British industries workplace learning is inbuilt, since to become fully qualified and experienced a period of apprenticeship is required (eg gas-fitters, plumbers and hairdressers). An individual is taken on by the company as an apprentice, with a specific focus on a learning and development programme that may lead to some form of qualification as well as practical experience. Many of the qualifications in the craft skills areas actually assess performance in the job as part of the qualification process. Training is given on the job by those who are actively employed in that field (undertaking real work), on the job in simulated or laboratory/workshop situations (so that skills can be practised), and in more theoretical classroom sessions. In other countries, apprenticeship and formal training is given more importance. In Germany, people are trained systematically for professions, and apprenticeship is very common even for jobs that are not usually regarded as needing one in Britain (sales, for instance).

Many apprenticeships in Britain are government-funded through, for example, Learning and Skills Councils (governed by the National LSC), and the learning and training undertaken is therefore closely monitored by government agencies as well as internally within the organisation by assessors and verifiers. These 'inspectors' will visit training centres and organisations from time to time with checklists to make sure that the training programme that has been sold to the individual and funded with government money is actually meeting the criteria that the government has set for the use of such funds.

VOCATIONAL AND COMPETENCY-BASED SCHEMES

Increasingly, British organisations are basing their performance management schemes upon competencies. Competencies define and describe the capacity actually to do something, such as change a lorry tyre. Competencies determine the key job activities, behaviours and knowledge that are required to undertake the job fully. They use descriptors to illustrate and exemplify how a performer in a specified role might show effectiveness (Favell, 2005). This inevitably leads to competencies being used for recruitment and selection for the various jobs, and to a focus upon developing the skills defined by the competencies as a main focus for learning and development activities. In some organisations and occupational areas (for example, the medical profession, airline flight crew instruction, and financial services) occupational competence is a requirement to get the licences that are legally required for operations in that arena. The whole area of apprenticeships (see above) also is focused around learning and development towards vocational and occupational competence.

In Britain, most occupational areas have National Standards, which detail the competencies needed for effectiveness in that arena. They are put together by standard-setting bodies (currently known as Sector Skills Councils – but from time to time names and organisations change).These bodies hold the responsibility for determining the National Standards in that occupational arena, and for confirming with, for example, the Qualifications and Curriculum Authority (QCA) their suitability for granting of awards, such as an NVQ (a National Vocational Qualification) in that subject.

PLACEMENTS, SECONDMENTS AND ATTACHMENTS

Many organisations, especially the larger ones, use placements, secondments and attachments as a key method of development for their staff. Although we have used three expressions here, they are all really one mechanism – that by which an individual is temporarily placed in (seconded or attached to) a department or team that does not do his or her usual work, sometimes in a very different discipline. The main idea is to enable the individual concerned to attain an insight into this particular new discipline and working arrangement, and into the wider issues and perspectives that this will bring to his or her experience. Secondments are often for three, six, nine or 12 months, according to how long the individual can be spared from his or her permanent job, and for how long the experience has to continue in order to achieve the optimum development aimed at.

Clearly, there are a range of important implications for this type of development activity. The work in the placed/seconded employees' own job role has to be covered in their absence, and this has to be accounted for as part of the development plan. What often happens is that someone else comes to the department on attachment/secondment, or perhaps an agency temp fills in.

Another consideration is how quickly the individual will be fully up to speed in the job he or she is now temporarily doing, and how any gaps will be covered during his/her development. Gaps are often covered by a permanent member of staff in that department doing work of a higher level than usual, as a way of developing them also, as well by giving them some responsibilities for things that they are fully capable of but normally do not have the opportunity to do. Monitoring the work during the attachment, to make sure that the incoming individual is progressing, and that the work is being done to a good standard, is also something that must be considered, to ensure that the secondment is effective. This is also likely to involve the question of how the individual on the attachment/secondment is to be trained in those areas where it is needed. Finally, any costs that might be involved, including the possible cost of temporary accommodation for the individual concerned, should also be taken into account during the planning stages. Good examples of this type of workplace learning and development are apprenticeships (see above) in which an apprentice might be assigned to different sections during a programme, and a graduate programme (see below) in which those on the programme might be rotated through a number of departments.

GRADUATE PROGRAMMES

Many larger organisations have graduate programmes so that each year they can take promising people into the organisation and train them in the ways of the business in readiness for a permanent position either at the end of the programme or as vacancies arise (Mumford, 1996). A programme usually involves a series of study days, both business- and management-focused, and placements in various sections of the organisation in real positions with real work to do, but under close guidance or a coach or mentor. Those on the programme are rotated through a range of areas to ensure that a broad experience is obtained of the business, but also to try to see if any area or type of work particularly suits the individual's skills and interests. Often a resource centre is available for further individual study, or open learning programmes carried out perhaps to obtain an appropriate qualification. Graduate programmes typically last one or two years, by which time the individual is thought suitable for permanent employment (or decides that the business is not for him or her and moves on).

RESOURCE AND LEARNING CENTRES

Organisations that are serious about the development of their staff often provide appropriate resources in support. In larger organisations this may take the form of a resource centre – a physical location that might resemble a small library – where these resources can be used or borrowed. A fully equipped resource centre might have available such things as books, magazines and journals, videos and DVDs, details of courses and programmes of study (both in-house and external), computers with Internet access for research or investigation, access to in-house intranet resources and information, and e-learning packages. The resources provided usually have a work focus but often also include other high-interest topics (for example, foreign-language-learning packages). In the largest of organisations there may even be a resident tutor or resource manager present to provide coaching and learning support, although with the arrival of e-learning this is becoming rarer in Britain.

FUNDING AND INSPECTION

One key aspect of workplace learning and development is that often it may be funded, part-funded or supported in some way by government funding bodies (for example, the Learning and Skills Councils). Also, where vocationally based qualifications are offered, awarding bodies have an interest in what takes place. Many work-based schemes are therefore subject to external inspection from time to time to ensure that the learning and development being provided is complete and to the standard required to meet the qualification of funding contract, and this is common in all European countries. In Britain, these Inspections or External Verification Visits are undertaken by government or awarding body inspection teams, generally working to the remit of QCA/SQA or QIA (the government bodies responsible for overseeing qualifications and quality of provision). Such an Inspection samples a range of things – for example, the work of all tutors, assessors and the learning environment, together with the administrative infrastructure of the organisation in respect of its training and development activity – to ensure that quality standards are being met, and therefore that government funds are being used appropriately.

REFLECTIVE ACTIVITY

Think about an organisation you know well.

Which training and development methods are used most frequently in the organisation? Why is it that they are used most frequently?

What issues promote or inhibit the selection of the methods in use?

Which other methods offer some advantages?

KEY ISSUES IN WORKPLACE LEARNING

We now pull together ten key points about workplace learning raised in this chapter:

- Within organisations, training, learning and development opportunities can take many forms and be very wide in approach and content.

- There are no real rules or boundaries to limit what is offered and how it takes place, so long as the organisation feels it is effective in achieving what is required, and the activity meets any legal requirements.

- The key must always be what it is that should be learned, and exactly how this can be best done bearing in mind the context, the nature of the work, the people involved, and the cost in both time and money.

- Getting the best fit between the form of training, the organisation and the individual is often a challenge, and each organisation should check the effectiveness of initiatives to ensure that the workforce is as skilled and knowledgeable as possible at all times in a way that disturbs the workflow the mimimum amount for maximum organisational achievement.

- Weak induction programmes can often prompt new staff to leave prematurely. An effective induction is a programme of study that is on-going and deals with key issues over a period of time, that slowly merges and leads naturally into the organisation's mainstream development programme.

- The exact nature of workplace learning and development might be affected by funding and associated inspection regimes that are specific requirements of a programme that is funded.

- Workplace learning and development is often linked to a robust and well-operating appraisal or performance management scheme. This enables each development activity to be planned and monitored as a natural part of everyday performance.

- The extent to which learners have access to resources in the form of materials and personal learning support often determines the effectiveness of the learning.

- Workplace learning can be associated with a wide range of qualifications, or be simply for the benefit of the organisation, the team and the individual.

- Learning benefits people and organisations. However, it may be more difficult to access in a smaller organisation or department.

Perhaps there are other key points that you would like to note for yourself.

Make an initial reading of the case study to gain an overview of the situation, and then read the questions that you will need to address. Now read the case study again, making notes of issues and facts that will help you in your analysis and responses to the questions. Remember to 'read between the lines' as well as picking out the obvious points, and also to consider what is not said as well as what is presented here.

MAIN CASE STUDY

The senior managers of a large financial institution recognise the importance of training and development for their staff. They have a clear policy that not only should staff be trained and developed to meet the licensing and legislative requirements that apply to their area of business, but that staff should also be encouraged and enabled to engage in other appropriate development activities. The middle managers, who largely look after staff performance and development, all welcome this policy. They have made it clear to all of their staff that development opportunities are available and can be applied for at any time. Many individual managers have therefore put together a list of courses that they think might be of interest to their staff, and make these available to staff so that individual members of staff can pick-and-mix the courses that they feel they would like to attend. There is no restriction on the number of courses that are allowed for each staff member, and it is up to each middle manager whether to allow attendance. Common practice is that staff just mention to the manager what they would like to do, and then a secretary books the place. The staff member then receives the letter from the training provider inviting him or her to the event, which he or she then attends when the due date arrives.

The staff appraisal system is good in that the process described in organisational paperwork is good practice, but in reality it does not happen, because managers do not have time and have not been properly trained. When an appraisal interview does take place, it is usually short, and development needs tend to be addressed at the appraisal interview with the question 'What do you want to do this year?', and then arrangements made after listing the responses. Costs have never been a barrier because money is said to be freely available for developmental purposes.

When staff are to attend a course, they are supposed to let their line manager know about their impending absence, but this does not always happen. Neither does the manager hold any pre- or post-attendance discussions, nor does the organisation have any mechanism for evaluating the effectiveness of any course (or, for that matter, any mechanism for checking that the member of staff actually attended). Some courses are held in-house for those areas of specialism where there is plenty of expertise, but these do not seem to be very effective. One employee recently missed half a day of a two-day course – and no one even noticed.

Some courses are particularly important to the organisation, especially those that re-license staff to enable them to operate in their specific financial area. However, staff are responsible for their own updates and re-licensing – the organisation does not keep records of when events are due or attended for any except the most essential staff. Rumour has it that many update courses are boring and inessential, so that it is not actually clear whether staff are or are not attending, and therefore may or may not be fully up to date.

Following a merger with a similar but slightly smaller concern, new staff are now to be incorporated into the wider organisation. In the smaller firm, training and development was of a very focused nature and a very high standard, as it had to be to keep the small firm competitive. The larger firm is now faced with some pressing issues. The recently arrived staff appear to be expecting detailed development discussions prior to training course attendance, and a debrief of what was learned following the course. They are also complaining about the appraisal system that appears to be blocking what they call proper discussion about their future, and the development needs that they have in order to position themselves to be ready when promotion opportunities arise. They have noted that training appears only to be courses, and are questioning this approach.

In the meantime, shareholders have begun to ask questions about the size of the training budget when compared to the size of the dividend budget that was recently set. Managers in the wider organisation, feeling suddenly under the spotlight, are now said to be unhappy with what they see as challenges to their way of doing things by both these newcomers and the shareholders. A further complication is that new legislation requires all of the professionals in one of the major fields of operation to be retrained and tested to ensure that they are advising customers in an appropriate way.

As a result of these growing challenges, the new bigger organisation has appointed a Head of Learning and Development to oversee the whole area of staff development, with the remit to obtain an overview of the key issues that have to be tackled, and to implement the most effective and cost-effective development scheme possible.

Your task

Imagine you are the new Head of Learning and Development.

1   Make a list of the issues that you should consider tackling.

2   Put that list in priority order, so that urgent business needs can be addressed first.

3   Consider how you might address the issues on your list.

4   Who else should be involved? Why them?

5   How will you know that the development activities are successful?

EXPLORE FURTHER

CIPD (2006) *Latest Trends in Learning, Training and Development*. London, CIPD
Excellent summary of the latest trends in workplace learning.

HARRISON, R. (2005) *Learning and Development*, 4th edition. London, CIPD
Textbook that provides a more extensive introduction to the concepts of workplace learning.

CHAPTER 15

Understanding coaching

Caroline Horner *and* Paul Ellis

INTRODUCTION

This chapter aims to help readers become more knowledgeable about coaching and its application within organisations.

LEARNING OUTCOMES

By the end of this chapter readers should be able to:

- explain what coaching is and is not
- describe the role of HR in putting in place coaching for an organisation
- consider some of the challenges faced.

This chapter is structured in two parts. Part 1 begins with the starter case study which, like the other case studies in this book, is based on a real-life situation. We then go on to look at the definition of coaching, and how coaching is distinctive. We also outline what coaching is used for and provide examples of when to use and when not to use it. Part 2 examines the three principal approaches to delivering coaching in the workplace. Throughout Part 2 the reader is asked to consider how to use the various coaching interventions, what the issues and challenges of each approach are, and the role of the HR professional in applying coaching within organisations.

The chapter concludes with the main case study.

Reference sources named within the chapter may be looked up in the *References and further reading* section at the end of the book.

Despite a run of good years, a large international financial services organisation was subject to a hostile takeover bid. The organisation successfully prevented the bid but discovered through the process that its leadership profile was perceived to be old-fashioned by being too rigid and instructional. An assessment of senior leaders across the organisation confirmed this. The CEO understood that the people issues had to be resolved if business results were going to be sustained in the future. A preliminary study showed that leadership development activities were being undertaken on an ad hoc basis and were evidently having limited impact. Coaches were being hired without reference to any organisational aims, in an unregulated coaching market that had no professional barriers to entry and no agreed measures for quality control. At the same time, the company wanted to fast-track the careers of minorities in the business and actively follow a strategy of diversity and inclusiveness.

Recognising the need to invest in its employees to resolve the problems it faced, the organisation decided to invest in the development of a leadership centre, including the development and implementation of a comprehensive coaching and mentoring framework to meet the needs of all its business units. Coaching was thought to be the most suitable method to ensure that new behaviours and learning from leadership development programmes were effectively carried through back in the workplace.

The company introduced a series of coaching interventions. Managers were encouraged to use and rewarded for using a coaching approach to help staff discover solutions for themselves, through posing powerful questions and providing 'in-the-moment' feedback. A peer-coaching network was started in addition to the existing mentoring scheme to assist new entrants to the organisation to pick up key skills and organisational processes. Team coaching was offered to large project teams, and external group process facilitators were employed to support teams to leverage the diversity of their teams to improve the quality and effectiveness of project work. Internal coaches were used to support individuals participating in leadership development programmes to effectively translate their learning into their day-to-day work as well as to provide a safe environment to explore their own leadership style and behaviours and to work at improving these behaviours. A group of external coaches was brought together through a rigorous assessment process to support senior leaders in a variety of challenges ranging from individual development areas to transition (taking on a significantly bigger role or project, moving to another country, managing a change programme for the organisation), and for a few executives to provide a safe supportive space in which to reflect and develop innovative thinking during an intense period of transition.

Coaching was the process that pulled multiple initiatives together across the organisation to shift old-style leadership behaviours and embed new skills and behaviours. There were many other elements – for example, the reward system and other organisation development initiatives – that supported the culture change. However, coaching was a key part of the mix, and today the organisation is beginning to be seen as a modern, innovative organisation that is a market leader and an attractive employer.

Questions for discussion

1 Why do organisations use coaching more frequently for the purposes described in the case study?

2 With reference to the case study, what are the main challenges of introducing coaching in an organisation?

1 UNDERSTANDING THE FUNDAMENTALS OF COACHING

DRIVING FORCES BEHIND COACHING

An increasing number of organisations are recognising the value of using coaching to support individuals to achieve sustained improvements in personal and organisational performance. In the CIPD learning and development survey 2006, eight out of ten respondents reported that they used coaching in their organisations (CIPD, 2007).

The increase has been driven by a number of organisational and societal trends, such as the globalisation of business and a fiercely competitive marketplace which experiences rapid and constant change (de Geus and Senge, 1997). Organisations have reacted by creating flatter, leaner structures that can respond more quickly to developments. However, these structures – along with increasing reliance on technology for business functions – mean that managers find it hard to know those who report directly to them, and therefore there are fewer opportunities to build a relationship between employees. Also, managers are often promoted into senior positions without the opportunity to develop their leadership skills over a series of roles. At the same time there is a growing recognition of the costs associated with executives who fail (Greco, 2001). Organisations now recognise the benefits of coaching to help key employees in developing appropriate leadership skills and behaviours.

Coaching is no longer seen as a remedial intervention triggered only when there is a problem. Leaders are expected to be challenged with tasks that they have never undertaken before or that may be entirely new to the organisation. Many coaching assignments are now initiated entirely to help the client's overall development as a leader.

WHAT EXACTLY DO WE MEAN BY COACHING?

Coaching draws on a variety of fields including psychology, leadership, organisational development, counselling and therapy; it is a vast topic. However, despite the fact that coaching is increasingly popular, there remains some confusion over what exactly coaching is and how it differs from other helping interventions such as mentoring and counselling (Kampa-Kokesch and Anderson, 2001; Kilburg, 1996).

The Chartered Institute of Personnel and Development (Jarvis, 2004; p.19) defines coaching as:

> Developing a person's skills and knowledge so that their job performance improves, hopefully leading to the achievement of organisational objectives. It targets high performance and improvement at work, although it may also have an impact on an individual's private life. It usually lasts for a short period and focuses on specific skills and goals.

Although there is no common definition, most coaching professionals agree on the following characteristics of coaching:

- It is frequently a one-to-one intervention in which the recipient of the coaching is referred to as the client (or coachee).

- The main purpose of coaching is individual learning and the expectation is that through this learning the current and future performance of the individual (and therefore team and organisational performance) will be improved; coaching is not about addressing the past.

- The client sets the agenda for the coaching and the role of the coach is to help the client in working through the issue, not to give advice or direct what the client should or should not do. That is, coaching is a non-directive intervention by which clients are helped to develop awareness and take responsibility for their own development.

- The client is seen as resourceful and is not engaging in coaching to be 'fixed' but rather supported to resolve his or her own issues.

- The coaching relationship is one of partnership in which coach and client are equals.

- The focus of coaching is to empower the client to manage his or her own learning and not to build dependency on the coach.

- It is a skilled activity which draws on skills such as active listening, effective questioning and feedback.

- Coaching is frequently time-limited and usually agreed for a specific length of time.

- The individual who receives coaching is psychologically healthy; he/she requires no clinical intervention.

REFLECTIVE ACTIVITY

Is there anything missing from this list of bullet points that you might have expected to see?

In the light of the CIPD definition above, how is coaching different from mentoring and counselling?

Clarity of understanding is important if the HR professional is to make sure that the individual and organisation use the right type of intervention, and it is useful to establish how coaching differs from the other helping disciplines.

The term 'mentoring' is often used interchangeably with 'coaching'. However, traditionally, mentoring is a relationship with someone who is older, more senior and experienced than the mentee. A mentor is also someone who transfers knowledge and gives advice often to those who are new to a role or the organisation. The mentoring relationship can extend over a long period, even years, and usually focuses on the professional and career development of the mentee. Organisations often have a formal mentoring programme whereby individuals who meet certain criteria – such as new entrants, employees with high potential and minority groups – are offered a mentor to help their development; such an arrangement is usually managed by HR departments (Clutterbuck, 2001; Garvey, 2004).

The difference between coaching and *counselling* is also not always clear. For the purposes of the HR professional, the key distinction to be drawn is that coaching is always for people who are psychologically well, but counselling may be used for both psychologically well and unwell people.

WHAT IS COACHING USED FOR?

One way to categorise the main ways in which coaching can be used in organisations is described by the following typology from Witherspoon and White (2004), who distinguished between coaching for skills, coaching for performance, coaching for development, and coaching for the executive agenda.

Coaching for skills is about helping the client to get knowledge and skills which are relevant to the individual's current role or work. The need for this coaching is often unambiguous, the goals being specific and clear. Such coaching is frequently delivered by peers, technical specialists or by the individual's line manager. This form of coaching is not usually outsourced to external coaches because of the need to apply a specific skill within a specific organisational context: it often includes more content because it recognises the stage of development of the client/coachee. Coaches may be more directional with those early in their development of the skill-sharing ideas, offering suggestions and where necessary providing advice. For some this level of coaching seems more like mentoring or one-to-one instruction.

Coaching for performance usually focuses on helping an individual to improve his or her performance in a current role. This coaching is normally the responsibility of the individual's line manager who works with the individual on a day-to-day basis and is ideally placed to give 'in-the-moment' feedback and ask questions that will help the individual to consider alternatives for delivering immediate results.

Coaching for development is focused on the future direction and development of an individual as he or she prepares for a new role or new responsibilities. The responsibility for development of direct reports is often that of the individuals' line manager. However, therein lies a conflict of interest because in times of pressure the line manager may focus on performance and results, and the time available to support individuals with development is limited. The focus is on 'stretch' learning goals and possibly behavioural change. Depending on the results that are targeted and the organisational culture, this coaching can be delivered by internal or external coaches. HR professionals must consider their role in the 'management' of the learning goals in this environment and the balance between controlling the coaching process to ensure consistency and quality against trusting individuals to manage their own development, and so empower them through coaching.

Coaching for the executive agenda is offered to support senior-level individuals usually with a wide variety of concerns. Leadership, especially at senior executive levels, can be an isolated role and coaching often offers a safe and confidential place in which individuals can be supported to explore new ideas, take time to reflect and be encouraged. This level of coaching is almost exclusively delivered by external coaches who are recognised to have the credibility required by the client population and also who maintain a level of confidentiality that should relieve concerns about privacy. HR professionals are often involved in the selection and assessment of coaches to work at this level. HR will also often provide a matching process to ensure an appropriate fit between coach and executive. After an effective relationship is established, the role of HR lessens and the process is frequently self-managed by the client. These interventions are often longer-term – ie lasting a year or more – and sessions may be ad hoc, set up in relation to specific client needs.

REFLECTIVE ACTIVITY

What would you use coaching for in an organisation?

What learning interventions might you use instead of coaching?

WHEN WOULD YOU USE COACHING?

Coaching is one of a range of interventions that organisations can use to meet identified learning and development needs. Deciding whether coaching is an appropriate intervention is a key responsibility of the HR professional. The benefits of a formal coaching intervention from an internal or external coach must be considered alongside other possibilities such as training courses, stretch assignments, mentoring or on-the-job training. It will also be important for the HR professional to work alongside the line manager of the individual in question so as not to displace the responsibility for day-to-day performance from the line manager. Should line managers be struggling with coaching people who report directly to them, HR professionals may have to consider training line managers to help them develop their own coaching skills, as opposed to removing the responsibility for managers to effectively coach their team members by getting help from outside.

Coaching for development is frequently offered together with other learning interventions such as training courses or leadership development programmes (see Chapter 14). This sort of coaching is often initiated with some assessments (such as 360-degree feedback or psychometrics) to raise awareness in individuals of their development areas and to draft an individual learning plan. The coaching then works alongside the learning plan, encouraging individuals to use the programme and opportunities in their work environment to experiment with new behaviours. Coaching can also be offered as a stand-alone intervention to support particular development needs – for example, individuals who are undertaking large projects and organisation change initiatives, and recently recruited or promoted individuals who may benefit from coaching to fast-track them in their new role. This ad hoc coaching is frequently organised through HR professionals, and thus it is important for the HR professional to understand the variety of purposes for coaching and have access to coaches who are specialised in delivering particular outcomes.

When NOT to use a coach

Coaching is not a panacea and there are situations which need a different intervention. Before engaging a coach, it is the responsibility of an HR professional to determine on behalf of individuals whether coaching is the appropriate intervention (Lee and Valerio, 2005). Common examples of where coaching may not be appropriate include:

- The individual is told to have a coach when he/she does not want coaching.

- Coaching is offered to an individual who has already been identified as no longer required in the organisation.

- The issue is more systemic in nature and outside the individual's control – this is where an organisational development intervention is required.

- The coachee has significant personal and emotional problems for which a different intervention may be more appropriate – for example, substance abuse, bereavement, marital breakdown, conflict resolution, etc.

- Specific advice or knowledge is required – a consultant may be more appropriate.

2 COACHING INTERVENTIONS AND THE ROLE OF HR

In recent CIPD research, Clutterbuck and Megginson (2005; p.19) describe a coaching culture as one in which

> coaching is the predominant style of managing and working together and where commitment to improving the organisation is embedded in a parallel commitment to improve the people.

Some 93% of respondents of the CIPD learning and development survey 2006 who then used coaching considered a coaching culture to be 'very important' or 'important' to the success of their organisation, and 72% identified improving individual and business performance as the core objective for developing a coaching culture.

There are a variety of activities that can be used to develop such a culture, and in this section we aim to explore three main approaches: the use of external coaches, the use of internal coaching, and the development of coaching skills in line managers. A core part of an HR professional's role is to decide the range of activities required for the specific organisation to meet its unique challenges. In the CIPD learning and development survey 2006, 47% said they were using training to develop coaching skills in line managers, whereas 18% said they were providing coaching through a network of internal and external coaches, and 35% said they were combining both of these approaches. These methods are examined in turn below.

EXTERNAL COACHING

An external coach is a professional who specialises in coaching and is separate from the purchasing organisation. External coaches frequently come to coaching after a career in business, psychology or counselling. Many have formal qualifications in coaching and related areas. External coaches may be dedicated full-time to coaching or have a portfolio career where they also offer services such as facilitation and consulting. External coaches are frequently reserved for senior-level leaders and executives because they are expensive. External coaches have a wide range of purposes for their coaching, and it is important for HR professionals to understand the specific niche of each external coach working in their organisation to effectively match an appropriate coach for the client's 'presenting issue' (a 'presenting issue' is what the client at first thinks the issue is). External coaches can be used for stand-alone interventions or to support leadership development and other programmatic interventions. HR professionals must consider what type of coaching they need and then find coaches who are informed by an appropriate philosophy and use an appropriate approach, and who can demonstrate their experience in delivering that type of intervention.

What are the advantages of using an external coach?

For senior-level clients, external coaches are often perceived as more 'credible' than internal coaches. This is because they are external to the organisation rather than because they necessarily have more coaching skills and experience than internal people. It may also be that external coaches offer clients a degree of confidentiality which a coach within the organisation may not be demonstrably able to offer.

The purpose of coaching for an individual at this level of the organisation often requires a shift in behaviours and perspectives to ensure a step-change in his or her own performance and in that of the organisation – so using external coaches can be helpful because they offer clients a fresh way of looking at existing issues which coaches and other colleagues within the organisational system may not see.

The challenge of using external coaching services

For the HR professional there are a number of challenges in using external coaching services. In particular, who is the client when the organisation pays for the coaching? It is common practice for coaches to treat what is discussed with the coachee as confidential, a model taken from the therapy professions. Yet this poses a conflict for a commercial organisation whose responsibility is to its shareholders. How does HR demonstrate value from procuring coaching? How should a coach employed by the company respond when a member of staff wants to be coached on leaving the company? And what of the coaches' ethical duty when they become privy to internal information which might, for example, be useful for insider trading (Peltier, 2001)?

To avoid potential problems and set up an ethical framework for coaching to take place that respects the needs of all parties involved, the initial agreement which outlines the contractual responsibilities and expectations is critical for ensuring a clear understanding for all those involved. The nature of coaching means that it is difficult to foresee every eventuality, in which case openness between the coach and client, and direct discussions about potential problem issues as they arise, are a useful guideline (Peltier, 2001; Lee and Valerio, 2005).

REFLECTIVE ACTIVITY

Should organisations dictate what employees focus on in coaching?

Selecting external coaches

Choosing an external coach who is fit for the purpose is an important task for the HR professional. A coach often works over a long period of time with key individuals in an organisation. In these relationships clients may talk about extremely sensitive and important issues for them and the organisation, and coaches are thus potentially in a very powerful position in which they can influence the behaviours, attitudes and decisions of the client and ultimately the organisation. Yet the coaching industry is currently unregulated. There are no barriers to entry for new coaches into the marketplace – anyone can become a coach. The early years of the twenty-first century saw a massive growth in the number of people offering coaching services, many with only a simple understanding of a coaching process, and often without any psychologically informed knowledge (Berglas, 2002; Freas, 2004). Who you choose as a coach is therefore very important: selecting a coach who is not appropriately skilled could harm your employees.

To develop the expertise to be able to choose the right coach, HR professionals must understand coaching and the organisational imperatives for using it. This can involve training in coaching techniques, networking with the coaching industry, attending conferences – and receiving coaching. Before you begin selecting coaches, establish what it is you are trying to achieve for your corporate clients, because that will often have a direct influence on the type of coach that you want. When you begin the selection, there can be a temptation to evaluate coaching companies, but best practice is to look at each individual coach. Critical areas to consider in assessing coaches' suitability include: the experience of the coaches, the level of seniority and the particular organisations, their coaching style, their supervisory arrangements, whether they practise continued professional development, and whether references are available.

Some organisations use a formal selection process to make sure they have coaches that are the correct 'fit' for their organisation and meet the standards they have set for coaches at that level (Horner and Dolny, 2006). The selection process also provides information to support the effective matching of coach to coachee. Such selection processes are time-consuming and costly and are usually undertaken only by larger organisations. However, given the variety of coaching styles (de Haan, 2005), approaches and backgrounds, an effective selection process ensures that you have access to a diverse group of coaches who meet the organisation's criteria for coaching at the level for which they are being recruited, and who share the philosophy of coaching and learning within your organisation. Where demand is sufficiently high, some organisations are now establishing a specific HR function as 'head of coaching' (Stern, 2007).

Supervision

Supervision is where a coach has regular structured opportunities to reflect with a more experienced coach or group of coaches to help him or her understand how he/she is working with his/her clients. The purpose of supervision is first to protect the clients, in that it provides the coach with a better understanding of the impact of his/her work and enhances the coach's self-awareness. These opportunities also help coaches to continuously develop their skills and provide coaches with support. Supervision can be an important quality-assurance activity for organisations as well as a useful source of learning for the organisation. In the light of its importance, the absence of regular supervision for internal or external coaches is a concern; participation in supervision is therefore often considered a prerequisite for employment of the coach. Recent research by the CIPD found that despite a dramatic growth in the use of coaching in organisations in recent years, very few firms are using supervision to support their coaches and to get the best value from their coaching services. Less than half (44%) of coaches say they are receiving regular supervision, and less than a quarter (23%) of organisations who use coaching are providing coaching supervision. Nevertheless, the picture has improved significantly in recent years, some 58% of those coaches who receive supervision having begun the process in the last two years (Hawkins and Schwenk, 2006).

REFLECTIVE ACTIVITY

How would you organise a selection process for external coaches?

How might you get insights from external coaches about the organisation without impinging on the confidentiality agreements they have with their individual clients?

INTERNAL COACHING

Given the cost of external coaching and the demand for this intervention, organisations are starting to develop internal coaches. Internal coaching is the same as external coaching with the obvious difference that the internal coach is a fellow-employee of the organisation. One definition (Frisch, 2001; p.242) is:

Internal coaching is a one-on-one developmental intervention supported by the organisation and provided by a colleague of those coached, who is trusted to shape and deliver a programme yielding individual professional growth.

Internal coaches tend to be outside the line management chain to differentiate from manager coaching on the job and avoid potential conflicts of interest.

There are many benefits in using internal coaches. An internal coaching service is likely to be more cost-effective than paying external coach fees. Being more affordable means that the coaching can be made more accessible across the organisation. Internal coaches know the organisational context, the culture and power relationships. They are more easily contactable and also have opportunities to observe the coachee and bring those observations into the coaching intervention (de Haan, 2005).

There are, however, some challenges in using internal coaching effectively. The main concern is about confidentiality and potential conflict of interests that arise in internal coaching, because the internal coach does not enjoy the same separation from the organisation as the external coach. Clear contracting between internal coaches and the client can address those concerns. Internal coaching requires organisational support to arrange training at a suitable level; to manage contracting and coaching relationships; to arrange supervision; to maintain continued professional development for the internal coaches; and to negotiate with management to allow the internal coaches to be used. The development of an internal coaching pool is therefore a significant investment. However, as well as the direct benefits of internal coaches, such a programme also provides evidence of the commitment to working towards a 'learning organisation' (Senge, 1990). Organisations that embrace internal coaching help model behaviours that individual managers have to adopt to enable cultural change.

REFLECTIVE ACTIVITY

What are the strengths and the limitations of using internal coaches?

What are the challenges for HR in managing a team of internal coaches?

COACHING SKILLS FOR LEADERS AND MANAGERS

The changing face of organisations has seen an increase in the need for a coaching culture in organisations by which managers and leaders adopt a different style of leadership. This is frequently because rapid change makes it difficult for managers to keep abreast of technical detail and they are thus all too frequently managing staff whose work they know too little about and so are unable to advise on technical aspects of the role. The use of coaching techniques is more useful in supporting leaders to deliver through others, rather than the old-style instructional 'Do as the boss says' approach. Although organisations have been slow to develop capacity among their leaders, this is changing as demand for leaders to deliver results through others and actively develop staff increases (Clutterbuck and Megginson, 2005). Training courses to build coaching skills in leaders are focused on supporting leaders to change from a leadership style which is directive (solving staff's problems for them) to a non-directive (helping staff to solve their own problems) approach. To reinforce this change, core coaching skills and techniques – for example, active listening, building rapport, open questions and effective feedback – are taught.

Whereas a coaching style may require a greater investment of time and effort on the part of the manager, the staff feel empowered because the manager does not seek to direct them but, by coaching, encourages them to solve their own issues. In the longer term staff become more productive, because a coaching approach encourages personal responsibility and promotes staff learning. This approach is also perceived as more attractive for a modern workforce because it recognises the independence and individuality of the employee.

The role for HR is to ensure that the managers have the appropriate skills to use coaching techniques in their daily work. HR should additionally be responsible for evaluating and choosing the training course and measuring any impact in such areas as organisational culture. It is also important to ensure that managers do not overstep the boundaries of their capabilities and start coaching at a level beyond their training. Explaining the purpose, approach and limits of the coaching skills provided is a useful way for the wider workforce to understand what it is their managers are trying to do, and why.

REFLECTIVE ACTIVITY

What is required to ensure the successful implementation of a programme to teach and/or improve coaching skills for managers?

How might you ensure that managers develop their coaching skills and actively use them with the people who report directly to them?

THE CENTRAL ROLE OF HR IN COACHING

Coaching's widespread popularity is a relatively recent phenomenon, and there is still considerable misunderstanding about what coaching is and how best to use it to be most effective. The lack of established standards, professional bodies and qualifications frameworks means that using coaching effectively is usually the responsibility of the HR department.

The role of the HR professional is critical to ensuring that coaching is used appropriately and that all the stakeholders involved understand, and are able to fulfil, their roles. HR professionals must understand the different types of coaching and know when it is the right intervention in preference to other learning and development options. They must understand how to select appropriately qualified coaches and then match them to both the organisational culture and the needs of the individuals. Finally, HR professionals are often responsible for setting up coaching contracts, ensuring that there are some means of quality control, and developing a way of evaluating the effectiveness of the coaching activities.

KEY ISSUES: COACHING

We now pull together ten key points about coaching raised in this chapter:

- Coaching draws on a variety of fields including, psychology, leadership, organisational development, counselling and therapy.

- There is no single definition of coaching, but most professionals would agree that its core purpose is individual learning that will contribute to the current and future performance of the individual – and therefore team and organisational performance. Coaching is not about addressing the past.

- Coaching is a skilled activity which relies on skills such as active listening, effective questioning and feedback. It is usually non-directional: the coach helps clients to find their answers to their issues, thus empowering the clients to be self-directed in their approach to performance and development.

- Coaching is normally time-limited.

- Organisational and societal trends have seen organisations increasingly use coaching techniques as a style of leadership and management to support

- their staff development, and to achieve better performance and enhanced self-direction.

- Although one-to-one coaching is mostly used by senior management because of the costs involved in its provision, it can be successfully used at all levels in an organisation.

- The three ways of implementing coaching are: external coaching, internal coaching, and the use of coaching skills by managers as part of day-to-day work conversations.

- Coaching can be used to address a number of issues, such as skills, performance, development, or for the client's own agenda.

- The role of HR is vital to ensuring that coaching is used appropriately and that all stakeholders involved understand and are able to fulfil their roles.

- HR professionals must understand the different types of coaching and know when it is the right intervention in preference to other learning and development options.

Perhaps there are other key points that you would like to note for yourself.

The main case study in this chapter now follows.

Make an initial reading of the case study to gain an overview of the situation, and then read the questions that you will need to address. Now read the case study again, making notes of issues and facts that will help you in your analysis and responses to the questions. Remember to 'read between the lines' as well as picking out the obvious points, and also to consider what is not said as well as what is presented here.

The Great Energy Business (GEB) is a large energy generation and supply company with a diverse and international workforce. Its leaders need a wide array of skills, and coaching is regarded as key in helping its leaders to deliver the highest levels of performance. Over the last few years the GEB has created a team of internal coaches to work with leaders across the business. It now has 50 trained coaches available. The GEB has used external executive coaches for a number of years with its board-level and directorate-level leaders, with some success. External coaching is a popular learning intervention, but seen across the business as a privilege for the executive community.

Having initially grown rapidly, the business has experienced below-market growth for a number of years. New companies have entered the market, competition for trained personnel is fierce, and new environmental regulation means that the industry is becoming a more challenging market to operate in. The arrival of a new CEO has led to a capability review of the organisation's management at all levels. This review has established that the old-fashioned directive style of leadership is unpopular with the workforce and leaders are perceived as unhelpful and unsupportive of employees. The cost implications of offering external coaches to all of the management team are far too high, so the head of HR has decided to create a pool of internal coaches to support a new leadership programme aimed at changing the leadership style and culture in GEB.

Coaching is viewed as essential because it offers a personal intervention which can be tailored to the requirements of the leader. The long-term nature of the coaching relationship, stretching over several months, also makes it an attractive method of learning because it is seen as having a greater chance of embedding new leadership styles and

behaviours. Because coaching focuses on future performance, it is perceived as sending out a positive message that the business is not going to dwell on the past but seek to move forward.

The challenge for the head of HR is to find people capable of performing as internal coaches. People with a sound understanding of the business, experience in the dynamics of change and a well-developed understanding of people are needed. Initially, the HR department, using its knowledge of the workforce, approached people who had a known interest in and passion for improving the organisation; this was then followed with a recruitment campaign which advertised the benefits for personal development in becoming a coach and asked for volunteers to become internal coaches

Selection of appropriate candidates was regarded as a crucial part of the programme. The HR department ran a selection and assessment process to screen out those people who did not demonstrate the potential to coach. The GEB used an external consultancy to help the department develop its own set of competencies to describe the behaviours of a trainee coach and meet the organisational requirements. Applicants had to have the support of their line managers because their role of internal coach was to be in addition to their normal duties. Applicants were asked to provide a presentation on what they understood about coaching and how they thought it could be applied within the organisation. This was followed by a criteria-based interview. Those who passed the assessment were offered a place on a training course.

Initially, a new programme started every eight weeks in order to quickly grow the pool of coaches; today, it runs once a year to maintain the pool. The course aims to equip GEB's internal coaches with the knowledge, skills and experience to coach effectively across the business, particularly, but not exclusively, in support of the leadership programme. The programme consists of taught elements, observed practice sessions and assessed fieldwork. Coach trainees also have an opportunity to undergo a series of coaching sessions with an external coach so that they can appreciate coaching from the client's perspective. The course lasts for six months, with the emphasis on skills development. At the end of the programme all trainees are formally assessed on a presentation on their understanding of coaching and how they have applied it, a demonstration of their coaching practice, and supporting evidence of the fieldwork undertaken.

Once in the internal coaching pool they are allocated clients on the leadership development programme. However, after they have completed six months of this coaching, they may be approached by anyone in GEB who wants coaching. This open market has created challenges for some coaches who are popular within GEB and has resulted in the HR department's having to negotiate with line managers to ensure that core work commitments are not compromised when certain internal coaches are doing several days of coaching a week.

Even as the internal coach programme was being launched, the HR department started to think about continuous professional development and supervision for the internal coaches. This was regarded as essential for the credibility of the programme. Continuous professional development ensured that coaches maintained their skill set and learned new techniques. The coaches were required to participate in continuous professional development as part of the right to practise, and quarterly workshops with outside speakers were offered. Supervision was vital in ensuring that the coaches could have a safe place to discuss their clients and learn about their coaching. In the first year as a coach, one-to-one supervision was mandatory for all coaches. There after, coaches went into a peer group of coaches supported by an external supervisor who ensured the independence of the discussions.

Despite a high initial cost in setting up the selection and training programmes, a cost-benefit analysis showed that by Year 2 of the programme it was offering better value for money than relying on external coaches. The use of internal coaches enabled coaching to be available at more management levels in the organisation. The long-term nature of the coaching – over several months in comparison to the traditional week-long training course – saw the learning become embedded because the coaching clients were supported in their changes through the coaching relationship. Those trained as internal coaches started to model coaching behaviour in their daily work, helping to implement a cultural change in the organisation.

Case study learning points

The GEB's internal coaching pool has now been operating for a number of years. Key learning points for HR were:

- Individuals receiving coaching must be committed to continuous learning.

- The board-level executives and some directorate-level leaders preferred to use external coaching because it was perceived to be more confidential.

- There must be clarity about how the coaching fits into the culture of the organisation. GEB HR now runs briefings on coaching, what it is, and how it works, for staff who are interested in receiving coaching.

- The internal coach volunteers must be prepared to put in considerable time and energy.

- A clear process has to be established for how internal coaches are selected, trained and then supported. HR must support and work with line managers to ensure that they are content for their staff to become internal coaches.

- Those who become internal coaches have found it to be a profound learning experience with considerable personal benefits for themselves, and a rewarding activity in supporting leaders and the organisation to develop.

Questions for discussion

1　Who in the business would be best placed to play the role of internal coach?

2　How might they be selected, developed and rewarded?

3　What support would be offered to them once they were in the internal coach pool?

4　How would the organisation establish a return on investment from the coaching skills programmes and the development of internal coaches?

5　What options are there to develop leaders' individual coaching skills?

6　How would you gather information from the coaches to benefit organisational learning without compromising the confidentiality of their clients?

7　How would the organisation measure the impact of coaching on its leadership development?

EXPLORE FURTHER

CIPD (2007) *Coaching at Work*, Magazine and online resource. London, Chartered Institute of Personnel and Development. Available online at:
http://www.cipd.co.uk/coachingatwork/ presales.htm
A bi-monthly publication which offers articles on current trends, developments and techniques in the coaching industry.

CLUTTERBUCK, D. and MEGGINSON, D. (2005) *Making Coaching Work: Creating a coaching culture*. London, CIPD
This work looks at the importance of creating an organisational culture that will effectively support the introduction of coaching.

JARVIS, J. (2004) *Coaching and Buying Coaching Services. A guide*. London, CIPD.
Available online at: **http://www.cipd.co.uk/guides**
A useful and succinct guide to the issues involved in procuring coaching services.

LEE, R. J. and VALERIO, A. M. (2005) *Executive Coaching: A guide for the HR professional*. San Francisco, Pfeiffer
One of the few published works on executive coaching written specifically for the HR professional.

WITHERSPOON, R. and WHITE, R. P. (2004) *Four Essential Ways That Coaching Can Help Executives*. Greensboro N.C., Center for Creative Leadership
A clear and concise guide to how coaching can be used within an organisation.

CHAPTER 16

People-related measures and high-performance HRM

Andrew Mayo

INTRODUCTION

HR departments want to be seen as 'business partners'. This means that they work with operating managers to help them with their objectives, but also that they are businesslike themselves. It is a general truth in business that 'Numbers speak louder than words.' This chapter provides a framework for distinguishing between the requirements for metrics for HR as a function, and separately for 'people in the organisation', and examines practical ways of meeting them. It also identifies the parameters for delivering high performance from the HR function.

LEARNING OUTCOMES

By the end of this chapter readers should be able to:

- explain the distinction between human capital management and HRM

- understand the types of measures appropriate to people

- define and link measures on human capital

- build an HR functional scorecard.

This chapter is in two parts – firstly, measures for managers to use; and secondly, measures for the effectiveness of the HR function's performance.

The chapter concludes with the main case study.

Reference sources named within the chapter may be looked up in the *References and further reading* section at the end of the book.

STARTER CASE STUDY

Extract from Shell Annual Report, 2005

Resourcing for the future
In 2005 we recruited more than 700 graduates and almost 2,000 experienced people from over 70 different nationalities, underlining our focus on recruiting from a wider range of countries and regions, especially Asia-Pacific and the Middle East. Our successful large-scale recruitment drive for experienced exploration and production professionals in 2005 means that Shell is well positioned to deliver on the increased level of investment in our upstream business. The recent appointment of chief scientists also demonstrates our continued commitment to technical excellence, and confirms the strength of Shell's career and development opportunities for technical staff. We place strong emphasis on local careers and employee development with 49 nationalities represented amongst our senior leaders.

Strengthening leadership and deepening professionalism
Shell's ability to capitalise on growth opportunities in emerging markets relies on the skills and professionalism of our employees. We continue to invest in training and development through a balance of on- and off-the-job learning. The establishment of Project and Commercial Academies will provide new opportunities for staff to develop expertise in these areas. Just as important is the ability to manage change effectively, and in 2005 we increased both resources and capability in support of business critical change initiatives. In addition, we are committed to the development of leadership capability through the integrated cross-business Shell Leadership Development programmes. These are delivered through strong partnerships with major international academic institutions, and in 2005 more than 7,000 people with leadership potential participated in these programmes.

Communication and involvement
The success of our business depends on the full commitment of all employees. We encourage the involvement of employees in the planning and direction of their work, and provide them with safe and confidential channels to report concerns. Employees in all countries where we operate have access to staff forums, grievance procedures or other support systems. A global Ethics and Compliance Helpline was introduced during December 2005, offering an independent, confidential and anonymous facility for reporting non-compliance and resolving dilemmas and concerns. The Shell People Survey is conducted every two years, and asks employees for their opinions on a number of topics relating to how they feel about working at Shell. The last survey in 2004 had a 78% response rate and showed an overall satisfaction rate of 64%. The next survey will take place in 2006. We seek to establish and maintain high-quality, direct and open dialogue with employees. Our staff are represented by collective labour agreements, unions and staff councils in many countries in which the group has operations.

Diversity and inclusiveness
Shell has had a long-standing commitment to the integration of diversity and inclusiveness into every aspect of our operations and culture. We set explicit expectations for all employees and leaders, underpinned by clear plans and targets. There are three global objectives: improving the representation of women in senior leadership positions to a minimum of 20% in the long term; improving the representation of local people in senior positions in their own countries; and improving the positive perceptions of inclusiveness in the workplace. At the end of 2005, women in senior leadership positions had increased to 9.9%, compared with 9.6% in 2004. In 36% of countries, local nationals fill more than half of senior leadership positions. The Shell People Survey (2004) reported that 64% of employees perceived workplace inclusiveness favourably. These results represent good progress, but further improvement is needed to meet our aspirations.

Questions for discussion

If you were an investor or potential investor in Shell, what would you conclude was good and bad about the organisation's people and about people management? What else would you like to know?

1 HUMAN CAPITAL MEASURES

WHAT DO WE MEAN BY 'HUMAN CAPITAL'?

It is important to start by understanding the difference between 'human resources' and 'human capital'. Both terms refer to the people in the organisation. People are of course costly resources – in most organisations today, the major cost that they have. But people are also the creators of value.

Why do organisations exist? Only for one purpose, and that is to create value – or benefits – for their stakeholders. A stakeholder is a person or group that has an interest in the organisation's being successful. Most organisations have at least three sets of stakeholders – their owners, their customers and their employees. In a commercial organisation the owners, or shareholders, want the organisation to be financially successful so that they receive a good return on their investment. But they can only do that if they have satisfied customers, and employees who are committed to their work and want to do a good job. In the public sector, the owners are policy-makers – usually the government – and the customers are the public.

Every organisation has two types of assets that it uses to create the value for its stakeholders. One type of assets is 'tangible' – these include money, buildings, equipment, machines and stocks of materials. They are regularly valued by accountants and from time to time a 'stocktake' is made of what the organisation has, what it owes to others and what it is owed itself – and this is carefully documented on what is called a 'balance sheet'. The second category comprises 'intangible' assets. These are not generally measured by accountants, but include things which a buyer would have to pay for (in addition to the tangibles) when buying the organisation. Intangible assets were first described by Swedish thinkers, and a comprehensive summary of them can be found in Edvinsson and Malone (1997). They may include a customer base, brand names, reputation, valuable contracts, systems, processes, knowledge and methodologies . . . and the people – their skills, experience, relationships and creativity. In fact, without people, nothing happens. That is why it is popular to say that 'People are our most important assets' – although in fact it is the *qualities* of people that are the actual assets. Just as money is often called 'financial capital', this aspect of people is called 'human capital'.

'Human capital management' is therefore to do with thinking about people as assets and not just costs. It is about the value they have as individuals and teams, and the value they create for others. 'Human resource management', we could say, is about administering the resource called people, and about processes, tools and programmes which maximise people's value and contribution.

REFLECTIVE ACTIVITY

Think of two different kinds of organisation that you are familiar with – maybe ones you have worked for, or ones you interact with as a customer.

Make a list of the kinds of tangible and intangible assets they have. For each organisation, rank approximately the importance of each type of asset.

If you were able to buy the organisation, what would you want to make sure you did not lose after the purchase?

WHY MEASURES ARE IMPORTANT

It is often said that 'What gets measured gets managed.' Managers all over the world are trained to work with numbers, and human capital management is therefore often associated quite rightly with people-related measures. However, Albert Einstein is quoted as saying 'What counts can often not be counted, and what is counted often does not count.' In other words, in looking for measures that relate to people we will not necessarily be looking through an accountant's lens, seeing everything as financial numbers – we have to be smarter than that and use a range of different kinds of measures.

We use a variety of different kinds of measures, such as:

- proportions, percentages and ratios
- indices, which weight and combine several measures
- ranking in order
- time-based trends
- perceptions of how people feel or see things
- levels of expertise
- costs and cost-based ratios
- the absence of negative events (like accidents and occupationally caused ill-health).

For a comprehensive survey of measurement options, see Becker, Huselid and Ulrich (2001).

Remember that all measures depend on the reliability of the measuring process. Perceptions of how people feel are particularly vulnerable to misinterpretation, unless the questions are phrased with careful and neutral objectivity. Whenever scales are used – such as estimating expertise – we have to be sure that the people who use them will all use them in exactly the same way, which will depend on how closely the scales are defined.

How do we know whether to be pleased with a particular measure or not? When is a measure 'a good result' and when is it 'a bad result'? Sometimes it is obvious, but often just a raw figure does not mean very much. There are three means of evaluation to help us answer the question:

- *By seeing if it is increasing or decreasing* compared to a previous figure. Whichever way it is going, we want to understand why. Some measures vary over short periods (for example, attrition rates may be quite different month on month) and we must look at trends such as three-month moving averages.

- *By comparison with similar measures* from other organisations – *benchmarking.* In fact, organisations like to make comparisons to see whether their figures are better or worse than those of competitors or sister organisations. Often third parties produce league tables, especially in the public sector.

- *By comparison against a target* we have set.

The different audiences for measures

The starter case study above was from the published Annual Report of Shell. It actually has much more information than most of this sort of report often does about people. The 'audience' for an annual report includes investors, journalists, academics, regulatory bodies and other external observers. It also includes competitors. What we choose to tell the world is governed by compliance with regulations, plus what we feel will give confidence in us as a good company in which to invest.

In 2003, the UK Government commissioned a report into what might be put about people in annual reports – it is known as the Kingsmill Report and is available online at **www.accountingforpeople.gov.uk**. It made a number of suggestions for data about people to be included in a section of an annual report called the Operating and Financial Review. As an input to this the CIPD produced a report of its own called *Human Capital: The external reporting framework* (Scarbrough, 2003). So far, nothing has been mandated for companies in law, although the best companies include a section on people which is most likely to be a narrative.

What is published externally must be separated from the need for management *within* an organisation to have good human capital management. We will inevitably use some of the same numbers, but in an annual report they are consolidated for the company as a whole. Just as we have to break down financial budgets into units and departments, so we must do the same for people measures for them to be useful. We may also want to focus on some detail that we might not want to make public.

There are four categories of measures we can have for our human capital (in Part 2 of this chapter we look at measures relevant to the work of the HR function itself), which are now considered in turn below. They are: statistics about the workforce and movements in it; the value of the people; the motivation of the people; and the productivity of the people.

STATISTICS ABOUT THE WORKFORCE

Consider the following exercise before reading any further.

REFLECTIVE ACTIVITY

A supermarket company has 32 stores and a total of 4,500 people.

What kind of breakdown of this population might we be interested in at any given point in time?

What kind of information would be useful over a specific period of time, such as three months?

For the first question we might look at the total company, or by area or individual store. We should then divide our data first into *job families* – this would include groups such as senior management, middle management, store management, store staff, professional support staff, buyers, and distribution operators. We could then be interested in the following distributions for each job family: length of service, time in job, age, disability, gender, ethnic origin, full-time/part-time, qualifications, vacancies, etc.

For the second question, we might be interested in the following:

- labour turnover, sometimes called attrition – this is the loss of people over a certain period (see Chapter 11)

- movements of people *in* to a job family or store over the period

- other transfers or promotions – all of these three measures might be consolidated into a 'headcount change report'

- the use of temporary or subcontract staff – again by job family or store

- absenteeism and sickness (see Chapter 11)

- accidents and ill-health (see Chapter 18).

REFLECTIVE ACTIVITY

Your monthly human capital (statistics) report has been produced. If you notice the following, what would you conclude, and what action would you consider taking?

Two stores show an unusually high loss of people occurring between three and six months of service.

Five stores have much worse absenteeism rates than the average.

In the job family of store managers, only 14% are women, and only 3% are from ethnic minorities.

There are three stores in which the age distribution shows 50% of the staff are aged over 50.

The ratio of HQ staff to store staff is 18% across the country – in a recent study of retail companies the average for the sector was given as 14%.

Note that we have here introduced the concept of *ratios* of one job family to another, or of one as a percentage of the whole workforce. These can be more revealing than simple statistics.

THE VALUE OF PEOPLE

We know the costs of people. But what do we know about their value? Is it the same? Clearly, it is not. We can have five different members of a team, all paid the same. But their manager knows they are all individuals, with different experience, knowledge, skills and attitudes. He or she would miss them in different ways if they left the team. There might indeed be an individual whose leaving would delight the manager because it meant that there was an opportunity for a *better* replacement. One of the problems for most organisations is that they are unable to balance the costs of people with any quantitative assessment of their value. 'Price is what you pay; value is what you get,' says one enlightened CEO. Whereas a team leader knows the unique and relative value of his or her people – and can describe it qualitatively – as we go above and beyond his or her level of management, that value is lost in a fog and those individuals just become 'headcount' and costs. As a result, poor decisions are often made and the value walks out of the door before we have finished counting the cost savings.

The great thing about people is they have the capacity to *increase* their value with time. They get new experience and new skills; they may be promoted and take higher responsibility. Provided we give the chance to people, most of them will grow with us – and we will reward them accordingly. If we are an organisation, it is in our interest to do this. Some academics have attempted to build formulae for the financial valuation of people (see, for example, Flamholz, 1999). We need not concern ourselves with these because they are not in any general use. We have to find a way of quantifying the *characteristics* of value that people bring to us. We can use a common framework but it is important that we do not assume that the same detailed components of value will fit all employees. What makes a call centre operator valuable to us is different from what makes an electrician or an HR business partner valuable to us.

Here we have two questions to ask. Firstly, what are the distinctive characteristics of these employees which epitomise their special value in the department of which they are part? There are some characteristics that we always value in any employee – positive attitudes, willingness, being a team player, reliability. But for each task there are additional abilities which distinguish one from another in the ability to achieve levels of performance. The kind of things we would look for might be (Mayo, 2001; pp80–1):

- *personal attitudes* – eg positive approach, flexibility, team member, takes initiative
  These are often to be found in competency frameworks. We are referring here to those which are more personality-oriented – ie are generally not developed through training. Most teams value people with these kinds of attitudes regardless of their work mission.

- *values alignment with the organisation* – its values, ethos, and mission
  People who comfortably align themselves to our values have particular worth. They become 'part of us' and are likely to be loyal to us.

- *job-relevant capability/expertise* – knowledge, skills, specialised experiences and people contacts
  Note: the widespread use of 'universal competency frameworks' – by which every employee at a certain level is expected to shine at a large number of behavioural competencies – makes no sense. It is more than behaviours: it is professional and technical expertise uniquely critical to the role in question that we want to identify.

- *productivity/contribution* – people vary in their ability to actually achieve things
  Some people are better at getting results than others – even with the same base level of knowledge and skill. It is to do with the way they prioritise time and effort. We always value more those who 'get things done'.

REFLECTIVE ACTIVITY

Think of a job that you know well.

What would be the characteristics of a really valuable person in such a job?

The second question to ask is: What additional characteristics does an individual have which indicate the promise of future value, beyond the current task? People may have previous experiences not used in the current job, or may just have the potential to grow and undertake a more demanding role in the future – higher or broader responsibilities. Another factor here may be 'mobility' – the willingness to take up positions in other locations or countries.

Compiling a 'human capital index'

Having identified the factors affecting high performance, we should then do the following. We need to weight the factors for relative importance; decide how to rate the factors as observed – both in terms of a scale and a process to apply it; design a display format for them; and summarise the data in an overall index of value. We may call this overall index by any suitable name. Elsewhere (Mayo, 2001; pp78–84) it is called the ' Individual Asset Multiplier', but we could use other terms such as 'Individual Value Index', 'Human Capital Index', or whatever suits the culture of the organisation best.

Table 35 shows a way to display the value of people in a team. It uses a rating scale of 0 to 2, where 1.0 represents 'a person who demonstrates the level of value we would expect for what we are paying'. This helps us do a number of useful things in human capital management. We can compare the value of different teams, and focus training on the characteristics that matter and recruitment on where we have gaps. The objective is to constantly increase the total index we have.

Table 35 Displaying the value in a group

Employee	Personal attitudes (20%)	Capability factor (20%)	Contribution factor (30%)	Values factor (15%)	Potential factor (15%)	Human capital index (100%)
A	1.7	1.6	1.8	1.6	1.9	1.725
B	0.7	1.0	0.8	0.8	0.7	0.805
C	1.4	1.1	0.8	1.6	0.9	1.115
D	1.6	1.7	1.5	1.0	1.5	1.485
E	1.0	0.8	0.9	1.1	1.0	0.945
Average per employee	1.28	1.24	1.19	1.22	1.20	1.215

THE MOTIVATION OF PEOPLE

We can have great people in our team or organisation, but creating the maximum value for stakeholders is not guaranteed just because of that. Extraordinary and well-qualified people can produce very little. The good news is that quite ordinary people can produce extraordinary results. What makes the difference? Their motivation – how the organisation (through its HR and other policies) and their manager inspires them, meets their personal needs, provides them with challenge and achievement, and so on.

We must define some terms here. *Satisfied* employees do not necessarily produce great results, but at least it is better than *dissatisfied* employees, so we have to know how employees are feeling about their work and the environment in which they perform it. The aspiration we have today is to have *engaged* employees – not just satisfied with the organisation but *committed* and keen to do the best job they can. Figure 21 names two types of motivation – 'intrinsic' and 'extrinsic'. The first is people's natural enthusiasm for what they do. It can be strengthened or sapped by 'extrinsic' factors – what the organisation or the manager does or does not do. What we want is for all the influences to be strong so that the end result is 'engaged employees'. And we want to know what is happening – to measure it, monitor it and manage it.

Figure 21 Motivation and engagement

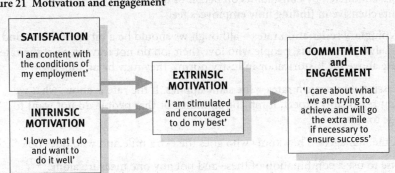

There are numerous surveys carried out by consultants on the levels of engagement of employees. Most of them find that between 10% and 20% of employees are 'highly engaged', between 10% and 15% are 'disengaged', and the remainder are 'somewhat engaged' (eg Corporate Leadership Council, 2004). Because engagement has direct and strong links to performance, the challenge for managements is to improve the first category. There are two things we want to measure. Firstly, 'Are people engaged or not?' And secondly, 'What are the factors that make them engaged?'

REFLECTIVE ACTIVITY

From your own experience, make a list of the kind of things in a work situation that a) make you frustrated and discontented, and b) make you enthusiastic and keen to do a great job.

How do we know people are engaged?

There are five ways to know whether people are engaged:

1   Ask the people. At this stage we are not interested in what makes people engaged or not, but just whether they *are* or not. Below are some statements to evoke responses which test that. As with all surveys the responses need a scale – typically a Likert-type scale ranging from 'Absolutely true for me' to 'Absolutely not true for me'.

  ● I would recommend my company to a friend as a good place to work.

  ● I am proud to tell others I work for the company.

  ● I really care about the future of my company.

  ● I am willing to put in a great deal of effort beyond what is normally expected to help my company succeed.

  ● I am personally motivated to help my company be successful.

2   Have an independent company ask the people. Surveys like The Great Place to Work conducted by consultants on behalf of the *Sunday Times* are very comprehensive in finding how employees feel.

  ● Voluntary resignation rates – although we should be a bit careful here and analyse the reasons, people who love their job do not leave it. So if the rates are above the historical or industry norms, they may be an indicator.

4   Excessive absenteeism rates – the same applies. If the rate is above what we might reasonably expect, it may be an indicator that people do not want to come to work.

5   Ask the managers. They know who goes the extra mile and who does not.

It is wise to use a combination of these and not any one measure alone.

How do we find out about the factors that make people engage or not?

As noted earlier, the answer to this question is different for different groups of people. We can take a compromise based on research of what *generally* makes a difference to people, or we can ask the group concerned and then draw up a survey based on what they said. Research into occupational psychology tells us fairly consistently about the things that motivate people in general. Factors include the nature of the work they do, whether they can feel a sense of achievement and whether they get recognition and opportunities for advancement. The most commonly used survey on engagement today is devised and copyrighted by Gallup (see **http://www.gallupconsulting.com/content/?ci=52**). It is known as the Q12™ (see the box below). It comprises 12 questions, and if the answer to a majority of them is 'yes', there is a strong chance that the employee is engaged. How do these relate to your answers to the previous apply your knowledge exercise?

The Gallup Q12™ Engagement Survey

1 Do I know what is expected of me at work?

2 Do I have the materials and equipment I need to do my work right?

3 At work, do I have the opportunity to do what I do best every day?

4 In the last seven days have I received recognition or praise for good work?

5 Does my supervisor, or someone at work, seem to care about me as a person?

6 Is there someone at work who encourages my development?

7 At work, do my opinions count?

8 Does the mission/purpose of my company make me feel my work is important?

9 Are my co-workers committed to doing quality work?

10 Do I have a best friend at work?

11 In the last six months have I talked to someone about my progress?

12 At work, have I had opportunities to learn and grow?

Now check on how these questions relate to your answers to the previous exercise.

Good organisations have always done employee opinion surveys. Usually, these are annual or even less frequent and cover many areas. Today they may be supplemented by local, short, frequent 'pulse surveys'. In the survey we need two to three questions which check whether people *are* engaged, plus a set covering the key influences such as in Q12.

Note: With all surveys of how people feel it is good to ask 'How important is this item for you?' in addition to asking for their scores on an item.

THE PRODUCTIVITY OF PEOPLE

People bring their value to organisations in order to create value for others. We need to know how successful they are – ie what they are creating. Each group of people should be linked to one or more stakeholders. Sales people add value to customers (through helping them get the right product and providing them with good service) and to the shareholders (by bringing in revenues). We would measure the value they add in terms of customer satisfaction and loyalty, *and* in sales revenues.

Productivity is defined as output over input – it is a ratio. The input is the denominator in the ratio, and we want it to relate to people. We can use:

- numbers of people (such as revenue per salesperson)
- time spent (such as customer satisfaction compared with time spent by salespersons in checking it)
- people cost (such as revenues in relation to total sales compensation cost).

A detailed study of ratios such as this can be found in Fitz-Enz (2000).

Remember, the output measure is a measure of value added. It is not mere activities. Take for example a public sector organisation. Our interest is not in the number of cases handled per person per week. It is the number of cases *resolved*. That is the value added.

REFLECTIVE ACTIVITY

For our chain of supermarkets, what measures of productivity might you have for one store?

What measures might you use for the purchasing and distribution departments?

PUTTING IT ALL TOGETHER

We now have four kinds of measures to form our human capital report. We do not want them to stand alone or just be bundled into a basket. We are interested in how they link together and their correlations, especially with performance (productivity). What is it about our people and what is it about their working environment that makes a difference to productivity? Some companies, especially in banking and retail, have been able to demonstrate a clear quantitative correlation between engagement and a business parameter. The 'human capital monitor' (Mayo, 2001; p.12ff) is one example of how the various measures can be shown together (see Figure 22). This kind of report is something we would compare with a previous one, to see in what areas we are making progress or otherwise.

Figure 22 A human capital (or 'people') monitor

The People Monitor – Group XX				
People as assets	**Commitment and engagement**		**Contribution to added value**	
GREAT PEOPLE The value of the people we have, using our chosen index	IN A GREAT PLACE TO WORK Input measures The factors that lead to engagement of this group	X (=)	GREAT RESULTS The measures of *value* for stakeholders or of productivity	
Maximising the value Measures of human capital management processes – both inputs and success indicators	**Success indicators** The measures of commitment and engagement			

Source: Mayo (2001)

Then, just as in looking at our money we create a balance sheet, we can create one for people. It is a summary at a point in time of where we are. Of course, the people balance sheet is not written in money. It is a summary of what is positive and what is getting better on one side, and what is negative or getting worse on the other (see Table 36).

Table 36 Example of a 'people balance sheet'

THE HUMAN CAPITAL BALANCE SHEET	
ASSETS	**LIABILITIES**
Factors on the Monitor that are at or ABOVE target	Factors on the Monitor that are BELOW target
OUR PEOPLE	OUR PEOPLE
. . . . .	. . . . .
. . . . .	. . . . .
MOTIVATION/ENGAGEMENT	MOTIVATION/ENGAGEMENT
. . . . .	. . . . .
. . . . .	. . . . .
VALUE ADDED	VALUE ADDED
. . . . .	. . . . .

Of course, organisations will find their own ways to present the data and information. It is not just the information that is important but the process and the action that follows it. HR in its 'business partner' role should play a key part in this process.

Final note: Whatever measures and presentation we use, it should feed into any organisational performance management systems such as the 'balanced scorecard' (Kaplan and Norton, 1996). Such a system focuses on the *most* important measures for supporting company strategy. They will not be enough in themselves to manage human capital – we need the detail we have discussed.

2 HIGH-PERFORMING HR MANAGEMENT

We noted on page 291 that there is considerable confusion under the heading of 'HR metrics' between measures of human capital and measures of the HR department's effectiveness. Often a mix of measures is presented in one freestanding report – a 'basket' of measures. These have little meaning if they are not connected together.

An HR department is a group of people in its own right, of course, and so the human capital measures apply to them – we are interested in their value, their motivation and the value they add. But professionally, we would want to go further into the activities and effect of what the department does. What should we want to know? Any support function has two roles. One is administrative – looking after the regulatory requirements and ensuring that people are properly paid, and so on. The other role is often described as 'strategic'. This is not a good word because nobody spends much time in a year thinking about strategy. A better term is 'value-adding'. The administrative side of HR is not really value-adding to any stakeholder – it is ensuring compliance with the law and with company policies, and providing good housekeeping. It has to be done well, and we come back to that later. However, HR – assuming it is more than just administrative personnel management – also has the capacity to add value to several stakeholders. It designs and owns a number of important people management processes, and it is there to support managers in achieving their own objectives.

THE VALUE THAT HR ADDS

So what should we want to know and measure? First, we want to understand and measure the value HR adds. Then there are two categories of effectiveness measures of *how* the value is delivered:

- *operating effectiveness* – This is how efficient we are; how well our processes achieve their purpose, how good a service we deliver, and what our productivity levels are.

- *project effectiveness* – This is whether we get a good return on what we spend on special initiatives and programmes.

Before we examine these in more depth, we must briefly consider the value added to stakeholders.

REFLECTIVE ACTIVITY

List the stakeholders for whom HR can add value.

What kind of value (or benefits) can/does HR add?

To check with your answer for the first part of the exercise above, there are three main stakeholders for HR. They are the owners (via senior management), managers and employees. Often there is a parent company to consider if the company is a division or subsidiary. HR may also provide benefits for suppliers, trade unions, communities, other functions such as IT and Finance, government departments and industry bodies. Can we measure the value HR adds? We start from the idea that everything can be measured if we try hard enough.

Financial value added is measured in money saved, or the return on money invested. We have to be careful we do not save money at the expense of benefits for other stakeholders. However, senior management is always pleased if we can save. Sometimes we have to spend to save – that is why we have to know how to do 'return on investment' calculations. Financial value added to employees is different – they want their salary, benefits and bonuses to be fair (so the measure is a perception), and we can also benchmark against market salaries and see which quartile of the salary ranges we are in.

Most of the other value-added items are measured by surveys of perceptions of one kind or another – of service provided, or of the value of a policy. Sometimes it is useful to measure 'negatives' or the extent to which things did *not* happen. Examples of this would be low rates of accidents or grievances. Having chosen how to measure what we are there to do, we move to measuring how well we do it, starting with operating effectiveness.

Table 37 The contribution of an HR function to stakeholder added value

HR stakeholders and areas of added value	Examples of practical contribution from HR and L&D initiatives
Senior management (and via them owners, shareholders, parent companies)	
• financial	• People management or people development projects with a good return on investment • Cost-saving initiatives
• reputational	• Employment brand • Handling of legal issues
• strategic	• Creating HR strategies and policies that support business strategy • Achieving employee alignment with company goals • Describing and achieving a cultural vision supporting the business goals
• continuity	• Talent and succession management • Retention strategies
• organisational effectiveness	• Organisational design • Communication strategies • People-related processes designed to make the organisation more effective
Operational management	
• strategic	• Creating people initiatives which support operational goals
• tactical	• Providing problem-based consultancy • Advising on legal and policy issues
• employee engagement	• Recognition programmes • Information on engagement • Performance management
Employees	
• financial	• Salary, bonus and benefit structures
• motivational	• HR policies and programmes • Good communications • Recognition programmes
• developmental	• Knowledge and skills enhancement • New experiences • Career planning and progression
• health and safety	• Absence of accidents • Employee health support

REFLECTIVE ACTIVITY

Look at Table 37.

In the light of what you have learned so far, what kind of measures would you use for each of the items in the right-hand column? Add another column to the right, and write in it the measures you suggest for each of those items.

OPERATING EFFECTIVENESS

We could deliver great added value, at least non-financially, but it could cost a fortune to do so. Every support function like HR must know whether it is good value for money. That is why we have to have some good 'internal' measures which we can monitor and manage. The four areas we now examine are: the quality of service provided for the cost; what our productivity is, and what value for money we give; how well HR processes work; and how time is utilised.

REFLECTIVE ACTIVITY

Jot down quickly all the things you look for in good service from a professional organisation.

Service

Many organisations today have 'service-level agreements' which describe how they will perform for their customers. They cover things like accuracy, timeliness, responsiveness, quality of advice, attitude of the people delivering the service, and ease of dealing. Which of these might require a survey? One might be done every quarter to see how customers of the HR service are experiencing it. Other things can be measured internally. For example, we can regularly track the time it takes to fill vacancies, or the number of mistakes in paying people, or how long it takes to process a benefit application.

Productivity and value for money

Earlier we examined the productivity of people (in a section of that heading). We are now looking for output measures of human effort. From Table 37 we could potentially have a lot of outputs. We could be selective or we could combine some into an index. If an HR person is dedicated to one type of added value (like training people, for example), we can just take his/her outputs (learning achieved index) and divide by his/her costs. Often HR professionals do many things – some service delivery, some projects, some other value-added contributions. So the only way we can fully comprehend our productivity is to have some division of people's time between various areas. Let us suppose that one thing we are trying hard to do is to improve the company's employment brand – its attractiveness to new employees. We would measure this in three ways – external league tables such as The Best Companies to Work For, the acceptance rate of offers made, and the number of employees leaving through dissatisfaction with the company (because they will tell other people). The productivity ratio is the increase in employment brand (as measured consistently) divided by the time spent on it. (If we have employed consultants, we must use the cost of time.) Of course Rome, and an employment brand, is not built in a day – so we might get quite low (or even negative) productivity levels in the short term.

'Value for money' is a very similar concept. One often-used ratio is the overall HR costs per employee in the organisation. This is not a good ratio, even though it is quick and easy to work out, because it depends what HR produces. So we have to combine it with service levels and value-added areas and ask 'Does this feel like value for money?' It is a judgement – but we can use benchmarking figures from other organisations to help us make that judgement.

How well HR processes work

HR owns, designs and either runs or helps run many processes that are to do with people management – many of which are discussed elsewhere in this book in detail. They include such areas as performance management, recruitment, development centres, promotion and absence management. They do not always run according to plan, often because managers do not play their full part (or we have made them too complicated). We need to be very clear about the *purpose* and *aims* of a process to be able to assess how well it is working. For example, there are actually several possible purposes of an appraisal system and people are often confused as to which they are.

Measures that can be used include:

- the 'penetration' of the process – What percentage of the people who are supposed to use it are actually doing so? For example, how many appraisals get done each year?

- the success of the process – To what extent are the intended outcomes achieved? In training it is one thing to measure the percentage of people who have training plans, but how many of them *complete* them?

- the time and/or cost taken for completion of a round of the process – Is it worth the goals achieved? For example, development centres are fun things for everybody involved, but very expensive. Is the time and cost justified by the achievement?

Someone should own every process – and they should be responsible for setting up and monitoring its success.

REFLECTIVE ACTIVITY

Take the process of recruitment – one (like many) that is designed by HR but shared in implementation with line managers.

What measures would you choose to monitor if the process was working well?

How well time is utilised

The truth is that very few people are productive (in terms of adding value) every minute of the day. We are not talking about rest breaks or the occasional chat, but about work itself. We all spend time doing internal and non-productive things (many of which really have to be done). We attend meetings, write reports, pass on communications, travel to meetings, have waiting time, read superfluous emails, comply with regulations, solve problems that should not have happened – and so on. All this is *non-value-added* work. It stops us spending our time directly contributing to one of the areas of value added we have identified. So from time to time we must take a rain check for a month or so and just ask people to jot down what their time is being spent on. The results are often quite disturbing. (For more on this, see Mayo, 2001, pp.221–5.)

PROJECT EFFECTIVENESS

Support functions like HR initiate projects and programmes for various reasons. Sometimes it is because senior management thinks it would be a good idea, or it may be that other organisations are doing it and HR thinks it would be beneficial to its own organisation. It could be that there is a problem to be solved – there are too many accidents, or too many people are getting stressed, or there is a quality problem in customer service. Remember that most operational difficulties have a people problem behind them.

It is important to register that it is no use going ahead and then later deciding we should find out whether there was a return on what we did, and try to evaluate its effectiveness. That is not what we do with financial capital investments. We first decide *whether* it will bring a return – we evaluate its anticipated effectiveness. All projects have some wishful thinking and optimism behind them, and this is why so many are an embarrassment and quietly forgotten afterwards. A problem in HR and training is that so many initiatives look naturally like good things to do. The question is whether they will make any difference.

It is not easy in HR because many of the projects have a lot more than purely financial benefits. But by now we are experts at understanding 'non-financial added value' and how we measure it. The simple formula for return on investment (ROI) is as follows (see Phillips, Stone and Phillips, 2001, Chapter 8, for a full explanation):

$$\% \text{ ROI} = \frac{\text{Financial benefits} - \text{Project costs}}{\text{Project cost}} \times 100 + \text{Non-financial benefits}$$

We may have to make an estimate of the financial benefits and sometimes can do that for the effects of a non-financial benefit. We might estimate that a 5% 'increase in engagement' affects productivity by 2%, which is worth £x. Or we can see what it looks like for just the financial benefits on their own. Does this itself show an acceptable rate of return? If so, the non-financial benefits are a bonus. Otherwise, we have to make a judgement – does this look like value for money? So there are two possible processes here: either preparing a case to justify an initiative or evaluating whether the initiative met its anticipated returns.

In making the case, we have four steps to go through:

1 Define the measurable objectives of the initiative.
2 Calculate the estimated costs of the project.

3 Estimate the returns (both financial and non-financial) to be expected from the initiative.

4 Balance the two and conclude that the initiative is or is not a worthwhile use of resources.

If we want to subsequently evaluate how right we were, we have to add some more steps (Mayo, 2004, p.187).

5 Make a data collection and evaluation plan.

6 Collect data before the initiative if before/after comparisons are to be made.

7 Collect data during the initiative as needed.

8 Collect data after implementation.

9 Calculate all costs involved at each stage.

10 Isolate the effects of the programme.

11 Calculate the financial impact of the data.

12 Compare with the costs.

13 Present together with the non-financial benefits.

14 Judge whether the actual ROI was satisfactory.

This is a lot of work – which is why it is often not done. You have to be good at understanding costs, and be realistic about the costs of implementation. Note Step 14, which is difficult – other factors may have influenced the benefits, especially if a long time period was involved. So we have to estimate how much of the benefits were actually *due to the programme*.

PUTTING IT ALL TOGETHER

As before, we have to make choices about exactly how many measures we choose to monitor. We do not have time to measure everything, so choose those that are preferably not difficult to do and that will have the biggest impact. Figure 23 shows a model format which would embrace all we have examined.

150 high-potential middle managers from 40 different operating companies of a multinational telecommunications company were sent, in groups of 25, on a three-day management conference. The management conference consisted of group discussions to work out how the company values could be practically implemented and how change was taking place within the organisation to achieve the strategic business objectives, together with exercises to identify and share best practice. The direct cost per three-day programme (including travel and accommodation) was £60,000. After the management conference, it was noticed that the turnover for this highly mobile group dropped from 12% to 8% (50% were replaced from outside – generally it was reckoned that the replacement of a middle manager from outside cost about nine months' salary). Also, motivation levels of two thirds of the group perceptibly increased. This was supported by anecdotal and written evidence from appraisals (managers often reported gaining 'significant motivation' from the programme) and was also measured as an increase in productivity of the teams being led. 50% of the managers were from sales teams whose annual revenues before the programme averaged £500,000 per team. The average cost centre had total costs of £200,000 per year. The productivity changes were an average of 10% per employee for the sales teams, and for the cost centres a decrease in 5% costs per employee. The average managerial salary (including benefits and bonuses) was £100,000. The average sales margin on revenues was 12%.

Your task

Using the information in the short case study above, calculate the value of the financial benefits, calculate the return on investment, and list other non-financial benefits that were probably achieved.

Figure 23 A model for an HR scorecard

THE VALUE WE ADD		OPERATIONAL EFFECTIVENESS		
Stakeholder	Value measure		targets	actuals
		Service delivery		
		Productivity measures		
PROJECT EFFECTIVENESS		Process measures		
Project	ROI expected	ROI actual		
		Percentage time 'value adding'		

KEY ISSUES: PEOPLE-RELATED MEASURES AND HIGH-PERFORMANCE HRM

We now pull together ten key points about the main issues raised in this chapter:

- There are two main areas of people-related measures – those to do with the human capital of the organisation and those to do with the HR function.

- 'Human capital' is linked in to the whole HRM concept, as distinct from personnel management. It is about seeing people as value-creating assets and managing them accordingly. It implies measurement as in any other part of a business, and is as valid for public sector organisations as well as private.

- There are four areas to consider in human capital measurement: workforce statistics, the value of people, the motivation of people, and finally their productivity.

- Statistics is about who we have and where – by job family and by department.

- We need to value people quantitatively in order to have a balance with the focus on costs – but we cannot do this in financial terms. We have to evaluate the characteristics of people that make them valuable.

- Satisfaction is not the same as engagement – we need to measure the latter using custom-made surveys.

- Productivity is the added value to stakeholders divided by some measure of the human input.

- When we look at the effectiveness of the HR function, we need to know the value it adds to its own stakeholders and quantify it.

- Then we look at 'operating effectiveness' – service delivery, process efficiency, productivity and value for money, and time utilisation – and finally 'project effectiveness' – return on investment for projects.

- For both sets of measures we need an integrated presentation of the measures – for human capital a 'monitor', for HR a 'scorecard'.

Perhaps there are other key points that you would like to note for yourself.

The main case study in this chapter now follows.

MAIN CASE STUDY

Make an initial reading of the case study to gain an overview of the situation, and then read the questions that you will need to address. Now read the case study again, making notes of issues and facts that will help you in your analysis and responses to the questions. Remember to 'read between the lines' as well as picking out the obvious points, and also to consider what is not said as well as what is presented here.

This case study concerns a university. The Summa cum Laude University has some 25,000 students and 3,750 staff, split approximately 50:50 between academic and support staff. It has six schools, mostly on one distributed city campus, but also with an outlying campus 40 miles away which serves part of two of the faculties. The schools differ in size but their functions are all similar – namely, to provide teaching for students and to undertake and publish research. Each school has a head and a group of senior department leaders, although strong hierarchical management is not a feature of academia and decisions are more taken by consensus. Each school has support staff – secretaries, administrators and technicians. These are managed by a facilities manager, and typically total 100–130 or so staff per school. The university centre houses corporate functions such as HR, finance, IT and estates (which looks after all the buildings).

In the faculty support department, measures of performance are not formalised. However, for administrators success is all about meeting deadlines in the faculty timetable – accuracy and efficiency. For the technicians it is the right materials in the right place at the right time, adherence to health and safety requirements, and housekeeping, stock-keeping and managing equipment maintenance.

It is a general problem in universities that support staff feel they are regarded as second-class citizens compared to the academics, and this makes a particular challenge for the manager. Technicians particularly often feel undervalued and strikes have not been unknown.

HR comprises some 25 people, located together in one building. Under the HR director (who sits on the university senior executive team) are two deputy directors who share responsibility for particular projects and initiatives. Each school has an HR adviser dedicated to them, plus an assistant. A service centre deals with all administration and recruitment. In addition, there are six

people working under a learning and development manager. They do a few basic training courses themselves but most staff training is outsourced and they manage the suppliers. As a department HR has enjoyed good stability of the key staff over the last five years although the absenteeism rate is about the public sector average.

HR keeps good data on attrition and absenteeism, although the breakdown of the reasons for each is very general. A comprehensive employee opinion survey is run every three years which covers many aspects of working for the university and is broken down by department in each school. HR is responsible for an appraisal system for all staff. Each year about 80% of appraisals are actually done. The appraisal links into a training planning system. There is no succession planning. HR is also responsible for internal communications and trade union negotiations.

Your task

You are a consultant who has been asked by the HR director to do two things. Firstly, she would like first a scorecard for the HR function to enable her to monitor the right indicators that will tell her the department is being effective.

What would you have in the scorecard and what measures would have to be built? Be specific and not general – you may have to be somewhat creative to think of what would be useful in this context.

Secondly, she would like a human capital monitor for the group of technicians.

Think about what makes such people valuable in the organisation, what is likely to motivate them, and how the result of their efforts can be measured in value added. How would you summarise clearly such a monitor for the manager?

In preparing the monitor and the scorecard, can you foresee any practical difficulties? Likewise in implementation?

EXPLORE FURTHER

BECKER, B. E., HUSELID, M. A. and ULRICH, D. (2001) *The HR Scorecard: Linking people, strategy, and performance*. Boston, MA, Harvard Business School Press
A book designed for HR business partners, from the most famous HR thinktank in the world. It discusses HR's strategic role and has an excellent chapter on measurement in general. It tells readers how to create and implement the HR scorecard and how to do cost-benefit calculations.

EDVINSSON, L. and MALONE, M. S. (1997) *Intellectual Capital*. London, Piatkus
From the founder of the intellectual capital movement while in Skandia Assurance, this gives the logic of intangible assets, why people are so important, and how people-related measures can be made and used.

FITZ-ENZ, J. A. C. (2000) *The ROI of Human Capital: Measuring the economic value of employee performance*. New York, Amacom
The father of HR metrics and founder of the Saratoga Institute provides lots of numerate ideas for measurement. This book shows how to gauge productivity and people costs at the levels of the organisation, a function and HRM. Essential reading for somebody going into the subject in more depth.

MAYO, A. J. (2001) *The Human Value of the Enterprise – Valuing people as assets, measuring, managing, monitoring*. London, Nicholas Brealey
This book provides an overview of human capital management and the measures associated with it. It argues why they are important and introduces the concept of 'the human capital monitor' for linking people, engagement and performance. It goes into detail in the possible measures for each area, and in so doing draws out the implications for 'value-based HRM'. It examines the impact on mergers and acquisitions of human capital management, and finally the issue of public reporting.

HRM and Employee Representation

CHAPTER 17

Employment relations

Paul Higgins *and* Richard Croucher

INTRODUCTION

This chapter is about employment relations – ie the *collective* relations between managers and employees and the influence that various actors have on the terms and conditions of employment, discipline and grievance.

LEARNING OUTCOMES

By the end of this chapter readers should be able to:

- identify the most important actors in employment relations
- recognise the importance of collective bargaining to the management of the employment relationship
- consider the impact of recent national and European legislation on unionised and non-unionised workplaces
- describe the appropriate grievance and discipline procedures for different employee issues.

The chapter is structured in three parts.

After the starter case study, designed to outline some of the issues that emerge in the employment relations field, the first part of the chapter endeavours to identify the characteristics and motivations of the key actors in employment relations. Attention then focuses upon trade union recognition and in particular the reasons why some organisations might choose to be pro- or anti-trade union. The section concludes by examining the prevalence of the two main forms of collective representation by workplace characteristics.

In the chapter's second section, we consider in more detail the interplay between the key employment relations actors by reference to two of the most important pieces of employment relations legislation in recent years. The first of these is the statutory recognition procedure introduced by the New Labour government in 1999. This is followed by an examination of 'partnership' between management and unions. The second piece of legislation is that which requires companies

This case study is based around a debate undertaken by four employees – Angela, Ashok, Charlene and Jim – regarding the virtues of joining and not joining a trade union. The debate subtly illuminates the complicated relationship between collectively organised employees, individual employees, union firms, non-union firms and government.

Charlene begins proceedings.

Charlene: I wouldn't join a trade union – they're troublemakers. Look at how trade unions caused havoc during the miners' strike in the 1980s and nearly brought the country to its knees. If it hadn't had been for the Conservatives, the country would never have changed. Look at all of the opportunities now! Much better jobs.

Jim: I agree – and besides, since Margaret Thatcher, trade unions haven't got much power anyway, so what's the point in joining them? In artificially raising wages they increased inflation, raised prices, made Britain uncompetitive and overburdened the taxpayer. I'm glad they've been disciplined.

Ashok: But can't you see it from the opposite perspective? Without trade unions wages would fall and employment conditions would worsen.

Charlene: No, not any more. Many organisations try to prevent union growth by offering better wages than agreed rates and also highly reward good individual performance – so if you work hard, you get paid more. That's fair. Look at some lazy people who fail to contribute to group work but get 'carried' by others and still get the same pay. It's a similar sort of thing. I'm an achiever. I don't want to be held back by others.

Angela: Actually, many professionals and well-paid people are members of trade unions as well – even professional footballers – so trade unions don't necessarily hold you back. On average, trade union members tend to be better paid than the average worker anyway. Ashok's right – you must also consider the situation of workers on lower pay without a trade union. They often have poor terms and conditions of employment, without protection. You only need to consider the work experience amongst retail staff, waiters and waitresses, bar staff, carers, call centre operatives . . . The list goes on.

Jim: Well, there's the minimum wage for them.

Angela: But that doesn't bring security nor necessarily mean good conditions of employment. You have to consider what each hour of work actually demands.

Ashok: I agree with Angela. People need a say at work, a countervailing power to management and capital. And anyway, in some organisations it might even be beneficial for both sides – employers and employees – to talk and improve matters for everyone. Employees are often closer to the user and can present management with good ideas that can help to achieve its goals. And if you treat staff well and pay them fairly, they will give back, too.

Jim: Yeah, but the conditions aren't there now. You can't treat waiters and waitresses or call centre staff too well because if you do, they'll lose their jobs. It's part of the global environment now. People will swear at you whatever. And there are plenty of people around the world who will accept inferior conditions, so if you don't put up, you shut up or leave.

Angela: And the employer loses someone with some ideas of their own, who's a bit more than just a 'yes' person and who can probably be used to help improve the ways things are done at work.

Questions for discussion

1. What can be learned from this debate?

2. Whose perspective do you most agree with, and why?

3. What would be your reasons for joining or for not joining a trade union?

with more than 50 employees to inform and consult with their staff on matters important to the employment relationship. The implications of both statutes for union and non-union organisations are carefully considered.

In the third section of the chapter we move on to consider the twin issues of discipline and grievance. These are vitally important issues for all HR professionals because they can be brought up in employment tribunals and courts of law. Taking each of these issues in turn we provide a definition of the terms, consider some trends in respect of their prevalence, and then go on to examine their statutory procedures.

The chapter concludes with the main case study.

Reference sources named within the chapter may be looked up in the *References and further reading* section at the end of the book.

1 KEY ACTORS IN EMPLOYMENT RELATIONS

WHO ARE THE KEY ACTORS?

The starter case study centred on the impact of trade unions, which are regarded as a key actor in employment relations. Trade unions are important to the study of employment relations because they represent an exclusively collective orientation to the employment relationship which might further entail representation and collective bargaining. Their existence and function within employment relations can therefore be contrasted with the more widespread individual forms of employee representation or even those conducted through unrecognised systems of collective representation.

Trade unions and individual employees are not, however, the only actors in employment relations, the complexity of which also includes the actions of the direct employer and its relationship with external employer associations and subcontractors and, of course, legislative authorities both domestic and, in the case of the United Kingdom, European. In this first section we consider the general characteristics and motivation of these various actors before focusing upon the issue of the importance of collective bargaining to the management of the employment relationship.

The key actors in employment relations can be identified as:

- the Government
- employers and management
- individually and collectively represented employees.

Government

The Government exerts a major influence on employment relations by enacting legislation, devising and executing economic policy and acting as an employer, directly or indirectly within the public sector. The Government is also involved to maintain order, to improve competitiveness, to redistribute wealth and to ensure social justice and fairness, to attract investment and to improve well-being. The Government can also pass direct employment relations legislation such as the Race Relations Act 1976 and the Sex Discrimination Act 1975 (see Chapter 5). It can also influence employment relations issues in indirect ways – for example, by its management of the economy, by passing other laws, by shaping the public mood through its politics and ideology, and by embarking upon the policies of nationalisation and privatisation. Over time, various governments in the United Kingdom have also created a number of independent employment relations agencies. These include employment tribunals, the Advisory Conciliation and Arbitration Service (ACAS), the Central Arbitration Committee (CAC) and the Certification Officer.

Although the Government is a key and overriding employment relations actor, there are no agreed limits to its actions because it intervenes for a number of reasons and in a number of ways. The Government has intervened strongly in employment relations since the 1960s, particularly, as suggested by the opening case study, during the Thatcher period (Wedderburn, 1991; Smith and Morton, 1993; Harvey, 2003). In more recent years, since the election of New Labour in 1997, some of the Government's most important legislative developments with respect to employment relations have included the establishment of the National Minimum Wage Regulations and the implementation of various European Union Directives such as the Working Time Directive and the Part-Time Workers Directive (Crouch, 2001; Smith and Morton, 2006).

Despite these broader regulatory shifts, however, Labour's approach to employment relations has not led to a radical departure from the approach adopted by the Conservatives. The reason for this is that New Labour shares its predecessor's enthusiasm for encouraging a flexible labour market, many of the more notable reforms, which might serve to regulate this, originating from the European Union rather than being purely domestic measures. This suggests that New Labour is not so much *responding* to the 'globalisation' threat but rather *creating* its very conditions. The following quote from former Prime Minister Tony Blair (1998) provides a good example of this:

> There will be no going back. The days of strikes without ballots, mass picketing, closed shops and secondary picketing are over. Even after the changes we propose, Britain will have the most lightly regulated labour market of any leading economy in the world.

Employers and management

Employers and management can relate either to those people responsible *in* organisations for carrying out the strategic and decision-making responsibilities or to those from *outside* the organisation who may have a direct or indirect influence on organisational goals. The second are subcontractors for the organisation, employers' associations and consultants.

In the first instance, we are referring to those organisational-based managers and employers responsible for the effective operation of the organisation. Precisely how these managers influence the employment relationship depends upon whether they, and particularly those specialists known as personnel officers or human resource managers, adopt a 'hard' or 'soft' approach to employment relations issues (Guest, 1987; Storey, 1992). The 'hard' approach takes its description from the perspective that the human resource is simply a factor of production together with land and capital and is largely treated as an expense to be cut rather than as potential for turning production into wealth. In contrast, the 'soft' model treats employees as valued assets, as a source of competitive advantage to be nurtured, trained and improved.

Our second instance includes subcontractors. At the extreme are organisations whose managers conduct employment relations through the medium of various forms of subcontracting. This involves employing the labour force indirectly or externally through an agent or subcontractor who deals with recruiting the workforce, monitoring production and paying workers (Grimshaw, Marchington, Rubery and Willmott, 2005). Subcontracting has the advantage to the host firm that labour issues are passed over to another organisation, and because of this it is easier to lay workers off as necessary. It has the disadvantage, however, that organisations using subcontracted labour have less direct control over the effort and compliance of workers.

Meanwhile, in more generally seeking to influence the employment relations landscape, employers and managers from different organisations sometimes organise together to collectively represent themselves through a employers' or management association. These associations are formed from representatives of firms within a particular industry and provide various services for member firms. They vary in size and influence from the very small with no full-time staff to large and highly influential organisations such as the Engineering Employers Federation, the Road Haulage Association and Retail Motor Industry Federation. These, along with consultants and lawyers, frequently advise companies about employment relations issues.

Individually and collectively represented employees

The final key actor in employment relations we can consider is employees. Employees are responsible for carrying out the day-to-day activities that lead to the achievement of organisational goals and might be employed on a full-time, part-time, temporary or casual basis. They might work for a single or for multiple employers and generally have other commitments outside of their paid work such as caring for dependants, specific ways of spending leisure time, consumption and studying. In terms of their paid work, employees may decide to represent themselves to their employer on either an individual or a collective basis. A number of the ways in which employees might individually represent themselves are examined in the chapter on communication (Chapter 19). For the purposes of this section, however, we are more concerned with employees who represent themselves collectively.

There are two main ways in which employees might decide to collectively represent themselves. The first is with the assistance of an independent trade union. The second is without trade union representation by setting up a body such as a joint consultative committee (JCC). These are usually organised within a single organisation and tend to involve consultation rather than negotiation.

Taking the latter first, there are numerous reasons why some organisations might not have trade union representation. For example, in smaller self-employed or family-run organisations no formally employed labour might be used and therefore there are no formal employment relations processes. Meanwhile, in smaller-scale organisations with few employees, staff often engage in interpersonal and face-to-face interaction without formal processes. However, at the same time, such organisations might instead be very autocratic in style such that The Boss compels employees to accept his/her commands. In contrast, for larger, medium-sized firms employing between 100 and 500 people a range of soft and hard human resource management styles are likely to be in evidence. However, unlike small businesses, most will operate with formal procedures and will have varying degrees of hierarchically organised control systems.

Finally, although there are only a few large non-union firms they do still, nonetheless, have a high profile in human resource textbooks. In the current climate, it is questionable what benefits such organisations that seek to avoid unions can achieve, particularly if they embark upon 'union substitution' strategies (Fiorito and Maranto, 1987; Guest and Conway, 1999). These are strategies that seek to gain the commitment of employees to corporate goals by, for example, paying above the union-negotiated pay (see below), and other employment conditions. In other words, in trying to keep unions out, non-union firms must in theory satisfy their workers in ways that independent trade unions would seek to do anyway. In turn, this means that such companies must have an interest in the outcome of collective bargaining (see below) although they are not direct parties to it.

For all of these reasons many non-union organisations are described as utilising 'best practice' HRM strategies which involve ensuring good pay and benefits, good complaints procedures, good job security and good communication. At the same time, a number of non-union firms might also display the characteristics of the 'ugly' face of non-unionism, with poor terms and conditions of employment and negligible or one-dimensional consultation strategies. This is particularly likely to be the case in low-skilled subcontracted work.

Meanwhile, the power of a trade union to actively influence the management of the employment relationship depends greatly upon whether it is 'recognised' by its members' employers for the purposes of collective bargaining. Unless otherwise compelled (see below), there are various arguments that an employer might put for and against choosing to recognise a trade union. In the first instance, an employer might choose to work with a union because it regards the union as an essential part of the communication process, particularly, as suggested above, in larger workplaces where it might be too time-consuming to talk to each employee separately. Similarly, such union-friendly organisations might think that by reaching agreement with union representatives, in contrast to imposing decisions, they will make superior decisions. On the other hand, employers are often concerned that trade unions make decision-making and communication in companies slow, cumbersome and inflexible. There is a view that unions tend to resist change and take a long time to get things done. The result is a reduction in the ability of managers to respond quickly and flexibly to market pressures and opportunities. In the light of these concerns, it might seem appropriate that they consider to what extent collective consent can be achieved by other means.

Either way, the step of 'being recognised' marks a very significant movement away from unilateral decision-making by management and involves the joint determination between management and trade union representatives of two sets of rules: substantive and procedural. Substantive rules establish terms and conditions of employment, such as pay, working hours, overtime arrangements, fringe benefits and holidays. Also included are training and promotion prospects. Procedural issues focus upon the issue of *how* the substantive issues are decided and relate to the rules and regulations determining decision-making at industrial, organisational and workplace levels.

In practice, the substantive outcomes of collective bargaining are not confined to union members. Unionised organisations apply collectively bargained terms and conditions of employment to their non-union employees as well as to their unionised ones. Equally significant to these collective rights, recognition imposes a duty on the employer to inform and consult about training, redundancy, pensions and health and safety.

Although there are various arguments that can be put for and against an employer's choosing to recognise a trade union, in the last 30 or so years the United Kingdom has moved from a position in which a large majority of people worked in establishments which recognised trade unions to one in which the large majority do not. The latest workplace employment relations survey, conducted in 2004 (Kersley, Alpin, Forth, Dix, Oxenbridge, Bryson and Bewley, 2006), details the percentage of workplaces that recognise a trade union and/or entertain a workplace-level JCC. The data is reproduced in Table 38.

Table 38 Percentage extent of trade union recognition and joint consultative committee coverage

	Trade union recognition	Workplace-level JCC
All workplaces	30	14
Organisation sector		
Private	16	11
Public	90	28
Industry		
Manufacturing	13	21
Wholesale retail	10	11
Hotels and restaurants	0	4
Financial services	72	5
Public administration	100	42
Education	81	30
Health and social work	41	13

Source: Kersley *et al* (2006)

Why do the substantive outcomes of collective bargaining apply to both union and non-union employees?

Why are the trade union figures for public sector organisations in Table 38 much higher than for private sector organisations?

Why are the trade union recognition figures for retail and restaurants so low?

The scale of difference between union recognition and JCC representation is low in some industries but high in others – how has this come about?

Note that we have here introduced the concept of *ratios* of one job family to another, or of one as a percentage of the whole workforce. These can be more revealing than simple statistics.

2 THE IMPACT OF NATIONAL AND EU LEGISLATION ON UNIONISED AND NON-UNIONISED WORKPLACES

So far we have considered the three most important actors in employment relations. It was explained that the Government, via requirements of the European Union, determines the overall legal framework and creates specific employment relations organisations such as ACAS. Then, from within these broad parameters managers, employers, employees and their representatives seek to influence organisational goals and outcomes.

Against this backdrop we now move on to consider in more detail the employment relationship between the key actors with respect to some of the most recent and important employment relations legislation. The first piece of legislation to be considered is the Employment Relations Act 1999, which introduced a statutory recognition procedure and paved the way for the development of social partnerships between employers and unions. The second is the Information and Consultation of Employee Regulations 2004, which compel qualifying employers to inform and consult with their workforce on a range of matters.

STATUTORY RECOGNITION PROCEDURE

Employers' attitudes to trade union organisation do not operate in a vacuum and depend on, among other things, a willingness for trade union participation and on government policy. In the first instance, as was suggested above, employees might feel safe in their jobs, with good terms and conditions of employment and thus not regard trade union membership and representation as necessary. Likewise, employers might work hard at both securing and maintaining employee consent and commitment through other means. Alternatively, sufficient numbers of employees might have a grievance at work (see below) and seek trade union representation to express this on more equal terms with their employer.

In the second instance, by passing legislation, the Government can have a tremendously important impact on employment relations. In recent years, government policy under the guise of New Labour has shifted with respect to collective representation via the passing of the Employment Relations Act 1999 (Waddington, 2003). This piece of legislation has provided trade unions with a legal right to trade union recognition provided the following conditions are met:

- the organisation has more than 20 employees

- the organisation has a minimum 10% 'threshold' union membership.

If these requirements are met, the following steps have to be taken for the union formally to secure recognition:

- Step 1: The union must formally approach the Central Arbitration Committee (CAC).

- Step 2: The employer must define the 'bargaining unit'.

- Step 3: The employer must allow the union access to canvass votes/members.

- Step 4: The vote must be taken, with due concern for confidentiality.

- Step 5: The union must receive a minimum of 50% of the vote, and at least 40% of those eligible to vote must have voted.

In fact, as Step 5 implies, if the trade union already has over 50% membership in the employer's organisation, recognition is largely automatic.

Since the passing of the Employment Relations Act 1999, cases of union recognition have increased, although much of this increase has occurred through voluntary recognition deals rather as a result of the statutory process. The reason for this is that by signing a voluntary deal, employers have much more influence over the content of the agreement and avoid a potentially damaging confrontation with their workforce. Lewis, Thornhill and Saunders (2003; p.159) adapt TUC data to show this trend in Table 39.

Table 39 The incidence of union recognitions by voluntary agreement 1996–2001

Period	Number of months	Number of voluntary agreements
Jan–Dec 1996	12	110
Jan 1997–Feb 1998	14	81
Mar 1998–Oct 1999	20	109
Nov 1999–Oct 2000	12	159
Nov 2000–Oct 2001	12	450

Source: Lewis *et al* (2003; p.159)

REFLECTIVE ACTIVITY

From Table 39 calculate the average number of recognition agreements per month.

What has been the trend over time, and what factors might account for this?

'Partnerships'

Given the difficulties that can be faced by some organisations over determining the terms and conditions of employment, a 'partnership approach' to the employment relationship has been adopted by some employers who have been faced with a claim for union recognition or who have decided to reassess and change their approach and relationship with employees and their representative bodies.

Many commentators view the adoption of a partnership approach to employment relations as being more reflective of a co-operative, joint problem-solving atmosphere where employers, employees and trade unions work together to achieve common goals such as fairness, competitiveness and job security (Ackers and Payne, 1998; Haynes and Allen, 2000). A variety of research suggests that partnerships might yield benefits for both parties. For the employer the beneficial outcomes might include higher employee commitment, a greater willingness to contribute, less absence, less labour turnover, less industrial conflict and superior performance. For the employees the benefits might include opportunities to exercise greater autonomy and direct participation, a more positive psychological contract, and an opportunity to share in the financial gains through employee share ownership. Likewise, other research has highlighted that there may also be gains for employee representatives, such as greater influence over employment issues and better representative organisational structures.

However, both the Confederation of British Industry (CBI) (Taylor, 1997) and the Chartered Institute of Personnel and Development (1998) have expressed concern that the onus of partnership is on employer–employment relations rather than employer–trade union relations. The basis for this argument is that employees' best interests are met when they can have some input into decisions which affect their day-to-day work activities, so long as these activities are restricted to work issues rather than wider organisational matters. It is suggested that 'communication programmes' geared to improve employee commitment to company goals and values might supplement such an approach.

Alternatively, there are trade union-sponsored approaches to partnership which embrace a central role for trade union representation, to help secure an independent employee voice in the workplace. This second approach centres on various forms of employee participation and involvement in everyday workplace activities. Indeed, a good way of distinguishing between the forms of communication that might prevail under the various forms of partnership is to utilise the terms 'employee involvement' and 'employee participation'.

Both methods assume that employees have a say at work, although the nature of such 'voice' differs tremendously. Put simply, employee involvement can be seen as enhancing the support and commitment of the organisation, and employee participation as providing employees with the opportunity to influence and take part in organisational decision-making. The key differences between the two are detailed in Table 40.

Table 40 Employee involvement and employee participation

Employee involvement	Employee participation
Inspired and controlled by management	Aims to harness collective employee inputs through market regulation
Oriented towards encouraging individual employee inputs through market regulation	Collective representation
Directed to responsibilities of individual employees	Management and organisational hierarchy's chain of command broken
Employees are often passive recipients of information and decisions already made	Active involvement of employee representatives
Decisions tend to be task-based	Decision-making at higher organisational levels
Assumes common interests between employer and employees	Plurality of interests recognised and machinery for their resolution provided
Aims to concentrate strategic influence among management	Aims to distribute strategic influence beyond management

REFLECTIVE ACTIVITY

Do you think it is possible for employers and employees to work together as a genuine partnership, or is there some underlying conflict of interest?

Which do you think requires better communication – involvement or participation? Why?

INFORMATION AND CONSULTATION

As a member state of the European Union, the UK is now subject to the terms of the Information and Consultation of Employee Regulations (ICE Regulations) 2004 (Hall, 2006), which began to take effect in 2005. The ICE Regulations are based on a framework agreed between the CBI and the Trades Union Congress. Under the standard provisions of these Regulations, qualifying employers must inform and consult with their workforce on measures that are expected to entail substantial changes in work organisation or contractual relations such as pay, redundancies and job transfers. Also included are training and development, equal opportunities, health, safety and environment and pension and welfare issues. Moreover, qualifying employers must inform and consult on recent and probable developments of the undertaking's activities and economic situation, such as profit and loss, sales performance, productivity, market developments and strategic plans. The implementation of the Regulations was staggered, beginning first by covering undertakings with more than 150 employees. From April 2008 the Regulations apply to undertakings with 50 or more employees.

The Regulations are intended to facilitate voluntary, rather than standard, agreements to emerge so that the characteristics of particular organisations can be accommodated, thus avoiding the laying down of detailed 'one-size-fits-all' rules that apply to everyone. Employers that have 'pre-existing' information and consultation agreements that cover all employees only have to consider making changes if they receive a request supported by 40% of employees to negotiate new arrangements. In such pre-existing and negotiated agreements it is possible for information and consultation arrangements to be either direct (between managers and employees) or indirect (through employee representatives) or a combination of the two.

In contrast, organisations that do not have formally approved information and consultation agreements may be vulnerable to having the Regulations' standard provisions for informing and consulting employees imposed on them if just 10% of employers make a request for new arrangements. Employers in this position will be required to negotiate new arrangements, but if agreement cannot be reached, the standard provisions apply. In particular, the Regulations' standard provisions allow for the election of employee representatives and the establishment of indirect methods of informing and consulting with the workforce.

The implications of the ICE Regulations for union and non-union organisations

The information and consultation regulations could potentially change the interface between employers and their employees substantially, whether trade unions are recognised or not. Because few organisations have 100% union membership or collective bargaining arrangements covering all employees, it is likely that strongly unionised occupational groups will be found alongside other groups with weak or non-existent union organisation. Many managers will have to decide whether to develop integrated or parallel systems of employee representation. Some commentators suggest that there is likely to be growth in the number of hybrid systems, and that the new legislation may test the degree of commitment that managers have for trade union-based collective bargaining. At the same time, the Regulations also give unions an opportunity to have structured contact with the non-unionised sections of the workforce, allowing the former to demonstrate to the latter the logic and benefits of union membership. Table 41, drawing upon WERS 2004, shows the types of issues, and their perceived importance, dealt with by union and non-union representatives over a 12-month period.

Table 41 Issues dealt with by employee representatives

Type of issue	Union representative		Non-union representative	
	Spent time on issue in past 12 months	Most important issue in past 12 months	Spent time on issue in past 12 months	Most important issue in past 12 months
Terms and conditions	79	38	65	31
Selection, development and staffing	69	18	77	31
Welfare issues	68	11	60	15
Individual disputes	73	16	44	6
Other issues	10	17	12	16

Source: Kersley et al (2006)

REFLECTIVE ACTIVITY

What differences in the significance of issues to union representatives and to non-union representatives can you spot in the figures as listed in Table 41?

To what extent do you think the figures in Table 41 support the argument that one feature of the ICE Regulations is that they allow union representatives to demonstrate to non-union employees the logic and benefits of union membership?

The impact of the ICE Regulations will be greater in organisations with no union recognition. The reason for this is that the preference among non-union employers is not to create any formal indirect structure of employee representation. Amongst such organisations, the Regulations mean that employers will find it more difficult to conduct their relationship with the workforce on a strictly 'need to know' basis. Instead, they will have to continuously inform and consult with employees on a broad range of issues and in a structured manner. Information and consultation agreements must not only be in writing and cover all employees of the undertaking, they must also set out how the employer is to give information to the employees or their representatives and to seek their views on such information. Employees will also be able to seek information from their employers rather than having to be content to receive whatever information management feels is in the best interest of the employees to receive.

In considering these requirements, it should finally be reiterated, however, that the practice of information and consultation is not the same as collective bargaining. Whereas the former is linked to the exchange of information and ideas, collective bargaining is the process by which employers and recognised trade unions jointly reach and negotiate decisions regarding the employment relationship such as pay and terms and conditions of employment. Moreover, although under the ICE Regulations employees will be given the opportunity to express their views and opinions about specific issues, the employer is not compelled to act upon them. The employer simply has to consider those opinions, provide feedback, and where necessary explain why actions have not been taken.

Having said that, organisations should ensure that they are compliant with the ICE Regulations or they could face a maximum penalty of £75,000. Organisations should also be aware that employees can challenge existing arrangements – and they may find that they are compelled to negotiate new arrangements.

3   DISCIPLINE AND GRIEVANCE

Thus far, we have considered the main actors in employment relations and, in particular, how national and European legislation has shaped the employment relations landscape in recent years and its impact on union and non-union forms of representation. Attention now turns to the twin issues of discipline and grievance, which form part of a two-way process that concerns complaints by managers and workers against one another. From 1 October 2004, the Employment Act 2002 made it a legal requirement for all organisations to follow minimum disciplinary, dismissal and grievance procedures in certain circumstances. These statutory procedures amount to a minimum standard that must be followed by all employers and employees, although many employers have more detailed and elaborate procedures than these minima. This section considers the implications of this Act for grievance and discipline procedures, and in addition presents a wider context because in issues of this sort HR managers need to know enough to speak with some authority.

GRIEVANCE

A grievance usually arises because an aggrieved individual regards some management decision (or act of indecision) or behaviour on the part of another employee (normally a manager) as unfair and unjust in its application to him or her. Grievances can be extremely serious, such as a sexual assault or a severe safety hazard. They may be less serious in totality but of serious concern to the employee, such as a new shift rota, a failure to consider for promotion, a critical appraisal report, a lack of opportunity for overtime or too much pressure of work. The types of grievance respondents mentioned to the 1998 and 2004 Workplace and Employment Relations Survey are provided in Table 42.

Most minor grievance and disciplinary matters can be dealt with in the day-to-day informal contact between employees and management, and in some respects this is perhaps the best way of dealing with them. There is something to be said for keeping things informal – the cost of formal hearings and the way that they 'raise the stakes' on the issue are two significant points here. However, there is also something to be said for formal procedures because these procedures enable everyone concerned to know exactly where they stand. For more serious cases, the Employment Act 2002 therefore sets out two statutory grievance procedures: standard and modified.

Table 42 Most common grievances raised in WERS 1998 and 2004

Grievance	Workplaces % 1998	Workplaces % 2004
Pay and conditions	25	18
Poor relations with supervisors, line managers	16	16
Work practices, pace of work	14	12
Working time, annual leave or time off work	13	10
Physical working conditions, health and safety	12	10
Promotion, career development	14	8
Bullying at work	3	7
Job grading or classification	13	6
Use of disciplinary sanctions, including dismissal	–	5
Performance appraisal	7	4
Sexual harassment	3	2
Selection for redundancies	–	2
Relations with other employees	–	2
Sex or race discrimination	3	1
Racial harassment	1	1
No grievances raised formally in past 12 months	44	53

Source: Kersley *et al* (2006)

The *standard procedure* has the following three steps:

- Step 1: the employee informs the employer of the grievance in writing
- Step 2: they meet to discuss the grievance
- Step 3: an appeal, if requested, is held.

The *modified procedure* is intended to apply where a dismissal has already occurred and comprises two steps:

- Step 1: the employee must set out the grievance and the basis of it in writing and send the statement or a copy to the employer
- Step 2: the employer must set out its response in writing and send the statement or a copy to the employee.

All grievance procedures, then, aim to ensure that the employee's case is heard quickly, that the employee concerned has a fair hearing with an opportunity for full discussion to take place, and that a response from management follows without too long a gap. The procedure should make clear to whom the grievance is to be addressed, who should accompany employees if they require somebody to help them in the process, and specific time limits for the meeting to be held and the decision given, plus the stages of any appeal. This really does mean at all times that people 'know where they stand'.

The right to appeal is important, and it must be noted here that the legal principle of natural justice requires that the person who hears the appeal should not be the person who previously heard the case at an earlier stage in the procedure. If this is not the case, the appeal may well not be regarded as valid at an employment tribunal and the employer is likely to lose this aspect of any case.

Failure to address grievances can be a serious matter and cause problems with motivation or demotivation – failure to address issues often leaves employees with 'residual anger' which can escalate into general unrest and disputes in the workplace. Thus, employees must know to whom they can turn in the event of a grievance and the support, such as counselling or sources of advice, that is available to them. Likewise, all line and senior managers must be familiar with their organisation's grievance procedure. HR managers need to impress this on line managers, and training can often be a useful way of doing this. Meanwhile, individuals should be encouraged to discuss ordinary, day-to-day issues informally with their line manager. This helps concerns to be heard and responded to as soon as possible.

The key risk for HR practitioners is not following the organisation's own procedures. It is this that most commonly causes employers to lose cases at employment tribunals. Perhaps more importantly, however, it can bring the procedures themselves into disrepute since employees are likely to notice breaches of procedure. Having procedures brought into disrepute is not likely to be positive for the HR department.

DISCIPLINE

One major consequence of employing people is that there must be a series of rules which regulates their behaviour. In many cases, disciplinary procedures are used to ensure compliance with these rules and a controlled and effective employee performance. This can, however, be one of the most difficult issues with which a manager has to deal because it brings to close attention matters relating to an individual's performance/capability and conduct.

In the first instance, all employers are likely to encounter some difficulties with the performance and capability of some of their employees (although such difficulties might derive from insufficient training and support). It is therefore good practice that such issues are addressed informally by managers via discussions which clarify what good performance 'looks like' and include goal-setting, support and timely positive feedback. Only when these options have been exhausted and where there is no alternative should managers enter a more formal disciplinary procedure.

In the second instance, employee conduct – or rather more accurately, *mis*conduct – could range from continued lateness or a failure to follow a reasonable management instruction through to theft, fighting and the committing of a more serious criminal offence. The most serious offences may constitute gross misconduct in the meaning of the disciplinary procedure, in which case the employee has clearly indicated that he or she has gone beyond the bounds of the contract and the employer has the right to instantly dismiss the employee. 'Gross misconduct' is a problematic term, however, in that there are often no solid safeguards that ensure that the allegation is actually proven. To draw an analogy: if someone is accused of a serious offence that may be punished with a serious penalty, the accusation is not tested according to *lower* standards of proof in a court of law. So for managers it is important to ensure that allegations are subjected to reasonably full investigation before dismissal. 'Gross misconduct' allegations are for this reason occasionally misused by managers seeking to impose strong penalties with little use of time-consuming procedures. HR managers must therefore monitor such situations closely, because their misuse can lead to demotivation on the part of those employees not disciplined who feel that a colleague has been treated unfairly and fear that the same could happen to them.

With misdemeanours, which are lesser offences, there is no right of dismissal for a first offence so warnings are the appropriate penalty. The practical distinction between gross misconduct and misdemeanours is, however, a delicate one and the boxes below provide a list of actions that would normally fall into either of the categories.

Examples of misdemeanours	**Examples of gross misconduct**
● Time-keeping not up to the required standard	● Fighting
	● Working under the influence of drink or drugs
● Attendance not up to the required standard	● Giving confidential information to competitors
● Performance not up to the required standard	● Theft
	● Fraud
● Inappropriate attitude towards management, fellow employees, customers or suppliers	● Sexual harassment
	● Deliberately damaging the organisation's property

As part of their employment, employees need to know what actions or lack of actions can lead to a formal disciplinary process being initiated, and ultimately, if serious enough, dismissal. Disciplinary practices, ranging from oral warnings to the termination of the employment relationship, aim to make employees' behaviour predictable and for those employers and managers with an autocratic style there is a framework of legal rights regulating the disciplinary process. Thus, disciplinary procedures are necessary:

● so that employees know what is expected of them in terms of standards of performance or conduct (and the likely consequences of continued failure to meet these standards)

● to identify obstacles to individuals' achieving the required standards (for example, training needs, lack of clarity of job requirements, lack of timely support) and to identify appropriate action to be taken

- as an opportunity to agree suitable goals and time-scales for improvement in an individual's performance or conduct

- as a point of reference for an employment tribunal should an employee make a complaint about the way he or she was dismissed

- to provide employees with clear guidance on what is acceptable in the workplace in terms of both behaviour and performance.

One of the main problems HR managers often encounter with these procedures is that different line managers see things differently, and as a result employees are not dealt with equitably across the organisation. That is, one employee receives a severe penalty in one case but another employee elsewhere receives a lesser penalty for what is essentially an identical case. A way of dealing with this is to maintain good, detailed records of cases and their outcomes.

Overall, a fair and effective disciplinary procedure is one that concentrates on improving or changing behaviour, rather than one that relies on the principle of punishment. It usually operates by a system of warnings – and an organisation's policy should outline exactly what warnings will be given and when. The following, in order of severity, are the most commonly used warnings:

- a formal oral warning (of which a record is kept)

- a first written warning

- a final written warning.

Any warning should specify a review period during which the individual receives appropriate support and during which his or her performance can be monitored. Similarly, a decision must also be made in relation to the length of time warnings will remain in place. This is sometimes called a 'slate clean' clause. The reason for this is that if it is too short a time, the employer runs the risk of achieving only short-term changes in behaviour. Yet if it is a long time, a sanction that remains on an employee's record for an excessive period of time relative to the original breach of discipline can act as a demotivating influence. Typical time-scales for the continued 'validity' of the three types of warning are:

- a formal oral warning: six months

- a first written warning: one year

- a final written warning: two years.

Where misconduct has been very serious, it may be appropriate for the warning to continue in force indefinitely.

More generally, employers have to be sure that any decision to dismiss an employee will be seen as 'reasonable' by an employment tribunal. Managers must be able to show that they have acted reasonably having regard to all the circumstances. As noted above, the employer must have followed the statutory and any other procedures in the organisation's procedural system prior to any dismissal and also have been fair. Other reasons employees might be dismissed include:

- they are employed under a fixed-term contract and that contract comes to an end without being renewed

- they are made redundant

- they lack the capability and qualifications to do the job – this covers the area of poor performance or the lack or loss of a necessary qualification

- they are in breach of statutory provision – such as the lack of a work permit or security clearance in parts of the public sector

- some other substantial reason – this covers areas such as making a false statement on their application form.

An individual is entitled to be accompanied by a work colleague or trade union official at formal disciplinary and grievance interviews, and for that purpose to select a companion of his or her choice. It is important to note that the right to be accompanied applies to every individual, not just union members, and it is of no consequence whether the organisation recognises unions or not.

REFLECTIVE ACTIVITY

List several employee actions/events each of what you think constitutes a) a misdemeanour and b) gross misconduct.

What disciplinary measures do you think are justified for the examples of grievance, misdemeanour and gross misconduct you have listed?

KEY ISSUES: EMPLOYMENT RELATIONS

We now pull together key points about the main issues raised in this chapter:

- Collective relations with employees remain important in many parts of the economy and large companies.

- Collective organisation of employees can bring benefits for companies as well as the employees.

- Trade unions are one important form of employee organisation, but not the only one. Employers also have to follow the law in consulting with employees by other methods.

- Relations with employee bodies can be partnership-based and need not be confrontational.

- HR managers have to be aware of the possibility of trade union recognition claims and how they operate.

- Following grievance and disciplinary procedures is vital for HR professionals, because the alternative is employment tribunals and court cases.

Perhaps there are other key points that you would like to note for yourself.

MAIN CASE STUDY

Look at the description of the case set out below. Then decide on the recommendations that you would make as an HR manager for dealing with the issues raised. Try to think beyond the level of a 'quick fix' or simple solutions by developing a longer-term strategy as well as responding to the immediate issue.

A large City financial services firm employs large numbers of very well-paid financial services staff in its plush offices in Canary Wharf in London. It has outsourced its office cleaning to a firm of contract cleaners. Most of the cleaning staff work when the offices are empty (or nearly empty, since some of the financial staff work very late and sometimes into the night). The contract cleaning staff come from many countries of the world. In fact, very few of the dozens of cleaners are British and almost all of them are women.

Recently, a Union sent a young organiser to work at the contract cleaners, and this young woman has interested many of the contract cleaning staff in joining the union. There are many grievances among the cleaners. Some allege that they are not being paid the National Minimum Wage because they are often asked to do more hours than they are actually paid for. If they refuse to do them, they can lose their jobs. Some of the cleaners also make allegations of sexual harassment. These allegations have been taken up by the union organiser with the contract cleaning company, but the company's representatives have said that they want nothing to do with the union and will not recognise it.

The large City firm was picketed by the Union one morning. The demonstrators handed out leaflets explaining the situation to City workers coming to work in the morning, and have attracted a good deal of press publicity. The firm is now embarrassed by the bad publicity, which has had even more impact than it otherwise might have done because the company has recently lost a high-profile case of its own involving a young woman stockbroker who won considerable damages because of the sexual harassment she suffered at the hands of male stockbrokers. The company is now in a dilemma. Although it has outsourced the cleaning work, it sees only problems coming from this direction in the future. Whatever the contract cleaners think, they find themselves in the position of having to try to get it to deal with the allegations made by the union.

Questions for discussion

1 What lessons do you think this case study holds for HR professionals in the financial services company?

2 What actions should the company take?

EXPLORE FURTHER

ACAS provides a wealth of up-to-date information concerning best practice employment relations. Its website is: **http://www.acas.org.uk**

The Involvement and Participation Association (IPA) is a centre of excellence for organisations developing world-class strategies for employee involvement and partnership. Its online searchable database provides free and instant access to over 150 examples of workplace partnership, over 100 examples of employee consultation arrangements, and over 550 other entries dedicated to employee involvement and participation in the workplace. Its website is: **http://www.ipa-involve.com/**

KERSLEY, B., ALPIN, C., FORTH, J., DIX, G., OXENBRIDGE, S., BRYSON, A., and BEWLEY, H., (2006) *Inside the Workplace: Findings from the 2004 Workplace Employment Relations Survey.* London, Taylor & Francis
The Work Employment Relations Survey (2004) provides a wealth of information concerning the state of employee relations in Britain.

The Information and Consultation of Employee Regulations 2004 (2004) SI 2004/3426. London, Stationery Office. Available online at: **http://www.opsi.gov.uk/si/si2004/ 20043426.htm**
Provides full details of the Information and Consultation of Employee Regulations 2004.

CHAPTER 18

Health and safety at work

Phil James

INTRODUCTION

This chapter is about the importance of managing health and safety at work effectively, and how such management can be achieved. It is a subject all HR professionals should understand because it strongly affects employee welfare and an organisation's costs, and cannot therefore simply be left to specialists.

LEARNING OUTCOMES

By the end of this chapter readers should be able to:

- explain why an organisation should see the issue of health and safety at work as a central part of its people management activities

- identify the main causes of workplace injuries and ill-health

- put an effective health and safety management system in place, and

- build into such a system legally required arrangements for workforce involvement in the identification and resolution of workplace health and safety issues.

The starter case study is followed by three sections which explore, in turn, the extent of work-related injuries and ill-health and the costs that organisations incur as a result of such harm, some of the main factors that cause such harm, how employers can adopt a systematic approach to the management of workplace health and safety, and the arrangements that organisations must put in place with regard to workforce consultation and more general involvement in health and safety matters. The chapter concludes with the main case study which focuses attention on the management of stress – one of the most important sources of work-related ill-health.

Reference sources named within the chapter may be looked up in the *References and further reading* section at the end of the book.

An experienced mechanical fitter was asked by her employer to remove the motor from an extractor fan located five minutes' walk from her department – a task which involved unscrewing the nuts on two rows of bolts. During this work the fitter, who had worked for this firm for 10 years, discovered that one of the nuts could not be unscrewed. She therefore decided to remove the nut by wedging a chisel between it and the bolt in order to create tension between them so that one could be turned without the other. However, when she tried to do this, by inserting the chisel and striking it with a hammer, a piece of metal flew into her right eye; she was not wearing protective goggles.

The employee knew that the risk of such an injury existed when hammering metal on metal, a task that she undertook on an almost daily basis. She also knew that although goggles had not been supplied to her as an individual, they were available on a communal basis in the department where she was based.

Questions for discussion

1 To what extent was the employee involved in this incident responsible for its happening?

2 Did the accident occur partly because of weaknesses in how health and safety was managed in the workplace?

3 What actions could management take to prevent a similar event from occurring in the future?

1   THE IMPORTANCE OF HEALTH AND SAFETY AT WORK

The scale of injuries and ill-health arising from work activities around the world is large. In 2005 there were 199 deaths in South African mines, but in China's mines the rate of deaths per tonne of coal mined is four times as high as in South Africa. Around 300 British workers die each year as a result of accidents, according to official statistics, and this figure does not include those deaths arising from road transport accidents that take place during employment (HSE, 2006). Survey data also suggests that around 1 million workers annually suffer an accident at work, and that there are currently over 2 million people in Britain who consider themselves to be suffering from a health condition caused or made worse by their work. By far the most common of these health conditions are not 'traditional' occupational diseases but musculo-skeletal disorders (MSDs) and stress, depression and anxiety.

It is clear, therefore, that health and safety problems can arise not only among manual workers and those working in 'heavy' industries, such as construction, mining and manufacturing, but also in non-manual occupations, and in private and public sector service organisations. In fact, those employed in the health and social work, public administration, and education sectors are among those that are most likely to report that their health has been damaged as a result of work.

Health and safety is therefore an issue of relevance to all organisations. It is also one that has potentially significant cost implications for employers. According to the British Health and Safety Executive over 20 million working days are lost each year through absences arising from occupational injuries and ill-health, and a further 300 million days' work activities are in some way limited by work-related health conditions. More generally, it has been found that accidents can incur considerable costs for organisations, including the management time spent on their investigation and payments on sick pay, the replacement or repair of damaged equipment and the employment of temporary staff to cover for those absent as a result of their injuries. It has been found that in one hospital these costs amounted to the equivalent of 5% of its total operating expenditure, and that in the case of a transport company they represented 37% of its annual profits.

These costs exist alongside potential legal liabilities. Two main sources of such liability exist: that arising from personal injury litigation brought by those harmed by their work activities, and that arising from non-compliance with legal health and safety duties (James and Walters, 2005).

Personal injury litigation involves common law actions for compensation, or what are legally called 'damages'. British law, like US law, is different from that in many other countries. There is 'common law' – ie law made by judges that has built up through decisions in the past – and statute law enacted by Parliament.

Legal actions under common law may be taken on the grounds that an employer has been negligent – that is, it has failed to comply with its common-law duty to take reasonable steps to protect employees from reasonably foreseeable risks. They may also take the form of actions for breach of statutory duty and involve claims for compensation based on the fact that an employer did not comply with a relevant duty and that this failure contributed directly to the harm suffered by an employee. Any compensation awarded as a result of either of these two types of action is usually paid by insurance companies because employers are legally required to purchase employers' liability insurance to cover it. Insurance premiums may rise if claims are made by employers.

Not carrying out their statutory health and safety duties can lead to employers' being served with Improvement Notices which require them, within a specified period of time, to make changes, or Prohibition Notices which stop them from carrying out activities involving a risk of serious personal injury or ill-health. They can also result in their being prosecuted before magistrates or, on indictment, in the Crown Court.

The statutory duties on which failure can bring these penalties and actions are extensive. The central ones take the form of general duties under the Health and Safety at Work (HSW) Act 1974. These require employers to ensure, so far as reasonably practicable, the health, safety and welfare of employees and similarly to protect all those who may be affected by the conduct of their undertaking, including non-employees and members of the public (Gunningham and Johnstone, 2000; James and Walters, 2005). Employers are also prohibited from charging employees for anything provided in order to protect them in pursuance of statutory requirements – a prohibition that, for example, applies to any protective equipment and clothing so provided.

These general duties are supplemented by an extensive range of duties contained in a large number of supporting regulations made under the 1974 Act, such as the Control of Substances Hazardous to Health Regulations 2002, the Health and Safety (Display Screen Equipment) Regulations 1992, the Control of Noise at Work Regulations 2005, the Workplace (Health, Safety and Welfare) Regulations 1992, the Personal Protective Equipment Regulations 1992, the Provision and Use of Work Equipment Regulations 1998, the Manual Handling

Operations Regulations 1992 and the Management of Health and Safety at Work Regulations 1999. The last of these sets of Regulations are of particular importance. Among other things, they require employers to:

- carry out, record and revise risk assessments in respect of both employees and non-employees

- appoint competent persons – that is, those possessing suitable skills, qualifications and competences – to provide management with health and safety assistance

- establish procedures for handling situations involving 'serious and imminent danger'

- provide various types of information for employees, fixed-term employees, non-employees and temporary workers

- supply various types of information to visiting employers and other employers sharing the same workplace and employment businesses, and

- give adequate training to employees.

These same Regulations also impose a number of specific duties on employers in relation to the protection of young workers and new or expectant mothers.

THE CAUSES OF WORKPLACE INJURIES AND ILL-HEALTH

A huge range of factors can lead to workers' suffering harm as a result of their work. An insight into some of the more important of them can be obtained by looking at those that are commonly associated with the occurrence of workplace accidents, work-related stress and MSDs.

Accidents

The most common sources of accidents are, on the face of it, fairly straightforward, including slips and trips, falls from a height or on the same level, being struck by a falling or moving object, and handling, lifting or carrying. The causes of them are, on the other hand, not necessarily straightforward since they can include a number of contributing elements. As a result, a distinction can often be drawn between the immediate event that 'triggers' or gives rise to an accident and more distant, but nevertheless important, causal factors (Turner and Pidgeon, 1997).

A clear illustration of this last point is the Clapham Junction railway disaster, which happened in 1988 and resulted in the death of 35 people and the injury of nearly 500 others (Hutter, 2001). The immediate cause was the failure of a worker, carrying out rewiring in a signal box, to remove a redundant wire from the fuse to a signal and cut back the other end of it so it could not come into contact with the electrical relay serving the fusebox concerned. The outcome of this was that when the wire was dislodged during later work it came into contact with the relay, and the signal, rather than staying at red while another train was on the stretch of track it regulated, therefore turned to green, causing another train to enter the same stretch and crash into the one already on it.

On detailed investigation, it was found that this failure by the worker had occurred against the background of a number of weaknesses in the structure and operation of the surrounding system of health and safety management. These weaknesses included:

- the fact that the worker had been allowed to work in the same way for some time without anybody telling him that it was incorrect
- a lack of clarity as to who in the supervisory and management structure was responsible for checking that his work had been done properly
- a failure to give him adequate training in correct working methods
- the time-scale for carrying out the overhaul of re-signalling in the area – an overhaul of which the worker's work formed part – that required high levels of overtime working (he himself had, in the three months prior to the accident, had just one day off work).

In short, what the Clapham disaster shows is that the causes of accidents can be multi-dimensional and that care must be taken to avoid too readily jumping to the conclusion that the event which immediately gives rise to them – say, a worker error – is the only, or even primary, cause of it. (This is a point that the earlier starter case study hopefully highlighted in the context of a rather more routine incident.)

Research done into the reasons underlying worker deviations from laid-down safety rules and procedures reinforces this point by showing that the factors causing such deviations can include (Turner and Pidgeon, 1997):

- time pressures
- an incompatibility between laid-down procedures and required work activities
- a desire by workers to carry out work tasks in a way which avoids or relieves boredom
- operational pressures stemming from production and broader financial considerations, including those associated with piecework payment systems intended to encourage workers to produce more and which cause supervisors to ignore, and even encourage, unsafe work practices.

Many factors can therefore contribute to the occurrence of an accident. Failures on the part of workers can clearly play an important role. So too, though, can broader management ones such as inadequate training and supervision, the use of poorly maintained and installed equipment, the imposing of excessive workloads, and the poor design of work tasks and processes – to name just a few.

Stress

Stress can give rise to behavioural responses that have negative implications for both the individuals affected and their employing organisations (Stansfeld et al, 1999). These responses can include increased alcohol consumption and smoking, drug use, poor eating habits, irritability and aggression, an inability to concentrate (resulting in 'presenteeism'), absence from work, and domestic conflict. (See also Chapter 11 on absenteeism.)

Some of these responses can have adverse health consequences for workers as a result of the physiological changes they cause (Cox et al, 2000). Amongst these outcomes are bronchitis, coronary heart disease, mental illness, thyroid disorders, obesity, peptic ulcers and certain forms of rheumatoid arthritis, skin diseases and diabetes.

Today, stress is most commonly conceptualised from a psychological perspective and as an outcome of some form of imbalance between the work environment and the physical and psychological characteristics of workers (Cox et al, 2000). Several aspects of the working environment have been identified as potentially contributing to this imbalance (Anderson-Connolly et al, 2002; Taylor et al, 2003). Some of the more important of these are:

- lack of control over work tasks

- negative work relationships, including bullying behaviour on the part of managers and other work colleagues

- inadequate information and support from colleagues and managers

- lack of role clarity and the perception of role conflict

- poor work–life balance

- excessive work demands arising, for example, from overly long working hours and too high workloads

- unchallenging work tasks

- poor management of change, often through failing to adequately consult staff and provide them with information on the changes taking place (see Chapter 19).

Also, the above factors can combine together in a negative way to increase the likelihood that stress occurs. A number of research studies have found stress to be particularly associated with a combination of high work demand and low task control.

It must be recognised, as pointed out earlier, that the precise impact that such factors have is influenced by the characteristics of those exposed to them – notably the nature of their personality and the emotional, coping, resources they are able to draw on. For example, some studies suggest that people who have a strong commitment to work and a high level of involvement in their job, a strong sense of urgency and a high degree of competitiveness are more vulnerable to work-related stress.

The role that these individual factors play draws attention to the fact that the management of work-related stress can include not only preventive strategies of the type discussed later but also 'secondary' ones aimed at increasing the ability of individual workers to cope better with their work situation through counselling and other support services, including training in the identification of stress symptoms and the management of stress. Such support is provided in some organisations via what are often called employee assistance programmes (EAPs) that provide not only access to stress counselling but also such forms of support as financial planning advice and 'marriage' guidance.

Musculo-skeletal disorders

Musculo-skeletal disorders (MSDs) are conditions that affect muscles, joints, tendons and other parts of the musculo-skeletal system. They therefore include low back pain, joint injuries and repetitive strain injuries of various types. MSDs can occur as a result of any activity that involves some movement of the body, including typing, lifting and repetitive manual activities, and so may arise among those working in a wide range of occupations and sectors. The likelihood of their occurring, however, is influenced not only by the nature of the work tasks done but also by the physical and psychological characteristics of workers and aspects of the work environment within which tasks are carried out (Buckle and Devereux, 1999). They can therefore be the outcome of the interaction that occurs between these three sets of factors, rather than just the nature of the work undertaken.

Certain types of work tasks have, nevertheless, been found to be particularly associated with the onset of MSDs. Those tasks include repeating the same sequence of movements many times (as may happen in production-line situations and in the case of high-speed data entry work), lifting or moving heavy loads, twisting or stooping when lifting or moving such loads, working with hands at or above shoulder height, exerting considerable force (as when pushing or pulling heavy items), repeated gripping and releasing between finger and palm, and, more generally, working at a fast pace. As a result, some of the forms of work that are particularly likely to give rise to MSDs are manufacturing assembly activities, packing or sorting components or products, driving, machine operations and keyboard work.

The strength and fitness of workers can act to increase or reduce the potentially harmful effects of some of these work tasks. The same is true of the degree of stress they are under, because muscular tension increases the likelihood that the effects will cause damage. It therefore follows from this last point that the type of psychosocial factors already identified as contributing to workers' suffering stress – such as high job demands, low task control and time pressures – can also play a role in the occurrence of MSDs. Other contributing factors include working in overly hot or cold temperatures, the former acting to increase the degree of physical effort that has to be expended on a task and the latter, in common with stress, reducing muscular flexibility; carrying out tasks in confined or otherwise unsuitable physical environments; and working too long and without adequate breaks.

REFLECTIVE ACTIVITY

Think of a job you have either done yourself or have observed.

In the light of the above sections of text, list the potential sources of risk to worker health and safety involved in it.

(The text suggested that such sources might be related to the personal characteristics of workers, the nature of the work tasks and processes they are engaged on, and aspects of the broader organisational environment within which they are employed.)

2 THE MANAGEMENT OF HEALTH AND SAFETY

The above review of some of the main causes of accidents, stress and MSDs has highlighted that their prevention can require employees to undertake a wide range of different types of preventive activities. In the case of accidents, for example, it points to the fact that these activities can include:

- the safe installation of plant and equipment, as well as their adequate maintenance
- the provision of preventive 'hardware', including machine guards and ventilation systems
- the appropriate design of work tasks and processes
- the clear communication of safety rules and procedures
- the adequate supervision of worker compliance with these rules and procedures
- the provision of training for workers and line managers on work-related risks and the actions necessary to control them.

In addition, and more generally, the review has highlighted the fact that accidents, stress and MSDs can be reduced by creating work environments, tasks and processes that are more compatible with the physical and psychological characteristics and capabilities of workers by, for example, making sure that:

- working hours are not excessive
- work pressures are not overly demanding
- manual handling tasks do not require the physical lifting or moving of too heavy loads.

It is now widely accepted that such preventive activities are likely to be most effectively undertaken as part of a systematic approach to the management of workplace risks containing the following central elements (Dawson *et al*, 1998; Health and Safety Executive, 1997):

- comprehensive assessment of workplace risks and the related identification of those that must be better controlled
- identification of the methods through which this control can be obtained, with priority given to removing risks and use being made of alternative solutions, such as the provision of protective equipment or the laying down of new rules and procedures
- the development of mechanisms such as training, giving relevant information and the laying down of required rules and procedures, to enable the effective implementation of these solutions
- the adoption of adequate arrangements to monitor and review the effectiveness of the control measures put in place.

Consequently, it is argued that what is needed is a dynamic – rather than a static, once-for-all – approach to health and safety management in which the adequacy of existing control measures undergoes a continuous process of monitoring and, where needed, subsequent adjustment. Such monitoring can be done in two ways: firstly, through the use of various 'output' measures which show how far the existing health and safety system has been successful in preventing (or not preventing) worker ill-health and injury; secondly, through the use of 'process' methods aimed at assessing the adequacy and operation of the health and safety arrangements in place. These are now examined in turn.

In relation to output measures, a number of different indices can be used to measure the scale of work-related harm caused by work activities. These include employee sickness absence records, occupational health records (including first-aid treatments and the results of health assessments), self-report data provided by workers, and accident statistics.

Commonly, these last statistics are used to calculate accident rates that (a) provide a way of tracking trends in accident performance that are not due to variations in hours worked or numbers employed, and (b) enable an understanding of variations in the severity of the injuries caused. Three of the most commonly used of these are accident frequency rates, accident incident rates and accident severity rates. These are calculated on the following bases:

Accident frequency rate

$$= \frac{\text{Total number of accidents}}{\text{Total number of person hours worked}} \times 1{,}000{,}000$$

ie accidents per 1,000,000 hours worked

Accident incident rate

$$= \frac{\text{Total number of accidents}}{\text{Total number of persons employed}} \times 1{,}000$$

ie accidents per 1,000 employees

Accident severity rate

$$= \frac{\text{Total number of days lost}}{\text{Total number of person-hours worked}} \times 1{,}000$$

ie the average number of days lost per 1,000 hours worked.

Accident statistics therefore not only provide a potentially valuable source of information on overall and comparative standards of safety performance but also can be used to spot areas of activity where remedial action is needed. At the same time, a potentially important limitation of them is that, by definition, they only relate to 'undesirable' events that have actually resulted in injury. They exclude from consideration other such events that, perhaps by chance, did not cause harm, and in doing so can potentially give a misleading picture of health and safety performance. It is for this reason that they can usefully be supplemented by the use of process measures that try to proactively assess the degree to which workplace risks are being managed.

Several different techniques can be used to more proactively assess the adequacy and operation of the existing health and safety management system. These include:

● workforce 'safety climate' surveys that give information on the adequacy of current policies, practices and attitudes

- the use of 'hardware' like noise meters to measure worker exposures to particular occupational health hazards, such as noise and fumes

- health surveillance aimed at monitoring whether workers' health is being affected by such exposures

- investigations into the causes of accidents and dangerous occurrences

- inspections and audits which systematically assess whether organisationally required and/or legally acceptable arrangements are in place and are adequately implemented and, more generally, identify areas where improvements must be made.

SYSTEMATIC MANAGEMENT AND STRESS

Work-related stress can be managed following the same systematic approach as that described above. Indeed, the use of such an approach is now encouraged by the Health and Safety Executive (HSE) through its Stress Management Standards. These Standards form part of a five-step risk assessment process which encompasses the identification of hazards, the making of a decision on 'who might be harmed and how', the evaluation of risk and the taking of relevant action, the recording of the assessment findings, and monitoring and review.

An Indicator Tool that can be used to more precisely gauge the extent and nature of the stress problems in an organisation is provided by the HSE, along with guidance on how to use employee focus groups to help find solutions to any problems that are discovered. The Indicator Tool is a self-completion questionnaire that can be given to all employees. Responses from the completed questionnaire can then be analysed through an accompanying Analysis Tool to compute average scores in relation to the Standards the HSE has specified in respect of the following six features of work tasks and environment: demands, control, support, relationships, role, and change (these tools, as well as more general information on the HSE's Stress Management Standards, are available at **http:// www.hse.gov.uk/stress/standards/sitemap.htm**). In this way, the HSE not only enables organisations to obtain an insight into their current situation regarding workforce stress and how far it is satisfactory, but also gives them a way of identifying where remedial action is most needed.

The challenges to systematic management

The value of adopting a systematic approach to health and safety management is clearly affected by the competence with which it is done and hence by the knowledge and skills of those involved in carrying out its central components (Dawson *et al*, 1998) – an issue that can be a source of difficulty in smaller organisations (Walters, 2001). The degree of commitment to health and safety amongst managers, and particularly senior ones, is important to how well these processes are undertaken.

Even if appropriate health and safety precautions are developed, it does not follow that they will be implemented effectively, particularly if no action is taken to define clearly the health and safety responsibilities of line managers and establish systems to hold them accountable for their performance in fulfilling them (Callagher, 2002). Unless there is such accountability, there is a clear danger that compliance with health and safety rules and procedures may suffer in the face of conflicting work pressures and a view that such compliance is of relatively little importance. For example, line managers may encourage workers to ignore safety rules in order to maintain production levels, workers can be tempted to cut corners as a way of protecting or enhancing their earnings, and workers may feel free to get round laid-down working methods in order to avoid the restrictions they impose on them.

In recent years and in recognition of the way in which such factors can adversely affect health and safety performance, increasing attention has been paid to taking actions to improve health and safety cultures or climates through the provision of training (Turner and Pidgeon, 1999). It must, however, be recognised that cultural change is difficult, particularly within a context of poor management support and commitment. Indeed, centrally driven culture change programmes may, by downplaying countervailing workforce views and values, actually generate conflict rather than consensus and therefore ultimately be counterproductive. Consequently, although programmes aimed at creating more positive attitudes to workplace health and safety may bring beneficial results, it is only likely where considerable care is taken with regard to their design and implementation.

REFLECTIVE ACTIVITY

Go online and find a substantial newspaper article that reports a major work-related accident.

In the light of the above sections of text on the management of health and safety, list the managerial factors that may have contributed to the accident's occurrence.

Note that we have here introduced the concept of *ratios* of one job family to another, or of one as a percentage of the whole workforce. These can be more revealing than simple statistics.

(The text suggested that such factors might include inadequacies in existing management systems and weaknesses in their implementation. Do these two categories of factors seem sufficient, in your view, to explain why the accident you have researched took place?)

3 WORKFORCE INVOLVEMENT

It has long been accepted that the involvement of workers in health and safety can make a positive contribution to the establishment of good health and safety standards (Walters and Nichols, 2007). In particular, such involvement is seen to:

- enable the detailed knowledge workers have of work tasks and processes, as well as the broader working environment, to be used to identify risks and what has to be done to control them

- engender worker ownership and support for laid-down preventive arrangements
- provide a platform for workers to voice their health and safety concerns and challenge current management actions.

The importance of workforce involvement to effective health and safety management is underlined by the fact that all employers in Britain are legally required to consult their workforces over health and safety matters. The relevant legal requirements are laid down in two sets of regulations: the Safety Representatives and Safety Committees (SRSC) Regulations 1977 and the Health and Safety (Consultation with Employees) Regulations 1996 (Walters and Nichols, 2007).

Under the SRSC Regulations, an independent trade union is entitled to appoint safety representatives from amongst the employees of an employer by whom it is recognised (see Chapter 17 on employment relations). Once appointed in accordance with the Regulations representatives have to be consulted by employers over a range of matters and are accorded a number of functions which entitle them to:

- investigate potential hazards and dangerous occurrences, and causes of accidents
- investigate complaints relating to an employee's health, safety or welfare at work
- make representations to employers on these and on general matters affecting the health, safety and welfare of employees
- carry out workplace inspections
- represent employees in consultation with health and safety inspectors
- receive information from such inspectors
- attend safety committee meetings.

In addition, safety representatives are entitled to the paid time off that is necessary for them to carry out their functions and to undergo such training as is reasonable in the circumstances. Employers are also obliged to make available information within their knowledge that is similarly necessary and to establish a safety committee, if requested to do so by two or more safety representatives.

The 1996 Regulations impose a duty of consultation on employers in relation to employees not covered by safety representatives appointed under the 1977 ones. This duty is the same as that which applies in the case of union safety representatives. However, employers may choose whether they consult employees directly or via elected representatives, known as representatives of employee safety (RES).

If this representative route is chosen, employers must provide the RES with adequate information for them to fully and effectively participate in consultations and to carry out their functions of making representations and consulting with inspectors. Representatives are also entitled to training, time off, and such other facilities and assistance as they may reasonably require to carry out their functions. However, in contrast to union-appointed safety representatives, they have no rights to carry out workplace inspections, to inspect statutory health and safety documents or to investigate employee complaints and accidents and dangerous occurrences that have to be legally reported. Nor are they able to require the establishment of a safety committee.

Table 43 below provides data, drawn from the Workplace Employment Relations Survey 2004, which shows how far employers do, in practice, consult over health and safety matters and the types of arrangements through which this consultation happens (Kersley *et al*, 2006). This data suggests that virtually all employers do so consult, that consultation is most commonly undertaken via direct, rather than representative, arrangements, and that arrangements of the latter type are more common where one or more unions are recognised.

Table 43 Health and safety consultation arrangements, 2004

Type of arrangements	All workplaces (%)	At least one recognised union (%)
Single or multi-issue joint consultative committees	20	41
Free-standing worker representatives	22	22
Direct methods	57	37
No arrangements	1	0

Base: All workplaces with 10 or more employees
Source: adapted from Kersley *et al* (2006; p.77)

Meanwhile, existing research evidence shows that the effectiveness of consultative arrangements is very much influenced by both the structures and broader organisational environment within which they operate (Walters *et al*, 2005). Research findings on the factors that affect the operation of health and safety committees illustrate this point clearly. For example, they suggest that committees are usually more effective where:

- there is a high level of commitment from employers, particularly through the appointment of at least one senior corporate officer who is able to exercise real authority and implement change in the workplace

- members have the information and knowledge to contribute effectively

- management–worker relationships are good

- worker representation operates through trade union channels.

In addition, committee effectiveness has been found to be influenced by such structural factors as the quality of communications between them and the workforce, the regularity of meetings and attendance at them, and the size of their membership.

REFLECTIVE ACTIVITY

The text in this section has suggested that workforce involvement can play an important role in supporting the effective identification and control of potential risks to worker health and safety.

Now re-read the earlier text section on the causes of work-related injuries and ill-health.

How far do you think that this earlier text provides support for these benefits of workforce involvement?

KEY ISSUES: HEALTH AND SAFETY AT WORK

We now pull together ten key points on health and safety at work as raised in this chapter:

- The scale of work-related injuries and ill-health is large and brings considerable costs on employing organisations, as well as on the economy as a whole.

- MSDs and stress-related conditions are the most common forms of occupational ill-health.

- The causes of accidents are often multi-dimensional and frequently include organisational failures beyond the immediate events that triggered them.

- Although the causes of MSDs and stress-related conditions are varied, their occurrence is often intimately connected to the way in which work activities are designed and managed.

- A failure to adequately manage health and safety can lead to prosecutions and the imposition of Improvement and Prohibition Notices, and also to the award of compensation to those harmed.

- It is widely accepted that a systematic and well implemented approach to the management of workplace health and safety is necessary if it is to be managed effectively.

- Such an approach needs to encompass the assessment of workplace risks and the related identification of those that need to be better controlled.

- Such an approach needs to encompass the determination of the methods through which this control can be obtained, and the development of mechanisms to enable the effective implementation of these solutions.

- Such an approach needs to encompass the adoption of adequate arrangements to monitor and review the effectiveness of the control measures so put in place.

- Worker consultation and representation can make an important contribution to the carrying out of these various processes.

Perhaps there are other key points that you would like to note for yourself.

The main case study in this chapter now follows. It gives an example of the effects of change both on the employees of an organisation and on the organisation itself in terms of productivity and cost-effectiveness caused primarily by health and safety factors.

MAIN CASE STUDY

Look at the description of the case set out below. Then decide on the recommendations that you would make as an HR manager for dealing with the issues raised.

In recent years competition facing this publishing company has been increasing and has impacted negatively on sales and profits. Against this background, senior management have been actively seeking to cut costs and increase efficiency. In the case of the editorial department, a key action taken to increase efficiency has been the purchase of an 'off-the-shelf' and more up-to-date computer system to store and transfer news stories. Meanwhile, in the production department the way in which its various activities are carried out has been changed. This change has entailed a move away from the previously existing system whereby individual staff were mainly responsible for carrying out all of them in relation to particular products to one where they specialise in just one of the department's central tasks – namely, subediting, typesetting or proofreading – a change that has further involved staff working, in a much less intensive way, with a much larger number of editors.

These changes were introduced without any real consultation with staff. They were also introduced in a way which sought to minimise the costs associated with making them. In particular, no adjustments were made to the office furniture of journalists to take account of the larger nature of the new desktop screens that they were now required to use and the implications that this had for the positioning of keyboards and work surface space. Nor was any action taken to develop and circulate detailed operational procedures relating to how production staff were to interface with each other, as well as with magazine editors, while carrying out their new 'sequential' system of working.

In the year that has passed since the changes significant rises in sickness absence and labour turnover have occurred. Much of these increases have, in turn, been found to be attributable to marked increases in the number of staff from both departments reporting stress-related problems and, in the case of the editorial department, an increase also in musculo-skeletal disorders affecting the lower back, arms, wrists, neck and shoulders. Furthermore, there are signs that the number reporting these conditions is increasing as a consequence of the higher workloads that the staff are bearing because of the increased level of sickness absence.

More generally, there are clear signs that staff morale and job satisfaction has been declining. Amongst journalists, an important factor underlying this decline has been the frustration caused by the new computer system's lack of suitability for use in respect of lengthy features, as opposed to short news items. As regards production staff, the chief factors at work would seem to be the way in which their work has become more repetitive and more vulnerable to disruption because of breakdowns in the flow of work in the new sequential method of working, and a perceived reduction in 'work quality' as a result of being far less able to identify with particular products and build up close working relationships with individual editors.

The upshot of all of this is that the changes made have neither led to the desired reductions in operational costs nor served to increase efficiency. Indeed, costs have actually risen because of the need to recruit and train more new staff as a result of the higher level of turnover, and to pay for more overtime working and to employ temporary staff to cover those on sick leave. These increased costs, moreover, exist alongside a growing concern amongst management that sooner or later they are likely to face legal actions from staff for the damage to health that they have suffered.

Your task

As an HR professional working in this company, prepare a report detailing a) what it should do to address the problems identified above, and b) how it should change its approach to the management of change in order to avoid similar problems occurring in the future.

EXPLORE FURTHER

DAWSON, S., CLINTON, M., BAMFORD, M. and WILLMAN, P. (1998) *Safety at Work: The limits of self-regulation.* Cambridge, Cambridge University Press
This book contains detailed case studies which shed light on health and safety management in a number of organisations and pinpoint the factors that influence it.

JAMES, P. and WALTERS, D. (2005) *Regulating Health and Safety at Work: An agenda for change?* London, Institute of Employment Rights
This report provides an overview and critical analysis of the legal framework for health and safety.

STANSFELD, S., HEAD, J. and MARMOT, M. (1999) *Work-Related Factors and Ill-Health: The Whitehall II study.* Research Report 266. Sudbury: HSE Books. Available online at: **http://www.hse.gov.uk/ research/crr_pdf/2000/crr00266.pdf**
This research report provides a good insight into how aspects of the psychosocial work environment can impact on worker health.

WALTERS, D., NICHOLS, T., CONNOR, J., TASIRAN, A. and CAM, S. (2005) *The Role and Effectiveness of Safety Representatives in Influencing Workplace Health and Safety.* Research Report 363. Sudbury: HSE Books. Available online at:
http://www.hse.gov.uk/ research/rrhtm/rr363.htm
This is a detailed study of the operation and impact of arrangements for worker representation in respect of health and safety, and the factors that influence their operation.

CHAPTER 19

Employee communication

Richard Croucher

INTRODUCTION

This chapter is about the HR aspects of communication from management to employees and vice versa.

LEARNING OUTCOMES

By the end of this chapter readers should be able to:

- explain the importance of HR's role in communication to employees in their workplace

- explain the growing significance of communication in British organisations in recent years

- describe the appropriate means of communication for different HR issues

- identify optimal communication methods to and from employees, and explain their potential advantages and difficulties.

The chapter is structured in two parts.

After the starter case study we define what exactly we mean by communication and discuss why it is important. Next, we look at the role of HR professionals in communication. Then we present some information on how British companies are making increasing use of communication to employees. We follow this with a section about who is communicating about what and with whom. In a third section of Part 1 we deal with an important new development in HR – that of communicating electronically with employees.

Part 2 discusses the potential advantages and difficulties involved in different forms of communication from employees: suggestion schemes, employee surveys and employee forums. This brings us to our main case study, which is about HR's role in trying to communicate with people doing work for the organisation but who are not directly employed by it.

STARTER CASE STUDY

The case study organisation is a financial services company in the City of London employing several thousand people. The best-paid employees are the salesmen directly involved in selling financial products to consumers, but these only constitute about 30% of the workforce. Most employees are 'back office' staff processing the business initiated by the salesmen; a majority of them are women, almost all of them less well paid than the mostly male salesmen. The company does not find it especially easy to recruit or retain staff in the 'back office' because although they are not especially highly skilled, there are reasonable opportunities for them to move on to work in other central London companies.

On 6 April 2003, working parents in the UK with young or disabled children gained the legal right to request flexible working arrangements; their employers acquired a statutory duty to give these requests serious consideration. The company HR director advised the board's employment subcommittee before the legislation became effective that although the legislation was intended for the parents of young children, this might prove rather divisive and demotivating for non-parents and that therefore consideration should be given to extending the right to all employees. However, this was rejected – operational managers were afraid that this would lead to a flood of requests and the company simply announced in the company newsletter for employees that it would follow the law.

In the event, after April 2003 many parents of young children – concentrated in the 'back office' – requested the right to work flexibly from their operational managers. The applications were dealt with by operational managers in consultation with HR. Several difficulties arose. Operational managers noticed, however, that employees thought that they had a right to work flexibly rather than (in fact, in law) a right to *request* to work flexibly. Secondly, a number of salesmen complained to their managers that they, too, wanted the right to work flexibly because at least parts of their work could be done at home. Thirdly, older people in the 'back office' put the same argument as that put by the salesmen.

The result in the spring and summer of 2003 was increased turnover throughout the central London operation, as employees felt that they were not getting their legal rights or saw that other companies had in fact extended the right to all employees.

Question for discussion

What can be learned from this real-life case study?

Readers should note that there are several important aspects of communication that we do not deal with in this chapter because they are tackled in depth in other chapters. So, for example, we do not deal with communications with prospective employees, nor do we deal with important types of communication with employees such as appraisals (see instead Chapter 12). A third very relevant subject dealt with elsewhere is that of communication to and from employee representatives (see Chapter 17). Nor do we deal with the important but different subject of communication *between* employees – an aspect that is closely related to organisational culture.

Reference sources named within the chapter may be looked up in the *References and further reading* section at the end of the book.

1 COMMUNICATION TO EMPLOYEES

WHAT EXACTLY DO WE MEAN BY 'COMMUNICATION'?

Everyone has their own 'common-sense' definition of 'communication'. But for the purposes of this chapter we must define it more precisely. We therefore define communication as a two-way process: it is communication by management *to* employees, and communication *from* employees to management.

In this chapter, we focus on the first aspect, communication *to* employees (sometimes known as 'downward' communication) in Part 1, and on communication *from* employees (sometimes known as 'upward' communication) in Part 2. Having said that, the distinction between the two is for convenience only because in the end most communication is really two-way. So, for example, briefings to employees about issues often provide opportunities for questions and feedback (Marchington, Wilkinson, Ackers and Dundon, 2001).

Managers have to communicate with employees all the time at work. It is impossible to imagine them doing their jobs without talking to the employees that they work with. Plentiful communication with employees has been shown to be linked to good company performance (Pfeffer, 1998). There are therefore both relatively informal as well as more formal communications to be considered under our general heading of 'communication'. Smaller companies often rely on informal methods and have few, if any, formal methods of communicating with employees, which they may perceive as 'bureaucratic'. In some cases, they prefer to encourage social events such as going to the pub for promoting mutual communication (Marchington, Wilkinson, Ackers and Dundon, 2001). In this chapter, although we do touch on informal channels, we deal mainly with the more formal methods. This does not mean that informal communications are unimportant (which is clearly not the case).

There are two reasons for our focus:

- First, formalised communications practices are linked to a positive 'psychological contract' between organisations and employees (see Chapter 11). This may be why they are also linked to high performance.

- Second, most organisations have a degree of formalisation in their practices, because not everyone wants to go to the pub with their manager.

In addition, we examine HR's role in advising and training other managers in communication – something that is relevant even where there are no formal communications practices.

More formal communication can take different forms, deal with different subjects, and be done by different groups of people and aimed at different groups within the workforce. These differences are an important theme of this chapter.

'Downward' communication (ie from management to employees) spans a number of different practices including:

- workforce briefings for all or part of the workforce on key issues

- quality circles, regular meetings with all or part of the workforce
- appraisal interviews
- newsletters, electronic circulars and DVDs
- electronic communication.

As noted above, some of these 'downward' methods may also involve some 'upward' communication (Marchington, Wilkinson, Ackers and Dundon, 2001). For example, appraisal interviews, workforce briefings or electronic communication may all also involve employees voicing their views.

'Upward' forms of communication (ie from employees to management) also include a number of different practices, such as:

- employee attitude surveys
- suggestion schemes
- employee forums
- project teams.

KEY ISSUES IN COMMUNICATION

There are a number of key issues in communication with employees. We summarise these under six main headings:

- *Subject*: What is communicated is perhaps the most important issue of all. Some information is regarded as sensitive. This is closely related to the issue of 'depth' (see below).

- *Quality*: This can also be subdivided into two aspects:
  – how good the information is, and especially how coherent
  – how credible it is. Bear in mind that some issues are both matters of debate and opinion and also vitally important to employees – information about employees' pensions, for example.

  If you recall the starter case study, you might already have thought that part of the problem was that the company did not really explain either the law or its own policy clearly or convincingly enough to employees.

- *Depth*: How many people in the organisation have access to the information? Many organisations now distribute information quite widely among employees. On the other hand, a lot of information is often distributed on a 'confidential' or 'need to know' basis in British organisations, and they have sometimes been criticised for being too restrictive with much information.

- *Timing*: Information may be released too early or too late for different stakeholders. A good example here is redundancy information. Stock market rules prevent listed companies from making internal announcements on this before the stock market is told, because it is 'price-sensitive' information. On the other hand, employees are themselves sensitive when they read about their own redundancy in the newspapers.

- *Receptiveness*: Employees should feel that they are being listened to. Action on their views may or may not be considered a good idea, but employees need feedback on them.

- *Regularity*: Employees learn to trust the communication if it is regular and tells them the good and the not-so-good news. Regular communication means it is less likely that rumours which are quite incorrect circulate in workplaces.

Let us examine some aspects of these key issues a bit more closely at this point. What problems can we foresee? Below, we raise a few issues under these six headings.

Subject

Organisations can send messages to employees only on subjects which they choose to communicate with them. For example, certain information such as commercially important material may not be passed on to certain employees because the organisations do not trust them with it.

Quality

The information may not be consistent with other information employees have. (For example, they may have read sensational articles in newspapers about employment law.)

Employees may simply not believe the information. (For example, on important matters they might only believe the most senior managers.)

There may be too much information so that employees have problems in digesting it.

The issues being communicated about may not in fact have been made clear to employees. Very often, managers think they have explained something whereas in reality employees are still quite unclear about the issues.

Depth

The information may not be fit for its purpose – for example, it may be too detailed and confusing for those it is aimed at. It may, say, have been initially designed as a management circular, re-worked slightly and then circulated to part-time workers.

Timing

Information may be released when leaked information has already reached employees as rumour, and it may then be treated with contempt.

Receptiveness

Employees may voice their ideas but feel that they are not listened to, creating a negative effect amongst them and actually demotivating them.

Regularity

A balance must be struck between giving people information so regularly that they are swamped with it, and too infrequently so that uncertainty arises.

REFLECTIVE ACTIVITY

What issues can you imagine arising in the subject, quality, depth, timing and regularity of information given by management to employees, or in receptiveness to their ideas?

THE ROLE OF HR PROFESSIONALS IN COMMUNICATION

In one sense, communicating with employees is the business of all managers. As we have already said, all managers have to communicate with employees all the time, and much of the communication is informal. In fact, HR professionals frequently see it as their job to communicate with employees (Croucher *et al*, 2006). But the important issue here is that it is the line manager's job, with help and support from HR (see Chapter 20). This help has to be with important, basic issues, and not just with complex ones.

REFLECTIVE ACTIVITY

So what is HR professionals' *particular* role in communicating with employees? Some important roles for HR professionals in communication are listed below. Read through the list and see if you can add to it.

- At the strategic level, the HR director, advised by other HR colleagues, will seek to influence corporate communications policies by advising on such matters as how and when major policy decisions (eg on family-friendly working practices, training policy, redundancies, etc) affecting employees are communicated.

- At the more day-to-day level, HR professionals will act as advisers to individual operational managers on how to communicate to employees on issues such as their pension or legal rights, or alternatively communicate directly with individual employees on such subjects. These matters are of vital importance to employees, for whom areas like pensions and benefits packages are central issues. Getting communication right in these areas is therefore also at the centre of HR professionals' jobs.

- HR professionals sometimes have to advise both senior and operational managers on employees' feelings on different subjects. It is usually HR professionals who are called on to run or at least to source and oversee employee attitude surveys, for example. To some extent, they may also try to act as employee advocates in order to maintain employee commitment and motivation. However, this role is in many ways difficult for HR professionals also trying to be business partners with senior management – they cannot substitute for elected employee representatives, who have less conflicting roles.

For the exercise above you may have added a number of different roles for HR professionals in communication. For example, one important additional role not listed in the exercise is in sourcing inputs from outside experts and/or themselves directly providing briefings for groups of other managers and groups of employees on a range of issues. Additionally, HR professionals are likely to play an important role in building other managers' presentational and communications skills, since operational managers are often appointed mainly for other skills that they have, such as technical capacities. They may not have thought very much about the nature of their exchanges with other employees and may sometimes need help in developing their interpersonal skills more generally. Some may never have asked themselves the important question 'Do my subordinates have reservations about talking to me?' Further, because HR professionals have people issues at the forefront of their minds, they may advise on where and when sensitive meetings such as appraisals or disciplinary meetings might best be held.

Overall, the role is a very significant one for HR professionals at all levels.

COMMUNICATION AS A KEY PART OF HIGH-INVOLVEMENT MANAGEMENT

Few people would deny that employees are at the centre of any organisation's capacities to operate effectively. Equally, it is one of the themes of this book that HRM should play a strategic role in organisations. There is therefore an important role for policies and practices that seek to involve employees in the organisation in a strategic way.

Intensive communication to employees is an important part of 'high-involvement management' (HIM), which seeks to win competitive advantage for the organisation by involving employees intensively in the organisation. Indeed, intensive communication is the cornerstone of HIM. HIM may include some or all of the following:

- first, increased information ('flow') down the organisation
- second, increased information ('flow') up the organisation
- third, changes in job design
- fourth, financial involvement or participation
- fifth, changes in leadership or management style towards a more participative approach.

For readers who want to know more, HIM is a major topic in Pfeffer (1998).

Intensive communication is important for several key reasons. These include:

- Communication by management to employees on certain key issues (organisational strategy and financial issues) has been shown to be linked to superior organisational performance (see Pfeffer, 1998).
- Communication can increase employee commitment to the organisation. Many employees prefer well-structured situations ('I like to know where I am' is often heard in organisations) to uncertainty. Cutting down on uncertainty helps people feel secure and to perform better.

- Inadequate or poor communication to employees can have a demotivating effect on them. Sending mixed messages (in which one statement apparently contradicts another) to employees is a common problem in organisations and means that employees are unclear as to what it is that the organisation wants of them, and what its priorities are.

- Some large companies may insist on it from small suppliers, anxious to ensure that the suppliers meet demanding quality standards.

- Employers may feel that these practices make it easier for them to make themselves an 'employer of choice'. Employees may feel more committed to the company and less inclined to leave it. In respect of certain highly skilled categories of employee, the costs of their leaving are especially high and employers try to minimise the possibility.

 REFLECTIVE ACTIVITY

List any other reasons you can think of for the importance of good communication.

THE INCREASE IN COMMUNICATION IN BRITAIN IN RECENT YEARS

Communication in British organisations has not historically been especially intensive in comparison with organisational communication in some other countries such as Germany (Hall and Soskice, 2001). The increased use of practices to facilitate communication between management and employees in the private sector was, according to a study carried out by Forth and Millward (2002) for the CIPD, one of the more striking developments in employment relations in the 1990s. Table 44 illustrates this by reproducing some of the study's figures. It shows the increased use of different types of communication to employees; two-way communication methods are included, as well as just 'downward' methods. The table highlights a number of quite dramatic developments in the 1990s, in particular a considerable increase in the incidence of workforce meetings. These were meetings where senior management met employees either all together or section by section. It also shows a great increase in the proportion of organisations that were using briefing groups, defined as regular meetings taking place at least once a month between junior managers or supervisors and all the workers for whom they were responsible. The same was true of problem-solving groups – ie regular work-group or team meetings taking place at least once a month to discuss aspects of performance (such as quality circles). These went from zero in the mid-1980s to a situation where almost half of the organisations surveyed reported using them. Even traditional methods of communication with employees, such as the company newsletter, were used more in 1998 than in 1984.

Table 44   The incidence of direct communication methods, 1984–1998

	1984	1990	1998
Two-way communication or consultation:			
Workforce meetings	34	41	48
Briefing groups	36	48	65
Problem-solving groups	–	35	49
Suggestion scheme	25	28	33
Downward communication:			
Management chain	62	60	6
Newsletters	34	41	50

Percentage of organisations employing 25 or more people
Source: Forth and Millward (2002; Table 2, p.4)

Table 45 shows the same developments, broken down by sector. It indicates that the public sector showed the greatest propensity to communicate with employees during the 1990s, although private sector organisations did move in a similar direction. This was true both of the percentage of organisations using any one of five communications practices, and of the number of these practices used. More recent data from organisations shows that the trend has continued since 1998.

Table 45   Use and breadth of direct communication by ownership sector, 1990–1998

	Private sector		Public sector	
	1990	1998	1990	1998
Use: Percentage of organisations using any one of five direct communication methods	74	84	92	94
Breadth: mean number of arrangements where they are used	2.4	2.7	2.6	3.2

Percentage of organisations employing 25 or more people
Source: Forth and Millward (2002; Table 3, p.7)

WHO IS COMMUNICATED TO ABOUT WHAT?

If, as suggested above, the purpose of communication is to increase the understanding and commitment of all who do work for organisations to overall goals, it follows that information about the organisation's strategy should be communicated to all these people. Yet if we look at the data on communication, we see that this is often not the case.

Cranet data shows that there is a hierarchy of information distribution in European organisations. In terms of formal briefings about business strategy and financial performance, managers are top of the information tree, followed by technical and professional workers (see Tables 46 and 47). These receive the best

Table 46 Briefing on business strategy for different employee categories

	UK	Sweden	Germany	Greece	Slovakia
Management	93%	97%	91%	94%	82%
Professional/technical	75%	79%	49%	46%	48%
Clerical	60%	77%	37%	23%	42%
Manual	46%	58%	23%	12%	23%

Source: Cranet-E (2003)

Table 47 Briefing on financial performance for different employee categories

	UK	Sweden	Germany	Greece	Slovakia
Management	93%	98%	93%	95%	80%
Professional/technical	78%	86%	78%	57%	40%
Clerical	64%	86%	70%	42%	48%
Manual	51%	70%	50%	21%	20%

Source: Cranet-E (2003)

information on business strategy, financial performance and work organisation. Next come clerical staff – and manual workers come last.

It is also important to remember here that other people who do work for organisations such as agency and subcontractors are not included in the survey, and almost certainly have even less information than those directly employed.

In many organisations, electronic communication plays an increasingly important role, and we turn now to this subject.

ELECTRONIC COMMUNICATION

What do we mean by 'electronic communication' here? We mean providing employees with information by electronic means. It is not, in other words, the electronic information systems used within HR departments. Its main feature is that the information is directed at employees. Electronic communication typically provides employees with information in the following areas: individual personal records/payroll/benefits/time-keeping and attendance/recruitment and selection/training and development/performance management/career planning/succession planning/work scheduling/health and safety. It is a part of 'e-HRM' (*Personnel Today*, 2005).

Electronic communication systems in HRM can typically take any of a number of different forms. The different forms depend on how interactive they are – in other words, how much employees can affect what information they can obtain from the system and how much they can affect that information themselves by changing it. Take for example 'downward' communication, which is probably the most common form. In this, employees can access some personal information (eg work schedules, current benefits they are entitled to). A more developed form allows two-way communication. In this form, an employee is able to update simple personal information such as address or bank details.

A third, even more developed form allows two-way communication in a more complex way. In this, the employee is able to perform intricate transactions and select items (such as the composition of benefits) which can be calculated by the system, approved or declined, and confirmed to the employee. So, for example, where 'cafeteria' benefits (ie benefits that award employees points, and allow them to use their points total by choosing whether they prefer to have childcare or health club membership, etc) are provided, the employee can personalise his or her mix of benefits and have it approved online. A few companies' systems allow even more complex transactions.

Why do organisations introduce electronic methods of communicating?

There are several key reasons why organisations do this:

- to reduce the administrative load on HR staff by cutting down on routine inquiries (Ulrich, 2002)
- to make sure that mistake-free, consistent information is given to all employees who ask the same question
- to become more focused on their internal (other managers, employees) and external (outsourced activities, employment agencies, customers) clients
- to cut costs.

These reasons are, of course, real benefits, and some companies have certainly succeeded in realising the first three even if the fourth has proved more difficult to achieve. There are several additional reasons for introducing or extending electronic methods. To take just one: there is an increasing demand from employees for career management information, some of which can be quite complex. But a further reason is especially important: it frees HR staff from more routine tasks and allows them to develop a more genuinely *strategic* role. HR staff can become more focused on the vital issues such as recruitment, staff development and retention or motivation rather than have always to be dealing with relatively routine inquiries.

The reasons for organisations' introducing these methods could be slightly contradictory; improving HR services for managers and other employees is not necessarily compatible with cutting costs. As in many areas, it is important for all organisations to be clear about the priorities they have when seeking to meet multiple aims: what is the order of importance of the different aims? It is often the case that cost savings do not materialise, or at least do not materialise in the medium term. In some cases, costs are effectively shifted within the organisation, so that fewer people are employed in HR and more of operational managers' time is taken up with answering employees' HR enquiries. The argument that savings would occur appears in some cases to have been put simply because it could help 'sell' the idea to senior managers.

What problems can arise with electronic methods of communication?

These methods may in some ways seem like an obvious and 'natural' development: people in society in general are using electronic methods, so why should employing organisations be any different? But this simple and optimistic view does not recognise that in society in general there are many people with little or no access to computers. In some companies, these people form a majority of the workforce. This means that the 'digital divide' between those with access to electronic information and those with little or none will be reproduced inside employing organisations. This in turn could mean that only part of the organisation's employees feel involved and committed to it. It is a considerable problem in some large manufacturing companies, where manual workers have little or no time or opportunity to use electronic information.

Secondly, many organisations that use these methods do not have a clearly defined strategy on which its introduction can be based. In other words, if organisations do not have clear strategies (including one for electronic communication), this is likely to become more obvious to employees when they are introduced. This is simply because the information will become more transparent to employees and they will see that the organisation is not sending them very clear messages through it.

Thirdly, electronic systems can overburden even the IT-literate employees, many of whom may only make use of a small proportion of the information available.

Fourthly, it can take employees years to catch up with the information that is available to them through electronic sources. In some companies, periods of over three years have been reported. This is not just because people take time to adapt to new things; it is also because line managers often have to pick up responsibilities that were previously those of HR, and have to accept this and learn to deal with it in practice. The problem is likely to be even more acute where people not directly employed by the organisation but who nevertheless need to know its policies and procedures (for example, contractors who need to know health and safety policies and procedures) are concerned (see Chapter 18).

 REFLECTIVE ACTIVITY

List ways in which you think the problems outlined above could be handled.

In answer to the exercise above, we have just three points to make. Firstly, our view is that all of the problem areas show that both the HR strategy and the reasons for introducing electronic communication, and the relationship between the two, need to be thought through thoroughly if electronic communication is to realise its promise. So, for example, if the strategic aim is to increase employee satisfaction rather than to reduce costs, it may be that only small to moderate amounts of key information are put on the website, backed up by a good telephone enquiry service. Secondly, in relation to the important 'digital divide' issue, it may be that it will have to be recognised in certain organisations that more HR communication will have to be done through conventional methods than they would ideally like. Finally, there is the issue of the uses of and attitudes to email. Many people see email and electronic communication more widely as overloading them. The ease with which emails can be sent probably encourages a huge amount of communication much of which used to be done on the telephone or in person. So the electronic information becomes too heavy, and much of it is ignored or regarded as low-grade information. In other words, increased volume may also have brought at least a perception of information overload of low-grade information much of which can be ignored.

In view of these points, it might be thought worrying that a small minority of organisations reported to the Cranet survey in 2003 that they *only* used electronic methods to communicate to employees. However, in most cases the same survey showed that the great majority of organisations were increasing communication through *every* available channel.

2 COMMUNICATION FROM EMPLOYEES

WHY EMPLOYEE VOICE?

Communication from employees to the organisations they work for (as opposed to day-to-day communication with their operational managers), sometimes called 'employee voice', is often not a conspicuously evident aspect of life in British organisations.

However, effective voice mechanisms can, as suggested at the beginning of this chapter, be a major source of competitive advantage for companies (Pfeffer, 1998) and can help improve service delivery in the public sector (Blumberg, 1976). Employees clearly know a lot about how work is done, and are often in customer-facing roles. They are therefore in a position to help improve efficiency. Sometimes, operational managers can feel that it is they who have to improve efficiency because it is central to their jobs and they may therefore resist 'employee voice'. But the HR professional has to recognise and overcome this resistance; it can be difficult.

In addition to the efficiency argument just made, employees can have valid and useful ideas about the organisation's strategic direction. However, many managers suggest the opposite and argue that employees' ideas are mainly in the operational area. We would suggest that this is in part because many employees have little opportunity to voice ideas about the organisation's overall direction. Good ideas are not necessarily the sole preserve of senior management. Opportunities for employees to voice their ideas on the subject are usually rare, however, and perhaps they should be encouraged.

Finally, for some this sort of communication is also about responding to employees' feeling that the organisation they spend much of their waking time working for should allow at least an element of democracy for employees.

REFLECTIVE ACTIVITY

Does the notion of democracy really have any place in an organisation that by definition has a hierarchy of authority? If you think it does, list some ways in which democracy might be expressed or made apparent.

One reason for giving all who do work for the organisation an opportunity to give their views on the organisation's strategic direction is that it tends to make employees feel positive about the organisation, and to increase levels of commitment and trust within it.

FORMS OF EMPLOYEE VOICE

Employee voice can take many different forms. Five of the most common forms, and the potential advantages and possible difficulties associated with them, are examined in some detail below. They are:

- 'open door' policies
- suggestion schemes
- employee attitude surveys
- employee forums
- work team, project team and general meetings.

'Open door' policies

Many companies operate 'open door' policies, whereby senior managers invite employees to voice individual concerns to them whenever they feel the need. Formal policies of this sort are particularly common in larger companies but many smaller companies suggest that the practice is common with them too even though it is not enshrined as a formal policy. 'Open door' policies are often advocated by senior managers as an 'ideal' way of dealing with employee concerns – and indeed they may be for them and for some employees – but there are at least three important difficulties to be considered.

First, individual employees often lack confidence in front of senior managers and may feel that if their views are considered 'off-message', they may suffer for them, so they therefore keep them to themselves. This is especially true of temporary staff. Organisations, including small companies, are hierarchies and those lower down the hierarchy are likely to have reservations about what they say to those higher up the hierarchy. Many managers in small companies have limited understanding of this and imagine that everyone speaks to them quite openly.

Second, many organisations have working patterns such as shiftworking that make 'open door' policies difficult to operate in practice.

Third, they can also be an excuse *not* to communicate. 'My door is always open to you' may be further interpreted as '. . . but don't come to me when I am busy or unless you have something really worthwhile to say' – which will put people off from trying the open door.

Suggestion schemes

Suggestion schemes are a long-standing method of seeking employee views on how savings may be made, or how improvements could be made in work organisation or service delivery. Typically, in formalised systems employees send their suggestions in to a central point, where they are evaluated for their usefulness. Employees are then sometimes rewarded for their suggestions. Organisations which claim to espouse continuous learning are likely to encourage people to suggest improvements rather than using a formal suggestion scheme. Japanese organisations may have more formal schemes but are less likely to pay for suggestions – on the basis that good ideas are part of what they expect/hope for from employees. That view has extended to some other manufacturing organisations.

In some companies, and especially in small ones, such practices may not exist as formal systems but are nevertheless there so that employees who make a good suggestion are given a reward of some type.

Suggestion schemes have obvious advantages for organisations seeking to improve efficiency. They are obviously very limited in that they only deal with ways of improving efficiency in a narrow sense. One potential disadvantage of them is that they can become a source of ill-feeling if a suggestion leads to employees' losing jobs.

Employee attitude surveys

Employee attitude surveys, like suggestion schemes, also have a long history and are becoming increasingly important in many organisations. They can have the advantage of getting a wide range of employee opinions on a range of subjects. There is now much more use of e-surveys as a means of collecting and analysing responses very quickly. These are commonly used where employees have access to email – but shopfloor employees can still join in through email kiosks on assembly lines. In other words, they can allow those people with less confidence to have a voice, and to have one across a wide range of issues.

They also have their problems. It is important to recognise that holding a survey raises employee expectations that something will be done. Also, although they are often used in organisations, they are also frequently only done once, or done irregularly. This means that employee satisfaction cannot be measured over time and particular problems identified. A less common but more serious problem can arise if they are in fact 'one-way' communication because management does not itself feed back the results to employees, or tell them what actions they propose to take on matters of concern. They can be demotivating if this is not done.

Employee forums

Many companies operate employee forums where small groups of employees meet with managers to discuss issues of mutual interest. Their scope can vary, from forums which deal only with production issues and are in reality close in nature to quality circles, to forums where no subject is ruled out of order. A number of these forums sometimes exist in each workplace, and these relate to an overall workplace forum. In some instances there are national employee forums. Employee forums may include union representatives in their participants (see Chapter 17). Readers can find more about communication with employees through unions and works councils in Brewster *et al* (2007) and Croucher *et al* (2006).

The strength of these methods can be that they allow employees a collective voice so that support can be offered to an individual voicing a general concern that some individuals might feel reticent about raising on their own. The disadvantages can be that some managers may think employees' concerns 'trivial'. Also, if managers do not themselves have the skills required to structure issues in a meaningful way, or to encourage people to speak and make them feel they are being listened to, this can disappoint employees and lead to a degree of cynicism.

Work team, project team and general meetings

This category includes many different types of meeting. Some work and project teams may be asked for their opinions on issues wider than just simple work problems as defined by management. Work teams are in some ways possibly the most important and successful form of employee communications, because this is where employees may be able to have the greatest impact on their daily working lives through chatting with their direct manager and making small suggestions for progress. They depend for their success on the skills of the line managers in drawing out employee suggestions.

General meetings may be held on a regular basis, and indeed in some workplaces are held as often as monthly. These methods have the advantages of collective systems already mentioned, and once again depend for their success to a great extent on the skills of the managers who run them. How well the facilitators can chair a meeting, how clearly they structure issues for discussion, how well they listen and how much feedback on previous discussions they provide are all significant issues.

KEY ISSUES: COMMUNICATION

We now pull together ten key points about communication raised in this chapter:

- Communication to employees is important because giving information to employees on issues such as business strategy and financial performance is linked to superior organisational performance.

- The subject, quality, depth and timing of information 'cascaded' down within organisations are important issues: information must be fit for purpose.

- In British organisations there has been a steady increase in the information flow to employees in recent years, but there is still a good deal of room for improvement in British organisations' information-giving to employees.

- Many managers in small companies rely mainly on informal communication, which they may or may not be skilled at. Managers may not have all the skills required for effective communication. Employees need to feel that they are being listened to even though their concerns may appear 'irrelevant' or 'trivial' to the manager concerned.

- Many who do outsourced or contracted work for organisations are given relatively little information compared to others who may be directly employed, even in 'lower' positions.

- HR has a key role to play in improving communication, including by providing training and coaching for other managers and workers which can improve their informal and formal communication.

- Electronic communication is playing an increasingly significant role in information-giving to employees. It can enable HR to increase its strategic role in organisations.

- Electronic communication faces the same problem as other forms of communication and indeed runs the risk of exacerbating existing inequalities between different types of worker in terms of the amount and quality of information they receive.

- Communication from employees is frequently done within strict limits imposed by management, and it is therefore important to recognise this and to provide opportunities for more wide-ranging expression of employees' views.

- Employee attitude surveys are often only done once, and how management acts on them is frequently not reported back to employees. This can lead to a negative effect on motivation.

Perhaps there are other key points that you would like to note for yourself.

The main case study now follows. It gives an example of how the increasingly important issue of communicating with people who do work for the organisation but are not directly employed by it can affect a company in practice.

Look at the description of the case set out below. Then decide on the recommendations that you would make as an HR manager for dealing with the issues raised. Try to think beyond the level of a 'quick fix' or simple solutions by developing a longer-term strategy as well as responding to the immediate issue.

The company (which we shall call Company A) is a major US-based data-handling company with a number of sites scattered throughout the UK, employing several thousand people. Its core business is processing data received from its customer organisations. The data arrives at the company in either paper or electronic form, and may (for example) be respondents' completed questionnaires to market surveys. It is then processed by entering it into data files in different forms, providing analyses and reports. In some cases, reports are then printed and bound for the customer companies. There are therefore three main types of employee: data entry clerks, data processing employees, and printers. Much of the data is confidential, some of it is highly confidential, and security of both the raw and processed data is an issue of commercial sensitivity for client companies, government departments and the National Health Service. Work is often carried out to demanding deadlines.

The company has two types of staff, making up about 15% of the workforce, who it does not directly employ. One type is agency staff, employed mainly for only short periods (up to six months) to carry out relatively routine tasks such as data entry. These staff are managed by Company A's managers. Agency staff are mainly employed because the company wants to retain some flexibility for dealing with peaks and troughs in demand, for which the agency staff offer a cheap, responsive and 'no commitment' service. The second type is staff employed by two external companies (Companies B and C), chosen for their technical expertise in their areas – for example, providing computer trouble-shooting services for core staff and other technical support services. Company B's staff are managed by Company B managers working on Company A's premises; Company C's staff are managed by Company C managers on a remote basis (ie they are not on Company A's premises unless they

feel they have to be for some specific reason). The company employs these staff for reasons that are mainly to do with the high quality of their work, their reliability and relatively low costs.

However, a range of difficulties and concerns associated with both agency and contracted-out staff has become increasingly evident.

First, the contractors' staff have sometimes been the cause of complaints recently not because of the general quality of their work (which is high) but rather because they sometimes appear not to understand what is vitally important work and what is of less importance. So they are reluctant to drop a trouble-shooting task of relatively low importance to go to deal with a problem that is holding up a job that is vital for the company. Recently, when a Company X manager approached them as a matter of urgency, two Company B employees asked him to 'hang on for a bit'. When he asked them to drop what they were doing, they told him to approach their Company B manager if he had a problem and wanted help straight away – they said they only had four hands between them. The Company B manager was himself not available at that time, and the delay required Company A employees to have to work late, causing annoyance to the women employees involved and costing the company overtime payments to them.

Second, although relations between agency and contract staff on the one hand and Company A staff on the other are generally good, there have been some problems between established Company A staff and both agency and Company B and C staff. So, for example, some non-core staff do not seem to know about Company A's health and safety policies. One Company C employee recently left a computer cable trailing across a gangway, allegedly causing a Company A employee to trip and bruise his arm. The

Company C employee refused to fill in an accident report form, saying it was not his fault and Company A's forms were nothing to do with him.

Third, fears have arisen among managers where highly confidential work has been involved, that non-core staff do not seem fully to appreciate the sensitivity of the data and how important this is to certain customers. Company B employees have, for example, recently taken highly confidential electronic records belonging to a government department out of Company A's building to work on them at home.

Your task

Imagine you are an HR professional or professionals working in Company A. Prepare a short report based on the facts you have been given above, making recommendations to your colleagues on how the situation can be improved.

EXPLORE FURTHER

FORTH, J. and MILLWARD, N. (2002) *The Growth of Direct Communication*. London, CIPD
This is a short British study of the communications reality in organisations, conducted for the CIPD and written in an accessible style.

HARLEY, B., HYMAN, J. and THOMPSON, P. (eds) (2005) *Participation and Democracy at Work*. Basingstoke, Palgrave Macmillan
This collection of essays discusses questions of 'industrial democracy' in an interesting and accessible way.

KERSLEY, B., ALPIN, C., FORTH, J., DIX, G., OXENBRIDGE, S., BRYSON, A., and BEWLEY, H., (2006) *Inside the Workplace: First findings from the 2004 Workplace Employment Relations Survey*. London, Taylor & Francis
This is the summary version of the most comprehensive survey of communications practices in Britain's private and public organisations. It is probably the best brief summary of what actually goes on in the country's organisations.

MARCHINGTON, M., WILKINSON, A., ACKERS, P. and DUNDON, T. (2001) *Management Choice and Employee Voice*. London, CIPD
This is a CIPD-commissioned report on British managers' use of different channels for employee voice (ie communication with employees through employee representatives).

PFEFFER, J. (1998) *The Human Equation: Building profits by putting people first*. Boston, MA: Harvard Business School Press
This is an important text, giving a US view of the subject in a clear way.

Contemporary and Critical Issues

CHAPTER 20

Changing roles in HRM

Chris Brewster

INTRODUCTION

This chapter looks at the changing nature of roles in HRM, exploring the various actors and their effects on the way that HRM is done within organisations. Different people play a part in HRM, and this chapter is about those different actors and their roles. HRM differs from traditional personnel management in that HRM tries in addition to personnel administration to take a more strategic role in the way people are managed. This is one of the main reasons why it involves more people in organisations than personnel management did: if HRM is 'strategic', it potentially at least involves more people, since 'strategy' describes the organisation's overall direction.

LEARNING OUTCOMES

By the end of this chapter readers should be able to:

- identify the most important actors in the area of HRM (HR specialists, line managers, employees, trade unions, outsourcers and consultants)

- recognise the impact of each of those actors and the changes effected by changes in their roles

- describe the effects of the changing roles on the way that HRM is done.

The chapter is linked to the strategic HRM debates (Chapter 3), the role of trade unions (Chapter 17) and international and comparative approaches to the study of HRM (Chapters 22 and 23). It considers only the parties immediately involved in organisational-level HRM. There are important changes going on amongst the parties external to HRM too, and these are covered in this chapter.

The chapter is structured in relation to the immediate parties to HRM – ie those most obviously and closely involved in it. After the starter case study we identify the most important actors in HRM and their key characteristics. We examine the role of the HRM department and those working in it. Attention is paid to the current debates about the strategic nature of HRM and the impact of e-HRM. We then address some of the other actors in HRM.

In the second part of the chapter we explore the important role of line managers in HRM.

STARTER CASE STUDY

Justine Doit, the relatively new CEO of Middlesex Educational and Support Services (MESS), recently attended a free seminar offered by one of the big consultancies at which she heard that modern organisations are moving towards a more strategic model of HRM in which small but powerful HRM departments work more or less directly for the CEO, as she understood it, and getting out of the low-value-added transactional work involved in the record-keeping and systems-operating role that old-fashioned personnel departments used to adopt.

MESS has until now been a fairly traditional education and training establishment, focused on the end product and with little real concern for management processes. The HRM department has undertaken a mixed role of supporting employees when they have problems, supporting line managers with problem employees, 'policing' the rules to make sure that systems operate as fairly as possible, and negotiating with the trade union.

Justine has organised an informal 'after-work meeting' with the consultants, Adam Cash and his new and apparently bright assistant, May Good: they have arranged that the meeting takes place in an upmarket restaurant recently featured in the Sunday papers.

Justine: I was very impressed with your presentation. I have to say that MESS is a long way from the sort of picture you present.

Adam: Well, that's not unusual. We have worked with a lot of organisations like yours, developing an added-value results-oriented approach to HRM.

Justine: Hmmm – but you know, it's not going to be easy. There are a lot of people with interests involved here. For a start, I wonder why our own HRM department hasn't been bringing these ideas to me. I'm not sure they would have the right competencies to manage the kind of HRM you were discussing.

May: Are you sure they haven't? We often find that the HRM people do put forward these ideas, but somehow they are not heard by the rest of the management team.

Adam: Well, whatever. The fact is that you have taken these ideas on board and, to be blunt, as the CEO you cannot ignore them. Like everyone responsible for results you have to be working on these kinds of issues.

Justine: Yes, but it's not just the HRM specialists. To be honest, I think they might even welcome some of this stuff. But what about my line managers? They expect the HRM department to be there to help them with the difficult and embarrassing people problems. And there will certainly be a reaction, too, from the trade union and from the employees.

May: Yes, somehow the employees always get left out of these debates.

Adam: Well, let's organise another meeting with some of your people and see how they react in practice. Another glass of this excellent Chilean Sauvignon?

Questions for discussion

1 What might be the reaction of the HRM department in MESS to the next meeting?

2 What is it that line managers expect from their HRM department?

3 Why might the trade union be opposed to a new strategically oriented HRM department?

In the third part we discuss the role of other important parties in HRM.

The chapter concludes with the main case study.

Reference sources named within the chapter may be looked up in the *References and further reading* section at the end of the book.

THE PARTIES TO HRM

At the start of this chapter we want to introduce the most important actors in HRM and their role (see Figure 24). Two parties are always and obviously involved in HRM, as indicated by the phrase itself: the human resources (the people working in the organisation) and the managers. In most larger organisations there are one or more HRM specialists, so we can split the management group into HRM specialists and the rest of the management group – usually called, in this context, 'line managers'. The HRM specialists may outsource some of their activities (such as, most commonly, payroll or training) to other people outside the organisation, and they may be advised by or work with HRM consultants. For their part, the employees may include trade union members and may call on the external union officers for help in their part of HRM (see Chapter 17). These 'internal' roles are the subject of this chapter.

Figure 24 The parties to HRM

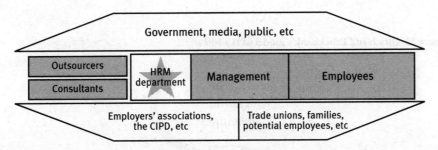

Around these roles, of course, no organisation is context-free (Brewster, 2007). What the government does in terms of the economy and of labour legislation has a big influence and some authors include the government as a party to HRM. Also influential is media coverage of the organisation and what the public thinks about it. If the organisation belongs to an employers' association, that will have an effect and so will the CIPD. The families of the employees and the potential employees and the general labour market also have an effect. But our focus in this chapter is on the people immediately concerned with HRM within the organisation.

1 THE ROLE OF THE HR DEPARTMENT

There have been many debates about the role of HRM departments and the specialists working in them. What is generally agreed is that there are several models of HRM determined largely by the relationship between two of the key factors that distinguish HRM from the older notion of 'personnel management': the link between HRM and corporate strategy, and the link between the HRM department and the line managers. HRM is assumed to include a closer link to corporate strategy and a focus on getting all line managers to act as people managers, with the HRM department establishing the appropriate environment and providing support for the line managers.

There is in some people's view a wish to see everyone in the department operating at the strategic level, but clearly that is not possible or desirable. The US guru Dave Ulrich and his colleague Wayne Brockbank (Ulrich and Brockbank, 2005) identify five main roles that have to be carried out within the HRM department (see Figure 25):

- the *employee advocate* focuses on the needs of today's employees, ensuring that people are paid appropriately, that their concerns are listened to and acted upon and, where relevant, dealing with the trade unions and the consultative arrangements

- the *human capital developer* focuses on ensuring that employees, are continually developing the skills and capabilities they will need to be successful in the future

Figure 25 Ulrich and Brockbank's model of HR roles

Source: Ulrich and Brockbank (2005)

- the *functional expert* deals with the administrative practices that are central to what the HR department offers the organisation (recruitment, selection, payroll, etc)

- the *strategic partner* has multiple dimensions: business expert, change agent, strategic HR planner, knowledge manager and internal consultant

- the *HR leader* pulls this all together, collaborating with other functions, setting and enhancing the standards for strategic thinking, and ensuring good corporate governance.

As Ulrich himself says, HR departments have to be good at all these things. In many cases, particularly in smaller organisations and in the less developed world, the department with responsibility for these areas is still most accurately entitled 'personnel administration'. That is what it does. The experts argue that this misses the roles that Ulrich's other categories represent: HRM departments should be more strategic in order to create value within organisations (Wright and McMahon, 1992). Further, many would go on to say that most of these administrative tasks can now be done more effectively through the use of information technology or through outsourcing (and we examine this shortly).

THE STRATEGIC INVOLVEMENT OF THE HRM DEPARTMENT

In many organisations the HR people do not have the credibility to play a strategic role. HR is not always represented at the top decision-making level of organisations (Brewster, Larsen and Mayrhofer, 1997). In some countries, HRM issues are taken into account anyway. Thus in Germany the law requires that many larger organisations have an employee representative on their supervisory board – even if the head of the HR function is not represented, HRM issues are discussed. In other countries, most senior HRM specialists are represented at the top level. In Britain about half the organisations with more than 200 people have an HRM representative on the main board or equivalent. In general, these figures seem to change very little over the years. It is clearly more likely that an organisation with an HRM specialist on the board will have a more strategic approach to HRM.

Other data from the Cranet research indicates that where there is no specialist presence at this level, the responsibility for HRM rests most frequently with the managing director or an administration manager. This could mean either that the topic is taken seriously, the top person seeing it as a crucial part of his or her responsibilities, or it could mean that it is not taken seriously at all, being swept into an 'and everything else' category. In either case it is not clear that the specialist input to decisions from the HRM angle is always going to be available when key strategic decisions are made.

The extent of strategic involvement of the HRM specialists varies by size and sector of organisations but also, significantly, by country (Brewster *et al*, 1997). The strategic implications of a management decision in Germany or the Netherlands are subject to the involvement of powerful works council representatives or the worker representatives on the supervisory board of the company. In these companies the knowledge that their decisions are subject to close examination – and can be reversed or varied – at that level means that managers tend to operate with HRM issues in mind (Wächter and Muller-Camen, 2002). Ideas that strategies are the preserve of senior managers (or even just managers) may be questioned too: in some countries employees have a much more significant input than in Britain. It is not a surprise, therefore, to find that the Cranet research shows that in some countries HRM is involved in the development of corporate strategy in more organisations than there are who have HR directors on the board. In Britain there is a close relationship between the two.

REFLECTIVE ACTIVITY

How might having an HR director on the main board help an organisation to develop competitive corporate strategies?

THE CHANGING NATURE OF THE HRM FUNCTION

The role of the HRM department is perhaps always ambiguous and dynamic. Like other functional specialists, HR professionals are constantly challenged to meet three competing aims: to make themselves more cost-effective through reducing the costs of services and headcount (the *operational* driver), to improve their services to meet the increasing demands of line managers and employees (the *relational* driver), and to address the strategic objectives of organisations (the *transformational* driver). The difficulty is that these drivers do not necessarily all point in the same direction. Indeed, often they cannot all be done at the same time.

As the CIPD has noted, in order to meet these challenges HRM departments are turning to changes in supply chain management and organisational restructuring policies including:

- greater use of electronic HRM
- downsizing the function
- allocating more responsibility to line managers
- outsourcing transactional or routine activities.

In each case, it is worth pointing out, the rhetoric may have moved ahead of the reality but there are clearly some kinds of development going on here. We examine these issues in turn.

ELECTRONIC HRM AND DOWNSIZING

In theory, at least, the extension of existing information and communications technology (ICT) systems, and the implementation of new ones, could transform the internal operations of the HRM department. This process, known as 'the e-enablement of HRM (e-HRM)', is qualitatively different from earlier applications of ICT to the information function of HR itself (known as HRIS). E-HRM refers to the application of ICT to HRM so that the process is changed from a face-to-face or paper relationship to an increasingly 'virtual' one. The concept is that line managers or employees can get from their computer all the information and advice they might otherwise get from the HRM specialists (Florkowski and Olivas-Lujan, 2006). In addition, the HRM department can do much more with the information that it has: checking the costs and effects of training more fully, linking pay and benefits costs more closely to output, and so on (Gueutal and Stone, 2005). According to those who take a very positive view of it, e-HRM has the potential to fundamentally transform the nature of the HRM function just as e-business has already done in sectors such as financial services and retailing.

Currently, the application of ICT to HRM accounts for a substantial element of the total technology-spend in organisations (as much as 10% of all ICT investment in British organisations, according to estimates). In 2006 one of the two main sellers of e-HRM systems, SAP, claimed that 9,500 companies worldwide used its applications to manage over 54 million employees, while the other main provider, Oracle, claimed that 76 of the US top 100 companies had adopted its software. Nevertheless, despite these claims, at present the use of e-HR technologies is uneven, varying between countries, sectors, sizes of organisations and showing marked differences even between organisations in the same country, sector and size. The effects are also unclear.

Little is known about the long-term cost-effectiveness of generic e-HR systems, whether they promote off-shoring and job losses in the UK (or whether this is offset by the creation of high-value jobs), or their overall contribution to organisational productivity and effectiveness. For every success story there is a horror story somewhere else. And, despite the claims of those who endorse them, it is not clear how generic systems will enable companies to obtain a competitive advantage if they all end up operating similar business processes to their competitors. We do know that the implementation of these systems has brought problems, in part because practitioners lack a sound body of theory and evidence on which to proceed. HRM specialists say that lack of guidance is one of the most important problems making the adoption of e-HR systems difficult. There are only a few studies, including some by the CIPD, that have systematically looked at the nature of e-HR technologies in use, the rationale for their adoption, problems influencing their implementation and their broader organisational effects. At this point in our knowledge, the consequences of e-HRM for HRM specialists, line managers and other employees are not well understood (Martin, 2005).

One particular area which is unclear is e-HRM's effect on the size of the HRM department. In theory, more e-HRM should lead to fewer people in the HRM function. In practice the relationship between organisational size, sector, national context and the size of the HR department within organisations is complex. Across Europe, the average ratio is about one and a half people in the HRM department for every 100 people employed, but this varies a lot (Brewster et al, 2006). Summarised, the proportion of staff engaged in the HR function tends to be smaller where the organisation is larger. It is lower in specific areas of the service sector, retailing and distribution – probably reflecting the importance of relatively low-value-added HR policies in this area – but HR departments are relatively large in the state sector, probably reflecting political pressures against excessive outsourcing. The impact of e-HRM so far seems to be very small.

REFLECTIVE ACTIVITY

Answer the following questions, and in each case relate your answer afterwards to the situation in your own organisation or an organisation you know well.

How might e-HRM assist in creating a cost-effective HRM department?

What changes would e-HRM mean to the capabilities required by the HRM department?

How would an organisation determine whether it had too many or too few people in the HRM department?

2 LINE MANAGEMENT RESPONSIBILITY FOR HRM

A crucial issue in HRM – one that is said to make it quite different from 'personnel administration' – is the responsibility placed on line managers for the management of their people. The balance of responsibilities for the management of people between the specialists in the HR department and the line managers who have day-to-day responsibilities for organising the work and the progress of their subordinates is unclear, contested and changing.

The British expert David Guest argued many years ago that because HRM is central to the well-being of an organisation and to its ability to perform effectively, the subject has to be central to the responsibilities of every single manager in an organisation. In a famous statement, Guest, 1997 argued that 'If HRM is to be taken seriously, personnel managers must give it away.' Others, however, have claimed that only a knowledgeable, experienced and influential HR department focused on nothing but HRM can provide the organisation with the expertise needed in this competitively crucial area of management. These commentators point to failures of line managers to manage their people effectively and argue that if the subject is not driven by a specialist department, the reality is that it gets ignored (at least until there is a crisis).

It seems that the trends in giving HRM responsibilities to line managers have been almost tidal, ebbing and flowing like the sea as the HR specialists move between opposition to the line, through the roles of power-holder, administrative centre, advocate for co-determination and change agent (Larsen and Brewster, 2003). Currently, there is a strong push to increase the degree of line management responsibility. The Cranet-E data shows that organisations across Europe have increased line management responsibilities. For each aspect of HRM and in each country, there are always significantly more organisations increasing line management responsibility than reducing it (Mayrhofer and Brewster, 2005). The evidence also shows that recruitment and selection, health and safety and the expansion and reduction of the workforce are more likely to have been given to the line managers, whereas industrial relations and training are more likely to stay with the HR function.

The reasons for these increases include the fact that line managers cannot avoid taking at least some responsibility for their subordinates. Perhaps the ability to give work to people, to make people enthusiastic about their work and to develop their potential are the marks of a good manager. Allocating time, money and energy to the management and development of subordinate staff is not only an investment in improved effectiveness and future success but a necessary precondition for that success. This is not a role that the HRM department can play. The HRM function is seen as playing the role of co-ordinator and catalyst for the activities of the line managers, working with line managers to deal with people-related business issues.

The emphasis on the line management role in HRM has come about for four closely linked reasons:

- There has been a trend towards managing organisations through the development of cost centre- or profit centre-based approaches. In such systems it does not make any sense to exclude from the managers' responsibilities the major operating cost of their centre: the cost of the people they employ.

- It is line managers, not the HRM specialists, who are in frequent, often constant, contact with employees, allocating tasks, making people enthusiastic about their jobs and monitoring performance.

- There is a growing emphasis on providing a responsive service for customers: line managers have to be able to respond quickly without having to get permission for changes to working hours or practices from the HRM department.

- There has been a widespread movement towards reducing the numbers in 'overhead' departments, such as HRM. In such circumstances the role of line management in HRM can be seen as an alternative to outsourcing the function – the 'internalising' shift. More responsibility taken by line managers should mean fewer people in the HRM department.

However, in many countries and in particular in the UK, the allocation of HRM responsibilities to the line has not got very far (Larsen and Brewster, 2003). There are six reasons why the assignment of HR responsibilities to the line has not gone further. These are that:

- Line managers are often not enthusiastic about taking on responsibility for HRM for the people in their area. They feel they have enough to do without that.

- Line managers under pressure often give HR responsibilities a low priority – they are often ignorant about legal requirements, trade union agreements and agreed practices or training.

- There is little evidence that organisations are providing any formal training to help their line managers handle the HR tasks that are being allocated to them.

- They are not particularly interested in HR issues and are unable to keep up to date with the latest HR thinking.

- Line managers are focused on their department and may not see the bigger picture (for example, when management development requires that one of their best people should move to another department, or when pay increases from their department could have a knock-on effect for others).

- Perhaps most significantly, the devolvement of HRM responsibilities to the line will not achieve the objectives hoped for if it is done in a policy vacuum, as it often is, just as a way of bringing costs down.

The balance of these different pressures means that the responsibility that line managers and HRM departments take over the next few years will continue to be discussed and will continue to change. Of course, allocating more responsibility for managing their people to line managers means, potentially, big changes in what line managers do and how they are judged – and equally big changes to the activities of the HRM departmental specialists.

The theoretical dividing line sometimes drawn between policy and practice is not so obvious on the ground. It is one thing to be asked to decide whether to recruit people for the immediately required work or for long-term careers with the overall organisation, or whether to recognise a union; it is another to place advertisements and to conduct negotiations. In practice, however, this distinction may be less clear and we should not make easy assumptions that the way forward would be to split the roles so that specialist HR directors set policies and line managers implement them. In practice, many of these less attractive tasks still have to be done, and there will in many cases be advantages in having them brought together under one specialist. Alternatively, with the spread of intelligent information and communications systems, much of this work will be available to the line manager without the intervention of an HR specialist.

In theory, HR specialists have to be closely involved with their line management colleagues if they want to perform their role successfully. As partners, the theory is, they share totally in the creation of policy and also in its implementation. They expect – and are expected – to contribute their specific expertise, knowledge and skill to the discussion. They will not be expected to agree with everything the line manager proposes, or expected to accept something when their professional expertise tells them that it is wrong to do so. To this extent they will not be such comfortable colleagues as the much-discussed 'internal consultants'. There is evidence that HR specialists can, indeed, be influential 'strategic change-makers'. On the other hand, it is clear that line managers as such are not a coherent group. Some senior executives may want their HR departments to take a strategic role, but many line managers just want their HR department to deal with the bureaucratic and sometimes difficult issues necessarily involved in managing people. They want a responsive operational partner, not a strategic one. Can partnering mean you ignore what your partner wants in order to do what you think is best for them?

REFLECTIVE ACTIVITY

Look back over

- the reasons for the growth of the allocation of HR responsibilities to line managers

- the reasons why that allocation has expanded no further.

How would you judge the importance of the two sets of explanations?

3 THE ROLE OF OTHER PARTIES IN HRM

It is worth taking a quick excursion now to mention the role of the people that work in an organisation as a factor in HRM. HRM is, after all, just another phrase for managing the people that the organisation uses. These may not, of course, be employees. Other people can contribute to an organisation – as self-employed contractors, as consultants (see below) and as agency workers. The majority are usually employees. But what is their role in HRM? People are the one resource that an organisation employs that is not a passive asset. All the other assets need people to give them value, but people are a value in themselves. The kind of people that an organisation can draw upon is very important: success depends not just on HRM policies or the capabilities of line managers – although they may make a critical difference – but also on the people the organisation has, the labour market they are drawn from, the educational characteristics they bring with them, their characters, their training, their attitudes and their values.

The people in every organisation are different. And that is one of the key things for the success of an organisation.

REFLECTIVE ACTIVITY

What kind of people does your organisation – or an organisation that you know well – employ?

What effect does that have on their HRM?

THE ROLE OF TRADE UNIONISTS

Trade unions include union members within organisations, activists (members who continue to be employed in an organisation but devote a lot of time and energy to the work of their union) and full-time trade union officials who do not work for anyone other than the union. For many organisations, therefore, the unions are not external players in their HR approach but internal actors. For others they are a mix of both. For HRM specialists the question of the role that the unions play is one to be managed in the same way that other aspects of the employer–employee relationship are managed: do we want to avoid the unions (is that a realistic option)? Do we want to fight them? Do we want to work with them? The employees' views, history, tradition and the behaviour of line managers are all important parts of this mix. Although it is not necessarily true that 'managers get the trade unions (and the industrial relations) that they deserve', it is certainly true that they get the trade unions (and the industrial relations) that history and the actions of managers up to and including the present group of managers deserve.

There are enormous numbers of examples from across the world of the effect of different approaches to trade unionism, to consultation and communication with and from managers and employees. Some organisations have developed individualistic relationships, so that the only real channel of communication is between management – particularly the immediate line manager – and employees. Some organisations have developed hard, antagonistic relationships with trade unions as the representatives of their employees, where there is so little trust that almost any action that the management takes is perceived as an attack on the employees or their unions. Some organisations have developed powerful partnership arrangements between themselves and their unions, so that the union sees its role as being to support but to challenge the management in order to make sure that the decisions that are taken actually deliver the best outcomes for the organisation so that the organisation remains successful and can deliver high pay levels and employment security. Like all simple pictures, these options emphasise certain characteristics and downplay others – but the truth of the picture is apparent.

Of course, the picture is complicated: some countries do not allow trade unions at all, some have government-controlled trade unions, and some allow the market to decide. The role that the trade union adopts in its relationship with the employers and their management representatives varies with country, sector, size of organisation and history. But whatever decisions are taken, the role that the trade unions adopt makes them more or less of an important player in the HRM scene.

REFLECTIVE ACTIVITY

Read through a fortnight's editions of a broadsheet newspaper and the current edition of *People Management*. See if you can find an article about an organisation in which a trade union is mentioned.

What role does the trade union have in that case?

THE PRESSURE TO OUTSOURCE

Outsourcing certain HRM activities – paying another organisation to carry them out for you – is part of the new rhetoric of HRM (CIPD, 2005; Paauwe, 1995). We should say that it is not actually new. Many management training institutions have existed for well over half a century, for example, and would not have been able to do that unless more than 50 years ago organisations had been outsourcing some of their training and development activities. Banks have long-established and profitable businesses in managing payroll for other organisations. What has happened is that there are now many new providers in the market and they are creating a demand for outsourcing and trying to talk up the changes that have gone on in order to improve their businesses. Many organisations remain resistant to the idea – and there is a clear country effect in that the 'outsourcers' are finding it very difficult to make any money in certain countries. The arguments for outsourcing include:

- HR departments should be freed from the boring low-value-added transactional work, so that they can focus on the strategic roles.

- Specialist organisations that do a lot of this work (management training centres, for example) can provide certain services better than the organisation itself.

- Economies of scale mean that the outsourcers may be able to provide the service more cheaply than the organisation can.

The opposition to outsourcing is built on arguments that:

- It does not make sense to put parts of the control of the organisation's most valuable resource (its people) in the hands of someone outside the organisation.

- The way that organisations manage their people gives them a competitive edge over other organisations that find it increasingly difficult to provide distinctive products, equipment or services, and outsourcers provide standard packages for all their (perhaps competitive) clients.

- E-HRM means that the advantages of using outsourcers may be less than the cost of developing an electronic in-house system to manage aspects of HRM – and those systems will be fully integrated with the rest of the organisation's HR policies and practices.

- In practice, it is often not cheaper to use outsourcers.

REFLECTIVE ACTIVITY

Have a discussion with others on the subject of outsourcing. No doubt there will be some arguments for and some arguments against the concept.

Which do you find the more convincing?

THE ROLE OF CONSULTANTS

There are now many large consultancy companies and a wide range of small independent consultants offering HRM services. Both offer two different kinds of service: they provide people who will do some activities in the place of, or sometimes alongside, people employed in the organisation; and they do activities aimed more at changing the policies of the organisation. Thus, consultancies offering redundancy services, expatriation services or headhunting tend to be doing activities that could be done by people within the organisation; consultancies that undertake culture change or organisational redesign projects are aiming to create or embed new policies. As elsewhere, the line between these two kinds of offerings is not clear, especially because many of the consultants and the people who employ them prefer to use the language of strategic change even when the task is just one of providing bodies to carry out an activity.

Why would organisations want to use consultants? There are a number of linked and overlapping reasons (we take here the example of a redundancy services consultant, but the same reasons could be applied to any other consultancy service):

- The consultants may have an expertise currently not available in the present HRM department: a redundancy services consultancy, for example, may be more up to date with the way the law has developed through the tribunals than the HRM department of an organisation that has never dealt with redundancies before. They may be more experienced and skilled at advising people in outplacement interviews of the alternative employment, financial and emotional implications.

- There may be good public relations reasons for using a consultant – 'We are taking the implications of this difficult situation for everybody very seriously: we have called in and will pay for experts to advise and assist us and to help you.'

- The consultants are temporary: they will soon be gone – any bad feeling that remains will, it is hoped, not attach to the permanent staff left behind, including those in the HRM department.

- Perhaps looking at the issue rather cynically, by employing consultants, managers can spread the blame – 'It wasn't my fault. We hired the most famous and expensive consultants and they advised us to do this . . .'

For whichever of these reasons, the use of consultants is now common and many consultancies make a lot of money from offering HRM services. For individuals, a few years in consultancy is either, at the start of a career, a good way to get experience of working in a wide range of different circumstances; in the middle of a career, a good way to make a comfortable income; or, at the end of a career, a good way to keep doing interesting things without the pressure and responsibility of working for a particular organisation.

REFLECTIVE ACTIVITY

At the top of a sheet of paper write 'As an HRM practitioner I would be in favour of using consultants because . . .' and list as many reasons as you can think of.

Then list an opposing argument against each of those reasons.

When might using consultants be especially helpful? In what circumstances might it be particularly problematic?

KEY ISSUES: CHANGING ROLES IN HRM

We now pull together ten key points about changing roles in HRM raised in this chapter:

- The roles of all the actors in HRM are changing greatly.

- The strategic involvement of senior HR specialists may be changing and new roles for these specialists as function leaders and contributors to strategic thinking in the business are being identified. The relationship between HR specialist and line manager is very important.

- The strategic partner and HR leader roles are complex and equivocal.

- Increasing pressure is being put on line managers to do a better job of people management. In many cases, good HR policies are of little value without effective line management implementation.

- The impact of outsourcing, e-HRM and consultancy operations are all being felt.

- The implications of e-HRM, outsourcing and the role of consultants remain to be resolved and in practice vary on a case-by-case basis.

- There are a number of implications in the changing roles of those involved in HRM for how we think about the subject, and significant implications in practice for the role of the HR function.

- The different roles that the specialists in HR departments can play are a useful way to look at some of the implications of the allocation of HR responsibilities. All the roles are important and all must be handled effectively and with credibility.

- The assumptions that people within an HRM department make about their role may not be shared by the other parties involved: they have to be continually tested.

- The 'interplay' between the many actors involved (corporate, national and plant-level HR specialists, line managers, trade unionists, consultants, outsourcers, etc) is complex and varies with context.

Perhaps there are other key points that you would like to note for yourself.

The main case study in this chapter now follows. It gives an example of what can happen when an organisation decides to restructure its HR function and operations.

Look at the description of the case set out below. Then decide on the recommendations that you would make as an HR manager for dealing with the issues raised.

Megaco is a service company based in Britain but with substantial overseas investments. It has been through a radical and massive downsizing process stretching across several years in order to cut costs. The company began with some 200,000 employees, mostly in Britain, but now only employs around half of that number. In the process it has lost many very experienced and well-trained people with a lot of understanding about their complex industry. Now that the process is nearing completion, there is very real pressure on the HRM department to downsize too, and to cut costs. The company's HR function has long been very traditionally structured and organised. Sub-departments within the HR department (recruitment, payroll, employee relations, training and other sub-departments) all reported up to the top of an organisational pyramid that ended with the Head Office HR department and ultimately the HR director.

Decisions were taken at board level drastically to reduce the size of the department. Many HR functions were devolved to mid-level managers for the first time. This enabled senior management to reduce the HR department and to focus the remaining HR professionals on 'lines of business' (ie different key products and services) rather than the HR functions (recruitment, training, etc) to get HR professionals reporting to the heads of these lines of business, not to Head Office HR and also to co-ordinate HR through 'centres of excellence'. These 'centres of excellence' are loose electronically connected groups of experts in each HR area who can respond

creatively to difficult problems and come up with new ideas. All relatively straightforward transactional work such as payroll, providing information on rates of pay, pensions and so on was to be outsourced to consultants. To facilitate all of this, the company bought expensive electronic information systems. Large numbers of HR people left as a result, disliking the changes. In fact, very few redundancies had to be made in the HR function because many left anyway.

There are now a number of problems as a result of this restructuring of the HR function. Many of the middle-level line managers are not happy with what has happened. They now have to deal with HR issues themselves, something they have not been trained for, and they feel they have to learn by costly and stressful trial and error. Meanwhile, the HRM department has the wrong skill set for the new roles it is being asked to perform. Many people in the company make cynical jokes about the 'centres of excellence'. In addition, it is widely rumoured in the company that consultants are working quite hard to get into positions where they can win large new contracts for advising middle-level managers.

Your task

Can you think of any wider consequences for the business of the decisions that were made to restructure the HR department?

If you were the HR director, how would you have responded to the board's demands to cut the costs of HR?

EXPLORE FURTHER

FARNDALE, E. and BREWSTER, C. (2005) 'In search of legitimacy: national professional associations and the professionalism of HR practitioners', *Human Resource Management Journal*, Vol. 15, No. 3, 33–48
This article presents the results of a worldwide survey of professional associations for personnel specialists, arguing that the function shows signs of professionalism but is not yet a profession.

GUEST, D. E. (1997) 'Human resource management and performance: a review and a research agenda', *International Journal of Human Resource Management*, Vol. 8, 263–76
A seminal, critical, study by one of the UK's leading thinkers about HRM on the link between HRM and firm performance.

MARTIN, G. (2005) *Technology and People Management: Transforming the function of HR and the HR function*. London, CIPD
A useful summary of the literature on developments in the technology available to, and increasingly used by, HRM departments and the implications that technology will have for the role of the function.

CHAPTER 21

The organisation of work

Martin Upchurch

INTRODUCTION

This chapter examines new ways of organising work in the modern workplace. The last 30 years have seen large changes in the organisation of work in workplaces all over the world. In the British workplace, change has been a direct product of new employer strategies to compete in an increasingly internationalised product market. The new wave of work organisation has included the development of both hard and soft techniques of HRM, has adapted to the Japanese production model, and has more latterly taken on the 'high performance' concept. The Government, in adapting to these developments, has also sought to encourage employers to work in partnership with their employees and trade unions in an effort to raise productivity in jointly agreed initiatives. This consensus-based approach is presented as an alternative to the confrontation between unions and employers in British industry. There is little disagreement amongst academics and practitioners that these changes have happened, although there remains considerable division as to the scale and scope of change, and probably more importantly, as to the effects the changes have had on the quality of working life and the intensity of work itself. All of this is important context for the HR professional.

LEARNING OUTCOMES

By the end of this chapter readers should be able to:

- appreciate the reason for change within a globalised economy
- describe government and employer strategies and reasons for reorganising work
- review the evidence of changing work organisation
- discuss the major points of debates and controversies associated with the organisation of work
- understand what all this means for the HR professional.

The chapter is in four parts. First, we consider the reasons for change, as they are located in a globalising economy. Then we review the importance of Japanese production methods and the concept of HRM for work organisation. Finally, we look at the high-performance work approach. Throughout we consider the debates and controversies around this new world of work.

The chapter concludes with the main case study.

Reference sources named within the chapter may be looked up in the *References and further reading* section at the end of the book.

STARTER CASE STUDY

Goos and Manning (2003) have produced evidence to suggest that a polarisation of job skills is taking place in Britain (reflecting the experience of the USA) between low-paid low-skilled jobs and high-skill knowledge-intensive jobs. Both sets of jobs are said to be growing faster in total than 'middling' types of jobs such as clerical, administrative and lower managerial jobs. Most of the low-skill jobs, however, are in service work in areas such as catering and tourism and in personal services in the caring sector, whereas in manufacturing there appears to be a decline in low-skill jobs in the USA and Europe as routinised jobs become automated. The pattern of job growth produced by these trends is reflected in a 'U-bend' profile.

The scenario described above has been questioned by other academic commentators. The starter case study is intended firstly to help understanding of the debate, and secondly to relate the recorded evidence to the situation in organisations.

Dorling and Thomas (2004), using 2001 Census data, record a relatively faster increase in 'associate professional' jobs (eg nurses, social workers, fire service operatives and police) than in any other jobs, and a second-fastest growth of 'elementary occupations' (such as those employed in shelf-stacking in retail and cleaning in the service sector). These trends would support a 'polarisation thesis', with a drift at the ends of the skills spectrum to low-skill poor-quality jobs at one end and to high-skill high-value-added jobs at the other, together with a stabilisation of middle managerial and administrative occupations.

However, using evidence from the Government's Annual Surveys of Hours and Earnings, the Director of Research at the Department of Trade and Industry Grant Fitzner (2006) shows that 'since 1998, the share of low-paid UK jobs has shrunk and the proportion of high-paid jobs has increased. The proportion of jobs paying around median earnings has remained relatively unchanged, contrary to the thesis of a "disappearing middle".' There seems also to have been a reversal in the managerial 'de-layering' process. A survey of 2,000 UK managers in 2002 showed that on average 22% of managers said that the proportion of managerial and professional staff had risen in the previous three years, against 8% who thought there had been a decline and 69% who reported little change.

Question for discussion

1 How can this seemingly contradictory evidence be explained?

2 Is it because there has been an increase in 'manager' jobs after two decades of managerial de-layering?

3 Does low-paid work by migrant labour (much of it illegal) register in the statistics? In your organisation or in one you know well, what trends can you observe which may confirm or refute the 'U-bend' profile?

4 What might these changes mean for the HR professional?

1 THE GLOBALISATION OF PRODUCTION AND SERVICES

The 1970s saw the end of the long period of post-war economic growth and stability. Rising oil prices added to inflationary tendencies and put extra strains on those advanced industrial nations, such as Japan, that were more dependent on imported oil than competitors. The economic downturn came with a crisis of profitability amongst corporations in the Western economies, leading them by the end of the 1970s to search for new production locations (to cut costs) and new markets (for sales of products).

The new era of globalisation started by this process was accompanied by changes in international political economy. Typically, it involved moves within supra-national institutions such as the International Monetary Fund, the World Bank, and later the World Trade Organisation (WTO), to pressurise the under-developed countries to lower tariff barriers and allow the free movement of capital, goods and services. This was thought necessary by the countries of the richer world to allow their enterprises access to the new markets in the form of foreign direct investment (FDI), the establishment of new production facilities, or the control and ownership of services.

The eventual reaction by countries of the developing South to this pressure from the industrialised North brought in the decline of their 'import substitution model' of national self-sufficient development and the creation of a new international division of labour. This division of labour was based on comparative advantage and free (but not necessarily fair) trade whereby the countries of the South produced goods and service for the world market linked either to commodity production or to cheap labour costs. The process of searching for ever-cheaper production locations has led many commentators to warn against a 'race to the bottom', which might negatively affect labour standards and conditions in both South and North. Table 48 shows the enormous gap which exists in wage costs for workers in manufacturing – workers in Sri Lanka, for example, earning just over half a US dollar an hour, whereas workers in Norway earn on average almost 35 dollars per hour. Even in the European Union, manufacturing wages vary from just over 7 dollars per hour (Portugal) to just over 34 dollars per hour (in what used to be West Germany).

In many ways globalisation is a double-edged sword. On the one hand the drive towards market liberalisation and downward regulation of labour and financial markets has created real fears about job insecurity, income inequality and declining democratic participation at work. On the other hand demands for some re-regulation to bring market forces under control have arisen in opposition. In terms of fears, the need to improve competitiveness in the world product market has clearly led employers to flexibilise their employment contracts and try reduce employment. This fear (real or perceived) is increased by the upturn in takeovers, mergers and alliances as capital restructures and consolidates on an international dimension.

Second, the expansion of corporate activity across national boundaries has weakened government ability to regulate corporate activity without fear of offending the very corporations whose investment decisions are seen by pro-

Table 48 Hourly compensation costs (in US dollars) for production workers in manufacturing, 2004

United States	22.87
Brazil	3.03
Canada	21.42
Mexico	2.50
Australia	23.09
Hong Kong (1,2)	5.51
Israel	12.18
Japan	21.90
Korea	11.52
New Zealand	12.89
Singapore	7.45
Sri Lanka	0.51
Taiwan	5.97
Austria	28.29
Belgium	29.98
Czech Republic	5.43
Denmark	33.75
Finland	30.67
France	23.89
Germany, former West	34.05
Germany, all	32.53
Hungary	5.72
Ireland, Republic of	21.94
Italy	20.48
Luxembourg	26.57
Netherlands	30.76
Norway	34.64
Portugal	7.02
Spain	17.10
Sweden	28.41
Switzerland	30.26
United Kingdom	24.71

(1) Hong Kong Special Administrative Region of China.
(2) Average of selected manufacturing industries.
Source: US Bureau of Labor Statistics, February 2006

market regimes to be important to national well-being and economic health. Corporate taxation, for example, has fallen by an average 3.5% in all advanced industrial countries since the mid-1990s, and tax rates on US MNCs in developing countries have dropped from an average 54% in 1986 to 28% in 1996. The UK economy is relatively highly exposed to the world market when compared to other advanced industrial nations. The UK has disproportionately high rates of both outward and inward investment, spread across both manufacturing and service industries, making the UK economy extremely dependent on decisions taken by non-UK owners abroad. Also, the UK has also experienced a higher rate of mergers, takeovers and strategic alliances than competitors. This is due in part to Britain's high exposure to the world economy and the consequent need for restructuring, and in part because of the Anglo-Saxon corporate governance regime with its emphasis on short-termism, shareholder value and propensity to hostile takeover.

Globalisation is also affecting provision of public services as regulatory regimes are liberalised to allow entry into national markets of foreign-owned service providers. The EU Services Directive will reinforce this trend by opening up public service markets within the EU, while the World Trade Organisation General Agreement on Trade in Services (GATS) has the same intention. What is highlighted by this evidence is the extreme volatility of investment and corporate ownership within the UK, which in turn makes both employee relations regimes and the labour market uncertain and unstable. This means that is hard for HR professionals to minimise redundancies and to avoid the negative effects described in Chapter 19.

Government strategy has responded to the high risks of a globalised economy by promoting both the high-performance workplace (see below) and partnership in the workplace between employers and employees. The aim is to improve UK productivity by building a consensus in the workplace on the need to modernise work practices through flexibility and skill training. Partnership is promoted as a method for such practice, by engaging employees through participation and establishing trust and job security (see Chapter 19).

The effects of these global processes on the organisation of work in the trading sector of advanced economies such as Britain are considerable.

Firstly, the pressures from stronger international competition have meant that *enterprises have reassessed their labour and production costs.* Low-skill labour-intensive industries in richer countries are less likely to survive, and employers will be tempted to shift production facilities or outsource production abroad to take advantage of lower labour costs. In the UK, for example, jobs needing degree-level qualifications have grown much faster than non-degree jobs in the last 15 years, while jobs needing low-level or no qualifications have declined sharply. According to WERS 2004, employers are also much more likely to provide off-the-job training than in the past, 64% of employers doing so in 2004 compared to 42% in 1998. Other enterprises may also re-examine their production operations and, if necessary, re-focus on core production while abandoning, subcontracting or outsourcing peripheral or lower-skill functions.

The textile and clothing industries show interesting examples of these processes. Cheaper labour costs in Morocco have led Courtaulds to move much of its textile production to that country, while the retailer Marks & Spencers has also moved where it gets a lot of its clothing brand away from the UK to Morocco. However, in some developed countries clothing production has been kept, due to government protectionist tariffs and cheap immigrant labour in the case of the Los Angeles area, or by marketing and cultural/networking links to the fashion industry in the case of the north Italian Emiglia-Romana industrial district. Considerable media attention has also been directed at companies' moving call centre operations abroad in cheaper labour locations such as India. However, surveys estimate that in 2004 only about 6% of call centre jobs have been offshored in this way.

Secondly, the nature of work itself is likely to change as *employers seek to restructure working methods,* either by using more creative and knowledge-based applications to production (eg robotics and computer-aided design), by intensifying levels of labour exploitation to cut down 'waste' time at work, by redesigning production processes with new technology, or by the introduction of more flexible working arrangements to allow multi-tasking and multi-skilling (see Chapter 10). The proportion of UK workers using information technology as part of their job, for example, is estimated to have risen from just over half in 1992 to almost three quarters in 2001.

Many commentators suggest that the two trends combined have led to a *polarisation* of job skills between those better jobs – MacJobs – which require an upgraded knowledge-based skill set, and those lower-graded routine-based-skill jobs in personal services, fast food and shops – McJobs (eg Goos and Manning, 2003). Other forms of flexibility – such as numerical, contract and temporal flexibility – may be used to create a tighter fit between organisational requirements and staffing. WERS 2004 records that some core employees have been trained to be functionally flexible in two thirds of UK workplaces with 10 or more employees. However, despite predictions in the 1980s and 1990s of the end of the 'job for life', the evidence shows that permanent full-time work is still the norm for the British worker, with 94% of employed men and 92% of employed women in permanent-contract jobs at the turn of the century. 96% of workers also have one job, rather than a 'portfolio' of different jobs, although portfolio working may exist within organisations as employees take on a range of tasks for a single employer.

One additional product of increased working with information technology has been a rise in working remotely from home as well as an increase in working via a laptop 'on the move'. According to the Government's *Labour Force Survey*, the proportion of people working mostly at or from home has risen to one in 10 (about 2.8 million people) in 2002 from one in 25 in 1981. IT has also encouraged the phenomenon of 'hot-desking' and open-plan offices. Hot-desking is now used by one in four employers, and most employers now use open-plan offices, often creating the appearance of office 'factories'.

Thirdly, because of the increased likelihood that new global companies will be able to enter product markets, *manufacturers and service providers have to be more responsive to consumer demands* if they are to retain and increase their market share. This will require production processes to be more functionally flexible. This need for *flexible specialisation* brings a 'new industrial divide' between the old mass production techniques and more flexible techniques based on cellular or alternative methods of production. More importantly, Japanese management and production techniques became increasingly seen as the way forward for production. British employers have tried to upgrade workers' skills as part of this process, particularly through work-based training.

Fourthly, there has been *an integration of tasks within the organisation*, achieved most importantly through teamworking. Teams are used to co-ordinate tasks between people in contrast to hierarchically based divisions of labour observed under Taylorist systems. WERS 2004 shows that 88% of public sector workplaces and 66% of private sector workplaces now operate with some core employees in formally designated teams. Teamworking might also involve some form of quasi self-governance (or autonomy) through which problem-solving can take place. A mixture of skills within teams can also remove the need for specialist individual operations such as quality checking and work allocation. The 2004 WERS survey showed that 21% of workplaces with more than 10 employees at that time had problem-solving groups amongst their core employees, up from 16% in 1998. The introduction of cellular teamworking in high-technology industries such as aerospace has also created opportunities for employers to outsource less profitable or lower-value-added production processes. Finally, as the classic Human Relations school of thought showed, teams have a distinct social role which may be used to integrate employees into the values and culture of the organisation, to reduce feelings of 'them' and 'us', and to facilitate the development of social capital through networking (see Chapter 24). Coaching and mentoring of employees is increasingly used as a way of instilling organisational culture and values (see Chapter 15).

Fifthly, many of the above changes *have social implications*. Although unemployment has fallen in the UK over the last decade, the proportion of inactive men in the labour market has stayed consistently high, reflecting a shift away from older traditional industries (in which men dominated) to newer information- and service-based industries with more women and younger employees. More workers are also coming from abroad, especially since the expansion of the EU into central and eastern Europe. Immigrant workers also show a polarised skill base – some are recruited to skilled jobs within industry and the public services, while others work in the informal economy. The net effect is to make the UK workplace and work regimes in general much more diverse.

REFLECTIVE ACTIVITY

What effect has globalisation had on an industry and/or organisation in which you work or which you know well?

What evidence is there of the industry's/organisation's outsourcing or shifting production to developing countries?

Has there been an upskilling of knowledge-based work in the industry/organisation?

What are the limits to working at home? Why might the office still live on as the core place of work?

2 JAPANESE METHODS

The 'Japanese production model' of the 1970s and 1980s was characterised by high-quality goods produced at low costs. Japan set new standards in production. Lower cost was a result not so much of cheaper basic wage costs but of lower *unit* wage costs which came from more efficient production methods based on teamworking, just-in-time production and business process engineering. High quality, according to the model, came from self-checking, quality circles and an ethos of continuous improvement (*kaizen*). Such was the power of the model that it led to a US-Government-commissioned enquiry by the Massachusetts Institute of Technology (MIT) to look at the nature, significance and possible use of the model in American manufacturing. The results of the study, written into book form as *The Machine that Changed the World* (Womack, Jones and Roos, 1990), praised the Japanese 'lean' production process and suggested that only a Toyotan 'best way' could solve the problems of US manufacturing competitiveness. Womack *et al* claimed that lean production meant working 'smarter, not harder', suggesting that the recommended new production methods should be a paradigm break with the alienating Taylorist methods of the past. Furthermore, they suggested (Womack *et al*, 1990; p.101) that the everyday experience of work would be better as a result:

> While the mass production plant is often filled with mind-numbing stress, as workers struggle to assemble unmanufacturable products and have no way to improve their working environment, lean production offers a creative tension in which workers have many ways to address challenges. This creative tension involved in solving complex problems is precisely what has separated manual factory work from professional 'think' work in the age of mass production.

As Japanese production methods began to be adopted in Western industrialised countries in the 1980s and 1990s, many studies tried to measure their impact. Oliver and Wilkinson (1992) produced an important work, *The Japanisation of British Industry*, in which they explained the prescriptions of the Japanese model designed to stop waste in production. They outlined Total Quality Management (TQM), continuous improvement (*kaizen*), just-in-time production (JIT), teamworking, job rotation and multi-skilling as key parts of the system and suggested that, in the UK context, such new methods might damage industrial relations. New techniques of HRM would be necessary to overcome labour resistance, including careful employee selection techniques, direct communications between the employer and employee, performance-related pay and longer-term job security. These practices thus combined both production methods and management techniques, and work was reorganised against the potential interests of collective labour but in favour of more satisfying work for the individual. By the end of the century, the impact of such work practices in UK workplaces was considerable. In 2000 quality circles covered three in ten workers – half as many again compared with 10 years earlier. The majority of UK workers now work in groups, an increase of 10% from the early 1990s.

REFLECTIVE ACTIVITY

Could the full range of Japanese practices be transferred to British factories and offices despite the great differences in cultural and institutional background?

Do Japanese production methods in fact mark a break with Taylorist mass production methods, or are they simply a revised and refined version of Taylorism?

Are workers liberated through self-checking of quality and through teamworking – or are they actually just working harder with extra surveillance?

Note that we have here introduced the concept of *ratios* of one job family to another, or of one as a percentage of the whole workforce. These can be more revealing than simple statistics.

In discussing the questions of the exercise above, many studies point to the enhanced effect on performance generated by worker peer pressure through teamworking, or highlight the autonomy of workers achieved under computer-aided teamworking. Labour-oriented perspectives are more critical. Garrahan and Stewart (1992), in their study of the Nissan transplant in Sunderland, focused on the ideological nature of control over workers in the factory, leading to intensified worker exploitation. Danford (1999), in his study of Japanese factories in South Wales, draws similar conclusions, and suggests that Japanese production methods intensify work through semi-Taylorist methods with limited opportunities for worker creativity and self-expression. A study for the Department for Education and Skills (DfES) by Felstead, Gallie and Green

CASE STUDY

'I must admit, a lot of the earlier ideas we were looking at were based on the idea that everybody would be encouraged to spend time off production on *kaizen* activity. But I'm afraid that's not reality, is it? Life isn't like that. We still want involvement from the shop floor, but our 100% priority – and I stress 100% – must be making parts. Therefore the direction we're moving in now is that team leaders, the unit managers, will be the problem-solvers and they will just involve team members in more of a consultative manner through effective communications with the employees.'

Personnel manager in car components factory, from Danford (1999) *Japanese Management Techniques and British Workers* (p.153)

Questions for discussion

1 What might explain the constraints on managerial ability to introduce full worker autonomy?

2 Should effective teamworking bring about the abolition of the role of team leader?

3 How might good performance for teamworking be rewarded?

(2002) reported that although responsibility might have increased, the amount of 'task discretion' in UK workplaces had decreased significantly for both professionals and skilled workers throughout the 1990s. Discretion and control for managers, however, seems to have increased, often with the use of remote surveillance techniques aided by information technology.

3 HUMAN RESOURCE MANAGEMENT AND THE ORGANISATION OF WORK

We now focus on how techniques of HRM may have reshaped the organisation of work in advanced economies such as Britain's. An important aspect of HRM has been the focus on individual value added, and its quantification by systems of performance measurement and appraisal (see Chapter 12). The measurement of performance is notoriously difficult. This is due to the sometimes contradictory pressures between the need for quantity and the need for quality; the inexact science of performance measurement itself (especially in public services); the likelihood of the creation of anomalies between jobs, grades and occupations; and the effects of bonuses on performance systems. In addition, no definite link has been confirmed between individual effort and the incentives (such as pay).

Despite these difficulties a move towards individual performance measurement has been a central feature of British workplace practice since the 1980s. According to WERS 2004 formal performance appraisal was conducted in 78% of British workplaces. The systems needed to conduct such performance review have been a major influence on the organisation of work.

- *New systems of financial control and accountability within organisations have been constructed*, including the creation of cost centres, budget centres and strategic business units and the marketisation of services between these units. Such units are made accountable not only for budgets but also for their value added or profitability. Because of this, the process of outsourcing activities which produce less value within the 'value chain' is encouraged, and the likelihood of organisational restructuring to maximise value added is increased. Techniques of HRM are subordinated to the process of financial accountability, leading to the development of 'hard' HRM and human asset accounting, as well as individual and group target-setting.

- Within the public sector, the development of '*new public management*' has tried to copy many of the features of divisional financial accountability seen in the private sector. However, the measurement of individual value added is much harder in the public sector than in the private sector due to the lack of profit imperative. A substitute for this has been the introduction by the Government of principles of marketisation through private finance initiatives, public–private partnerships and internal trading of services. This has had a parallel effect on organisational restructuring and the creation of organisational targets in sectors such as the NHS and education.

- In many organisations performance measurement has moved beyond quantitative assessment towards *softer competency objectives* such as the ability to work in teams, leadership, etc. A good deal of competency assessment reflects TQM processes whereby attitudinal structuring is undertaken by HRM-led initiatives to promote ideas of customer consciousness. Teamworking has been especially encouraged, both to reflect 'Japanese' best practice and to encourage commitment through employee task participation.

- Other occupationally specific competencies include concepts of emotional and even aesthetic labour. Both *emotional and aesthetic labour* measurement is justified by organisational needs to satisfy customer demand. As well as the employee 'selling' manual effort to the employer (manual labour) and intellectual effort (intellectual labour) the need might also be to 'sell' positive aspects of personality (emotional labour) or how one looks (aesthetic labour).

 REFLECTIVE ACTIVITY

What are the main purposes of creating flatter spans of control in organisations by de-layering managerial jobs?

Why might methods of performance-related pay be more contested in public sector employment?

How can teams be used to create a greater customer or consumer consciousness?

JOB REDESIGN AND BUSINESS PROCESS ENGINEERING

In looking at the above developments some commentators suggest that HRM techniques represent a return to motivational theory popularised by theorists of the Human Relations school such as Maslow, Herzberg and McGregor. This is in reaction to the alienation of workers associated with Taylorist and Fordist principles of scientific management and automated mass-assembly production. For these reasons renewed efforts to revisit *job design* (eg job rotation, job enrichment, job enlargement) through teamworking processes do not just fulfil the needs of lean production but also employees' needs for and desires for intrinsic and extrinsic motivation. Allied with these developments are debates about contract status and content, as job boundaries and job descriptions are deliberately blurred or even absent and the 'new psychological contract' is open-ended, with greater expectation of self-initiative and lower expectation of paternalistic and heavily regulated employment relationships.

Alongside new contractual expectations are efforts to reorganise hierarchical structure within organisations through business process engineering. Such new organisational design allows more horizontal communication between employees and networking to complete specified tasks and projects. Traditional structural boundaries are by-passed or abolished in order to generate employee creativity and initiative. The resulting organisational form can be described as the 'virtual corporation'. The blurring of contract boundary is potentially negative for employee interests, as organisational control may adversely affect controls over health and safety, and working hours, whereby the 'norm' expectation of the eight-hour working day disappears and a long hours culture of 'presenteeism' is substituted. Business process re-engineering has also often resulted in substantial de-layering of managerial and other jobs, as organisational redesign happens. Because of this, the process has often been criticised for forgetting the 'human dimension' of working life.

This has been recognised by Michael Hammer, the computing academic and business consultant who first coined the phrase 'business process re-engineering', when interviewed for an article in the *Wall Street Journal* in 1996.

> *Dr Hammer points out a flaw: He and the other leaders of the $4.7 billion re-engineering industry forgot about people. 'I wasn't smart enough about that,' he says. 'I was reflecting my engineering background and was insufficient appreciative of the human dimension. I've learned that's critical.'*

REFLECTIVE ACTIVITY

How might the 'virtual corporation' differ in organisational design from a traditional hierarchically organised enterprise?

What extra skills might be required of employees in a task-based networking organisation?

What would be the consequences for HR professionals working in 'virtual corporations' or in task-based networking organisations?

The difficulties of organisational redesign experienced in the 1990s, combined with the structural limitations to continued productivity improvement through lean production techniques, have led commentators to refer to a 'crisis of HRM'. Sparrow and Marchington (1998) talk about a *contribution dilemma* of HRM which questions the technical validity of many HRM techniques, argues for a need to define the link between HRM and organisational performance, and refers to the growing sophistication of the role of HRM within organisational strategy. Out of such reflection new approaches have emerged centred on the notion of the 'high-performance work system', which is examined below.

4 HIGH-PERFORMANCE WORK SYSTEMS

In the early 1990s, there was increasing concern on the part of employers and US political leaders that productivity growth in America was possibly suffering from the aftershocks of a decade of de-layering of jobs within corporations. One potential byproduct of increasing job precariousness was a decline in workplace trust seen as necessary in business process engineering to develop a spirit of creativity and innovation. Applebaum, Bailey, Berg and Kallenberg (2000) argued that a shift in management–employee relations was now needed if organisations were to overcome lack of trust and create the conditions for increased productivity. Their book *Manufacturing Advantage: Why high-performance work systems pay off* makes an argument for the high-performance work system (HPWS) that placed job security, management–worker trust, worker participation and upskilling as central features:

- direct worker participation in decisions over operational functions – sharing power with management rather than individual worker empowerment

- agreement to increase worker skills

- creation of incentives for worker participation

- facilitation of co-ordination and communication between employees.

It is argued that the above high-skill model must be based on management's willingness to devolve power within the organisation, if necessary in consultation/negotiation with trade unions (see Chapter 17). Such an approach leads, it is suggested, to a win/win situation based on mutual gains for both employers and employees. Earlier experiments at the 'high-performance' approach were introduced at the Volvo car factory in Kalmar, Sweden, in the form of *semi-autonomous teams* (although it should be noted that the factory has since been closed).

CASE STUDY

Volvo defined five levels of group-working at its Kalmar plant. Level 1 is simply working as a group. Level 5 (the highest level) allows for the increased possibility that the group can make its own decisions. Payments to each group are linked both to training and to the consequent level of attainment.

Level 1 – working as a group

Level 2 – job enlargement

Level 3 – increases in responsibility for planning

Level 4 – job rotation

Level 5 – increased possibility of making own decisions.

Questions for discussion

1 Why might it be argued that such job re-design will increase worker productivity?

2 How might such changes in the organisation of work affect managerial authority and control?

The central proposition of HPWS is that previous efforts to drive workers to work harder by lean production, peer pressure, surveillance and control are inferior to systems which allow more worker discretion and greater autonomy. The ideas of HPWS have since been taken up by the UK Government in its publications on the subject (DTI, 2002; 2004) as well as the CIPD (2004). The Engineering Employers' Federation (EEF) also promotes the concept and in its pamphlet *Catching Up with Uncle Sam: The final report on US/UK manufacturing productivity* (2001) a link is made between more responsible and discretionary working methods and improved productivity. A joint CIPD/EEF Report (2003) argues that in introducing HPWS:

> Job design is very influential. Where people have some influence over how they do their job, and where they find their job interesting and challenging, they are much more likely to have job satisfaction, be motivated and be more committed to the organisation.

The CIPD (2004) report produced by David Guest lists 18 high-performance work practices associated with HPWS, which may be introduced as bundles of practices and which have implications both for the organisation of work and for HR practice. Examples are shown in the box below.

Flexible job descriptions
Open-ended job description with lack of precise roles and expected tasks. Implication of continual skill upgrading

Work improvement teams
Task-based semi-permanent multi-skilled teams enacted to boost quality and design more efficient and less wasteful working method

Problem-solving groups
Ad hoc (often voluntary) multi-skilled groups drawn from different work departments with the aim of suggesting methods of overcoming design problems and improving quality; similar to quality circles

Single status
System of awarding equal benefits to all occupational groups in the workplace – such as pension entitlement, holiday entitlement, sick leave entitlement, car-parking spaces, etc, but excluding pay and remuneration

Harmonisation
Process of moving to single status or near single status

Job redesign
Job rotation to allow employees to utilise a greater range of skills on a greater range of tasks, thus reducing alienation
Job enrichment to allow employees to expand their skills and responsibilities

Continuous learning
Promotion of learning and development within organisation through formal and informal means and through permanent and semi-permanent organisational structures

In particular flexible job descriptions, multi-skilling, work improvement teams, problem-solving groups, single status and harmonisation are all considered important factors within an environment of continuous learning. However, central to the HPWS approach is the important role of employee discretion in improving organisational performance. Purcell *et al* (2003), in their case study research on behalf of the CIPD, emphasise this link, and suggest that for organisational performance to improve employees must not only do their job but act 'beyond contract' to do more. Their willingness to do so is in turn a function of improvements in job satisfaction and the consequent supposed link between job satisfaction, organisational commitment and individual performance. It follows that for such discretionary behaviour to really work well, organisations must relax supervisory and hierarchical control.

REFLECTIVE ACTIVITY

List examples of high-performance working in organisations you are familiar with.

What barriers might there be in organisations to the introduction of HPWS?

How might such barriers be overcome?

The concept and operational effects of HPWS have been criticised. Although Appelbaum *et al*'s (2000) US-based study appeared to show positive outcomes of HPWS for employees in terms of trust and job satisfaction, some other studies have been less enthusiastic. Both White, Hill, McGovern, Mills and Smeaton (2004a) and Danford, Richardson, Stewart, Tailby and Upchurch (2005) in surveys conducted for the Economic and Social Research Council's Future of Work Programme found that HPWS can negatively affect employees' work–life balance and intensify work. Discretion is often limited to management grades, and does not reach down to lower-grade occupations. Danford *et al* (2005; p.8) further argue that many of the constraining and controlling aspects of lean production 'have been cannibalised most successfully in the current ideology of the high-performance workplace'.

The difficulties of introducing effective HPWS are recognised by practitioners. Porter and Ketels' (2003) report into UK competitiveness suggested that UK companies are less likely to adopt modern management techniques than their competitors. The role of line managers in implementing the process is crucial, and it is here that some resistance to relaxing control may take place. Findings from WERS 2004 seem to confirm the pessimism, as the proportion of workplaces using a combination of high-involvement practices has shown only a 'marginal increase' since the 1998 survey. Most importantly, there appeared to be a continued lack of trust between employers and employees. Trust appeared in only 'a minority' of workplaces. Because of this the Government has been keen to link up HPWS with 'partnership'-based practices, emphasising the micro-institutional benefits of employee–employer consensus and joint problem-solving. The Government has since established a Partnership Fund to encourage joint problem-solving initiatives between employees, their unions and employers. Both the TUC and the CBI have also embraced the concept of partnership at work, seeing it as both a route to higher productivity and of mutual benefit to employers and the workforce. However, important differences exist between the US, UK and the 'European Social Model' institutional environments. The European 'social partnership' model offers greater institutional support for employee voice and representation than that of the USA. Partnership in Britain appears a hybrid case lying between the US mutual gains model and the EU social model.

KEY ISSUES IN WORK ORGANISATION

We now pull together ten key points about the organisation of work raised in this chapter:

- Increased internationalisation of the world economy has intensified product market competition and has been a major driver of outsourcing and industrial restructuring. In an attempt to remain competitive and increase productivity, employers have turned to new production methods and business process engineering and sought to focus on core activities which maximise value added for the organisation. Value chains have expanded across national boundaries and a new international division of labour has emerged.

- As for the workplace itself, evidence points to an intensification of work as wasteful production is gradually eliminated and time porosity in the working day is squeezed by self-disciplinary processes induced by teamworking, surveillance and monitoring of performance, and multi-skilling and tasking of the workforce.

- An associated effect appears to have been a polarisation of skills within the workforce as lower-skilled jobs are automated and routinised and 'knowledge'-based jobs are credited with more discretion and autonomy.

- A rejoinder to this process has been the new paradigm of high-performance working and partnership, with an emphasis on organisational trust and employee consultation constructed to channel workers' creativity into the production regime.

- Within the non-trading public sector many of the processes associated with manufacturing and service provision have

been replicated. Encouraged by marketisation and privatisation, a new disaggregation of function has emerged within organisations which has encouraged cost-consciousness and relaxed hierarchical controls in favour of a networking-based organisational culture.

- Much of the discussion of high performance has been framed within concerns over a 'crisis of HRM' by which doubts have arisen over the usefulness of HRM techniques in enhancing organisational performance.

- Workplace-based evidence also suggests that increased discretion appears to have been focused on managers, while staff remain subject to continuing and new forms of control.

- As we move from the present to the future it is clear that no simple picture of work and the workplace will emerge.

- Employers in advanced industrial nations such as Britain will have enormous pressure placed on them to move up the value chain in order to compete in the world economy. Such a move will not only define the type of jobs that are available in the labour market, but will also define the ideal 'type' of worker that is required to fill the job.

- More innovative production will require a more innovative workforce, and this may continue to challenge both employers and workers alike.

Perhaps there are other key points that you would like to note for yourself.

The main case study in this chapter now follows. It reflects the context of the finance sector in the UK over the last decade – a sector that might be said to have undergone more than its fair share of restructuring during that period.

Make an initial reading of the case study to gain an overview of the situation, and then read the questions that you will need to address. Now read the case study again, making notes of issues and facts that will help you in your analysis and responses to the questions. Remember to 'read between the lines' as well as picking out the obvious points, and also to consider what is not said as well as what is presented here.

The finance sector in the UK now represents about 19% per cent of all UK employment. In the past, divisions between the three sub-sectors (banking, insurance and building societies) in the UK were fairly well established but since the 1980s boundaries within the sector have become blurred as they have undergone the 'financial services revolution'. The sector has been especially affected by mergers, acquisitions and takeovers alongside de-regulation and then re-regulation of financial markets and de-mutualisation within the sector. This process has been a response to increased competition, as organisations seek to develop economies of scale and secure an increased market share.

The restructuring of the industry has also adversely affected job security as cost efficiency and capital concentration has taken its toll. New forms of delivery based on call centre operation followed the telephone-based creation of *Direct Line* in the 1980s and this has been followed in turn by Internet and digital television access as well as new entrants into the product market. New technology has also allowed much of the administration and case work to be computerised, and as a consequence many jobs are now routinised and closely monitored for output. The introduction of cash machines, for example, has eliminated the need for so many front desk staff in retail banks, but increased the need for 'white-collar factories' of staff processing the transactions. Those that do work in the high street banks are now also expected to be able to sell the bank's products over the counter. All new insurance claims or applications are usually scanned in the post room and then sent electronically to a claims or new business handler via the computer network. Once one claim is completed, the next one simply pops up on the screen. At the other end of the spectrum, insurance advisers, for

example, are expected to have knowledge of a range of products that could be made available to a customer or client. Because of this, their own knowledge of a company's products (and its competitors' products) is likely to add value to the employing organisation.

In terms of staff representation the sector exhibits the complete range of relationships from non-union (or indeed anti-union), through recognition of dependent staff association, independent staff associations, to independent trade union. The independent unions representing the sector (predominantly Amicus through its old MSF section, and UNIFI) have traditionally recorded low levels of militancy. This has been explained in the past with particular reference to banking, as a reflection of the conservative organisational culture of the industry. More recently, commentators have noted a change in bank workers' attitudes towards a more collective and pro-union orientation driven by work intensification and regimentation, which may be a precursor of similar developments in the rest of the finance sector. Employer strategy in response includes the development of partnership arrangements – 14 signed in the sector between 1997 and 2000.

Alongside capital concentration have been major changes to the organisation of work as employers have sought to become more cost-efficient in an increasingly competitive product market. Both de/re-regulation and de-mutualisation are reasons for the emergence of a new management 'model' whereby the old model based on paternalism, conservatism and bureaucracy has given way to a new model of sales and performance orientation and technocracy. However, evidence from the banking sector and from insurance suggests that this new model has not always been successfully translated into creation and consolidation of softer HRM techniques based on employee involvement and participation. This is partly because of a continuation of the old management culture and partly because of the background of staff reductions and low trust of management motives fed by job insecurity. De-layering of management jobs has been accompanied with the break-up of the whole business into separately accountable business divisions. Restructuring of work has been driven by the perceived need to cut operating costs, leading to work intensification through computerisation and increased case-loading. New forms of pay are prevalent in the sector, based on individual performance and sometimes linked with job evaluation to accommodate shifting skills in relation to new technology. Competency-based pay is also common, emphasising the ability to work in teams, and sales and customer consciousness. Some organisations within the sector also have market-based pay systems, with pay rates set to the ability to recruit and retain staff within a localised labour market. As with much UK industry, teamworking has been introduced throughout the sector and operational targets have been introduced for these teams based on sales performance, completed case work, or other quantifiable measures.

Case study adapted from: Upchurch, M., Richardson, M., Tailby, S., Danford, A. and Stewart, P. (2006) 'Employee representation and partnership in the non-union sector: a paradox of intention?', *Human Resource Management Journal*, Vol. 16, No. 4, 393–410

Qustions for discussion

1 In the light of this background to recent developments in the finance sector, what do you consider to be priority areas for the management of human resources in the sector?

2 What problems might an HR practitioner envisage with the introduction of widespread teamworking?

3 In what ways might jobs in such organisations be subject to enlargement or rotation?

EXPLORE FURTHER

APPELBAUM, E., BAILEY, T., BERG, P. and KALLENBERG, A. L. (2000) *Manufacturing Advantage: Why high-performance work systems pay off*. Ithaca, Cornell University Press
This is an excellent description of a high-performance workplace in the USA.

DANFORD, A. (1999) *Japanese Management Techniques and British Workers*. London, Mansell
This provides a critique of Japanisation in the UK.

GOOS, M. and MANNING, A. (2003) 'McJobs and MacJobs: the growing polarisation of jobs in the UK'. In R. Dickens, P. Gregg and J. Wadsworth (eds) *The Labour Market Under New Labour: The state of working Britain*. New York, Palgrave Macmillan
This study illustrates the polarisation of work-based skills in the UK economy.

WHITE, M., HILL, S., MCGOVERN, P., MILLS, C. and SMEATON, D. (2004a) *Managing to Change?* Basingstoke, Palgrave
A useful survey of UK workplaces from the ESRC's Future of Work programme.

WOMACK, J. P., JONES, D. T. and ROOS, D. (1990) *The Machine That Changed the World: The triumph of lean production*. New York, Rawson Macmillan
This is a seminal account of lean production conducted at the request of the US Government.

CHAPTER 22

International HRM

Michael Muller-Camen *and* Chris Brewster

INTRODUCTION

This chapter is about the HRM issues faced by companies operating internationally.

LEARNING OUTCOMES

By the end of this chapter readers should be able to:

- describe factors that encourage international firms to standardise or globalise HR practices
- discuss the extent to which HR practices can be globally standardised
- list the different approaches to transfers of employees
- evaluate the ways multinational firms can select, prepare, compensate and reintegrate expatriates.

This chapter is in two parts. The first part deals with the 'global versus local' dilemma and discusses whether and how multinational companies (MNCs) can standardise HR policies and practices across their subsidiaries. We analyse the contradictory pressures towards global integration and local responsiveness faced by multinationals and describe some examples of their impact on HRM. The second part deals with HR issues to do with the transfer of employees abroad. We explore some of the ways that the process has been analysed and then work round the 'expatriate cycle' of selecting them, preparing them, managing them and bringing them back.

The chapter concludes with the main case study.

Reference sources named within the chapter may be looked up in the *References and further reading* section at the end of the book.

IT Company is a large multinational corporation that has more than 100 years of history, a global workforce of more than 100,000 employees and is headquartered in the USA. Up until the early 1990s, the corporation was structured around geographical areas, each of which was afforded relatively powerful independence. So, for example, the UK headquarters in London had high decision-making autonomy in relation to the US headquarters in New York and the European headquarters in Paris. One outcome of this so-called area structure was that hardly any global HR policies existed, so that HR practices in areas such as pay, training and flexitime differed widely between countries. Nevertheless, a strong corporate culture ensured that some core values applied throughout the organisation. For example, since its foundation IT Company has been known for its strong anti-union stance. Combined with an emphasis on sophisticated and innovative HR policies, the parent company has been able to defeat several recognition campaigns by trade unions. The same has happened in the UK, where local management prided itself on defeating a strong union recognition campaign in the 1970s. However, in other countries IT Company does recognise trade unions. For example, the German subsidiary has a powerful body of elected employee representatives (as encouraged by German law), some of whom are trade union members, who have a strong say in any decisions affecting the workforce. Up to the early 1990s the company also participated in industry-wide bargaining which determined pay and conditions for the large majority of its workforce.

In the early 1990s, IT Company – which had enjoyed a near monopoly status in its markets until then – encountered economic problems due to higher global and domestic competition. A new CEO made far-reaching changes to the business strategy and the organisational structure. In particular, the decision-making authority of local managers was reduced and responsibility transferred to regional headquarters such as Paris and to the US headquarters. Furthermore, the company was structured around business units, each responsible for a certain range of products such as printers or IT solutions. Business units were encouraged to standardise management functions such as finance, marketing and human resources as far as possible on a worldwide basis.

Question for discussion

You are in charge of HR for the global business unit printer of IT Company which has production and distribution organisations in almost 100 countries.

1 Which HR practices would you standardise on a global basis?

2 Where would you allow different approaches?

3 How would you ensure that global policies are implemented by the subsidiaries?

4 Why would you choose these options?

1 STRATEGY, STRUCTURE AND STANDARDISATION OF HR POLICIES

THE 'GLOBAL VERSUS LOCAL' DILEMMA

The issues facing IT Company in the starter case study are to some extent experienced by all organisations that operate in more than one country. On the one hand there are pressures for global integration and standardisation. Among these are global competitors and products that can be sold throughout the world, meaning that customers can compare prices across national borders, rapid technological change (which must be transferred across borders as quickly as possible), and the need to achieve economies of scale (which means doing things in a similar way in every location). On the other hand there are pressures for local responsiveness and differentiation due to differences in consumer preferences, distribution channels, workforce cultures and national institutions, such as legislation, labour markets and taxation. This tension is often called the 'global versus local' dilemma (Evans, Pucik and Barsoux, 2002). Unfortunately, the consultants' advice to 'think global and act local' sounds good but is in practice rather meaningless. Furthermore, where an organisation stands on this issue depends on factors such as the competitive situation which the business faces, how integrated its business is (whether goods, for example, are manufactured from parts supplied from different countries), how easily its business can be moved to different countries, how globalised its branding is, etc. It may well be that an organisation such as IT Company might reach different answers for different parts of its operation.

REFLECTIVE ACTIVITY

In which industries are pressures for global integration very strong, and in which is local responsiveness very important? How can international firms deal with such differences?

Among the industries that face high pressures for global integration and in which it is important to achieve high economies of scale you may, in your answer to the above exercise, have included sectors where manufacturing is integrated across borders and moving the process is very expensive: engines, construction equipment, semi-conductors and industrial chemicals, for example. Although there is, due to the demands cited earlier, a general trend towards global standardisation, there are still some industries where local responsiveness is a key requirement for business. You may have thought about industries such as food, healthcare and household appliances.

Clearly, the type of global environment a multinational organisation is facing should have an impact on its business strategy. Bartlett and Ghoshal (1989) developed a typology of three strategies that are appropriate for a particular combination of local and global pressures an organisation faces. We now briefly introduce three of these:

● the multi-domestic strategy

● the global strategy

● the transnational strategy.

The *multi-domestic strategy* is recommended for firms in industries that are under high pressure for local responsiveness, but that only face low pressure for global integration. Firms in such industries have to customise product offering and marketing to local conditions. This means that they have to have a complete set of value-creation activities in all major markets. Although there are some businesses for which such a strategy makes sense – similar to IT Company portrayed in the starter case study – growing global competition, and perhaps fashion, has made a multi-domestic strategy less popular and many international firms have attempted to adopt a global strategy.

A *global strategy* aims to standardise product offering and marketing strategy across different markets. Value-creation activities such as production and R&D are in a few favourable locations to achieve economies of scale.

The *transnational strategy* corresponds to the central argument of Bartlett and Ghoshal – that irrespective of industry, businesses have to be globally integrated and locally responsive at the same time, and to move from a headquarters-subsidiary approach to a truly 'stateless' approach, in which the location of headquarters is incidental. We might question how many companies are truly transnational (Dickmann and Muller-Camen, 2006). Can you think of a major multinational company where you are not sure which country dominates its policies?

One means to make sure that the strategy chosen is implemented is to adopt an appropriate structure. Similar to IT Company up to the early 1990s, firms that follow a multi-domestic strategy often have a global area division structure. This means they are organised geographically on the basis of countries or regions that report directly to the main headquarters. In contrast, businesses with a global strategy are usually organised in product divisions that have worldwide responsibility for a certain product. For firms with transnational strategies, Bartlett and Ghoshal foresee a matrix structure within which each manager has two reporting lines – for example, one to the product division to ensure that global integration is as high as possible, and one to the area to ensure that local responsiveness is achieved.

REFLECTIVE ACTIVITY

You are the HR manager of an MNC's foreign subsidiary.

How much autonomy in decision-making would you like to have? What arguments would you put forward to localise decision-making? How might headquarters justify attempts to centralise decision-making?

Irrespective of the structure that a business has or intends to introduce, a crucial issue is the allocation of responsibility between headquarters and subsidiaries. We now examine this issue in the context of centralisation and decentralisation of HR policies and practices.

CENTRALISATION AND DECENTRALISATION OF HR POLICIES

You may have argued, in your response to the exercise above, that high autonomy of the subsidiary in strategic HR decisions would reduce the burden on headquarters and increase motivation at lower levels. It should also lead to better decisions locally by the people directly involved and, last but not least, increase accountability. In contrast, amongst other arguments you may have suggested that the corporate HR function will argue that centralised decision-making will make global co-ordination easier. It will ensure consistency between global strategies and local decisions. If headquarters take decisions and just inform local managers, duplication of efforts will be avoided. However, instead of such very broad answers you may have concluded that it depends on the specific HR practice whether this is best decided for the organisation as a whole or locally.

At the extremes the arguments are clear: pay levels for locally recruited and employed staff are determined locally; management development systems for those selected as future organisational leaders should be worldwide. Relevant pay rates within the local community will be unknown to specialists at the headquarters of the organisation. They can only make such decisions by drawing on and then second-guessing the local specialists – a waste of resources. Paying people the same salaries wherever they work makes little sense in a world where living standards vary considerably between countries. Reward issues other than levels of pay may be subject to worldwide policies – for example, that the top quartile always includes a performance-related salary element.

On the other hand, the organisation must retain the right to promote and encourage its best and brightest, beyond the local unit if necessary, wherever they are found. An organisational objective, common to many MNCs, of drawing on the best talent available irrespective of country of origin, requires that the management development systems have some cross-border coherence. Identifying the best people in each country will be of maximum benefit if there is some way of comparing these individuals across countries. Here, too, reality is not as simple as this statement implies. For example, one very successful international bank, Citicorp, has a uniform system throughout the world. This, the company argues, facilitates identification of the best wherever they are in the world – and its results would seem to suggest that they are good at it. Another equally successful international bank, and a direct competitor, the Hong Kong and Shanghai Banking Corporation, has different systems in different regions and countries, and compares leading individuals after they have been identified by these different systems. This company argues that the different cultural environments in which it operates mean that imposing a worldwide system would cause it to overlook people who may not be brought forward by a uniform, and therefore probably culturally biased, system (see Chapter 23). And this company too has good people coming through at the senior levels.

Between these extremes there is considerable uncertainty and significant problems arise (Harris, Brewster and Sparrow, 2004). Should there be a local performance assessment system, so that performance can be related to the local pay scales and take account of local cultures? Or should the performance assessment system be international, so that it can identify likely future leaders wherever they are found in the organisation? And should the organisation communicate with its employees individually or through trade union or representative structures (see Chapter 17)?

A few examples highlight these problems. Taking performance appraisal first, we have enough knowledge of the effects of culture (see Chapter 23) to know that there is no easy answer to this question. The US-style performance appraisal process assumes that employees will work jointly with their boss to set targets, to assess their own performance, to comment on the extent to which their boss has helped them with achieving their targets – or made things more difficult for them. It also assumes that they will do much of this through a face-to-face interview. It is not likely that such performance appraisal systems will work in the same way in many Eastern societies, where open responses to seniors are discouraged, where challenging the boss's expectations of what is possible would be seen as insubordination, where admitting faults amounts to a loss of face, and where, for example, the idea of criticising the boss's work in front of that boss would be seen as a sort of organisational suicide.

The organisation will try to ensure the objectives which appraisals are seen as meeting: encouraging improved performance, assessing career options and identifying training needs. But how to do this? The more the organisation attempts to enforce a worldwide system, the more likely it is that managers will bend the system to their local requirements (Ferner et al, 2004). Often this will involve exaggerated or incomplete reports or even reporting back on interviews that never in fact took place. So what appears to be exactly comparable data may be very misleading. The more the organisation is responsive to these cultural issues, the less likely it is to have information that it can use to assess people across national boundaries.

The question of communication channels (see Chapter 19) is complicated by national institutions. In Europe, for example, employers are required to recognise trade unions for collective bargaining in different circumstances in different countries – when certain thresholds (usually the existence of a certain number of union members among employees) are reached, when employees request it, or, exceptionally, when unions win ballots. In many European countries employers are required to establish and pay for employee representation committees that may have extensive powers, including, for example, the right to review appointments or to be consulted prior to major investment decisions. Of course, national laws and institutions are in part a reflection of and a support to national cultural values.

MNCs therefore have a series of decisions to make. Will they deal with trade unions? Will they refuse to? Will they check the legislation carefully and do the minimum necessary to comply with the legislation? Or will they embrace the law and the purposes behind it on the grounds that such behaviour will show them as good citizens and that other MNCs in that country have been successful while adopting the local employment systems in full? Or will they allow individual countries (and, by extension, individual country management teams) to make their own decisions (Almond et al, 2005)? At the extreme, will they – as Walmart, a famously anti-union US company, is reputed to have done – simply refuse to open operations where they would have to recognise a union? (Note, however, the pull of profits. When Walmart was told it could not open in China without recognising the union, the potential profits were too big to be overridden by policy, and in 2006 Walmart signed an agreement with the Chinese trade unions – possibly because they are not internationally recognised as independent trade unions.)

Overall, every international organisation will always have a continual tension between the costs of and the advantages to be gained by standardisation, and the costs of and the advantages to be gained from being locally responsive. This applies to all aspects of an MNC's operations but is particularly relevant for HRM, where local sensitivities are most pronounced. Recently, standardisation has become not only more popular but also more possible. The development of significantly improved telecommunications, the Internet and intranets have allowed organisations to develop shared services and centres of excellence which are often virtual – drawing together the best experts they have from across the globe and generalising the messages across their various operations in all countries (Tregaskis, Glover and Ferner, 2006). Employees logging in with a question about their training provision might (sometimes unrealised by them) be getting their answers from the company's top development expert half a world away. Obviously, for these systems to work well an increased degree of standardisation is required.

CONTROL MECHANISMS

Research has shown that there is a potential conflict of interest between the wish of headquarters to control affiliates and the subsidiaries' managers' desire for autonomy. Foreign managers in particular can use various strategies to obstruct the implementation of global policies. For example, they can argue that local trade unions prevent them from introducing a global pay policy (Ferner *et al*, 2004). This raises the question of how an MNC can make sure that all its units are committed to common goals.

REFLECTIVE ACTIVITY

You are employed in the HR department of a UK MNC, and you have to ensure that foreign units implement HR practices.

How are you going to do that?

There are four possible methods of control. One means of control is to *measure and benchmark results and outputs*. For example, your HR strategy might be to have a fair representation of females in management positions. In order to achieve this you may set and measure the goal of increasing the ratio of female managers by 2 percentage points until this strategic aim is achieved. A second type of control is rules and regulations. This is *bureaucratic control* (Ferner, 2000). For example, you could produce manuals that specify in detail how certain HR processes such as resourcing should be organised. A third type of control is social or cultural control. For example, Bartlett and Ghoshal (1989) suggest that senior managers in MNCs should have a matrix in their mind so that for every decision they take they have in mind the needs of global standardisation and local responsiveness. In this way, without being explicitly told, managers strive to implement organisational goals. Such control mechanisms may work well in organisations that have a strong organisational culture and that make great use of training and development to socialise managers into the behaviours and values expected of them. For the remainder of this chapter we concentrate on another means of control which is arguably the most important one in any organisation. This is our fourth method, *control through personnel*.

2   INTERNATIONAL STAFFING AND EXPATRIATION

INTERNATIONAL STAFFING

Staffing is a crucial issue for all organisations and it is certainly important for MNCs (Harzing, 2001). One option is for the international organisation to transfer its people between different countries: such transferees are usually referred to as 'expatriates'. Research suggests that there are important strategic issues that can be addressed by long-term international assignments. Most importantly, expatriates are supposed to improve the performance of the subsidiary they are assigned to. They can do this by solving technical problems, developing local talent, opening new international markets and by developing, sharing and transferring best practices. They can also help to improve the communication between headquarters and subsidiary and assure that global policies are implemented by a particular subsidiary. They can do this by fostering the parent corporate culture in the subsidiary, by developing networking processes and by controlling financial results. Where expatriates are sent from the headquarters operation to the subsidiaries, this operates as a powerful – perhaps the most powerful – form of control.

Some 40 years ago, Perlmutter (1969) identified four main approaches used by MNCs. First, there is the *ethnocentric* staffing approach. In firms that rely on this approach, foreign subsidiaries are managed by employees sent from the parent company, who are usually parent-country nationals (PCNs). This approach is perhaps the most common, even if in theory it should only be used in firms with a global strategy that aim to centralise decision-making and are interested to implement global policies and practices. Second, there is the *polycentric* approach. MNCs that favour a polycentric approach normally rely on managers recruited locally, who are usually host-country nationals (HCNs). This can normally be found in firms that pursue a multi-domestic strategy and where each subsidiary has relatively high decision-making autonomy. For example, the senior management of a UK firm in Germany consists mainly of German nationals. Third, there is the *geocentric* approach, by which firms emphasise passport diversity and employ PCNs, HCNs and third-country nationals (TCNs) in their subsidiaries, as well as managers from the subsidiaries in their headquarters. This is normally favoured by MNCs that aim to pursue a transnational strategy. It could, for example, mean that the board of a Swedish electronics firm in the UK consists of managers with British, Canadian, German and Swedish passports. The fourth and final approach is the *regiocentric* staffing policy. Similar to the geocentric approach, it favours passport diversity, but TCNs only move within a region such as Europe or Asia.

REFLECTIVE ACTIVITY

What are the advantages and disadvantages of the ethnocentric staffing approach outlined above?

Among the advantages of an ethnocentric staffing approach you may have noted, in your response to the exercise above, that parent-company employees or PCNs are familiar with the products, technology and culture of the MNC. Some of this knowledge is tacit (ie knowledge that people have but cannot fully explain or transfer to others – see Chapter 14 on HRD) and cannot be transferred except by people. Employees from the parent company can therefore play a vital role in implementing corporate-wide quality standards, business strategies or styles of management. They can facilitate communication between headquarters and subsidiaries and are an important means of control for headquarters. Finally, they may also compensate for the inadequacy of local managerial skills.

However, an ethnocentric strategy also has severe disadvantages. If most senior management positions are filled with PCNs, as is the case in many Japanese MNCs, local staff lack opportunities for promotion, which may lower morale. At least initially, PCNs may be unfamiliar with the local culture, which could lead to costly mistakes in dealings with co-workers, customers and governments. Most importantly, if holding a passport of the country where a MNC has its worldwide headquarters is a criterion for promotion, that may not only be considered discrimination but the firm may also be wasting a large share of its pool of talent (see Chapter 6 on diversity).

A similar advantages and disadvantages analysis could be applied to each of Perlmutter's approaches. Clearly, what is going to be the best approach will vary between, and perhaps even within, MNCs.

THE EXPATRIATE ASSIGNMENT CYCLE

Although research demonstrates that expatriation can bring significant benefits to business, it also shows that this will only be achieved if expatriates are managed properly. There is therefore a need to manage the expatriate cycle properly. Its key elements – which are discussed in more detail in the next section – can be seen in Figure 26.

Figure 26 The expatriate assignment cycle

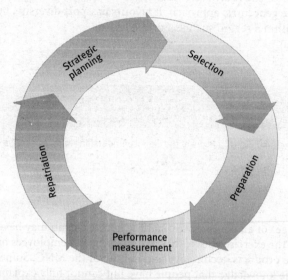

Source: Harris *et al* (2004; p.148)

Expatriate selection

Many MNCs have no formal system for selecting employees whom they send on an international assignment. Expatriates are often chosen in an informal way and at short notice. The employees selected have usually demonstrated high technical competence and good managerial skills. Because there is often an underlying assumption that managerial skills are universal, it is assumed that the candidate will be similarly successful in a foreign context. However, research has shown that technical ability is not enough and that interpersonal and cross-cultural skills are also important for expatriates.

Mendenhall and Oddou (1985) identified four key attributes of successful expatriates. *Self-orientation* suggests that expatriates should have high self-esteem, self-confidence and psychological well-being. At the same time, they should also exhibit a high degree of *others-orientation* in order to be able to develop relationships with host-country nationals. In this respect, knowledge of the local language is also important. A third desired attribute is *perceptual ability* – the capacity to understand why host-country nationals behave the way they do. Finally, and particularly if there is a high degree of cultural distance between home country and country of assignment, *cultural toughness* is required. This can help the expatriate to deal with factors such as loneliness, crime and language difficulties.

So far we have only talked about the expatriate. However, particularly if they are senior managers, they may well have a partner, and also perhaps children, who may or may not follow them on the assignment. Some organisations therefore also consider the cross-cultural adaptability of the spouse when selecting an employee for a foreign assignment.

Preparation

Employees who are going abroad can be prepared, at least to some extent, for the cross-cultural interactions they are likely to encounter. Some organisations therefore offer pre-departure training or other preparation with the objective of reducing misunderstanding, inappropriate behaviours and culture shock when expatriates (and families) arrive in their new location.

Preparation can consist of the following elements:

- Environmental briefings can give documentary information about the host country's political system, economics and history, management processes, markets, etc.

- Cultural awareness training aims to help expatriates to understand cultural differences between their own culture and the host country's culture. For this purpose, cultural assimilators are a useful tool. These use programmed learning approaches to provide the trainee with intercultural encounters. For example, South Americans would learn that punctuality for meetings is essential in Germany. Germans would learn that being seen as a rounded person, and not just being business-focused, is vital for doing business in South America. In order to communicate effectively with host-country nationals it is also recommended that expatriates learn the language of the new culture.

- There is also a need for training in the laws, institutions and common practices of the host country.

- If time permits, a prospective expatriate should visit the country of assignment. Such a preliminary visit can also be a final test of the suitability of an employee for a particular assignment.

- Perhaps the cheapest and most effective form of preparation is to get the transferee to meet with people who are from, or who have worked in, the country that will be their new home.

Some firms also involve the spouse and children of an expatriate in the preparation. In addition they provide not only training but also practical assistance for the relocation, which could include the organisation of housing.

REFLECTIVE ACTIVITY

In the light of the challenges of managing performance (see Chapter 12), what do you think are the major issues facing international firms that want to assess the performance of employees working abroad?

Assessing performance

International organisations are concerned with the performance of their subsidiary operations and the key expatriates in them. Accurately measuring the performance of an employee who may be thousands of miles away and who is operating in a different context from most of the other employees in the system is not easy. Most large MNCs operate some form of formal performance measurement system. Some corporations have standardised this worldwide to facilitate the exchange of people. However, even in such cases it may be difficult to judge the performance of an expatriate due to unintentional bias. If the expatriate is assessed by a home-country manager, this person may lack knowledge of the local situation and thus might not be able to appreciate issues that may have adversely affected performance. In such circumstances, the appraiser may rely on the information from the expatriate himself/herself or on hard data such as market share and profitability that are likely to reflect factors outside the control of the expatriate. In either case the understanding is likely to be partial. In contrast, host-nation managers may not understand that expatriates transfer home-country standards and expectations to the subsidiary. In addition they may have performance standards that differ from those of the parent firm. One solution is to have multiple people (raters) in the home and host country who assess the expatriate.

Compensation

Rewarding, or compensating expatriates is more complicated than the always problematic issue of pay and rewards in one country (Perkins, 2006). This is largely for two reasons. Firstly, there are large differences in salaries, cost of living, taxes and benefits between countries. On top of this there are the difficulties created by differences in tax regimes, currency movements, etc. Secondly, as noted, most MNCs try to link at least some element of pay to performance – and that is going to be difficult.

MNCs usually try to make sure not only that their expatriates maintain their standard of living when going abroad, but that they also compensate for any additional costs incurred, or for the level of perceived hardship involved. The most common method to ensure this is the balance sheet approach. Its first element is the base salary. This is the same as in the home country, but adjusted for differences in cost of living and the currency exchange rate. A UK manager (TCN) working for a US MNC in Germany will therefore have a base salary that is tied to the salary structure of the British subsidiary. Benefits such as pension plans and stock options are equalised as well. Besides the base salary and benefits, expatriates usually receive various allowances for relocation, housing, private education of children or the hardships incurred. Finally, the MNC has to equalise any differential tax effects that are caused by the relocation. All these costs make an expatriate much more expensive than if a host-country national is employed. An additional factor, of course, is that many employees who accept a foreign assignment do it not only because they hope to gain additional experience and to boost their careers but also because they are aware of the generous allowances and incentives so that even if they take their families with them they expect to be much better off than at home. For any HRM specialist, juggling costs, labour market requirements and expectations is fundamental to all reward packages (see Chapter 13). In the case of expatriates the pressures are high.

Repatriation

The final element in the expatriate assignment cycle is repatriation, which is the process of returning home from the foreign assignment. Research shows that many expatriates leave their organisation shortly after their return. This is a significant loss to the organisation. As we have seen, the costs of each expatriate are considerable and the learning that they have achieved will be substantial. Researchers find that expatriates are almost always very positive about the experience and its effects on their knowledge and their careers – but between a quarter and a third of them do not continue their careers in the organisation that has paid for that experience. From the organisation's viewpoint, not only does this mean a loss of a valuable resource, it means (because people tend to stay in the same industry or occupation) that these people tend to get picked up by their competitors. It also reduces the organisation's ability to internationalise thinking in the company. For these reasons, this wastage is currently occupying the time of many international HR specialists.

A number of factors account for this high level of turnover. Organisations may, either because of poor HR planning or through practical changes that have occurred in the meantime, not have an adequate re-entry position that makes use of the international experience of the repatriate. Combined, often, with a loss of status and pay, initial expectations that an international assignment would lead to rapid career progression are often disappointed. In addition, the expatriate and the family, if unprepared, may find that readjusting to 'home' is not as smooth or as comfortable as they had expected. In short, a lot of problems come together to make these, now more knowledgeable and hence more marketable, employees consider their employment position. This may be unsatisfactory for the repatriate, but certainly means that critical knowledge is lost to the organisation.

To avoid this level of wastage, international HR specialists in MNCs have begun to set up repatriation programmes. One element can be a repatriation agreement which, before the start of the assignment, stipulates the type of job that will be given to the expatriate upon returning. Of course, in the current rapidly changing situation, few companies feel confident enough to give such guarantees. More promisingly, it seems that ongoing communication and contacts with the home organisation during the assignment is linked to retention. For this purpose it is increasingly common, at least amongst the larger MNCs, to assign coaches or mentors to the soon-returning expatriate (see Chapter 15). The role of the mentor is to ensure that career and performance are on track and that discussions about a suitable re-entry position start in good time

REFLECTIVE ACTIVITY

In the light of the costs and difficulties of sending employees abroad on a long-term assignment, what alternatives can you suggest?

As you may have considered in response to the exercise above, long-term expatriates are only one of a number of different types of international assignment (Harris *et al*, 2004). Expatriates can be on short-term assignments of less than one year. Then there are international commuters who travel on a regular weekly or fortnightly basis between their home country and an operation of the MNC in another country. Frequent flyers, who undertake regular international business trips, are a third assignment type. Among the problems associated with these assignments are work–life balance issues, travel fatigue and the difficulty of dealing with foreign cultures to which one is only exposed for short intervals. There is also the increasing growth of 'virtual assignments' in which people use modern communication technologies to work in international teams although they may rarely, or in some cases never, meet face to face. All these different types of assignment have become more widespread recently – but then, so has the typical, standard, expatriate assignment. International working is just becoming more common.

KEY ISSUES: INTERNATIONAL HRM

We now pull together ten key points about international HRM raised in this chapter:

- IHRM covers all the same topics as HRM generally, but is inevitably more complex.

- International organisations are always dealing with the twin pressures of standardisation across the organisation and responsiveness to the local environment.

- There is increasing pressure for organisations to standardise, and modern technology is making it possible to move further in that direction.

- Different approaches to IHRM are likely to be relevant for different kinds of organisations and for different organisational structures and philosophies.

- MNCs would benefit from close alignment of their IHRM with their corporate strategy. Often it is not aligned at all.

- Controlling local operations is a key to success for MNCs. Transfer of individuals from one country to another is a powerful mechanism for such control.

- International transfers also bring benefits in internationalising the thinking of MNCs.

- But international assignees are an expensive option: they are, post for post, the most expensive people that MNCs employ.

- Many employees assigned to other countries leave their organisation just before or after they are due to return home, with a consequent loss of the organisation's investment.

- Better management of the expatriate cycle will benefit the expatriates and the organisation they work for.

Perhaps there are other key points that you would like to note for yourself.

The main case study in this chapter now follows. It gives an example of the professional and work–life balance issues faced by expatriates.

MAIN CASE STUDY

Look at the description of the case set out below. Then decide on the recommendations that you would make as an HR manager for dealing with the issues raised. Try to think beyond the level of a 'quick fix' or simple solutions.

Sonja has a senior position in an investment bank in London, which recently opened a branch in Moscow. Shortly after starting the foreign operation, the manager selected to head the subsidiary was poached by another bank. Sonja was asked to step in at short notice, although she had had no previous international exposure. The main reasons for choosing her were her excellent track record and experience in setting up and managing a new department in the home office. It was suggested to her that after the successful completion of the assignment in Russia she would be a major factor in any future promotion decisions. Given the urgency of the situation, Sonja was given three days to decide whether she would accept the offer. Intensive discussions with her partner, who is a freelance IT consultant, and their 10-year-old child followed. Although both were sceptical about the move, eventually Sonja was able to persuade them to move with her to Moscow.

Sonja and her family were housed in a gated compound in an expensive suburb of Moscow, where many of Russia's new millionaires have their homes. A driver took her to work and collected her each day. During the first month in Moscow, which was in August, Sonja and her family enjoyed working and living in a different world, made friends with other expatriates who lived near by and her husband and daughter spent a lot of time in exploring the city. Within a few weeks, Sonja's daughter was established in the local 'international school' and her partner began to pick up some work from their new friends. However, shortly after this initial honeymoon, problems started to develop.

Sonja became increasingly aware that Russia is a hard place to do business. Much of the country seems to operate without the attention to standards, ethics, the following of regulations and the honouring of contracts that she was used to in London. She was often told that she was expected to socialise (which seemed to mean get drunk) with key clients and that she 'had to adjust to the Russian way' when it seemed to her that she was being asked to go beyond good business practice.

It was difficult to establish good relationships in the office. Because she did not speak Russian she had asked the staff, all of who had been selected partly because they could, to speak English in the office. Nevertheless, a lot of the work was conducted in Russian, and she did not feel that she was fully in control of what was being done. The staff often worked late, as she did herself, but whereas some of them then went out for a drink or a meal, she was driven back to her family.

After the first few projects for other expatriates, her partner found it difficult to get much work because he could not speak Russian. He did not spend much time with the other expatriates' non-working partners, mostly women (although Sonja was beginning to worry that he was spending too much time with one of them). He spent a lot of time at home working on his computer.

The winter had set in. The centre of Moscow, where the office was, became particularly dirty and unpleasant. Going out in the evenings or weekends became a major expedition.

Sonja and her partner had begun to fall out increasingly frequently. The only one who seemed to be adapting well was their daughter.

The combined effect of all of these problems was irritation and hostility. On a business trip to London, Sonja asked for a meeting with the international HR specialists. The Bank's senior managers, who had recently visited Moscow, suspected that she might be about to ask to return home. They made it clear to the HR department that this assignment was already costing them more than they wanted to see spent and they didn't want to see their investment wasted.

Your task

Imagine you are one of the international HR professionals working for this multinational firm. Prepare a short report based on the facts you have been given above, making recommendations to your colleagues. Analyse what went wrong and how the situation can be improved.

EXPLORE FURTHER

BARTLETT, C. A. and GHOSHAL, S. (1989) *Managing Across Borders: The transnational solution*. Boston, MA: Harvard Business School Press
An excellent analysis of the global environment faced by multinational enterprises and how this is influencing strategic choices.

HARRIS, H., BREWSTER, C. and SPARROW, P. (2004) *International Human Resource Management*. London, CIPD
A very useful analysis of the many important issues involved in IHRM.

PERKINS, S. J. (2006) *International Reward and Recognition*, Research Report. London, CIPD
Clear and concise presentation of new qualitative and quantitative research results in this contentious area by one of the specialists in the field.

PERLMUTTER, H. V. (1969) 'The tortuous evolution of the multinational corporation', *Columbia Journal of World Business*, Vol. 4, 9–18
A classic of the IHRM literature – still a much-used starting point, even if later critics have pointed to a lack of supporting evidence and the rather simplistic unitary assumptions of organisational structures.

SPARROW, P. R. (2006) *International Recruitment, Selection and Assessment*, Research Report. London, CIPD
Thorough and up-to-date analysis of this critical topic drawing on new research and previously published data.

CHAPTER 23

Instead of HRM: a cross-cultural perspective

Terence Jackson

INTRODUCTION

HRM is mainly a concept developed in the Anglo-Saxon world and applied to other cultural contexts, often unsuccessfully. To think of people as a 'resource' may be at odds with many non-Western cultures, and this is where problems might arise. This chapter critically examines the transfer of HRM to other cultures. It explores alternative cultural models, and looks at the future of HRM in a multicultural world.

This chapter therefore aims to develop an understanding of the cultural boundedness of the concept of human beings as a resource; to explore the nature of HRM in a global world; to discuss the problems encountered by international companies when transferring HRM practices abroad; and to look at alternative ways of thinking about the value of people in organisations, and the implications for people management. It does this mainly within the context of so-called 'developing' countries.

LEARNING OUTCOMES

By the end of this chapter readers should be able to:

- explain the cultural origins of human resources management
- describe different concepts of the value of people in organisations across cultures
- analyse the problems of transferring Western HRM practices across cultures
- identify alternative approaches to managing people in different countries
- develop a critical attitude towards HRM principles in a cross-cultural context.

The chapter has five parts. The first part deals with the origins of HRM as an American concept. The second part looks at how we might break out of this culturally bound concept of managing people. The third part looks at how we might compare approaches to managing people across cultures. The fourth considers the transfer of HRM approaches to other countries. Finally, the fifth part considers how we might develop international approaches to managing people by considering stakeholders and their different values and concepts of people.

The chapter concludes with the main case study.

Reference sources named within the chapter may be looked up in the *References and further reading* section at the end of the book.

STARTER CASE STUDY

Johnny Mbeki was late for work again. He had already had a couple of warnings from the HR manager, not simply for being late but because he was slow at his job. He had a lame leg. He'd had it since birth. On the whole he coped with it, but sometimes it affected his work. On this occasion, he was called into the HR manager's office.

'I'm afraid that this has gone a bit too far. I've tried to make allowances, but you are affecting overall production. If I have to speak to you again, I will have to let you go.'

The next morning the HR manager received a delegation from the workforce – colleagues of Johnny. They asked that he be given special treatment. They explained that Johnny had an extended family that depended on him. His were the only wages coming in. They lived in a township far from the factory. It takes him a long time to get to work, depending on public transport that is not always reliable. Sometimes when a family member is sick, he has to stay behind, and this can make him late for work.

They asked the HR manager to give Johnny another chance. They, as members of his work team, promised to cover for him, to make up for his slowness and his sometimes coming in late. Overall production in the work group would not be affected. The HR manager agreed.

Questions for discussion

1   Do you agree with the HR manager's decisions?

2   Johnny has been given due warning, and is not very productive. It doesn't matter that his work mates stick up for him – he should be sacked on the next occasion. Do you agree?

3   This incident takes place in South Africa. Does this make any difference to the decision? Should Western standards of HRM apply in this instance?

1   THE ORIGINS OF HRM: AN AMERICAN CONSTRUCTION?

The term 'human resource management' (which arose originally in the United States, and is now almost universally accepted), and the concept behind it, is laden with value. Values are part of the fabric of culture and are specific to countries or communities. That human beings are a resource to further the executive ends of an organisation is a concept that is against the values of many non-Western cultures. Perhaps in its most extreme or instrumental conceptualisation – ie one that really does look at people as a way of meeting organisational aims – this may also be against the values of many 'Western' cultures. Certainly, the ideas behind what constitutes the principles, policies and practices of managing people in organisations differ even among and within Western European countries, and certainly between US and most Western European countries.

From its origins in the individualistic achievement-oriented management culture of the United States, the term 'human resource management' has spread in a globalised world. Particularly in writing about the management of people, it is very difficult not to use this term. Sometimes little thought is given to the implications of its underlying concept, or of its manifestations in the policies and practices that multinational corporations use across different countries.

This is not to denigrate the contributions to global managing that HRM in many of its principles – such as the competences approach (Boyatzis, 1982) – can often make. The point here is to place HRM in its cultural context, and to examine its appropriateness in other cultural contexts. Before doing this we must first situate the concept of HRM in its original cultural setting.

The importance of the contribution of the HRM function to the bottom line and to shareholder value is a key issue in US and other Western-based human resource management (Becker, Huselid, Pickus and Spratt, 1997). The cultural perception that human beings are a resource to be used in the pursuit of shareholder value may be challenged by a view that people have a value in their own right. For example, a developmental approach that sees people as an integral part of the organisation, and as the subject for organisational objectives, seems to be implicit within Japanese people management policies and practices (Allinson, 1993).

This may be reflected in practices that seek to integrate employees as key stakeholders in the organisation and to gain commitment to the corporate endeavour. Human resource practices among corporations in Japan such as employment security, extensive job rotation, continuous on-the-job training, evaluation of the total person, seniority-/ability-based wage structure and promotions, welfare facilities and even the cooperation with 'enterprise unions' or trade unions limited to the company, are used to build a *moral* involvement of staff as part of a corporate community (Ishido, 1986).

This contrasts with 'Western' practices that may only try to gain a *calculative* involvement of staff based on an exchange where the organisation is seen by the employee as a means to an end, and where employees will work spontaneously and cooperatively if that is seen as benefiting them directly, but will leave the organisation if a better opportunity occurs outside.

This is reflected in HRM practices that take a 'competencies' approach. Job descriptions are defined by specific duties, and by the competencies needed to perform those duties well. This reflects operational requirements, which in turn reflects the strategic objectives of the corporation. The best person is recruited to the specific position, and is seen as a resource to achieve the executive ends of the organisation. Hence, HRM practices have competency- and objectives-based appraisal systems that determine pay and promotion.

REFLECTIVE ACTIVITY

Think about the differences in the way you are valued, as a person, in different situations and by different groups of people – in your family, in your community, within a social group, at university, in the workplace.

Are there major differences between the way you (or people you know) are valued in work and non-work situations? In your culture, are you valued within your local community like a family member? If so, does this contrast with the way people are valued in work situations? Is it possible to value people in the work situation the same as in the family or community situation? Should work be completely separate from the community?

2 HARD AND SOFT APPROACHES TO HRM: BREAKING OUT OF THE PARADIGM?

STAKEHOLDER APPROACHES AND 'SOFT' HRM

There has increasingly been an emphasis in Western HRM literature on the stakeholder approach to managing organisations (perhaps driven by the interest in Japanese approaches). A hard *instrumental* approach had already been challenged in a limited way within the context and conceptual framework of Western human resource management (Legge, 1989). This caused a distinction to be drawn in the strategic human resource management literature between the 'hard' perspective reflecting utilitarian instrumentalism, which sees people in the organisation as just a resource to achieving the ends of the organisation, and the 'soft' developmental approach, which sees people more as valued assets capable of development, worthy of trust, and providing inputs through participation and informed choice (Storey, 1992; Tyson and Fell, 1986).

Yet the concept of human resource management is itself a product of a particular Anglo-US culture, as we noted above. It is likely that the 'hard' and 'soft' approaches taken within Western organisations are both a reflection of an inherent cultural concept that perceives human beings in organisations as a means to an end. They are simply two poles representing high to low *instrumentalism*.

If managers and human resource professionals are unable to break out of this concept or paradigm, it is likely that when they, or managers educated in the Western tradition, try to implement 'Western' human resource practices in cultures which have a different concept of people, and a different regard for people in organisations, incompatibilities will be shown through employees' lack of motivation and alienation leading to low productivity and labour conflicts (see Chapter 17 on employment relations).

For example, the current author has carried out many interviews in many different organisations in sub-Saharan African countries. Many times he has been told by employees, and managers, that when going into work in the morning they are stepping out of their own culture and going into a foreign culture. And when they go home in the evening, they step back into their own culture (Jackson, 2004).

WESTERN AND INDIGENOUS APPROACHES: TRANSITIONAL AND DEVELOPING ECONOMIES

The importance of cultural values to organisational life is well established in the literature. The most well-known theory in this area is that of Hofstede (1980; 2003). From a survey of managers and staff of IBM in more than 50 countries, he identified four cultural values that varied among the cultural groups. These are:

- *Power distance* – This is the extent to which inequalities among people are seen as normal. This dimension stretches from equal relations being perceived as normal to wide inequalities being viewed as normal.

- *Uncertainty avoidance* – This refers to a preference for structured situations versus unstructured situations. This dimension runs from being comfortable with flexibility and ambiguity to a need for extreme rigidity and situations with a high degree of certainty.

- *Individualism/collectivism* – This looks at whether individuals are used to acting as individuals or as part of cohesive groups, which may be based on the family (which is more the case with Chinese societies or the corporation as may be the case in Japan).

- *Masculinity/femininity* – Hofstede distinguishes 'hard values' such as assertiveness and competition, and the 'soft' or 'feminine' values of personal relations, quality of life and caring about others, where in a masculine society gender role differentiation is emphasised.

Yet Hofstede's original study published in 1980 included very few developing countries. What his theory did rather well was to provide a critique of Western (particularly American) management applied in other countries, and it has opened up a great debate in this area.

More recently there is growing interest in the relationship between indigenous and foreign (mainly Western) cultures in the practice and development of management and organisation in the transitional economies of the former Soviet bloc, in China, and to a lesser extent in the so-called 'developing' countries of South Asia, Africa and Latin America. These issues have also been explored in the newly industrialised countries of East Asia, as well as in the 'hybrid' East-West cultures of the economies of Hong Kong and Singapore. This literature on the whole challenges the assumptions upon which human resource management is based in the Western world, and its applicability to managing people in countries of which the economies have more recently been launched into the global marketplace (Jackson, 2002a).

REFLECTIVE ACTIVITY

Have another look at the starter case study. To what extent do you think the HR manager is stuck within the Western paradigm of human resource management? He has conceded the point to Johnny's work colleagues – but does he understand the real differences between the Western/Anglo-Saxon approaches he has been trained in, and the rather different community-based values the African employees have been brought up with? Think about this for a while . . . and then read on.

3   THE INSTRUMENTAL AND THE HUMANISTIC LOCUS OF HUMAN VALUES: OPPOSITES OR COMPLEMENTARY?

The differences in perspectives towards the value of people in organisations, and the validity of human resource management, particularly in non-Western countries, is best understood in terms of the concept of *the locus of human value*.

We can define the locus of human value as the way, culturally, people place a value on other people. Two main orientations or *loci* have been discussed in the literature (Jackson, 2002b):

- *Humanism* is a regard for people as an end in themselves, and having a value for themselves and of themselves within an organisational context. So the locus of value or worth of persons in a work organisation is towards those persons in themselves rather than towards organisational objectives as appropriate ends. In other words, the question might be asked, what can the organisation do for its people? The organisation can be used in a developmental way to develop talents in a holistic way.

- *Instrumentalism* is defined as a regard for people as a means to an end, where the locus of value or worth is towards the ends (objectives) of the organisation. In other words, the question might be asked, what can this person do for the organisation? The person is seen as a resource (albeit a valuable one), like any other resource: money, plant, machinery, etc. He or she is recruited because of his/her specific set of competences that can help meet the objectives of the organisation.

INDIVIDUALISTIC AND COLLECTIVISTIC CULTURAL VALUES

This way of conceptualising the perceived value of human beings has its roots in the distinction between *individualistic* and *collectivistic* cultures (Hofstede, 1980 and 2003; discussed above). There seems to be a simple split between the individualistic Western cultures in which individuals are brought up in nuclear families and where individualism and individual achievement is often emphasised, and collectivistic non-Western cultures in which people are more likely to be part of an extended family and group involvement is emphasised. The lifetime protection of people which collectivism affords (either in corporations as in traditional Japanese companies, or within extended family groups such as in communities as different as those in China, India and the African continent) would seem to indicate a valuing of people in their own right, and as part of a collective. The expectation of people in individualistic cultures of having to look after themselves would indicate a more instrumental view of people in organisations.

But the connection between humanism and collectivism, and instrumentalism and individualism is not as straightforward as it might at first appear. Firstly, collectivism is target-specific and obligatory in nature. Japanese men may be more psychologically involved with their organisations, and Chinese more involved with their families, but at the expense of those outside the collective (Hui, 1990). Hence, those outside the in-group may be regarded instrumentally (as a means to an end). This is often shown in the large numbers of casual workers on short-term contracts employed by Japanese corporations. These workers can be 'let go' at short notice in times of economic downturn, and thus protect the jobs of the 'salarymen': those within the corporate in-group who have a lifetime commitment for employment.

Secondly, the work of cross-cultural researcher Shalom Schwartz (1999) in the 1990s contrasts 'conservatism' and 'egalitarian commitment'. 'Conservatism' correlates negatively with Hofstede's individualism, and 'egalitarian commitment' correlates positively with it. So, while the socio-centric values linked to 'conservatism' are those that would be expected to be associated with collectivism, 'egalitarian commitment' expresses going beyond selfish interest (loyalty, social justice, responsibility and equality), but places a voluntary rather than an obligatory aspect on this towards the in-group. In other words, it could be possible that individualism might give rise to humanistic values.

Instrumentalism and humanism may not relate, therefore, in a *direct* way to the level of individualism and collectivism in a society, because there may be different cultural influences in different societies that lead to a lessening of a humanistic locus of human value within the organisation and/or a softening of an instrumental locus of human value. We can look at some examples of this from around the world.

EXAMPLES OF HUMANISM-INSTRUMENTALISM IN DIFFERENT COUNTRIES

Australia has an individualistic 'Western' culture, yet has also been seen as having a 'humanistic' orientation that leads to a concern for the well-being of the workforce and for quality of work life. More accurately (in Schwartz's research), this may reflect a moderately high level of egalitarian commitment, and in terms of the popular management literature, the 'mateship' of Australian society (Westwood and Posner, 1997).

More recent research has suggested that Americans are not as individualistic as Hofstede's original 1980 study has suggested. The GLOBE (House *et al*, 2004) study undertaken in the late 1990s and early 2000s is worth noting in this respect. This view is reflected in the USA's moderately high scores on Schwartz's 'egalitarian commitment' scale.

Yet Australian and US values towards people in organisations may still be different. With Australia having a higher historical level of protectionism of both business and of the workers in the labour market, American work culture may be expected to show a higher level of individual achievement orientation than that of Australia. However, both countries have similar moderately high scores on Hofstede's 'masculinity' values dimension, which in part measures the level of competitiveness and results focus, and Australia has more recently gone through a time of economic liberalisation and increase in competitiveness and less worker-friendly labour markets (Tixier, 2000).

Both Australian and American organisations have been shown to have a command-and-control orientation with a top-down management approach (Wheeler and McClendon, 1998). Again, this may be a factor that promotes the view that employees may be used instrumentally towards the objectives of the organisation's executive. Yet there are other reasons, apart from the recent conceptualisation of 'egalitarian commitment' within the cross-cultural values literature, why the harder forms of instrumentalism are being 'softened' in the Anglo-Saxon countries and probably also in Western Europe, but also why the 'harder' versions may be being adopted uncritically in the rather short-term orientation of transitional countries in the former Soviet bloc, and in the newly industrialised countries of East Asia.

There are influences on HRM policies and practices in Anglo-Saxon countries that appear to have given rise to a 'softer' instrumentalism. These include the maturation of Western HRM systems, the influence of Human Relations theory, and influences from Japanese management.

CULTURAL 'CROSSVERGENCE': DEVELOPING HYBRID MANAGEMENT

This brings us to the issue of 'crossvergence' of cultural influences, where different cultures come together to form specific 'hybrid' management approaches. Hong Kong is a good example of this. One study of crossvergence in Hong Kong found Hong Kong managers closer in their values to those from America than managers from the nearby Guangzhou Province in mainland China (Priem, Love and Shaffer, 2000). Another study of Hong Kong notes the different treatment of employees of in-group members and out-group members in Chinese family firms (Hui, 1990). Hong Kong society is culturally complex. It has been at the interface of Eastern and Western society for many years. The evidence in the literature in terms of its level of individualism-collectivism and the way it is changing is contradictory (Ho and Chiu, 1994). So because of both cultural crossvergence and differential treatment of employees within a 'hybrid' collectivist management, both instrumentalism and humanism will be modified by the influence of the other.

THE INFLUENCE OF WESTERN INSTRUMENTALISM ON TRANSITIONAL AND NEWLY INDUSTRIALISED COUNTRIES

The influence of instrumentalism on transitional and newly industrialised countries should also be mentioned. Studies of Russia have noted a tendency of corporations to adopt uncritically imported HRM solutions, which underestimate the complexities of the 'free market' economy in the context of the Russian situation (May, Bormann Young and Ledgerwood, 1998). Also noted is the lack of commitment by employees to the organisation, a lack of managerial responsibility, disregard for health and safety issues, and strained labour-management relations. This would seem indicative of a high level of instrumentalism.

This may also be the case in Eastern and Central European post-Soviet countries. Yet countries such as the Czech Republic and Poland are historically different from Russia, with traditions of pre-Soviet industrialisation and entrepreneurship, and relative efficiency under the Soviet system (Koubrek and Brewster, 1995). They may be far closer to Western Europe than Russia in their cultural orientation, yet suffer from a lack of maturity of their HRM systems.

Russia may also have a stronger tradition of collectivisation, and perhaps even 'Asiatic' humanistic orientations than Poland and the Czech Republic. Russian cultural values appear much higher on conservatism and lower on egalitarian commitment than Poland (Smith, Dugan and Trompenaars, 1996).

The newly industrialised countries in East Asia are also likely to come under influences of the older industrialised countries to adopt short-term measures that have been successful elsewhere in order to effectively compete in the global economy. They may be influenced by both Japanese models of industrialisation and US models (Chen, 1995).

In one study, Korean organisations have been shown to be different from those of Japan in terms of the level of solidarity shown by employees towards their co-workers (Bae and Chung, 1997). Although Korean employees expect a higher level of commitment from their companies towards them, and from them to the company, the corporation shows a lower level of solidarity to workers than both their Japanese and American counterparts. Korean people management appears to be less consultative than Japanese firms, and have a lower loyalty downwards. Yet loyalty is expected upwards. This represents a more authoritarian system than that of Japan. Hard instrumentalism may therefore be a feature in the newly industrialised countries of East Asia as well as of transitional countries. However, there will also be humanistic influences on such countries.

DIFFERENCES BETWEEN COLLECTIVISTIC AND INDIVIDUALISTIC COUNTRIES

If organisations are seen as meeting collective social needs such as providing full employment as in the case of the former Soviet bloc, or serving the needs of people as part of a collective in-group as in the case of Japan and Korea, this may reflect in the level to which people see their organisation fulfilling the needs of its people. A view of contractual obligations only within individualistic societies may work against this type of view. In a society with such collectivistic socio-cultural values, individuals may be valued as part of the wider collective.

This may be different from the values implicit within 'egalitarian commitment' and the 'human relations school' in Western society where a consideration of the 'valuing' of people may still be oriented towards a particular end that is separate from the individual. In a collectivist society, the 'end' may not be separate from the individual. It may also be the case that the relationship between the collectivism and a humanistic locus in organisations may be more simple than the relationship between individualism and instrumentalism. In other words, humanistic approaches may be appropriate in both collectivistic and individualistic culture, but instrumental approaches will be against the humanistic values of collectivistic cultures. Attempting to transplant Western HRM practices directly to collectivist societies will therefore be problematic. Yet collectivistic societies can be quite different in the type of people management systems adopted.

'CAPTURING' THE WIDER SOCIETAL COLLECTIVISM IN THE CORPORATION

The difference noted in the literature between the lower loyalty of the Korean corporation and the higher loyalty of the Japanese corporation has already been noted (Bae and Chung, 1997). This may affect the degree of concern of managers for employees with a value in themselves (humanism). Unlike in other collectivist cultures, such as India and African countries, Japanese corporations have been successful in using a wider societal collectivism for the corporation by 'utilising social and spiritual forces for the organisation's benefit, and in accepting the responsibilities to their employees' in the words of the classic study on Japanese management by Pascale and Athos (1981). Although people management practices arising from this (eg lifetime employment, payment by seniority) have come under increasing pressure, there still seems to be a people and relationship focus that is important in obtaining employees' moral commitment to the organisation.

This relationship focus is also found in Chinese business organisations where familial relations are important both internally and in *guanxi* relations in business dealings (Chen, 1994). Although there are differences in the ways corporations capture this societal collectivism in people identifying with the corporation and the corporation identifying with its people, the mindset or locus of human value is still likely to be humanistic in a collectivist society. Where corporations cannot or do not use and work with this, alienation between people's 'home' culture and the alien culture they step into when they go to work in the morning is likely.

REFLECTIVE ACTIVITY

This section has mainly been about the different, often hybrid, approaches to valuing and managing people in various emerging economies. Most of your training and education so far in HRM has no doubt been from a Western perspective. However, how much of this would you be able to apply in countries that are quite different from Anglo-Saxon ones?

For example, at this stage you could review theories you have learned about motivating staff. How does practice vary in Japan and Korea?

How could the HR manager in our starter case study better motivate staff? (We will return to this issue later in our main case study at the end of this chapter.)

4 LOOKING AT HRM IN A CROSS-CULTURAL PERSPECTIVE: DOES IT WORK OVERSEAS?

THE RELATION BETWEEN HOME AND WORK: DIFFERENT SOLUTIONS

The contradictions between life outside and inside the world of work organisations have been investigated in various ways since the Industrial Revolution in the West, from the concept of 'alienation' in the Marxist tradition onwards.

Organisations in different cultural settings may have different responses to this contradiction. These include:

- the calculative/contractual responses of US HRM systems which recognise and work within the instrumental relationship between employer and employee (trying to humanise this through quality of work-life initiatives and employee involvement while firmly focusing on the bottom line)

- the moral, spiritual and obligatory responses (such as creating an internal labour market – ie ways of helping people to rise inside the organisation) of traditional Japanese organisations which capture the collectivistic and humanistic orientations within the wider society (humanistic approaches).

There seems little doubt that between these different approaches, which have been represented here as *humanism* and *instrumentalism*, policies and practices are being shared across cultures through the processes and activities of firms who are internationalising through different types of strategies and expatriates' activities and functions in host countries.

This may not be through convergence (the coming together of value systems) but by *crossvergence* (developing of hybrid value systems as a result of cultural interactions), as we outlined above. Hence raw 'Taylorism' (the instrumental, stop-watch approach of the American Frederick W. Taylor publicised in the early twentieth century), concerned with finding the most efficient methods and procedures for co-ordination and controlling work and workers, may not be a feature of the mature HRM systems in, for example, the United States as a result of the influences discussed above, but may be seen in the policy manifestations of organisations in Russia and other post-Soviet countries, identified in the post-Soviet system as a move towards greater efficiency, higher workforce discipline, less paternalism and more instrumentalism and a decline in human contact – as well as short-termism and deterioration in employee–manager relations.

THE HEGEMONY OF WESTERN PRACTICES

In HRM practice this means borrowing from the West. In Russia one study (Lawrence, 1994) suggests that HRM systems are built more explicitly around business objectives, with formal systems of staffing, career planning, management development, skills training and appraisal systems with 'management by objectives' (MBO).

This tendency may also be the case in Korea (Chen, 1995), with workers putting a strong emphasis on extrinsic (such as pay) rather than intrinsic factors of motivation (such as inherent satisfaction drawn from the job), and some organisations having MBO systems and focusing more on wages and conditions, and performance being seen as an important factor (see Chapter 13 on reward). Yet there appears in addition to be retention of seniority systems. Western-style appraisal systems also seem to be used, but include other considerations apart from performance, and an emphasis on harmony militating against negative judgements and reflecting tolerance and appreciation of people's best efforts.

THE COMPETENCES APPROACH IN WESTERN HRM

The manifestations of an instrumental locus of value are best explained by the competences approach to human resource management. A competence has been defined as 'the ability to demonstrate a system or sequence of behaviour as a function related to attaining a performance goal' (Boyatzis, 1982). The required competences are therefore determined by operational objectives, which are related to strategic objectives, and link the various human resource functions such as selection, training and reward, in seeking organisational objectives. It is also supported by a systems concept of organisation, where people (as resources) are organised in the best way, and having the best skills, to ensure efficient throughput through the system (see Chapter 2 on the systems approach). For example, job descriptions would identify appropriate persons for particular positions within the system, ensuring the required competences.

This may be one of the more important implications and manifestations of an instrumental locus of control, which may remain although certain features of a 'softer' instrumentalism such as quality of work–life initiatives may resemble features of a 'harder' humanism. This may be an appropriate response of HRM policies in getting higher levels of mutual contractual involvement of employees in cultures that show an instrumental locus of human value.

A DEVELOPMENT APPROACH IN HUMANISTIC CULTURES

In cultures that have a humanistic locus of human value, the development of a moral commitment may be more appropriate. So Japanese firms may show a higher commitment to people and community welfare by keeping (in-group) employees in work through economic downturns, which in turn encourages stability, commitment and a sense of belonging.

This element of social welfare and responsibility was also shown in the Soviet countries, as well as obtaining the commitment of workers through ideological means. However, it is likely that the two systems are different on the level of commitment to developing people, although the same opportunities may have presented themselves through longer-term planning and a lack of pressure from a concern for shareholder value in the case of Japan and the Soviet economy.

Rather than based on a competences approach which links individuals to the operational and strategic objectives of the organisation, a developmental approach based on job flexibility and rotation (rather than fitting a person to a job), and promotion based on experience through seniority seems to show a more holistic approach to the person. So the organisation, and experience within it, tries to develop the person as a committed part of the human organisation.

The concept of locus of human value (Jackson, 2002b) may therefore be helpful in understanding an inherent contradiction between the world outside work organisations and life inside. The different attempts at reconciling these two worlds, and the possible effects of crossvergence through global cultural interaction, may bring the two loci into conflict or contradiction. Yet they may come together to form a hybrid people management system.

Through crossvergence, management systems may be borrowed and adapted, rather than the cultural orientations of those being managed substantially changing. Hence, it is the managers from emerging and transitional economies who are trained and influenced by Western traditions, rather than the workers who staff the enterprises.

Similarly, the literature on international and comparative HRM practices in different countries reflects those policies and practices being introduced, rather than telling us very much about how employees react to such policies, and how successful they might be in the long term. The wholesale adoption of Western HRM principles, albeit with necessary adaptations, in Russia, for example, may ultimately be ineffective as inappropriate ways to manage people within a culture that may reflect a humanistic locus of human value.

This view is currently being reflected in the growing management literature in at least two parts of the world: South Africa (eg Mbigi, 1997) and India (eg Rao, 1996):

● In practice this is reflected in the *Ubuntu* movement in South Africa (this comes from a phrase that means 'people are only people through other people'), where enlightened corporations are trying to integrate indigenous African approaches within their people management systems.

● In India an Indian approach to human resource development is providing a synthesis of Western and Indian approaches, but the spiritual/holistic/developmental aspects of humanness are emphasised.

It may also be the case that the so-called K-type management of Korea may reflect an effective synthesis of indigenous Korean with Japanese and American approaches (Chen, 1995).

In developing effective international and cross-cultural systems, managers should learn to think outside the parochial box of HRM. Blindly introducing Western HRM practices that reflect an *instrumental* view of people may be ineffective, if not an affront to the humanity of people outside Western traditions. Yet managing globally goes further than simply adapting effectively practices from one culture to another. Managers should ask themselves what could be learned from the *humanism* of South Asia and from Africa in managing global enterprises successfully. What can be learned from the attempts of reconciling instrumental and humanistic approaches in the countries where this is becoming more successful?

5   MANAGING PEOPLE INTERNATIONALLY: STAKEHOLDERS, HUMAN VALUE AND INTERNATIONAL STRATEGY

In summary, from the above discussion, it is possible to draw three interdependent conceptual threads – stakeholder consideration, the locus of human value, and multicultural/strategising oppositions – that must be considered in managing people internationally. Firstly, an understanding and consideration of stakeholders is important in any enterprise. Within the context of corporate life, two categories of stakeholder may be identified: corporate and community. In many societies, these two sets of stakeholders may be quite distinct. For example, a high regard for shareholder value in societies emphasising a free market economy may see the local community within which it operates as only a source of labour (see Chapter 25). Where there is a high governmental or institutional involvement in the finances and control of enterprises, government and local communities may be high-profile stakeholders in the enterprise.

Secondly, one of the major jobs of the management of people within the enterprise is to reconcile the distinctions between these two sets of stakeholder groups, and the lives of people in the community, and their lives in the enterprise. Across cultures, there are different ways in which this is approached. A major cultural influence in how this is approached is the way in which people are seen in organisations (the locus of human value). An *instrumental* cultural perspective may therefore bring a contractual relationship with the employee who provides his or her time in exchange for wages. A *humanistic* cultural perspective may bring an obligatory relationship of commitment amongst members of the corporation.

Thirdly, as a result of the often competing local and global forces in international management, which on the one hand leads to local cultural adaptation and adoption, and on the other leads to universalisation of management principles through international strategies, there are different combinations of solutions to this issue – some highly adaptive and successful, and some not so successful. So hybrid solutions adopted in Korea may be regarded as successfully reconciling corporate and community life, whereas solutions in many sub-Saharan African countries have not adapted well to the situation.

KEY ISSUES: COMPARATIVE HRM

We now pull together ten key points showing the main lessons that can be learned from the above discussion for HRM professionals working across cultures:

- Seeing people in organisations as just a means to an end may be an affront to human dignity in many non-Western countries including Japan, Korean and Russia and other transition countries in Central Europe and Asia, and emerging countries in Africa, Latin America and South Asia.

- Inappropriate HR policies and practices in countries with humanistic cultures may lead to alienation, poor motivation and labour conflict.

- Staff may see themselves as stepping out of their own culture into an alien one when they go to work in the morning where approaches to managing people in the organisation are different from the way people are valued in their own communities.

- HR practices based on the competences approach may be interpreted in humanistic cultures as fitting a person to the requirements of the job and the organisational objectives, rather than developing a person around a number of jobs and developing him or her holistically. This may be contrary to practices reported in Japanese organisations, and may lead to a lack of identification with the organisation and a lack of commitment.

- Thought should therefore be given to introducing a more developmental/holistic approach in other collectivistic societies such as in sub-Saharan Africa.

- Payment by results and performance-related reward may also be inappropriate in humanistic cultures, and may be seen as reflecting an instrumental perception of people.

- In these circumstances it may be better to reward people on the basis of their commitment to the group and the organisation, and their development as a valued group member.

- Instrumental approaches may be appropriate in instrumentally oriented cultures, but humanism also has value as a concept and approach toward people.

- Developing moral commitment and involvement, aiming corporate resources towards the advancement of its people, focusing on the whole person rather than as a resource with a set of competences may also bring positive results in instrumental cultures.

- A 'soft' instrumental approach does not equal a humanistic approach. To break out of the parochial box needs an understanding of the cultural differences between an instrumental and a humanistic locus of human value. This represents the difference between aiming people as a resource towards executive goals of the organisation, and aiming the resources of the organisation towards achieving the development of human capacity of people with a value in their own right.

Perhaps there are other key points that you would like to note for yourself.

The main case study in this chapter now follows. Returning to South Africa, the case study presents different sets of value systems for a Western manager and African staff: readers are asked to consider how these might be reconciled.

MAIN CASE STUDY

Cashbuild, a supplier of building material mainly to the home market, was set up in 1978 by Albert Koopman (see Koopman, 1991). Despite initial problems, he was able to quickly turn these around and it became a successful business. It has since been sold by Koopman as a highly profitable going concern. It is quoted on the Johannesburg Stock Exchange, operates in a number of southern African countries, and is today a household name in South Africa. At the beginning it struggled with very high turnover of staff and low motivation. Koopman, a white Afrikaans-speaking businessman brought up within Western management traditions, had to do some hard thinking about the value systems of his predominantly Zulu workforce. He had to address these differences and gain the commitment of the African workforce if he was to turn the company around.

He conceptualised the differences between what he sees as his own 'individual' value system and that of his 'communal' workforce. Some of the distinctions that he drew are as follows.

INDIVIDUAL

- I control my life: I therefore say that I missed the bus
- I want to show you who is in charge by gripping your hand hard when I greet you – I am your opponent
- I am self-reliant
- I like job descriptions, status and rank because I know who has to be in which place; I like to alienate people
- I pay bonuses to motivate you to work harder because this works for me; I like to compete against my fellow man through higher earnings
- I will only support my brother for a short while in case of his financial embarrassment, then he must find a job
- I normally have a small family so that we can have a better quality of life and hopefully avoid financial destitution
- The more I have, the more I am
- My concern is for production
- I am driven by merit and reward for individual effort
- I am individually competitive – everyone is my opponent

COMMUNAL

- Outside forces control me – therefore I say the bus left without me
- I want to show my connectedness to you by greeting you with a soft hand and hold it longer – I am your friend
- I am cooperative and emotional
- I prefer operating in a team working towards a common goal and not divided from my human being – I like solidarity amongst people
- As part of a group, I dare not separate myself from my group by earning more through hard work; you will therefore be throwing good money after bad because I don't want to be separated through money
- The more I earn, the more I tend to care for my brothers and sisters for as long as necessary
- I have an extended family to help me during times of destitution
- I am, therefore the more I am prepared to give and share
- My concern is for people
- I am driven by group reward for group effort
- I am cooperative – we're all in this together and should assist one another

Your task

Look at these differences in values, and recommend how they can be reconciled. In particular, how can people management systems and practices be developed to gain commitment and motivate people?

Now look below at what Koopman did, and what he recommends.

What Koopman did

Koopman describes how in Cashbuild, shared values were built mainly by getting people together in order to develop an understanding of values and principles upon which they might wish to work. He goes on to make recommendations on how motivational systems may be developed, drawing on his experience in Cashbuild, in order to take account of the more communal orientation of managers and staff. Basing reward on a belief that people do not work purely for money, and that the need for dignity, pride, belonging and freedom should be fulfilled first, they addressed those needs first at Cashbuild before any additional rewards for money were introduced. Maintenance factors were also addressed as they were raised, such as funeral policies, housing loans and educational assistance – although these were only addressed once additional productivity and wealth, as well as 'human freedom' had been created.

What Koopman recommends

His recommendations from his experience were:

- Avoid rewarding staff for something they do not have control over. This involves avoiding long-term goals (over 12 months) and things beyond the workplace. This addresses the orientation towards an external locus of control.

- Only share profit if profitability is raised. If not, this is tantamount to paternalism. Loyalty is difficult to buy in this way if staff see through this.

- Giving staff share ownership is not meaningful when, for example, food prices are a main concern in Africa. Their ability to sell their shares defeats the objective.

- Avoid rewarding communally oriented staff on an individual basis that will separate them into classes by money and grading systems, and avoid the principle of capitalist meritocracy, because it does not apply in Africa.

- Develop communal reward schemes for communal effort, for example, by group or section.

- Reward only those things that people feel they can control and measure themselves.

- Reward for upward movement of productivity indices.

- If share schemes are created, do so via a collective, with people gaining a meaningful proportion of shares that can directly influence their voting rights on issues within the organisation.

Your task

These recommendations represent at least one organisation's attempt to introduce motivational measures that address the issue of rewarding more communally minded staff. How can this now be applied to resolving the situation in the starter case study? How can motivational people management practices be introduced?

EXPLORE FURTHER

JACKSON, T. (2002a) *International HRM: A cross-cultural approach*. London, Sage
This book is a fairly comprehensive overview of different approaches to people management in a wide range of countries.

JACKSON, T. (2002b) 'The management of people across cultures: valuing people differently', *Human Resource Management*, Vol. 41, No. 4, 455–75
This article discusses the concept of the locus of human value and provides some empirical data for country differences.

JACKSON, T. (2004) *Management and Change in Africa: A cross-cultural perspective*. London, Routledge
This book provides a comprehensive study of people management in sub-Saharan Africa, and discusses many of the issues raised in the current chapter.

KOOPMAN, A. (1991) *Transcultural Management*. Oxford, Basil Blackwell
This book provides additional information on the main case study of this chapter.

PASCALE, R. T. and ATHOS, A. G. (1981) *The Art of Japanese Management*. New York, Simon & Schuster
This is a classic study of Japanese management which had tremendous influence on management in the United States and the UK.

CHAPTER 24

Creating corporate capability: a new agenda

Peter Critten

INTRODUCTION

The aim of this chapter is to help readers understand how the role of human resource development (HRD) is changing from being a deliverer of training solutions to being a facilitator of learning. In the newer role, it better builds 'intellectual capital' as part of the wider HR strategy.

LEARNING OUTCOMES

By the end of this chapter readers should be able to:

- describe the defining characteristics of an HRD strategy designed to build corporate intellectual capital

- recognise the difference between such an HRD strategy and a more traditional 'training-oriented' approach

- appreciate how such a strategy is part of a corporate-wide approach to knowledge management

- recognise what role HR professionals can play in contributing to such an HRD strategy.

This chapter offers another view of workplace learning, also outlined in Chapter 14. It makes a case for a new approach to HRD in the context of a developing knowledge economy, in which 'strategies have to be dynamic, changeable and, to an extent, opportunistic' (Garvey and Williamson, 2002). It argues that HRD has never been able to decide whether its focus should be on individual needs (personal development as well as skills and knowledge improvement) or the organisation's business and strategic needs. But to understand this tension – still a factor in most companies' approach to HRD – it is necessary to understand how thinking about HRD has changed over the last 50 years.

The chapter is in four sections which chart the key developments in HRD in Britain from the 1960s until now. Part 1 gives an insight into the legislation of the 1960s that was pivotal in shaping attitudes to what was called 'systematic training', which was overseen by Government-appointed Industry Training Boards. Part 2 moves on to the 1980s. Then, again, a Government initiative – Investors in People – focused attention onto seeing training and development as an investment in rather than as a cost to the business. The third part describes the principles behind the idea of the 'learning organisation', which was introduced in the early 1990s and is still an espoused vision for many organisations today. The final section, Part 4, moves the agenda on from the mid-1990s to now and, we suggest, the future. This is the agenda of 'knowledge management'.

As well as being a 'historical' journey, it might be seen also as 'developmental' in that all of the approaches to HRD we highlight are still with us.

The chapter concludes with the main case study.

Reference sources named within the chapter may be looked up in the *References and further reading* section at the end of the book.

STARTER CASE STUDY

An expanding chain of DIY shops called DIY Solutions was started in the early 1980s by John Miles, an engineer by profession who took early retirement to indulge his passion, DIY. He opened a shop in a leafy London suburb with a particular mission in mind.

Now, in the early 1990s, he is genuinely retiring and about to hand over the business as a successful going concern to an employee, Matt Dyson, who is to take on a new role as MD. On his last day at work, John Miles is being interviewed by a reporter from a local paper.

Interviewer: Can you tell us, John, what made you start up this business in the first place?

John Miles: Well, I'd spent about 30 years working as an engineer in various construction companies and got to a point when I'd had enough working for other people so I decided to retire early and invest in a shop which allowed me to indulge my secret passion, DIY.

Interviewer: Wasn't that the time when the big chains like Homebase and B&Q were also recognising the DIY boom and beginning to capitalise on it? How did you expect to compete with them?

John Miles: That's the point – I wasn't going to compete but could provide something

none of the big stores could provide – friendly practical advice which was available to local householders, on their doorstep, as it were.

Interviewer: Well, you certainly read the market well at the time, because over the last 10 years you've grown from one shop to 10. And one of the benefits that I know all your customers talk about (including me) is the expertise of your staff. Did you start by recruiting staff who already had such expertise, or did you train them yourself?

John Miles: A bit of both, actually. When I started my first shop I was lucky to still be in contact with former colleagues, engineers, who were practical people, like me, and who had all been trained and developed themselves in ways which which I'm sorry to say have passed away. When I was a young engineer, I had an apprenticeship with a firm that made sure I learned my craft but also allowed me time to attend the local college where I took my City and Guilds qualifications so I understood the theory as well as the practice. I was lucky that one or two of my colleagues also decided to take retirement a year after me and they joined me in a partnership which meant the business could expand – plus I knew I had people in charge who knew what they were talking about.

But as we expanded we had to take on new staff who hadn't the same background as ours and needed developing. Here I was also lucky, and was able to draw on experience working with engineering companies. In the 1970s the Government introduced what were called Industry Training Boards (ITBs) to monitor the training given by different industries and provide financial incentives for effective – what they called 'systematic' – training. At first we did not like interference from our own ITB, the Engineering Industry Training Board (EITB), but after a while we realised they could teach us a lot about how to get the best out of our people by systematic development. Beforehand we'd wasted a lot of money sending staff on courses that added nothing to the business. But the concept of 'systematic' training meant we were able to draw up individual plans for each employee based on what knowledge/skill they needed to acquire to be effective at a particular task.

Despite Maggie Thatcher's destruction of the ITBs in the late 1980s – I liked her support for individual enterprise, but she didn't understand how the ITBs were beginning to help business add value to itself – I've remembered the lessons learned and now have a full-time 'training officer' who was made redundant from the EITB whose job it is to develop training plans for all our new (and old) employees.

Interviewer: That's quite unusual, isn't it, to have a training officer in such a small company?

John Miles: Maybe it is, but you've remarked yourself on how customers value our expertise, and that's all down to training. But we don't stop with initial training – which Derek, my training officer does himself in each of the shops. All our staff are

encouraged to keep up to date with the latest developments in our field by attending courses and subscribing to trade journals. And this applies to my managers as well.

Interviewer: So in conclusion, John, what's the legacy you would say you're handing over to your successor?

John Miles: Matt comes from the same background as me. He was one of my former colleagues I told you I took on in a partnership in the early years. I know he will make sure our staff are as up to date on latest developments to match any training that the big chains can provide. But we have the advantage in having staff who are dedicated to giving quality advice which they believe in.

Interviewer: Thanks very much, John. Enjoy a 'proper' retirement now, and I look forward to interviewing Matt after another 10 years have passed.

Questions for discussion

1 How would you compare the way staff were helped to perform their jobs by the training officer, Derek, in the DIY Solutions of the 1980s and early 1990s with your understanding of how staff are 'trained' and 'developed' in organisations today?

2 In fact, what exactly is your understanding of the terms 'development' and 'training', and do you see any difference between their meanings?

Note: At the end of this chapter, in the main case study, we return to the business 15 years later. That case study features a report by an outside consultancy into how effective Matt Dyson has been in growing and developing the workforce of DIY Solutions. Your task after reading the report will be to recommend just how you would put the consultancy's recommendations into action based on what you have learned about HRD in the chapter.

1 THE LEGACY OF THE LEGISLATION OF THE 1960s AND 1970s

In 1986 the Institute of Personnel Management published *Training Interventions* by John Kenney and Margaret Reid, which replaced a former publication, *Manpower Training and Development* first published in 1972. In 2004, the seventh edition of 'Training Interventions' was published by the CIPD under a new title *Human Resource Development: Beyond training interventions* (Reid, Barrington and Brown 2004). The change in titles over the last 30-plus years reflects the transition from 'Training' to 'Learning' to 'HRD', which is the subject of this chapter.

Our story begins in the 1960s when the Government was concerned about the need to improve skills level of those in work – not such a different story from today. It was also concerned that bigger companies were taking, or 'poaching' experienced staff from other companies and not undertaking training themselves. These were the main reasons for the passing of the Industry Training Act in 1964 whereby each of the major industries had to establish its own Industry Training Board to set and monitor training standards for their industry sector. In our case study, John Miles remembered the influence of the Engineering Industries Training Board.

The Industry Training Act gave each Training Board the right to collect a payment called a levy (based on a percentage of a company's payroll) of companies of a certain size in their industry. With this money they were then able to reward companies that did train according to specified standards – what became known as 'systematic training'. In the way that each industry specified its own standards, it was in fact similar to the German training system that still largely works in this way today. The British ITB system followed the cycle of four stages shown in Figure 27.

Figure 27 The systematic training cycle

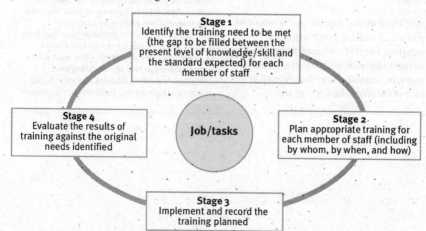

REFLECTIVE ACTIVITY

How does the four-stage cycle shown in Figure 27 compare with how you described your understanding of how staff are 'trained' and 'developed' to perform effectively above?

(If you read the interview with John Miles again – in the starter case study – you will see that this is probably the way the training officer Derek trained new staff. He would have most likely followed the 'systematic training cycle' as practised by his own Industry Training Board of the time, the Engineering Industry Training Board.)

CHANGING VIEWS OF TRAINING

Reid *et al* (2004; p.2) remind us of a definition of training that was first proposed in the Manpower Services Commission's *Glossary of Training Terms* in 1981:

> *Training is a planned process to modify attitude, knowledge or skill behaviour through learning experience to achieve effective performance in an activity or range of activities. Its purpose, in the work situation, is to develop the abilities of the individual and to satisfy the current and future needs of the organisation.*

Ten years before that a slightly different definition had been proposed by the then Department of Employment in its *Glossary of Training Terms* of 1971:

> *Training is the systematic development of the attitude/knowledge/skill behaviour pattern required by an individual to perform adequately a given task or job.*

REFLECTIVE ACTIVITY

Look at the 1971 and 1981 definitions of training as cited and list what you think are significant differences between them.

In these two definitions we may consider that there are three significant differences of emphasis:

- The 1971 definition talks about 'systematic development' whereas in the 1981 definition it becomes a 'planned process'.

- The most important addition in the 1981 definition is a focus on 'learning experience'; learning plays no part in the 1971 definition.

- The 1981 definition talks about the purpose of training (albeit in the work situation) as being not just for the benefit of the organisation but for that of the individual as well – whereas the context of training in the 1971 definition is firmly within the organisation in a given task or job.

As we go on to argue in this chapter, these are important distinctions which reflected changing views in society. But for those practising training in the 1960s and 1970s, like the starter case study DIY Solutions' training officer Derek, these principles would underpin their practice for all time. So although the starter case study interview was conducted in the early 1990s, Derek's approach to development of staff was *still* based on a 'systematic approach to training' as reflected in the 1971 definition: 'Training is the systematic development of the attitude/knowledge/skill behaviour pattern required by an individual to perform adequately a given task or job.'

In fact, this attitude towards training 'the workers' to enable companies to achieve their business objectives has its roots in the early twentieth century with the American Frederick W. Taylor's concept of 'scientific management'. Harrison (2002; p.18) points out that:

> If we locate the true origins of organisational HRD here, we can more easily understand those tensions in purpose and values that still bedevil the learning and development process in many organisations today. They arise from trying to combine a business imperative with a genuine concern for the well-being and development of the individual.

To be fair to Derek, his plans went beyond training as such, as John Miles remarked to the interviewer in the starter case study:

> But we don't stop with initial training – which Derek, my training officer does himself in each of the shops. All our staff are encouraged to keep up to date with the latest developments in our field by attending courses and subscribing to trade journals. And this applies to my managers as well.

This reflects more the principles of the 1981 definition with a move towards the importance of learning experience and, just as importantly, the professional needs of the individual as well as goals of the organisation. Today we would call this 'continuous professional development' (CPD).

In Figure 27, note that Stage 4 of the systematic training cycle focuses on 'evaluation'. During the 1960s and 1970s 'evaluation' of training meant little more than how the 'trainees' on a training course/programme rated the 'training experience' on what became known as a 'happy sheet' given out at the end. But towards the end of the 1960s, Kirkpatrick introduced a model which helped trainers collect evidence of 'value' not just according to a favourable or unfavourable comment about the training experience, but at higher levels. What had they learned from the training? And at a higher level still, how had their behaviour changed? And then the final level which really opened up a debate which continues until today: what evidence is there that the training has led to real, concrete, tangible results like reduction of costs, increase in profits? (More information about models of evaluation that followed soon after is to be found in Reid *et al*, 2004; pp200–1.)

The move to thinking about training in a more strategic way that had implications not just for the individual and his or her job but for the enterprise as a whole leads us into Part 2 of the chapter and a description of a more strategic approach to development put forward at the end of the 1980s that set the agenda for the 1990s.

2 THE INVESTING IN PEOPLE ERA: ADDING VALUE TO THE ORGANISATION

Towards the end of the 1980s the training initiatives of the 1960s and 1970s were perceived not to have created the skilled workforce that had been hoped for, and in 1988 the Government White Paper *Employment for the Nineties* set out a strategy for the next ten years. This meant the end of the ITBs and the creation of a National Training Task Force which spent a year talking to business about what were the 'people' factors that made one company more effective than another. They identified key criteria which successful companies used, to show that investment in people made a difference to an organisation's performance. These criteria became the basis for a National Award of 'Investor in People' (IiP) to those companies that met them. Over the years, the criteria have been reviewed, as has the institution administering the scheme. The current criteria are divided into three categories (see the box below). These are the criteria companies have to show they can meet if they are to be given the national 'kite-mark' proudly displayed in the reception area of many organisations today. Originally run by the Department of Education and Employment, the scheme is now run by a private company: Investors in People UK (see the website for further information: **www.investorsinpeople.co.uk**).

Investors in People criteria

Developing strategies to improve the performance of the organisation

An investor in People develops effective strategies to improve the performance of the organisation through its people.

1 **A strategy for improving the performance of the organisation is clearly defined and understood.**

2 **Learning and development is planned to achieve the organisation's objectives.**

3 **Strategies for managing people are designed to promote quality of opportunity in the development of the organisation's people.**

4 **The capabilities managers need to lead, manage and develop people effectively are clearly defined and understood.**

Taking action to improve the performance of the organisation

An Investor in People takes effective action to improve the performance of the organisation through its people.

5 **Managers are effective in leading, managing and developing people.**

6 **People's contribution to the organisation is recognised and valued.**

7 **People are encouraged to take ownership and responsibility by being involved in decision-making.**

8 **People learn and develop effectively.**

Evaluating the impact on the performance of the organisation

An Investor in People can demonstrate the impact of its investment in people on the performance of the organisation.

9 **Investment in people improves the performance of the organisation.**

10 **Improvements are continually made to the way people are managed and developed.**

Source: **www.investorsinpeople.co.uk**

REFLECTIVE ACTIVITY

Look at the Investors in People criteria listed in the box above and note down the ways in which they differ from the definitions of training and development that shaped HR development strategies over the previous 30 years.

One difference is that in the IiP criteria the word 'training' does not appear anywhere. In the same way as 'training courses' were understood to be methods by which companies met the demands of ITBs in the 1970s and 1980s, many organisations claimed to meet the criteria of IiP by showing evidence of the number of training courses they were running – which is still true of many organisations trying to meet the criteria today. And that is why a note published by the Department of Employment in 1990 clearly (if slightly plaintively) stated:

> Investors in People is not just one more training programme scheme or initiative. Nor is it simply about persuading companies to spend more on training. It's about helping companies to realise the value of their most potent investment – their own people.

There are other definitions of HRD in the latter half of this chapter – but the above is as good as any.

The focus is on how 'learning and development' can help improve the **business** as a whole and not on training. This is also the focus of HRD. But how do you show the link between HRD and performance? This has been at the centre of 'evaluation' for decades and was what the ITBs were trying to achieve. The ten criteria for the Investors in People Award come closest to measuring some of the 'activities' organisations might undertake to make the link possible.

REFLECTIVE ACTIVITY

Look once more at the ten Investors in People criteria listed in the box above and note down the kind of evidence that you might look for in a company that is seeking IiP accreditation.

If you look at the Investors in People website and go to the Investors in People Standard, you will find evidence of the following kind listed against the criteria:

- People are clear about the business strategy and are involved in the decision-making process.

- People's ideas for improvement are welcomed and rewarded.

- People can describe how their learning and development has contributed to improvement in themselves, their teams and the organisation overall.

Clearly, this is good HRM practice and reflects principles of communication and performance management which appear in other chapters in this book (see Chapters 19 and 12 on communication and performance management). But is this enough to show that the business has really changed? What if a business is to be defined not by the product it sells or profit it makes but by its capacity to learn? A former CEO of IBM is said to have remarked that the business of his company was learning – the design and selling of computers was a by-product of that learning. This brings us to the third stage in our journey, which explores the practical value of what has been called 'the learning organisation'.

Again, in the UK at least, this concept was championed by a state-sponsored organisation. In 1986 the Director of the Manpower Services Commission said that 'If we are to survive – individually or as companies, or as a country – we must create a tradition of "learning companies"'. Thus was begun the Learning Company Project the results of which we examine in the next part of the chapter.

REFLECTIVE ACTIVITY

List ways in which you think an organisation might be said to *learn*. What evidence would you be looking for to prove it?

3 THE COMING OF THE 'LEARNING ORGANISATION'

If your response to the above exercise was to question the question – to say that it is difficult to imagine how an organisation could be said to learn – you are in good company. Although it is reasonable to think of individuals and even teams of individuals learning, somehow it is difficult to see how an organisation can be said to be learning. Yet if we can talk about an organisation 'changing', what is learning if it is not about changing? The Learning Company Project led to the publication in 1991 of *The Learning Company* in which Mike Pedlar, John Burgoyne and Tom Boydell explained their strategy for what steps could practically be taken to create a 'learning organisation', which they defined (Reid *et al*, 2004; p.274) as:

an organisation which facilitates the learning of all its members and continuously transforms itself.

They provided guidelines under five key headings:

Strategic

- a learning approach to strategy – company policy and strategy continuously being revised as a result of feedback from all members of the organisation

- participative policy-making – everyone encouraged to participate in decision-making and facilities made available for this to happen.

Looking in

- information – the empowerment of everyone through the use of ICT to share information

- formative accounting and control – the opening up of bureaucratic control procedures to review and change by all who use them

- internal exchange – the encouragement of cross-departmental exchange and projects which bring together a variety of business functions and expertise

- reward flexibility – the encouragement of creative ways of rewarding innovating thinking and learning.

Structures

- enabling structures – the breaking down of top-down control structures in favour of a more flexible network wherein information and knowledge can be more easily shared.

Looking out

- boundary workers as external scanners – the encouragement of all staff to be the 'ears and eyes' of the organisation in their interaction with the external world and ensuring that the organisation 'learns' from their feedback

- inter-company learning – the encouragement of all staff to interact with other companies and again ensure that the organisation learns from their feedback.

Learning opportunities

- a learning climate – the creation of an internal culture which supports learning and the exchange of information and knowledge resulting from that learning

- self-development for all – the encouragement of everyone to take ownership of their own learning and development.

Like the 10 criteria for Investors in People, the above 11 principles would be a good basis for any HRD strategy. They would certainly help to bring about the goal expressed in the first half of the definition proposed by Pedlar, Burgoyne and Boydell (1991) – ie 'the facilitation of learning of all its members' – but would they necessarily lead to the second requirement, continuous transformation of the organisation? This is the difference between good HR *transactions* – which the 11 criteria put forward – and a change in what Peter Senge calls our 'mental models' which shape the way we see the world and can thereby lead to a *transformation* of the world (see Reid *et al*, 2004, pp273–4 for another view of learning organisations, which Peter Senge introduced in the early 1990s and which is based around 'systems thinking').

To be fair, Pedlar and his colleagues (1991) recognised that

We can't take you to visit a learning company or bring in a blueprint of what worked elsewhere – it's not like that. The magic of the Learning Company has to be realised from within. The key word is 'transformation' – a radical change in the form and character of what is already there.

The paradox is that since the publication of these guidelines there have been very many other publications with titles like 'Twenty Steps to Becoming a Learning Organisation', suggesting, in contradiction to Pedlar *et al*'s advice, that there is a blueprint to be had.

REFLECTIVE ACTIVITY

You have an opportunity to create from scratch an organisation that meets all 11 criteria listed by Pedlar, Burgoyne and Boydell as those of the learning organisation. What will it look like? Describe how it is structured and give suggestions for its culture, vision and values.

Hint: Start with a structure very different from the familiar top-down hierarchical one regarded as standard. Think of the organisation as a network.

If I were a visitor to the organisation you have been asked to describe in the exercise above, what might I see happening around me? Examples of what I might see, listed under each of the headings cited, could include:

Strategic

- Organisation policies reflect the value of all members, not just those of top management.
- Organisation regularly conducts surveys to take account of both customers' and staff's views.

Looking in

- Accountants and finance people act as consultants and advisers as well as score-keepers and 'bean counters'.
- Organisation recognises the value of teamwork by appropriate rewards.

Structures

- Organisation encourages and supports the creation of informal networks that cut across organisation silos.
- Roles and career paths are flexibly structured so that cross-department working is encouraged.

Looking out

- Staff are encouraged to engage in and learn from activities/projects outside work.

- Regular meetings are held with customers, suppliers and community members to agree on common areas of interest which impact on company policy.

Learning opportunities

- Every member of staff has a self-development plan which is regularly updated, and a budget allocated to them to be spent on personal as well as professional and vocational development.

- Everyone is encouraged to develop coaching and mentoring skills to help and develop colleagues and staff.

If I saw these kinds of activities taking place, it would show that the organisation certainly valued learning, which would meet the requirements of the first half of Pedlar *et al*'s definition of a learning organisation – namely, that it can be seen 'to facilitate the learning of all its members' – but would this be enough to meet the second criterion so that it 'continuously transforms itself'? The capacity of an organisation to change is also at the heart of Peter Senge's definition of a learning organisation, which he sees as one that is 'continually expanding its capacity to create its future'.

In the 1990s the car company Rover were enthusiastic supporters of the concept of the 'learning organisation' and supported staff's learning in many ways – but this was clearly *not* a 'sustainable' development for them because they failed to use that learning to create their own future. The next and final part of the chapter looks at what was the missing link and what any HRD strategy needs if it is to help its organisation survive into the future – ie the translation of learning into corporate knowledge.

REFLECTIVE ACTIVITY

Write down your own definition of 'knowledge'.

What form or forms do you think it might have in an organisation?

4 THE AGE OF THE KNOWLEDGE COMPANY AND THE KNOWLEDGE ECONOMY

The term 'knowledge society' is much in use today but it was first used over 50 years ago by the Daddy of all management gurus, Peter Drucker (see Reid *et al* 2004; p.267). He first suggested that an organisation's health in the future would depend more on its 'intellectual assets' rather than the traditionally valued assets like machinery, land, property and money. This must have sounded very strange to his colleagues 50 years ago, but today the Internet has meant that 'intellectual capital' is seen as a key competitive advantage. As the CEO of Hewlett-Packard said: 'If HP knew what HP knew, it would be unbeatable.' Helping an organisation become aware of what it knows and how it can know more is the central role of HRD.

Philosophers have argued about what knowledge is for thousands of years and in the definitions you have come up with in response to the exercise above you have no doubt added to the debate. We are not about to join in here, but it *is* important to distinguish between 'information' and 'knowledge', which are often used interchangeably, and 'data'. As the word's etymology suggests, 'data' means 'what are given' – ie symbols, some form of record which requires interpretation and only then has meaning or significance. Information is data which has been given a meaning or conveys a message. This word's etymology implies 'what has been given shape'. It is the receiver of the message who gives it shape, meaning. But to do that he/she needs 'knowledge', some form of personal framework within which new information is processed and evaluated (Stewart, 1997; Davenport and Prusak, 1998).

It is generally accepted that what has become known as 'knowledge management' dates from 1995 with the publication of Nonaka and Takeuchi's *Knowledge Creating Company* (see Reid *et al*, 2004; p.275). This brought to public attention the notion of 'tacit' knowledge which was first expressed by a social philosopher, Michael Polanyi, nearly 40 years earlier. Polanyi (1966) said that *all* knowledge (including so-called objective facts of science) involves a personal and subjective component – tacit knowledge. But for this knowledge to be realised and shared it has to be made explicit. Nonaka and Takeuchi suggest that companies can make such knowledge explicit by a process of socialisation, externalisation, combination and internalisation.

Personal knowledge, or what became known as *human capital*, is just one part of what has been described as 'intellectual capital'. The term 'intellectual capital' emerged out of the belief of the then CEO of Sweden's company Skandia in the 1980s that a knowledge-intensive service company's competitive strength in the future would rely less on traditional accounting assets (eg property, equipment, etc) than on less concrete, intangible factors like individual talent, skills and competencies. By the early 1990s it had created an Intellectual Capital function under the direction of Leif Edvinsson, who defined intellectual capital as having two parts: human capital (similar to personal knowledge) and structural capital. In our starter/main case study, human capital would be the knowledge each employee has. But this knowledge would also include what Polanyi calls 'tacit knowledge' as well as the 'explicit knowledge' that might be outcome of a training course, for example. As we will see, it is this kind of knowledge that most organisations are unaware their organisation possesses but which may be vital to them (see Mayo, 2001).

A few years later, as a result of a collaboration between Hubert Saint-Onge of the Canadian Imperial Bank of Commerce and Leif Edvinsson of Skandia, a third component – *customer capital* – was identified as being necessary to define the capital that emerges from synergistic relationships with customers. We give examples of this when we return to our case study at the end of the chapter.

The task of knowledge management is helping individuals and organisations to make explicit what they know (this is often called 'codifying') and to share it in such a form that others can not only use but add to. In our view this provides a bridge to bring individual and organisational learning together. We suggest that a knowledge management strategy provides a much stronger HRD strategy by providing a process whereby individual and collective learning can be codified and shared in such a way as to add value to an organisation's intellectual capital. So the HRD strategy for the future might be more closely linked with valuing people as assets (see Chapter 4).

However, although 'knowledge management' might be thought a step forward in the link between individual and organisational learning, there is an underlying assumption that knowledge somehow exists 'out there' as a 'thing' to be captured. The mainstream view is of knowledge being located in people's heads. Some years ago some organisations appointed so-called 'knowledge officers' whose job it was to 'extract' knowledge essential to the organisation's survival and 'codify' it in some way – ideally in some form of database – but that was never going to work.

REFLECTIVE ACTIVITY

From what you have learned above about the distinctions between data, information and knowledge, think about and/or discuss with colleagues what it is that can be 'captured' in the ways suggested.

Depending on what Senge calls your 'mental model' you might – as your answer to the exercise above – have said that knowledge, information or even data can be captured. If you believe that knowledge can be stored in people's heads, it is likely that you think it can be stored in a computer. But there is another view of knowledge, which is that it is a *social* phenomenon and comes out of our relationships with each other. In such a context 'knowledge' is not an 'it' but a *process*. This leads to the fourth part of 'intellectual capital', the idea of *social capital*, which is the knowledge that comes out of our sharing ideas and knowledge with each other. It is a process that in turn generates *new* knowledge. We suggest that this process is the missing link whereby individual learning becomes group learning, which becomes organisational learning.

It is also the process which is at the heart of the next generation of the WorldWide Web, which goes beyond individual access to information, which may or not become knowledge, but which can become knowledge when shared with others. The best example of this is the notion of 'wikis' and 'wikipedia' through which anyone can contribute to shared knowledge. So knowledge becomes a shared property which can not only be accessed but *changed* and so lead to the kind of transformation that should be the goal of a learning organisation. It should also be the goal of an HRD strategy. But for that to happen we need to 'see' organisations in new ways. This kind of sharing will not happen where organisations operate in top-down control-oriented hierarchies where 'information' (**not** knowledge) is filtered down on a 'need to know' basis. In our starter case study, John Miles and his training officer operated in such a world. This was fine when it was a small operation – but we shall soon see (in the main case study) what happens when it grows and has to meet changing demands both from the inside (diversity of staff) and outside (changing customer expectations).

At this stage the organisation has to be run on more 'organic' principles, and the way staff are developed has to take into account the need for them to continually update themselves. But taking a lesson from above, the organisation must recognise that in developing themselves the staff have knowledge to share which can change the way the organisation operates. In this way every member of staff can help to 'co-create' corporate capability.

Often staff can build what have been called 'communities of practice' in which professional staff meet informally to discuss ways in which they can improve their professional practice (Wenger, 1998). In contrast to 'training', which is often imposed, communities of practice are entered into voluntarily by staff looking to develop themselves through reflection on their practice. The trick for HRD is to encourage such communities, provide them with the support mechanisms they need, and above all, provide the means whereby lessons learned can be spread throughout the organisation. (For more about communities of practice, see Harrison and Kessels, 2004, and Wenger, 1998.)

Finally, here is the definition given to HRD by Harrison and Kessels (2004; pp4–5) who describe it as 'an organisational process' which:

> comprises the skilful planning and facilitation of a variety of formal and informal learning and knowledge processes and experiences, primarily but not exclusively in the workplace, in order that organisational progress and individual potential can be enhanced through the competence, adaptability, commitment and knowledge-creating activity of all who work for the organisation.

KEY ISSUES IN HRD

We now pull together ten key points raised in this chapter:

- An organisation's current approach to HRD may have its roots in the past where the priority was to 'train' staff to meet company objectives by observing 'systematic training' principles.

- HRD has to balance nurturing and 'developing' individuals' skill and knowledge on the one hand and 'training' staff to meet the company's objectives on the other.

- An important contribution to the development of current HRD good practice was emphasis in the 1980s on individuals' 'learning experience'.

- The notion of an organisation also having the capability to learn created a new context in which individuals' learning could have a 'transforming' impact on the organisation itself.

- The structure of the organisation can help or disable learning, thus affecting an HRD strategy's effectiveness.

- For learning to be spread and shared, organisations must be structured like organic networks rather than in the more typical hierarchy.

- For an organisation to be able to 'value' its learning it has to be translated into knowledge which can be shared and codified in such a way as to contribute to an organisation's 'intellectual capital'.

- Knowledge is created and shared through social exchange.

- A key role of an HRD practitioner is to encourage the creation of 'communities of practice' within which knowledge is shared and good practice codified to contribute to an organisation's 'structural capital'.

- In this way an HRD strategy for the future will be to develop an organisation's 'corporate capability' by encouraging the 'co-creation' of new knowledge.

Perhaps there are other key points that you would like to note for yourself.

The main case study in this chapter now follows. It continues the story narrated in the starter case study, although the action now takes place 15 years later. It comprises a report from an HRD consultancy group that the Chief Executive Matt Dyson has brought in to examine the company's development needs and to recommend an appropriate HRD strategy. The recommendations give examples of principles that reflect the themes addressed in the final part of this chapter.

Look at the structure of the organisation as it is currently (as shown in Figure 28), reflecting a growth over the 15 years from 10 outlets to 20, and then read the consultant's report.

Figure 28 DIY Solutions organisation chart

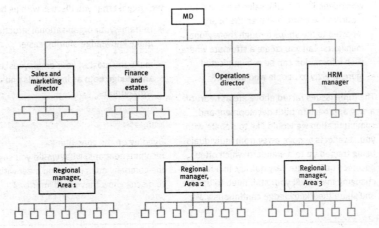

Report to the MD of DIY Solutions

Thank you for the opportunity of spending time with a range of employees in your organisation over the last two months. We have begun to form a better picture of your business, how your current employees fit into this picture, and how they and future employees ought to be developed.

In no order of importance, we list below three observations on your business, how it has changed and how your staff feature. At the end of each observation we have raised one or more questions we would like to discuss further with you.

Observation 1

Growth in number of employees from 20 ten years ago to 150 now. Growth primarily in shop staff as you continue to open up new premises. Units are organised within three geographical areas each under a regional manager who reports directly to you.

- Does the organisation structure best serve your needs, and does it serve the relational and development needs of your staff?

Observation 2

Change in the age, experience of staff recruited to your shops. Over the last ten years recruitment has primarily been in the hands of the three area managers who have the same background as John Miles and yourself – ie engineering. But over the last ten years you have not been able to recruit experienced engineers (which was your former recruitment strategy). According to your regional managers, you seem to be going for previous experience in retail rather than recruiting staff with engineering or indeed DIY expertise. In some outlets there is tension between those with broader retail experience – who also tend to be younger – and the older staff with engineering/DIY experience.

- Can you use the new mix of skills and talent to your advantage?

Observation 3

The directional flow of information is 'top-down'. There have been recent occasions when information needed in the shops has taken some time to percolate down via the regional managers. For example, your sales team recently attended a sales exhibition where they made an important link with an outside company who had developed a new type of patio heater which was fraction of the price of those currently on the market. A number of your shops have been approached recently by local customers stocking up on equipment for the barbecue season. Had this information been available earlier, you could have capitalised on this new market earlier.

- This new information faced two hurdles before it was communicated to the people who needed it. First the sales team had to report to the board and then the board reported to the shops through the regional managers. Can you create a structure where such information can be communicated more directly to people who need it?

The three issues raised above are at heart of a new approach to both development and communication we would like to debate with you. It reflects a move away from individuals being trained up to a standard which often becomes out of date very quickly. In a rapidly changing market all your staff need to update and share their knowledge continuously. We suggest that you think about how you develop your staff in terms of sharing 'knowledge' rather than training individuals against individual standards of competence.

We suggest that you discuss with us how to:

- re-frame your organisational structure to make knowledge-sharing easier
- make the most of your employees' existing knowledge both as individuals and as work-groups.

Your task

Building on the consultant's recommendations, what would you suggest the company does when you meet with them to discuss how they could improve?

EXPLORE FURTHER

Davenport, T. H. and Prusak, L. (1998) *Working Knowledge: How organisations manage what they know.* Boston, MA, Harvard Business School Press
This book is a good introduction to the concept of 'knowledge management'.

Garvey, B. and Williamson, B. (2002) *Beyond Knowledge Management – Dialogue, creativity and the corporate curriculum.* London, FT/Prentice Hall
This book takes a pragmatic approach to HRD emerging out of learning in the workplace. It provides useful case studies to illustrate principles introduced.

Harrison, R. and Kessels, J. (2004) *Human Resource Development in a Knowledge Economy – An organisational view.* London, Palgrave Macmillan
This book makes a case for HRD to be seen as a separate discipline in its own right and for the HRD practitioner to be the catalyst for the creation of new knowledge.

Reid, M. A., Barrington, H. and Brown, M. (2004) *Human Resource Development – Beyond training interventions,* 7th edition. London, CIPD
This book is a good introduction to how HRD has developed from being seen as 'training', and is a good source of reference for a variety of HRD practices.

Wenger, E. (1998) *Communities of Practice: Learning, meaning and identity.* Cambridge, Cambridge University Press
This book introduces the concept of 'communities of practice' and how they can be enabled to grow in an organisation.

CHAPTER 25

Corporate social responsibility and sustainable HRM

Mary Hartog, Clive Morton *and* Michael Muller-Camen

INTRODUCTION

In this chapter we examine the growing importance of corporate social responsibility and the implications that concepts such as sustainability have on HRM and the HR function.

LEARNING OUTCOMES

By the end of this chapter readers should be able to:

- understand the business rationale for corporate social responsibility (CSR)
- describe links between CSR and HRM
- evaluate the role HR departments have in developing CSR
- examine ethical issues that can arise when operating globally.

This chapter is structured in five parts. The first part introduces sustainability issues facing organisations. The second examines links between CSR and HRM. We then in the third part consider the role HR departments can play in developing CSR by implementing the process and in the fourth part by making it sustainable. The final, fifth part of the chapter examines ethical issues that are faced by companies that operate internationally.

The chapter concludes with the main case study.

Reference sources named within the chapter may be looked up in the *References and further reading* section at the end of the book.

A UK water company had been in the public sector until privatisation, and thereafter the goals of profit and shareholder value loomed large in the mind of top management. Although in the public sector the dominant theme had been 'service', many employees had joined the organisation to pursue professional goals and standards. After privatisation, top management had changed their focus rapidly towards commercial requirements, but further down the organisation the public sector values and culture remained rooted in 'how we do things around here'. There was a desire for change at the top but a feeling of insecurity below, leading to inflexibility and rigidity.

An ambitious change programme was launched, designed to introduce flexibility, working across boundaries and a commercial outlook. 'Transformation Journey' teams were formed composed of 'diagonal-slice multi-disciplined' groups to unite levels in the hierarchy and departments. They were encouraged to choose their own projects and given the freedom to do so. Management were disappointed when 90% of the Journey teams chose community-based projects such as redecorating a hostel for the homeless or producing a children's garden at a hospice when the expectation had been that they would choose ways of reducing costs, improving efficiency and increasing profit. However, having given groups the choice, there was no going back and the project continued.

Some four years later top management wished to diversify the business and brought in consultants to advise on the feasibility of selling other products to the existing (monopoly) customer base. The consultants duly reported to the board that they had been pleasantly surprised by their surveys. 'Your customers trust you and this gives a good base for further business initiatives.' The executives congratulated themselves, assuming the credit for efficient and effective management of water resources and disposal of sewage. 'No, no!' the consultants quickly responded. 'Your customers expect that as part of paying their water bills – the source of the trust is the work your employees do in the community!'

The company went ahead with the new venture. What was an unexpected by-product of a successful change programme became a new business. The view of the outside, for those participating in the Transformation Journey teams, encouraged flexibility and teamwork. A win/win/win all round!

Questions for discussion

1 What lessons can management learn about the relationship between society and business from this example?

2 What would you say to shareholders of the company to convince them that 'community work' can contribute to the bottom line?

1 CORPORATE SOCIAL RESPONSIBILITY AND SUSTAINABLE ORGANISATIONS

Over recent years the concept of corporate social responsibility (CSR) that first emerged in the 1950s and 1960s in the USA has become widely accepted by multinational corporations and governments. This is because of the recognition of sustainability as a management concept, the increasing importance of non-government organisations, the growth of socially responsible investment, consumer pressure and recent corporate scandals. It is expected that CSR has, and will have, a strong impact on corporate reporting practices, investment strategies, the management of supply chains and public relations (Matten and Moon, 2007).

But what is CSR? For the purpose of this chapter we have chosen the following definition, which acknowledges that firms serve a broad range of stakeholders and which highlights the importance of striking a balance between economic performance, meeting the stakeholders' expectations and responsibility towards society (Hopkins, 2006; p.214):

> CSR is concerned with treating the stakeholders of the firm ethically or in a socially responsible manner. Stakeholders exist both within a firm and outside. The aim of social responsibility is to create higher and higher standards of living, while preserving the profitability of the corporation, for its stakeholders both within and outside the corporation.

THE LINK BETWEEN CSR, SUSTAINABILITY AND HRM

The PWC Global Survey 2003 of 1,000 CEOs entitled *Leadership Responsibility and Growth in Uncertain Times* defines 'sustainability' in the following terms:

> We prefer the single word 'sustainability' – borrowed from the world of sustainable development and in this context to mean adding economic, environmental and social value through a company's core business function. Another way of saying it is 'Doing business with your grandchildren's interests at heart.'

The link between sustainability, CSR and HRM is aptly demonstrated in the following quote (Etzioni, 2001):

> The challenge in any multicultural society is to gain a shared framework in order to flourish.

Etzioni argues that

> the most profound problems that plague modern societies will be fully addressed only when those whose basic needs have been met shift their priorities up Maslow's scale of human needs. That is, only after they accord a higher priority to gaining and giving affection, cultivating culture, becoming involved in community service and seeking spiritual fulfilment.

Etzioni was aiming this at individuals in society. This chapter will argue that the same applies to organisations that make up the institutions in our society and as was demonstrated in *Beyond World Class* (Morton, 1998), which suggested that the individual, the organisation and the community needed each other for growth. The thesis was that 'No organisation or company is an island and can hope to maintain or go beyond being world-class unless it operates in partnership with the world outside the factory gates.'

WHAT IS THE BUSINESS RATIONALE FOR CSR?

CSR is closely linked to the sustainability of organisations. Research has shown that three conditions must be in place for organisations to demonstrate sustainability. Firstly, organisations need world-class practices to ensure efficiency, effectiveness and competitiveness. Secondly, the organisation must be 'extrovert' and continually scan the horizon taking in data on trends, customer needs, community views and supplier interaction. Thirdly, agility is important. Based on the first two conditions the organisation is in a position to change or modify direction to ensure sustainability. The premise is that it is 'in the business interest' to pursue CSR policies within this model (Morton, 2003).

Alternative models take as their premise that businesses have to be forced by law or 'licence to operate' to act on behalf of 'stakeholders' or society as a whole. They are guided by external pressures such as industry and market standards, the media, industry reputation, pressure groups and public opinion. Other models point to the perceived need of businesses to advertise their CSR credentials to gain reputation. This may be a product of the first premise, 'the business case', which suggests 'I don't mind doing the right thing if it pays!'

The growth of CSR cannot be separated from the 'stakeholder philosophy'. Only a generation ago businesses saw themselves as solely responsible to shareholders. Indeed, even today, some business leaders would agree with this, protesting that others outside the business have no influence on the conduct of business. In contrast, the stakeholder philosophy assumes that an organisation has not only shareholders but a number of key relationships with groups such as employers, customers and the community (see Figure 29).

Figure 29 What are our key relationships?

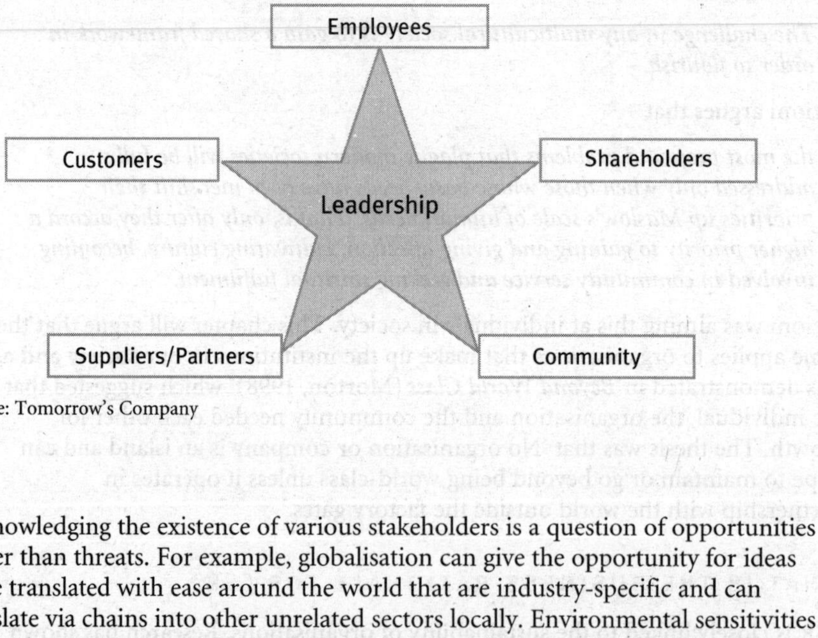

Source: Tomorrow's Company

Acknowledging the existence of various stakeholders is a question of opportunities rather than threats. For example, globalisation can give the opportunity for ideas to be translated with ease around the world that are industry-specific and can translate via chains into other unrelated sectors locally. Environmental sensitivities can with positive approaches lead to new business (for example, BodyShop) or at least prevent losses (such as the consumer reaction against Shell over Brent Spar). Consumer groups can help rather than hinder, and knowledge-based companies have 70 to 80% of their assets (intellectual capital) 'owned' in the brains of their employees. Taken together, on the one hand there are more demanding employees, customers and communities who expect their individual needs and values to be respected, but on the other hand this gives an opportunity for greater dialogue and contribution that can aid the objectives of the enterprise.

The approach is not without its critics (see, for example, Stoney and Winstanley, 2001). The term 'stakeholder' is open to misinterpretation in that the only people who *own* the business are shareholders and therefore are the only 'stakeholders' to be able, by policy, to grow the business or cease trading. The main criticism of the stakeholder approach is the supposed possibility of confusion and possible removal of concentration on the 'bottom line'. One answer might be that the results can be seen over the long term from stakeholder or 'inclusive' companies such as Marks & Spencer and Boots – the bottom line is the winner over the long term rather than just the short-term horizon.

TOMORROW'S COMPANY

In 1995, the Royal Society of Arts and Manufactures developed the concept of 'Tomorrow's Company'. Such a company would compete at world-class levels through the adoption of an inclusive approach. In terms of vision 'Tomorrow's Company' places a positive value on each of its relationships. Firstly, it works in partnership with stakeholders and maintains a healthy reputation – in other words, a strong licence to operate. Secondly, it has an inclusive approach to business leadership. This means accepting the need for change and rating long-term 'trust' relationships higher than short-term low-trust relationships as a source of competitive advantage, thus reinterpreting directors' duties – that is, to stakeholders not just shareholders – and producing annual reports that mean something to all stakeholders, not just obeying company law. Thirdly, an inclusive approach to people is recommended, which is discussed in more depth below. Fourthly, an inclusive approach to investment needs is required, which avoids an exclusive concern with immediate returns and puts a higher emphasis on fundamentals and future prospects. Finally, there has to be an inclusive approach to society. For example, business leaders can help create a climate for success, by developing community partnerships, by working with the government, by improving business representation and networking structures, and by clearing the way for the growth of small businesses. Overall, these elements will create value as indicated by Figure 30.

REFLECTIVE ACTIVITY

In respect of an organisation or a business with which you are familiar, think through the rationale behind CSR and dealing with stakeholders.

Is it the moral case – ie should we be treating those external to the firm in this sort of way?

Is it the 'licence to operate' – ie if we do not maintain a good reputation, we go out of business?

Is it the 'business case' where good relationships built by CSR bring additional business and good publicity?

Or is it a mixture of all three?

Figure 30 What does success look like?

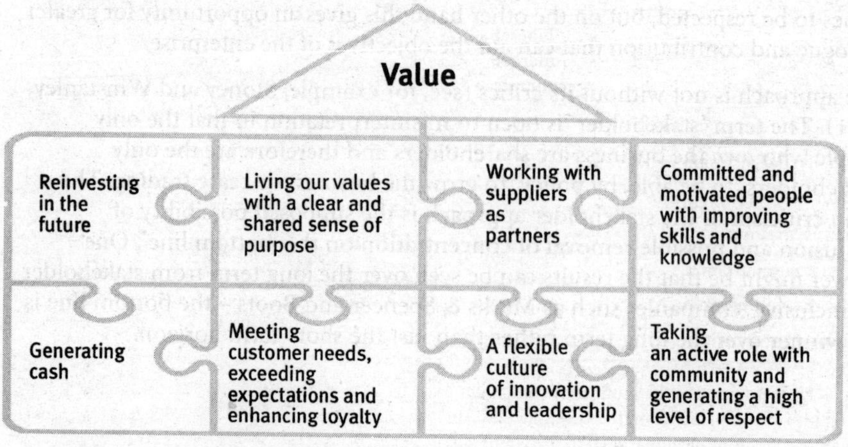

Source: Tomorrow's Company

2 CSR AND EMPLOYEES

After examining how it can be positive for an organisation to engage in CSR, we now want to look at the implications for HRM. According to 'Tomorrow's Company' the following people issues are preconditions for success. 'Tomorrow's Company':

- anticipates and responds to changes in employment patterns and in individuals' expectations

- supports individuals in developing their capabilities

- motivates people to make the best possible contribution

- adapts its organisational structure to enable people's contributions to be used fully

- participates in exploring the future of work.

What can this mean in practice? Because there is so far hardly any literature about the link between CSR and HRM, we now turn to the results of a study of HR issues in CSR reported by Muller-Camen *et al* (2008). Over recent years most global firms have started to publish CSR reports annually although their names reflect different ways of saying that – for instance, we have a Global Citizenship Report (eg Microsoft), a Corporate Responsibility Report (eg GlaxoSmithKline), a Human Resources and Social Report (eg Deutsche Post), a Social Environment Report (eg British Telecom), a Sustainability Report (eg Johnson & Johnson) and similar titles. The study, based on an analysis of 59 reports of the world's 100 largest corporations, found that five HR practices are commonly reported and, at least for these companies, are compatible with CSR. We now discuss each item separately according to how often they are disclosed in the reports (see Table 49). In our analysis, we differentiate between companies

Table 49 Social disclosure on selected items in CSR reports by Fortune 100 companies

	Liberal market economies+	%	Cooperative market economies+	%	All	%
Number of reports analysed	26		33		59	
Diversity and inclusion policy	26	100	25	76	51	86
Health and safety reporting	22	85	30	91	52	83
Extensive training	21	81	28	85	49	82
Direct communication	19	73	23	70	42	71
Indirect communication	12	46	26	79	38	64
Employment stability	3	12	14	42	17	29

Notes: + Figures represent the number of companies in each category. Liberal market economies includes CSR reports of companies from the USA, the UK, Australia and Canada. Cooperative market economies includes corporations headquartered in the Netherlands, Belgium, Germany, Switzerland, France, Japan and Italy.

Source: Muller-Camen *et al* (2006)

from 'liberal market' economies and those from 'cooperative market' economies (Hall and Soskice, 2001). The former consists of organisations from Anglo-Saxon countries and the later of companies from continental Europe and Japan.

DIVERSITY AND INCLUSION POLICY

The large majority of companies analysed disclose information on diversity and inclusion (see Table 49). For example, in its Global Citizenship Report 2004, Hewlett-Packard gives statistics on the ethnic and gender balance of its US workforce, states its diversity policy, and gives an overview of the programmes to promote diversity and the awards it has received. One reason for the popularity of diversity is the high importance attached to diversity management and equal opportunity in Anglo-Saxon countries. This is not only because of legal pressure but also because there is a business case for diversity management (see Chapter 6). In contrast, diversity management is still not fully accepted in continental Europe and Japan. This is also shown by our data, in that only 76% of companies from these regions – and thus significantly less compared to Anglo-Saxon firms – have a diversity management and inclusion policy. Some of those not disclosing information about diversity, however, give data on gender equality and disability (Muller-Camen *et al*, 2008).

HEALTH AND SAFETY REPORTING

Health and safety together with diversity and inclusion are the most frequently disclosed social indicator according to the CSR reports analysed (see Table 49). Most of the firms that do not disclose information on this item are banks and insurance companies where it is less of an issue. In contrast to industry, differences between business systems are minor. A good example for health and safety reporting is BP's Sustainability Report 2003, which describes safety policies, provides data on safety performance and reports on the improvement of standards. In contrast to diversity, international differences are not obvious (Muller-Camen *et al*, 2008).

TRAINING

Most CSR reports provide data on training initiatives and data on expenditure and number of employees covered. International differences are not obvious. Nevertheless, in the absence of standardised reporting practices it is difficult to estimate the extent to which they are committed to extensive training and to compare and contrast this data between firms (Muller-Camen *et al*, 2008).

DIRECT COMMUNICATION

Employees will contribute to enhancing organisational performance if the company shares with them information on issues such as financial performance, strategy and operational measures (see Chapter 19 on communication). Only very few CSR reports disclose information on this aspect. Nevertheless, what they do is provide insights into methods of employee communication. For example, BP's Sustainability Report 2003 shows results from an attitude survey and introduces BP's intranet-based worldwide complaints tool OpenTalk. Whereas there is no major difference between business systems in the disclosure of direct communication efforts, a difference exists with indirect communication (Muller-Camen *et al*, 2008).

INDIRECT COMMUNICATION

International CSR standards suggest that businesses should respect the the right to join unions and the right to collective bargaining (see Chapter 17 on employment relations). It is therefore not surprising that 64% of the reports disclose information on how the respective corporations deal with trade unions and employee representatives. However, whereas such information was found in 79% of the CSR reports from continental European and Japanese firms, only 46% of Anglo-Saxon firms, and thus significantly less, disclose information on this item. This applies in particular to those US MNCs that are non-union firms in the United States. They either do not touch this issue or state that although they respect the law, they prefer direct communication (Muller-Camen *et al*, 2008). An example of this is IBM, which expresses such a view in its Corporate Responsibility Report 2002 (p.36):

> *Throughout the company's history, IBM has respected the rights of employees to organise, and has made managers at all levels aware of those rights. It is our long-standing belief, however, that the interests of IBM and its employees are best served when managers and employees deal directly with each other. However, IBM complies with legal requirements worldwide regarding employee and third-party involvement.*

IBM's report does not show any examples of dialogue with trade unions. This is in strong contrast to many continental European and Japanese MNCs who describe negotiations with employee representatives (eg the European Works Council) and offer a much more positive view of social partnership with works councils and unions (Muller-Camen *et al*, 2008). An example is the following statement from the Belgian/Dutch finance firm Fortis (Fortis Sustainability Report 2004, p.34):

> At Fortis we attach great importance to smooth and effective consultations with works councils and unions. We ensure that employee representatives receive the time and resources necessary (meeting-rooms, electronic communication, etc) to fulfil their role properly. Their role is twofold: joining in deliberations and talks on strategy, growth of profitability and employment opportunities at the different Fortis entities and at Fortis as a whole and, additionally, protecting the interests of employees collectively and individually. They also make sure that employees who find themselves in conflict with their superior possess a published and documented procedure for lodging an appeal. Senior management all the way up to the CEO and COO exercise their personal efforts to provide relevant company information first-hand to the local works councils and the European Works Council of Fortis.

STABLE EMPLOYMENT

Stable employment is not generally perceived as part of CSR by multinational companies, as demonstrated by the relatively low reporting. The rationale for employment stability is that otherwise a high-trust relationship will not develop and workers will not fully cooperate in becoming more efficient and productive, if their jobs are at risk. The Japanese car producer Toyota is one of the few firms that state explicitly in their CSR reports that they offer stable employment (Toyota Environmental and Social Report 2004, p.72):

> Stable employment that avoids simple layoffs and terminations is a key pillar in the relationship of mutual trust between labour and management. In addition, the Toyota management system is based largely on bringing out to the greatest extent employee abilities, reasoning skills and creativity. Consequently, the simple disposal of human resources, a major management asset, not only damages the relationship of trust but also hinders the spontaneous display of ability by employees. Accordingly, Toyota always takes a medium- to long-term management perspective and has made the realisation and continuation of stable employment through all possible employment policies the fundamental basis of its management philosophy.

Although other CSR reports are not as explicit as Toyota, a high percentage of European/Japanese corporations (42%) report on how they have tried to downsize and restructure in a socially responsible manner. For example, the Dutch ABN Amro Bank explicitly discusses in its Sustainability Report 2004 (p.59) the dilemma a major workforce reduction in 2004 caused and the communication, consultation, training, outplacement advice and internal redeployment activities that were taken in order to minimise the impact on the workforce. In contrast, Anglo-Saxon firms usually do not report on the handling of restructuring in their CSR reports and/or seem to offer much less assistance than continental European firms. This difference also affects operations of the same firms. For example, the Dutch insurance company AEGON disclosed in its Corporate Responsibility Report 2003 that staff reductions in the Netherlands will be achieved via natural attrition whereas in the USA and UK reorganisation will involve compulsory redundancies (Muller-Camen *et al*, 2008).

3 HOW CAN CSR BE IMPLEMENTED?

The Centre for Tomorrow's Company has shown that those companies that are inclusive in their relationships inside and with their communities are consistently more profitable and more able to make strategic choices for the future. We know that individuals need organisations in which to develop and that communities need both companies and people to contribute for mutual benefit. Organisations benefit from being active in the community and HR needs to champion such policies. Looked at deeply, HR can see that its own strategies can benefit from linking with and supporting CSR policies.

The challenge for HR today is to define their role in ways that will give the best contribution to the sustainability of the organisation that employs them. We have seen that HR practices must contribute to organisational sustainability and environmental sustainability. This implies that there should be a shared responsibility between employer and employee concerning their contribution to sustainability – hence a linking together on vision, values, ethos and ethics, purpose (of the enterprise, its worth and products). We know that HRM practices that involve and engage employees improve productivity and individual well-being. Similarly HR practices that encourage protection of the environment have multiple benefits – eg a 'cycle to work' scheme where the employee benefits from an interest-free loan, and via salary sacrifice, reduces tax liability, and the employer gains through less car parking and fitter employees.

If the initial premise for a sustainable organisation is accepted, HRM policies should be focused on engaging employees towards those mutually beneficial goals. Creating and maintaining the 'extrovert' organisation requires employers to be continually scanning the horizon for opportunities and relationships for the organisation, feeding back perceptions and measures on how the organisation is succeeding in markets and sectors, with suppliers and customers and in wider CSR terms within the communities that it operates. If employees can be encouraged to be proactive in their commitments, a sustainable virtuous cycle can exist. This is shown in Figure 31.

The greatest HRM policy and practice contribution towards success in this area is encouraging change in a supportive atmosphere of trust. The values of the sustainable organisation should include 'openness, transparency, honesty and integrity'. In this, the approach taken here links closely with the evolved approach of corporate governance and should come naturally to the organisation that pursues the approach outlined in this chapter. The trust that is the necessary ingredient for change is a product of how an organisation treats others – whether employees, suppliers, customers or communities. Again, this is the 'oil' for a sustainable virtuous cycle which should be reflected in the HR policies and practice.

Figure 31 Products of the three-legged stool: mission accomplished – sustainability

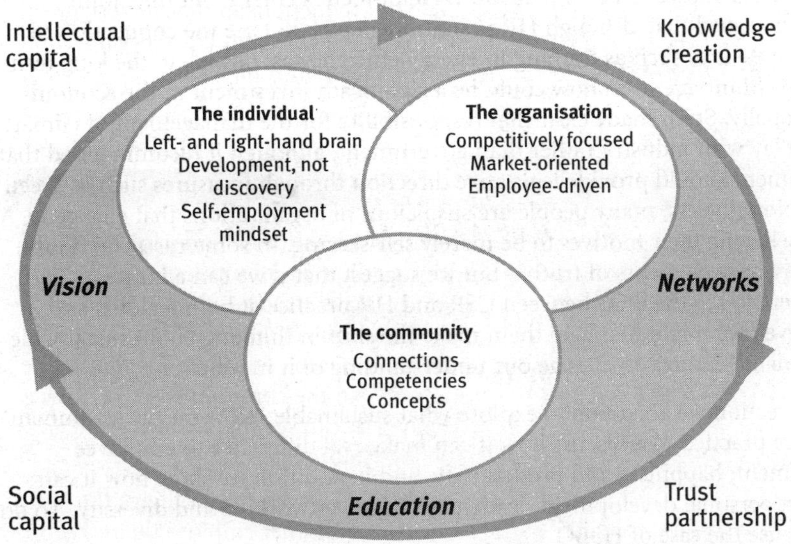

Intellectual
capital

Knowledge
creation

The individual
Left- and right-hand brain
Development, not
discovery
Self-employment
mindset

The organisation
Competitively focused
Market-oriented
Employee-driven

Vision

Networks

The community
Connections
Competencies
Concepts

Social
capital

Education

Trust
partnership

Source: Morton (1998; p.276)

REFLECTIVE ACTIVITY

Is the idea of sustainable human resource management just the latest fad or does it have any enduring substance to it? Indeed, is it just another idea or does it have something practical to offer? (Some might even say it is a contradiction in terms.)

Brainstorm your ideas and share them with a friend. Then make a note of your key thoughts before reading on.

At the end of this chapter come back to them and see if you have changed your point of view.

4 SUSTAINABLE HRM AND THE HR FUNCTION

Cynics might say that corporate social responsibility has little or nothing to do with human resource management – after all, most HR practitioners have enough to do tackling the day-to-day jobs of recruitment, absence management, disciplinary matters and training and development without having to worry about saving the planet as well. In any case, most CSR departments are separate from HR and have a role more in common with the marketing department and the task of brand management. Indeed, some would go so far as to say that saving the planet is not the job of business, let alone the HR department. However, the Stern Report (2006) might change a few minds. It forecast that climate change has the potential to shrink the economy by 20%. In response, the Chartered Institute of Personnel and Development's chief economist John Philpott argued that although HR practitioners may not see the connection or regard measures such as training in energy efficiency as 'hassle', in the long term this type of intervention now could be a significant investment in the economy. Additionally, Stern made clear that responsibility for the management of climate change lay with industry rather than government, although it recommended that government should provide legislative direction through measures such as green taxes. Nonetheless, many people are suspicious of organisations that engage in CSR, believing their motives to be merely self-serving. In some cases, no doubt, this may have elements of truth – but we suggest that if we can educate managers to see the links between CSR and HR practice at both a global and local level, we might just help them make the shift in thinking about sustainable HRM viable enough to change our understanding of it in practice.

In this section we are going to explore what sustainable HRM means for human resource practice. We discuss how it can make real difference to employee engagement, happiness and productivity, and in addition we show how it can support personal development, leadership and teamworking and diversity. To do this we use the case of HSBC.

HSBC is a global bank which decided five years ago to take a global approach to CSR – one that would serve to join up its global workforce. To do this it took up the concept of business partnership with three charitable organisations working with global environmental projects: Botanical Gardens Conservation International, The World Wildlife Fund and Earthwatch. HSBC donated in the region of £25 million to help fund the work of these new business partners. Partnership was also developed in a practical way with over 2,000 HSBC employees sponsored to take part in two-week educational field trips to work on environmental projects in places like Amazonia and Belarus, with scientists and conservationists. Significantly, the learning experience did not stop there. Taking the learning back home has become an important feature of this project, and although not initially planned for, it serves to demonstrate the potential benefits of this type of global CSR for people and organisation development generally. And it is this potential we would argue that HR has to pay attention to and actively support.

Based on the experience that HSBC participants had working on a global environmental project, it was thought that this would motivate them to set up local projects when they returned home. And indeed, approximately 50% of participants were sufficiently motivated to do something either in their local community or in their workplace that improved or contributed to environmental sustainability on their return. But more significantly, the project brought surprises in respect of personal and organisational development. For example, an employee who was known to be particularly shy, returned self-confident and able to share her learning with her colleagues. Other examples included employees gaining a better understanding of other cultures, having met people of different nationalities in the global CSR project teams, while others reported that they were more able to work with people who had strong personalities, and able to recognise and work more effectively with people who had different learning styles. These outcomes were commonly reported, and although one might expect participants to return full of enthusiasm for environmental concerns and a greater appreciation of CSR, what had not been expected was the extent to which it would engage teams.

An evaluation was undertaken by the Cambridge Programme for Industry to look at the programme's impact on both individual development and organisation development. This discovered that for many participants the experience had been deep and transformative. One explanation is that the experience of taking part in the project had been a meaningful activity for many employees, linking with their personal passions for the environment. People met others and had important new experiences. This type of learning process is believed to help loosen our mental models – in other words, our perspectives of how we see the world. In this case it helped employees see the link between the global environmental issues and our day-to-day lives and work practices.

By linking into the personal values of employees through the CSR project and creating awareness of the links between global issues and local practice, the company had created an opportunity to align personal values with espoused corporate values, and in the process improved the psychological contract between employees and the employer (see Chapter 19). It also created a feel-good factor, raising employee satisfaction and pride in the organisation, all of which have a positive impact on employee retention and productivity.

The CPI survey showed that 74% of participants reported increased development of skills and competencies in team work and leadership following their experience in the CSR project. Another 84% reported building and maintaining relationships. They further noted that line managers had not been prepared for the potential impact this project had for team engagement and thus they could not always take the opportunity to embed the learning that this CSR project generated.

CSR projects like that of HSBC's have the potential to impact on organisation development and learning – but this potential will only be fully realised if work is done to make sure that the transfer of learning from the project to the workplace is made easier by creating and maintaining a culture of learning and support. This will entail training those in line management with skills in coaching and facilitation if the benefits of such interventions are to help the development of the organisation. This is a job for the human resource development practitioner. It is this appreciation of human capital theory in practice that will help a company capitalise on learning opportunities that this type of CSR intervention can create, effectively facilitating the process of individual and organisational learning and change. In so doing, it will help create many changes in attitudes, and further understanding in the culture of the organisation towards what CSR can achieve and what sustainable HRM means in practice. Finally, as well as the benefits this type of CSR activity can bring in terms of brand management, with added value created through employee engagement, it will be positive for the reputation of the company itself as an employer of choice. For HR practitioners getting on the inside of the CSR agenda and using it to facilitate sustainable HR can add value and improve HR's contribution to the organisation as a strategic business player (Redington, 2005).

We can understand this in the following way. We are all connected to one another and live interdependent lives, pooling resources from the same planetary source. To understand sustainability in this fashion connects the planet to all our lives in communities and workplaces in a way that goes further than what we traditionally think of as the role of business and management.

So what does all this mean for the relationship between HRM, CSR and their respective tasks and functions? Firstly, we would suggest that these functions ought to be strategically integrated into the business. Although CSR is perceived mainly to have an external or extrovert function and HR is seen to serve an internal function, we suggest that these traditional divisions are in part to blame for a lack of integration and joined-up thinking. Better communication between HR teams and CSR implementers could make sure that HR issues figure prominently within CSR planning, reporting and target-setting, and in turn HR could better support and complement the efforts of CSR departments in terms of recruitment, people management and individual and organisational learning. Also, companies could include communication between management and staff, staff associations, works councils and unions within the scope of CSR stakeholder dialogue, with the aim of fostering environmental sustainability. Selection criteria for HR staff and general managers might include consideration of environmental knowledge and skills and/or commitment to developing corporate socially responsible work practices. Compensation and reward policies should aim to encourage eco-initiatives by employees, particularly initiatives that would have relevance and add value to the workplace and local communities in which the business operates. Job descriptions could include responsibilities for environmental goals and training and development provided to increase ecological awareness and foster eco-centric values appropriate to and in support of the vision and mission of the company (Ramus and Steger, 2000). The HRD practitioner has a particular job to support the creation of an ethical learning culture – one that is itself sustainable and contributes beyond the bottom line. Taken together, CSR could encourage companies to develop more long-term HR strategies that create win/wins for employees and employers alike.

5 MNCS, CSR AND ETHICS

So far we have argued that any organisation should at least to some extent fulfil the expectations of its stakeholders and behave in a socially responsible way. However, there may be different standards of acceptable or desirable behaviour in different countries (Jackson, 2000). Over the last decades, MNCs have been in the headlines for and been accused of not fulfilling ethical requirements. For example, well-known firms such as British Aerospace and the German electronic group Siemens have been involved in corruption scandals. In particular, they were accused of paying bribes to government officials to get large contracts. Another problem, which has become particularly obvious in the textile and footwear industries, is sweat-shops and child labour. Companies such as Levi-Strauss and Nike have been accused of exploiting workers in Third World countries by working with suppliers that violate labour standards. This particularly applies to plants that use child or forced labour, have an unsafe working environment, do not allow workers to unionise, require extensive working weeks and pay wages that do not meet employees' basic needs (Kolk and van Tulder, 2004). A final issue is discrimination. For example, in many countries gender discrimination is still common and often not challenged by the subsidiaries of multinational firms.

There are basically three approaches that MNCs can take to deal with these issues. The first one is ethical relativism. Basically, this means adapting corporate practices to the ethical standards of the host country. However, these vary widely. For example, the Corruption Perception Index of Transparency International shows that although in some countries such as Finland and Denmark there is almost no corruption amongst public officials and politicians, corruption is rampant in Nigeria and Bangladesh. The second option of dealing with moral obligations is ethical ethnocentrism. Firms that follow such an approach will apply ethical standards common in the home country to their operations abroad. In some cases this can lead to subsidiaries of multinational companies following higher standards and being more socially responsible than local companies. The downside is, however, the imposition of HR practices that do not fit host-country requirements. For example, a US MNC may forbid the recruitment of relatives of current employees, which could be normal practice in other countries. The third approach is ethical universalism. This assumes that there are worldwide standards that can be applied universally. A manifestation of this approach is the international code of conduct from organisations such as the OECD, the UN and the International Labour Organisation (ILO). For example, the ILO suggests that MNCs should follow HR practices such as stable employment, equal opportunities, recognition of the right to form and belong to a union, and training and consultation with employee representatives (Dowling, Welch and Schuler, 1999).

Today, most large MNCs try to impose global standards based on one or more of the internationally accepted codes of conduct. They draw up their own code of conduct and often introduce a monitoring system. In addition, employees are trained how to deal with ethical dilemmas.

KEY ISSUES: CSR AND HRM

We now pull together ten key points about CSR and HRM raised in this chapter:

- CSR takes a stakeholder approach that recognises the overlapping interests of stakeholders – ie the business, the community, employers and employees – and pays equal regard to them, and it takes both an external and an internal focus on its affairs.

- CSR is in the interest of the business to pursue. CSR can support the business brand and reputation and help the business become an employer of choice.

- Organisations need to prepare fully to use the potential impact that involvement in CSR can achieve for the business.

- Tomorrow's Company tells us that successful companies adopt partnership, stakeholding, inclusivity and trust, and commitment to the long term.

- HR practices such as diversity, health and safety, training, direct and indirect communication and stable employment are compatible with CSR.

- Values of sustainable organisations include openness, transparency, honesty and integrity.

- If HR practitioners see the link between global issues and local concerns of running the business, it will make a significant investment in the economy.

- Sustainable HRM requires joined-up thinking – the concept that CSR looks outward and HR looks inward is no longer helpful.

- Sustainable HRM supports responsive long-term policies and practices that promise to create win/wins for all.

- Major ethical issues facing international firms are bribery, gender discrimination and child labour.

Perhaps there are other key points that you would like to note for yourself.

The main case study in this chapter now follows. It gives an example of an HR/CSR issue faced by many organisations that has strong ethical implications for developing the business in a global economy.

MAIN CASE STUDY

Look at the description of the case set out below. Then decide on the recommendations that you would make as an HR manager for dealing with the issues raised. Try to think beyond the level of a 'quick fix' or simple solutions and to draw on the lessons learned from this chapter.

The Wellness at Work Foundation is an established private sector health company that has provided services for business organisations in the United Kingdom for the past 25 years. Although it does not provide private medical insurance, it supplies a range of services that support companies in achieving their occupational health and well-being policies, such as employee counselling and assistance programmes, and return-to-work services for staff who have suffered serious illness. In recent years it has opened more than ten small hospitals providing minor surgical procedures and optical and dental services for employees and companies who have private health insurance. More recently, it has opened corporate gymnasiums in five companies in the South-East, and has devised corporate training programmes and published advice on topics such as stress management, keeping fit, and managing absence and retention through well-being for HR practitioners and line managers. In 2003 it decide to expand the business by setting up a partnership company in an emerging market in one of the international emerging economies.

A small hospital has been established in Tiger City in the free-trade zone, which allows international business to set up with local partners who hold a minimum of a 51% share in the business. This has proved to be an attractive proposition for local entrepreneurs who can stand to make considerable profits from partnering with international companies – businesses that are well established without having the expertise of running the business..

When the company was set up in Tiger City, a senior executive was sent by the UK business partner to work alongside an appointed executive for the local entrepreneur. In addition, several key staff with a range of experience including marketing and sales, hospital management and administration, and nursing and ancillary services were also sent out from the UK on fixed-term two-year

contracts to establish the business. It was anticipated that these employees would return to the UK after that time to resume their posts. The aim was that once the business was established, it would employ local staff and international staff employed on local contracts.

Whereas multinationals traditionally offered high salaries, rewards and status for expatriate workers, this is no longer guaranteed. There is growing competition for jobs and an increasing desire fuelled by national legislation to employ locals wherever possible. However, it is still a period of transition in which some locals hold senior positions based on who they are and who they know, rather than on merit, and the gap between rich and poor is so great that many locals who would want to work lack the education and skills required to do the job. The cost of living is also rising, with a property boom to match business growth. This has led to a steep rise in rental accommodation in the past year.

In the four years in which the business has been operating, it has successfully established a number of its products in Tiger City and is beginning to establish a healthy client base. It has yet to break even in terms of the investment that has gone into establishing the business in this international market, but with predicted growth it is on target to do so by 2012. With the exception of the senior executive, all the original UK employees have now returned to the UK. None, however, has remained with the company; all have chosen to move on.

A common point of feedback in exit interviews has been that 'The profit-before-service position demanded by the local entrepreneur created tension and concerns of a professional nature.' In this environment individuals felt unable to voice their concerns and felt they had to keep their heads down and try to get on with their jobs. This, they claimed, created stress because they felt at times that professional integrity and quality of service was being compromised, and indeed, they expressed the view that the reputation of the company itself might also have been damaged. Deeply affected by the experience, these employees reported a need for 'a fresh start somewhere else' on their return to the UK.

With high turnover of both UK staff before or on return to the UK and a 25% turnover in new hires since 2005 of international staff that have joined this venture, the UK partner decided to conduct a confidential employee opinion survey similar to its UK Quality of Working Life survey to elicit feedback from employees. Additionally, it sent a quality inspection team to Tiger City to undertake a quality audit of practices and procedures. The inspection quality team has yet to report back its findings and recommendations, but in the meantime the HR department has analysed the results of the employee survey. Some of the key findings are:

- 60% of staff describe feeling stressed at work and confirm the feeling that there is a tension between service and profit that is causing anxiety.

- A number of staff report being made to feel uncomfortable by a memo sent out by the local entrepreneur's representative prior to the visit of the quality audit team which stated: 'You can say what you like – please feel free to express your opinions: you will not be fired.'

- International staff (many of whom had been recruited from the UK by way of Internet recruitment and telephone interview) reported that their expectations with regard to pay, resettlement allowance, help with accommodation, employment visas, holiday entitlement and hours of work were not as good as presented in the recruitment process. For example, the resettlement allowance was not sufficient to cover the recent rise in rents in the local area, which is booming, and even where the company had provided accommodation in property that it owned, the allowance did not cover replacement of worn or soiled furniture and broken equipment.

Holiday entitlement was calculated on a seven-day week as opposed to a five-day week as in the UK. The consequent 45 days' holiday per annum, with only one day for Christmas and no bank holiday allowance, left staff feeling that what initially looked generous was misleading, leaving insufficient time to visit home and have proper breaks. Several members of staff reported that they had been called in to the manager's office by a representative of the local entrepreneur to 'talk through their concerns'. The manner in which the interview was conducted was reported as intimidating and not at all reassuring, and the management style of the local partner's representative was described as brusque. Indeed, one new hire said she felt powerless to discuss her expectations freely because they were dismissed from the first with comments such as 'We know how you are feeling – you have ex-pat syndrome.' Unable to go home for fear of conspicuously failing, a number of new hires reported adopting the strategy of making the best of it until such time as they could find a better offer – but because visas were issued by employers, this was easier said than done.

- Working hours were described as problematic by over 50% of employees. The local contract specifies a 47-hour week. In light of the long hours culture in the UK, compared to the rest of Europe, at first international employees from the UK were not concerned about this – but as the expectations became clearer about the work schedules and expectations, this changed. In Tiger City the normal operating hours for business are 8:30 am to 5:30 pm, but the business was also open in the evenings and at weekends. It was in addition the local custom that most employees worked a shift during the weekend. Thus, six-day working patterns were frequently the case. With staff numbers limited while the business was growing, staff were expected to service the rising demands of the business, and several said that although in theory they could take time off in lieu, the clause

'Additional hours may be required to accommodate the needs of the business at the employer's discretion' was invoked all too often.

- 40% of staff reported that their journey to work caused them stress. Because of the very high rents in Tiger City, many staff could not afford to live in the centre of town or within easy commuting distance of the business. Indeed, many of them lived several kilometres away in a satellite city so that the journey-to-work time was regularly in the region of two hours by car, which meant leaving before 6 am if they were to be at work by 8:30am. The return journey met with similar delays. Because this was the only means of transport since the city's infrastructure was still under construction and the transport system had yet to be established, staff found the journey stressful and said this impacted on their performance once they reached the workplace.

- Over 40% of staff reported that they felt professionally challenged by their work. Because the business was growing, staff numbers were still relatively low compared to those in the UK, and staff were frequently asked to take on duties and responsibilities that stretched their professional competence and experience. Without adequate training and experienced and senior colleagues to call on for advice, this led to increased anxiety and stress.

- 60% of staff reported that they had no induction and were just left to get on with it when they arrived.

- Over 50% of staff reported that they did not know about or understand the business strategy, and that there was little or no indirect or direct communication.

- 30% of staff said that they often felt embarrassed that the company was promoting some services that it couldn't yet deliver and that it fell to them to put customer expectations right about what services actually were currently available.

- 30% of staff revealed that they found noise pollution a problem, saying that they could not get away from the constant noise of construction either at home or at work in daylight hours.

Your task

You are the HR manager who has been asked to advise on this case. Prepare a short report based on the facts you have been given above, making recommendations to your colleagues on how the ethical dilemma presented can be solved. Bear in mind the recommendations of Tomorrow's Company and the findings of Muller-Camen *et al* (2008) in making your case. The goal is to achieve recommendations for sustainable HRM while achieving good bottom-line results.

EXPLORE FURTHER

HOPKINS, M. (2006) *CSR and International Development – Are corporations the solution?* London, Earthscan
One of the best introductions into CSR with a special emphasis on developing countries.

MORTON, C. (2003) *By the Skin of our Teeth*. London, Middlesex University Press
This book argues that businesses that pay only lip service to the idea that their people are a key source of sustainability survive only 'by the skin of our teeth'. It shows how to create sustainable organisations through people.

MULLER-CAMEN, M., HARTOG, M., HENRIQUES, A., HOPKINS, M. and PARSA, S. (2008) 'Corporate social responsibility and human resource management', *Human Resource Management Journal*, under review
One of the first studies that empirically examines the relationship between HRM and CSR.

REDINGTON, I. (2005) *Making CSR Happen: The contribution of people management.* London, CIPD
This CIPD report is one of the first analyses of the link between CSR and HRM and how the HR function can become actively involved in CSR.

Conclusion

CHAPTER 26

Potential future developments in HRM

Richard Croucher *and* Andrew Mayo

This textbook has covered the great variety of activities that engage the HR practitioner, and some of the inevitable tensions and dilemmas inherent in satisfying a range of different stakeholders. We now briefly point to some of the main complexities in the role, and to some of the continuing issues that come from the HR professional's position.

As the HR function has steadily shifted from being only concerned with employees and employment to a greater involvement in the overall business direction, so the tensions and dilemmas have become greater. Today's HR practitioner has to be able to advise managers on a wide range of different HR issues and to develop lawful policies that are felt fair by employees. They have to ensure that these policies are followed by line managers in order to ensure that organisational performance is maximised and that relevant legislation is adhered to. In addition, an HR practitioner is expected to understand and contribute to other aspects of the business outside of the traditional sphere of HR. In some cases additional tensions have been caused by a sense of inferiority in the perceived lack of recognition of the value that HR can potentially deliver.

One important issue is the enduring effort to establish the importance of people management issues – often described as 'soft' matters – with other managers. This is shown in the current concern with 'strategic' HRM, but has been around for many years. Everyone has heard the assertion that 'People are our greatest asset', but this may appear glib and can often draw a cynical response. Understandably, managers primarily concerned with providing a product or service at as low a cost as possible and often to demanding deadlines are not always receptive to declarations that training, supporting and motivating people are organisational priorities. How HR professionals show their understanding of other business issues is also relevant here. Although there are positive signs that in many cases they have been showing a greater awareness of wider business matters recently, having to deal with the daily weight of relatively non-strategic (but essential) personnel administration tasks as well as maintaining a strategic and business-oriented perspective is always a challenge.

Nevertheless, products and services are ultimately provided by people, and although 'labour' is undoubtedly a 'factor of production' like raw materials or data, it is not a factor of production like any other. A second enduring theme is therefore the changing role of HR professionals in relation to employees. In the past, what we call HR today was called 'welfare'. HR professionals are also very mobile today and spend little time building up relationships at all levels in an organisation. Ulrich (1997) suggested one of the four key roles is that of 'employee champion', but HR seems more obsessed with 'strategic partnership' with other managers today. Nevertheless, few things can be more important than engagement, productivity and 'well-being'. The key bottom-line calculations that derive from absenteeism and attrition (labour turnover) are largely related to motivation. It is one of the responsibilities of HR professionals to ensure that the creation and maintenance of a positive psychological contract is taken seriously by line managers and supervisors because it is one of the key factors producing the desired outcomes. There are both possibilities and tensions between this and another trend, in the form of the move away from 'consistency = fairness' to 'flexibility = fairness'. This is matched by personalised flexible benefit packages – a sea-change from the rigidity of HR's historic approach. A further challenge is that of managing those who do work for the organisation but are not employed by it. HR managers increasingly have to manage across organisational boundaries, trying to ensure that organisational goals are met by those who are not the organisation's employees.

HR always feels it is in a maelstrom of crisis. In fact the evidence is that there is a strong and remunerative market for highly professional and experienced players in HR, plus a growing recognition that intangible assets drive value in modern organisations. The contribution that HR can make is increasingly relevant, but it must embrace more consultancy skills and business knowledge. Ulrich described four areas of HR capability – business mastery, change and process mastery, professional knowledge, and personal credibility. The editors hope at least that this text has contributed to providing the third of these. The first two have to be learned too, and the last is all about the ability to create high-trust relationships. In the end it is this that counts most of all.

References and further reading

ACKERS, P. and PAYNE, J. (1998) 'British trade unions and social partnership: rhetoric, reality and strategy', *International Journal of Human Resource Management*, Vol. 9, No. 3, 529–50

ADAMS, J. S. (1965) 'Inequity in social exchange'. In L. Berkowitz (ed.) *Advances in Experimental Social Psychology*, Vol. 2, pp267–99

ALLEN, R. and KILLMANN, R. (1999) 'The role of the reward system for a total quality management-based strategy', *Journal of Organizational Change and Management*, Vol. 14, No. 2, 110–31

ALLINSON, R. (1993) *Global Disasters: Inquiries into management ethics*. New York, Prentice Hall.

ALMOND, P., EDWARDS, T., COLLING, T., FERNER, A., GUNNIGLE, P., MULLER-CAMEN, M., QUINTANILLA, J. and WÄCHTER, H. (2005) 'Unraveling home and host country effects: an investigation of the HR policies of an American multinational in four European countries', *Industrial Relations*, Vol. 44, No. 2, 276–306

ANDERSON, N. and SHACKLETON, V. (1993) *Successful Selection Interviewing*. Oxford, Blackwell

ANDERSON-CONNOLLY, R., GRUNBERG, L., GREENBERG, E. and MOORE, S. (2002) 'Is lean mean? Workplace transformation and employee well-being', *Work, Employment and Society*, Vol. 16, No. 3, 389–413

ANSOFF, H. I. (1986) *Corporate Strategy*. New York, McGraw-Hill

APPELBAUM, E., BAILEY, T., BERG, P. and KALLENBERG, A. L. (2000) *Manufacturing Advantage: Why high-performance work systems pay off*. Ithaca, Cornell University Press

ARMSTRONG, M. (2002) *Employee Reward*. London, CIPD

ARMSTRONG, M. and BARON, A. (2005) *Managing Performance – Performance Management In Action*. London, CIPD

ARMSTRONG, M. and BARON, A. (2002) *Strategic HRM*. London, CIPD

ARNOLD, J., COOPER, C. L., ROBERTSON, I. T. (1995) *Work Psychology – Understanding human behaviour in the workplace*, 2nd edition. London, Pitman

ASHTON , C. (2001) *E-HR: Transforming the HR function*. London, Business Intelligence

ATKINSON, J. (1984) 'Manpower strategies for flexible organisations', *Personnel Management*, August, 28–31

BAE, K. and CHUNG, C. (1997) 'Cultural values and work attitudes of Korean industrial workers in comparison with those of the United States and Japan', *Work and Occupations*, Vol. 24, No. 1, 80–96

BALL, K. S. (2001) 'The use of human resource information systems: a survey', *Personnel Review*, Vol. 30, No. 6, 677–93

BARON, J. and COOKE, K. (1992) 'Process and outcome: perspectives on the distribution of rewards within organizations', *Administrative Science Quarterly*, Vol. 37, No. 2, 191–7

BARTLETT, C. A. and GHOSHAL, S. (1989) *Managing Across Borders: The transnational solution*. Boston, MA: Harvard Business School Press

BECKER, B. E., HUSELID, M. A. and ULRICH, D. (2001) *The HR Scorecard: Linking people, strategy, and performance*. Boston, MA, Harvard Business School Press

BECKER, B. E., HUSELID, M. A., PICKUS, P. S. and SPRATT, M. F. (1997) 'HR as a source of shareholder value: research and recommendation', *Human Resource Management*, Vol. 36, No. 1, 39–47

BENNISON, M. and CASSON, J. (1984) *The Manpower Planning Handbook*. Maidenhead, McGraw-Hill

BERGLAS, S. (2002) 'The very real dangers of executive coaching', *Harvard Business Review*, June, 86–92

BERGMANN, T. J. and SCARPELLO, V. G. (2002) *Compensation Decision-making*. Cincinnati, OH: South Western Publishing

BILSBERRY, J. (1996) *The Effective Manager: Perspectives and illustrations*. London, Sage

BLUMBERG, P. (1976) *The Sociology of Participation*. New York, Schocken

BLUNDELL, B. and MURDOCK, A. (1997) *Managing in the Public Sector*. London, Butterworth-Heinemann

BLYTON, P. (1996) 'Workplace flexibility'. In B. Towers (ed.) *The Handbook of Human Resource Management*. Oxford, Blackwell

BOLSTER, B. I. and SPRINGBETT, B. M. (1961) 'The reaction of interviewers to favourable and unfavourable information', *Journal of Applied Psychology*, Vol. 45, 97–103

BOXALL, P. and PURCELL, J. (2003) *Strategy and Human Resource Management*. Basingstoke, Palgrave Macmillan

BOYATZIS, R. E. (1982) *The Competent Manager*. New York, John Wiley & Sons

BPS (2002) *Code of Good Practice for Psychological Testing*. Available from: **www.psychtesting.org.uk**

BREWSTER, C. (2007) 'Comparative HRM: European views and perspectives', *International Journal of Human Resource Management*, Vol. 18, No. 5, 769–87

BREWSTER, C. (1995) 'Towards a European model of human resource management', *Journal of International Business Studies*, Vol. 26, No. 1, 1–21

BREWSTER, C. and HEGEWISCH, A. (1993) 'Methodology of the PriceWaterhouse Cranfield project on European human resource management', *P+Journal of the European Foundation for the Improvement of Living and Working Conditions*

BREWSTER, C., LARSEN, H. H. and MAYRHOFER, W. (1997) 'Integration and assignment: a paradox in human resource management', *Journal of International Management*, Vol. 3, No. 1, 1–23

BREWSTER, C., WOOD, G., BROOKES, M. and VAN OMMEREN, J. (2006) 'What determines the size of the HR function? A cross-national analysis', *Human Resource Management*, Vol. 45, No. 1, 3–21

BREWSTER, C., WOOD, G., CROUCHER, R. and BROOKES, M. (2007) 'Are works councils and joint consultative committees a threat to trade unions? A comparative analysis', *Economic and Industrial Democracy*, Vol. 28, No. 1, 49–77

BROOKS, I., WEATHERSTON, J. and WILKINSON, G. (2004) *The International Business Environment*. Harlow, Prentice Hall/Financial Times

BROWN, D. (1996) 'Team rewards: lessons from the coal face', *Team Performance Management*, Vol. 2, No. 2, 12

BUCKLE, P. and DEVEREUX, J. (1999) *Research on Work-Related Neck and Upper Limb Musculo-Skeletal Disorders*. Luxembourg, Office for Official Publications of the European Union

CABINET OFFICE (2007) *Transformational Government Enabled by Technology*, Annual Report. Online version available at: **www.cio.gov.uk/documents/annual_report2006/trans_gov2006.pdf** [accessed July 2007]

CACCIOPE, R. (1999) 'Using team-individual reward and recognition strategies to drive organizational success', *Leadership and Organization Development Journal*, Vol. 20, No. 6, 322–31

CALLAGHER, C. (2002) 'Occupational safety and health management systems in Australia: barriers to success', *Policy and Practice in Health and Safety*, Vol. 1, No. 2, 67–81

CAPELLI, P. (2005) 'Making the most of online recruiting', *Harvard Business Review*, Vol. 79, 139–46

CARDY, R. L. and MILLER, J. S. (2003) 'Technology implications for HRM'. In D. Stone (ed.) *Advances in Human Performance and Cognitive Engineering Research*. Greenwich, CT: JAI Press

CARDY, R. L. and MILLER, J. S. (2005) 'E-HR and performance management: a consideration of positive potential and the dark side'. In H. G. Gueutal and D. L. Stone (eds) *The Brave New World of e-HR: Human resource management in the digital age*. San Francisco, Jossey-Bass

CARRAHER, S. M., HART, D. E. and CARRAHER, C. E. (2003) 'Attitudes towards benefits among entrepreneurial employees', *Personnel Review*, Vol. 32, No. 6, 683–93

CASCIO, W. F. (2006) *Managing Human Resources: Productivity, quality of work life, profits.* New York, McGraw-Hill

CEDAR (2002) *Human Resources self-services/postal survey.* Available from: **www.cedar/com**

CHAPMAN, D. S. and WEBSTER, J. (2003) 'The use of technologies in the recruiting, screening and selection process for job candidates', *International Journal of Selection and Assessment*, Vol. 11, No. 2/3, 113–20

CHEN, M. (1995) *Asian Management Systems.* New York, Routledge

CIO (2007) *IT Skills Framework and the Focus of the Council.* Online version available at: **http://www.cio.gov.uk/about_the_council/index.asp** [accessed July 2007]

CIPD (2007) Performance management factsheet. Online version available at: **http://www.cipd.co.uk** [accessed March 2007]

CIPD (2007) *HR and Technology: Impact and advantages.* London, CIPD

CIPD (2007) *Coaching at Work*, Magazine and online resource. London, Chartered Institute of Personnel and Development. Available online at: **http://www.cipd.co.uk/coachingatwork/ presales.htm**

CIPD (2006) *HR and Technology: Beyond delivery*, Change Agenda. London, CIPD

CIPD (2006) *The Changing HR Function: The key questions*, Change Agenda. London, CIPD

CIPD (2006) *Recruitment*, Factsheet. London, CIPD

CIPD (2006) *Induction*, Factsheet. London, CIPD

CIPD (2006) *Latest Trends in Learning, Training and Development.* London, CIPD

CIPD (2006) *Recruitment, Retention and Turnover survey.* Available from: **http://www.cipd.co.uk/surveys**

CIPD (2006) *Public Policy Perspectives: People, productivity and performance.* Online version available at: **http://www.cipd.co.uk/subjects/maneco/ecolabmrkt/_smrtwrk.htm** [accessed March 2007]

CIPD (2005) *Technology and People Management: The opportunity and the challenge.* London, CIPD

CIPD (2005) *On-Line Recruitment*, Factsheet. London, CIPD

CIPD (2005) *Performance Management*, CIPD Survey Report. London, CIPD

CIPD (2005) *Performance Appraisal.* London, CIPD

CIPD (2005) *HR Outsourcing: The key decisions.* London, CIPD

CLUTTERBUCK, D. (2001) *Everyone Needs a Mentor*. London, Chartered Institute of Personnel and Development

CLUTTERBUCK, D. and MEGGINSON, D. (2005) *Making Coaching Work: Creating a coaching culture*. London, CIPD

COHEN, A. (2001) 'Corporate e-ducation', *PC Magazine*, 2 January, 137

COLLINS, J. and PORRAS, G. (1994) *Built to Last*. New York, Harper Business

CONNOCK, S. (1991) *HR Vision*. London, IPM

COOK, M. (2004) *Personnel Selection. Adding value through people*, 4th edition. Chichester, John Wiley & Sons

CORPORATE LEADERSHIP COUNCIL (2004) *Driving Performance and Retention Through Employee Engagement*. London, CLC

COX, T., GRIFFITHS, A. and RIAL-GONZALEZ, E. (2000) *Research on Work-Related Stress*. Luxembourg, Office for Official Publications of the European Union

CRANFIELD SCHOOL OF MANAGEMENT (2006) *Selection Methods Letting Employers Down*. Available from: **http://www.manufacturingtalk.com/news/can/can166.html**

CROUCH, C. (2001) 'A third way in industrial relations?' In S. White (ed.) *New Labour: The progressive future?* Basingstoke, Palgrave

CROUCHER, R. and KELLIHER, C. (2005) 'The right to request flexible working in Britain: the law and organisational realities', *International Journal of Comparative Labour Law and Industrial Relations*, Vol. 21/3, 503–20

CROUCHER, R. and SINGE, I. (2005) 'Consultation in a British utilities company: reinforcing the hierarchy?', *Journal of Industrial Relations*, Vol. 47, No. 4, 471–5

CROUCHER, R. and WHITE, G. (2007) 'Enforcing a national minimum wage: the British case', *Policy Studies*, Vol. 28, No. 2, 145–61

CROUCHER, R., GOODERHAM, P. and PARRY, E. (2006) 'The influences on direct communication in British and Danish firms: country, "strategic HRM" or unionization?', *European Journal of Industrial Relations*, Vol. 12, No. 3, 267–86

DANFORD, A. (1999) *Japanese Management Techniques and British Workers*. London, Mansell

DANFORD, A., RICHARDSON, M., STEWART, P., TAILBY, S. and UPCHURCH, M. (2005) *Partnership and the High-Performance Workplace: Work and employment relations in the aerospace industry*. Basingstoke, Palgrave Macmillan

DANIELS, K. and MACDONALD, L. (2005) *Equality, Dversity and Discrimination*. London, CIPD

DAVENPORT, T. H. and PRUSAK, L. (1998) *Working Knowledge: How organisations manage what they know*. Boston, MA, Harvard Business School Press

DAVIES, R. (1993) 'Making strategy happen: common patterns of strategic success and failure', *European Management Journal*, Vol. 11, No. 2, 210–13

DAWSON, S., CLINTON, M., BAMFORD, M. and WILLMAN, P. (1998) *Safety at Work: The limits of self-regulation.* Cambridge, Cambridge University Press

DBA (2002) *360-Degree Feedback,* Training Handbook Bulletin by Diane Bailey Associates. London, GEE Publishing

DE GEUS, A. and SENGE, P. M. (1997) *The Living Company.* Boston, MA, Harvard Business School Press

DE HAAN, E. and BURGER, Y. (2005) *Coaching With Colleagues.* Basingstoke, Palgrave Macmillan

DIBBEN, P., JAMES, P., ROPER, I. and WOOD, G. (2007) *'Modernising' Work and Employment in Public Services: Redefining roles and relationships in Britain's changing workplace.* London, Palgrave

DICKINSON, J. (2006) 'Employees' preferences for the bases of pay differentials', *Employee Relations,* Vol. 28, No. 2, 164–83

DICKMANN, M. and MULLER-CAMEN, M. (2006) 'A typology of international human resource management strategies and processes', *International Journal of Human Resource Management,* Vol. 17, No. 4, 580–601

DOMBERGER, S. and JENSEN, P. (1997) 'Contracting out by the public sector: theory, evidence, prospects', *Oxford Review of Economic Policy,* Vol. 13, No. 4, 67–78

DORLING, D. and THOMAS, B. (2004) *People and Places: A 2001 census atlas of the UK.* Bristol, Polity Press

DOWLING, P. J., WELCH, D. E. and SCHULER, R. S. (1999) *International Human Resource Management,* 3rd edition. Cincinnati, OH, South-Western College Publishing

DRUKER, J. and WHITE, G. (1997) 'Constructing a new reward strategy', *Employee Relations,* Vol. 19, No. 2, 128–46

DTI (2005) *Equality and Diversity, Coming of Age: Consultation on the Employment Equality Regulations 2006.* London, Department of Trade

DTI (2001) *Work–Life Balance: The business case.* London, Department of Trade and Industry

DWP (2005) *Opportunity Age.* London, The Stationery Office

ECU (2007) *Dignity at Work: Final project report.* The Equality Challenging Unit. Online version available at: **https://www.ecu.ac.uk** [accessed April 2007]

EDVINSSON, L. and MALONE, M. S. (1997) *Intellectual Capital.* London, Piatkus

EDWARDS, J. R. (1991) 'Person–job fit: a conceptual integration, literature review, and methodological critique'. In C. L. Cooper and I. T. Robertson (eds) *International Review of Industrial and Organisational Psychology,* Vol. 5, 283–357. New York, Wiley

EEF/CIPD (2003) *Maximising Employee Potential and Business Performance: The role of high performance working.* London, EEF/CIPD

ETZIONI, A. (2001) *Sustaining the Community of Communities*. Demos Collection, Vol. 16

EUROPEAN COMMISSION (2005) *Lisbon Action Plan incorporating EU Lisbon programme and recommendations for actions to member states for inclusion in their national Lisbon programmes*

EVANS, A. and WALTERS, M. (2002) *From Absence to Attendance*, 2nd edition. London, CIPD

EVANS, P., PUCIK, V. and BARSOUX, J.-L. (2002) *The Global Challenge*. New York, McGraw-Hill

FARNDALE, E. and BREWSTER, C. (2005) 'In search of legitimacy: national professional associations and the professionalism of HR practitioners', *Human Resource Management Journal*, Vol. 15, No. 3, 33–48

FAVELL, I. (2005) *The Competency Toolkit*. London, Fenman

FELSTEAD, A., GALLIE, G. and GREEN, F. (2002) *Work Skills in Britain 1986–2001*. London, DfES

FERNER, A. (2000) 'The underpinnings of "bureaucratic" control systems: HRM in European multinationals', *Journal of Management Studies*, Vol. 37, No. 4, 521–40

FIORITO, J. and MARANTO, C. (1987) 'The contemporary decline of union strength', *Contemporary Policy Issues*, Vol. 5, No. 4, 12–27

FITZ-ENZ, J. (2002) *How to Measure Human Resources Management*. New York, McGraw-Hill

FITZ-ENZ, J. A. C. (2000) *The ROI of Human Capital: Measuring the economic value of employee performance*. New York, Amacom

FLAMHOLZ, E. G. (1999) *Human Resource Accounting: Advances in concepts, methods and applications*, 3rd edition. Norwell, Kluwer

FLEETWOOD, S. (forthcoming)

FLORKOWSKI, G. W. and OLIVAS-LUJAN, M. R. (2006) 'The diffusion of human resource information technology innovations in US and non-US firms', *Personnel Review*, Vol. 35, No. 6, 684–710

FLYNN, M. and McNAIR, S. (2007) *Managing Age: A guide to good employment practice*. London, CIPD/Trades Union Congress

FORTH, J. and MILLWARD, N. (2002) *The Growth of Direct Communication*. London, CIPD

FOWLER, A. (1996) *Employee Induction: A good start*. London, CIPD

FRAME, P., HARTOG, M. and WILSON, D. (2005) 'Productive diversity: capitalising on human resources. How can we harness our knowledge of diversity?', *International Journal of Knowledge Culture and Change Management*, Vol. 4

FREAS, A. and SHERMAN, S. (2004) 'The Wild West of executive coaching', *Harvard Business Review*, November

FRENCH, R. (2007) *Cross-Cultural Management in Work Organisations*. London, CIPD

FRISCH, M. H. (2001) 'The emerging role of the internal coach', *Consulting Psychology Journal*, Vol. 53, No. 4, 240–50

FURNHAM, A. and HEAVEN, P. (1999) *Personality and Social Behaviour*. London, Arnold

GALANAKI, E. (2002) 'The decision to recruit online: a descriptive study', *Career Development International*, Vol. 7, 243–51

GARRAHAN, P. and STEWART, P. (1992) *The Nissan Enigma: Flexibility at work in a local economy*. London, Mansell

GARVEY, B. (2004) 'The mentoring/counselling/coaching debate', *Development and Learning in Organizations*, Vol. 18, No. 2, 608

GARVEY, B. and WILLIAMSON, B. (2002) *Beyond Knowledge Management – Dialogue, creativity and the corporate curriculum*. London, FT/Prentice Hall

GOODERHAM, P.N., NORDHAUG, O. and RINGDAL, K. (1999) 'Institutional and rational determinants of organisational practices: human resource practices in European firms', *Administrative Science Quarterly*, Vol. 44, 507–31

GOOS, M. and MANNING, A. (2003) 'McJobs and MacJobs: the growing polarisation of jobs in the UK'. In R. Dickens, P. Gregg and J. Wadsworth (eds) *The Labour Market Under New Labour: The state of working Britain*. New York, Palgrave Macmillan

GRATTON, L. (2000) *Living Strategy*. London, Prentice Hall/Financial Times

GREENGARD, S. (1999) 'Web-based training yields maximum returns', *Workforce*, Vol. 78, No. 2, 95

GRIMSHAW, D., MARCHINGTON, M., RUBERY, J. and WILLMOTT, H. (2005) 'Introduction: fragmenting work across organisational boundaries'. In M. Marchington, D. Grimshaw, J. Rubery and H. Willmott (eds) *Fragmenting Work, Blurring Organisational Boundaries and Disordering Hierarchies*. Oxford, Oxford University Press

GUEST, D. E. (1997) 'Human resource management and performance: a review and a research agenda', *International Journal of Human Resource Management*, Vol. 8, 263–76

GUEST, D. (1987) 'Human resource management and industrial relations', *Journal of Management Studies*, Vol. 24, No. 5, 503–21

GUEST, D. and CONWAY, N. (2000) *The Psychological Contract in the Public Sector*. London, CIPD

GUEST, D. and CONWAY, N. (1999) 'Peering into the black hole: the downside of the new employment relations in the UK', *British Journal of Industrial Relations*, Vol. 37, No. 3, 367–89

GUEST, D. and CONWAY, N. (1997) *Employee Motivation and the Psychological Contract*, IPD Report. London, IPD

GUEUTAL, H. G. and FALBE, C. M. (2005) 'E-HR: trends in delivery methods'. In H. G. Gueutal and D. L. Stone (eds) *The Brave New World of e-HR: Human resource management in the digital age.* San Francisco, Jossey-Bass

GUEUTAL, H. G. and STONE, D. L. (2005) *The Brave New World of e-HR: Human resource management in the digital age.* San Francisco, Jossey-Bass

GUNNINGHAM, N. and JOHNSTONE, R. (2000) *Regulating Workplace Safety: Systems and sanctions.* Oxford, Oxford University Press

HALL, M. (2006) 'A cool response to the ICE regulations? Employer and trade union approaches to the new legal framework for information and consultation', *Industrial Relations Journal*, Vol. 37, No. 5, 456–72

HALL, P. A. and SOSKICE, D. (eds) (2001) *Varieties of Capitalism: The institutional foundations of comparative advantage.* Oxford, Oxford University Press

HANDY, C. (1993) *Understanding Organisations.* London, Penguin

HARLEY, B., HYMAN, J. and THOMPSON, P. (eds) (2005) *Participation and Democracy at Work.* Basingstoke, Palgrave Macmillan

HARRIS, H., BREWSTER, C. and SPARROW, P. (2004) *International Human Resource Management.* London, CIPD

HARRISON, R. (2005) *Learning and Development*, 4th edition. London, CIPD

HARRISON, R. and KESSELS, J. (2004) *Human Resource Development in a Knowledge Economy – An organisational view.* London, Palgrave Macmillan

HARVEY, C. P. and ALLARD, M. J. (2005) *Understanding and Managing Diversity*, 3rd edition. London, Pearson/Prentice Hall

HARVEY, D. (2003) *The New Imperialism.* Oxford, Oxford University Press

HARZING, A. W. (2001) 'Who's in charge? An empirical study of excecutive staffing practices in foreign subsidiaries', *Human Resource Management*, Vol. 40, No. 2, 139–58

HASLAM, C., NEALE, A. and JOHAL, S. (2000) *Economics in a Business Context.* Cornwall, Thompson Learning

HASLAM, C., WILLIAMS, K., JOHAL, S. and WILLIAMS, J. (1994) *Cars: Analysis, history, cases.* Oxford, Berghahn Books

HAWKINS, P. and SCHWENK, G. (2006) *Coaching Supervision: Maximising the potential of coaching. A guide.* London, CIPD

HAYNES, P. and ALLEN, M. (2000) 'Partnership as union strategy: a preliminary evaluation', *Employee Relations*, Vol. 23, No. 2, 164–87

HEALTH AND SAFETY EXECUTIVE (2006) *Health and Safety Statistics 2005/06.* Sudbury, HSE Books

HEALTH AND SAFETY EXECUTIVE (1997) *Successful Health and Safety Management.* Sudbury, HSE Books

HEERY, E. (1996) 'Risk, reward and the New pay', *Personnel Review*, Vol. 25, No. 6, 54–65

HIGHWAYS AGENCY (2007) *Business Plan.* Online version available at: **http://www.highways.gov.uk/aboutus/1283.aspx**; general access: **http://www.highways.gov.uk/default.aspx** [accessed July 2007]

HO, D. Y-F. AND CHIU, C-Y. (1994) 'Component ideas of individualism, collectivism and social organization: an application in the study of Chinese culture'. In U. Kim, H. Triandis, C. Kagitcibasi, S.-C. Choi and G. Yoon, *Individualism and Collectivism: Theory, method and application.* Thousand Oaks, Sage

HODGE, G. and GREVE, C. (2005) *The Challenge of Public–Private Partnerships: Learning from international experience.* Cheltenham, Edward Elgar Publishing

HOFSTEDE, G. (2003) *Culture's Consequences,* 2nd edition. Thousand Oaks, Sage

HOFSTEDE, G. (1980) *Culture's Consequences.* Thousand Oaks, Sage

HOLBECHE, L. (2001) *Aligning Human Resources and Business Strategy.* London, Butterworth-Heinemann

HOPKINS, M. (2006) *CSR and International Development – Are corporations the solution?* London, Earthscan

HORNER, C. and DOLNY, H. (2006) 'Choosing the right coaches for your company', Paper presented at i-Coach Academy and Standard Bank, Knowledge Resources Conference, Johannesburg, South Africa

HOUSE, R., HANGES, P. J., JAVIDAN, M. and DORFMAN, P. W. (eds) (2004) *Leadership, Culture and Organizations: The GLOBE study of 62 societies.* Thousand Oaks, Sage

HUANG, J. H., JIN, B. H. and YANG, C. (2004) 'Satisfaction with B2E benefit systems and organisational citizenship behaviour: an examination of gender differences', *International Journal of Manpower,* Vol. 25, No. 2, 195–210

HUI, C. H. (1990) 'Work attitudes, leadership styles and managerial behaviour in different cultures'. In R. W. Brislin (ed.) *Applied Cross-Cultural Psychology.* Newbury Park, Sage

HUTTER, B. (2001) *Regulation and Risk: Occupational health and safety on the railways.* Oxford, Oxford University Press

ICHNIOWSKI, C. and SHAW, K. (2003) 'Beyond incentive pay', *Journal of Economic Perspectives,* Vol. 17, No. 1, 155–80

ILMARINEN, J. (1999) *Ageing Workers in the European Union: Status and promotion of workability, employability and employment.* Helsinki, Finnish Institute of Occupational Health

IPD (1998) *The Future of Employment Relations,* a Position Paper. London, IPD

ISHIDO, H. (1986) 'Transferability of Japanese human resource management abroad', *Human Resource Management,* Vol. 25, No. 1, 103–20

JACKSON, T. (2004) *Management and Change in Africa: A cross-cultural perspective.* London, Routledge

JACKSON, T. (2002a) *International HRM: A cross-cultural approach*. London, Sage

JACKSON, T. (2002b) 'The management of people across cultures: valuing people differently', *Human Resource Management*, Vol. 41, No. 4, 455–75

JACKSON, T. (2000) 'Management ethics and corporate policy: a cross-cultural comparison', *Journal of Management Studies*, Vol. 37, No. 3, 349–69

JAMES, P. and WALTERS, D. (2005) *Regulating Health and Safety at Work: An agenda for change?* London, Institute of Employment Rights

JANSEN, E. and VON GLINOW, M. (1985) 'Ethical ambivalence and organizational reward systems', *Academy of Management Review*, Vol. 10, No. 4, 814–22

JANZ, J. T. (1989) 'The patterned behavior description interview: the best prophet of the future is the past'. In R. W. Eder and G. R. Ferris (eds) *The Employment Interview: Theory, research, and practice*. Newbury Park, CA: Sage

JARVIS, J. (2004) *Coaching and Buying Coaching Services. A guide*. London, CIPD. Available online at: **http://www.cipd.co.uk/guides**

JOHNSON, A. (2006) 'Orange blossoms', *People Management*, Vol. 12, No. 21, 57–60

JOHNSON, G. and SCHOLES, K. (1999) *Exploring Corporate Strategy*. London, Prentice-Hall

KALETSKY, A. (2006) 'Why the sun is rising over Britain, not Japan', *The Times*, 10 November

KAMPA-KOKESCH, S. and ANDERSON, M. Z. (2001) 'Executive coaching: a comprehensive review of the literature', *Consulting Psychology Journal*, Vol. 53, No. 4, 205–28

KAPLAN, R S and NORTON, D. P. (1996) *The Balanced Scorecard*. Boston, MA: Harvard Business School Press

KEHOE, J. K., DICKTER, D. N., RUSSELL, D. P. and SACCO, J. M. (2005) 'E-selection'. In H. G. Gueutal and D. L. Stone (eds) *The Brave New World of e-HR: Human resource management in the digital age*. San Francisco, Jossey-Bass

KERR, S. (1975) 'On the folly of rewarding A, while hoping for B', *Academy of Management Journal*, Vol. 18, No. 4, 769–83

KERRIN, M. and OLIVER, N. (2002) 'Collective and individual improvement activities: the role of reward systems', *Personnel Review*, Vol. 31, No. 3, 320–37

KERSLEY, B., ALPIN, C., FORTH, J., DIX, G., BRYSON, A. and BEWLEY, H. (2005) *Inside the Workplace: First findings from the 2004 Employment Relations Survey*. London, Routledge

KERSLEY, B., ALPIN, C., FORTH, J., DIX, G., OXENBRIDGE, S., BRYSON, A. and BEWLEY, H. (2006) *Inside the Workplace: Findings from the 2004 Workplace Employment Relations Survey*. London, Taylor & Francis

KILBURG, R. R. (1996) 'Towards a conceptual understanding and definition of executive coaching', *Consulting Psychology Journal*, Vol. 48, No. 2, 134–44

KOCH, M. and McGRATH, R. (1996) 'Improving labor productivity: human resource policies do matter', *Strategic Management Journal*, Vol. 17, 335–54

KOLK, A. and VAN TULDER, R. (2004) 'Ethics in international business: multinational approaches to child labor', *Journal of World Business*, Vol. 39, 49–60

KOOPMAN, A. (1991) *Transcultural Management*. Oxford, Basil Blackwell

KOUBREK, J. and BREWSTER, C. (1995) 'Human resource management in turbulent times: HRM in the Czech Republic', *International Journal of Human Resource Management*, Vol. 6, 223–47

KRISTOF, A. L. (1996) 'Person–organization fit: an integrative review of its conceptualizations, measurement, and implications', *Personnel Psychology*, Vol. 49, No. 1, 1–49

LADO, A. and WILSON, M. (1994) 'Human resource systems and sustained competitive advantage', *Academy of Management Review*, Vol. 19, No. 4, 699–727

LARSEN, H. H. and BREWSTER, C. (2003) 'Line management responsibility for HRM: what's happening in Europe?', *Employee Relations*, Vol. 25, No. 3, 228–44

LAWRENCE, P. (1994) 'German management: at the interface between Eastern and Western Europe'. In R. Calori and P. de Woot (eds) *A European Management Model: Beyond diversity*. London, Prentice Hall

LEE, R. J. and VALERIO, A. M. (2005) *Executive Coaching: A guide for the HR professional*. San Francisco, Pfeiffer

LEGGE, K. (1989) 'Human resource management: a critical analysis'. In J. Storey (ed.) *New Perspectives on Human Resource Management*. London, Routledge

LEPAK, D. P. and SNELL, S. A. (1998) 'Virtual HR: strategic HRM in the 21st century', *Human Resource Management Review*, Vol. 8, No. 3, 215–34

LEWIS, G. (2000) *Mentoring Manager*. London, Prentice Hall

LEWIS, P. (1998) 'Exploring Lawler's New pay theory through the case of Finbanks' reward strategy for managers', *Personnel Review*, Vol. 29, No. 1, 10–32

LEWIS, P., THORNHILL, A. and SAUNDERS, M. (2003) *Employee Relations: Understanding the employment relationship*. London, FT/Prentice-Hall

LEWIS, S. (2003) 'Flexible working arrangements: implementation, outcomes and management'. In C. L. Cooper and I. Robertson (eds) *International Review of Industrial and Organisational Psychology*. London, John Wiley & Sons

LEWIS, S. and COOPER, C. (2005) *Work-life Integration: Case studies of organisational change*. London, John Wiley & Sons

LEWIS, S., WATTS, A. and CAMP, C. (1996) 'The Midland Bank experience'. In S. Lewis and J. Lewis (eds) *The Work Family Challenge: Rethinking employment*. London, Sage

LEWIS, S. *et al* (forthcoming)

LOCKE, E. A. and LATHAM, G. P. (1990) *A Theory of Goal-Setting and Task Performance.* Cited in J. Arnold, C. L. Cooper and I. T. Robertson (1995) *Work Psychology – Understanding human behaviour in the workplace,* 2nd edition. London, Pitman

LORETTO, W., VICKERSTAFF, S. and WHITE, P. (2006) 'What do older workers want?', *Social Policy and Society,* Vol. 5, No. 4, 479–83

LORETTO, W., VICKERSTAFF, S. and WHITE, P. (2005) *Older Workers and Options for Flexible Work.* Manchester, Equal Opportunities Commission

LUCAS, R., LUPTON, B. and MATHIESON, H. (2006) *Human Resource Management in an International Context.* London, CIPD

LUNDY, O. and COWLING, A. (1996) *Strategic Human Resource Management.* London, Routledge

McCALL, M., LOMBARDO, M. and MORRISON, A. (1998) *The Lessons of Experience.* Lanham, Lexington Books

McCLELLAND, D. C. (1971) *Motivational Trends in Society.* Cited in M. Steers and L. W. Porter (1987) *Motivation and Work Behaviour,* 4th edition. New York, McGraw-Hill

McMANUS, M. A. and FERGUSON, M. W. (2003) 'Biodata, personality and demographic differences of recruits from three sources', *International Journal of Selection and Assessment,* Vol. 11, No. 2/3, 175–83

McNAIR, S. and FLYNN, M. (2005) 'The age dimension of employer practices: employer case studies'. Department of Trade and Industry, Vol. 42

McNAIR, S., FLYNN, M., OWEN, L., HUMPHREYS, C. and WOODFIELD, S. (2004) *Changing Work in Later Life: A study of job transitions.* Guildford, University of Surrey

MARCHINGTON, M. and WILKINSON, A. (2005) *Human Resource Management at Work.* London, CIPD

MARCHINGTON, M., WILKINSON, A., ACKERS, P. and DUNDON, T. (2001) *Management Choice and Employee Voice.* London, CIPD

MARTIN, G. (2005) *Technology and People Management: Transforming the function of HR and the HR function.* London, CIPD

MATTEN, D. and MOON, J. (2007) '"Implicit" and "explicit" CSR: a conceptual framework for a comparative understanding of corporate social responsibility', *Academy of Management Review.* Forthcoming

MAY, R., BORMANN YOUNG, C. and LEDGERWOOD, D. (1998) 'Lessons from Russian human resource management experience', *European Management Journal,* Vol. 16, No. 4, 447–59

MAYO, A. J. (2006) *What's the Future for Human Capital? Measuring and reporting – the fundamental requirement for data.* London, CIPD

MAYO, A. J. (2004a) *Understanding HR Return On Investment.* One Stop Guide Series. London, *Personnel Today* Management Resources

MAYO, A. J. (2004b) *Creating a Learning and Development Strategy*. London, CIPD

MAYO, A. J. (2001) *The Human Value of the Enterprise: Valuing people as assets – monitoring, measuring and managing*. London, Nicholas Brealey

MAYO, A.J. (1994) *Managing Careers – Strategies for Organisations*. London, IPM

MAYRHOFER, W. and BREWSTER, C. (2005) 'European human resource management: researching developments over time', *Management Review*, Vol. 16, No. 1, 36–62

MBIGI, L. (1997) *Ubuntu: The African dream in management*. Cape Town, Knowledge Resources

MENDENHALL, M. and ODDOU, G. (1985) 'The dimensions of expatriate acculturation: a review', *Academy of Management Review*, Vol. 10, 39–47

MEYER, C. (1994) 'How the right measures help teams excel', *Harvard Business Review*, Vol. 72, No. 3, 95–103

MORRISON, J. (2006) *The International Business Environment: Global and local marketplaces in a changing world*. Basingstoke, Palgrave Macmillan

MORTON, C. (2003) *By the Skin of our Teeth*. London, Middlesex University Press

MULLER-CAMEN, M., HARTOG, M., HENRIQUES, A., HOPKINS, M. and PARSA, S. (2008) 'Corporate social responsibility and human resource management', *Human Resource Management Journal*, under review

MULLINS, L. (2007) *Management and Organisational Behaviour*. Harlow, Prentice Hall/Financial Times

MUMFORD, A. (1996) 'Special needs, different solutions'. In J. Bilsberry (ed.) *The Effective Manager: Perspectives and Illustrations*. London, Sage

NEEDLE, D. (2004) *Business in Context*. London, Thomson Learning

NEWELL, S. and SHACKLETON, V. (2000) 'Recruitment and selection'. In S. Bach and K. Sisson (eds) *Personnel Management: A comprehensive guide to theory and practice*. London, Blackwell

NONAKA, I. and TAKEUCHI, H. (1995) *The Knowledge Creating Company*. Oxford, Oxford University Press

OECD (2003) *Ageing and Employment Policies (Vieillissement et politiques de l'emploi)*. Stockholm, OECD

OLIVER, N. and WILKINSON, B. (1992) *The Japanisation of British Industry*. Oxford, Blackwell

OLVE, N., ROY, J. and WETTER, M. (2001) *Performance Drivers: A practical guide to using the balanced scorecard*. London, John Wiley & Sons

ORGAN, D. W., PODSAKOFF, P. M. and MACKENZIE, S. B. (2006) *Organizational Citizenship Behavior: Its nature, antecedents, and consequences*. Thousand Oaks, Sage

OWEN, L. and FLYNN, M. (2004) 'Changing work: mid to late life transitions in employment', *Ageing International*, Vol. 29, No. 4, 333–50

PAAUWE, J. (1995) 'Personnel management without personnel managers: varying degrees of outsourcing the personnel function'. In P. Flood, M. Gannon and J. Paauwe (eds) *Managing Without Traditional Methods*. Wokingham, Addison-Wesley

PARVIS, L. (2007). *Understanding cultural diversity in today's complex world.* Available from: **www.lulu.com/browse/search.php?fkeywrds= diversityparagraph1**

PASCALE, R. T. and ATHOS, A. G. (1981) *The Art of Japanese Management.* New York, Simon & Schuster

PEARCE, J., BRANYICZKI, I. and BAKACSI, J. (1994) 'Person-based Reward Systems', *Journal of Organizational Behavior*, Vol. 15, 261–82

PEARN, M. and KANDOLA, R. (1993) *Job Analysis.* London, IPM

PEDLAR, M., BURGOYNE, J. and BOYDELL, T. (1991) *The Learning Company.* London, McGraw-Hill

PELTIER, B. (2001) *The Psychology of Executive Coaching: Theory and application.* Hove, Brunner-Routledge

PERKINS, S. J. (2006) *International Reward and Recognition*, Research Report. London, CIPD

PERLMUTTER, H. V. (1969) 'The tortuous evolution of the multinational corporation', *Columbia Journal of World Business*, Vol. 4, 9–18

PERSONNEL TODAY (2005) *UK Makes Use of e-HRM.* 12 April

PFEFFER, J. (1998) *The Human Equation: Building profits by putting people first.* Boston, MA: Harvard Business School Press

PHILLIPS, J. J. and PHILLIPS, P. P. (2005) *Proving the Value of HR.* Alexandria, SHRM

PHILLIPS, J. J. and PHILLIPS, P. P. (2002) *Measuring Intellectual Capital.* Alexandria, VA, ASTD

PHILLIPS, J. J., STONE, R. D. and PHILLIPS, P. P. (2001) *The Human Resources Scorecard.* Boston, MA, Butterworth-Heinemann

PILBEAM, S. and CORBRIDGE, M. (2006) *People Resourcing: HRM in practice.* London, Prentice-Hall/FT

POLANYI, M. (1966) *The Tacit Dimension.* New York, Doubleday

PORTER, M. and KETELS, C. H. M. (2003) *UK Competitiveness: Moving to the next stage.* DTI Economics Paper No. 3. London, DTI

PRIEM, R. L., LOVE, L. G. and SHAFFER, M. (2000) 'Industrialization and values evolution: the case of Hong Kong and Guangzhou, China', *Asia-Pacific Journal of Management*, Vol. 17, No. 3, 473–92

RAMUS, C. A. and STEGER, U. (2000) 'The roles of supervisory support behaviours and environmental policy in employee "eco-initiatives" at leading-edge European companies', *Academy of Management Journal*, Vol. 43, No. 4, 605–26

RAO, T. V. (1996) *Human Resource Development: Experiences, intervention, strategies.* New Delhi, Sage

RAPOPORT, R., BAILYN, L., FLETCHER, J. and PRUITT, B. (2002) *Beyond Work–family Balance: Advancing gender equity and workplace performance.* London, Jossey-Bass/John Wiley

REDINGTON, I. (2005) *Making CSR Happen: The contribution of people management.* London, CIPD

REID, M. A., BARRINGTON, H. and BROWN, M. (2004) *Human Resource Development – Beyond training interventions,* 7th edition. London, CIPD

ROBERTS, G. (2005) *Recruitment and Selection,* 2nd edition. London, CIPD

ROBERTSON, I. T. (1994) 'Personality and personnel selection'. In C. L. Cooper and D. M. Rousseau (eds) *Trends in Organisational Behaviour.* London, John Wiley & Sons

ROBERTSON, I. T. and SMITH, M. (2001) 'Personnel selection', *Journal of Occupational and Organizational Psychology,* Vol. 74, No. 4, 441–72

RODRIQUEZ, R. (2006) 'Diversity finds its place', *HR Magazine,* Vol. 51, No. 8

RUEL, H. J. M., BONDAOUK, T. and LOOISE, J. C. (2004) 'E-HRM: innovation or irritation? An expansive empirical study in five large companies on web-based HRM', *Management Review,* Vol. 15, No. 3, 364–81

RUGMAN, A. and COLLINSON, S. (2006) *International Business.* Harlow, Prentice Hall/Financial Times

SADLER, P. (1993) *Managing Talent.* London, Economist Books

SCARBROUGH, H. (2003) *Human Capital: The external reporting framework,* Change Agenda. London, CIPD

SCHMIDT, F. L. and HUNTER, J. E. (1998) 'The validity and utility of selection methods in personnel psychology and theoretical implications of 85 years of research findings', *Psychological Bulletin,* Vol. 124, 262–74

SCHULER, R. S. (1992) *Linking the People with the Strategic Needs of the Business.* American Management Association

SCHWARTZ, S. H. (1999) 'A theory of cultural values and some implications for work', *Applied Psychology: An International Review,* Vol. 48, No. 1, 23–47

SCOTT, S. and DEAN, J. (1992) 'Integrated manufacturing and human resource management: a human capital approach', *Academy of Management Journal,* Vol. 35, No. 3, 467–504

SEARLE, R. H. (2003) *Recruitment and Selection: A critical text.* Milton Keynes, Palgrave/Open University Press

SENGE, P. M. (1990) *The Fifth Discipline: The art and practice of the learning organization.* London, Random House

SENGE, P., ROSS, R., SMITH, B., ROBERTS, C. and KLEINER, A. (1994) *The Fifth Discipline Fieldbook: Strategies and tools for building a learning organisation.* London, Nicholas Brealey

SLOMAN, M. (2007) *The Changing World of the Trainer*. Oxford, Butterworth-Heinemann

SLOMAN, M. and ROLPH, J. (2003) *E-learning*, Change Agenda. London, CIPD

SMITH, P. and MORTON, G. (2006) 'Nine years of New Labour: neoliberalism and workers rights', *British Journal of Industrial Relations*, Vol. 44, No. 3, 401–20

SMITH, P. and MORTON, G. (1993) 'Union exclusion and the decollectivisation of industrial relations in contemporary Britain', *British Journal of Industrial Relations*, Vol. 31, No. 1, 97–114

SMITH, P. B., DUGAN, S. and TROMPENAARS, F. (1996) 'National culture and values of organizational employees: a dimensional analysis across 43 nations', *Journal of Cross-Cultural Psychology*, Vol. 27, No. 2, 231–64

SNELL, S. (1992) 'Control theory in strategic human resource management', *Academy of Management Journal*, Vol. 35, No. 2, 292–327

SNELL, S. A., STUEBER, D. and LEPAK, D. P. (2002) 'Virtual HR departments: getting out of the middle'. In R. L. Henneman and D. B. Greenberger (eds) *HRM in Virtual Organisations*. New York, NY: Information Management Publishing

SPARROW, P. R. (2006) *International Recruitment, Selection and Assessment*, Research Report. London, CIPD

SPARROW, P. AND MARCHINGTON, M. (1998) 'Is HRM in crisis?' In P. Sparrow and M. Marchington (eds) *Human Resource Management: The new agenda*. London, FT/Pitman

STANSFELD, S., HEAD, J. and MARMOT, M. (1999) *Work-Related Factors and Ill-Health: The Whitehall II study*. Research Report 266. Sudbury: HSE Books. Available online at: **http://www.hse.gov.uk/research/crr_pdf/2000/crr00266.pdf**

STERN, S. (2007) 'The rise of the listening guru', *Financial Times*, 19 July, 14

STEWART, T. A. (1997) *Intellectual Capital – The new wealth of organizations*. London, Nicholas Brealey

STONE, D. L., STONE-ROMERO, E. F. and LUKASZEWSKI, K. (2003) 'The functional and dysfunctional consequences of human resource information technology for organisations and their employees'. In D. Stone (ed.) *Advances in Human Performance and Cognitive Engineering Research*. Greenwich, CT: JAI Press

STONEY, C. and WINSTANLEY, D. (2001) 'Stakeholding: confusion or Utopia? Mapping the contextual terrain', *Journal of Management Studies*, Vol. 38, No. 5, 603–26

STOREY, J. (1992) *Developments in the Management of Human Resources*. Oxford, Blackwell

STREDWICK, J. and ELLIS, S. (2005) *Flexible Working Practices*. London, CIPD

STROHMEIER, S. (2007) 'Research in e-HRM: review and implications', *Human Resource Management Review*, Vol. 17, No. 1, 19–37

TAILBY, S. (2003) 'Flexibility'. In G. Hollinshead, P. Nicholls and S. Tailby (eds) *Employee Relations*, 2nd edition. Harlow, Pearson

TANNENBAUM, S. I. (1990) 'Human resource information systems: user group implications', *Journal of Systems Management*, Vol. 41, 27–32

TAYLOR, P. (2006) *Employment Initiatives for an Ageing Workforce in the EU-15*. Luxembourg, Office for Official Publications of the European Communities

TAYLOR, P. J. and SMALL, B. (2002) 'Asking applicants what they *would* do versus what they *did* do: a meta-analytic comparison of situational and past behaviour employment interview questions', *Journal of Occupational and Organizational Psychology*, Vol. 75, No. 3, 277–94

TAYLOR, P., BALDRY, C., BAIN, P. and ELLIS, V. (2003) 'A unique working environment: health, sickness and absence management in UK call centres', *Work, Employment and Society*, Vol. 17, No. 3, 435–58

TAYLOR, R. (1997) 'CBI chief signals support for partnership with unions', *Financial Times*, 11 September

TAYLOR, S. (2005a) *The Employee Retention Handbook*. London, CIPD

TAYLOR, S. (2005b) *People Resourcing*, 3rd edition. London, CIPD

TEO, T. S. H., SOON, L. G. and FEDRIC, S. A. (2001) 'Adoption and impact of human resource information systems', *Research and Practice in Human Resource Management*, Vol. 9, No. 1, 101–17

TIXIER, M. (2000) 'Communication and management styles in Australia: understanding the changing nature of its corporate affairs', *Cross-Cultural Management: An International Journal*, Vol. 7, No. 1, 12–22

TREGASKIS, O., GLOVER, L. and FERNER, A. (2006) *International HR Networks in MNCs*, Research Report. London, CIPD

TREGASKIS, O., MAHONEY, C. and ATTERBURY, S. (2004) 'International survey methodology experiences from the Cranet Network'. In C. Brewster, W. Mayrhofer and M. Morley (eds) *Human Resource Management in Europe: Evidence of convergence?* London, Butterworth-Heinemann

TUCKMAN, B. and JENSEN, N. (1977) 'Stages of small group development revisited', *Group and Organisational Studies*, Vol. 2, 419–27

TURNER, B. and PIDGEON, N. (1997). *Man-Made Disasters*. London, Wykeham

TWOMEY, D. and QUAZI, H. (1994) 'Triangular typology approach to studying performance management systems in hi-tech firms', *Journal of Organizational Behaviour*, Vol. 15, No. 6, 561–73

TYSON, S. and FELL, A. (1986) *Evaluating the Personnel Function*. London, Hutchinson

ULRICH, D. (1997) *Human Resource Champions*. Boston, MA: Harvard Business Press

ULRICH, D. and BROCKBANK, B. (2005) *The HR Value Proposition*. Boston, MA: Harvard Business

ULRICH, D. and BROCKBANK, W. (2005) 'Role call', *People Management*, Vol. 16, June, 24–8

ULRICH, S. (2002) 'From e-business to e-HR', *International Human Resource Information Management Journal*, Vol. 5, 90–7

VROOM, V. H. (1964) *Work and Motivation*. Cited in J. Arnold, C. L. Cooper and I. T. Robertson (1995) *Work Psychology – Understanding human behaviour in the workplace*, 2nd edition. London, Pitman

WÄCHTER, H. and MULLER-CAMEN, M. (2002) 'Co-determination and strategic integration in German firms', *Human Resource Management Journal*, Vol. 12, No. 3, 76–87

WADDINGTON, J. (2003) 'Annual review article: heightening tension in relations between trade unions and the labour government in 2002', *British Journal of Industrial Relations*, Vol. 41, No. 2, 335–58

WALKER, A. (1999) 'Ageing in Europe – challenges and consequences', *Zeitschrift für Gerontologie und Geriatrie*, Vol. 32, No. 6, 390–7

WALTERS, D. (2001) *Health and Safety in Small Enterprises*. Oxford, PIE Peter Lang

WALTERS, D. and NICHOLS, T. (2007) *Worker Representation and Workplace Health and Safety*. Basingstoke, Palgrave Macmillan

WALTERS, D., NICHOLS, T., CONNOR, J., TASIRAN, A. and CAM, S. (2005) *The Role and Effectiveness of Safety Representatives in Influencing Workplace Health and Safety*. Research Report 363. Sudbury: HSE Books. Available online at: **http://www.hse.gov.uk/_research/rrhtm/rr363.htm**

WALTERS, M. (2005) *People and Performance: Designing the HR process for maximum performance delivery*. London, CIPD

WEDDERBURN, L. (1991) 'Freedom of association and philosophies of labour law', *Employment Rights in Britain and Europe: Selected papers in labour law*. London, Lawrence & Wishart

WEEKES, S. and BEAGRIE, S. (2002) *E-People*. Knoxville, TN: Capstone Publishing

WENGER, E. (1998) *Communities of Practice: Learning, meaning and identity*. Cambridge, Cambridge University Press

WESTWOOD, R. J. and POSNER, B. Z. (1997) 'Managerial values across cultures: Australia, Hong Kong, and the United States', *Asia-Pacific Journal of Management*, Vol. 14, 31–66

WHEELER, H. N. and MCCLENDON, J. A. (1998) 'Employment relations in the United States'. In G. J. Bamber and R. D. Lansbury, *International and Comparative Employment Relations*. London, Sage

WHITE, M., HILL, S., MCGOVERN, P., MILLS, C. and SMEATON, D. (2004a) *Managing to Change?* Basingstoke, Palgrave

WHITE, M., HILL, S., MCGOVERN, P., MILLS, C. and SMEATON, D. (2004b) '"High performance" management practices, working hours and work–life balance', *British Journal of Industrial Relations*, Vol. 41, No. 2, 175–95

WILLEMS, I., JANVIER, R. and HENDERICKX, E. (2006) 'New pay in European civil services: is the psychological contract changing?', *International Journal of Public Sector Management*, Vol. 19, No. 6, 609–21

WITHERSPOON, R. and WHITE, R. P. (2004) *Four Essential Ways That Coaching Can Help Executives.* Greensboro, NC, Center for Creative Leadership

WOMACK, J. P., JONES, D. T. and ROOS, D. (1990) *The Machine That Changed the World: The triumph of lean production.* New York, Rawson Macmillan

WOOD, G. and SELA, R. (2000) 'Making human resource development work', *Human Resource Development International*, Vol. 3, No. 4, 451–64

WOOD, G., HARCOURT, M. and ROPER, I. (2006) 'The limits of numerical flexibility. Continuity and change'. In G. Wood and P. James (eds) *Institutions, Production and Working Life.* Oxford, Oxford University Press

WRIGHT, P. and MCMAHON, A. (1992) 'Theoretical perspectives for strategic human resource management', *Journal of Management*, Vol. 18, No. 2, 295–320

WWP DEVELOPING PEOPLE (2007) *Managing diversity.* Available from: **www.wwp.co.uk/ diversity _ cultural _ equality _workplace.htm?gclid=COP8V**

ZUSMAN, P. R. and LANDIS, R. S. (2002) 'Applicant preferences for web-based vs traditional job postings', *Computers in Human Behaviour*, Vol. 18, No. 3, 285–96

Index